FILM
AWARDS

Volume Three
1980 – 1999

About the Author

Brian Lindsay was awarded a PhD from the University of New South Wales for his thesis "Darkening Frontier, Vanishing Outback: Film, Landscape and National Identities in Australia and the United States". His articles about the Academy Awards have appeared in *The Sydney Morning Herald* and *The Australian*. Passionate about film and theatre history, he lives in Sydney, Australia with his partner, Simon.

His previous publication, *Category Fraud*, examined how studios have gamed the Oscar nominations for decades by campaigning for lead performances to be nominated in the supporting categories, and argued that it was past time the Academy reformed its rules to end the practice and restore integrity to the Oscars. *Category Fraud* was published by Tranter Ward Books in 2016.

The first and second volumes of *Film Awards: A Reference Guide to US & UK Film Awards*, the only film awards reference book to cover the annual awards season category by category, were published in 2017 and 2018. The fourth volume will be published by Tranter Ward Books in 2020.

FILM
AWARDS

A Reference Guide to
US & UK Film Awards

Volume Three
1980 – 1999

Brian Lindsay

TRANTER WARD BOOKS

Tranter Ward Books
Sydney NSW Australia
www.tranterward.com

First Edition 2019

ISBN: 978-0-9804909-6-1

Cover design by Simon Moore, Elton Ward Creative

A catalogue record for this book is available from the National Library of Australia

To Matt, Stephen,
Michael and Adam

Introduction

Each year the Academy Awards ceremony is the culmination of a season of award presentations by critics' associations, industry guilds and other prestigious organisations. As the season unfolds, debate invariably ensues as to whether each set of accolades portend Oscar glory or are merely curious anomalies.

There are numerous books and websites that diligently list the various nominees and winners, many providing commentary on which films were favoured by the critics and which swept the Globes on the way to the Oscars. Without exception, they chronicle the annual awards season the same way, taking each set of awards in turn – the New York Film Critics Circle winners, then the National Board of Review winners, then the Golden Globe Award nominees and winners, and so forth, concluding with the Academy Awards.

It's only on rare occasions, however, that we want an overview of an entire awards season or even a snapshot of all the winners of the Los Angeles Film Critics Association prizes from a given year. More often, we reach for such reference books because, at that moment, we are interested in a certain film, director or performance. Having just watched *Pulp Fiction*, for example, you're curious to see how Quentinn Tarantino fared during that year's awards season. Which groups nominated him? Who was he up against? Which accolades did he win? Who did he lose out to? When you have such questions, this is the book to grab.

Film Awards takes a fresh and long overdue approach to the annual awards season: category by category. No more looking up the Best Director winner from one critic's group, then turning the page to look up the winner from a different critic's group later in that season, then flicking to another page to find out who was nominated for the Golden Globes, and then finally turning to yet another page and scanning through a list of all the Academy Award nominees to find out who was in contention for the Oscar. In this book, the nominees and winners for Best Director from all the major awards groups in a given year are listed together in one quick-reference table on the same page. At a glance, you can see which awards Quentin Tarantino won for *Pulp Fiction*, who he was nominated alongside and to whom he lost.

Reference tables are compiled in *Film Awards* for Best Picture, Director, Actor, Actress, Supporting Actor and Supporting Actress. In this third volume, covering the years 1980 through to 1999, the tables include the nominees and winners of the Academy Awards, Golden Globe Awards, British Academy Awards, Producers Guild of America Awards, Directors Guild of America Awards, Screen Actors Guild Awards, New York Film Critics Circle Awards,

Los Angeles Film Critics Association Awards, the London Film Critics Awards, the National Board of Review Awards, the National Society of Film Critics Awards and the Critics' Choice Awards where relevant in each instance (depending on which year the awards commenced and in which categories they were presented). Information about major film festival prize winners are not included as only a small number of selected candidates are eligible rather than all the films released throughout the year as is the case with the major annual awards.

The reputation of a film can diminish or become enhanced with the passage of time. In 2012, for example, leading film critics and academics polled by the British Film Institute's Sight & Sound magazine placed David Lynch's *Blue Velvet* among the top one hundred films of all time. While the film won one of the major Best Picture prizes for the year of its original release, it was not even nominated for the top prizes at the Academy Awards, the British Academy Awards or the Golden Globes. In 1986, reaction to *Blue Velvet* was decidedly mixed. The New York Times called it "startling [and] powerfully imaginative" and declared it to be "an instant cult classic" while the New York Post dismissed it as "one of the sickest films ever made". To better understand why certain films and performances garnered awards recognition while others were overlooked, *Film Awards* quotes from leading film critics in the United States, the United Kingdom and Australia to reveal the critical opinion contemporaneous to each film's initial release. Such quotes are reproduced with original spellings.

Throughout the book, films are referred to by the title under which they were originally released in their country of origin. Alternate titles by which a film was known in the United States are included in parentheses.

References to directors and performers in the index relate only to instances when the individual was an awards season contender. For example, only instances when Meryl Streep is listed or referred to as a winner, nominee or contender for Best Actress or Best Supporting Actress appear in the index. Other incidental references to her in the book, such as when she was a presenter of the Best Actor statuette or was the star of a Best Picture nominee are omitted.

Film Awards has been designed to place the annual Oscar winners for Picture, Director and Acting into historical context alongside the other winners and nominees from that season as well as the opinions of the leading newspaper and magazine film critics of the day. Hopefully it will be an interesting and informative companion as you discover (or rediscover) the lauded films and performances of the years 1980 to 1999.

Abbreviations

AMPAS	Academy of Motion Picture Arts and Sciences
BAFTA	British Academy of Film and Television Awards
DGA	Directors Guild of America
HFPA	Hollywood Foreign Press Association
NBR	National Board of Review
NSFC	National Society of Film Critics
SAG	Screen Actors Guild
BFCA	Broadcast Film Critics Association
BG	Boston Globe
CST	Chicago Sun-Times
CT	Chicago Tribune
FC	Film Comment
FQ	Film Quarterly
G	The Guardian
HRp	The Hollywood Reporter
LAT	Los Angeles Times
MFB	Monthly Film Bulletin
NYDN	New York Daily News
NYer	The New Yorker
NYP	New York Post
NYT	The New York Times
PDN	Philadelphia Daily News
PI	The Philadelphia Inquirer
S&S	Sight & Sound
SFC	San Francisco Chronicle
SFX	San Francisco Examiner
SMH	The Sydney Morning Herald
TT	The Times
TGM	The Globe and Mail
V	Variety
WP	The Washington Post

Note on income figures quoted for Best Picture Academy Award nominees: Figures quoted are for North American box office gross during period of original release.

BEST PICTURE

ACADEMY AWARDS

Coal Miner's Daughter
(Schwartz, Universal, 125 mins, 6 Mar 1980, $67.1m, 7 noms)
The Elephant Man
(Brooksfilms, Paramount, BW 125 mins, 2 Oct 1980, $26.0m, 8 noms)
• *Ordinary People*
(Wildwood, Paramount, 124 mins, 18 Sep 1980, $54.8m, 6 noms)
Raging Bull
(Chartoff-Winkler, United Artists, BW & C 129 mins, 13 Nov 1980, $49.0m, 8 noms)
Tess
(Société Française, Columbia, 170 mins, 11 Dec 1980, $20.1m, 6 noms)

GOLDEN GLOBE AWARDS

(Drama)	(Comedy/Musical)
The Elephant Man	*Airplane!*
The Ninth Configuration	• *Coal Miner's Daughter*
• *Ordinary People*	*Fame*
Raging Bull	*The Idolmaker*
The Stunt Man	*Melvin and Howard*

BRITISH ACADEMY AWARDS

Being There
• *The Elephant Man*
Kagemusha (The Shadow Warrior)
Kramer vs Kramer

NEW YORK – *Ordinary People*
LOS ANGELES – *Raging Bull*
BOARD OF REVIEW – *Ordinary People*
NATIONAL SOCIETY – *Melvin and Howard*
LONDON – *Apocalypse Now*

The year's biggest box office hit was *The Empire Strikes Back*, the sequel to the 1977 science-fiction blockbuster *Star Wars* which, at the time, was the highest-grossing film of all-time (NYT "expands on the first film, but never outstrips it"; LAT "a hugely accomplished and exciting follow-on"; CT "excellent entertainment … a sequel that lives up to and expands upon its original"; WP "a stunning successor … a tense and pictorially dazzling science-fiction chase melodrama … thrilling, witty, inventive"; V "a worthy sequel"). Despite its commercial success and positive reviews, *The Empire Strikes Back* did not emulate the original by scoring a Best Picture nomination from the Academy. "The only blockbuster attraction of 1980," reported Gary Arnold in The Washington Post, "was brushed off by the Academy voters with nominations in three craft categories, although the board of governors announced last week that it would receive a special achievement award for visual effects."

Instead, the front-runners for the Best Picture Academy Award were the films honoured by the New York Film Critics Circle and the Los Angeles Film Critics Association.

The Los Angeles critics had chosen *Raging Bull*, a biopic directed by Martin Scorsese and starring Robert De Niro as the 1948 middle-weight boxing champion Jake LaMotta, which had received glowing reviews from most leading critics (NYT "ambitious ... a movie with a resonant life and style of its own"; LAT "superior"; CT "one of the best American films of the year"; WP "a ponderous work ... a uniquely alienating movie"; BG "a masterpiece"; V "unsatisfactory"; MFB "powerful"). Following its Los Angeles win, *Raging Bull* finished as runner-up for the National Board of Review and National Society of Film Critics prizes and placed third in the voting by the New York critics. It was an unsuccessful nominee for the Golden Globe (Drama), but was one of two films to top the list of Oscar contenders with eight nominations.

In New York, the critics selected *Ordinary People*, a drama about a Chicago family struggling to cope with a son's death which had been the runner-up in the voting in Los Angeles (NYT "moving, intelligent and funny"; LAT "a strongly emotional and beautifully written and performed family drama ... intimate and demanding ... outstanding ... a fine and touching piece of work"; CT "excellent"; WP "an earnest, engrossing, faithfully shallow movie ... given the source material, the film is as good as respectful adaptation could make it"; BG "extraordinary ... the movie is flawed, it's too careful ... but its fierce determination to avoid sentimentality redeems it"; V "powerful"; Time "powerful"; TGM "earnestly boring"). The directorial debut of former Best Actor Oscar nominee Robert Redford, *Ordinary People* was also named Best Picture by the NBR and won the Globe (Drama). Redford had been honoured by the Directors Guild of America which normally indicated success at the Academy Awards, but *Ordinary People* had only garnered six nominations in five categories, and three other Best Picture nominees were in contention for more statuettes.

Equalling *Raging Bull* with eight nominations was the black-and-white British drama *The Elephant Man*, directed by American film-maker David Lynch (NYT "haunting ... a handsome, eerie, disturbing movie"; LAT "artistically daring [and] emotionally overwhelming ... extraordinary"; CT "not perfect, but very good and profoundly sad ... makes us ache with empathy"; BG "a bizarre, baroque film"; V "moving"; S&S "fascinating"; MFB "a fascinatingly hybrid piece of movie-making"). Less than a fortnight before the Oscar ceremony, *The Elephant Man* was named Best Film by the British Academy, outpolling a field of nominees that included *Kramer vs Kramer*, the previous year's Best Picture Oscar winner.

The other two nominees were the Globe (Comedy/Musical) winner *Coal Miner's Daughter*, a biopic about country and western singer Loretta Lynn (NYP "entertaining [and] ... mighty good ... delightful, unexpectedly moving ... American Dreamstuff of a most charming order"; LAT "an affecting and folksy portrait"; CT "at its core is pretty much your standard Hollywood show-biz biography"; WP "admirable"; V "a thoughtful, endearing film") and the literary adaptation *Tess* which had placed third in the voting by the Los Angeles critics (NYT "a lovely, lyrical and unexpectedly delicate movie"; LAT "a masterpiece of the film art ... stunningly beautiful ... one of the few nearly perfect translations of the spirit and substance of a literary classic into the different language of film"; V "sensitive, intelligent [but] fails to achieve the accumulative emotional power of the book"). *Tess* was considered a non-starter by many because of the controversy surrounding director Roman Polanski, who had fled the United States three years earlier after being charged with having sex with a minor. The chances of *Coal Miner's Daughter*, meanwhile, appeared to be limited by its omission from the Best Director category – no film had won Best Picture without a nomination for its director since 1931/32. Furthermore, some leading film critics openly questioned whether it deserved the nomination. "As much as one can admire the performance of Sissy Spacek for which she has been nominated as best actress, it does seem that the film, though perfectly acceptable in its way, deserves its best picture nomination far less than 'Airplane' and far, far less than a couple of other films that were mostly cold-shouldered in the year's Academy voting," said Vincent Canby in The New York Times. In the Boston Globe, Bruce McCabe wrote, "'Coal Miner's Daughter' was one-third of a good film subverted by the other two-thirds, a soap opera about show-biz riches and fame not bringing happiness". McCabe concurred with Canby that he found the film's inclusion in the Best Picture category "a nomination that mystifies".

In addition to the hugely popular Globe-nominated spoof *Airplane!* (released in some territories as *Flying High*) (NYT "hilarious ... marvelous ... thoroughly satisfying"; LAT "the year's nuttiest, funniest comedy"), the films Canby cited as more deserving of a Best Picture nomination were: John Huston's *Wise Blood* (NYT "possibly the most successful screen adaptation of a major work to come along in a very long time ... exuberant ... one of the finest, most heartfelt films Mr Huston has ever made"; WP "painful and touching and grimly comic"; BG "resonates with a multi-layered intelligence ... a remarkable achievement"; FQ

"a brilliant mixture of painfully lucid and tantalizingly inexplicable elements");
Brian De Palma's *Dressed to Kill* (NYT "most entertaining ... a witty, romantic,
psychological horror film"; LAT "a stunning film"; WP "fresh, ominously
satisfying ... sleek"; MFB "the masterpiece of Brian De Palma's gratuitous
cinema"); and NSFC prize-winner and Globe nominee *Melvin and Howard*
(NYT "sharp, engaging, very funny"; LAT "an amusing fable – and a nice,
modest little movie"; CT "one of the year's best"; WP "remarkably appealing
but perhaps a shade too wistful for its own good"; BG "mild, quirky and
idiosyncratic"; V "more engaging than compelling"; S&S "affectionately good-
humoured"; MFB "highly engaging").

All five of the Academy's Best Picture nominees had, meanwhile, featured
on a list of the year's ten best movies compiled by film critic Charles Champlin
in the Los Angeles Times. The other films on his list were: the Australian dramas
Breaker Morant (NYT "genuinely, surprisingly affecting and unspeakably sad";
LAT "a vivid, highly dramatic and engrossing story, beautifully made ... [a] taut
and impassioned court-martial drama"; WP "admirable"; BG "compelling";
TGM "solidly entertaining and thoughtful") and *My Brilliant Career* (LAT "not
just timeless but sharply contemporary"; CT "noteworthy"; BG "it's hard to
imagine a film filled with more quiet integrity, intelligent passion, realistic
drama and genuine entertainment"; WP "a beautiful production"; TT "a gifted
piece of film-making"); *Fame* (NYT "hugely entertaining"; LAT "it's
impossible not to feel exhilarated [but it's] by no means an unmitigated
triumph"; CT "hackneyed ... too obvious"; WP "an example of potentially
stirring movie material gone woefully astray"; MFB "comes unstuck"); Woody
Allen's *Stardust Memories* (NYT "scathing, audacious ... provocative ... fine,
funny ... a marvelous movie"; LAT "a brilliant, uncomfortable work"; WP "has
no dramatic shape or resonance and the incidental laughs are few and far
between ... seems washed-out and cheerless ... misguided"; BG "one of Allen's
most accessible films ... [and] his wittiest"; TGM "wholly embarrassing ...
much of what is meant to be funny is not and much of what is meant to be serious
is hilarious, and a great deal of the film is simply witless"; FQ "quite good");
and the extremely low-budget film *The Return of the Secaucus Seven* (NYT
"sweet and engaging ... an honest, fully realized movie"; LAT "the sleeper film
of the year, engaging and greatly affecting ... one of the year's most enjoyable
and pertinent pictures"; WP "delightful ... a witty, affectionate and thoroughly
modern comedy of manners"; BG "a poignant romantic comedy").

Other notable exclusions included: Akira Kurosawa's *Kagemusha (The
Shadow Warrior)*, a Best Film nominee at the British Academy Awards (NYT
"the director's most physically elaborate, most awesome film ... majestic,
stately, cool"; NYP "impressive"; LAT "splendid ... unfolds as one stunning,
stylized image after another"; WP "the year's most impressive spectacle"; V "a

sweeping epic"; CT "a remarkable film ... a grand film that entertains at many levels"; BG "a stunning film of epic proportions and incisive sensitivity"; TGM "unwieldy but moving, simultaneously grandiose yet unadorned"; G "spectacular"; FQ "conceptually bold"); *The Stunt Man*, a film completed in 1978 but not released until 1980 for which Richard Rush was a Best Director nominee (NYT "sometimes entertaining" but "largely uninviting ... a second-rate picture ... simple trickery remains its prime concern"; LAT "vigorous, spellbinding and provocative ... a virile and ribald whoop-up [which] plays very entertainingly"; CT "the year's most clever film, an exhilarating piece of flim-flam that turns out to be a genuine thriller"; TGM "the best movie about making a movie ever made"; FQ "unbelievable ... gets simplistic"); Venice Film Festival winner *Gloria* (NYT "a very peculiar, lumpy mixture"; CT "fascinating"; WP "just a hell of a lot of fun"; BG "a fascinating film ... totally visceral cinema ... exhilarating"); and the previous year's Oscar winner as Best-Foreign Language Film *Die Blechtrommel (The Tin Drum)* (NYT "stunning ... compels attention"; WP "there is a beastly stylishness to this film, and a crude humor belying the solemnity, but this version is no complicated masterwork"; BG "a masterpiece ... a brilliant, devastating portrait of a state of mind ... fascinatingly rich, dense and complex"; S&S "remarkable").

Unsurprisingly, the Academy ignored *Heaven's Gate* (director Michael Cimino's first film since *The Deer Hunter*), a disastrously expensive flop which critics had savaged (NYT "fails so completely ... pretentious ... awful ... an unqualified disaster"; NYP "lacking ... more colorful than understandable"; V "overlong" and "incoherent"; TT "an expansive, badly told Western"; Time "a four-hour fiasco") as well as Nicolas Roeg's *Bad Timing* which won the People's Choice Award at the 1980 Toronto International Film Festival but received only a limited, independent commercial release after an executive at its distributor in the U.K., the Rank Organisation, slammed it as "a sick film made by sick people for sick people" and it earned an X rating in the United States (LAT "superior ... moody and elliptical"; CT "finally just an exercise in telling a shallow and crude story in a sophisticated and complicated way").

On Oscar night, *Ordinary People* prevailed, collecting the Best Picture prize along with three other statuettes. Surprisingly, *Kagemusha (The Shadow Warrior)* was outpolled by *Moskva Slezam ne Verit (Moscow Does Not Believe in Tears)* for the Best Foreign-Language Film trophy (NYT "seems endless"; WP "often entertaining though sometimes drags"). "That it should be so honoured by the Academy is incredible," exclaimed Vincent Canby in The New York Times when the winner was released in North American cinemas three weeks later. The Washington Post film critic Gary Arnold, meanwhile, said that "there was more condescending good will than esthetic discrimination behind the Oscar voted to 'Moscow'".

BEST DIRECTOR

ACADEMY AWARDS
David Lynch for *The Elephant Man*
Roman Polanski for *Tess*
• **Robert Redford for *Ordinary People***
Richard Rush for *The Stunt Man*
Martin Scorsese for *Raging Bull*

GOLDEN GLOBE AWARDS
David Lynch – *The Elephant Man*
Roman Polanski – *Tess*
• **Robert Redford – *Ordinary People***
Richard Rush – *The Stunt Man*
Martin Scorsese – *Raging Bull*

DIRECTORS GUILD AWARD
Michael Apted
  – *Coal Miner's Daughter*
David Lynch – *The Elephant Man*
• **Robert Redford – *Ordinary People***
Richard Rush – *The Stunt Man*
Martin Scorsese – *Raging Bull*

BRITISH ACADEMY AWARDS
Robert Benton – *Kramer vs Kramer*
• **Akira Kurosawa**
  – *Kagemusha*
  (*The Shadow Warrior*)
David Lynch – *The Elephant Man*
Alan Parker – *Fame*

NEW YORK – **Jonathan Demme** – *Melvin and Howard*
LOS ANGELES – **Roman Polanski** – *Tess*
BOARD OF REVIEW – **Robert Redford** – *Ordinary People*
NATIONAL SOCIETY – **Martin Scorsese** – *Raging Bull*
LONDON – **Nicolas Roeg** – *Bad Timing*

The major critics' prizes were each won by a different director.

On 18 December 1980, the National Board of Review gave their award to actor-turned-director Robert Redford for his acclaimed directorial debut, *Ordinary People* (NYT "[a] very real achievement"; NYP "directed with a sure touch"; LAT "by no means perfect … [but] assured and affecting"; CT "crisply directed"; WP "an auspicious, if conventional, directing debut … demonstrates that he's more capable and sensitive than 90 percent of the directors in the business"; BG "an astonishing debut"; V "a remarkably intelligent and assured directorial debut"; TGM "workmanlike"; TT "unobtrusive" direction).

1980

Two days later, the Los Angeles Film Critics Association honoured Roman Polanski for *Tess*, a lauded adaptation of Thomas Hardy's late nineteenth century novel, 'Tess of the d'Urbervilles' (NYT "has achieved the impossible"; LAT "the best work yet of a master of the screen ... a film of remarkable maturity"; V "falters in some crucial scenes"). Tied in second placed in the voting were Martin Scorsese for *Raging Bull*, a biopic about boxing champion Jack LaMotta (NYT "his finest [film] ... an achievement"; LAT "Polanski has made a masterful film"; CT "a superior achievement of film art ... beautifully filmed ... [and] the film's supporting cast is equally distinguished which is a tribute to Scorsese's ability"; WP "an opaque interpretation"; BG "superb ... an extraordinary accomplishment") and Richard Rush for *The Stunt Man* (NYT "Rush keeps the film moving busily, sometimes entertainingly, forward but he seldom offers his audience enough incentive to puzzle through a wild overabundance of riddles"; V "impressive").

At the end of the month, the New York Film Critics Circle presented their plaudit to Jonathan Demme for the comedy *Melvin and Howard* (LAT "a work of confident nonchalance"; CT "absolutely charming"; S&S "[the] unpretentious certitude in Demme's handling marks him as a director well worth watching"; MFB "fluid stylistic assurance"). Scorsese once again finished as runner-up, while Los Angeles prize-winner Redford placed third. Also garnering votes from the New York critics were NBR winner Polanski and Brian De Palma for *Dressed to Kill* (LAT "a directorial tour de force"; CT "excellent filmmaking by De Palma"; WP "enhance[s] De Palma's reputation as the most exciting and distinctive manipulator of suspense since Alfred Hitchcock ... [he is] in smooth command of a fluid, baroque visual imagination ... a tour de force of pictorial exposition").

Early in the new year, the National Society of Film Critics honoured Scorsese ahead of Demme, while the Film Section of The Critics' Circle in London selected Nicolas Roeg for the controversial drama *Bad Timing*, a film completed in 1979 and given only a very limited, independent commercial release late the following year (TT "creates a perfectly coherent and intriguing central narrative and relationship").

On 12 January, the Hollywood Foreign Press Association short-listed Polanski, Redford, Rush and Scorsese for the Best Director Golden Globe but overlooked Demme in favour of American film-maker David Lynch for the British drama *The Elephant Man* (LAT "Lynch now joins a growing list of AFI graduates who will leave a mark on film history ... [he] deploys all the resources of image and montage to create a spiritual biography ... tosses caution aside"; V "commendable"). Demme was also an unexpected omission from the list of Directors Guild of America finalists which featured Michael Apted for the biopic *Coal Miner's Daughter* (NYT "effortless ... [has] a gentle touch"; WP "astutely crafted ... Apted's restraint is laudable [but] while the procession of sequences remains vivid and absorbing, one often feels that climactic episodes have been muffled or shortchanged – the movie has a peculiar way of drifting away from you") alongside Lynch, Polanski, Redford and Scorsese.

Demme was also excluded at the Academy Awards, becoming the third New York critics prize-winner in a row to be omitted from Oscar consideration. Instead, for the second time in four years, Oscar voters short-listed the same five nominees as the HFPA. Lynch, Redford, Rush and Scorsese were all mentioned for the first time, while Polanski received the second Best Director nomination of his career just three years after fleeing the United States while awaiting sentencing for statutory rape.

In addition to Demme, the other notable omission from the Oscar ballot was Japanese director Akira Kurosawa for the Best Foreign-Language Film frontrunner *Kagemusha (The Shadow Warrior)* (NYT "so elegantly directed that even perfunctory shots seem integral to the film's ritual"; LAT "there's no question that with this film we're in the presence of a work by a master"; WP "splendidly visualized"; BG "compelling"; V "impressive handling"). Less than a fortnight before the Oscars, Kurosawa was named Best Director by the British Academy, outpolling a field of nominees that included Oscar nominee Lynch and the previous year's Oscar winner, Robert Benton for *Kramer vs Kramer*.

Also by-passed were: DGA nominee Apted for *Coal Miner's Daughter*, one of the year's Best Picture candidates; previous winner John Huston for *Wise Blood* (WP "the restrained artistry with which the director and actors have translated O'Connor's literary vision into a film is amazing ... Huston's straightforward, sardonic direction reinforces a compact, unusually literate screenplay"; BG "proves that, in the right hands, superior novels can be made into superior films"); John Cassavetes for *Gloria* (LAT "infuses the plot with a street-scene veracity"; BG "does a great job keeping his rollercoaster on its slippery tracks": MFB "cleverly negotiates this plot"); Bruce Beresford for *Breaker Morant* (NYT "crisp"; LAT "beautifully made"; BG "Beresford's stiff-upper-lip direction never stoops to melodrama ... he handles the courtroom scenes with the same artistic crispness as the exciting battle sequences ... sensitive directorial touch"); and Gillian Armstrong for *My Brilliant Career* (LAT "beautifully directed"; CT "directed with understated wit and sympathy"; WP "impressive ... establishes her instantly as the most sensitive and accomplished woman director in the English-speaking world"; BG "the film is nurtured by [her] provocative attention to meaningful detail"; TT "[an] extraordinary debut").

Redford triumphed at the Golden Globes and won the Guild accolade, making him the overwhelming favourite for the Academy Award. On Oscar night, he took home the Best Director statuette.

1980

BEST ACTOR

ACADEMY AWARDS
• **Robert De Niro as 'Jake LaMotta' in *Raging Bull***
Robert Duvall as 'Bull Meechum' in *The Great Santini*
John Hurt as 'John Merrick' in *The Elephant Man*
Jack Lemmon as 'Scottie Templeton' in *Tribute*
Peter O'Toole as 'Eli Cross' in *The Stunt Man*

GOLDEN GLOBE AWARDS

(Drama)
• **Robert De Niro – *Raging Bull***
John Hurt – *The Elephant Man*
Jack Lemmon – *Tribute*
Peter O'Toole – *The Stunt Man*
Donald Sutherland – *Ordinary People*

(Comedy/Musical)
Neil Diamond – *The Jazz Singer*
Paul Le Mat – *Melvin and Howard*
Tommy Lee Jones
  – *Coal Miner's Daughter*
Walter Matthau – *Hopscotch*
• **Ray Sharkey – *The Idolmaker***

BRITISH ACADEMY AWARDS
Dustin Hoffman – *Kramer vs Kramer*
• **John Hurt – *The Elephant Man***
Roy Scheider – *All That Jazz*
Peter Sellers – *Being There*

NEW YORK – Robert De Niro – *Raging Bull*
LOS ANGELES – Robert De Niro – *Raging Bull*
BOARD OF REVIEW – Robert De Niro – *Raging Bull*
NATIONAL SOCIETY – Peter O'Toole – *The Stunt Man*

Critics showered Robert De Niro with praise for his portrayal of 1948 middleweight boxing champion Jake LaMotta in Martin Scorsese's *Raging Bull* (NYT "remarkable ... may well be the performance of his career"; LAT "probably the best of his remarkable career to date"; CT "superior ... shockingly well acted"; BG "[a] shattering characterization ... unforgettable, one of the more brilliant performances on the screen in recent years"; Time "always absorbing and credible"; TT "brilliant"). At the end of the year De Niro won three of the four major critics' prizes. The Los Angeles Film Critics Association named him Best Actor for the second time in five years, as did the New York Film Critics Circle, who had also given him their supporting award in 1973. De Niro also received his first award from the National Board of Review and his first Golden Globe. The Chicago Tribune declared, "De Niro has to be the odds-on favorite to win the Academy Award as best actor, which will cap an already extraordinary career for the 37-year-old star."

The only group not to honour De Niro was the National Society of Film Critics who had given him a supporting accolade in 1973 and the Best Actor trophy in 1976. Instead the NSFC rewarded Peter O'Toole for his performance as a domineering film director (apparently based on David Lean) in *The Stunt Man* which won him acclaim in the United States (NYT "magnificent"; LAT "[a] tour de force ... at the peak of his extravagant form ... this beguiling vaudeville turn should remind [audiences] that O'Toole is one of the very best in his craft"; CT "played to flamboyant perfection"; V "excellent"; FQ "acts up a witty storm"; Time "daring and hilarious") but was largely condemned in Britain (TT "has now definitely abandoned acting for mannerism"; S&S "at his most irritatingly mannered"; MFB "tiresomely mannered"). O'Toole claimed the NSFC award by single point over De Niro.

Both men were recognised by the Academy (previous Best Supporting Actor winner De Niro for a fourth time in seven years and O'Toole for a sixth time). Also nominated were: Robert Duvall, the runner-up in the New York voting and third-place getter in the NSFC balloting, as a Marine pilot in *The Great Santini* (NYT "splendid"; LAT "performed with a brave intensity"; CT "brilliantly played ... a wonderful performance ... Duvall is totally into his character and never patronizes the character or us"; WP "played with dubious bravado"; V "excellent"; TT "wonderful"; MFB "excellent"; Time "splendid"); Los Angeles prize runner-up John Hurt as the disfigured John Merrick in *The Elephant Man* (NYT "extraordinary ... truly remarkable"; NYP "amazing"; LAT "gives a performance that was arduous and self-denying, and is unforgettable"; BG "an intriguing, sensitive performance"; V "[a] virtuoso performance"; FQ "[an] eloquently vulnerable performance"); and previous winner Jack Lemmon (short-listed for a seventh time) for reprising his stage success as a dying New York press agent reconnecting with his son in *Tribute* (NYT "Lemmon gives a desperate performance, though what he's aiming at, all too obviously, is a bravura one"; LAT "flamboyant and ruinously vulnerable ... he is terrific, and I suspect and hope the Oscar crowd will agree ... [he] has been as good before, but rarely any better"; CT "not once did I accept the two principal players as real characters ... it was more of a pleasure to watch [Lemmon] but believe that his character exists? No"; MFB "Lemmon's performance is, in most ways, a 'tour de force' of past performances").

The most surprising omission was Canadian actor Donald Sutherland as the father in *Ordinary People* (NYT "splendid"; LAT "truly poignant"; CT "well-acted ... turns in his best work since 'M*A*S*H' a decade ago"; WP "excellent"; BG "superb ... deftly and discreetly plays [the father]"; TT "exemplary"). He was the only Globe (Drama) nominee overlooked and the only member of the film's four principals not to be recognised. Arguably the most deserving candidate to be snubbed for a nomination, however, was Japanese performer Tatsuya Nakadai in dual roles in the epic *Kagemusha (The Shadow Warrior)* (LAT "perfectly cast, expressing with equal effectiveness the confident authority of [the mighty lord] and the vulnerability of the thief"; V "extraordinary"; CT "a remarkable performance"; WP "brilliantly acted ... [a] marvelous performance ... Nakadai is a riveting, unexpectedly funny presence ... he maintains human contact even when the director's formality threatens to become suffocating"; TGM "played exquisitely").

Among those also by-passed were: Globe nominee Tommy Lee Jones as Loretta Lynn's husband in *Coal Miner's Daughter* (NYT "extraordinary ... has a strength and humour that brings the film's love story to life... quietly outdoes his past performances"; CT "exceptional"; WP "smartly impersonated ... should be a decisive popular break-through for [him]"; V "superb"; LAT "admirable"; TT "stunningly good"; MFB "superbly played"); Globe (Comedy/Musical) winner Ray Sharkey as a music promoter based on Bob Marcucci in *The Idolmaker* (NYT "funny, fanatical, and energetic in a way that makes sense of [the character] ... flamboyant but still Mr Starkey seems even fresher and more idiosyncratic than anything he does or sees"; CT "wildly overacts his role, lending an air of farce to the whole film ... Sharkey renders the film inconsequential with his mannered acting style that makes him come off as a halting, tepid version of Robert De Niro ... all we see is an actor chewing the scenery"; WP "Starkey, energized but unglamorous, seems an astute choice for [the role] ... Starkey brings off a difficult lyric assignment that gives the story an emotional lift"; BG "Starkey never gets under the skin of [his character]. His nervous mannerisms suggest the neurosis of the character but not the substance. You have a hard time believing"; V "believable"; MFB "'The Idolmaker' is convincingly anchored in Ray Starkey's performance ... [his] raw energy renders [the story] entirely believable"); previous winner Jack Nicholson in *The Shining* (NYT "one of his most razor-sharp performances ... [a] vibrant characterization, furiously alive in every frame [and] devilishly funny"; LAT "the film belongs to Jack Nicholson ... you're likely to be dazzled"; WP "hauntingly played ... Nicholson's performance gathers power as the movie progresses"; BG "goes a long way to redeeming the movie ... he transcends the creep-like characterization that gives so many horror films their bad smell"; V "idiotic ... it's hard to believe he's taking any part of this role seriously"; MFB "exactly right"); Globe nominee Walter Matthau in *Hopscotch* (NYT "beautifully played"; LAT "[the film is] a sensational showcase for the debonair Mr Matthau"; CT "laconic yet charming [but] even Matthau's slumping shoulders can't carry the weight of Ronald Neame's heavy-handed direction";

WP "amusing enough"; TGM "a surprisingly low-key and funny performance"); Brad Dourif as the preacher in *Wise Blood* (NYT "first-rate"; WP "a frighteningly fine performance ... remarkable ... it's impossible to imagine an actor being more in character"; BG "[a] sterling performance"; FQ "extraordinary ... perfectly modulated ... [he] is the physical embodiment of the character described by [the author of the original novel]"; MFB "[a] brilliant performance"); Edward Woodward in *Breaker Morant* (NYT "excellent"; CT "first-rate"; BG "superlative"; Time "[a] fine, full-throated performance"); James Caan in *Hide in Plain Sight*, a film which he also directed (NYT "Caan's performance is the key to the picture's consistent style. He is excellent ... the best work he's done since 'The Godfather'"; CT "needlessly mannered"; WP "a double triumph for Caan as star and director"; MFB "a not unsympathetic directorial debut by James Caan, somewhat hampered by his own over-indulgent performance [with] somewhat pretentious mannerisms"); Frank Langella in *Those Lips, Those Eyes* (NYT "if there's any reason to see [the film] it's to appreciate Mr Langella's work"; LAT "dazzling ... splendidly histrionic as a struggling summer stock actor"; CT "[the film is] half of a winner, thanks primarily to Langella, who in scene after scene communicates his obvious love for his chosen profession"; WP "Langella gives the role a knowing and sometimes dashing interpretation ... [but his] acting ability doesn't overcome the disillusioning aspects of his sallow appearance and famished crooning"; BG "the film is redeemed by the presence and performance of Frank Langella, who simply overpowers the material"); and Bruno Ganz in *Messer im Kopf (Knife in the Head)* (NYT "Ganz is extraordinary"; LAT "his most harrowing portrayal ... utterly convincing"; BG "create[s] an indelible image through subtle gestures"; TGM "the performance is masterly"; MFB "[the film is] consistently convincing (and affecting), largely thanks to Bruno Ganz's muscular performance ... he succeeds in making Hoffman not only a believable individual but also one profoundly weary with all the people interfering in his life").

At the British Academy Awards, two weeks prior to the Oscars, Hurt was rewarded for his role in *The Elephant Man*. He won the BAFTA over three of the previous year's Oscar nominees, including winner Dustin Hoffman for *Kramer vs Kramer*.

At the Academy Awards, the Oscar, as expected, went to De Niro. Even one of his rivals, nominee Jack Lemmon, admitted to having voted for De Niro. "This year, there was no better performance than Robert De Niro's in 'Raging Bull', he told the Chicago Tribune's Gene Siskel.

The following year, De Niro was outpolled for the British Academy Award by Burt Lancaster in *Atlantic City*, a frontrunner for that year's Best Actor Oscar. At the 1981 Venice Film Festival, meanwhile, the Best Actor prize was presented to Lemmon for his performance in *Tribute*.

BEST ACTRESS

ACADEMY AWARDS
Ellen Burstyn as 'Edna Mae McCauley' in *Resurrection*
Goldie Hawn as 'Judy Benjamin' in *Private Benjamin*
Mary Tyler Moore as 'Beth Jarrett' in *Ordinary People*
Gena Rowlands as 'Gloria Swenson' in *Gloria*
• **Sissy Spacek as 'Loretta Lynn' in *Coal Miner's Daughter***

GOLDEN GLOBE AWARDS

(Drama)
Ellen Burstyn – *Resurrection*
Nastassja Kinski – *Tess*
• **Mary Tyler Moore**
   – *Ordinary People*
Deborah Raffin – *Touched by Love*
Gena Rowlands – *Gloria*

(Comedy/Musical)
Irene Cara – *Fame*
Goldie Hawn – *Private Benjamin*
Bette Midler – *Divine Madness*
Dolly Parton – *9 to 5*
• **Sissy Spacek**
   – *Coal Miner's Daughter*

BRITISH ACADEMY AWARDS
• **Judy Davis – *My Brilliant Career***
Shirley MacLaine – *Being There*
Bette Midler – *The Rose*
Meryl Streep – *Kramer vs Kramer*

NEW YORK – Sissy Spacek – *Coal Miner's Daughter*
LOS ANGELES – Sissy Spacek – *Coal Miner's Daughter*
BOARD OF REVIEW – Sissy Spacek – *Coal Miner's Daughter*
NATIONAL SOCIETY – Sissy Spacek – *Coal Miner's Daughter*

For a second year in a row, an actress won all the major end-of-year Best Actress accolades: the New York Film Critics Circle, Los Angeles Film Critics Association, National Board of Review and National Society of Film Critics prizes, a Golden Globe and the Academy Award. Thirty-one-year old Sissy Spacek was honoured with the clean sweep for her portrayal of country and western singer Loretta Lynn in *Coal Miner's Daughter*, for which critics had praised both her acting and her singing – she had chosen to re-record the star's hits herself rather than have Lynn's vocals dubbed over the film (NYT "captivating ... extraordinary ... creates a character of immense steadfastness, gumption and humor ... luminous"; NYP "uncanny"; LAT "a smashing portrayal ... real rather than cosmetic ... a dazzling piece of portraiture"; CT

"Spacek turns 'Coal' into film gold ... [an] extraordinary portrait ... the role is a genuine roller coaster, and Spacek is equal to its every turn ... the film's success is due first and foremost to Spacek"; WP "smartly impersonated ... it's impossible to find fault with her acting or singing"; V "superb"; TT "stunningly good"; LAT "absolutely marvelous ... astonishingly fine ... smashing"; S&S "gets right under the skin of country singer Loretta Lynn"; MFB "superbly played"; Time "convincing"). It was Spacek's second Oscar nomination.

Despite Spacek's impressive haul of trophies in the lead up to the Oscars, some observers thought a victory at the Academy Awards was not a foregone conclusion. "A close race for best actress looms between Sissy Spacek and Mary Tyler Moore," declared Gary Arnold in The Washington Post when the nominations were announced. Acclaimed and beloved for her starring role on one of American television's most lauded, popular and long-running series, the situation comedy 'The Mary Tyler Moore Show', Moore was mentioned by Academy members for playing a role that sharply contrasted with her established image – the cold-hearted mother in the drama *Ordinary People* (NYT "remarkably fine, simultaneously delicate and tough and desperate"; LAT "a stunning portrayal"; CT "superb"; WP "excellent ... plays the part so skilfully, it's possible to take a better view of this character than the creators intended"; BG "superb ... Moore's conception of the character is compelling"; V "brilliantly observed"; TT "exemplary"; MFB "exemplary"; Time "deserves some kind of award"). Moore won the Best Actress (Drama) Golden Globe for her performance and finished as the runner-up to Spacek for the New York and NSFC accolades. The score in New York was 37 points to 20, while the NSFC chose Spacek over Moore 48 points to 27. In the balloting by the Los Angeles critics, Moore finished in third place.

In New York, Moore shared the runner-up position with Goldie Hawn (who finished outright third for the NSFC prize) as a wealthy woman who joins the army in *Private Benjamin*, a comedy on which she was also Executive Producer (NYT "totally charming ... she's an enthusiastic farceur, but her characterization is so firmly based that she can slip from slapstick to romantic comedy and back without losing a beat"; LAT "confirm[s] her status as the screen's top comedienne, scoring a major personal triumph"; Time "does not play with much conviction"; TGM "always enchanting ... never overplaying her hand, she adroitly combines the zaniness of her performance in 'Cactus Flower' with the maturity of 'Shampoo' [and so] convincingly manages the delicate feat of converting a weak girl into an independent woman without sacrificing the character's vulnerable charm"; TT "puts rather a lot of strain on her po-eyed, rag-doll charm"; MFB "Hawn's performance lacks the edge necessary to cut through the enveloping flim-flam"). A previous Best Supporting Actress Oscar winner, Hawn received her second Oscar nomination for her performance.

Also under consideration for the Academy Award were Los Angeles prize runner-up Ellen Burstyn (short-listed for a fifth time) as a woman who discovers she has healing powers in *Resurrection* (NYT "the kind of performance that makes all the odd events in the screenplay seem perfectly plausible ... outstanding"; LAT "a lovely portrayal"; BG "played deftly (and deftly underplayed)"; V "genuinely moving"; TT "plays it with strenuous conviction") and Gena Rowlands who earned her second nomination as a woman protecting a child from the Mafia in *Gloria*, a film directed by her husband John Cassavetes (NYT "Rowlands has a lot of talent and realizes with gusto"; LAT "a wonder ... creating a character of infinite richness and interest"; CT "a marvel ... truly impressive"; WP "Rowlands turns in a Grade-A performance that outshines every flaw the movie has"; BG "brought to life in bravura fashion"; V "excellent"; MFB "a marvellous coup de théâtre ... superlative").

"It's difficult to take exception to any of the nominees for the best actress award," wrote Vincent Canby in The New York Times, "but it does seem a pity that Shelley Duvall was not recognized for her work as Olive Oyl, the performance of her career so far." Duvall had portrayed the beloved cartoon character in *Popeye*, a costly live-action musical comedy adaptation that was one of Hollywood's biggest flops (NYT "Duvall was fated to be the definitive Olive Oyl ... [an] unexpected treasure ... superb"; LAT "highest praise to Shelley Duvall for her deliciously addled, uncoordinated, petulant but finally endearing Olive Oyl. She is exactly the translation from newsprint to film that the whole picture had in mind ... [a] first-rate performance ... absolute high-voiced perfection"; CT "cast perfectly"; WP "she outdoes herself with fluttery, goosey, endearing slapstick solicitude"; BG "perfectly characterized"; S&S "it's hard to imagine anyone but Shelley Duvall as the corncrake Olive Oyl").

Also overlooked were: Nastassja Kinski in *Tess* (NYT "Polanski makes perfect use of her [such that] her placidity and reserve work very beautifully"; NYP "exquisitely acted"; LAT "a performance that is unhistrionic to the point of being anti-histrionic"; WP "[a] fundamentally inadequate performance ... the turbulent emotional reality of Tess remains muted and incomprehensible"); Deborah Raffin in *Touched by Love* (NYT "offers no surprises, and none of the details that might make [the character] interesting"; LAT "persuasive"; V "[a] well-judged, unemphatic performance"); Irene Cara in *Fame* (V "[a] strong performance"; TGM "stunning and impressive"); Dyan Cannon in *Honeysuckle Rose* (CT "credit to Dyan Cannon for pulling off the film's best acting job. She is absolutely convincing"; S&S "[a] rich, earthy performance"; MFB "beautifully played"); Jodie Foster in *Foxes* (NYT "makes 'Foxes' worth seeing ... stunningly direct"; CT "a fine performance"; V "shows more talent than ever in a difficult role"); and Theresa Russell in *Bad Timing* (CT "astonishingly powerful").

1980

In his review in The New York Times of the 1978 Norwegian drama *Formynderne (The Guardians)*, Harold C. Schonberg described Vibeke Løkkeberg's portrayal of the artist Else Kant as "brilliant" and said, "a kind of gleaming intelligence and dedication characterize her work". The film, however, only screened twice as part of the 'Scandinavia: New Film' series at the Museum of Modern Art in New York City in early November 1980. With no qualifying commercial run in Los Angeles County cinema, Løkkeberg's performance was ineligible for Oscar consideration.

The most glaring omission from the list of Oscar nominees, however, was Australian actress Judy Davis for her film debut as the novelist Miles Franklin in the 1979 Australian period drama *My Brilliant Career* (NYP "brilliant"; LAT "sensationally fine ... beautifully acted ... a performance that is so affecting and so right that she appears to be the character rather than to be acting"; CT "convincing ... [the] modest story [is] made memorable by Davis' earnestly engaging and wholly winning performance"; WP "impressive"; BG "her ebullient energy awakens the latent meaning from [the] screenplay and infuses the simple story with appropriate complexity ... she conveys desperation and elation with authentic restraint"; V "fine"; TT "[a] rounded, sympathetic portrait"; S&S "a winning performance"). Less than two weeks before the Oscars, the British Academy awarded Davis the Best Actress BAFTA ahead of a field of candidates that included one of the 1979 Best Actress Oscar nominees and the 1979 Best Supporting Actress Oscar winner. On the eve of the Academy Awards ceremony, in an article in which he picked the favourites from among the nominees in the top categories, Gary Arnold bemoaned in The Washington Post that "the wonderful performance of Judy Davis in 'My Brilliant Career' [is] out of the competition" for the Best Actress statuette.

On the eve of the Oscar ceremony, with *Ordinary People* firming as the favourite for Best Picture among pundits, Bruce McCabe in The Boston Globe declared, "The Academy will go for Moore, hands down. A more deserving choice would be Rowlands, who created a real modern woman out of little more than air in 'Gloria'. Ellen Burstyn struggled heroically to portray an improbable faith healer in 'Resurrection', but was defeated by a deficient and superficial conception, as were Spacek in 'Coal Miner' and Hawn in 'Private Benjamin'." Concurring with this prediction was Gary Arnold who wrote in The Washington Post, "Moore's impersonation of a cold unloving mother after so many years as an endearing comedy star on television represents the sort of about-face comeback that often proves irresistible to Academy voters."

On the big night, however, it was critics' prize-winner Spacek who was chosen by the members of the Academy. The following year, she was among the unsuccessful BAFTA nominees for her work in *Coal Miner's Daughter*.

BEST SUPPORTING ACTOR

ACADEMY AWARDS
Judd Hirsch as 'Dr Tyrone Berger' in *Ordinary People*
• **Timothy Hutton as 'Conrad Jarrett' in *Ordinary People***
Michael O'Keefe as 'Ben Meechum' in *The Great Santini*
Joe Pesci as 'Joey La Motta' in *Raging Bull*
Jason Robards as 'Howard Hughes' in *Melvin and Howard*

GOLDEN GLOBE AWARDS
Judd Hirsch – *Ordinary People*
• **Timothy Hutton – *Ordinary People***
Michael O'Keefe – *The Great Santini*
Joe Pesci – *Raging Bull*
Jason Robards – *Melvin and Howard*

NEW YORK – **Joe Pesci** – ***Raging Bull***
LOS ANGELES – Timothy Hutton – *Ordinary People*
BOARD OF REVIEW – **Joe Pesci** – ***Raging Bull***
NATIONAL SOCIETY – **Joe Pesci** – ***Raging Bull***

Joe Pesci had given up acting and was managing an Italian restaurant when his former co-star Robert De Niro contacted him about playing the brother of boxing champion Jake LaMotta in *Raging Bull* (NYT "superb … remarkable"; LAT "superb"; CT "is equal to De Niro in every scene they have together"; BG "played superbly"). It proved to be the role of a lifetime, garnering Pesci critical acclaim and a slew of accolades including the New York Film Critics Circle, National Board of Review and National Society of Film Critics prizes. Pesci was also the runner-up in the voting by the Los Angeles Film Critics Association and earned a Golden Globe nomination for his portrayal.

Many favoured Pesci to take home the Oscar ahead of the Golden Globe winner Timothy Hutton for his role as the troubled son in *Ordinary People* (NYT "excellent"; NYP "touching"; CT "excellent"; WP "Hutton's performance is the most plausible claim to distinction [for the film] … although the explanation for Conrad's shaky emotional state seems contrived, Hutton's acting never fails to arouse sympathy, and makes the character's anxiety vividly concrete"; BG "superb"; TGM "can be caught calculating his effects"; TT "exemplary"; MFB "exemplary"). Key observers such a Vincent Canby in The New York Times, believed the performances of Hutton and his co-star and fellow nominee Judd Hirsch as the psychiatrist (NYT "splendid"; CT "a workmanlike, no-nonsense performance"; WP "excellent") would "cancel each other out in the final voting". The other nominees were Michael O'Keefe as a domineering Marine pilot's son in *The Great Santini* (NYT "splendid"; LAT "likable"; Time "splendid"; V "terrific"; TT "astonishing"; MFB "excellent") and previous winner and New York prize runner-up Jason Robards for his cameo appearance as Howard Hughes in *Melvin and Howard* (NYT "Robards is not on the screen very long but he is the mythical figure that gives point to the entire fantasy"; LAT "engaging ... delightful"; CT "Robards convinces us that we really are seeing Howard Hughes"; WP "brilliant"; S&S "excellent").

According to Aljean Harmetz of The New York Times, the most surprising omission from the ballot was musician Levon Helm as the father in *Coal Miner's Daughter* (NYT "extraordinary"; WP "submerge[s] so completely in the role") while Vincent Canby wrote that it was "inconceivable but true that 'The Elephant Man' should be nominated for eight awards, including best picture, best direction and best actor, while the performance of Anthony Hopkins is overlooked." Hopkins' work as Dr Treves in *The Elephant Man* had drawn strong praise from critics (NYT "played with humane, quirky compassion"; NYP "[a] performance of rare quality"; LAT "taut and restrained, understated"; WP "[an] agitated performance"; BG "plays Treves sensitively"; V "splendid"; Time "a scrupulously restrained performance")

Other notable absentees were: Cannes honoree Jack Thompson in *Breaker Morant* (NYT "excellent"; LAT "superb"; BG "superlative"; V "[a] standout"; Time "well played"); Leigh Lawson in *Tess* (V "excellent"); Keith Gordon in *Dressed to Kill* (NYT "most appealing"); both Sam Shepard (NYT "excellent"; LAT "a fine, feral performance"; WP "exceptional"; BG "superb"; TT "sharply sketched") and Richard Farnsworth (NYT "succeeds beautifully") in *Resurrection*; Harry Dean Stanton in *Wise Blood* (NYT "first-rate"; FQ "extraordinary"); Slim Pickens in *Honeysuckle Rose* (NYT "[a] strong supporting performance"; LAT "at the peak of his mature powers and a wonder to watch"); and co-stars Robert Morley (WP "a miscalculation"; TGM "especially delightful"), Richard Attenborough (WP "admirable") and Derek Jacobi (WP "particularly impressive"; TGM "played rather spectacularly") in *The Human Factor* (NYT all three "superb ... have never been better"; BG "the acting is sublime").

On Oscar night, there was no split between the *Ordinary People* nominees. The statuette was won by Hutton, the youngest male actor to win an Academy Award. The next day in the Chicago Tribune, Gene Siskel wrote, "the young actor's triumph was marred only by a controversy over whether he belonged in the supporting category when his role clearly was the centre of the movie."

1980

BEST SUPPORTING ACTRESS

ACADEMY AWARDS
Eileen Brennan as 'Capt. Doreen Lewis' in *Private Benjamin*
Eva Le Gallienne as 'Grandma Pearl' in *Resurrection*
Cathy Moriarty as 'Vickie LaMotta' in *Raging Bull*
Diana Scarwid as 'Louise' in *Inside Moves*
• **Mary Steenburgen as 'Lynda Dummar' in *Melvin and Howard***

GOLDEN GLOBE AWARDS
Lucie Arnaz – *The Jazz Singer*
Beverly D'Angelo – *Coal Miner's Daughter*
Cathy Moriarty – *Raging Bull*
• **Mary Steenburgen – *Melvin and Howard***
Debra Winger – *Urban Cowboy*

NEW YORK – Mary Steenburgen – *Melvin and Howard*
LOS ANGELES – Mary Steenburgen – *Melvin and Howard*
BOARD OF REVIEW – Eva Le Gallienne – *Resurrection*
NATIONAL SOCIETY – Mary Steenburgen – *Melvin and Howard*

Mary Steenburgen dominated the awards season with her role in *Melvin and Howard* (NYT "enchanting"; LAT "endearing"; V "gives the picture a very welcome center of warmth and humanity"; S&S "excellent"; MFB "superb"). She collected the New York Film Critics Circle, Los Angeles Film Critics Association and National Society of Film Critics awards, as well as the Golden Globe and the Academy Award.

The only prize Steenburgen didn't collect was the National Board of Review plaudit, which was presented to Eva Le Gallienne for her performance as the grandmother of a faith healer in *Resurrection* (NYT "excellent"; G "superb"; TT "sharply sketched").

Both women were recognised by the Academy along with: Eileen Brennan as an army captain in *Private Benjamin* (NYT "she's never been seen to such good effect in a film"; MFB "[her] performance is pitched so high that all credibility soon evaporates"); Diana Scarwid as a waitress in *Inside Moves* (NYT "excellent"; LAT "marvelous"; WP "[the role is] ideally embodied by the attractive, forthright young actress Diana Scarwid"; V "hits the right notes") and Cathy Moriarty for her film debut as boxer Jack LaMotta's second wife in *Raging Bull* (NYT "superb ... comes across with the assurance of an Actors Studio veteran"; LAT "just about perfect"; CT "a true discovery"; V "never adequately fills in the blanks of the character"). Moriarty was a most unlikely Academy Award contender having had no acting experience of any kind prior to being cast in *Raging Bull*. She landed the role after three months of script readings for the director opposite Robert De Niro and Joe Pesci, who had discovered the teenager after seeing her photograph in a slide show at a disco in Mt Vernon, New York. "They told me that I fit the role, I fit the character" she later explained to Judy Klemesrud in an interview for The New York Times, "The real Vickie had a deep voice and a Bronx accent, and so did I. They wanted someone like that. And they also wanted someone whose reactions would be natural and real, and I think the fact that I had never acted before helped me to be that way."

Overlooked were: Blythe Danner as a marine's wife in *The Great Santini* (NYT "lovely work"; LAT "affecting"; CT "a fine, necessarily understated performance"; Time "splendid"; TT "extraordinary"; MFB "excellent"); Charlotte Rampling as an actress in *Stardust Memories* (NYT "excellent"; S&S "a handsome performance"); Elizabeth McGovern as the girlfriend in *Ordinary People* (NYT "makes memorable the small role of the troubled son's girlfriend"; LAT "[a] good portrayal"); Shelley Duvall as the terrified wife in *The Shining* (CT "[she] is wasted in scene after scene in which she's required to play a typical burnt-out American housewife."; BG "Nicholson is supported superbly by Shelley Duvall"); Helen Mirren in the poorly received *Caligula* (NYT "truly seems to be acting when all around her are merely performing"); Pamela Reed in both *Melvin and Howard* and *The Long Riders* (WP "impressive … is so good as Belle Starr that it seems a pity she never evolves into a major character"); both Mary Nell Santacroce as the landlady (NYT "first-rate") and Amy Wright as the teenage girl (NYT "first-rate"; MFB "brilliant") in *Wise Blood*; Lois Smith in *Resurrection* (NYT "excellent"); and Angela Winkler as the mother in *Die Blechtrommel (The Tin Drum)* (NYT "remarkable").

The most glaring omissions, however, were two of the Globe nominees: Beverly D'Angelo as singer Patsy Cline in *Coal Miner's Daughter* (NYT "extraordinary [in] a brief but astonishingly sharp impression"; LAT "notable"; CT "exceptional [and] compelling"; WP "a dazzling impersonation"; V "a stellar performance") and New York and NSFC runner-up Debra Winger in *Urban Cowboy* (NYT "splendid"; LAT "very impressive"; V "outstanding"; TGM "she is exactly right for the kinda-cute, kinda-sexy, independent Sissy"; MFB "an attractive performance"). Vincent Canby in The New York Times declared Winger "may turn out to have been the movie find of 1980".

BEST PICTURE

ACADEMY AWARDS

Atlantic City
  (Paramount, 104 mins, 3 Apr 1981, $12.7m, 5 noms)
• *Chariots of Fire*
  (Enigma, The Ladd Co., Warner Bros., 124 mins, 25 Sep 1981, $58.9m, 7 noms)
On Golden Pond
  (ITC, IPC, Universal, 109 mins, 22 Jan 1982, $119.3m, 10 noms)
Raiders of the Lost Ark
  (Lucasfilm, Paramount, 115 mins, 12 Jun 1981, $242.4m, 8 noms)
Reds
  (JRS, Paramount, 194 mins, 4 Dec 1981, $40.4m, 12 noms)

GOLDEN GLOBE AWARDS

(Drama)	(Comedy/Musical)
The French Lieutenant's Woman	**• *Arthur***
• *On Golden Pond*	*The Four Seasons*
Prince of the City	*Pennies from Heaven*
Ragtime	*S.O.B.*
Reds	*Zoot Suit*

BRITISH ACADEMY AWARDS

Atlantic City
• *Chariots of Fire*
The French Lieutenant's Woman
Gregory's Girl
Raiders of the Lost Ark

NEW YORK – *Reds*
LOS ANGELES – *Atlantic City*
BOARD OF REVIEW – *Chariots of Fire* and *Reds*
NATIONAL SOCIETY – *Atlantic City*
LONDON – *Chariots of Fire*

The frontrunner for the Best Picture Academy Award was *Reds*, Warren Beatty's three-hour drama about journalist John Reed and writer Louise Bryant at the time of the Russian Revolution (NYT "an extraordinary film, a big romantic adventure movie [and] a commercial movie with a rare sense of history"; NYP "marvelous"; LAT "big and beautiful ... [an] intimate epic"; CT "instead of being a history lesson, 'Reds' is much more a tempestuous love story ... a mammoth production that at its core is really just an extended on-screen romance"; WP "an earnestly muddled mish-mash ... an intriguing, ambitious disappointment"; BG "a crock ... a pretentious, over-blown, tedious soap opera"; V "too ponderous and unwieldy"; Time "entertaining"). The film won the New York Film Critics Circle's Best Picture prize, shared the National Board of Review award and claimed the Directors Guild of America honour for Beatty. It also had a leading tally of Oscar nominations. The film's twelve mentions included nods in all top seven categories (Picture, Director, Screenplay and the four acting categories and was a greater tally than garnered by any film since 1966). *Reds*, however, was not a runaway favourite. Also nominated were the Golden Globe (Drama) winner, two other prize-winning films, and the year's box office champ.

The sentimental favourite for the Oscar was *On Golden Pond*, the film version of a popular Broadway play, in which Hollywood veterans Henry Fonda and Katharine Hepburn co-starred for the first time (NYT "a mixed blessing"; LAT "[an] unstrident, gentle film"; CT "a beautiful film"; WP "the shallowest heartwarmer in recent memory ... presumes far too smugly and ineptly on moviegoing good will and nostalgia"; V "a class act"; TGM "unapologetically sentimental"). The film had outpolled *Reds* to win the Globe (Drama) and had received ten nominations from the Academy.

The two dark horses were *Atlantic City* and *Chariots of Fire*, two foreign-made dramas that had been contenders for the Best Foreign Film Golden Globe. *Atlantic City* was an independent Canadian-French film shot in Canada under the direction of Frenchman Louis Malle. It starred another Hollywood veteran, Burt Lancaster, as an ageing mobster fascinated by an aspiring croupier (NYT "a rich, gaudy cinema trip ... sometimes rueful and sometimes funny"; LAT "captivating ... an off-beat love story and an affectionate satire of American pop culture, past and present"; CT "distinguished"; WP "a cleverly contrived and sweetly realized romantic fable"; BG "a diverting interesting film [with] an offbeat luminosity"). It had first won acclaim at the 1980 Venice Film Festival where it was named Best Picture. It finished third in the New York voting, and was awarded Best Picture by the Los Angeles Film Critics Association and the National Society of Film Critics. It was, however, the least nominated of all the Best Picture contenders. *Chariots of Fire*, meanwhile, was a British drama about athletes at the 1924 Olympic Games (NYT "unashamedly rousing ... emotionally involving ... an exceptional film"; LAT "majestic ... masterful, exultant, triumphant and joyful"; CT "a breath of fresh air"; WP "moving"; BG "glorious ... a rich, dense, textured story ... one of the best films of recent years ... an emotionally invigorating, inspiring and even exhilarating cinematic experience"; V "a winner"; TT "a film of substance and intelligence"; S&S "curiously affecting"). *Chariots of Fire* finished fourth in the New York voting and unexpectedly shared the NBR honour with *Reds*. In the week before the Oscars, it outpolled *Atlantic City* for two awards: the Best Foreign Film Globe and then, in the middle of the Oscar voting period, the British Academy Award for Best Film.

The Oscar long-shot was Steven Spielberg's box office hit *Raiders of the Lost Ark* (NYT "one of the most deliriously funny, ingenious and stylish American adventure movies ever made"; LAT "hurrah and hallelujah! ... unabashedly wide-eyed and exaggerated"; CT "entertaining ... full of upbeat thrills ... a cheerful, thrilling adventure ... most likely will become one of your all-time favourite entertainments"; WP "sensational ... awesomely entertaining ... a transcendent blend of heroic exploits, cliffhangers and wit"; BG "a rip-snorting action-adventure movie ... an exciting roller-coaster ride ... consistently entertaining and diverting"; V "a cracker jack fantasy-adventure ... a perfect balance between escapist fun and hard-edged action").

The most glaring absentee from the list of Oscar contenders was Sidney Lumet's *Prince of the City*, a drama about police corruption which had been the runner-up for the top New York prize and had polled third in the NSFC balloting (NYT "a crisp, thrilling adventure ... begins with the strength and confidence of a great film, and ends merely as a good one ... but it's exciting and impressive all the same"; LAT "this beautifully photographed, rich, dark, somber work balances somewhere between lecture and moral lesson"; WP "extremely powerful"; BG "a sensational film ... fascinating, gripping and quite compelling"; V "a powerhouse, emotionally-charged drama ... strong critical kudos and major awards loom assuredly on the horizon"). The other notable absentee was Milos Forman's *Ragtime*, which had garnered eight Oscar nominations in minor categories (NYT "sorrowful, funny and beautiful [yet] also, finally, very unsatisfactory ... a major disappointment, but it's a lively, provocative one"; LAT "[a] rich, intricate, often bewildering film"; CT "a great movie ... one of the very best of the year ... an extraordinarily rich tapestry of America"; WP "picturesque but tedious"; BG "except for the evocative sets and upbeat musical score, 'Ragtime' is better read than seen").

Other films by-passed for consideration were: the Globe (Comedy/Musical) winner *Arthur* (NYT "a terrifically engaging, high-spirited screwball comedy"; LAT "simply top-flight ... an eminently satisfying movie ... irresistible"; WP "charming ... witty and adroit ... the biggest little sleeper of the season"; CT "particularly disappointing"; BG "a delightful comedy"); *Body Heat* (NYT "a gritty, steamy, amoral and thoroughly satisfying melodrama"; LAT "has two qualities rarely found in movies with a steambath sexual content: intelligence and fun"; WP "absorbing entertainment"; BG "a pretentious, predictable film noir melodrama ... extraordinarily cold"; TGM "a respectable resurrection of classic suspense melodrama"; MFB "the pleasures it affords are undeniable [but] it is equally obvious that nothing new is being offered beneath the gloss"); *True Confessions* (NYT "the year's best mystery film [and] quite simply one of the most entertaining, most intelligent and most thoroughly satisfying commercial American films in a very long time"; LAT "as engrossing, as rich in detail, and as fascinating a portrait of corruption and ethnicity as we have had from an American director in years"; WP "remains an anticlimactic story in the last analysis"; BG "a fine, slick, moody and polished piece of work that insinuates itself subtly and ambiguously into your consciousness"); Globe nominee *Pennies from Heaven* (NYT "startlingly bold and risky ... [but] not easy to respond to"; LAT "fascinating to watch ... [but] cold"; WP "a rejuvenating, landmark achievement in the evolution of Hollywood musicals ... certainly the finest American movie of 1981"; BG "one of the best films of the year"; V "hopelessly esoteric ... virtually no artistic payoff"; TGM "disappointing"; MFB "remarkable"); Globe and BAFTA nominee *The French Lieutenant's Woman* (NYT "astonishingly beautiful ... an immaculately visualized adaptation"; CT "conventionally entertaining but also a serious piece"; WP "an unfailing visual treat ... handsome and evocative ... absorbing"; BG "intriguingly ambiguous and intriguing enough to be diverting"; V "ultimately most affecting"; FQ "exceptional ... easily one of the best movies of the year"); the Australian war film *Gallipoli* (NYT "has an uncommon beauty, warmth and immediacy"; LAT "a singularly intelligent entertainment"; CT "unimpressive"; BG "not a great work of art or an innovative war movie ... but succeeds because you care what happens to the main characters"; V "highly entertaining"; S&S "undeniably impressive"); the Brazilian drama *Pixote: A Leido Mais Fraco (Pixote)* (NYT "uncompromisingly grim"; LAT "a great and anguishing film ... extraordinary"; CT "a film that gains its greatness from urgency and truthfulness"; BG "a devastating film, one with compelling – and sometimes distasteful – imagery"; V "social exposé of the first order ... vivid"; MFB "little more than titillation"); and François Truffaut's *Le Dernier Métro (The Last Metro)* (NYT "dazzling"; CT "puzzling and beautiful"; WP "undramatic"; BG "elegant and exquisite ... triumphs as an homage to the theater"; MFB "does not resonate").

Atlantic City was the only Best Picture nominee to go unrecognised on Oscar night. *On Golden Pond* and *Reds* each collected three statuettes. *Raiders of the Lost Ark* garnered four awards and a special Oscar for sound effects editing. Surprising all the pundits was *Chariots of Fire*, which claimed four Academy Awards, including the Best Picture statuette. The Times in London described the Best Picture result as "the stunning surprise of the evening." It was the first time that a non-American film had claimed the Best Picture Oscar since *Oliver!* in 1968. As Beatty had won Best Director for *Reds*, the win also marked the first occasion that the Best Picture and Director statuettes had been presented to different films since 1972.

BEST DIRECTOR

ACADEMY AWARDS
• **Warren Beatty for** *Reds*
Hugh Hudson for *Chariots of Fire*
Louis Malle for *Atlantic City*
Mark Rydell for *On Golden Pond*
Steven Spielberg for *Raiders of the Lost Ark*

GOLDEN GLOBE AWARDS
• **Warren Beatty** – *Reds*
Milos Forman – *Ragtime*
Sidney Lumet – *Prince of the City*
Louis Malle – *Atlantic City*
Mark Rydell – *On Golden Pond*
Steven Spielberg – *Raiders of the Lost Ark*

DIRECTORS GUILD AWARD
• **Warren Beatty** – *Reds*
Hugh Hudson – *Chariots of Fire*
Louis Malle – *Atlantic City*
Mark Rydell – *On Golden Pond*
Steven Spielberg
   – *Raiders of the Lost Ark*

BRITISH ACADEMY AWARDS
Bill Forsyth – *Gregory's Girl*
Hugh Hudson – *Chariots of Fire*
• **Louis Malle** – *Atlantic City*
Karel Reisz
   – *The French*
   Lieutenant's Woman

NEW YORK – **Sidney Lumet** – *Prince of the City*
LOS ANGELES – **Warren Beatty** – *Reds*
BOARD OF REVIEW – **Warren Beatty** – *Reds*
NATIONAL SOCIETY – **Louis Malle** – *Atlantic City*
LONDON – **Andrzej Wajda** – *Czlowiek z Zelaza (Man of Iron)*

For the second year in a row, a previous Best Actor nominee was the favourite to win the Academy Award for Best Director. Three years after becoming the second person in Oscar history (after Orson Welles in 1941) to receive simultaneous nominations in the acting, writing and directing categories and as the producer of a Best Picture nominee, Warren Beatty achieved the feat again with four mentions for the historical drama *Reds*, his second outing as a director, which was the year's most nominated film and the frontrunner for the Academy's Best Picture statuette (NYT "the film's scenes of epic events are stunning, but so are the intimate moments"; LAT "gives [the history] full weight

... [and] serves his fellow actors marvelously well"; CT "theatrical and phony"; WP "the movie is undermined by his failure to rise to the peculiar grandeur of the love story"). During the award season Beatty won the Los Angeles Film Critics Association and National Board of Review prizes, the Golden Globe Award and the Directors Guild of America honour.

Beatty only finished fourth, however, in the voting by the New York Film Critics Circle (with 20 points). Outpolling him were: Sidney Lumet, who took the prize, for the police corruption drama *Prince of the City*, with 33 points (NYT "delineated beautifully ... Lumet's economy in parts of this film is simply dazzling"; WP "scrupulous in avoiding simplistics ... as a director, Lumet is clinical and methodical [and] virtually every characterization, down to the most minor, is meticulously and earthily detailed"; BG "a virtuoso showcase for the talent and energies of writer-director Sidney Lumet"); Louis Malle for the independent film *Atlantic City*, with 26 points (LAT "astute"; WP "sweetly realized ... keeps a discreetly observed distance, allowing the performers to interact and the setting to reinforce their scheming and dreaming"; BG "what Malle has done in 'Atlantic City' is to transform a tacky, seedy, but highly resonant resort area and its used, somewhat soiled inhabitants and habitués into a film that is far more compelling than it has any right to be"); and Hugh Hudson for the British historical drama *Chariots of Fire*, with 25 points (NYT "it's to the credit of Mr Hudson that [the film] is simultaneously romantic and commonsensical, lyrical and comic"; LAT "masterful"; CT "an immaculately made film ... impressive"; BG "a quite splendid piece of work ... fully realized, fully integrated ... Hudson makes a brilliant debut as a feature film director"; TT "limited"). The New York winner and runner-up were also the main contenders for the National Society of Film Critics accolade, but finished in a different order. Malle claimed the honour ahead of Lumet by 40 points to 27. Trailing Lumet in third place by just a single vote was Brazilian director Hector Babenco for *Pixote: A Leido Mais Fraco (Pixote)* (NYT "finely made"; WP "rambles").

Although he was short-listed by the Hollywood Foreign Press Association, in a major surprise, Lumet was excluded from Oscar consideration. It was the fourth year in a row that the New York winner had been overlooked. Others shut-out by the Academy were: Los Angeles runner-up Lawrence Kasdan for his directorial debut *Body Heat* (NYT "extraordinarily accomplished direction ... emerges as a member of the American directing elite"; WP "an impressive directing debut"; BG "takes a detached approach ... he dispassionately records the characters ... it's this contradiction between style and content that irrevocably leads to the film's destruction"); previous winner and Globe nominee Milos Forman for *Ragtime* (LAT "patchy"; BG "he misinterprets essential segments of the novel"; V "superbly crafted"); Australian director Peter

Weir for *Gallipoli* (WP "Weir's solemnity becomes so exaggerated that the entire presentation is robbed of human interest"; BG "Weir understands the key to drama is character [so] he creates likeable human beings with whom audiences can identify, instead of the metallic figures that zip and zap around in the heads of many American filmmakers"; V "admirable"); Ulu Grosbard for *True Confessions* (NYT "Grosbard's direction is just about flawless"; WP "confirms Grosbard's admirable concentration on the nuances of performance and setting [and] expands his range by evoking a fascinating period setting"; BG "the film's alternatingly oblique and neon style and tone combine to keep it interesting and unpredictable"; TGM "[his] style is in opposition to the content"; MGB "heavy-handed"); BAFTA nominee Karel Reisz for *The French Lieutenant's Woman* (CT "beautifully made"; BG "a clever, skilful, original interpretation of a literary enterprise"; Obs "carefully crafted"; FQ "crucial to the success of the project"; S&S "Reisz's direction remains too strictly detached"); and François Truffaut for *Le Dernier Métro (The Last Metro)* (NYT "at his very best"; CT "beautifully made"; BG "signifies the return to the front rank of one of the great directors ... inspired ... Truffaut's attention to the intricate fabric of his film that makes it such a pleasure to watch"; TGM "perfect moviemaking").

Instead the Academy selected the same five directors that had been short-listed for the Guild prize. Beatty earned his second mention as a director by Oscar voters, while Steven Spielberg was also named for a second time for the box office hit *Raiders of the Lost Ark* (WP "Spielberg's timing always keeps him ahead of the audience"; BG "an assured, relaxed, impressive work"; V "deft"). Hudson was included for the first time, as was Mark Rydell for *On Golden Pond* (NYT "the gooiness of Mr Rydell's direction, which, when in doubt, cuts to lyrical shots of the sun-dappled waters, of loons paddling and lily petals glistening with dew ... one more drop of dew and this movie would have drowned"; LAT "may initially have seemed an outside choice [but he has] surprised everyone [as] the film's emotional sequences are perfectly realized"). Also acknowledged for the first time was New York runner-up and NSFC champion Malle, the French husband of previous Best Supporting Actress nominee Candice Bergen. It was the first time since 1964 that the five directors of the five Best Picture Oscar nominees were all under consideration for the Best Director statuette.

The Academies in London and Hollywood both gave their top awards to *Chariots of Fire*. Neither, however, honoured Hudson, the film's director. The British Academy honoured Malle for *Atlantic City*, while on the other side of the Atlantic, Beatty was presented with the Academy Award for *Reds* (he was unsuccessful at his three other nominations on Oscar night).

BEST ACTOR

ACADEMY AWARDS
Warren Beatty as 'John Reed' in *Reds*
• **Henry Fonda as 'Norman Thayer, Jr.' in *On Golden Pond***
Burt Lancaster as 'Lou' in *Atlantic City*
Dudley Moore as 'Arthur Bach' in *Arthur*
Paul Newman as 'Michael Gallagher' in *Absence of Malice*

GOLDEN GLOBE AWARDS

(Drama)
Warren Beatty – *Reds*
• **Henry Fonda – *On Golden Pond***
Timothy Hutton – *Taps*
Burt Lancaster – *Atlantic City*
Treat Williams – *Prince of the City*

(Comedy/Musical)
Alan Alda – *The Four Seasons*
George Hamilton
   – *Zorro, The Gay Blade*
Walter Matthau
   – *First Monday in October*
• **Dudley Moore – *Arthur***
Steve Martin – *Pennies from Heaven*

BRITISH ACADEMY AWARDS
Robert De Niro – *Raging Bull*
Bob Hoskins – *The Long Good Friday*
Jeremy Irons – *The French Lieutenant's Woman*
• **Burt Lancaster – *Atlantic City***

NEW YORK – **Burt Lancaster** – *Atlantic City*
LOS ANGELES – **Burt Lancaster** – *Atlantic City*
BOARD OF REVIEW – **Henry Fonda** – *On Golden Pond*
NATIONAL SOCIETY – **Burt Lancaster** – *Atlantic City*

The early frontrunner for the year's Best Actor accolades was sixty-eight-year old Hollywood veteran Burt Lancaster for his performance as an ageing gangster fascinated by an aspiring young croupier in *Atlantic City*. His performance garnered praise at the 1980 Venice Film Festival and was further lauded when the film was released in the United States the following April (NYT "excellent ... one of Mr Lancaster's most remarkable creations, a complex mixture of the mingy and magnificent"; NYP "superb"; LAT "has imparted dignity to the man he plays so very well ... Lancaster catches us completely in the man's dreams"; CT "perfectly cast"; WP "the most satisfying single aspect of the film ... a disarmingly beautiful characterization, an elderly grace note to an exceptional starring career ... Lancaster is at once believable and endearing"; BG "the film is illuminated by [his] performance").

In early December, however, another Hollywood veteran emerged as a contender for the end of year prizes: seventy-six-year old Henry Fonda as a retired university professor in *On Golden Pond*, a film that also starred his daughter, Jane Fonda, and another veteran Hollywood star, Katharine Hepburn, neither of whom he had previously appeared with on screen (NYT "one of the great performances of his long, truly distinguished career ... film acting of the highest order"; LAT "may be Henry Fonda's finest screen performance ... in this straightforward, deceptively simple performance there's the distillation of everything Fonda has mastered"; CT "excellent"; V "superb"; TGM "impressive ... a great performance"; TT "devastating").

The two men dominated the critics' prizes. Lancaster was named Best Actor by the National Society of Film Critics, both the New York Film Critics Circle and Los Angeles Film Critics Association, and the British Academy Award. Fonda, meanwhile, won the National Board of Review plaudit and the Golden Globe as Best Actor (Drama), and finished as the runner-up in New York (Lancaster won convincingly 58 points to 27).

Lancaster was nominated for the Oscar for a fourth time (he had last been included in 1962). Fonda earned a second nod, having gone unrecognised since he had been the unsuccessful favourite for *The Grapes of Wrath* in 1940 (the gap of forty-one years between consecutive nominations was a new record). While both were considered strong candidates for the statuette, Fonda was seen as the favourite. "Even though the Academy members have yet to cast a vote, many critics are convinced that Henry Fonda will walk away with this year's Best Actor award," said Chris Chase in The New York Times, "Given the pure, burning quality of the Fonda performance, it isn't surprising that an Oscar should be predicted for him. What *is* surprising is that it would be his first." Lancaster was already an Oscar winner while Fonda had never won, although he had been presented with an honorary award from the Academy "in recognition of his brilliant accomplishments and enduring contribution to the art of motion pictures" at the 1981 ceremony.

Overshadowed by the two veteran Hollywood stars were the other three nominees: Warren Beatty, who received his third nomination as Best Actor for his turn as a communist journalist in *Reds*, the film for which he won the Best Director statuette (NYT "fine"; LAT "what you don't get from Beatty's performance is Reed's pain or his complexity"; CT "his acting style, which can slip into a narcissistic pose now and then, serves the film poorly"; WP "too lightweight to impersonate [his] literary character ... it's dismaying to find the leading performance so deficient in animal or intellectual magnetism"; BG "a stereotype"); Dudley Moore, the winner of the Globe (Comedy/Musical), as a drunken millionaire playboy in *Arthur* (NYT "uninhibitedly comic [and] his timing is magical"; LAT "manages to engender true empathy for a millionaire ... [his] timing [is] perfection"; CT "simply Dudley Moore getting bombed"; WP "the most ingratiating role of [his] film career"; BG "played with absolutely devastating insouciance ... a virtuoso performance of light comedy"; V "a delightful riot throughout"); and Paul Newman, who was mentioned for a fifth time, for his performance as a Florida businessman in *Absence of Malice* (NYT "one of Mr Newman's better characters in years"; NYP "good"; CT "[the film] is not totally without appeal, which can be found principally in the characterization turned in by Newman, his best [in years] ... manages to keep his character's motivation nicely under wraps, and the drama of what's going to happen to him does capture our attention"; BG "the strongest aspect of the film is Paul Newman's superb performance ... Newman is actually a revelation in this film"; TGM "artificial").

The Los Angeles Times reported the selection of Newman was considered by industry insiders as "something of a surprise", a view shared by Gene Siskel in the Chicago Tribune. "Newman was the best thing about the frequently preposterous 'Absence of Malice'," Siskel wrote, "but [his] nominated performance doesn't compare to the much more sophisticated work of Treat Williams in 'Prince of the City' ... Williams avoided turning his character of narcotics cop Danny Ciello into a simple good-guy-against-the-bad-guys role. Williams portrayed a character filled with vanity, naiveté, fear and courage ... His performance was so dark and uptight that Ciello came across realistically." Widely praised by critics, Williams' performance in *Prince of the City* had been considered by many to be certain to receive a nomination (NYT "competent and plausible throughout the film and sometimes much better than that, never brings to Danny's lonely moments the depth or importance that might make him more tragic than confused ... he does his best work in the early part of the story"; LAT "in the exhausting central role, Williams is adequate in most of the nuts and bolts scenes but he never conveys implacable authority and he simply isn't up to the technical demands of Ciello's increasingly pressured outbursts"; WP "summons his battery of resources to give Ciello volatility and depth on the screen ... one might be able to find false notes or over-exertions in this performance, but nobody could say it wasn't absolutely relentless"; BG "a blistering, brilliant performance"; V "outstanding").

Prior to the announcement of the nominations, meanwhile, Ivor Davis, the Hollywood correspondent for The Globe and Mail, had likewise considered Robert Duvall to be a "strong contender" for the Oscar for his performance as the cynical cop in *True Confessions* (NYT "marvelously acted"; LAT "[a] performance of the greatest intelligence, understatement and elegance"; CT "a delight"; BG "[a] subtle but exquisite, powerful and superbly realized performance ... Duvall illuminates the cliché of the tired, tainted cop with his own intriguing brand of compressed energy"; V "excellent"; TGM "much of [the film's] fascination is due to Robert Duvall, who gives what would be the performance of any other actor's career [but for him is] just another perfect pearl on what has become an extremely long string"; MFB "strong"). Duvall had finished third in the voting by the critics' circle in New York but was ignored by the Actors Branch of the Academy, as was his co-star Robert De Niro as the priest (NYT "marvelously acted"; CT "compelling [and] riveting "; WP "it's peculiarly satisfying to see De Niro playing a controlled, intellectual personality ... he brings absolute conviction to [the role]"; BG "gives one of his best – and most compressed – performances ... [his] performance is chiefly in his eyes and his canny facial expressions"; MFB "strong"). Perhaps Oscar voters were simply unable to choose between the two actors. As critic Sheila Benson had opined in the Los Angeles Times, "Somehow, De Niro and Duvall seem to have achieved a blended performance, to share the same genes, tics and little familial gestures. It is a memorable duet." It was a view echoed by Vincent Canby in The New York Times who wrote, "Mr De Niro and Mr Duvall are at the peak of their talents here. They work so beautifully together it sometimes seems like a single performance, two sides of the same complex character."

Others overlooked by the Academy were: previous winner and NSFC runner-up Gene Hackman in *All Night Long* (LAT "a charming and appealing performance"; CT "a decent low-key portrayal of a man having a mid-life crisis"; WP "the most endearing role of his career ... reflects the reawakening of pride, humor and vitality in George subtly"; BG "underplayed with gratifying deftness"; TGM "a flawless characterization"); Globe nominee Steve Martin in *Pennies from Heaven* (NYT "Martin is something of a revelation as a dance-man"; LAT "though he learned to dance admirably and performs with likable earnestness, stays confusingly unfocused as the central figure"; WP "played with riveting intensity ... [his] performance figures to astonish both fans and detractors"; BG "extraordinary"; TGM "does a little bit of everything (sings, dances, cracks jokes) without doing any of it more than a little bit well"); BAFTA nominee Jeremy Irons in *The French Lieutenant's Woman* (NYT "completely convincing"; BG "a fine job ...[he and Streep] bring to life what is essentially a literary conceit"; V "remarkable"); William Hurt as the slow-witted Florida lawyer in *Body Heat* (NYT "does a wonderful job of bringing Nick to life ... Hurt establishes himself as an instantly affable screen star"; BG "a splendid performance"; TGM "Hurt is so good at capturing the charming and chilling Ned that he almost makes up for the film's weaknesses"; MFB "[a] flawless performance"); Marcello Mastroianni in *La Citta delle Donna (City of Women)* (NYT "has never been better ... a supremely accomplished performance, modest and grand, broadly comic at times, even touching in its details"; LAT "impeccable"; WP "endows [the character] with an endearing foolishness that invites far-reaching human sympathy"); Nick Mancuso as the man drawn into a religious cult in the Canadian horror film *Ticket to Heaven* (NYT "Manusco makes [the character's] transformation disturbing and understandable"; LAT "Manusco' performance is surely among the year's best. It comes so deeply from within that before our eyes he seems transformed from a husky, darkly good-looking young man into terrified, ascetic shell of his former self"; CT "beautifully performed"; WP "a phenomenal job, sustaining a complex, turbulent portrait"); Christopher Walken in *The Dogs of War* (NYT "unusually convincing in a difficult, hermetic kind of role ... [a] haunted, severely unsentimental performance"; LAT "lacks the starry magnetism essential to make us care much about the character"; CT "[the film] is fired by Christopher Walken's compressed performance ... the movie is redeemed by Walken who understands the character's fundamental drive to kill ... plays the amoral anti-hero with a precise touch of paranoia and never gives in to any indulgent impulses"; WP "impenetrable"; TGM "given nothing to hang his character on, he simply hides behind those high cheek bones and that glazed stare"); previous winner Richard Dreyfuss as a quadriplegic sculptor in *Whose Life is It Anyway?* (NYT "the film is measurably diminished every time he leaves the screen ... [the film is] held chiefly together by the wit and animation Mr Dreyfuss brings to his role ... [he is able] to bring power and pathos to the rest of the drama"; BG "a superb, memorable performance"; MFB "thoroughly competent"); Jeff Bridges in *Cutter's Way* (also released as *Cutter and Bone*) (LAT "another fully realized portrait"; CT "continues to be impressive in film after film"; WP "[character is] brilliantly embodied in the film by Jeff Bridges"; BG "[a] first-rate performance"); Alan Bates in *Quartet* (NYT "remarkably interesting characterization"; LAT "excellent"; WP "effective [and] remarkable"; BG "the performances of Bates and Smith crackle with acerbic wit"); and Gérard Depardieu in *Le Dernier Métro (The Last Metro)* (NYT "splendid"; CT "first rate ... acquits himself well here"; BG "Depardieu's portrayal of an instinctive and sensitive stage actor is rich, subtle and luminous"; TGM "[he] is a good actor but he's not able to play one; his miscasting is woeful").

On Oscar night, over four decades after he had first been favoured to do so, Fonda finally won the Best Actor Academy Award. Too ill to attend the ceremony, the statuette was collected by Jane Fonda. "Oh Dad," she said at the podium as she held her father's award, "I'm so happy and proud for you." Just five months later, Henry Fonda passed away. He was posthumously nominated for *On Golden Pond* by the British Academy the following year, but was outpolled by the winner of that year's Best Actor Oscar, Ben Kingsley in *Gandhi*.

BEST ACTRESS

ACADEMY AWARDS
• **Katharine Hepburn as 'Ethel Thayer' in *On Golden Pond***
Diane Keaton as 'Louise Bryant' in *Reds*
Marsha Mason as 'Georgia Hines' in *Only When I Laugh*
Susan Sarandon as 'Sally' in *Atlantic City*
Meryl Streep as 'Sarah Woodruff' and 'Anna' in *The French Lieutenant's Woman*

GOLDEN GLOBE AWARDS

(Drama)
Sally Field – *Absence of Malice*
Katharine Hepburn – *On Golden Pond*
Diane Keaton – *Reds*
Sissy Spacek – *Raggedy Man*
• **Meryl Streep – *The French Lieutenant's Woman***

(Comedy/Musical)
Blair Brown – *Continental Divide*
Carol Burnett – *The Four Seasons*
Jill Clayburgh
  – *First Monday in October*
Liza Minnelli – *Arthur*
• **Bernadette Peters
  – *Pennies from Heaven***

BRITISH ACADEMY AWARDS
Mary Tyler Moore – *Ordinary People*
Maggie Smith – *Quartet*
Sissy Spacek – *Coal Miner's Daughter*
• **Meryl Streep – *The French Lieutenant's Woman***

NEW YORK – Glenda Jackson – *Stevie*
LOS ANGELES – Meryl Streep – *The French Lieutenant's Woman*
BOARD OF REVIEW – Glenda Jackson – *Stevie*
NATIONAL SOCIETY – Marília Pêra – *Pixote: A Leido Mais Fraco (Pixote)*

Two years after winning the Best Supporting Actress Oscar for *Kramer vs Kramer*, Meryl Streep was the early favourite to win the Best Actress statuette for her dual roles as a nineteenth century English woman and the contemporary actress portraying her in a movie, in *The French Lieutenant's Woman* (NYT "acted to the elegant hilt ... has never been more in command of her talent as she switches back and forth between the lightweight movie actress and the tragic Sarah"; NYP "remarkable"; LAT "luminous ... both a theatrical performance and a naturalistic characterization"; WP "film critics are overrating Meryl Streep's performance as this ambiguous cipher"; BG "a fine job ... [she and Irons] bring to life what is essentially a literary conceit"; V "never a false note in the sharply contrasting characterizations"; FQ "exceptional ... in both roles"; Obs "brilliantly played"). Streep was named Best Actress by the Los Angeles Film Critics Association (her second plaudit from the group), but was out-polled for the other three critics' awards.

In a highly unusual scenario, both the New York Film Critics Circle and the National Board of Review Best Actress accolades were won by an actress whose performance had been nominated for the Golden Globe (Drama) three years earlier: Glenda Jackson as the late English poet Stevie Smith in the British drama *Stevie* (NYT "splendid ... extraordinary [and] profoundly moving"). The film had been screened in Los Angeles in 1978 in order to qualify for Globe and Oscar consideration, but did not play in a New York City cinema until June 1981. At the end of the year, Jackson was recognised by the New York critics and the NBR but was ineligible for the Academy Award having already been overlooked three years earlier.

In another surprise, the National Society of Film Critics selected Marília Pêra as Best Actress for her turn as a prostitute in Hector Babenco's Brazilian drama *Pixote: A Leido Mais Fraco (Pixote)* (NYT "splendid"; LAT "[an] astonishing, unsparing performance"; WP "unforgettable"). Although top-billed, she really played a supporting role and finished as the runner-up for the Best Supporting Actress honour from the New York critics.

With neither Jackson nor Pêra in contention for the Oscar, Streep's main rivals for the statuette appeared to be two previous Best Actress Oscar winners who had finished as runners-up for the critics' awards. Finishing second to Streep in Los Angeles, and then third for both the New York and NSFC prizes, was Diane Keaton as feminist writer Louise Bryant in *Reds* (NYT "nothing less than splendid ... the best work she has done to date"; LAT "hardest of all for audiences may be Louise Bryant [who] is alienating and exasperating and actress Keaton spares her nothing. Bryant's emotional dishonesty is a problem"; CT "Keaton attempts to play Bryant [but] in my opinion doesn't even come close"; WP "too lightweight to impersonate [her] literary character ... compromised by confused, expedient tendencies in the script"; BG "Annie Hall in a babushka ... [an] undefined woman whose development and growth consists chiefly of her dawning realization that she loves John Reed and must live with him"). Narrowly out-polled by Jackson for the New York honour and then finishing as runner-up for the NSFC plaudit as well, was Faye Dunaway for her portrayal of previous Best Actress Oscar winner Joan Crawford in *Mommie Dearest* (NYT "uncanny ... Dunaway's work here amounts to a small miracle, as one movie queen transforms herself passionately and wholeheartedly into another ... stunning ... ghoulishly affecting ... a serious caricature, done in bold, simple, risky strokes ... Dunaway often achieves a series of fascinating, contradictory effects in a single moment"; LAT "terrific ... [she] does have a good go at Crawford, capturing her paradoxical essence, which was that she could seem formidable and vulnerable simultaneously ... [it is a] compassionate portrayal"; CT "part of our fascination with the film is Dunaway's extraordinary physical impersonation"; WP "a triumph of droll costuming, makeup and hair-styling rather than inspired, sympathetic acting ... exposes Dunaway as a preposterously limited acting instrument"; BG "a wild, uninhibited and quite fascinating performance ... compelling"; S&S "magnificently over-the-top").

When the Golden Globe nominees were announced, both Streep and Keaton were included in the Best Actress (Drama) category but Dunaway was overlooked. Included instead were: Sally Field as a reckless reporter in *Absence of Malice* (NYT "misplaced"; NYP "good"; LAT "enormously effective"; TGM "artificial"); Katharine Hepburn as the wife of a retired university professor in *On Golden Pond* (NYT "in fine form"; LAT "in every way, she is the perfect counterpoint for Fonda ... she gives the film a core of tenderness ... magnificent"; CT "the best performance in the film ... a performance without gimmicks or 'great scenes' ... communicates so much of the film's emotional power ... Hepburn delivers another honest portrayal that doesn't contain a single false gesture"; V "superb"; TGM "a non-mannered, first-rate performance ... built into the character is a shift in direction which Hepburn navigates superbly"; TT "magical ... [with] intimations of infinite depths of feeling beneath the eccentric surface"); and Sissy Spacek as a divorcee with two sons in *Raggedy Man*, the feature directorial debut of her husband, Jack Fisk (NYT "her film from start to finish"; NYP "does not know how to give a bad performance"; LAT "a performance both sensible and lyric, sturdy and surrendering"; CT "appealing ... obviously knows her character well"; BG "so earthily understated that she blends into the dusty Texas environment"; V "excellent"; TGM "[a] resourceful, intentionally modest performance"; S&S "a beautifully modulated performance"). Streep won the Globe at the end of January.

Less than two weeks later, Streep received her third nomination from the Academy in four years (her first in the Best Actress category). Previous winner Keaton was also included (for the second time), as was previous winner Hepburn, who made history as the first person to receive a twelfth nomination in the acting categories. Three other recent previous winners – Dunaway, Field and Spacek – were all passed over, however, in favour of Marsha Mason as a recovering alcoholic actress trying to start over in *Only When I Laugh* (NYT "excellent ... played with quite remarkable, edgy, self-mocking charm ... she has never given a performance equal to this one. She is very, very fine"; CT "the major problem is Mason"; V "a bravura performance"; MFB "serviceable") and Susan Sarandon as a woman aspiring to be the first female croupier in a Monte

Carlo casino, in *Atlantic City* (NYT "excellent"; NYP "superb"; CT "has her most appealing role yet"; BG "the film is enhanced by [her] intelligent personification"). Mason and Sarandon had neither featured in the voting for the critics' prizes nor been on the lists of Globe nominees. In a Washington Post article about 'For Your Consideration' advertisements on the day that the Oscar nominations were due to be announced, Gary Arnold had cited Columbia's campaign for Mason's performance in *Only When I Laugh* as an example of "when a studio pushes hard for a film with only a slim chance of success" while Aljean Harmetz, the Hollywood correspondent for The New York Times commented the next day, "The biggest surprise in the acting categories was the nomination of Susan Sarandon, as a waitress with her eye on better things, for best actress for 'Atlantic City'. The nomination was particularly surprising since Paramount, the studio that released 'Atlantic City', had been pushing Miss Sarandon for supporting actress. A flabbergasted Miss Sarandon said today that even she had voted for herself in the supporting-actress category."

Globe nominee Spacek and New York and NSFC runner-up Dunaway were both notable omissions from the Academy ballot paper, although the exclusion of Dunaway had been widely predicted. A fortnight before the announcement of the Oscar nominations, for example, Ivor Davis, the Hollywood correspondent for The Globe and Mail, had written, "Dunaway got a lot of mileage out of her hysterical, look-alike portrayal of Joan Crawford in 'Mommie Dearest' but is not considered a serious best actress contender." She had the misfortune, Davis explained, of appearing in a film lambasted by critics and considered by studio officials as "the laughing stock of Hollywood." Dunaway's chances were also dealt a blow when Christina Crawford, the daughter of Joan, told journalists, "Faye Dunaway's portrayal was absolutely ludicrous!"

In addition to Spacek and Dunaway, the Academy by-passed: Globe (Comedy/Musical) winner Bernadette Peters in *Pennies from Heaven* (NYT "funny and charming"; LAT "as created and as performed, she's the most interesting character in the film"; WP "Peters contributes the strongest performance in the film"; TGM "[an] extremely attractive performance"); Liza Minnelli in *Arthur* (NYT "a performance richly comic and assured"; LAT "the least forced, most engaging performance from Minnelli in ages, in what is almost a supporting role"; CT "doesn't seem to be able to get into her character ... it's a very patronizing performance"; BG "excellent ... gives a toned-down but totally appropriate dimension to her character"); BAFTA nominee Maggie Smith in *Quartet* (NYT "[a] remarkably interesting characterization"; LAT "excellent"; WP "effective [and] remarkable"; BG "the performances of Bates and Smith crackle with acerbic wit"); Kathleen Turner for her film debut as the socialite who uses a lawyer to murder her husband in *Body Heat* (NYT "looks like the quintessential 40s siren, but sounds like the soap-opera actress she is";

LAT "has a stillness, a concentration and a sexual directness that lets her throw off the film's more purple prose, savor it and get the maximum mileage from it while not appearing a damn fool"; CT "impressive"; BG "a mechanical doll ... delivers her lines in a consistent monotone"); Simone Signoret in *Chère Inconnue (I Sent a Letter to My Love)* (NYT "an immensely rich and funny characterization"; WP "[the film is] a disarming triumph for Signoret ... stunning"; BG "makes everything she says seem like a grandmotherly truth"); and Catherine Deneuve in *Le Dernier Métro (The Last Metro)* (NYT "a star performance ... splendid"; CT "first rate ... creating her finest character since 'Tristana' ... proves here she is more than a perfume ad or pretty face"; BG "handsomely played"; TGM "she walks, albeit beautifully, through the role").

Just prior to the Academy Awards, Streep won the BAFTA in London, but the result did little to bolster her faltering status as the early Oscar frontrunner. "An unprecedented fourth Oscar may be presented to Hepburn this year – for perhaps the silliest performance of a great career – because the competition is considered trifling," wrote Gary Arnold in The Washington Post the day before the Academy Awards ceremony was scheduled to take place, "Meryl Streep was regarded the favorite months ago on the basis of her imposing Time cover story and elusive emoting in 'The French Lieutenant's Woman'. In recent weeks Diane Keaton has become the touts' favorite on the basis of her Newsweek cover story and splendid performance in 1982's 'Shoot the Moon'. There's a slight hitch, of course, because she's been nominated for a less impressive outing as the inexplicable Louise Bryant in 'Reds'. Nevertheless, rumor has it that 'Shoot the Moon' may win for her tomorrow night anyway, since it surpasses the five nominated performances, and who can be sure Academy members won't forget it a year from now? I'm also informed that it's Common Knowledge in Hollywood that the release of 'Shoot the Moon' was delayed as a favor to Keaton, who didn't want to compete with herself in 'Reds'."

On Oscar night, Katharine Hepburn became the first person to win a fourth statuette in the acting categories (all of them as Best Actress). "It became clear midway through the show that the academy members had been as apt to vote *against* certain choices as *for* others," wrote Janet Maslin in The New York Times the day after the telecast, "Certainly, Katherine Hepburn was not named best actress because of any groundswell among academy members who felt she needed a fourth Oscar; she won because the voters lacked enthusiasm for Diane Keaton or Meryl Streep, the true leading contenders in that category."

The following year, Hepburn repeated her win at the British Academy Awards while at the Oscars, Streep was victorious for her performance in *Sophie's Choice*. Despite receiving a Golden Globe nomination, Keaton was not among the Academy Award contenders that year for her performance in *Shoot the Moon*.

BEST SUPPORTING ACTOR

ACADEMY AWARDS
James Coco as 'Jimmy Perino' in *Only When I Laugh*
• **John Gielgud as 'Hobson' in *Arthur***
Ian Holm as 'Sam Mussabini' in *Chariots of Fire*
Jack Nicholson as 'Eugene O'Neill' in *Reds*
Howard E. Rollins, Jr. as 'Coalhouse Walker' in *Ragtime*

GOLDEN GLOBE AWARDS
James Coco – *Only When I Laugh*
• **John Gielgud – *Arthur***
Jack Nicholson – *Reds*
Howard E. Rollins, Jr. – *Ragtime*
Orson Welles – *Butterfly*

BRITISH ACADEMY AWARDS
Denholm Elliott – *Raiders of the Lost Ark*
John Gielgud – *Arthur*
Nigel Havers – *Chariots of Fire*
• **Ian Holm – *Chariots of Fire***

NEW YORK – John Gielgud – *Arthur*
LOS ANGELES – John Gielgud – *Arthur*
BOARD OF REVIEW – Jack Nicholson – *Reds*
NATIONAL SOCIETY – Robert Preston – *S.O.B.*

"A priceless performance," said Variety about John Gielgud as the sarcastic butler of a drunken millionaire in the hit comedy *Arthur*, "truly the kind that wins best supporting actor Oscars." The Washington Post's Gary Arnold agreed, writing, "If the Motion Picture Academy has any smarts the membership ought to resolve that this year's Oscar for best supporting actor rightfully belongs to John Gielgud." The veteran English thespian's work was the most wildly praised of the year (NYT "the seriously comic weight of the movie … splendid … provides the film with its comic backbone." LAT "[his] timing [is] perfection"; CT "Gielgud is so good that this movie would have been a lot more interesting and funny if it had been about his character"; WP "when it comes to impeccable timing and delivery, nothing in 'Arthur' can surpass John Gielgud's explosively funny performance … [the writer] may have earned a special place in theatrical history by providing Gielgud with a great comic valedictory"; BG "breathes life into a cliche"). At the end of the year, the seventy-seven-year old Englishman received Best Supporting Actor accolades from both the New York Film Critics Circle and Los Angeles Film Critics Association. He subsequently won the Golden Globe as well, and became the strong favourite for the Academy Award.

The strongest challenger for the year's supporting accolades was Jack Nicholson for his portrayal of playwright Eugene O'Neill in *Reds* (LAT "superlative"; CT "convincing ... submerges himself into the role of O'Neill by underplaying the part ... allows the marvelous dialogue to speak for itself"; WP "a commanding performance ... projects a smoldering sexual intensity and cynical charm that remain the strongest single identity in the film"; BG "has been given the best dialogue in the film"; V "a major delight"). Nicholson won the prize from the National Board of Review (his second award from the group), finished as runner-up to Gielgud in the voting in both New York (36 points to 29) and Los Angeles, and polled third for the National Society of Film Critics trophy. Some observers believed that he would be carried to a win on Oscar night in a sweep by the Best Picture frontrunner.

Nicholson was nominated by the Academy for a seventh time, while Gielgud was mentioned for a second time (he had been in contention in 1964). The rest of the Oscar field, however, were first-time nominees: James Coco as an unemployed gay actor in *Only When I Laugh* (NYT "excellent"; LAT "endearing"; CT "fits his role ... possess the innate theatricality that is needed to make Simon's stage-bound dialog work on the screen"; TGM "noteworthy ... [he and Hackett] all but transform caricatures into people"; MFB "astonishingly restrained"); Ian Holm as the coach of an Olympic athlete in the British drama *Chariots of Fire* (NYT "runs off with one of the fattest roles in the film"; CT "the most memorable [character] in the film ... this is truly a case of an actor disappearing into a role"; WP "expertly acted"; V "scene-steals every time"; TT "an astoundingly rich performance"); and Howard E. Rollins, Jr., who had finished fourth in the New York voting, in Milos Forman's *Ragtime* (NYT "astonishingly good [and the] most noteworthy in the huge cast"; LAT "takes charge of the film"; CT "played with an exciting mixture of spunk and pride"; WP "well played"; BG "tries his best to add flesh and bones to his skinny role"; V "staggeringly effective").

"The biggest surprise of the nominations was a name that was not on the list," reported Gene Siskel in the Chicago Tribune, "that of James Cagney, 77, who made his acting comeback in 'Ragtime' after 20 years away from the movies. He has been thought to be a shoo-in for the best supporting-actor category." (NYT "doing a lot with very little"; LAT "he brings integrity as well as stirring remembrances of things past"; CT "what a comeback it is ... it's great to see him on the screen again"; WP "a cheerful bonus").

Also left out of the running for the statuette were: Globe nominee Orson Welles in *Butterfly* (NYT "has two brief, funny scenes as a small-town judge"; LAT "florid, flamboyant"; TGM "sleazily hilarious"); NSFC winner Robert Preston in the satire *S.O.B.* (NYT "splendid ... has his best screen role in years"); NSFC runner-up Jerry Orbach in *Prince of the City* (WP "a revelation ... Orbach is so good and so imposing that many people may wish the movie had been all about him"; BG "superb"); Jonathan Pryce in the punk music movie *Breaking Glass* (NYT "an outstanding brief turn as Kate's saxophone player, turning an almost comic figure into the film's most touching one"); Wilford Brimley in *Absence of Malice* (NYT "extremely good ... scene-stealing"; LAT "marvelous"); Jack Weston as a dentist who considers himself a great chef in *The Four Seasons* (NYT "hilarious"; LAT "fine"; WP "wacky"); BAFTA nominee Denholm Elliott in the box office smash *Raiders of the Lost Ark* (LAT "absolutely perfect"); Nigel Havers in *Chariots of Fire* (LAT "effortless"; WP "expertly acted"); Heinz Bennent in *Le Dernier Métro (The Last Metro)* (NYT "noteworthy"); and both Tom Berenger (LAT "lively"; WP "could also help to turn [him] into a pinup, which may or may not secure the starring roles he probably deserves") and Colin Blakely (LAT "lends some color") in *The Dogs of War* (NYT both "excellent support").

Just prior to the Oscars, Cannes honoree Holm emerged as a potential dark horse when he was named Best Supporting Artist by the British Academy. The gender-blind category had been introduced a year after the British Academy had scrapped its supporting prizes. All four nominees were men.

Although *Chariots of Fire* won the Best Picture Oscar in a huge upset, Holm was not carried to a surprise win. As expected, the Academy Award went to Gielgud. Nicholson's performance in *Reds* did not go without any recognition, however. At the following year's British Academy Awards, he won the Best Supporting Actor trophy.

BEST SUPPORTING ACTRESS

ACADEMY AWARDS
Melinda Dillon as 'Teresa' in *Absence of Malice*
Jane Fonda as 'Chelsea Thayer Walker' in *On Golden Pond*
Joan Hackett as 'Toby Landau' in *Only When I Laugh*
Elizabeth McGovern as 'Evelyn Nesbit' in *Ragtime*
• Maureen Stapleton as 'Emma Goldman' in *Reds*

GOLDEN GLOBE AWARDS
Jane Fonda – *On Golden Pond*
• Joan Hackett – *Only When I Laugh*
Kristy McNichol – *Only When I Laugh*
Maureen Stapleton – *Reds*
Mary Steenburgen – *Ragtime*

NEW YORK – Mona Washbourne – *Stevie*
LOS ANGELES – Maureen Stapleton – *Reds*
BOARD OF REVIEW – Mona Washbourne – *Stevie*
NATIONAL SOCIETY – Maureen Stapleton – *Reds*

As the aunt of English poet Stevie Smith in *Stevie*, Mona Washbourne won the 1978 Best Supporting Actress prize from the Los Angeles Film Critics Association and was a Golden Globe nominee following the film's limited, awards-qualification release in Los Angeles. Washbourne was not, however, considered by the other three major American critics' groups until *Stevie* was screened in New York City for the first time in June 1981 (NYT "marvelously well-played"). Surprisingly, she collected the New York Film Critics Circle and National Board of Review awards, and finished as the runner-up for the National Society of Film Critics accolade. Despite the plaudits, however, having been eligible for Oscar consideration in 1978 and overlooked, Washbourne was not a contender for the statuette in 1981.

The favourite for the Academy Award was fifty-six-year old Maureen Stapleton, who received her fourth Oscar nod as early twentieth century anarchist Emma Goldman in *Reds* (NYT "marvelous"; NYP "memorable"; LAT "a fierce-eyed, impassioned performance"; WP "[a] treasure"). Prior to the Oscars, Stapleton won plaudits from both the Los Angeles critics and the NSFC, and finished as one of the joint runners-up for the New York accolade.

The dark horse for the statuette was Joan Hackett as the best friend of a recovering alcoholic actress in *Only When I Laugh* (NYT "excellent"; LAT "especially good"; CT "so mousy that there is no way one can accept her as having been beautiful"; V "tersely funny" TGM "noteworthy ... [she and Coco] all but transform caricatures into people"). Hackett, a respected stage actress, had unexpectedly out-polled Stapleton for the Golden Globe.

Also nominated for the Oscar were: Melinda Dillon (for the second time) as a woman driven to suicide in *Absence of Malice* (NYT "extremely good"); Elizabeth McGovern, who had finished fourth in the voting in New York, as the former chorus girl in *Ragtime* (NYT "superbly acted"; LAT "wonderfully dippy and off-center"; CT "plays Nesbit with great charm and energy and resourcefulness"; V "deft"); and previous Best Actress Oscar winner Jane Fonda (her sixth nomination) as the daughter of a retired university professor in *On Golden Pond* (NYT "very good"; LAT "the trickiest role [in the film which she makes work] by the raw-nerve sincerity of her performance ... it is the deepest, truest performance she has achieved since 'Klute'"; V "superb"; TGM "remarkable"; S&S "miscast").

Overlooked for consideration were: the other New York runner-up (and NSFC Best Actress prize-winner) Marília Pêra as a prostitute in *Pixote: A Leido Mais Fraco (Pixote)* (NYT "splendid"; LAT "[an] astonishing, unsparing performance"; WP "unforgettable"); Lisa Eichhorn, who finished third in the NSFC vote, in *Cutter's Way* (also released as *Cutter and Bone*) (WP "impersonated with maddening monotony"; BG "[a] first-rate performance"); Geraldine Fitzgerald as the grandmother in *Arthur* (NYT "a standout ... how great it is to see her raising a little hell in a comedy role!"; LAT "played perfectly"); Lynsey Baxter in *The French Lieutenant's Woman* (NYT "splendid"; WP "makes the spoiled, immature, temperamental Ernestina a savory, coherent bundle of contradictions ... the most striking and affecting performance in the film"); and the previous year's winner Mary Steenburgen in *Ragtime* (NYT "astonishingly good ... plays Mother with a strength of will not allowed in her comic performance in 'Melvin and Howard'"; LAT "a subtle and delicious performance"; CT "with this small but sweet role solidifies her claim to being a major screen talent").

The year after abolishing its supporting prizes, the British Academy introduced a new gender-blind category, Best Supporting Artist. All four nominees were men, and so the BAFTAs made no contribution to the Best Supporting Actress Oscar contest for the second year in a row.

On Oscar night, the widely-anticipated sweep by *Reds* did not eventuate; the film was even upset in the Best Picture category. There was, however, no surprise in the Best Supporting Actress race. The statuette was presented to Stapleton, a Hollywood veteran who had first been nominated in 1958.

The following year, Stapleton shared the Best Supporting Actress BAFTA with Indian actress Rohini Hattangadi for her performance in *Gandhi*.

1982

BEST PICTURE

ACADEMY AWARDS

E.T. – The Extra-Terrestrial
   (Universal, 115 mins, 11 Jun 1982, $399.8m, 9 noms)
• *Gandhi*
   (Indo-British Films, Columbia, 188 mins, 8 Dec 1982, $52.7m, 11 noms)
Missing
   (Universal, Polygram, 122 mins, 12 Feb 1982, $14.0m, 4 noms)
Tootsie
   (Mirage, Columbia, 119 mins, 17 Dec 1982, $177.2m, 10 noms)
The Verdict
   (Zanuck-Brown, Twentieth Century-Fox, 129 mins, 8 Dec 1982, $54.0m, 5 noms)

GOLDEN GLOBE AWARDS

(Drama)
• *E.T. – The Extra-Terrestrial*
Missing
An Officer and a Gentleman
Sophie's Choice
The Verdict

(Comedy/Musical)
The Best Little Whorehouse in Texas
Diner
My Favorite Year
• *Tootsie*
Victor/Victoria

BRITISH ACADEMY AWARDS

E.T. – The Extra-Terrestrial
• *Gandhi*
Missing
On Golden Pond

NEW YORK – *Gandhi*
LOS ANGELES – *E.T. – The Extra-Terrestrial*
BOARD OF REVIEW – *Gandhi*
NATIONAL SOCIETY – *Tootsie*
LONDON – *Missing*

Two very different films, both acclaimed by critics, were the main contenders for the Best Picture Academy Award. One was a science fiction fairy tale that had become the biggest box office smash of all time, the other an epic biography of a celebrated historical figure. Both won major Best Picture prizes.

The Los Angeles Film Critics Association gathered first, on 11 December 1982, and gave their Best Picture prize to the year's biggest commercial success,

1982

Steven Spielberg's *E.T. – The Extra-Terrestrial* (NYT "an enchanted fantasy … may become a children's classic of the space age"; NYer "genuinely entrancing"; LAT "so full of love and wonder, of pure invention and the best kind of screen magic, that it's not only the film of the summer, it may be the film of the decade"; CT "enchanting … a pure delight"; WP "[a] masterpiece … a catharsis for adults and a triumph for children"; BG "the best cinematic fairytale since 'The Wizard of Oz' … [a] touching drama"; V "captivating, endearingly optimistic and magical").

The New York Film Critics Circle cast their votes nine days later and *E.T. – The Extra-Terrestrial* finished in third place (with 28 points). The winner (with 36 points) was *Gandhi*, Richard Attenborough's expensive, three-hour homage to the pacifist revolutionary Indian leader Mahatma Gandhi. *Gandhi* had only entered US cinemas a few weeks earlier but had already won the National Board of Review prize despite mixed reviews from leading critics. (NYT "a big, amazingly authentic-looking movie … [and] a perfectly reverent if unexceptional film about an exceptional man"; NYP "simply the movie of the year"; NYer "[has] no dramatic center … it isn't a disgrace – it just isn't much of anything"; LAT "emotional empathy is the crucial missing element"; CT "a solid, traditional work … impressive"; WP "a tediously prestigious biography [of] smothering solemnity"; BG "a sprawling epic filled with gorgeous scenery, excellent performances and historical pageantry … old-fashioned … engaging entertainment"; PI "an epic of stunning dimension"; V "eloquently expressive and technically exquisite … near perfect"; HRp "a cinematic event"; TT "a major contribution … personal, delicate, dedicated and uncompromised"; Sp "an important film [but] an opportunity has been missed"). *Gandhi* did not appear on The New York Times list of the year's twenty best films.

The two Oscar frontrunners did not compete against one another at the Golden Globes. At the time, the Hollywood Foreign Press Association excluded non-American movies from the two Best Picture categories and so *Gandhi* was nominated for the Best Foreign Film award, which it won. Meanwhile, *E.T. – The Extra-Terrestrial* claimed the Best Picture (Drama) Globe. The Best Picture (Comedy/Musical) trophy was won by *Tootsie*, which many regarded as the year's Oscar dark horse (NYT "[a] rollicking, hip new comedy"; NYP "an absorbing, rollicking success"; LAT "radiant … a generous, wonderfully funny entertainment with a backbone of intelligence"; CT "a rich comedy with a gentle message … a terrific piece of American commercial moviemaking"; WP "rowdy, inconsequential fun [and] a lucky tightwire act"; BG "the funniest, most revealing comedy since 'Annie Hall'"; V "remarkably funny and entirely convincing"). *Tootsie* had finished as the runner-up in the voting in New York (with 32 points) and had won the National Society of Film Critics Best Picture prize ahead of *E.T. – The Extra-Terrestrial*.

When the Academy announced its list of nominees, the three Globe winners were all mentioned for both Best Picture and Best Director. *Gandhi* topped the list of contenders with eleven nominations, followed by *Tootsie* with ten and *E.T. – The Extra-Terrestrial* with nine. Two other acclaimed American films completed the list of Best Picture candidates. Receiving five nods, including a mention in the Best Director category, was the courtroom drama *The Verdict*, which had been the runner-up for the NBR award (NYT "a solidly, old-fashioned courtroom drama … a clever, suspenseful, entertaining movie"; LAT "absorbing"; WP "pushes viewer patience … [an] imbecilic courtroom melodrama"; BG "guilty of blowing what should have been an airtight case"; TGM "a manipulative, rabble-rousing, liberal crowd-pleaser"). Nominated four times, but surprisingly excluded from Best Director consideration, was the political drama *Missing*, one of two films to share the Palme d'Or at the Cannes Film Festival earlier in the year (NYT "a suspense-thriller of real cinematic style … a striking cinematic achievement"; LAT "an extremely important if not entirely successful film"; BG "one of the most entertaining, insightful films so far this year"; TGM "one of the year's best films"; V "highly interesting, constantly absorbing"; TT "uncompromised").

The German war drama *Das Boot (The Boat)* received six mentions, including Best Director, more than any non-English language film had received previously. It was, however, overlooked for the Best Picture category (NYT "another moving testament to the wastefulness of battle"; NYP "amazingly authentic and realistic … it ranks with the great war films … a masterpiece"; LAT "thrilling, claustrophobic and unremittingly exhausting … superb"; CT "undeniably exciting"; WP "this brilliant, claustrophobic thriller is destined to become a classic … sensational"; BG "as natural and real as a documentary"; TGM "technically, it is superb").

Other notable omissions were: the drama *Sophie's Choice* (NYT "deeply affecting … casts a powerful, uninterrupted spell"; NYP "a haunting, lyrical film of great emotional and intellectual stimulation"; NYer "an infuriatingly bad movie"; WP "compelling … brilliant"); the romantic hit *An Officer and a Gentleman* (NYT "first-rate … [a] thoroughly involving romance"; CT "exceptional entertainment"; V "deserves a 21-gun salute"; TGM "shamelessly manipulative"; MFB "an old-fashioned, regressive, right-wing fantasy"); the musical comedy *Victor/Victoria* (NYT "a marvellous fable … splendid … both romantic and bone-crushingly funny"; CT "a hugely unsatisfying film"; WP "ought to sink from the weight of its implausibility"; BG "an astonishingly uninspired pastiche of slapstick clichés"; V "sparkling, ultra-sophisticated entertainment"; TGM "there is almost nothing about this comedy that is not funny … marvellous vaudeville"; MFB "rather bland"); the low-budget release *Diner* (NYT "entertaining … fresh, well-acted and energetic … the happiest surprise of the year"; LAT "a fresh and personal wonder"; CT "full of memorable moments"; BG "extremely clever ... ultimately blossoms into a moving film"; V "dark and depressing ... an interesting picture difficult for most audiences to watch"); the Hungarian drama *Mephisto* which had won the Best Foreign-Language Film Oscar the previous year (NYT "lacks an essential clarity"; LAT "[an] elegant and subtle study"; CT "a film full of visual power"; WP "stilted and didactic"; BG "brilliant metaphorical filmmaking"; TGM "powerful"; TT "stunning"); the New Zealand movie *Smash Palace* (NYT "something out of the ordinary ... a 'modern' film that doesn't take sides ... extraordinary"; NYer "amazingly accomplished"; LAT "it's hard to become emotionally caught up in the action"; CT "challenging";); the French comedy *Le Beau Mariage (A Good Marriage)* (NYT "charming ... a witty, halcyon entertainment"; LAT "enchanting ... rueful, funny and compassionate ... a small-scale masterpiece"; WP "goes peculiarly amiss"; BG "too oblique"; TGM "sparkling and garrulous"); and the Turkish drama *Yol*, which had been the other Palme d'Or winner (NYT "ponderous ... a film whose political and ethnic concerns are likely to be equated – wrongly – with cinematic achievement"; LAT "almost unbearably painful to watch ... stunning"; WP "sprawling and diffuse"; BG "unforgettable ... [a] masterpiece"; V "deeply felt and often harrowing").

Decades after its release, Ridley Scott's science fiction film noir *Blade Runner* is now acclaimed as a masterpiece which has influenced the design and style of numerous films. It was not a contender for Best Picture honours at the time of its release, however, because the original version released by Warner Bros. earned only faint praise from critics (NYT "muddled yet mesmerizing"; LAT "an extraordinary-looking film ... an exercise in visual sensuality"; WP "pictorially stunning ... at best a freakish success"; V "riveting ... brilliantly imagined"). It was the release of the film on home video that earned it a cult following, and the emergence of Scott's original workprint edit and subsequent director's cuts that has secured its reputation.

In the lead up to the Oscars, Attenborough won the Directors Guild of America honour and the Golden Globe and *Gandhi* was named Best Film by the British Academy in London over a field of contenders that included both *E.T. – The Extra-Terrestrial* and *Missing*, the winner of the top accolade from the London critics. These victories made the epic biopic the favourite for the Oscar according to a majority of Hollywood observers. Surprisingly, however, book-makers in the UK favoured Spielberg's popular science fiction hit over Attenborough's worthy historical drama, perhaps believing that Hollywood would not embrace a foreign film as Best Picture two years in a row.

On Oscar night, however, *Gandhi* not only triumphed as Best Picture but collected a total of eight statuettes. It subsequently became a modest success at the North American box office, finishing among the top twenty earners of 1983.

BEST DIRECTOR

ACADEMY AWARDS
• **Richard Attenborough for** *Gandhi*
Sidney Lumet for *The Verdict*
Wolfgang Petersen for *Das Boot (The Boat)*
Sydney Pollack for *Tootsie*
Steven Spielberg for *E.T. – The Extra-Terrestrial*

GOLDEN GLOBE AWARDS
• **Richard Attenborough –** *Gandhi*
Constantin Costa-Gavras – *Missing*
Sidney Lumet – *The Verdict*
Sydney Pollack – *Tootsie*
Steven Spielberg – *E.T. – The Extra-Terrestrial*

DIRECTORS GUILD AWARD
• **Richard Attenborough –** *Gandhi*
Taylor Hackford
  – An Officer and a Gentleman
Wolfgang Petersen
  – Das Boot (The Boat)
Sydney Pollack – *Tootsie*
Steven Spielberg
  – E.T. – The Extra-Terrestrial

BRITISH ACADEMY AWARDS
• **Richard Attenborough –** *Gandhi*
Constantin Costa-Gavras – *Missing*
Mark Rydell – *On Golden Pond*
Steven Spielberg
  – E.T. – The Extra-Terrestrial

NEW YORK – Sydney Pollack – *Tootsie*
LOS ANGELES – Steven Spielberg – *E.T. – The Extra-Terrestrial*
BOARD OF REVIEW – Sidney Lumet – *The Verdict*
NATIONAL SOCIETY – Steven Spielberg – *E.T. – The Extra-Terrestrial*
LONDON – Constantin Costa-Gavras – *Missing*

For the third year in a row, the Best Director Academy Award was won by an actor: Richard Attenborough for *Gandhi* (LAT "[the subject] is more than decently served by Attenborough's self-effacement; it is illuminated sensitively and intelligently"; CT "well-crafted"; WP "Attenborough may stop short of shameless, nostalgic hero worship, but he can often be detected sanitizing Gandhi's story"; PI "compelling ... manages the epochal events [and] the moments of intimacy with equal aplomb"; V "a triumph"). Prior to his Oscar win, Attenborough collected the Directors Guild of America accolade, the

Golden Globe and the British Academy Award. Surprisingly, however, he received none of the major critics' prizes.

Steven Spielberg collected the Los Angeles Film Critics Association and National Society of Film Critics awards for *E.T. – The Extra-Terrestrial* (NYT "slick"; WP "he never lets us down, not once … a simple premise, plotted and timed to perfection"; BG "unless another unforeseen masterpiece is released, Spielberg and his crew will wear out the carpet at the Dorothy Chandler Pavilion during the [next] Oscar ceremony"). He also finished as the runner-up for the New York Film Critics Circle prize, which was won by Sydney Pollack for *Tootsie* (NYT "[maintains] the discipline that keeps 'Tootsie' on track from start to finish"; CT "commercial American moviemaking at its best … moves the intricate story briskly"; BG "never allows the story to degenerate into slapstick"; V "beautifully sustained direction"). The National Board of Review, meanwhile, chose Sidney Lumet for *The Verdict* (NYT "utterly unobtrusive [but in parts] uncharacteristically awkward"; LAT "an amazingly restrained job"; WP "a good deal of the composition is so deliberately static that you're compelled to conclude Lumet wanted to make a film that looked stagey"; BG "[the film] is mortally wounded by his tendency toward overstatement"; V "distant, almost episodic approach"). Finally, the London Film Critics rewarded Constantin Costa-Gavras for *Missing* (NYT "beautifully achieved"; LAT "has an unerring eye and ear"; CT "no small achievement"; V "excels").

The four critics' honourees were nominated alongside Attenborough for the Globe. The fifth nominee for the Academy Award, meanwhile, was Wolfgang Petersen for *Das Boot (The Boat)* (NYT "brings to this film a careful, thoughtful, sympathetic tone, and a great deal of verisimilitude … his direction powerfully fosters the impression that you are there"; TGM "[directs] with a deft and terrifying touch").

By-passed were: Taylor Hackford for *An Officer and a Gentleman* (NYT "brings to this film a warmth and meticulousness that shows in every aspect"; WP "less than inspired"; BG "burdens the film with a series of gratuitous subplots that merely dilute the drama"); Blake Edwards for *Victor/Victoria* (NYT "his cockeyed, crowning achievement"; BG "tediously paced"; TGM "still [a] master of farce"); Barry Levinson for *Diner* (NYT "uneven"; LAT "sure"; BG "an impressive debut"); Ridley Scott for *Blade Runner* (LAT "if the story is frail and unhelpful, it is certainly drenched in atmosphere"); Alan J. Pakula for *Sophie's Choice* (WP "remarkably accomplished … [shows] exquisitely balanced restraint"; TT "sensitive"; MFB "filmed with an exactitude and beauty of detail"); and István Szabó for *Mephisto* (LAT "superb"; CT "bravura staging"; BG "[his] austere, incisive approach cuts to the heart of every scene, illuminating his theme"; V "exemplary"; TGM "vividly conveys an atmosphere of uncertainty and paranoia").

BEST ACTOR

ACADEMY AWARDS
Dustin Hoffman as 'Michael Dorsey' and 'Dorothy Michaels' in *Tootsie*
• **Ben Kingsley as 'Mahatma Gandhi' in *Gandhi***
Jack Lemmon as 'Ed Horman' in *Missing*
Paul Newman as 'Francis P. Galvin' in *The Verdict*
Peter O'Toole as 'Alan Swann' in *My Favorite Year*

GOLDEN GLOBE AWARDS

(Drama)
Albert Finney – *Shoot the Moon*
Richard Gere
   – *An Officer and a Gentleman*
• **Ben Kingsley – *Gandhi***
Jack Lemmon – *Missing*
Paul Newman – *The Verdict*

(Comedy/Musical)
• **Dustin Hoffman – *Tootsie***
Peter O'Toole – *My Favorite Year*
Al Pacino – *Author! Author!*
Robert Preston – *Victor/Victoria*
Henry Winkler – *Night Shift*

BRITISH ACADEMY AWARDS
Warren Beatty – *Reds*
Albert Finney – *Shoot the Moon*
Henry Fonda – *On Golden Pond*
• **Ben Kingsley – *Gandhi***
Jack Lemmon – *Missing*

NEW YORK – Ben Kingsley – *Gandhi*
LOS ANGELES – Ben Kingsley – *Gandhi*
BOARD OF REVIEW – Ben Kingsley – *Gandhi*
NATIONAL SOCIETY – Dustin Hoffman – *Tootsie*
LONDON – Ben Kingsley – *Gandhi*

In January, Albert Finney impressed critics with his performance as the husband in a disintegrating marriage in the family drama *Shoot the Moon* (NYT "superb … [an] anguished, biting, full-length performance"; NYP "wonderful"; LAT "superficially drawn"; CT "first-rate"; WP "Finney [is] reborn as a forceful screen actor … brings a seething psychological conviction to his role"; Time "serves his befuddled character perfectly"; TGM "affected … [a] walking-dead performance"; MFB "excellent"). Despite the film's release so early in the year, Finney's performance garnered nominations from several key awards organisations during the awards season.

A few weeks later, just a day after the Academy had announced the previous year's Oscar nominees, Jack Lemmon emerged as another serious Best Actor contender for his portrayal of a political conservative whose beliefs and patriotism are shaken during his search for his missing son in a repressive South American country in *Missing* (NYT "superb ... acted with immense authority"; NYP "has never been better"; BG "his best performance since 'Save the Tiger' ... convincingly subtle"; V "superior"; TGM "his finest performance since 'Some Like It Hot' ... he has rigorously eschewed excess and has in the process created the performance of a lifetime"; TT "admirably played"). Soon after its US premiere, the film screened at the Cannes Film Festival where Lemmon received the festival's Best Actor prize.

Over the next few months several other performances caught the attention of critics: Jürgen Prochnow as the Captain of a German submarine in *Das Boot (The Boat)* (LAT "excellent ... carries the film's ruthless energy while suggesting humanity underneath"; CT "striking"; WP "intensely controlled"); Klaus Maria Brandauer as a German actor who associates himself with the Nazi regime in order to further his career in *Mephisto* (NYT "brilliant"; LAT "[a] magnetic, exhausting performance"; CT "to anyone's list of great movie performances you must now add one more: Klaus Maria Brandauer as actor Hendrik Hofgen in 'Mephisto' ... without chewing up the scenery and becoming obnoxious in the process, Brandauer at times seems to leap off the screen and grab our attention"; BG "one of the more memorable film-acting performances in recent years ... extraordinary, seldom less than compelling ... [a] virtuoso performance"; V "extraordinary"; TGM "[a] magnificent, paradoxical performance"); Al Pacino as a playwright deserted by his wife, in the comedy *Author! Author!* (NYT "handles [the role] appealingly and comfortably"; LAT "isn't the much-touted change of pace for Pacino because he's still playing hollow-eyed drama, not comedy [while] the story keeps going off around him like a hand grenade"; WP "illustrates his inability to lighten up an emphatically gloomy, brooding screen presence"; BG "superb"; V "Pacino's warmest performance to date ... superb"; TGM "looks unaccountably dissipated ... Pacino's lugubriousness sabotages whatever infinitesimal chance the movie might have had for success"); Richard Gere as a marine in the popular *An Officer and a Gentleman* (NYT "has never been this affecting before"; LAT "simple and direct"; CT "just right"; BG "too offbeat"); Peter O'Toole as an alcoholic former matinee idol in *My Favorite Year* (NYP "wildly wonderful"; LAT "superb ... makes the most lasting impression ... O'Toole makes Swann elegantly self-knowing"; CT "has no difficulty playing a legendary actor whose time has passed ... he is enjoying a second wind in his career"; WP "brilliantly inspired and professionally transformed ... [a] sublimely funny performance"; BG "manages to put up a marvelous struggle ... while he's on screen, the film is a bright, funny mixture of pathos and self-parody [but] when he's off, so is the film ... O'Toole confirms his stature as one of the finest actors of our time"; V "stylish"; TT "a generous display of self-parody"; MFB "conducts himself with attractively crazed grandeur"); 1980 Cannes winner Michel Piccoli as the magistrate in the comedy *Salto nel Vuoto (A Leap into the Void)* (NYT "extraordinarily well acted"); and Paul Newman as a lawyer in *The Verdict* (NYT "[both] a measured performance [and] a dazzling movie-star turn ... as shrewd and substantial a performance as he has ever given, although it may not be his most entirely credible"; LAT "pungently acted ... digs down deep, rejecting flashiness and easy tricks, to show us the painful rebirth of a decent man"; WP "the idea of his finally winning his Oscar on this sad-sack showing is sad to contemplate ... one of his wrong numbers"; CT "commendable [but an] overhyped performance"; BG "excellent ... through his well-crafted performance, Newman captures the essence of a man who has one last shot at self-respect ... will probably receive a Best Actor Oscar nomination"; TGM "his acting in the second half is safe and self-assured, while his acting in the first is not only shy of good, it's downright bad. It would be ironic but predictable if he were to win an Oscar for his weakest performance in years"; V "a studied, multi-layered portrait ... extraordinarily realistic"; TT "very decently acted").

The two most serious challengers for the year's prizes, however, appeared in films released at the very end of the year.

On 8 December 1982, Richard Attenborough's epic biopic *Gandhi* was released in the United States and earned praise for the portrayal of the eponymous Indian spiritual and political leader by the Indian-English actor Ben Kingsley (NYT "a splendid performer who discovers the humor, the frankness, the quickness of mind that make the film far more moving than you might think possible ... a lively, searching performance that holds the film together"; NYP "overwhelming ... [in] the year's finest achievement by an actor"; LAT "[a] magnificent central performance ... Kingsley doesn't traffic in impersonation but in the illumination of Gandhi's strength and spirit"; CT "an elemental, thoughtful, finely chiselled performance ... extraordinary ... the performance of a lifetime"; WP "one feels grateful for the playful, fallible human dimensions Kingsley brings to Gandhi's goodness"; BG "excellent ... remarkable"; PI "the cohesive force in the film"; V "a masterfully balanced and magnetic portrayal"; Time "nothing short of astonishing"; TT "wholly real and believable"; FQ "wonderful"; Sp "a bravura performance ... brings an intelligence to his interpretation ... the wit, the shrewdness, the compassion which characterised Gandhi are convincingly depicted ... impressive is the actor's subtle refusal to engage in hyperbole").

Nine days later, critics were also taken with Dustin Hoffman's turn in the hit comedy *Tootsie* as a struggling actor who lands a role on a daytime soap opera by pretending to be a woman (NYT "splendid ... an important part of [the film's] success is Mr Hoffman's grand performance as both the edgy, cantankerous Michael Dorsey and the serenely self-assured Dorothy Michaels"; CT "exceptional ... creates two fully realized characters ... this role, played wrong, played too much for laughs, could be a sewer in actor's career. For Dustin Hoffman, it's another triumph"; WP "brings it off convincingly"; BG "grabs the title role and turns it inside out ... his portrayal vibrates with intensity ... Hoffman should be the odds-on favorite to cop another Best Actor Oscar"; V "triumphs in what must stand as one of his most brilliant performances").

Kingsley and Hoffman dominated the critics' prizes. Hoffman narrowly collected the National Society of Film Critics award (for the second time in four years) while Kingsley was honoured by the National Board of Review, the Los Angeles Film Critics Association and the New York Film Critics Circle (he won the latter on the first ballot by 14 votes to 5 over Hoffman). The two men also each won a Best Actor Golden Globe.

When the Academy Award nominations were announced in mid-February, Kingsley was short-listed for the first time and was soon declared the favourite by both observers and book-makers. His competition were men who had each been in contention for the prize on at least four previous occasions. Previous winner Hoffman, mentioned for the fifth time, was regarded as Kingsley's main challenger. Also recognised were previous winner Lemmon (for the eighth and final time), Newman (for a sixth time and the second year in a row), and O'Toole (for a seventh time).

Kingsley's status as the Oscar favourite was consolidated when he was named Best Actor by the British Academy ahead of Lemmon in *Missing*, Finney in *Shoot the Moon* and two of the previous year's Oscar nominees: Warren Beatty in *Reds* and the late Henry Fonda in *On Golden Pond* (who had died only five months after winning his golden statuette).

On Academy Awards night, there was no upset in the Best Actor category: Kingsley received one of the eight statuettes collected by *Gandhi*. As a result, O'Toole went home empty-handed for a seventh time, equalling Richard Burton's losing streak.

Hoffman's performance in *Tootsie*, meanwhile, received the Best Actor prize from the British Academy the following year.

1982

BEST ACTRESS

ACADEMY AWARDS
Julie Andrews as 'Count Victor Grezhinski' and 'Victoria Grant' in
    Victor/Victoria
Jessica Lange as 'Frances Farmer' in *Frances*
Sissy Spacek as 'Beth Horman' in *Missing*
• **Meryl Streep as 'Sophie Zawistowska' in *Sophie's Choice***
Debra Winger as 'Paula Pokrifki' in *An Officer and a Gentleman*

GOLDEN GLOBE AWARDS

(Drama)
Diane Keaton – *Shoot the Moon*
Jessica Lange – *Frances*
Sissy Spacek – *Missing*
• **Meryl Streep – *Sophie's Choice***
Debra Winger
    – *An Officer and a Gentleman*

(Comedy/Musical)
• **Julie Andrews – *Victor/Victoria***
Carol Burnett – *Annie*
Sally Field – *Kiss Me Goodbye*
Goldie Hawn – *Best Friends*
Dolly Parton
    – *The Best Little Whorehouse
    in Texas*
Aileen Quinn – *Annie*

BRITISH ACADEMY AWARDS
• **Katharine Hepburn – *On Golden Pond***
Diane Keaton – *Reds*
Jennifer Kendal – *36 Chowringhee Lane*
Sissy Spacek – *Missing*

NEW YORK – Meryl Streep – *Sophie's Choice*
LOS ANGELES – Meryl Streep – *Sophie's Choice*
BOARD OF REVIEW – Meryl Streep – *Sophie's Choice*
NATIONAL SOCIETY – Meryl Streep – *Sophie's Choice*

In an article in The New York Times in mid-December, Vincent Canby described 1982 as "a vintage year for exceptional performances by film actresses." From films released over the preceding months, he picked out: Diane Keaton as a woman in a disintegrating marriage in *Shoot the Moon*, for which she was later the runner-up for the New York Film Critics Circle prize (NYT "superb ... terrific"; NYP "wonderful"; LAT "superficially drawn"; WP "demonstrating impressive new range and authority as a dramatic actress"; BG "superbly played"; TGM "a minor acting epiphany ... memorable"; MFB

62

"excellent"); Anna Jemison in the New Zealand drama *Smash Palace* (NYT "strong"; LAT "Jemison is multifaceted with lovely emotional timbre"; BG "Jemison's portrayal of Jacqui burns with frustrated intensity"); Debra Winger as a factory worker in *An Officer and a Gentleman* (NYT "beautifully acted ... has such emotional immediacy that she positively glows"; LAT "[a] beautifully drawn performance"; BG "brings a wonderful sensitivity to her role"; TGM "surprisingly powerful"); Barbara Sukowa as a singer and prostitute in *Lola* (NYT "smashing"); Béatrice Romand in *Le Beau Mariage (A Good Marriage)* (NYT "a comedienne of the first order"); 1980 Cannes winner Anouk Aimée as the magistrate's sister in *Salto nel Vuoto (A Leap into the Void)* (NYT "extraordinarily well-acted"; LAT "cast dramatically against type as a middle-aged, virginal spinster, she rises to demands never before placed upon her as an actress"; WP "totally boring, all film long"); Claudia Cardinale in *Fitzcarraldo* (NYT "not on screen as long as one might wish, but she lights up her role"); and Julie Andrews as a drag cabaret star in *Victor/Victoria*, a musical comedy directed by her husband, Blake Edwards (NYT "the performance of her career ... at peak form both as a comedienne and as a singer"; NYP "not spectacularly convincing"; CT "on the emotional scale she's pretty much a two-note actress here [and] as a result, she undermines the comic spirit of the picture"). "As if that weren't enough," wrote Canby, the opening of two films within a week of one another in early December, "added two more names to be considered when the time comes to pick the best of the year's best. It's not going to be easy."

The first of the two additional Best Actress contenders was Jessica Lange. Canby said her portrayal of 1930s Hollywood starlet Frances Farmer in *Frances* was "astonishing ... remarkable" and "exhilarating". Other leading film critics were equally enthusiastic (NYT "magnificent [in] a performance so unfaltering, so tough, so intelligent and so humane that it seems as if Miss Lange is just now, at long last, making her motion picture debut ... genuinely memorable ... consistently splendid ... both funny and heart-breaking"; NYP "can only be described as miraculous [in] a brilliant, intricately polished piece of work full of irony, pain, and energy"; V "quite an accomplishment"; TT "[the] one strong saving grace in this scrambled film"; MFB "admirable throughout").

Garnering even greater acclaim was Meryl Streep as a Polish survivor of the Holocaust in *Sophie's Choice* (NYT "accomplishes the near-impossible, presenting Sophie in believably human terms ... in a role affording every opportunity for overstatement, she offers a performance of such measured intensity that the results are by turn exhilarating and heart-breaking"; NYP "the performance of the year ... positively mesmerizing ... so natural and full of unexpected insights that she makes each scene a marvelous adventure"; LAT "incandescent [in a] bravura performance ... she has slipped under the skin of her diabolically difficult character perfectly [giving a] complex, glowing performance"; CT "a striking performance ... achieves greatness"; WP "extraordinary ... [a] magnificent performance [which] involves feats of linguistic mimicry and modulation that are formidable ... the expressive effects she rings from that accented, halting English are phenomenal"; V "convincing [and] effective"; Time "fine and beautiful and a little heartbreaking"; S&S "tremendously sensitive"; MFB "splendidly detailed"). In his article, Canby called Streep's work "stunning ... riveting" and "a ravishing combination of technical skill and mysterious artistry." The Times, meanwhile, summed up the critical consensus by declaring "this may be a performance that wins an Oscar."

Ordinarily, Lange and Streep may have split the critics' prizes and closely contested the Academy Award. However, Lange also received praise from critics for another film released at Christmas time, the comedy *Tootsie*. Her role in this second release was promoted for the year's supporting accolades. As a result, Lange won the New York Film Critics Circle honour, the Golden Globe and the Oscar in the secondary acting category and Streep was left to collect a clean sweep of the six major end of year Best Actress awards.

Streep claimed the Academy's statuette with her fourth nomination. Lange was recognised by the Academy for the first time with nominations in each of the acting categories. From Canby's list of Oscar-worthy candidates both Andrews and Winger also made the list – Andrews, a previous winner and the year's Globe (Comedy/Musical) champ, was included for a third time, while Winger was mentioned for the first time. The fifth nominee was previous winner Sissy Spacek (her third nomination) as the wife of a missing journalist in *Missing* (NYT "superb ... acted with immense authority"; NYP "extraordinary emotional depth and control"; CT "does a much better job than Lemmon of disappearing into character"; BG "in contrast with her theatrical performance in 'Coal Miner's Daughter', Spacek neatly underplays her character in deference to both the script and Lemmon"; TGM "compelling"; V "fully believable").

On the eve of the previous year's Oscar ceremony, Gary Arnold wrote in The Washington Post, "In recent weeks Diane Keaton has become the touts' favorite on the basis of her Newsweek cover story and splendid performance in 1982's 'Shoot the Moon' ... she's been nominated for a less impressive outing in 'Reds' [but] rumor has it that 'Shoot the Moon' may win for her tomorrow night anyway, since it surpasses the five nominated performances, and who can be sure Academy members won't forget it a year from now?" Although nominated for a Golden Globe, Keaton's performance in *Shoot the Moon* was indeed forgotten by Academy members. "Keaton's failure to get a nomination as best actress for 'Shoot the Moon', despite critical raves, was undoubtedly because of the movie's box-office failure when it was released in January 1982," explained Aljean Harmetz in The New York Times, "Box-office success and failure have certain – although not infallible – relation to Academy nominations."

1982

BEST SUPPORTING ACTOR

ACADEMY AWARDS
Charles Durning as 'The Governor' in *The Best Little Whorehouse in Texas*
• **Louis Gossett, Jr. as 'Sgt. Emil Fowley' in *An Officer and a Gentleman***
John Lithgow as 'Roberta Muldoon' in *The World According to Garp*
James Mason as 'Ed Concannon' in *The Verdict*
Robert Preston as 'Toddy' in *Victor/Victoria*

GOLDEN GLOBE AWARDS
• **Louis Gossett, Jr. – *An Officer and a Gentleman***
Raul Julia – *Tempest*
David Keith – *An Officer and a Gentleman*
James Mason – *The Verdict*
Jim Metzler – *Tex*

BRITISH ACADEMY AWARDS
Frank Finlay – *Return of the Soldier*
Edward Fox – *Gandhi*
• **Jack Nicholson – *Reds***
Roshan Seth – *Gandhi*

NEW YORK – John Lithgow – *The World According to Garp*
LOS ANGELES – John Lithgow – *The World According to Garp*
BOARD OF REVIEW – Robert Preston – *Victor/Victoria*
NATIONAL SOCIETY – Mickey Rourke – *Diner*

As a transsexual former football player in *The World According to Garp*, John Lithgow won the Best Supporting Actor awards from both the New York Film Critics Circle and the Los Angeles Film Critics Association (NYT "excellent"; LAT "played tenderly ... Lithgow endows the most intricately layered of the film's characters with lasting poignance and dignity"; WP "played with extraordinary sensitivity"; BG "superb ... Lithgow transforms Muldoon's transsexuality into a nonissue, a study in personality and character transcending gender-orientation"; V "funny and often moving"; MFB "perfectly judged"; Time "fails to give his usual gifted portrayal of an eccentric").

The National Board of Review gave their supporting accolade to Broadway veteran Robert Preston for his turn as an ageing gay cabaret artist in *Victor/Victoria* (NYT "if Mr Preston doesn't get an Oscar for this film, he never will ... the richest, wisest, most rambunctious performance he's given since his

65

triumph in 'The Music Man' ... most refreshing"; LAT "[a] deft, inventive performance ... masterful"; V "most impressive [in] a shimmering portrait"; TGM "a terrific comic creation").

The National Society of Film Critics, meanwhile, selected Mickey Rourke for his performance as a hairdresser in *Diner*, writer-director Barry Levinson's nostalgic film about growing up in the late 1950s (NYT "plays [the role] superbly"; LAT "has the film's charismatic role ... memorable"; CT "excellent"; WP "attractively performed ... a decisive starring opportunity").

Surprisingly, none of these three critics' prize-winners appeared on the ballot for the Best Supporting Actor Golden Globe. Preston was nominated in the Best Actor (Comedy/Musical) category and both Lithgow and Rourke were overlooked entirely.

Instead the Globe candidates were: both Louis Gossett, Jr. as a tough Marine officer (NYT "always a good supporting player, is this time a star ... [he acts with] subtlety and spark ... the kind of performance that wins awards, being a seamless blend of actor and material"; LAT "an energized, exhausting performance"; CT "it's tempting to say that Gossett steals the show, and certainly he will be remembered at Academy Awards time"; BG "excellent"; V "does more with his eyes and a facial reaction than others can accomplish with pages of dialogue") and David Keith as one of the officer candidates (NYT "unusually memorable"; LAT "manages real poignance ... emerges as one of the screen's strongest young supporting actors ... his performance in a complex role is one of the film's solid assets"; BG "excellent") in *An Officer and a Gentleman*; Raul Julia as Kalibanos in *Tempest*, a comic reworking of the William Shakespeare play (NYT "ordinary"; LAT "[a] surprisingly amusing if spotty performance ... Julia is right out there teetering on the edge again, too far over for some, giving others a ripely generous characterization"; BG "energetic"); James Mason as a ruthless lawyer in *The Verdict* (NYT "does a wonderful job"; LAT "brilliantly performed"; BG "Newman is well supported by James Mason's polite but insidious portrayal of the defense lawyer ... Mason could garner [an Oscar nomination] as Best Supporting Actor"; CT "a fine piece of work"; TGM "especially memorable"; V "nearly steals the whole show"; TT "very decently acted"); and Jim Metzler as the older brother in *Tex* (NYT "gives a superb performance"; CT "the backbone of the film ... exceedingly well-played"; WP "attractively played"; V "impressive"). Gossett, Jr. emerged as the winner at the ceremony in late January.

"Perhaps the hardest choices that had to be made by the members of the Academy's acting branch," wrote Aljean Harmetz in The New York Times upon the announcement of the annual Oscar nominees, "becomes obvious in the supporting actor category, which was considered a particularly rich category this year." The Academy short-listed: Globe winner Gosset, Jr., New York and Los

Angeles prize-winner Lithgow and NBR winner Preston (each for the first time), Globe nominee Mason (for the third time) and Charles Durning for his performance as a singing and dancing Governor of Texas in the musical comedy *The Best Little Whorehouse in Texas* (V "show-stopping"). Durning also appeared that year in *Tootsie* as the father of a young soap opera star (V "wonderful").

In addition to NSFC winner Rourke, Academy members overlooked: both New York award runner-up George Gaynes as a pompous, lecherous soap star (NYT "priceless"; WP "too bad there isn't more for Gaynes to do – he's great fun") and Los Angeles prize runner-up Bill Murray as the lead character's best friend in *Tootsie* (NYT "splendid ... [has never] appeared to such rich advantage"; LAT "a droll delight"; BG "excellent"); Kevin Kline for his film debut as the title character's unstable lover in *Sophie's Choice* (NYT "appealing [but] less than fully convincing"; WP "extraordinary"); Richard Bradford as a retired naval officer in *Missing* (LAT "a wonder ... a small revelation ... excellent"); Peter Weller in *Shoot the Moon* (NYT "superb ... strong and fully realized"; TGM "memorable"); Scott Glenn as the trainer in *Personal Best* (NYT "very good ... the role is far more revealing played than written"; LAT "wonderful"; WP "played so smartly"); and Rutger Hauer as a renegade android leader in the science fiction film noir *Blade Runner* (NYT "[Ford] is often upstaged by Rutger Hauer ... [he] is properly cold-blooded here, but there is something almost humorous behind his nastiness ... he is by far the most animated performer in a film intentionally populated by automatons ... [a] brutal, moving performance"; WP "majestic"; V "intriguing and charismatic").

Both Edward Fox (LAT "stands out"; BG "superior") and Roshan Seth were nominated by the British Academy for their performances in *Gandhi*, the year's most Oscar nominated film, but neither made the list in Hollywood.

While there was strong sentimental support for veterans Mason and Preston, on Oscar night, as expected, Gossett, Jr. won the Academy Award. He was only the third African American to win a statuette in the acting categories (and the first since 1963).

BEST SUPPORTING ACTRESS

ACADEMY AWARDS
Glenn Close as 'Jenny Fields' in *The World According to Garp*
Teri Garr as 'Sandy' in *Tootsie*
• **Jessica Lange as 'Julie' in** *Tootsie*
Kim Stanley as 'Lillian Farmer' in *Frances*
Lesley Ann Warren as 'Norma' in *Victor/Victoria*

GOLDEN GLOBE AWARDS
Cher – *Come Back to the Five and Dime, Jimmy Dean, Jimmy Dean*
Lainie Kazan – *My Favorite Year*
• **Jessica Lange –** *Tootsie*
Kim Stanley – *Frances*
Lesley Ann Warren – *Victor/Victoria*

BRITISH ACADEMY AWARDS
Candice Bergen – *Gandhi*
Jane Fonda – *On Golden Pond*
• **Rohini Hattangadi –** *Gandhi*
• **Maureen Stapleton –** *Reds*

NEW YORK – Jessica Lange – *Tootsie*
LOS ANGELES – Glenn Close – *The World According to Garp*
BOARD OF REVIEW – Glenn Close – *The World According to Garp*
NATIONAL SOCIETY – Jessica Lange – *Tootsie*

In December, Jessica Lange won acclaim from critics for two contrasting performances: as the troubled 1930s film star Frances Farmer in the drama *Frances* and as a daytime soap opera star in the hit comedy *Tootsie* (NYT "a total delight"; BG "excellent"; V "displays a talent for relatively realistic romantic comedy"). In order to increase her chances of winning an Oscar, Columbia campaigned for Lange to be considered for the supporting prize for *Tootsie*, while Universal advertised her performance in *Frances* as a Best Actress contender. When the Oscar nominations were announced on 17 February 1983, Lange became the first person to receive nominations in both the lead and supporting acting categories in nearly four decades. The three previous double Oscar nominees – Fay Bainter in 1938, Teresa Wright in 1942 and Barry Fitzgerald in 1944 – all claimed statuettes in the supporting category. Lange was a strong favourite to preserve this record. In the lead up to the Oscars, she won the Best Supporting Actress awards from the New York Film Critics Circle and the National Society of Film Critics, and also claimed the Golden Globe.

The only other serious contender for the Oscar was Glenn Close as the eponymous character's feminist mother in *The World According to Garp* (NYT "excellent ... performs miracles with the toughest of the story's many difficult roles"; NYP "marvelously played"; LAT "an extraordinary debut ... triumphant"; BG "[a] virtually impeccable performance ... Close's firm, even-handed performance provides a persuasive counterpoint to Williams"; WP "splendid ... an extraordinary, indeed perfect, casting choice ... Close embodies [Jenny] with uncanny effectiveness"; V "perfect"; TT "convincing"). Close won both the Los Angeles Film Critics Association and National Board of Review prizes, and finished as the runner-up to Lange for both the New York and NSFC honours. Surprisingly, she was not a Globe nominee.

Also nominated by the Academy were: Teri Garr as a struggling actress in *Tootsie* (NYT "splendid ... [has never] appeared to such rich advantage"; WP "her greatest movie scene yet"; BG "excellent"; V "fine"); Kim Stanley (her second and final nomination) as the mother in *Frances* (NYT "vivid"; NYP "there is greatness in Stanley's performance"; V "fine"); and Lesley Ann Warren as a gangster's moll in *Victor/Victoria* (NYT "enchantingly self-possessed and very comic").

Overlooked for consideration were: Mary Beth Hurt as Garp's wife in *The World According to Garp* (NYT "excellent"; NYP "marvelously played"; LAT "she has one of the most difficult roles"; BG "good"; V "excellent"; TT "cannot be faulted"); both Dana Hill as the eldest daughter (LAT "[a] shattering performance"; TGM "memorable") and Karen Allen as the girlfriend (NYT "superb ... strong and fully realized") in *Shoot the Moon*; Lainie Kazan in *My Favorite Year* (WP "brilliantly inspired and professionally transformed ... [a] sublimely funny performance"); Lindsay Crouse as the nurse in *The Verdict* (LAT "superb and almost unrecognizable"; V "bravura"); Dee Wallace as the mother in *E.T. – The Extra-Terrestrial* (LAT "splendid"); and Phoebe Nicholls as the fiancée in the British comedy *The Missionary* (NYT "a particular revelation ... [she] is delightfully dense").

Surprisingly, although *Gandhi* was the year's most Oscar nominated film, BAFTA co-winner Rohini Hattangadi (LAT "glowingly warm"; WP "well-played, as far as the elusive material allows") went unrecognised in Hollywood for her performance in the biographical epic.

On Oscar night, Lange was outpolled for the Best Actress award by Meryl Streep. As expected, however, she received the statuette as Best Supporting Actress for *Tootsie*. Lange went on to win the Best Actress statuette twelve years later.

1983

BEST PICTURE

ACADEMY AWARDS

The Big Chill
  (Carson, Columbia, 105 mins, 30 Sep 1983, $56.2m, 3 noms)
The Dresser
  (Goldcrest, World Film Services, Columbia, 118 mins, 6 Dec 1983, $5.3m, 5 noms)
The Right Stuff
  (Chartoff-Winkler, Ladd Company, Warner Bros., 193 mins, 9 Sep 1983, $21.5m, 8 noms)
Tender Mercies
  (EMI, Universal, 92 mins, 4 Mar 1983, $8.4m, 5 noms)
• *Terms of Endearment*
  (Brooks, Paramount, 132 mins, 23 Nov 1983, $108.4m, 11 noms)

GOLDEN GLOBE AWARDS

(Drama)	(Comedy/Musical)
Reuben, Reuben	*The Big Chill*
The Right Stuff	*Flashdance*
Silkwood	*Trading Places*
Tender Mercies	• *Yentl*
• *Terms of Endearment*	*Zelig*

BRITISH ACADEMY AWARDS
• *Educating Rita*
Heat and Dust
Local Hero
Tootsie

NEW YORK – *Terms of Endearment*
LOS ANGELES – *Terms of Endearment*
BOARD OF REVIEW – *Betrayal* and *Terms of Endearment*
NATIONAL SOCIETY – *La Notte di San Lorenzo (Night of the Shooting Stars)*
LONDON – *The King of Comedy*

When the Academy announced its list of nominees on 16 February 1984, the comedy-drama *Terms of Endearment* led the field of contenders (with eleven nominations), followed by the patriotic drama *The Right Stuff* (with eight mentions) and Ingmar Bergman's final movie *Fanny och Alexander (Fanny and Alexander)* (with six nominations). Of these three films, *Terms of Endearment* was the overwhelming favourite for the Best Picture Oscar.

1983

Adapted from Larry McMurtry's novel about a stormy mother-daughter relationship, *Terms of Endearment* was the directorial debut of James L. Brooks, and starred Shirley MacLaine and Debra Winger, with Jack Nicholson in a supporting role. It opened in November to acclaim from critics and enjoyed notable box office success (NYT "not a perfect movie [but] one of the most engaging films of the year ... funny, touching, beautifully acted"; NYP "perfect and unforgettable ... ultimately heartbreaking"; NYDN "utterly captivating"; LAT "pungent and beautifully observed ... fascinating, tender, hilarious ... [an] extraordinary picture"; CT "one of the year's finest films"; WP "one of the most remarkable and satisfying tear-jerkers ever achieved by American filmmakers ... will loom very large in the Academy Awards picture, possibly as the eventual favorite in most of the major categories"; BG "endearing ... that uncommon kind of American movie, the kind that doesn't just manipulate our feelings, but releases them"; V "enormously enjoyable"; S&S "a crassly constructed slice of anti-feminism"). Although not listed by The New York Times as one of the year's top twenty films, *Terms of Endearment* was named Best Picture by both the New York Film Critics Circle and Los Angeles Film Critics Association and won both the National Board of Review prize (which it shared) and the Golden Globe (Drama). Its status as the Oscar favourite was confirmed when Brooks won the Directors Guild of America accolade in early March.

Directed by Philip Kaufman, *The Right Stuff* was an adaptation of Thomas Wolfe's novel about the early days of the American space programme. It earned positive reviews, but struggled to attract an audience (NYP "entirely too long [and] fragmented"; LAT "a brash, beautiful, deeply American film"; V "full of beauty, intelligence and excitement"; HRp "the picture of the year"). At the end of the year, *The Right Stuff* finished runner-up in the voting in New York, but its Oscar chances were dashed when Kaufman was unexpectedly overlooked for a Best Director nomination. No film had won the top statuette without a nomination for its director since *Grand Hotel* in 1931/32.

An intimate epic about children growing up in Sweden in the early twentieth century, Bergman's *Fanny och Alexander* was the director's most commercially successful release and amongst his most acclaimed projects (NYT "a big, dark, beautiful, generous, family chronicle ... [a] triumph"; NYP "something of a miracle ... a masterpiece"; LAT "magic [and] deeply moving"; CT "serene ... crowns Bergman's career ... watching this film is like diving into a long, rich novel"; BG "glorious"; PI "a masterpiece"; V "a rich tapestry of childhood memoirs"; S&S "a sustained triumph"; FQ "a lush, sprawling, glowing work"). It finished as runner-up for the National Society of Film Critics prize and won a clean sweep of the major American accolades for Best Foreign-Language Film. Despite six Oscar nods, including one for Bergman as Best Director, *Fanny och Alexander* was not included as a Best Picture contender.

1983

Nominated ahead of *Fanny och Alexander* for the Academy's top award were: *The Big Chill*, a popular film about a group of 1960s college students re-united years later at a friend's funeral (NYT "[a] sweet, sharp, melancholy comedy ... represents the best of mainstream American film making"; LAT "deft, witty, marvelously entertaining"; CT "has its incidental pleasures along with some major flaws"; WP "slick but superficial"; PI "remarkable"; V "amusing, splendidly-acted but rather shallow"; TT "a skilful social comedy"); *The Dresser*, a British drama about an ageing theatre star and his personal assistant (NYT "isn't satisfying in a conventional way, but it is great fun if you are moved by actors and acting"; LAT "[a] splendid, funny and eye-misting film"); and *Tender Mercies*, a drama about a former singer's relationship with a widow (NYT "funny, most appealing and most sharply observed"; NYP "wonderful"; LAT "has the feel of an American classic"; WP "simply fails to take care of fundamental dramatic business"; BG "a quietly magnificent movie"; V "outstanding"; TGM "minimal in everything but its impact"; MFB "a quietly, inoffensively bad film"). *Tender Mercies* had been the runner-up for the Los Angeles critics' top accolade.

Along with *Fanny och Alexander*, the most notable omission from the Oscar list was the Globe (Comedy/Musical) winner *Yentl*, a musical directed by Barbra Streisand (NYT "a vanity production, but even at its kitschiest it seems to be heartfelt"; NYP "not only wonderful: it's a blooming miracle"; LAT "fascinating"; CT "a surprisingly emotional musical"; WP "endearing ... [but has an] uninspired score and other shortcomings"; PI "pleasant, solid entertainment"; "V "ultimately bogs down due to repetitious musical numbers and overly methodical telling of a rather predictable story"; FQ "brilliant").

Also by-passed for consideration were: NBR co-winner *Betrayal*, a British adaptation of Harold Pinter's acclaimed play (NYT "a riveting film ... moving and immaculate"; LAT "sinuous, sophisticated, humorous and disturbing ... a darkly thrilling film"; CT "one of the year's finest films"; BG "so dense in its structure and so rich in character that the eternal love triangle is given new meaning"; V "absorbing"); BAFTA winner *Educating Rita* (LAT "warm and ingratiating ... one of the most thoroughly enjoyable films of the season"; CT "the fresh and funny movie turns into a lifeless, symmetrical set piece"; WP "charming"; TGB "an air of theatrical contrivance hovers over the proceedings"; MFB "a workmanlike if not entirely inspired adaptation"); the drama *Silkwood* which finished third in New York and for which Mike Nichols was a Best Director nominee (NYT "highly emotional"; NYP "powerful and honest [but] depressing"; LAT "haunting and deeply disturbing"; CT "isn't much fun to watch, but when a list of the best American movies about the working class is compiled, 'Silkwood' should be near the top"; WP "a jumbled account"; BG "a brilliant movie that puts art above polemics, and the facts above speculation ...

quite simply, one of the best films of this, or any, year"; PI "[a] troubling, brilliant drama"; V "very fine"; FQ "a complex portrait"); London Film Critics prize-winner *The King of Comedy* (NYT "not an absolute joy by a long shot [but] very funny [and] exhilarating"; LAT "a weird, obsessive film ... does not work [yet] still has more to keep us fascinated than any other American film released [this year] ... compelling"; CT "a most unhappy film"; PI "[a] masterful and daring film"; V "a royal disappointment"); BAFTA nominee *Heat and Dust* (NYT "haunting, beautiful [and] thoroughly satisfying ... demonstrating a sort of literary complexity that seldom works well on screen"; LAT "attempts too much [but] is rewarding ... casts its spell upon the viewer"; WP "fails"; BG "[a] subtly brilliant movie ... dazzling"; MFB "a likeable patchwork"); *To Be or Not to Be* (NYT "smashingly funny ... scarcely misses a comic beat right from the opening sequence"; WP "only succeeds in establishing a remarkable new low in remakes"; BG "appealing"; PI "[a] riotous remake ... turns out to be one of the year's most accomplished comedies"; V "very funny"); BAFTA nominee *Local Hero* (NYT "quirky, disarming [and] appealingly odd"; LAT "effortlessly charming"; CT "charming"; WP "a delightfully evocative movie ... enchanting"; BG "genuinely gracious and heartwarming ... [a] magnificent movie"; Sp "a touching and graceful and funny film"); *La Nuit de Varennes (That Night in Varennes)* (NYT "great historical pageant"; LAT "imaginative, absorbing and beautiful"; CT "immediately commands our interest"); *Le Retour de Martin Guerre (The Return of Martin Guerre)* (NYT "beautiful and moving"; LAT "superbly made, constantly surprising ... a film of notable freshness and vitality ... well-nigh flawless ... one of the most satisfying entertainments, serious yet captivating, of the year"; WP "a remarkably involving and touching period drama ... admirable [and] compelling"; BG "one of the best films of the year ... a work of art"; PI "an engrossing and beautifully made movie"; TGM "the film is thoughtful, graceful, gorgeously detailed, witty and effortlessly entertaining"); and surprise National Society of Film Critics prize-winner *La Notte di San Lorenzo (Night of the Shooting Stars)* (NYT "not a work that makes one think a lot ... the film has a studied, picturesque quality that makes it all seem self-congratulatory and a tiny bit condescending"; LAT "a jagged, amazing film, both breathtaking and satisfying ... warmhearted and earthy [and] constantly surprising ... an extraordinary film"; WP "magnificent ... an epic mosaic on the theme of a small-scale exodus ... one of the greatest human documents and emotional odysseys ever contrived for the medium ... [an] indispensable, indelible moviegoing experience"; BG "magnificent ... an exquisitely detailed, marvelously unaffected movie"; TGM "a work of popular art in the best sense").

On Oscar night, *Terms of Endearment* received five statuettes, including Best Picture. Bergman's *Fanny och Alexander*, meanwhile, collected the Academy Award for Best Foreign-Language Film.

BEST DIRECTOR

ACADEMY AWARDS
Bruce Beresford for *Tender Mercies*
Ingmar Bergman for *Fanny och Alexander (Fanny and Alexander)*
• **James L. Brooks for *Terms of Endearment***
Mike Nichols for *Silkwood*
Peter Yates for *The Dresser*

GOLDEN GLOBE AWARDS
Bruce Beresford – *Tender Mercies*
Ingmar Bergman – *Fanny och Alexander (Fanny and Alexander)*
James L. Brooks – *Terms of Endearment*
Mike Nichols – *Silkwood*
• **Barbra Streisand – *Yentl***
Peter Yates – *The Dresser*

DIRECTORS GUILD AWARD
Bruce Beresford – *Tender Mercies*
Ingmar Bergman
  – *Fanny och Alexander*
  (Fanny and Alexander)
• **James L. Brooks**
  – *Terms of Endearment*
Lawrence Kasdan – *The Big Chill*
Philip Kaufman – *The Right Stuff*

BRITISH ACADEMY AWARDS
• **Bill Forsyth – *Local Hero***
James Ivory – *Heat and Dust*
Sydney Pollack – *Tootsie*
Martin Scorsese
  – *The King of Comedy*

NEW YORK – Ingmar Bergman – *Fanny och Alexander (Fanny and Alexander)*
LOS ANGELES – James L. Brooks – *Terms of Endearment*
BOARD OF REVIEW – James L. Brooks – *Terms of Endearment*
NATIONAL SOCIETY – Paolo Taviani and Vittorio Taviani – *La Notte di San Lorenzo (Night of the Shooting Stars)*
LONDON – Andrej Wadja – *Danton*

"It would constitute a Hollywood scandal if Barbra Streisand were denied an Oscar nomination for her direction" said Gary Arnold in The Washington Post in relation to *Yentl*, the musical drama about a Jewish woman who poses as a man in order to study Talmudic Law which was the previous Best Actress Oscar winner's directorial debut (NYT "while there's no mistaking the fact that Miss

Streisand has lavished great attention on some of the film's details, her carelessness about others is perplexing ... a technical sloppiness is evident throughout the movie"; CT "her direction is more than adequate"; WP "an endearing triumph for Barbra Streisand ... [her] directing ability, perhaps most impressive and surprising in the way it generously showcases the work of fellow cast members, may transform her movie career"; BG "her intense conviction carries [the film] past the bloated Hollywood style in which it's made, saves it from being sunk by stylistic inappropriateness"; PI "proves that she is a fine and inventive director"; V "thoroughly professional [and a] perfectly creditable job"). There was outcry from the National Organization for Women at the end of January when Streisand was overlooked for a nomination by the Directors Guild of America, a snub that appeared all the more glaring when, just three days later, she became the first woman to win the Best Director Golden Globe. The furore intensified further on 16 February 1984 when Streisand was also left off the ballot for the Academy Award but all five of the male directors she had outpolled for the Globe received Oscar nominations.

Recognised by the Directors Guild, the Hollywood Foreign Press Association and the Academy were: Australian filmmaker Bruce Beresford for his first American film, *Tender Mercies* (NYT "the success of [the film is due to his] secure sense of what he wants to see on the screen and his ability to put it there"; BG "unobtrusive ... Beresford's major attributes – his concentration on character over plot and his excellent sense of lighting and composition – serve him well"); and the Swedish master film-maker Ingmar Bergman for *Fanny och Alexander (Fanny and Alexander)* (NYT "another triumph in the career of one of our greatest living film makers"; LAT "his most generous and life-affirming work"; CT "this is the work of a director who has found his way to serenity"; WP "sometimes heavy-handed"; BG "a glorious exclamation point on the illustrious career of the best director of our time").

Also making the Globe and Oscar ballots were previous winner Mike Nichols for *Silkwood* (NYT "the most serious work Mr. Nichols has yet done in films"; WP "monotony of Nichols' inert, detached pictorial style"; BG "understated"; V "impressive") and Peter Yates for *The Dresser* (NYT "directed with immense affection").

Nichols and Yates were included ahead of first-time DGA finalists Lawrence Kasdan for *The Big Chill* (NYT "it's a particular achievement for Mr Kasdan"; WP "flows smoothly and sustains a professionally glib, polished style"; PI "accomplished") and New York Film Critics Circle prize runner-up Philip Kaufman for *The Right Stuff* (NYT "succeeded in bringing a verisimilitude to the movie"; WP "has assembled a terrific group of character actors and emerging young stars, and then orchestrated moments that will leave their work permanently imprinted on the sentiments of moviegoers ... Kaufman is so good with actors and social contexts"; PI "has steadfastly resisted taking the easy way out ... has made a film that is patriotic on a deeper level").

Other notable absentees from the Oscar list were: Martin Scorsese for *The King of Comedy* (NYT "confirms his reputation as one of the most original voices of his film generation"; LAT "Scorsese may be incapable of making an uninteresting film"); Lewis Gilbert for *Educating Rita* (NYT "ponderous"; LAT "deft"; WP "thoughtfully paced"; V "a marvelous job"; TGM "if you were ever curious how a bad director can destroy the work of two talented actors and a slight, but funny, script, you need look no further than 'Educating Rita' ... Gilbert simply matches the verbal cliches with visual ones ... plodding, listless direction"; MFB "workmanlike"); BAFTA winner Bill Forsyth for *Local Hero* (NYT "film-making that is thoroughly original in an unobtrusive way ... he has developed a dryly whimsical style"; WP "Forsyth's disarming, wry, whimsical outlook has ripened into a personal style of extraordinary deftness and enchantment"; MFB "is at full and masterful stretch"; Sp "deft"); BAFTA nominee James Ivory for *Heat and Dust* (NYT "graceful"; BG "effortlessly cuts back and forth [between the two parts of the story]"); Daniel Vigne for *Le Retour de Martin Guerre (The Return of Martin Guerre)* (LAT "superbly made"; WP "has sustained a fascinating illusion of period authenticity"; BG "exquisite direction"; PI "beautifully made"); and surprise National Society of Film Critics prize-winners brothers Paolo Taviani and Vittorio Taviani for the war film *La Notte di San Lorenzo (Night of the Shooting Stars)* (NYT "studied"; LAT "seem to have transcended their own material to create an extraordinary film"; WP "[it's] a great movie subject [and] the fraternal filmmaking team never lose their grip on an exceptional opportunity"; BG "[has an] exquisite and sustained tone"; PI "the Tavianis have hit upon a marvelous method of telling their story"; TGM "technically distinguished ... there are sequences of bravura filmmaking").

Although *Terms of Endearment* was favoured for the year's top Best Picture accolades, many observers believed that the Guild and the Academy would follow the example of the New York critics and honour Bergman for *Fanny och Alexander*, which he had announced would be his final film as director. Despite this, however, the Guild and the Academy both gave their plaudits to Brooks, who had previously collected the National Board of Review and Los Angeles Film Critics Association awards (he won the latter ahead of Beresford).

BEST ACTOR

ACADEMY AWARDS
Michael Caine as 'Dr Frank Bryant' in *Educating Rita*
Tom Conti as 'Gowan McGland' in *Reuben, Reuben*
Tom Courtenay as 'Norman' in *The Dresser*
• **Robert Duvall as 'Mac Sledge' in *Tender Mercies***
Albert Finney as 'Sir' in *The Dresser*

GOLDEN GLOBE AWARDS

(Drama)
Tom Conti – *Reuben, Reuben*
• **Tom Courtenay – *The Dresser***
• **Robert Duvall – *Tender Mercies***
Richard Farnsworth – *The Grey Fox*
Albert Finney – *The Dresser*
Al Pacino – *Scarface*
Eric Roberts – *Star 80*

(Comedy/Musical)
Woody Allen – *Zelig*
• **Michael Caine – *Educating Rita***
Tom Cruise – *Risky Business*
Eddie Murphy – *Trading Places*
Mandy Patinkin – *Yentl*

BRITISH ACADEMY AWARDS
Michael Caine – *Beyond the Limit (The Honorary Consul)*
• **Michael Caine – *Educating Rita***
Robert De Niro – *The King of Comedy*
• **Dustin Hoffman – *Tootsie***

NEW YORK – Robert Duvall – *Tender Mercies*
LOS ANGELES – Robert Duvall – *Tender Mercies*
BOARD OF REVIEW – Tom Conti – *Merry Christmas, Mr Lawrence* and *Reuben, Reuben*
NATIONAL SOCIETY – Gérard Depardieu – *Danton* and *Le Retour de Martin Guerre (The Return of Martin Guerre)*

As a former country and western singer who begins a romance with a widow in *Tender Mercies*, Robert Duvall was named Best Actor by both the New York Film Critics Circle and the Los Angeles Film Critics Association, shared the Golden Globe (Drama) and earned his fourth Oscar nomination (NYT "great ... thoroughly transformed"; LAT "absolutely shattering ... seems to have willed himself into another body"; BG "there isn't a trace of artifice in a performance that is brilliantly understated"; V "dignified and moving"; TT "beautifully played"; HRp "a performance that should win him the Oscar"; MFB "heartfelt").

Duvall was favoured to win the Academy Award over four British actors: both Albert Finney as a mentally unstable theatre actor (NYP "dazzling ... a tumultuous performance"; V "startling [in an] indelible screen performance"; TGM "the most flamboyant, delightfully theatrical male performance of the year"; TT "consummate technique ... [a] marvel"; MFB "showily brilliant [but] does not quite convince in the crucial scene"; Time "a revelation") and Globe (Drama) co-winner Tom Courtenay as the star's personal assistant (NYP "dazzling"; V "delicately shaded"; TGM "technically impeccable, but entirely external"; TT "skilful"; Time "perfectly polished") in *The Dresser* (NYT "riveting ... the two actors give you a very flashy run for your money"; LAT "they are the all-stops-out characters that actors cherish, and Courtenay and Finney do them full justice"); Globe (Comedy/Musical) winner Michael Caine as an alcoholic university professor in *Educating Rita* (NYT "superior"; NYP "his best work in years"; LAT "convincing ... a career high point"; PI "at his world-weary best"; TGM "a superlative performance ... first-rate"; TT "expertly played"); and National Board of Review winner Tom Conti as a poet in love with a student in *Reuben, Reuben* (NYT "Conti is fine in a big, rich role ... stylishly acted"; LAT "brilliant ... one of the more electrifying performances of the year"; PI "externalizes his emotions with amazing control ... he's a joy to watch"; V "a tour de force"). The NBR also cited Conti for his turn as a PoW in *Merry Christmas, Mr Lawrence* (NYT "has some fine moments"; LAT "the film's true star"; CT "fine ... is particularly well cast"; WP "quietly stalwart in a performance that would probably seem irresistibly noble and sensitive in a less sluggish picture"; PI "in the thankless role, his rueful asides are the best line-readings in the movie").

The most glaring absentee from the Oscar list was another foreigner: Frenchman Gérard Depardieu, who won the National Society of Film Critics prize ahead of Duvall by 34 points to 26, and was the runner-up in the voting in New York, for his performances in *Le Retour de Martin Guerre (The Return of Martin Guerre)* (NYT "superb ... a beautifully executed performance, its power always controlled"; NYP "has never been better"; LAT "[the film] affords Depardieu one of the most engaging and heroic roles of his career"; CT "impeccably performed"; BG "[a] masterful performance"; PI "played with startling virtuosity") and *Danton* (NYT "played with all stops out"; WP "if there's a heroic, tragic dimension to Depardieu's characterization, it eludes me"; BG "a star turn, not an instance of an actor getting inside [a character's] skin"; PI "some of [his] best work, surpassing even his excellent performance earlier this year [as Martin Guerre]"; MFB "plays unashamedly to the gallery").

Several Golden Globe nominees were bypassed by Academy members, including: Richard Farnsworth in the 1982 Canadian drama *The Grey Fox*, for which he'd share the London Film Critics prize the following year (NYT "a delight ... remarkably appealing"; NYP "a great performance"; LAT "proves absolutely his power as the star of a film"; CT "certainly worthy of some kind of acting award"; PI "sets just the right tone of vulnerable toughness ... is especially adroit"); Al Pacino in *Scarface* (NYT "played with such mounting intensity that one half expects him to self-destruct before the finale ... a busy performance [but] not a mannered one"; LAT "is best in the earlier sections"; CT "another major disappointment from Al Pacino"; WP "[a] vivid portrayal"; BG "misfires"; V "extremely effective"); Eric Roberts in *Star 80* (NYT "acted with great flamboyant intensity ... initially riveting [in] a technical tour de force ... [but] the performance becomes a little bit aimless"; LAT "in Eric Roberts' hands, the flashy, obnoxious Snider becomes someone you watch with horrified fascination"; CT "played with a rabid, imploding energy ... walks away with the movie"; WP "he's obviously trying very hard, but there's not much commanding ferocity in his rages"; BG "one of the best performances of the year"; V "a startlingly fine performance"; TGM "extraordinary ... the most imaginative performance any actor has given this year"); Eddie Murphy in *Trading Places* (NYT "[a] lithe, graceful, uproarious performance"; CT "marking himself as a major comedy talent"; WP "doesn't provide [him] with a significantly enhanced showcase, but it does allow him to confirm [his] exhilarating comic authority ... [he] makes the most of every moment"; BG "shines"); and Mandy Patinkin in *Yentl* (CT "the linchpin of the movie ... never overplaying his hand"; WP "emerges as a powerful combination of leading man and character actor").

Also overlooked were: both Jeremy Irons (NYT "extraordinary ... dazzling"; LAT "hits precisely the right tone"; WP "splendid"; BG "astounding") and the previous year's winner Ben Kingsley (NYP "distinguished ... emerges as a real artist of stunning versatility"; LAT "holds center stage"; WP "splendid"; BG "as close to perfection as one can expect"; PI "mesmerizing"; V "an immaculate performance, brimming with subtle shadings"; MFB "a chilling portrait") in *Betrayal*; BAFTA nominee Robert De Niro in *The King of Comedy* (NYT "one of the best, most complex and most flamboyant performances of his career"; LAT "he has transformed himself"; BG "a bravura performance"; PI "has the task of making a totally unsympathetic character hold the screen for nearly two hours ... he summons every ounce of his awesome gift, and brings it off in a piece of acting virtuosity that would be a triumph even if the rest of the film were a failure"; V "another virtuoso performance"); and both Marcello Mastroianni (NYT "dazzling"; LAT "[an] unsparing and gallant performance") and Jean-Louis Barrault (NYT "superb"; LAT "a great, intelligent performance ... remarkable") in *La Nuit de Varennes (That Night in Varennes)*.

On Oscar night, as expected, Duvall won the Academy Award. The following year, Finney was honoured at the Berlin Film Festival while both he and Courtenay were unsuccessful nominees for the Best Actor BAFTA.

1983

BEST ACTRESS

ACADEMY AWARDS
Jane Alexander as 'Carol Wetherby' in *Testament*
• **Shirley MacLaine as 'Aurora Greenway' in *Terms of Endearment***
Meryl Streep as 'Karen Silkwood' in *Silkwood*
Julie Walters as 'Susan "Rita" White' in *Educating Rita*
Debra Winger as 'Emma Horton' in *Terms of Endearment*

GOLDEN GLOBE AWARDS

(Drama)
Jane Alexander – *Testament*
Bonnie Bedelia – *Heart Like a Wheel*
• **Shirley MacLaine**
  – *Terms of Endearment*
Meryl Streep – *Silkwood*
Debra Winger – *Terms of Endearment*

(Comedy/Musical)
Anne Bancroft – *To Be or Not to Be*
Jennifer Beals – *Flashdance*
Linda Ronstadt
  – *Pirates of Penzance*
Barbra Streisand – *Yentl*
• **Julie Walters – *Educating Rita***

BRITISH ACADEMY AWARDS
Jessica Lange – *Tootsie*
Phyllis Logan – *Another Time, Another Place*
Meryl Streep – *Sophie's Choice*
• **Julie Walters – *Educating Rita***

NEW YORK – Shirley MacLaine – *Terms of Endearment*
LOS ANGELES – Shirley MacLaine – *Terms of Endearment*
BOARD OF REVIEW – Linda Hunt – *The Year of Living Dangerously*
NATIONAL SOCIETY – Debra Winger – *Terms of Endearment*

"I have wondered for twenty-six years what this would feel like," said Shirley MacLaine as she stood at the podium on Oscar night, holding the Best Actress statuette, "Thankyou for terminating the suspense." First nominated for her role in *Some Came Running* in 1958, forty-nine-year-old MacLaine won at her fifth nomination for *Terms of Endearment* (NYT "played with perfect composure ... a lovely mixture of longing, stubbornness and reserve ... if the gods are attending, [this performance] will win her not only an Oscar nomination, but the award itself"; NYP "literally lights a match to the screen"; LAT "that MacLaine can give us every one of Aurora's facets and still make her infinitely compassionate is the measure of the actress' art"; WP "memorably represented"; Time "a brave, bravura performance").

In addition to winning the Academy Award (just two years after her younger brother, Warren Beatty, received the Best Director Oscar for *Reds*), MacLaine also collected the New York Film Critics Circle and Los Angeles Film Critics Association prizes and the Golden Globe (Drama). It was her third Globe, having won in the Comedy/Musical category in 1960 and 1963. A year after her Oscar victory, MacLaine was an unsuccessful nominee for the Best Actress award at the British Academy Awards in London where she was outpolled by an actress who did not even receive a nomination in Hollywood that year: Maggie Smith in the British war-time comedy *A Private Function*.

The main challenger for the Academy Award was MacLaine's co-star, Debra Winger, who received her second consecutive Oscar nomination for her performance as the dying daughter in *Terms of Endearment* (NYT "stunning"; NYP "awesome"; LAT "inhabits every scene she is in with a perception and a believability that are extraordinary"; CT "impressive"; WP "marvellous ... the crowning achievement [of the] movie ... Winger establishes a claim [on the Best Actress Oscar] that may be as difficult to challenge as Meryl Streep's a year ago"; BG "convinces"; PDN "Winger is a revelation"). Winger was named Best Actress by the National Society of Film Critics and was only very narrowly outpolled by MacLaine in the voting by the circle in New York, losing on the fifth ballot 32 points to 30.

Some observers believed that MacLaine and Winger would split the vote between them, thus handing the Oscar to one of the other nominees. Some observers thought the most likely beneficiary in this scenario would be the runner-up for the prize in Los Angeles, Jane Alexander, who was nominated for a fourth time as a mother looking after her family following a nuclear holocaust in *Testament* (NYT "powerfully acted ... convincing"; NYP "devastating"; LAT "in a role that could have become morbid or neurotic, Alexander reveals an unfolding warmth, an endurance and strength that ultimately becomes noble ... it is a side of Alexander than no one has caught before, not even in her finest work"; CT "one can't fault the performance"; BG "we don't feel her anguish with appropriate intensity"; PI "a beautiful, low-key performance"; V "an understated performance that deserves Academy Award consideration"; TT "played with fine unsentimentality"). "Three times, Alexander has been nominated for Academy Awards," observed Rick Lyman in The Philadelphia Inquirer, "but she has never won one. Maybe this time."

Another potential winner in the event of a split vote was the previous year's winner Meryl Streep, who garnered her fifth nod in six years, and her third consecutive Best Actress mention, for her portrayal of nuclear safety activist Karen Silkwood in *Silkwood* (NYT "another stunning performance ... a tour de force as funny as it is moving ... superb"; NYP "too calculatedly studied to be totally real"; WP "Streep's portrayal of Silkwood sustains a relentlessly droopy pathos"; CT "once again a wonder here ... seemingly effortless acting"; BG "confirms her status among the best of contemporary actresses [with an] excellent performance"; PI "it's getting a little boring to hail each new Streep performance as the best she has ever given; problem is, it's true again ... creates the character from ground zero without self-conscious gestures or little bits of business. She is able to convey on the strength of her skill alone the specter of a contradictory, real person"; V "another career triumph ... her performance is a thrill to behold"; TT "proves what a ranging actress she is"; FQ "embodying the role with accustomed professionalism ... makes her character breathe [by revealing] the emotional complexity behind her actions").

The real dark horse, other critics believed, was English actress Julie Walters who made the list for her turn as a working class hairdresser who attends university in *Educating Rita*, a role she had originated on stage in London (NYT "superior"; NYP "a joy"; LAT "a splashy screen debut ... captivating"; CT "would be routine, conventional entertainment save for [her] energetic performance"; WP "a buoyant, joyous performance"; PI "engaging"; V "certainly ranks as one of the top femme performances so far this year"; TGM "first-rate ... [a] superior performance ... marvelously upbeat"; TT "expertly played"). In the lead-up to the Oscars, Walters won both the Globe (Comedy/Musical) and the Best Actress BAFTA. Her victory in London came over a field of nominees that included the previous year's Oscar winner, Meryl Streep in *Sophie's Choice*.

The most glaring omission from the Academy's list was Bonnie Bedelia as a championship drag-racer in *Heart Like a Wheel* (NYT "a fine performance, combining flintiness and strength with a gentler sensibility ... [a] strong, funny, sharply observed performance"; NYP "[an] inspired performance ... beautifully structured ... painfully real ... three-dimensional"; LAT "wonderful"; V "a terrific performance"; S&S "Bedelia's understated performance is magnificent"; MFB "beautifully understated"; Time "quite spectacular"). The film's initial April release had floundered after poor preview screenings in the American mid-west, but the movie was given a wide release and an awards season campaign after Tom Sherak took over as President of Distribution at Twentieth Century-Fox and it earned a positive reception at the New York Film Festival. The studio's efforts garnered Bedelia a Best Actress (Drama) Golden Globe nomination, but not recognition from the Academy.

Also overlooked were: Mariel Hemingway as the murdered model Dorothy Stratten in *Star 80* (NYT "a true performance, as fully realized as the somewhat limited circumstances allow"; LAT "makes a gallant stab at playing her [but] Stratten's unique quality eludes her"; WP "gives a performance that's profound ... playing [the role] without a false note"; V "does a fine job throughout"; TGM "radiant"); Barbra Streisand as a Jewish woman who disguises herself as a man in order to study Talmudic Law in the musical *Yentl*, a film which she also directed, produced and co-wrote (NYT "brings a disarming humility to her performance"; NYP "vulnerable [and] appealing"; WP "Streisand's recovery of her original form is almost complete in 'Yentl' though there's a self-conscious side to her performance"; PI "reconfirms that she is a marvelous farceur, a great singer and an actress who knows her range and works beautifully within it"); Globe nominee Anne Bancroft in *To Be or Not to Be* (NYT "the revelation for film audiences is that Miss Bancroft is such a wildly gifted comedienne ... an equal partner who never fails to meet Mr Brooks's comic challenges ... terrific"; CT "radiant"; WP "contributes an acceptable reprise of the [Carole] Lombard role"; PI "a delightful concoction of femme fatale and prima donna ... makes a fine foil for [Mel] Brooks' backstage posturing"); Cannes honoree Hanna Schygulla as the lady-in-waiting in *La Nuit de Varennes (That Night in Varennes)* (NYT "brings an astonishing composure to her performance"; LAT "brilliant"); Mary Steenburgen in *Cross Creek* as novelist Marjorie Kinnan Rawlings, upon whose novel was based the 1946 Oscar-nominated film *The Yearling* (NYT "[Rawlings'] triumphs, however contrived or sentimentalized, really do feel like triumphs here [and] much of the credit for that is attributable to Miss Steenburgen who manages to seem more authentically of the place and of the period than anything or anyone else [in the film] ... Steenburgen eloquently embodies the self-sufficiency and determination [the film] means to eulogize"; NYP "a performance of quiet strength and lyrical sweetness"; LAT "Steenburgen has only one [scene] in which [her character] is even alive; the rest of the performance is stiff, removed and emetic"; WP "sleepwalks through her role ... oddly affected"; PI "played with spunky candor"; TGM "has fashioned a delightful career portraying eccentrics; that her performance here proves she cannot compete with Sally Field should not do her any long-term harm"; MFB "good"); Patricia Hodge in *Betrayal* (NYT "extraordinary ... dazzling"; LAT "marvellously felicitous"; WP "splendid"; BG "astounding ... as close to perfection as one can expect ... performs brilliantly ... through subtle gestures and appropriate pauses, interprets Pinter's character with absolute confidence"; PI "magnificent"); and Greta Scacchi in *Heat and Dust* (NYT "dominates [in] a good role, exceptionally well played"; LAT "captivating"; BG "first-rate").

MacLaine reprised the role of Aurora Greenway in *The Evening Star*, a 1996 sequel to *Terms of Endearment* (based on McMurtry's follow-up novel), but did not garner recognition from the Academy for her performance.

1983

BEST SUPPORTING ACTOR

ACADEMY AWARDS
Charles Durning as 'Colonel Ehrhardt' in *To Be or Not to Be*
John Lithgow as 'Sam Burns' in *Terms of Endearment*
• **Jack Nicholson as 'Garrett Breedlove' in *Terms of Endearment***
Sam Shepard as 'Chuck Yeager' in *The Right Stuff*
Rip Torn as 'Marsh Turner' in *Cross Creek*

GOLDEN GLOBE AWARDS
Steven Bauer – *Scarface*
Charles Durning – *To Be or Not to Be*
Gene Hackman – *Under Fire*
• **Jack Nicholson – *Terms of Endearment***
Kurt Russell – *Silkwood*

BRITISH ACADEMY AWARDS
• **Denholm Elliott – *Trading Places***
Bob Hoskins – *Beyond the Limit (The Honorary Consul)*
Burt Lancaster – *Local Hero*
Jerry Lewis – *The King of Comedy*

NEW YORK – Jack Nicholson – *Terms of Endearment*
LOS ANGELES – Jack Nicholson – *Terms of Endearment*
BOARD OF REVIEW – Jack Nicholson – *Terms of Endearment*
NATIONAL SOCIETY – Jack Nicholson – *Terms of Endearment*

The character of former astronaut Garrett Breedlove does not appear in Larry McMurtry's popular novel 'Terms of Endearment'. In adapting the book, writer-director James L. Brooks decided that the central character of Aurora Greenway needed to be softened, and so invented Breedlove as a love interest for her. The part was to have been played by Burt Reynolds, but conflicting work commitments meant that the role went to Jack Nicholson instead. Upon the movie's release he won rave reviews (NYT "possibly the best performance [he has] ever given ... a masterly comic invention, with a magnificent repulsiveness that [he] turns into pure hilarity"; LAT "entirely endearing ... brilliant"; CT "a delight"; BG "[he] takes the biggest gamble, using virtuosic understatement to hold his own against MacLaine's flamboyance ... he draws us into a character we never feel is very deep, yet he makes us think he's worth knowing anyway"; Time "a joyously comic display"; MFB "a fine performance").

1983

As the awards season unfolded, Nicholson collected accolades from all six of the major American prize-giving groups, all of whom had honoured him before. He was the first man to win a clean sweep since the sixth group, the Los Angeles Film Critics Association, had begun handing out prizes in 1975. Surprisingly, despite his clean sweep of the American-based accolades, Nicholson was not even nominated for the Best Supporting Actor BAFTA when *Terms of Endearment* was released in Britain the following year. Nicholson's second Oscar win came from his seventh nomination in fifteen years.

Nominated by the Academy for the second consecutive year were both Charles Durning, as a Nazi officer in the remake of *To Be or Not to Be* (LAT "the one actor who towers over the circumstances is Charles Durning, who manages to make his dense and bombastic Gestapo chief a figure of hilarity ... [he] is far superior to the rest of the picture"; BG "awful, [just] a caricature"; V "a standout"; TT "fine") and John Lithgow as the bank employee in love with Aurora's daughter in *Terms of Endearment* (NYT "there are some lovely supporting performances in [the film], most notably John Lithgow's as the bashful Iowa banker"; LAT "superlative"; BG "fills the screen with squashed decency as the Iowa bank manager"). Lithgow had been the runner-up in the voting in Los Angeles for his performances in *Terms of Endearment* and as a disturbed passenger in *Twilight Zone - The Movie* (NYT "[he] is both legitimate and comic"; LAT "Lithgow begins roughly at the intensity of King Lear's storm scene and builds, touchingly and exhaustingly, from there"; WP "plays [the role] with spellbinding, feverish intensity"; BG "[a] manic performance").

Each considered by Oscar voters for the first time were actor-writer Sam Shepard as the first man to break the sound barrier in *The Right Stuff* (CT "playwright Sam Shepard is movie-star-memorable as Yeager"; WP "swaggering with country confidence and sex appeal"; PI "plays him with an almost symbolic force as the man who defines an almost indefinable quality") and Rip Torn as a struggling Florida farmer in *Cross Creek* (NYP "thrilling"; LAT "the film's great jolt of electricity comes from Rip Torn's backwards gentleman ... every breath Torn takes is in character ... touching [with] heartfelt, free-wheeling dimensions"; PI "one of the best supporting performances of the year ... a luscious piece of screen acting"; V "thoroughly watchable and entertaining"; TGM "played archly and convincingly"; TT "forceful"; MFB "good"). Torn, the cousin of previous Oscar winner Sissy Spacek, and the husband of previous Oscar nominee Geraldine Page, was nominated for portraying the man on whom was based the character played by Gregory Peck in *The Yearling*.

It was little surprise that New York Film Critics Circle prize runner-up Ed Harris failed to make the Oscar ballot for his acclaimed portrayal of astronaut and politician John Glenn in *The Right Stuff* as Warner Bros. had promoted his work for consideration in the Best Actor category (CT "absolutely apple-pie likeable as John Glenn ... [he] is definitely an actor to watch"; WP "[a] magnetic portrayal"; PI "in Ed Harris' fine reading of Glenn there are many humanizing touches"; TGM "when Ed Harris brings John Glenn to life, the feat is impressive, but what the audience is admiring is less an act of artistry than an act of impersonation; it's an artful impersonation, but there's no room for an actor's imagination"). Leonard Klady in The Washington Post felt the category designation left Harris with "little chance for [a] nomination".

It was something of a surprise to many, however, when Burt Lancaster was excluded from both the Golden Globe and Academy Award ballots for his turn as a billionaire oil tycoon obsessed with star-gazing in *Local Hero* (CT "his presence gives 'Local Hero' an urgency and importance that such a delicate film needs"; BG "his self-assured dignity leavens his wacky portrayal with just the right measure of genuine insanity"; S&S "[a] nicely judged performance"; Sp "performs extraordinarily well"). "The 69-year-old Lancaster, who just gets better with age, was denied the Best Actor Oscar for his performance in 'Atlantic City', but he should be the early favourite for a Best Supporting Actor award in next year's competition," had opined Michael Blown in The Boston Globe when the film opened in North America in March. Lancaster's performance garnered him a BAFTA nomination, but no awards season recognition in Hollywood.

Academy members also overlooked three performers short-listed for the Golden Globe: Steven Bauer in *Scarface* (NYT "excellent"; LAT "most notable"; WP "[a] seemingly effortless portrayal ... impressive"); Gene Hackman in *Under Fire* (LAT "nicely authoritative"; CT "acted meticulously"; PI "[a] Grade-A contribution"); and Kurt Russell in *Silkwood* (NYT "very, very good"; BG "effective"; PI "excellent").

Excluded from consideration for both the Globe and the Oscar were: both Jeff Goldblum and William Hurt in *The Big Chill*; Allan Hubbard in *Tender Mercies* (NYT "does a convincing job"; V "almost steals the show"); Leon Ames in *Testament* (V "[a] deeply felt portrayal"); BAFTA nominee Jerry Lewis in *The King of Comedy* (NYT "played with brilliant solemnity"; LAT "faultless"; CT "a surprisingly restrained performance"; BG "a surprisingly evocative portrayal"); Ed Asner as the defence lawyer in *Daniel* (NYT "the kind of heavy, sturdy performance that is the order of the day here"; LAT "fine ... a humble, self-effacing, honest performance"; BG "understated"); Jean-Louis Trintignant in *La Nuit de Varennes (That Night in Varennes)* (NYT "superb"); and all four of the actors recognised by the British Academy, including winner Denholm Elliott as the butler in *Trading Places* (NYT "quite good").

1983

BEST SUPPORTING ACTRESS

ACADEMY AWARDS
Cher as 'Dolly Pelliker' in *Silkwood*
Glenn Close as 'Sarah Cooper' in *The Big Chill*
• **Linda Hunt as 'Billy Kwan' in *The Year of Living Dangerously***
Amy Irving as 'Hadass' in *Yentl*
Alfre Woodard as 'Geechee' in *Cross Creek*

GOLDEN GLOBE AWARDS
Barbara Carrera – *Never Say Never Again*
• **Cher – *Silkwood***
Tess Harper – *Tender Mercies*
Linda Hunt – *The Year of Living Dangerously*
Joanna Pacula – *Gorky Park*

BRITISH ACADEMY AWARDS
• **Jamie Lee Curtis – *Trading Places***
Teri Garr – *Tootsie*
Rosemary Harris – *The Ploughman's Lunch*
Maureen Lipman – *Educating Rita*

NEW YORK – Linda Hunt – *The Year of Living Dangerously*
LOS ANGELES – Linda Hunt – *The Year of Living Dangerously*
BOARD OF REVIEW – Linda Hunt – *The Year of Living Dangerously*
NATIONAL SOCIETY – Sandra Bernhard – *The King of Comedy*

The Los Angeles Times declared the Best Supporting Actress Oscar race as "the toughest category of the year with no clear winner."

The critics' choice had been Linda Hunt, a four-foot-nine-inch tall New York theatre actress, for her performance as a male Chinese-Australian photo-journalist in *The Year of Living Dangerously* (NYT "not exactly dominating [her co-star's] performances, but providing the film with its dramatic center, is Miss Hunt's haunted Billy Kwan"; LAT "Hunt's Kwan is an inspired creation ... complex and compelling ... the kind of performance that wins Oscars"; CT "arresting ... a woman plays a man, and quite convincingly"; WP "manages to upstage [the two] stars ... [an] extraordinary [and] marvelous performance ... this tiny, brilliantly elusive actress has submerged herself in another sexual identity ... it's unlikely that anyone who sees [the film] will ever forget Hunt's performance"; BG "[a] magnificent performance"; V "an astonishing feat of acting"; Time "[a] star-making performance"; Sp "a most remarkable performance – both touching and sinister"). Hunt was honoured by the New York Film Critics Circle, the Los Angeles Film Critics Association and the National Board of Review.

Another actress favoured by the critics' groups was singer and former television personality Cher as Karen Silkwood's lesbian housemate and nuclear power plant co-worker in the drama *Silkwood* (NYT "very, very good"; NYP "excellent"; LAT "touching and funny"; BG "effective"; PI "excellent ... startling"; V "has some wonderful moments"). Cher was runner-up for both the east and west coast plaudits and the National Society of Film Critics prize. She lost the voting for the New York circle's accolade to Hunt by just a single point. Cher was also the winner of the Best Supporting Actress Golden Globe.

Nominated by the Academy for the first time were both Amy Irving as the innocent young Polish Jew who is deceived into marrying the title character in *Yentl* (WP "portrayed with dreamy mock-naïve seductiveness") and Alfre Woodard as Marjorie Kinnan Rawlings' housekeeper in *Cross Creek* (LAT "a fine debut"; PI "a lovely performance"; V "registers strongly"; TGM "terrific"; TT "touching"; MFB "good"). Woodard tied with Cher as the runner-up for the Los Angeles circle's plaudit. The only previous nominee on the list was Glenn Close as one of the reunited college friends in *The Big Chill* (PI "marvelous"; V "splendidly-acted").

Warner Bros. pushed for Barbara Carrera to be recognised for her turn as Fatima Blush in the James Bond movie *Never Say Never Again* (NYT "awfully overwrought [and] extravagantly in love with the idea of evil [but nonetheless] a major part of the fun"; WP "foremost among the enthusiastic cast is gorgeous antagonist Barbara Carrera, who was just born to be bad; she's deliciously vicious ... each entrance by Carrera is a special comic event ... [ends up] stealing the show"; MFB "rather strident"). However, leading film critic Leonard Klady dismissed the campaign in The Washington Post reporting that no one in Hollywood took the ads seriously and it was merely additional publicity for the film. Carrera was nonetheless among the Golden Globe nominees. An Oscar nomination, however, eluded her.

Also overlooked by the Academy were: NSFC winner Sandra Bernhard as the insane fan in *The King of Comedy* (NYT "impeccable ... unforgettably alarming [in a] fine performance"; LAT "a startling original ... she gives an exhausting, unique performance that is so personal it's impossible to imagine another young actress in the role"; CT "the Masha character [is] a total cartoon, and Bernhard's performance didn't increase Masha's credibility"); Globe nominee Joanne Pacula in *Gorky Park* (LAT "Pacula is beautiful, and certainly up to the demands of the role, which calls for her to be sullen and angry 97% of the time"; BG "projects doe-eyed dissident desperation"); Mary Jo Deschanel as

Annie Glenn in *The Right Stuff* (LAT "outstanding"; WP "a nearly mute but moving performance"); previous Best Actress nominee Carroll Baker in *Star 80* (LAT "deft"; WP "an impressive comeback"); Amanda Plummer in *Daniel* (NYT "brings a frightening urgency to the role of Daniel's troubled sister, but she's almost too real and unpredictable for her surroundings here"; LAT "finds her full power"; WP "sustains a pitch of craziness so high that it tends to inhibit pathos"); Michelle Pfeiffer in *Scarface* (NYT "will not be easily forgotten"; LAT "most notable"; WP "good supporting work"); both Ellen Barkin (NYT "superb") and Tess Harper (NYT "superb ... brings a beautifully understated dignity to the role"; BG "excellent support"; V "most affecting"; TGM "makes Rosa Lee, her first film role, believable"; TT "beautifully played"; MFB "heartfelt") in *Tender Mercies*; both Zena Walker as the actor's wife (NYP "excellent") and Eileen Atkins, a BAFTA nominee the following year, as the stage manager (LAT "it is [her] quietly sane Madge who lingers longest in your memory and in your affections") in *The Dresser*; and British Academy Award winner Jamie Lee Curtis in *Trading Places* (NYT "quite good ... manages to turn a hard-edged, miniskirted prostitute into a character of unexpected charm"; WP "a cheerful comic discovery ... better than the material warrants"; BG "brings another dimension to the stereotype").

Despite the various critics' prizes, the relatively unknown Hunt was considered less likely to claim the statuette than either Cher, the high-profile winner of the Globe, or Close, who was nominated for a second year in a row for her part in a box office hit. Thus, when Hunt won the Oscar, The Times described her as a "surprise" winner.

BEST PICTURE

ACADEMY AWARDS
• *Amadeus*
(Zaentz, Orion, 158 mins, 19 Sep 1984, $51.6m, 11 noms)
The Killing Fields
(Goldcrest, Warner Bros., 141 mins, 2 Nov 1984, $34.6m, 7 noms)
A Passage to India
(GW Films, Columbia, 163 mins, 14 Dec 1984, $26.4m, 11 noms)
Places in the Heart
(Tri-Star, 112 mins, 21 Sep 1984, $34.7m, 7 noms)
A Soldier's Story
(Caldrix, Columbia, 101 mins, 14 Sep 1984, $22.1m, 3 noms)

GOLDEN GLOBE AWARDS
(Drama)
• *Amadeus*
The Cotton Club
The Killing Fields
Places in the Heart
A Soldier's Story

(Comedy/Musical)
Beverly Hills Cop
Ghostbusters
Micki and Maude
• *Romancing the Stone*
Splash!

BRITISH ACADEMY AWARDS
The Dresser
• *The Killing Fields*
Paris, Texas
A Private Function

NEW YORK – *A Passage to India*
LOS ANGELES – *Amadeus*
BOARD OF REVIEW – *A Passage to India*
NATIONAL SOCIETY – *Stranger Than Paradise*
LONDON – *Paris, Texas*

Controversy made *Once Upon a Time in America*, Sergio Leone's historical epic about Jewish gangsters in New York City, the most eagerly anticipated screening at the Cannes Film Festival. Daunted by the film's nearly-four-hour running time and its convoluted, non-linear structure, Warner Bros. and the Ladd Co. had seized control of the picture and announced plans to cut the film by a third and release a version with a chronological narrative. Leading critics slammed this shorter version when it opened in cinemas. In the New Yorker, Pauline Kael called the short version "incoherently bad" and declared "I don't believe I've ever seen a worse case of mutilation." Many critics joined her in pointing to the studio's interference as the key reason for the movie's failure (NYT "plays like a long, inscrutable trailer for what might have been an entertaining movie [due to] the chaos of the editing"; NYP "sprawling, pretentious"; LAT "at times compressed into near incomprehensibility"; CT "a mess ... [the film] becomes barely intelligible after a while in this short version"; PI "misshapen ... without question the biggest disaster of the season ... the whole thing is full of holes"; V "a disappointment of considerable proportions ... surprisingly deficient in clarity and purpose"). Leone's original longer version screened in selected cinemas in a handful of American cities and internationally, earning positive reviews (LAT "mesmerizingly beautiful, brutal, always absorbing"; CT "a very powerful, beautiful epic"; MFB "extraordinary"; SP "very impressive ... unstoppable and rolls over any misgivings which might arise"). At the end of the year, Leone's full version of *Once Upon a Time in America* finished as the runner-up for the Los Angeles Film Critics Association's Best Picture accolade, but the damage caused by the studio's interference all but ruled it out of Oscar contention.

The early frontrunner for the Best Picture Academy Award was *Places in the Heart*, a drama about a widow struggling to save her farm in the Depression (NYT "one of the best films in years about growing up American ... moving and often funny"; NYP "magnificent"; LAT "an extraordinary, restorative, deeply American film"; CT "one of those rare films that earns its emotional honesty"; WP "a distinguished film that is both moving and provocative"; V "a loving, reflective homage"; TGM "a nostalgic and soft-hearted yet hard-headed memoir"; TT "outrageously sentimental"; S&S "sentimental"). At the end of the year, however, the New York Film Critics Circle and the Los Angeles Film Critics Association each snubbed *Places in the Heart* and instead embraced a pair of films that later emerged as the main Oscar contenders.

In a major surprise, the west coast group awarded their top accolade to *Amadeus*, an adaptation of a successful Broadway play about the rivalry between composers Antonio Salieri and Wolfgang Amadeus Mozart. Released two days before *Places in the Heart*, *Amadeus* sharply divided critics, and later was a notable absentee from the annual New York Times list of the year's ten best films (NYT "exhilarating ... a major achievement ... extraordinary"; NYP "a big yawn"; LAT "an enthralling film"; WP "a remarkable movie"; V "a disappointment"; TT "spectacular"; Time "grand, sprawling entertainment").

When the New York critics voted just three days later, *Amadeus* did not receive a single vote for Best Picture (sixteen films were supported by the members of the circle on the initial ballot). With 42 points, the winner was *A Passage to India*, an adaptation of E. M. Forster's novel, which was the first film directed by David Lean since the critically savaged release of *Ryan's Daughter* in 1970 (NYT "moving ... wonderfully provocative"; NYP "genuine movie greatness"; LAT "affecting, humorous, surprising, ironic, intelligent [and] an intense six-character drama"; CT "achieves an additional measure of greatness by showcasing our lack of understanding of both man and nature"; TGM "gorgeously packaged ... but where there should be insight, there is only obfuscation"; MFB "notably spectacular"; Time "superb").

The runner-up in the New York balloting, finishing with 27 points, was *The Killing Fields*, a drama about the horrors of the Khmer Rouge regime in Cambodia (NYT "diffuse and wandering ... less effective as a personal story than as an indictment of the Communists' brutality"; NYP "an exhausting but memorable experience ... profoundly heartbreaking"; LAT "utterly, grippingly mesmerizing ... must simply not be missed ... shattering"; CT "unquestionably is one of the year's most powerful and important motion pictures"; V "admirable, if not entirely successful"; TGM "rarely has a nightmare been so convincing"; MFB "fundamentally unsatisfying").

Finishing third in the New York voting with 18 points was the independent road-trip comedy *Stranger Than Paradise* (NYT "the year's most original American film ... immensely invigorating ... something quite special"; LAT "probably the freshest, most clear-eyed and certainly one of the funniest American films of 1984"; CT "an odd movie that works ... it's the freshness of the film that is captivating"; BG "the comedy surprise of the year"; V "bracingly original"; TGM "a plaintive, intelligent, laconic comedy").

The National Board of Review also embraced *A Passage to India*, while the National Society of Film Critics selected *Stranger Than Paradise* ahead of *Un Dimanche à la Champagne (A Sunday in the Country)* (NYT "exquisite from beginning to end"; LAT "superb"; CT "magnificent ... luminous"; WP "a glistening, ornately constructed movie"; BG "remarkable"; PI "exquisite ... [a] remarkable film"; TT "could hardly have been bettered ... a quiet classic"; MFB "undeniably a charmer"; S&S "prettily evocative, but a bit thin").

At the Golden Globes, *Amadeus* was named Best Picture (Drama) while *A Passage to India* won the Globe for Best Foreign Film. When the Academy Award nominations were announced, these two films led the list of contenders with each garnering eleven nominations, including nods for Best Picture and Best Director. *The Killing Fields* and *Places in the Heart* followed, both receiving mentions in seven categories, including Best Picture and Best Director.

The final Best Picture Oscar nominee was *A Soldier's Story*, Norman Jewison's film version of Charles Fuller's 1981 Pulitzer Prize winning play about the investigation of an African-American army officer's murder (NYT "a tense drama"; NYP "marvelous"; CT "excels ... poignant"; WP "powerful"; V "taut, gripping"; TGM "powerful"; S&S "fascinating"). It was overlooked in the Best Director category and only received three nominations.

In addition to *Once Upon a Time in America* and *Stranger Than Paradise* the Academy overlooked: *Greystoke: The Legend of Tarzan, Lord of the Apes* (NYT "the season's most unexpected, most invigorating surprise ... unusually intelligent and serious entertainment ... breathtaking"; NYP "ultimately preposterous"; LAT "a great spectacle [with a] sting of real emotion"; CT "by no means a disaster, but it also is not the very special film that one had hoped it would be"; BG "so ambitious in scope that its minor sins must be forgiven"; PI "splendid"; V "generally absorbing but dramatically uneven"); the Globe (Comedy/Musical) winner *Romancing the Stone* (NYT "mostly charmless"; LAT "lots of fun"; CT "genuinely funny ... a remarkably winning, appealing movie"; BG "has no artistic merit but it's a great way to kill an evening"; TT "a jolly affair"); *Broadway Danny Rose*, for which Woody Allen was a Best Director nominee (NYT "endearing ... sweet and funny"; LAT "a gorgeous time to be had by all"; CT "light, congenial and very funny"; WP "endearing"; V "amusing"; TT "wonderful"); the Palme d'Or winner and NBR runner-up *Paris, Texas* (NYT "initially promising [but ultimately] awful"; LAT "mysterious, magnificent [and] deeply affecting"; CT "[a] frustrating but ultimately rewarding film"; BG "no landmark film ... has wonderful things in it, but it's also severely flawed"; V "beautiful ... refined arthouse cinema"); *Under the Volcano* (NYT "mesmerizing"; LAT "beautifully sad ... rich, ripe, subtle"; CT "fails ... and yet strangely riveting"; PI "mesmerizing"; TGM "fascinating"); *The Bostonians* (NYT "a rare delight ... one of the best adaptations of a major literary work ever to come onto the screen"; LAT "eminently satisfying"; CT "thoroughly satisfactory"; BG "one of the best films of the year"; PI "an honorable disappointment"); the cult spoof *This is Spinal Tap* (NYT "the funniest film of 1984 ... a witty, mischievous satire"; BG "a scathing satire"; CT "hilarious"; V "vastly amusing"; TT "[a] delightful spoof"; MFB "consistently convincing, generally hilarious"); *All of Me* (NYT "genuinely funny"; LAT "fitfully funny ... only occasionally lives up to the promise of its premise"; WP "a mighty good time"); *Entre Nous (Between Us)* (NYT "moving ... perfectly realized"; NYP "a depressing French soap opera"; LAT "astonishing"; CT "exceptionally fine"; WP "impressive"); and the 1983 drama *L'Argent (Money)* (NYT "[a] beautiful, astringent film"; LAT "a masterpiece"; CT "a most serious film ... shocking and thrilling").

In early March, the Directors Guild of America named Milos Forman as Best Director for the second time, thus positioning *Amadeus* as the favourite for the Academy Award. Two weeks later, on Oscar night, *Amadeus* collected eight statuettes, including Best Picture and Best Director for Forman.

At the British Academy Awards, *The Killing Fields* was named Best Film. The following year, *Amadeus* and *A Passage to India* were both unsuccessful nominees for the top BAFTA.

1984

BEST DIRECTOR

ACADEMY AWARDS
Woody Allen for *Broadway Danny Rose*
Robert Benton for *Places in the Heart*
• **Milos Forman for *Amadeus***
Roland Joffe for *The Killing Fields*
David Lean for *A Passage to India*

GOLDEN GLOBE AWARDS
Francis Ford Coppola – *The Cotton Club*
• **Milos Forman – *Amadeus***
Roland Joffe – *The Killing Fields*
David Lean – *A Passage to India*
Sergio Leone – *Once Upon a Time in America*

DIRECTORS GUILD AWARD
Robert Benton – *Places in the Heart*
• **Milos Forman – *Amadeus***
Norman Jewison – *A Soldier's Story*
Roland Joffe – *The Killing Fields*
David Lean – *A Passage to India*

BRITISH ACADEMY AWARDS
Roland Joffe – *The Killing Fields*
Sergio Leone
  – *Once Upon a Time in America*
• **Wim Wenders – *Paris, Texas***
Peter Yates – *The Dresser*

NEW YORK – David Lean – *A Passage to India*
LOS ANGELES – Milos Forman – *Amadeus*
BOARD OF REVIEW – David Lean – *A Passage to India*
NATIONAL SOCIETY – Robert Bresson – *L'Argent (Money)*
LONDON – Neil Jordan – *The Company of Wolves*

The Oscar frontrunners were previous winners Milos Forman for *Amadeus* (NYT "has preserved the fascinating heart of Mr Shaffer's play, and made it available to millions who might never enter a legitimate theater … well done"; NYer "trudges through the movie as if every step were a major contribution to art"; LAT "[the] interpolation [of Mozart's music] into the action is subtle and masterful"; CT "has been beautifully mounted by Forman") and David Lean (his seventh and final nod) for *A Passage to India* (NYT "his best work since 'The Bridge on the River Kwai' and 'Lawrence of Arabia'"; LAT "stunningly fine"; CT "has the discipline to tell both the full story of a great novel and yet leave us with a sense of mystery"; V "magnificently crafted"; TGM "Lean's craft has not deserted him with age but his weakness for the emptily pictorial has

94

overwhelmed him ... bombastic"). Lean had collected his third New York Film Critics Circle accolade and his fourth National Board of Review plaudit, while Forman garnered his first Los Angeles Film Critics Association prize and his second Golden Globe before becoming the Oscar favourite when he was named by the Directors Guild of America for the second time.

Also nominated for the Oscar were: previous winner Woody Allen for *Broadway Danny Rose* (LAT "confident direction"); previous winner Robert Benton for *Places in the Heart* (LAT "has now grown into an exceptional film maker"; V "flawlessly crafted"; TGM "there are no false notes"); and Roland Joffe for *The Killing Fields* (NYT "gives this film a realistic and involving visual style"; LAT "extraordinary [and] electrifying"; CT "directed as convincingly as a documentary").

Overlooked were: National Society of Film Critics winner Robert Bresson for the 1983 drama *L'Argent (Money)* (NYT "at the top of his very idiosyncratic form ... serenely composed"; LAT "draws upon his formidable powers of expression in leading us to see the same old thing in a new way"; PI "Bresson's manner is clinical, unsparing and totally relentless"); Cannes winner and New York and NSFC runner-up Bertrand Tavernier for *Un Dimanche à la Champagne (A Sunday in the Country)* (NYT "particularly graceful ... the film's painterly style is well attuned to its characters; WP "extraordinary"); BAFTA winner Wim Wenders for *Paris, Texas* (CT "tends to use his actors and the Texas landscape interchangeably so that his film outshines any individual star"); Los Angeles runner-up Sergio Leone for *Once Upon a Time in America* (Sp "an impressive command of filmic techniques"); previous winner John Huston for *Under the Volcano* (NYT "it ranks with the best work [he] has ever done"; LAT "ranks with [his] mightiest works"; PI "splendid"); James Ivory for *The Bostonians* (NYT "[the film] unfolds elegantly but not always smoothly ... the pacing is much less graceful than the material itself"; BG "painterly direction"); DGA nominee Norman Jewison for *A Soldier's Story* (NYT "most commendably, he has let the drama speak for itself, applying the skills of a film maker to polish the facets that lend such substance to the drama"; LAT "he stages and photographs [this film] in giant, heavy, oppressive detail ... the flashbacks are elaborate, old-fashioned, heavily underlined ... [at times] ham-handed"; WP "[the story] is unfolded by Jewison with methodic thoroughness"); and Diane Kurys for *Entre Nous (Between Us)* (NYT "extraordinary assurance ... wonderfully sustained artistry"; LAT "charts the most delicate course imaginable"; WP "should elevate [her] to the highest echelon of the profession"; BG "Kurys' artistry is never more apparent than in her ability to move the story without conventional plot devices or superficial resolutions").

On Oscar night, it was Forman who emerged victorious, claiming his second Best Director statuette.

1984

BEST ACTOR

ACADEMY AWARDS
• **F. Murray Abraham as 'Antonio Salieri' in** *Amadeus*
Jeff Bridges as 'the Starman' in *Starman*
Albert Finney as 'Geoffrey Firmin' in *Under the Volcano*
Tom Hulce as 'Wolfgang Amadeus Mozart' in *Amadeus*
Sam Waterston as 'Sydney Schanberg' in *The Killing Fields*

GOLDEN GLOBE AWARDS

(Drama)
• **F. Murray Abraham** – *Amadeus*
Jeff Bridges – *Starman*
Albert Finney – *Under the Volcano*
Tom Hulce – *Amadeus*
Sam Waterston – *The Killing Fields*

(Comedy/Musical)
Steve Martin – *All of Me*
• **Dudley Moore**
  – Micki and Maude
Eddie Murphy – *Beverly Hills Cop*
Bill Murray – *Ghostbusters*
Robin Williams
  – *Moscow on the Hudson*

BRITISH ACADEMY AWARDS
Tom Courtenay – *The Dresser*
Albert Finney – *The Dresser*
• **Haing S. Ngor – The Killing Fields**
Sam Waterston – *The Killing Fields*

NEW YORK – **Steve Martin** – *All of Me*
LOS ANGELES – **F. Murray Abraham** – *Amadeus* and **Albert Finney** –
    Under the Volcano
BOARD OF REVIEW – **Victor Banerjee** – *A Passage to India*
NATIONAL SOCIETY – **Steve Martin** – *All of Me*
LONDON – **Albert Finney** – *Under the Volcano*

When the Oscar nominations were announced, Steve Martin became only the fourth winner of the New York Film Critics Circle's Best Actor award to be overlooked by the Academy. Martin had been cited for his performance as a lawyer possessed by the spirit of an ill-tempered heiress in *All of Me* (NYT "astonishing ... the film's most conspicuous asset ... his best work in films thus far"; LAT "magnificent"; WP "a tour-de-force"; TT "shows a distinct talent for physical comedy"; MFB "brilliant"). Martin also won the National Society of Film Critics plaudit, but was surprisingly outpolled at the Golden Globes.

In addition to Martin, Oscar voters also by-passed all the other Globe (Comedy/Musical) candidates including: the unexpected winner Dudley Moore in *Micki and Maude* (NYT "restores [his] comic credibility"; LAT "manages to make irresistible a man that in lesser hands would seem merely a cad"; CT "wonderful"; WP "demonstrates genuine spontaneity here"); Eddie Murphy in *Beverly Hills Cop* (NYT "inspired clowning ... [he] knows exactly what he's doing, and he wins at every turn"; LAT "[he] gives this movie its bite and flash, its heart and soul"; CT "just playing himself"); and one of the joint NSFC runners-up, Robin Williams in *Moscow on the Hudson* (NYT "plays with fine comic intensity"; LAT "has captured the bittersweet twin tastes of freedom and homesickness beautifully"; CT "his most controlled performance on film ... manages to present a genuine character"; V "a superbly sensitive portrayal").

Unsurprisingly, Robert De Niro's performance in *Once Upon a Time in America* was also omitted from the various awards season ballots. Having seen the original, longer version of the gangster epic, Gene Siskel praised De Niro in the Chicago Tribune for "a spectacular performance that solidifies his reputation as the actor of his era". When the studio's drastically edited version opened in North American cinemas, however, Vincent Canby wrote in The New York Times, "Mr De Niro and Mr Woods might well be giving good performances, but it's impossible to tell from the evidence being shown here."

Also by-passed for Oscar consideration were: Howard E. Rollins in *A Soldier's Story* (NYT "an arresting performance"; WP "highly restrained ... [he] is not without charisma, but his performance is strangely the least exciting of the lot"; TGM "does his best with a remote role"); Woody Allen in *Broadway Danny Rose* (NYT "unusually self-effacing"; LAT "a whirlwind of cheer"; CT "delightfully frantic"; PI "his finest screen performance"; V "perfect"); Harry Dean Stanton in *Paris, Texas* (NYT "marvelous"; LAT "his combination of innocence and anguish [is] breathtaking ... a performance that demands attention"; BG "Stanton, whose laconic pain always seems real, seems to be playing in a vacuum"); Rupert Everett in *Another Country* (NYT "good"; BG "the best thing in the film"; V "marvelously acted"; Sp "excellent"); John Hurt in *1984* (NYT "splendid ... the film's center of gravity"; LAT "ravaged and intense, Hurt is perfectly cast"; CT "makes palpable the drudgery of [his character's] daily existence"; SFC "extraordinary"; PI "unforgettable"; V "holds center stage throughout"); Peter Coyote in *A Stranger's Kiss* (NYT "outstandingly good"; CT "plays him quite well"); and both Nicolas Cage (NYT "excellent ... very sympathetically captures Al's urgency and frustration"; V "sensitive") and Matthew Modine (NYT "exceptionally sweet and graceful [and] terrifically affecting"; V "skilfully essays the offbeat troubled character") in *Birdy* (NYT "together these actors work miracles with what might have been unplayable"; LAT a pair of "beautifully sustained performances").

Next to Martin, the most glaring omission from the list of Oscar contenders, however, was National Board of Review winner Victor Banerjee as the accused doctor in the Best Picture nominee *A Passage to India* (NYT "at the film's center is Mr Banerjee's superb performance"; CT "[his] performance as Dr Aziz is no less impressive than say, Ben Kingsley's Gandhi ... [but] Aziz is not a holy man, and so bringing alive his character isn't the sort of thing that wins plaudits"; V "excellent"; Time "electrifying"; TGM "hopeless ... ruined by what may well be the director's patronizing attitude").

Instead, the Academy short-listed all five men earlier nominated for the Best Actor (Drama) Golden Globe: both F. Murray Abraham, the Globe winner and one of the two Los Angeles honourees, as composer Antonio Salieri (NYT "played with immense, tragic humor and passion"; NYP "a quiet, studied performance"; LAT "exceptional"; CT "Abraham 'out-acts' Hulce ... a fine choice [for the part]"; V "quietly excellent"; TT "impresses immediately") and Tom Hulce as composer Wolfgang Amadeus Mozart (NYT "gets better and better as the drama progresses"; LAT "if he is never exactly credible as the assured conductor/creator, he is certainly touching in the film's last third"; TT "builds in strength and sensitivity as the film proceeds") in *Amadeus;* Sam Waterston as a reporter in *The Killing Fields* (NYT "acted with self-effacing honesty"; LAT "played with strength and honesty"; CT "absolutely credible"); Jeff Bridges as an alien in *Starman* (NYT "a role that, played by anyone else, might seem preposterous ... [but in his hands] becomes the occasion for a sweetly affecting characterization"; LAT "exceptional"; CT "excels ... touching ... a fine acting job"; WP "[a] quirky, effective portrayal"); and Albert Finney as an alcoholic diplomat in *Under the Volcano* (NYT "brilliant ... a performance of extraordinary delicacy ... superb"; LAT "masterly [in a] towering portrayal ... I wonder when we'll have a performance to equal this one in the sum of its intelligence and execution"; CT "at times we think he's blowing his credibility, that his performance is much too big to be realistic; but minutes later, it all seems quite calculated ... striking"; BG "magnificent"; PI "breathtaking ... exquisite and accurate in the petty details"; V "simply extraordinary [in an] extremely difficult role"; S&S "plays [the role] with something approaching virtuosity: he pulls out all his many stops"). Finney had been the other winner in Los Angeles, and had finished as runner-up for both the NSFC and New York prizes (he had led the voting in New York after the first round).

The day before the Globe nominations were announced, Vincent Canby commented in The New York Times that Abraham was "expected to be a cinch to win an Oscar nomination [and] has a very good chance of winning the top award." Abraham went on to win both the Globe and the Academy Award. The following year, he and Banerjee were nominated for the British Academy Award, but were outpolled by that year's Oscar winner.

BEST ACTRESS

ACADEMY AWARDS
Judy Davis as 'Adela Quested' in *A Passage to India*
• **Sally Field as 'Edna Spalding' in *Places in the Heart***
Jessica Lange as 'Jewell Ivy' in *Country*
Vanessa Redgrave as 'Olive Chancellor' in *The Bostonians*
Sissy Spacek as 'Mae Garvey' in *The River*

GOLDEN GLOBE AWARDS
(Drama)
• **Sally Field – *Places in the Heart***
Diane Keaton – *Mrs Soffel*
Jessica Lange – *Country*
Vanessa Redgrave – *The Bostonians*
Sissy Spacek – *The River*

(Comedy/Musical)
Anne Bancroft – *Garbo Talks*
Mia Farrow
    – *Broadway Danny Rose*
Shelley Long
    – *Irreconcilable Differences*
Lily Tomlin – *All of Me*
• **Kathleen Turner**
    – *Romancing the Stone*

BRITISH ACADEMY AWARDS
Shirley MacLaine – *Terms of Endearment*
Helen Mirren – *Cal*
• **Maggie Smith – *A Private Function***
Meryl Streep – *Silkwood*

NEW YORK – Peggy Ashcroft – *A Passage to India*
LOS ANGELES – Kathleen Turner – *Crimes of Passion* **and** *Romancing the Stone*
BOARD OF REVIEW – Peggy Ashcroft – *A Passage to India*
NATIONAL SOCIETY – Vanessa Redgrave – *The Bostonians*

On consecutive days in mid-December, the New York Film Critics Circle and the National Board of Review each named seventy-seven-year old English theatre veteran Peggy Ashcroft as Best Actress for her performance as the elderly chaperone in David Lean's *A Passage to India* (NYT "splendid"; LAT "when she is off the screen here, the hole is almost too much to bear … dazzlingly adept"; V "a constant source of delight"; TGM "scene-stealing … delivers Fosterisms with priceless panache"). Just days earlier, however, Ashcroft had been named Best Supporting Actress by the Los Angeles Film Critics

Association for the same performance. Columbia had been promoting the actress in the supporting category, but following her New York and NBR wins, the studio switched strategy and launched a new campaign for recognition by the Academy in the Best Actress contest. Despite this, Ashcroft appeared on both the Golden Globe and Oscar ballots in the secondary category.

The other two main contenders for the critics' prizes were Vanessa Redgrave, as a nineteenth century feminist in *The Bostonians* (NYT "astonishing ... a character Vanessa Redgrave was born to play ... among the finest things she's ever done"; NYP "quite impressive"; LAT "a great and unforgettable portrait"; BG "remarkable") and Kathleen Turner, both as a romance novelist in *Romancing the Stone* (NYT "can't carry this burden by herself"; LAT "here she has a chance to display considerably more personality"; PI "terrific ... she pulls it off beautifully") and as a prostitute in *Crimes of Passion* (CT "[a] risky performance [that has] gone to waste"; WP "her most aggressive performance"). Turner claimed the Los Angeles award ahead of Redgrave, but this result was reversed in the National Society of Film Critics voting which saw Redgrave win by 31 points to 23. Redgrave led the voting in New York after the initial round, but ultimately finished runner-up to Ashcroft, the veteran winning by 39 points to 31 on the fourth ballot. At the Golden Globe Awards, Redgrave was a nominee in the Drama category and Turner won the Comedy/Musical trophy for *Romancing the Stone*. Surprisingly, however, while Redgrave earned her fifth nomination from the Academy, Turner was left off the list of candidates.

Also overlooked for consideration by Academy voters were: previous winner Diane Keaton in *Mrs Soffel* (NYT "utterly convincing"; LAT "creates [a] quite complex character ... convinces"; WP "struggles mightily to make Mrs Soffel more than a prop in an argument"); Cannes Best Actress winner Helen Mirren in *Cal* (NYT "through a layer of reserve, makes Marcella a woman of unexpected substance"; CT "does an adequate job"; TGM "extraordinarily subtle"; MFB "acutely and economically suggests a character slowly overcoming her fear of revealing herself"; G "a particularly good portrait ... requires the sort of careful understatement not usually asked of her"); previous winner Anne Bancroft in *Garbo Talks* (NYT "played with great verve"; LAT "played with bracing wit and illuminating tenderness"); Mia Farrow in *Broadway Danny Rose* (NYT "her comic talents here are a revelation ... almost steals the show"; LAT "a bravura turn"; CT "truly unrecognisable ... this is an Academy Award nomination-caliber performance"; V "wonderful ... terrific all the way"; TT "almost unrecognizable"); Shelley Long in *Irreconcilable Differences* (NYT "Long's talents as a comedienne shine through"; LAT "slightly mannered"; CT "very good"; TGM "convincing ... never loses her air of vulnerability [or] to be straining after effect"); 1983 BAFTA nominee Phyllis Logan in *Another Time, Another Place* (NYT "[a] luminous presence ...

exciting"; G "memorable"); Hanna Schygulla in *Eine Liebe in Deutschland (A Love in Germany)* (NYT "a triumphant performance ... [she] transforms the movie into a cinematic event"; LAT "does what perhaps only a great actress can do, which is to play total abandon without looking silly"; WP "you can't help but be seduced by [her]"; TGM "astonishingly unpredictable but never mannered or theatrical ... her warmest and most expansive performance to date"); and Isabelle Huppert in *Entre Nous (Between Us)* (NYT "superb, better than she has been in years – strong, funny, self-assured ... splendid"; LAT "impeccable"; CT "comes across as a complete person ... her transformation as a character provides a rich dramatic arc"; BG "superbly acted").

The surprise nominee in the field of Best Actress Oscar contenders was Peggy Ashcroft's co-star in *A Passage to India*, twenty-nine-year old Australian Judy Davis, who played the role of the naive and sexually repressed heroine (NYT "has a particular presence that helps make the film work"; LAT "Davis, in this pivotal, difficult role, is Adela exactly"; CT "excels in the difficult role of Miss Quested"; V "outstanding"; TGM "performs a near-miracle in the pivotal role of Adela ... Davis is admirable not because she is able to make the actions of Miss Quested believable, but because she is able to retain the audience's interest in, and sympathy for, the character"). Despite glowing reviews, Davis had not featured in the voting for any of the critics' prizes and had not been a Globe nominee. She was the only actress in the category not to have previously won an Academy Award.

In addition to Davis and Redgrave, Oscar voters short-listed three American actresses for their performances as farmers' wives struggling to save their family farms in three different films: Sally Field in *Places in the Heart* (NYT "beautifully played"; NYP "no praise can be high enough ... a performance of Oscar calibre"; LAT "the film's superb center"; CT "it's a role that was made to order for the diminutive Field"; WP "subtle [yet] vivid"; TGM "[a] gritty, no-nonsense portrayal"; TT "magnificent"; Time "luminously portrayed"); Jessica Lange in *Country* (NYT "a good, tough performance"; NYP "honest and dedicated"; WP "gives attractive stamina and grit to Jewell Ivy, but as an actress she is better equipped for communicating vulnerability and victimization on the screen"; S&S "excellent"; MFB "excellent"); and Sissy Spacek in *The River* (NYP "breathtakingly vital and alive"; LAT "it's Spacek who brings the authenticity [to the film]"; CT "[the director] uses her as much as a prop as a character"; WP "brings her usual sensitivity and intelligence to a role that's far from the center of the movie"; MFB "[a] perfectly judged performance").

The frontrunner in the list of nominees was Field, who had won her second Globe (Drama) for her performance. On Oscar night, Robert Duvall opened the evening's second last envelope and declared Field as the winner. It was her second Best Actress statuette in six years.

BEST SUPPORTING ACTOR

ACADEMY AWARDS
Adolph Caesar as 'Master Sergeant Vernon C. Waters' in *A Soldier's Story*
John Malkovich as 'Mr Will' in *Places in the Heart*
Noriyuki 'Pat' Morita as 'Mr Miyagi' in *The Karate Kid*
• **Haing S. Ngor as 'Dith Pran' in *The Killing Fields***
Ralph Richardson as 'the Sixth Lord Greystoke' in *Greystoke: The Legend of Tarzan, Lord of the Apes*

GOLDEN GLOBE AWARDS
Adolph Caesar – *A Soldier's Story*
Richard Crenna – *The Flamingo Kid*
Jeffrey Jones – *Amadeus*
Noriyuki 'Pat' Morita – *The Karate Kid*
• **Haing S. Ngor – *The Killing Fields***

BRITISH ACADEMY AWARDS
• **Denholm Elliott – *A Private Function***
Michael Elphick – *Gorky Park*
Ian Holm – *Greystoke: The Legend of Tarzan, Lord of the Apes*
Ralph Richardson – *Greystoke: The Legend of Tarzan, Lord of the Apes*

NEW YORK – Ralph Richardson – *Greystoke: The Legend of Tarzan, Lord of the Apes*
LOS ANGELES – Adolph Caesar – *A Soldier's Story*
BOARD OF REVIEW – John Malkovich – *Places in the Heart*
NATIONAL SOCIETY – John Malkovich – *The Killing Fields* and *Places in the Heart*

The "special achievement" of Roland Joffe's *The Killing Fields*, wrote Gene Siskel in the Chicago Tribune, "is the amount of screen time turned over to Pran's survival story. Racism affects the ways movies are edited, and in less confident hands far less time would be allotted to Pran's story. A producer or studio might be fearful that audiences would prefer to see the white hero to a yellow hero." In London, the British Academy recognised that Sam Waterston and Haing S. Ngor were co-leads in *The Killing Fields*, nominating both men in the Best Actor category. Ngor, a Cambodian doctor who had escaped to the United States after years of persecution and imprisonment by the Khmer Rouge regime, went on to win the accolade for his portrayal of Cambodian interpreter

Dith Pran, his first role as an actor (NYT "reveals an extraordinary screen presence"; NYP "unforgettable"; LAT "played with strength and honesty"; CT "surprisingly convincing for a first-time actor"; V "carries the weight of the film's most important sequences"). In the United States, however, apparently fearful that the members of the Academy would not reward an Asian performer (no performer of East Asian heritage had ever received a nomination in the leading categories to that date), Warner Bros. promoted Ngor for recognition in the supporting category. He emerged as the surprise winner of the Golden Globe and two months later became the second non-professional actor to receive the Best Supporting Actor statuette from the Academy.

Among the nominees outpolled for the Oscar was one of Ngor's co-stars, John Malkovich. For his performances as a war photographer in *The Killing Fields* and as the blind boarder in *Places in the Heart* (NYT "stunning"; LAT "[a] performance so rich, intelligent and many-layered [it] can only be called triumphant"; WP "proves in his screen debut that he is an actor of great depth, but has a contemporary speech pattern that seems out of place here"; PI "one of the year's standout supporting performances ... an electrifying movie debut"; V "totally believable"), Malkovich was named Best Supporting Actor by the National Society of Film Critics and finished runner-up for the Los Angeles Film Critics Association prize. For his turn in *Places in the Heart* he won the National Board of Review prize, finished runner-up in New York and received his first Oscar nomination.

Also nominated by the Academy were: Los Angeles winner Adolph Caesar reprising his stage success as a tough African-American army sergeant murdered during the Second World War in *A Soldier's Story*, a role he had previously played on stage (NYT "expert"; LAT "plays with a harrowing strength that projects to the back row of the theater"; CT "the best performance I've seen in an American movie this year ... absolutely mesmerizing ... his performance is full of finely-controlled anger and humor and blindness and wisdom"; WP "although he is clearly accustomed to the largeness of a stage performance, he is fascinating on the screen"; V "extraordinary"; TGM "expertly played"; TT "outstanding"); Noriyuki 'Pat' Morita as a karate instructor in the box office hit *The Karate Kid* (NYT "charming ... throughout the film, [he] sustains a scene-stealing, if hokey, eccentricity"; LAT "the role of a lifetime ... Morita's portrait, in all its richness and humor, is the film's significant and original contribution"; CT "[a] fine, credible performance ... makes the often predictable story worth sitting through ... [his] performance also is a model of restraint"; WP "beautifully played ... the kind of tough-fibered, eccentrically sentimental characterization that can exalt a career"; V "simply terrific ... makes him a memorable character"); and the late Ralph Richardson, who was posthumously mentioned for his final screen appearance as Tarzan's senile, aristocratic grandfather in *Greystoke: The Legend of Tarzan, Lord of the Apes* (NYT "dominates the film in one of his most moving and wise performances ... tumultuously entertaining"; LAT "memorable ... a rousing exit role in an exceptional career"; CT "his performance is more entertaining than the role"; PI "a touching valedictory performance"; V "dignified and moving"; TT "enriches the film with his miraculous ease both in comedy and pathos"). Richardson had won the accolade in New York (his second honour from the east coast circle, following his Best Actor prize in 1952) and had finished as the NSFC runner-up. It was his second Oscar nod.

Richardson and his co-star Ian Holm were also nominees for the British Academy Award, but were outpolled by Denholm Elliott, who won his second consecutive BAFTA as Best Supporting Actor for his turn in the war-time comedy *A Private Function*, a performance that would go unrecognised in Hollywood the following year.

The surprise omissions from the Academy's list were both Globe nominees: Richard Crenna in *The Flamingo Kid* (NYT "extremely funny"; WP "as he mugs and gesticulates, he's an actor playing a fraud playing a role"; PI "most of the interest in the film lies in watching [him] struggle against the constructions and clichés of the screenplay"; V "hits the right notes") and Jeffrey Jones as the Emperor in *Amadeus* (NYT "especially good"; LAT "exceptional in a performance both humorous and sly"; V "[a] striking performance"; TT "wonderfully alive").

Also overlooked were: the late Richard Burton in his final screen appearance in *1984* (NYT "fine"; LAT "Burton's final film performance is one of his very best, crisp and disciplined"; CT "[a] muted performance"; SFC "[an] extraordinary performance"); both James Fox and Nigel Havers in *A Passage to India* (NYT "equally good"; V both "fine"); Howard da Silva in *Garbo Talks* (NYT "quite wonderful"; LAT "wonderful"); both Julian Beck (NYT "noteworthy") and Bob Hoskins (NYT "especially effective ... in a class by himself") in *The Cotton Club*; Larry Riley reprising his stage success in *A Soldier's Story* (WP "seems destined for stardom ... Riley is illuminating as the simple, slow-talking country boy ... in lesser hands [the part] could have been merely an ignorant and superstitious backwards hick; Riley reveals the gentleness and artless honesty of the man"; TGM "demands compliments ... [his] portrait is virtually an anthropological essay"); and Darren McGavin in *The Natural* (LAT "superb"; V "excellently played"),

BEST SUPPORTING ACTRESS

ACADEMY AWARDS
• **Peggy Ashcroft as 'Mrs Moore' in** *A Passage to India*
Glenn Close as 'Iris' in *The Natural*
Lindsay Crouse as 'Margaret Lomax' in *Places in the Heart*
Christine Lahti as 'Hazel Zanussi' in *Swing Shift*
Geraldine Page as 'Mrs Ritter' in *The Pope of Greenwich Village*

GOLDEN GLOBE AWARDS
• **Peggy Ashcroft** – *A Passage to India*
Drew Barrymore – *Irreconcilable Differences*
Kim Basinger – *The Natural*
Jacqueline Bisset – *Under the Volcano*
Melanie Griffith – *Body Double*
Christine Lahti – *Swing Shift*
Lesley Ann Warren – *Songwriter*

BRITISH ACADEMY AWARDS
Eileen Atkins – *The Dresser*
Cher – *Silkwood*
• **Liz Smith** – *A Private Function*
Tuesday Weld – *Once Upon a Time in America*

NEW YORK – Christine Lahti – *Swing Shift*
LOS ANGELES – Peggy Ashcroft – *A Passage to India*
BOARD OF REVIEW – Sabine Azéma – *Un Dimanche à la Champagne (A Sunday in the Country)*
NATIONAL SOCIETY – Melanie Griffith – *Body Double*

The four major American critics' groups were divided over whether or not to consider Peggy Ashcroft in the leading or supporting category for her performance as the chaperone in *A Passage to India* (NYT "splendid"; LAT "when she is off the screen here, the hole is almost too much to bear ... dazzlingly adept"; V "a constant source of delight"; TGM "[Judy Davis] is ably supported (and then some) by a scene-stealing Ashcroft, who delivers Fosterisms with priceless panache"). The New York Film Critics Circle and the National Board of Review each named the seventy-seven-year old theatre legend as the year's Best Actress. The Los Angeles Film Critics Association and the National Society of Film Critics, however, voted for Ashcroft in the secondary category.

She won the prize from the west coast group, and finished as the runner-up for the NSFC plaudit. Columbia studio executives attempted to resolve the confusion by launching a campaign for Ashcroft as a Best Actress Oscar contender. Despite this, she received nominations for both the Golden Globe and the Academy Award as Best Supporting Actress.

The runner-up to Ashcroft in Los Angeles was Christine Lahti, as a nightclub dancer turned factory worker in *Swing Shift* (NYT "so good that she turns a secondary role into a major one"; LAT "[a] smashing performance ... by sheer, seemingly effortless force of personality and technique, the willowy Lahti [becomes] the center of our attention"; WP "seems to reduce the leading lady to Lilliputian dimensions ... she tends to enthral the camera and diminish anyone else in the immediate vicinity"; BG "superb"; FQ "[an] emotionally vivid performance"). With Ashcroft considered in the major category, Lahti won the Best Supporting Actress award in New York and later earned her first Globe and Oscar nominations.

The other actress to benefit from the classification of Ashcroft's performance by certain critics' groups as that of a leading lady was Sabine Azéma, who claimed the NBR prize for her turn in *Un Dimanche à la Champagne (A Sunday in the Country)* (NYT "particularly adroit"; CT "injects the excitement of life into [the film]"; WP "plays the antique-dealer daughter with a brassy crassness"; MFB "excellent").

Interestingly, the only actress to outpoll Ashcroft was Melanie Griffith, as a porn star in the comedy-thriller *Body Double* (NYT "the movie's real focal point ... a perfectly controlled comic performance that successfully neutralizes all questions relating to plausibility"; LAT "the picture's catalyst ... she is able to elbow her way through a terrifically funny portrait [and] when the last quarter of the film ricochets into near incomprehensibility, it's Griffith you miss most"; WP "played nicely ... original and witty"). Runner-up to Lahti in New York, Griffith won the NSFC award 36 points to 19 over Ashcroft. In a major surprise, however, Griffith was not among the list of Oscar candidates even though she had been a Globe contender.

Also by-passed for Oscar consideration were: BAFTA nominee Tuesday Weld in *Once Upon a Time in America* (NYT "only Miss Weld's performance seems to survive the chaos of the editing"); Drew Barrymore in *Irreconcilable Differences* (NYT "too studiously adorable"; LAT "touching"); both Hermione Gingold (NYT "quite wonderful"; LAT "wonderful"; WP "amusing"; BG "overcooked") and Carrie Fisher (LAT "deliciously funny") in *Garbo Talks*; 1983 BAFTA nominee Rosemary Harris in *The Ploughman's Lunch* (NYT "[a] superlative performance"); Jacqueline Bisset in *Under the Volcano* (LAT "masterly ... the very finest work Bisset has done"; CT "[a] fine performance ... holds her own with Finney [and] does it with her sincerity"; TGM "the salient failing [of the film]"); Amy Madigan in *Places in the Heart* (TT "magnificent"); and Lily Tomlin in *All of Me* (NYT "her best work in films thus far"; LAT "you keep feeling there should have been more done to put Tomlin's industrial-strength talent to better use"; WP "Tomlin is restricted to the status of an adornment, but a charming one"). Universal had promoted Lily Tomlin for Best Supporting Actress honours, but the Hollywood Foreign Press Association had instead included her among the nominees for the Best Actress in a Comedy or Musical Golden Globe. Academy members did not include her on the ballot in either category.

Alongside Ashcroft and Lahti, Academy members short-listed: Glenn Close (for the third consecutive year) in *The Natural* (LAT "superb"; WP "Redford and Close suggest a rapport that's always a gesture away from consummation"); Lindsay Crouse in *Places in the Heart* (NYT "especially noteworthy"; LAT "exactly right"; WP "adept"); and Geraldine Page in *The Pope of Greenwich Village* (NYT "walking away with what there is of the movie, though she is seen in just two brief scenes, is Geraldine Page, who is splendidly funny and sad as the tough, whisky-sodden mother of a crooked cop"; LAT "gives the film its showiest scene"; CT "overplays her role as a cop's widow, but there is good will in her performance, too"; WP "takes command of the camera and one's emotions in her two scenes with an authority that somehow eludes the leads").

Ashcroft won the Globe in late January, and entered the Oscar race as the overwhelming favourite. Sadly, however, she was not present at the ceremony at which she won the statuette as she had been forced to return suddenly to England for the funeral of Michael Redgrave. Ashcroft's victory resulted in Geraldine Page joining Richard Burton and Peter O'Toole as the only actors to have gone home empty-handed from the Oscars seven times. The following year, however, Page finally claimed an Oscar (as Best Actress) while Ashcroft was named Best Actress by the British Academy in London for her turn in *A Passage to India*.

BEST PICTURE

ACADEMY AWARDS
The Color Purple
(Warner Bros., 152 mins, 18 Dec 1985, $94.1m, 11 noms)
Kiss of the Spider Woman
(H B Films, Sugarloaf, BW & C 119 mins, 26 Jul 1985, $17.0m, 4 noms)
• *Out of Africa*
(Universal, 150 mins, 18 Dec 1985, $87.1m, 11 noms)
Prizzi's Honor
(ABC Motion Pictures, Twentieth Century-Fox, 130 mins, 14 Jun 1985, $26.7m, 8 noms)
Witness
(Feldman, Paramount, 112 mins, 8 Feb 1985, $65.5m, 8 noms)

GOLDEN GLOBE AWARDS

(Drama)
The Color Purple
Kiss of the Spider Woman
• *Out of Africa*
Runaway Train
Witness

(Comedy/Musical)
Back to the Future
A Chorus Line
Cocoon
• *Prizzi's Honor*
The Purple Rose of Cairo

BRITISH ACADEMY AWARDS
Amadeus
Back to the Future
A Passage to India
• *The Purple Rose of Cairo*
Witness

NEW YORK – *Prizzi's Honor*
LOS ANGELES – *Brazil*
BOARD OF REVIEW – *The Color Purple*
NATIONAL SOCIETY – *Ran*
LONDON – *The Purple Rose of Cairo*

The early frontrunner for the year's Best Picture accolades was *Prizzi's Honor*, a black comedy about a Mafia hitman released in North American cinemas in June (NYT "exhilarating ... a breathless rollercoaster ride [and] ferociously funny, satirical melodrama"; NYP "a marvelous treasure on every level"; LAT "a resoundingly comic love story with sobering underpinnings ... the treasure of the year ... a rich, dense character comedy"; CT "a charmer ... a classic piece of moviemaking"; WP "[a] delightful black comedy"; PI "[a] definitive and devastating satire on corporate life"). As the awards season unfolded, however, the critics' prizes were divided between numerous acclaimed contenders throwing open the race for the Best Picture Oscar.

The first major critics' award for Best Picture was won by a film that had not even been released. On 14 December 1985, the Los Angeles Film Critics Association selected *Brazil*, a fantasy which had been shelved by Universal when director Terry Gilliam had refused to re-edit his final cut to make it more accessible and optimistic. Following the accolade from the west coast circle (which also gave the film their Best Director and Best Screenplay kudos), the studio reluctantly opened the film on Christmas Day in cinemas in Los Angeles and New York for a one-week Oscar qualification run (NYT "superb ... may not be the best film of the year, but it's a remarkable achievement"; LAT "you cannot help but be impressed"; CT "a remarkably unsettling fantasy ... often very funny and dazzling throughout ... tends to leave audiences in a state of shock"; V "chillingly hilarious").

The runner-up for Best Picture in Los Angeles was *Out of Africa*, an epic adaptation of the memoirs of the Danish writer Isak Dinesen (NYT "a big, physically elaborate but wispy movie"; NYP "a cold, passionless motion picture ... too long, too slow and too ponderous"; LAT "there doesn't seem to be enough electricity to power a love story 2½ hours long"; CT "sumptuous ... beautiful and haunting"; BG "long and languid"; V "a sensitive, enveloping romantic tragedy"; TGM "a panoramically satisfying, old-fashioned middle-brow epic"; TT "magnificent"; MFB "a superlative picture of romantic loss").

Out of Africa subsequently finished as runner-up again in the voting by the National Board of Review. The winner was *The Color Purple*, an adaptation of the popular Pulitzer Prize winning novel by Alice Walker (NYT "uneven ... some parts are rapturous and stirring, others hugely improbable"; NYP "a noble, compelling, powerfully acted, magnificently photographed, richly textured film of heart-rending impact"; WP "dull, maudlin and misconceived – in short, a failure, however noble"; V "not a great film ... marred by overblown production"; CT "[a] triumphantly emotional and brave adaptation"; TT "[a] chain of slick, mostly shallow set-pieces, staged with an eye to prettification ... the symbols and embellishments do little to foster a sense of reality").

Prizzi's Honor polled sixth in the NBR vote, but two days later won the Best Picture, Director and Actor accolades from the New York Film Critics Circle. It won the top prize with double the number of points of the runner-up, Woody Allen's *The Purple Rose of Cairo* (NYT "pure enchantment ... a sweet, lyrically funny, multi-layered work ... splendid"; LAT "a sweet film, funny, smart, lovely, sad ... hilarious"; WP "a wonderfully inventive, blithely entertaining movie – it's just plain fun"; CT "delightful ... a classic film ... one of the finest movies about movies ever made"; BG "surrealistic, neat and sweet"; PI "magical ... not so much a movie as a delicate bubble that floats before your eyes"; V "a light, almost frivolous treatment of a serious theme"; TT "technical perfection"). *Out of Africa* finished third, and *Brazil* polled in fourth place.

On 2 January 1986, the New York prize-winner finished second in the National Society of Film Critics vote, behind *Ran*, Akira Kurosawa's historical epic (NYT "a visual masterwork"; LAT "superb ... a heroic saga of human destiny, a war movie with some of the greatest battle scenes in the history of cinema, a costume drama of the utmost magnificence"; CT "the year's best film ... a mighty triumph ... a rousing, epic piece of moviemaking"; BG "magnificent ... a great film"; V "dazzlingly successful"; TT "unique ... takes film spectacle to new heights ... literally breath-taking ... a masterpiece"). *Ran* had previously been named Best Foreign Film by the NBR and both the New York and Los Angeles critics.

At the Golden Globes, *Out of Africa* finally emerged as a winner when it claimed the Best Picture (Drama) award and two other trophies. The evening's biggest winner, however, was *Prizzi's Honor* which claimed four Globes, including Best Picture (Comedy/Musical), Best Director and Best Actor (Comedy/Musical). In the Best Foreign Film category, *Ran* was surprisingly outpolled by the film with which it had shared the Los Angeles critics' award: *La Historia Oficial (The Official Story)*, an Argentinian drama about a family torn apart by revelations about the past (LAT "elegantly persuasive and haunting ... a film of surpassing subtlety and insight"; CT "remarkably moving"; WP "crude craftsmanship"; BG "one of the best films of the year ... raises the art of political drama to a new high"; TGM "enlightening"; MFB "involving").

There were major surprises when the Academy Award nominations were announced in early February. Leading the field with eleven nominations each were *The Color Purple* and *Out of Africa*, neither of which had appeared on The New York Times list of the year's twenty best films. *Prizzi's Honor* followed with eight nods, a tally matched by the drama *Witness* (NYT "it's not really awful, but it's not much fun"; LAT "beautifully looking and beautifully played, but essentially hollow"; CT "both exciting and thoughtful [and] a genuinely gripping thriller"; PI "evocative").

All were short-listed for the Best Picture Oscar, along with *Kiss of the Spider Woman*, an independent drama about a gay man and a political activist sharing a prison cell (NYT "a brilliant achievement ... extraordinarily moving ... one of the best films in a long while"; LAT "succeeds on a deep, emotional level and as spellbinding entertainment as well"; CT "[a] fine film ... never less than compelling"; WP "a bore ... a flaccid gabfest from beginning to end that manages to both undermine politics and trivialize art"; BG "brilliant ... one of the best directed, best written and best acted films of this, or any, year"; V "partially successful"; FQ "engrossing"; MFB "seductively brilliant").

While the directors of the other four Best Picture nominees were recognised, Steven Spielberg, in a major shock, was excluded for *The Color Purple* which all but ruled it out of contention as no film had won Best Picture without a nomination for its director since 1931/32. In early March, the Directors Guild of America presented their annual accolade to Spielberg, thus failing to offer Oscar observers the usual indication of Oscar night success. Spielberg's place in the Best Director category was taken by Kurosawa, but *Ran* was a glaring omission from the list of Best Picture nominees.

Other films overlooked were: Los Angeles winner *Brazil*, which received nominations only for Best Original Screenplay and Best Art Direction; *The Trip to Bountiful* (NYP "a moving, unforgettable experience ... works perfectly as a small, richly detailed film"; LAT "[a] stunning film ... precise, delicate"); *After Hours* (NYT "at best, an entertaining tease, with individually arresting sequences ... [but] there is no satisfying resolution to the tension"; LAT "sweetly ominous"; CT "a successful tonic for tired souls"; WP "dazzles but falls apart ... fails to satisfy ... much of what's wrong with [the film] stems from the loose, episodic script"; TGM "good and grisly and fun ... equal in quality to the best that American movies have to offer"); *Cocoon* (LAT "the summer's nicest surprise"; WP "a mishmash"; BG "isn't without a few problems [but] comes as close to enchantment as any movie this summer"; V "mesmerizing"); box office hit *Back to the Future*, a Globe and BAFTA nominee (NYT "appealing ... takes [its] sweet, ingenious premise and really runs with it"; LAT "big, cartoonish and empty, with an interesting premise that is underdeveloped and overproduced"; CT "one of the most endearing and accomplished of entertainments ... a classic"; WP "a whirling, merry-go-round of a movie ... a wildly pleasurable sci-fi comedy, filled with enchantment and sweetness and zip"); *Desperately Seeking Susan* (NYT "[a] terrifically genial, stylish farce"; LAT "endearingly hilarious"; TGM "a tightly controlled farce"); the Berlin Film Festival winner *Wetherby* (LAT "darkly brilliant ... [a] quietly stunning work"; CT "[a] riveting drama [and] the year's best mystery ... a shattering, empathetic portrait of English reserve ... flawless"; BG "powerful and remarkable [despite] the occasional portentousness of the dialogue"; TGM "suffers from saying too much"); the British comedy *A Private Function* (NYT "stylish ... a comedy of immense charm"; CT "wonderful ... a classic comedy of class struggle ... delightful"; WP "an amusing farce [but] it never quite ignites"; PI "hilarious"; TT "a classic of British comedy"); and the Palme d'Or winner *Otac na Sluzbenom Putu (When Father was Away on Business)* (NYT "warmly appealing ... a humorous, richly detailed portrait ... a gentle, touching film"; LAT "superb ... has an incredible richness of incident and depth of emotion"; CT "it's not a bad film and there are a number of affecting moments, but taken as a whole the picture seems like a very loosely constructed, second-rate imitation of [other's films]"; WP "superb").

As the Academy Awards approached, the momentum for the early favourite stalled, despite its win at the Golden Globes. With the cinematic run ended and the home video rental rights already sold to Vestron outright, ABC Motion Pictures no longer had a financial incentive to arrange cinema screenings of *Prizzi's Honor* for Academy members or take out expensive advertisements in the industry trade papers on behalf of the film. "'Prizzi' is dead!" Ashley Boone, President of Distribution at Lorimar declared in a New York Times article by Aljean Harmetz at the end of January. During the critical Oscar voting period, only the film's distributor, Twentieth Century-Fox, mounted a campaign for *Prizzi's Honor*, and even then, the ads focussed mainly on the performance of Jack Nicholson. The studio was hoping the star would appear in one of their upcoming projects, Harmetz disclosed. On Oscar night, *Prizzi's Honor* collected just one statuette.

It was the winner of the Globe (Drama) which ended up triumphant at the Academy Awards. *Out of Africa* won seven statuettes, including Best Picture and Best Director. *La Historia Oficial* was named Best Foreign-Language Film while *The Color Purple* joined the 1977 drama *The Turning Point* as the most nominated films in Oscar history to completely strike out on awards night.

In London, the British Academy gave their Best Film prize to a film that the Academy had not even nominated for the Best Picture Oscar: *The Purple Rose of Cairo*. Woody Allen's film won over a field of nominees that included the previous year's Oscar winner *Amadeus*. It had earlier been chosen as Best Film by the London Film Critics. Like *Prizzi's Honor*, Allen's comedy was another film which had completed its cinematic run and become available for home video rental prior to the Academy Awards.

The following year, the British Academy did not even nominate either *The Color Purple* or *Out of Africa* for the Best Film BAFTA, even though both were eligible.

BEST DIRECTOR

ACADEMY AWARDS
Hector Babenco for *Kiss of the Spider Woman*
John Huston for *Prizzi's Honor*
Akira Kurosawa for *Ran*
• **Sydney Pollack for *Out of Africa***
Peter Weir for *Witness*

GOLDEN GLOBE AWARDS
Richard Attenborough – *A Chorus Line*
• **John Huston – *Prizzi's Honor***
Sydney Pollack – *Out of Africa*
Steven Spielberg – *The Color Purple*
Peter Weir – *Witness*

DIRECTORS GUILD AWARD
Ron Howard – *Cocoon*
John Huston – *Prizzi's Honor*
Sydney Pollack – *Out of Africa*
• **Steven Spielberg – *The Color Purple***
Peter Weir – *Witness*

NEW YORK – **John Huston** – *Prizzi's Honor*
LOS ANGELES – **Terry Gilliam** – *Brazil*
BOARD OF REVIEW – **Akira Kurosawa** – *Ran*
NATIONAL SOCIETY – **John Huston** – *Prizzi's Honor*
LONDON – **Roland Joffe** – *The Killing Fields*

"The seventy-nine-year old John Huston is the favourite for Best Director," declared The New York Times in the lead up to the Oscars. Huston had won his third award from the New York Film Critics Circle, his second Golden Globe, and the National Society of Film Critics honour for *Prizzi's Honor* (NYT "directed with a humanely funny gusto ... demonstrates the extraordinary, continuing vitality of this amazing film maker"; LAT "guides [his cast] in immaculate style"; CT "the special charm of [the film] grows out of the mixture of whimsy and heartbreak concocted by master director John Huston"; WP "has composed [the film] mostly with a clinical, unobtrusive camera [which] lends the movie a kind of grandeur [and] keeps it from descending into farce"; PI "shrewdly organized and subtle").

The other major contender for the critics' accolades had been Akira Kurosawa for *Ran* (LAT "bravura ... awe-inspiring"; CT "absolute command"; BG "he retains sweep and surehandedness, filling the screen with unforced panoramic grandeur and vivid, painterly closeups"). The veteran Japanese director had received the National Board of Review plaudit and finished runner-up for New York and Los Angeles prizes and the NSFC.

The Academy nominated both Huston and Kurosawa along with Hector Babenco for *Kiss of the Spider Woman* (NYT "staged with perfect control and fierce originality ... never falters"; CT "polished ... his talent is undeniable"; WP "stuttering pace"; BG "one of the best directed films of the year"), Sydney Pollack for *Out of Africa* (TGM "may be [David] Lean's disciple in the painstaking fabrication of mindful pop epics"; MFB "too many grand gestures and too little metaphor") and Peter Weir for *Witness* (NYT "perfunctory"; BG "Weir gets remarkable things from his actors"; PI "well-directed").

None of these candidates were presented with the Directors Guild of America accolade, however. The Guild winner was Steven Spielberg for *The Color Purple* (NYT "uneven ... he's over his head here"; LAT "his almost every decision has been disastrous"; CT "can be viewed as Spielberg's successful attempt to enlarge his reputation"; WP "falls short ... there's no intimacy, or sincerity ... an obvious bid for the Oscar"; TGM "heavy-handed"). There had been an outcry when Spielberg had been overlooked by the Academy despite his film receiving a leading tally of eleven nominations. It was the first time that the Guild winner was not in contention for the Oscar.

Others by-passed for Oscar consideration were: Los Angeles Film Critics Association winner Terry Gilliam for *Brazil* (LAT "richly visionary"); Woody Allen for *The Purple Rose of Cairo* (NYT "as fine as anything he's done"; LAT "he has taken the gimmick to its limits and made it live"; WP "masterfully managed"; BG "artistry raised to wizardry"; PI "consummate skill and ingenuity"; TT "comic genius"); Ron Howard for *Cocoon* (NYT "directed in [his] charming, personable style ... brings a real sweetness to his subject"); Martin Scorsese for *After Hours*, for which he was named Best Director at Cannes the following year (LAT "dazzling movie making"; CT "radical changes in tone are difficult to pull off, and it is only in [the] last segment of the film where he fails"); and Emir Kusturica for *Otac na Sluzbenom Putu (When Father was Away on Business)* (NYT "[his] expert, measured direction is able to weave disparate elements together into a gentle, touching film"; CT "plodding"; WP "[he] is able to make subtle shifts seamlessly ... striking").

With the DGA winner excluded from the field and the British Academy not presenting a prize, Oscar observers predicted a win for Huston. However, in what Variety later called "a shock", the winner was Pollack for *Out of Africa*.

BEST ACTOR

ACADEMY AWARDS
Harrison Ford as 'John Book' in *Witness*
James Garner as 'Murphy Jones' in *Murphy's Romance*
• **William Hurt as 'Luis Molina' in *Kiss of the Spider Woman***
Jack Nicholson as 'Charley Partanna' in *Prizzi's Honor*
Jon Voight as 'Manny' in *Runaway Train*

GOLDEN GLOBE AWARDS

(Drama)

Harrison Ford – *Witness*
Gene Hackman – *Twice in a Lifetime*
William Hurt
  – *Kiss of the Spider Woman*
Raul Julia – *Kiss of the Spider Woman*
• **Jon Voight – *Runaway Train***

(Comedy/Musical)

Jeff Daniels
  – *The Purple Rose of Cairo*
Griffin Dunne – *After Hours*
James Garner – *Murphy's Romance*
Michael J. Fox – *Back to the Future*
• **Jack Nicholson – *Prizzi's Honor***

BRITISH ACADEMY AWARDS
F. Murray Abraham – *Amadeus*
Victor Banerjee – *A Passage to India*
Harrison Ford – *Witness*
• **William Hurt – *Kiss of the Spider Woman***

NEW YORK – Jack Nicholson – *Prizzi's Honor*
LOS ANGELES – William Hurt – *Kiss of the Spider Woman*
BOARD OF REVIEW – William Hurt – *Kiss of the Spider Woman*
NATIONAL SOCIETY – Jack Nicholson – *Prizzi's Honor*
LONDON – Richard Farnsworth – *The Grey Fox* and James Mason – *The Shooting Party*

At the Cannes Film Festival in May, William Hurt was named Best Actor for his performance as an imprisoned gay man in *Kiss of the Spider Woman*. When the film was released in July, Hurt's performance was met with almost universal acclaim by critics (NYT "a performance that is crafty at first, carefully nurtured, and finally stirring in profound, unanticipated ways ... exquisitely poised ... succeeds in making the campy, flamboyant aspects of Molina's homosexuality seem credible and metaphorical in equal measure"; NYP "[a] magnificent, three-dimensional performance"; LAT "[a] rapturous characterization ... a performance both generous and acute"; CT "memorable ... Hurt never makes the movie less than compelling ... he'll be difficult to beat at Oscar time"; BG "brilliant ... never crosses the dangerous border between the acceptably outrageous and outright camp"; TT "brilliant [and] without fault"; S&S "[acts with] authority and passion"; MFB "practically perfect"). Among the few dissenting voices were The Washington Post which called his performance "superficial" and "a homosexual caricature" and Variety which said that he "falls somewhere between the hypnotic and the monotonous". Interestingly, Variety was more enthusiastic about Hurt's co-star, Raul Julia, commending him for "a strong, straight and believable performance" as the other prisoner. Despite his screen time and Globe (Drama) nomination, most observers expected Julia to earn a place on the Academy's ballot for Best Supporting Actor.

In June, Jack Nicholson won acclaim for his portrayal of a slow-witted Mafia hit man in the black comedy *Prizzi's Honor* (NYT "terrific ... as good as anything he's ever done"; LAT "memorable"; CT "eminently watchable" but his Brooklyn accent "doesn't work – it's the film's only flaw"; WP "a definitive comic performance"; PI "gives a dazzling virtuoso display"; V "fascinating"; MFB "exemplary as well as very funny").

At the end of the year, Hurt and Nicholson split the critics' prizes. Hurt outpolled Nicholson to win the Los Angeles Film Critics Association and National Board of Review awards, while Nicholson claimed both the New York Film Critics Circle and National Society of Film Critics plaudits ahead of Hurt.

The only major prize claimed by another actor was the Golden Globe (Drama) which, in a major shock, was won by Jon Voight as an escaped prisoner in *Runaway Train* (NYT "a fiery performance ... entirely different from anything else he has done on screen"; LAT "mixes humanity and blood lust [to make] his murderer explicable, then sympathetic"; CT "delivers a wonderful speech about survival, but it's only one of many such monologues"; WP "completely over the top"; PI "a terrific, manic presence ... it may be his best screen performance – he's way over the edge – but at the same time it's a hard, deft kind of hamminess"; V "brilliant"). In the Comedy/Musical category, meanwhile, Nicholson added to his haul for the season. It was his fourth Globe.

When the Academy announced its list of nominees, Globe winners Nicholson and Voight were mentioned for an eighth and third time, respectively. Hurt was mentioned for the first time, as were both Harrison Ford as a police officer in *Witness* (NYT "good"; LAT "beautifully played"; CT "without calling undo attention to himself, once again proves to be a fine, workmanlike actor ... he probably won't win any awards for this performance, but he should"; PI "a casual, disciplined performance that draws on the kind of self-deprecating humor he's best at"; V "excellent") and James Garner as a widower in *Murphy's Romance* (LAT "[his] super-relaxed style works wonderfully here"; CT "effortlessly good ... the key to the film"; V "sincere").

According to Jack Mathews in The Los Angeles Times, Garner was a surprise inclusion ahead of Gene Hackman in *Twice in a Lifetime* (CT "his best performance since 'Under Fire'"; BG "superior acting"; PI "shows his range by bringing an essentially limited man and his dilemma to life"), Danny Glover in *The Color Purple* (NYT "manages to be terrifically winning"; WP "while [he] glowers impressively, he's too hateful to be believed"; CT "worthy of special comment ... horrific while remaining credible") and Michael J. Fox in *Back to the Future* (NYT "played winningly"; CT "played appealingly"; WP "projects intelligence and a self-confidence that can be unprepossessing, but he's found the character's timidity in the script and brings it out").

Also overlooked for consideration were: Jeff Daniels in *The Purple Rose of Cairo* (PI "wholly convincing, and there's none of the over-playing that the dual roles must have invited"); Griffin Dunne in *After Hours* (NYT "well-acted"; CT "brings a convincing touch ... there is an ordinariness to Dunne's characterization that is just right"; TGM "[a] seamless performance in the dauntingly difficult lead"); Jonathan Pryce in *Brazil* (V "played with vibrant comic imagination"; TT "amiably effective ... marvellously appealing"); Klaus Maria Brandauer in *Oberst Redl (Colonel Redl)* (NYT "a good performance ... but he has nothing much to work with"; LAT "brilliantly played ... totally convincing"; CT "superb ... brilliantly conveys the rising anxiety that haunts Redl"; PI "[a] visceral performance"; V "superb"; TT "a tour de force"; S&S "[a] powerhouse performance"); Sean Penn in *The Falcon and the Snowman* (NYT "dominates the screen ... arresting"; CT "special ... absolutely lifelike"; WP "plays the role for all his worth"; V "superb"; TGM "a performance that should earn him [an] Oscar nomination"; Sp "good and bravely restrained"); Albert Brooks in *Lost in America* (LAT "painting an agonizingly accurate portrait of a man imprisoned in his own fantasies"; CT "wildly funny"); the late James Mason in his last film appearance in *The Shooting Party* (NYT "[a] secure, wise and utterly relaxed performance ... ranks with the best work of his career"; LAT "Mason gives us the man in his entirety"; CT "memorable"; BG "pure quality ... immensely touching ... unforgettable"; PI "commands the camera in every scene"; G "he manages to suggest a great deal more than he might had he walked through the part"; S&S "superb"); and the previous year's co-honoree at the Cannes Film Festival, Alfredo Landa in *Los Santos Inocentes (The Holy Innocents)* (NYT "arouses great compassion ... acted in a plain, utterly convincing style"; LAT "glorious, understated acting"; WP "a heartwarming performance"; BG "[a] masterwork of understatement"; TGM "superb").

In late March, the Academies in Hollywood and London declared Hurt to be the year's Best Actor. For the BAFTA, he outpolled a field of nominees that included the previous year's Oscar winner, F. Murray Abraham in *Amadeus*. Hurt was a contender for the Best Actor Oscar in both of the next two years.

BEST ACTRESS

ACADEMY AWARDS
Anne Bancroft as 'Mother Miriam Ruth' in *Agnes of God*
Whoopi Goldberg as 'Celie' in *The Color Purple*
Jessica Lange as 'Patsy Cline' in *Sweet Dreams*
• **Geraldine Page as 'Mrs Watts' in *The Trip to Bountiful***
Meryl Streep as 'Karen, Baroness Blixen' in *Out of Africa*

GOLDEN GLOBE AWARDS
(Drama)

Anne Bancroft – *Agnes of God*
Cher – *Mask*
• **Whoopi Goldberg**
  – *The Color Purple*
Geraldine Page – *The Trip to Bountiful*
Meryl Streep – *Out of Africa*

(Comedy/Musical)

Rosanna Arquette
  – *Desperately Seeking Susan*
Glenn Close – *Maxie*
Mia Farrow
  – *The Purple Rose of Cairo*
Sally Field – *Murphy's Romance*
• **Kathleen Turner**
  – *Prizzi's Honor*

BRITISH ACADEMY AWARDS
• **Peggy Ashcroft – *A Passage to India***
Mia Farrow – *The Purple Rose of Cairo*
Kelly McGillis – *Witness*
Alexandra Pigg – *Letter to Brezhnev*

NEW YORK – Norma Aleandro – *La Historia Oficial (The Official Story)*
LOS ANGELES – Meryl Streep – *Out of Africa*
BOARD OF REVIEW – Whoopi Goldberg – *The Color Purple*
NATIONAL SOCIETY – Vanessa Redgrave – *Wetherby*

The Best Actress prize at the Cannes Film Festival was shared by Norma Aleandro as a woman who suspects that her adopted daughter is the orphan of murdered political dissidents in *La Historia Oficial (The Official Story)* (NYT "luminous ... conveyed with remarkable subtlety"; LAT "[a] towering and deeply affecting performance"; CT "there isn't a false moment in a role that has a wide emotional range"; WP "impressions register almost imperceptibly in her face; her performance is less notable for the times she emotes than for the times she chooses not to – a tapestry of eloquent silences"; BG "in one of the great performances of the year, she conveys the heartfelt intensity of a mother torn by personal and political revelations"; TGM "[a] monumental performance"; TT "outstanding") and Cher as the mother of a disfigured teenager in *Mask* (NYT "played with a good deal of skill"; LAT "ferociously fine"; CT "another fine performance"; BG "brings many subtle dimensions to a film that's otherwise lacking this essential virtue"; V "beautifully acted"; MFB "insufficient"). At the end of the year, Aleandro was named Best Actress by the New York Film Critics Circle and Cher was nominated for the Globe (Drama), but both were overlooked for the Oscar. As nominations for foreign-language performances were rare, few were surprised by the absence of Aleandro, but many were stunned by Cher's exclusion. Just days before the nominations were announced, Anne Thompson had written in Film Comment, "The unanimous shoo-in [in this category] is Cher for her stops-out turn in 'Mask'".

The Cannes honorees were not the only prize-winners left off the list of Oscar contenders. The Academy also ignored: Kathleen Turner in *Prizzi's Honor*, for which she won her second consecutive Best Actress (Comedy/Musical) Globe (NYT "terrific"; NYP "played with a crisp, stylish freshness"; LAT "slightly overmatched [by Nicholson] but she never seems to notice"; CT "eminently watchable ... she is carrying more than half the load [of the film] in fleshing out her various characters [and] she plays them all brighter than we expect"; WP "the great flaw of [the film] ... never seems to get a handle on her role"; MFB "superlative"); Maggie Smith in *A Private Function*, for which she won the previous year's Best Actress BAFTA (NYT "deliciously funny"; LAT "pungently entertaining"; CT "expertly performed"; WP "sharp satire"; V "topnotch"; S&S "marvellous"); National Society of Film Critics winner Vanessa Redgrave in *Wetherby* (NYT "[her] warm, credible performance is very much the heart of the film"; CT "remarkable"; BG "dominates the film, but subtly"; V "excellent"; TGM "gives us an authentic character ... certainly one of the most impressive performances of her screen career"; MFB "excellent"); and Rosanna Arquette in *Desperately Seeking Susan*, for which she won the Best Supporting Actress BAFTA (NYT "[a] delight"; LAT "skilfully carries the film"; TGM "charts [her character's path] with unerringly amusing directness").

Notable performances by several previous Best Actress Oscar winners were also overlooked, including: Jane Fonda in *Agnes of God* (NYP "riveting"; CT "gets into character convincingly"; V "tiresome"); Sissy Spacek in *Marie* (NYT "gives yet another guileless, radiant performance of unusual immediacy"; LAT "superb ... a burningly committed performance"; CT "there's nothing wrong with Spacek's performance; it's her one-note character who is a bore"; BG "splendid"; V "excellent"); and Glenda Jackson in *Return of the Soldier* (NYT "splendid"; CT "[provides] a series of acting lessons"; WP "never connects with anything real"; BG "it's a tribute to [her] skill that she overcomes the director's simplistic, stereotypical approach and creates a woman of extraordinary depth").

Other notable omissions from the Academy's list were: Mia Farrow in *The Purple Rose of Cairo* (NYT "[a] glowing, funny performance"; LAT "radiant"; CT "a revelation ... utterly convincing"; PI "excels here"; V "excellent"; TT "unflawed"; Time "[a] lovely performance"); Miranda Richardson in *Dance with a Stranger* (NYT "a striking performance [and] a smashing film debut"; NYP "magnificent"; LAT "[her] grasp of her character is triumphant"; CT "mesmerizing ... a raw performance ... seems to be giving a part of herself on the screen without tearing up the scenery"; WP "a bravura debut ... pours her soul into [the character]"; PI "brilliantly realized"; V "riveting"; TT "beautifully played"; Sp "in every way, a most extraordinary performance"); Theresa Russell in *Insignificance* (NYT "exceptionally good"; LAT "puzzling; within a single scene she can vary from inspired to abysmal, and back again"; CT "[a] fine performance, except for a wavering accent"; V "subtle ... skilfully counterpoints a cheery exterior to inner despair"; G "at times this looks a rather rehearsed performance, a little too mannered to be entirely true [but then her] acting takes wing and develops a momentum of its own"); Glenn Close in both *Maxie* (LAT "reveals lovely gifts as a sexy romantic comedienne ... [the film's box office hope] seems to rest on the attention [she] deserves for an Academy Award nomination"; WP "never really becomes a flapper ... works a little too hard at proving what a gosh-darn versatile actress she is") and *Jagged Edge* (NYT "convincing"; LAT "glowing but daft"; WP "[a] handsome performance ... shows more grit in her performance here than there's been in the past"); and Laura Dern in *Smooth Talk* (NYT "an award-calibre performance"; LAT "one of the finest, most sustained and most shatteringly observed [performances] this year"; WP "a performance of quiet depth and intensity ... stunning").

Nominated for the Oscar, but considered by observers to be only outside chances to claim the statuette, were previous winner Anne Bancroft as the mother superior in *Agnes of God* (NYT "forceful"; NYP "riveting"; CT "subdued and not maudlin"; V "highly engaging"; TT "a fiery, rounded performance") and NSFC runner-up Jessica Lange in *Sweet Dreams* (NYT "extraordinary"; V "Lange's portrayal of country singer Patsy Cline [is] certainly equal to Sissy Spacek's Oscar-winning recreation of Loretta Lynn"; S&S "a marvellously fluid and vivacious performance"; MFB "superlative").

The three nominees considered by pundits to have a genuine chance of claiming the Oscar were all actresses whose films had been released, within three days of one another, in the midst of the voting by the major critics' groups.

Meryl Streep won her fourth Los Angeles Film Critics Association plaudit (her third as Best Actress), finished runner-up in the voting in New York and was nominated for the Globe (Drama) for her portrayal of Baroness Blixen in *Out of Africa* (LAT "can pretty nearly do anything; she can certainly make all the facets of the infinitely complex Baroness Blixen sparkle like crystal"; CT "once again uses her voice as an instrument of deception, creating a convincing Danish character out of little more than a voice and period costumes"; BG "fills the screen with Dinesen's strength and eccentricity ... revels in Blixen's powerfulness ... Streep clearly has another Oscar in her sights"; V "another engaging performance"; TGM "[a] luminous performance"; TT "remarkable ... compelling ... impressive"; MFB "detailed mimicry"). It was the sixth Oscar nomination in eight years (and the fourth time in five years in the lead category) for Streep, who'd already won in both categories. Earlier in the year, she had earned mixed reviews for *Plenty* (NYT "doesn't help [the film] ... does all the right things technically but the character remains chilly and distant"; LAT "the most beautifully modulated performance of her career ... [her] work is rich and complex [and] for the first time, completely free of her trademark mannerisms"; WP "her work here has all the meticulous details of her other performances [but] for the first time she's really able to breathe"; BG "seems miscast").

Runner-up to Streep in Los Angeles, Whoopi Goldberg received the National Board of Review award as the mistreated heroine in *The Color Purple* (NYT "wonderful ... compelling"; NYP "magnificent ... it's no wonder the buzz about Oscars is already circulating around her mesmerizing performance"; LAT "compelling ... a most touching debut"; CT "a natural talent who does not overact"; WP "unfortunately, is no actress, but essentially a clown, with a clown's range of emotions ... she never gets at anything beyond generalized emotion ... her Celie is a heroic victim, but never a character"; TT "the film's one great strength"; MFB "[a] truly remarkable performance which carries the film"). Goldberg subsequently became the first African American woman to win the Globe (Drama), and soon after, received her first Oscar nomination.

In *The Trip to Bountiful*, Geraldine Page played an ageing widow who travels back to her hometown, a part originated on television and then on Broadway by Lillian Gish in the 1950s (NYT "exquisitely performed ... has never been in better form ... ranks with the best things Miss Page has done on the screen"; LAT "magnificent [and] moving [in] an unforgettable portrayal ... a precisely conceived and calculated turn by a gifted professional always aware of what she is doing and the effects she's creating"; CT "inhabits the role with authority and vinegar"; SFC "the sort of tour de force that actresses – and Academy Award voters – smack their lips over"; V "the performance of a lifetime ... excellent throughout"; Time "Page is overwhelming in the worst sense of the word, a steamroller of tics, tricks and mannerisms"; TT "triumphant [in a] tour de force"; MFB "[the film] becomes a vehicle for [a] grande dame's virtuosity"). The Academy nominated Page for an eighth time in thirty-two years.

On Oscar night, *Out of Africa* won seven awards, including Best Picture, but Streep missed out on a third statuette. After going home empty-handed seven times previously, Geraldine Page finally received the Academy Award.

1985

BEST SUPPORTING ACTOR

ACADEMY AWARDS
• **Don Ameche as 'Art Selwyn' in** *Cocoon*
Klaus Maria Brandauer as 'Bror, Baron Blixen' in *Out of Africa*
William Hickey as 'Don Corrado Prizzi' in *Prizzi's Honor*
Robert Loggia as 'Sam Ransom' in *Jagged Edge*
Eric Roberts as 'Buck' in *Runaway Train*

GOLDEN GLOBE AWARDS
• **Klaus Maria Brandauer – *Out of Africa***
Joel Grey – *Remo Williams: The Adventure Begins...*
John Lone – *Year of the Dragon*
Eric Roberts – *Runaway Train*
Eric Stoltz – *Mask*

BRITISH ACADEMY AWARDS
• **Denholm Elliott – *Defence of the Realm***
James Fox – *A Passage to India*
John Gielgud – *Plenty*
Saeed Jaffrey – *My Beautiful Laundrette*

NEW YORK – Klaus Maria Brandauer – *Out of Africa*
LOS ANGELES – John Gielgud – *Plenty* and *The Shooting Party*
BOARD OF REVIEW – Klaus Maria Brandauer – *Out of Africa*
NATIONAL SOCIETY – John Gielgud – *Plenty* and *The Shooting Party*

Four years after winning the Best Supporting Actor Oscar for *Arthur*, John Gielgud was a strong contender for the prize again. He was named Best Supporting Actor by the Los Angeles Film Critics Association for the second time and also won the National Society of Film Critics prize for his performance as an elderly diplomat in *Plenty* (NYT "fun to watch ... plays [the part] with a certain comic rigor"; WP "his seigneurial timing bolsters the movie's best comic lines ... splendid"; BG "grandly impeccable") and his cameo as an animal rights activist in *The Shooting Party* (NYT "simply cannot do wrong"; CT "plays superbly"; WP "dotters endearingly about"; TGM "peerless").

Other strong contenders were Klaus Maria Brandauer as the aristocratic husband in *Out of Africa* (NYT "beautifully played"; NYP "easily steals the film"; V "well played"; CT "well-acted"; BG "seems a shoo-in for the best supporting Oscar"; TT "wickedly clever") and fifty-seven-year old William

Hickey as the ageing head of a Mafia family in *Prizzi's Honor* (NYT "terrific ... the performance of [his] career"; NYP "colorful"; WP "gives a bravura comic performance ... he moves delicately like a precious marionette, and delivers his lines in a singsong as scary and hilarious as a roller coaster"; V "colorful"). Brandauer outpolled Gielgud by 34 points to 21 to win the plaudit from the New York Film Critics Circle and also received the National Board of Review prize. Hickey, meanwhile, finished as runner-up to Gielgud for both the Los Angeles and NSFC honours (Gielgud won the latter, 27 points to 18).

Surprisingly, both Gielgud and Hickey were overlooked for the Golden Globe. In the absence of his main rivals, Brandauer emerged as the winner ahead of previous winner Joel Grey as the Korean martial arts tutor in *Remo Williams: The Adventure Begins...* (LAT "unrecognizable ... walks off with the highest honors [though] probably not without protest from the Korean-American community that a Korean-American actor was not cast"); John Lone in *Year of the Dragon* (LAT "dominates his every scene ... it is almost not possible to watch another actor when Lone is on the screen"; CT "effective"); Eric Roberts as a young prison escapee in *Runaway Train* (NYT "borders on the absurd"; LAT "works another brilliant turn"; CT "tiring in his frantic reactions"; WP "presented with Voight's [own overacting], Roberts has no choice but to follow ... goes two hours on the edge of mania"; PI "gives another overblown, bogus performance ... his line readings are all several notches too emotional ... he becomes an embarrassment to watch"; V "impressive"); and Eric Stoltz as a teenage boy afflicted with a disfiguring disease in *Mask* (LAT "beautifully played ... simply amazing"; CT "played memorably"; V "beautifully acted"; MFB "[a] dedicated impersonation").

When the Academy Award nominations were announced, Gielgud was again overlooked. Oscar voters instead short-listed five first-time nominees: Globe champ Brandauer; critics' contender Hickey; Globe nominee Roberts; Robert Loggia as a foul-mouthed private investigator in *Jagged Edge* (LAT "giving vivid life to [a] weary cliche"; WP "priceless ... shambling imperially, [he] breathes life into a familiar character"); and Don Ameche as one of the elderly people rejuvenated by aliens in *Cocoon* (NYT "marvelous"; WP "there are few treats equal to watching Ameche"; BG "marvelous").

In addition to Gielgud and the overlooked Globe candidates, the Academy also passed over: 1984 BAFTA winner Denholm Elliott in *A Private Function* (NYT "first-rate ... marvelous"; LAT "[a] pungently entertaining performance"; CT "expertly performed"; WP "fine"); Treat Williams in *Smooth Talk* (NYT "comes very close to stealing the picture ... an award-calibre performance"; LAT "the very best he has been in years"; WP "stunning ... his best role since 'Prince of the City'"; TT "wonderful"); Alan Arkin in *Joshua Then and Now* (NYT "it is Mr Arkin whose appearances, however infrequent, really enliven the movie ... the apparent effortlessness with which [he] inhabits this character makes him all the more winning"; LAT "when Arkin is on the screen there's almost no better place to be"; CT "a performance worthy of an Oscar nomination"; BG "hilarious ... [but his] mugging is allowed to throw the film off kilter"); David Suchet in *The Falcon and the Snowman* (NYT "very good"; TGM "especially admirable"); Armin Mueller-Stahl as Archduke Franz Ferdinand of Austria in *Oberst Redl (Colonel Redl)* (NYT "the most interesting character in the film ... played with chilly charm"; LAT "brilliant ... he makes evil so palpable that one's flesh crawls at the sight of his cold eyes"; S&S "[a] powerhouse performance"); and the previous year's co-honoree at the Cannes Film Festival, Francisco Rabal in *Los Santos Inocentes (The Holy Innocents)* (LAT "glorious, understated acting"; WP "memorable"; BG "naturalistic ... [a] masterwork of understatement"; TGM "superb").

Also absent from the Academy's short list was Raul Julia as the other prisoner in *Kiss of the Spider Woman* (NYT "has never been so restrained ... the performance of his career"; CT "Julia's is the less showy role by far and he wisely resists any competitive temptation to chew the scenery in an effort to upstage Hurt ... wonderful ... gradually reveals a poetry that makes the whole movie work"; WP "Julia brings all his charisma to the role, but he's pouring it down a sinkhole"; BG "appropriately understated"; V "a strong, straight and believable performance"). Despite his considerable screen time and Globe (Drama) nomination, most observers had expected him to earn a place on the Academy's ballot for Best Supporting Actor.

Most critics favoured Brandauer to win the Oscar because *Out of Africa* was one of the year's two most Oscar nominated films and his lead performance in *Oberst Redl* had been so widely acclaimed by critics yet overlooked by the Academy. "We can only assume that the citations that Brandauer has been receiving for best supporting actor in Sydney Pollack's 'Out of Africa' (from the New York Film Critics Circle and the Los Angeles Film Critics Association) are partly in recognition for his much larger and more impressive work here," said Rick Lyman in his review of *Oberst Redl* in The Philadelphia Inquirer a couple of days before Christmas. Others, however, predicted that the Academy would choose Ameche, the seventy-seven-year old sentimental favourite who had never been recognised despite a Hollywood career of over fifty years.

On Oscar night, sentiment prevailed. Ameche was presented the statuette. He reprised the role of Art Selwyn three years later in the sequel, *Cocoon: The Return*, but never received a second nomination from the Academy.

At the British Academy Awards, Gielgud received a nomination for *Plenty*, but was outpolled by Denholm Elliott, who collected his third consecutive Best Supporting Actor BAFTA for *Defence of the Realm*. Elliott's performance was eligible for Oscar consideration the following year.

BEST SUPPORTING ACTRESS

ACADEMY AWARDS
Margaret Avery as 'Shug' in *The Color Purple*
• **Anjelica Huston as 'Maerose Prizzi' in *Prizzi's Honor***
Amy Madigan as 'Sunny Mackenzie' in *Twice in a Lifetime*
Meg Tilly as 'Sister Agnes' in *Agnes of God*
Oprah Winfrey as 'Sofia' in *The Color Purple*

GOLDEN GLOBE AWARDS
Sonia Braga – *Kiss of the Spider Woman*
Anjelica Huston – *Prizzi's Honor*
Amy Madigan – *Twice in a Lifetime*
Kelly McGillis – *Witness*
• **Meg Tilly – *Agnes of God***
Oprah Winfrey – *The Color Purple*

BRITISH ACADEMY AWARDS
• **Rosanna Arquette – *Desperately Seeking Susan***
Judi Dench – *Wetherby*
Anjelica Huston – *Prizzi's Honor*
Tracey Ullman – *Plenty*

NEW YORK – Anjelica Huston – *Prizzi's Honor*
LOS ANGELES – Anjelica Huston – *Prizzi's Honor*
BOARD OF REVIEW – Anjelica Huston – *Prizzi's Honor*
NATIONAL SOCIETY – Anjelica Huston – *Prizzi's Honor*

Anjelica Huston was the unanimous choice of the four major American critics' groups as Best Supporting Actress for her performance as the daughter of a Mafia boss in *Prizzi's Honor*, a black comedy directed by her father John Huston (NYT "a riveting presence … if Miss Huston doesn't get an Oscar nomination for this performance, I'll be very surprised … terrific"; NYP "a smoldering, raunchy portrait"; LAT "terrific"; CT "a most pleasant surprise … stealing many of the scenes … played magnificently … her final scene is a piece of minimalist acting that deserves to win awards"; WP "brings subtle effects to a character that's broadly written – she's alternately cynical and seductive, satirical and sad, but you never hear the gearbox"; SFC "simply stunning"; MFB "superlative").

The critics' accolades made Huston the overwhelming favourite for the Academy Award, but her frontrunner status was shaken when she was outpolled for the Golden Globe in a major upset. The winner was Meg Tilly as the naive and troubled nun in *Agnes of God* (NYT "radiant"; NYP "riveting"; LAT "sweetness and torment [are] so well embodied by Tilly"; CT "as other-worldly as one could want"; BG "[the film] is stolen by Tilly ... she convinces"; V "brings a convincing innocence and sincerity to the role that would be hard to match"). The Globe result was all the more surprising given that *Prizzi's Honor* won more Globes than any other film that night, including Best Picture (Comedy/Musical) and Best Director for John Huston.

Huston and Tilly were each short-listed by the Academy alongside Amy Madigan as the angry and unforgiving elder daughter in the family drama *Twice in a Lifetime* (NYT "plays her role with a fierce, riveting conviction"; LAT "almost incandescent in her fury ... brilliant"; CT "terrific ... [her] performance is the most vibrant in the movie"; BG "superior acting"; TGM "good") and two actresses for their debut performances in *The Color Purple*: Margaret Avery as the singer who befriends the heroine (NYT "warmly magnetic"; NYP "beautifully acted"; LAT "electrifying"; V "[a] standout") and Oprah Winfrey as the strong-willed Sofia (NYT "handles [the role] gracefully"; NYP "played with robust force ... stunning"; LAT "in Winfrey's hands, Sofia is indomitable and unforgettable"; CT "a shockingly good film debut ... [she is] always in character here, and the range of performance is the sort that wins Oscar nominations in the supporting category"; V "[a] standout").

While Huston remained the Oscar favourite, several observers started talking about upset wins by either Globe champ Tilly or Los Angeles Film Critics Association runner-up Winfrey.

On Oscar night, the expected Best Picture and Director wins by *Prizzi's Honor* did not occur. The only statuette the film claimed was for Best Supporting Actress. Anjelica Huston's Oscar win came thirty-seven years after her father and grandfather, John and Walter Huston, won statuettes as Best Director and Best Supporting Actor for *The Treasure of the Sierra Madre*. "This means a lot to me," she told the audience at the Dorothy Chandler Pavilion, "since it comes from a role in which I was directed by my father. And I know it means a lot to him."

In London, Huston was nominated for the Best Supporting Actress BAFTA, but was outpolled by Rosanna Arquette, who had strangely been included in the secondary category for *Desperately Seeking Susan*. Arquette's co-lead performance in *Desperately Seeking Susan* had been nominated for the Globe (Comedy/Musical), but overlooked by members of the Academy.

Contenders overlooked for the Oscar were: National Society of Film Critics runner-up Mieko Harada as the vicious Lady Kaede in *Ran* (NYT "by far the most interesting figure in this drama ... memorable"; LAT "electrifying"; BG "a force of nature ... the one character who does have personality"; V "unforgettable"); 1984 BAFTA winner Liz Smith as the dotty old mother in the British comedy *A Private Function* (NYT "first-rate ... marvelous"; CT "expertly performed"; WP "fine"; TGM "magnificently mannered"); both Rosanna Arquette (LAT "has just the right edge as Marcy who, in the space of five minutes, can be open, seductive, hysterical, vague, trusting and dangerous") and Linda Fiorentino (NYT "very good"; LAT "splendid"; WP "gives her best performance yet"; TGM "impossible to imagine how [she] could be better") in *After Hours*; Rebecca de Mornay in *The Trip to Bountiful* (NYT "superb ... a particular treat ... holds her own with one of the great scene-stealers of her age"; NYP "excels"; V "delightful"; S&S "the real acting honours belong to a touching cameo by Rebecca de Mornay"; MFB "appears completely overwhelmed by [Page's] virtuosity"); Sonia Braga in *Kiss of the Spider Woman* (NYT "hilarious"; CT "called upon to satirize bad acting, makes a perfect spider woman"; MFB "wonderfully apt"); Judi Dench in *Wetherby* (NYT "very fine"; V "excellent"; TGM "strong"); Judi Bowker in *The Shooting Party* (NYT "especially charming"; BG "touching"); and Ann-Margret in *Return of the Soldier* (NYT "splendid ... a surprise"; WP "wears no make-up, which is our clue that this is a Serious Performance, but without her glamor, there's not much there").

BEST PICTURE

ACADEMY AWARDS
Children of a Lesser God
(Sugarman, Paramount, 110 mins, 3 Oct 1986, $31.8m, 5 noms)
Hannah and Her Sisters
(Rollins-Joffe, Orion, 103 mins, 7 Feb 1986, $40.0m, 7 noms)
The Mission
(Goldcrest, Kingsmere, Warner Bros., 126 mins, 31 Oct 1986, $17.2m, 7 noms)
• *Platoon*
(Hemdale, Orion, 120 mins, 19 Dec 1986, $137.9m, 8 noms)
A Room with a View
(Merchant Ivory, Cinecom, 117 mins, 7 Mar 1986, $20.9m, 8 noms)

GOLDEN GLOBE AWARDS

(Drama)	(Comedy/Musical)
Children of a Lesser God	*Crimes of the Heart*
The Mission	*Crocodile Dundee*
Mona Lisa	*Down and Out in Beverly Hills*
• *Platoon*	• *Hannah and Her Sisters*
A Room with a View	*Little Shop of Horrors*
Stand by Me	*Peggy Sue Got Married*

BRITISH ACADEMY AWARDS
Hannah and Her Sisters
The Mission
Mona Lisa
• *A Room with a View*

NEW YORK – *Hannah and Her Sisters*
LOS ANGELES – *Hannah and Her Sisters*
BOARD OF REVIEW – *A Room with a View*
NATIONAL SOCIETY – *Blue Velvet*
LONDON – *A Room with a View*

The National Board of Review began the major awards season by presenting its Best Picture award to *A Room with a View*, a British adaptation of E. M. Forster's novel, directed by James Ivory (NYT "quite an achievement … delicious … blithely, elegantly funny"; LAT "a virtually irresistible film … [an] airy, delectable adaptation … glorious"; CT "a rich comedy of Victorian English manners [and] a great love story"; WP "there's no real narrative here and no substance either ... [the film is] amusing [but] little more than a lark, a series of skits, a two-hour tribute to the rich British eccentric"; V "thoroughly entertaining"; TT "irresistibly charming ... a masterpiece"; G "shines bright"; MFB "near-perfection").

Two days later, the Los Angeles Film Critics Association honoured *Hannah and Her Sisters*, a comedy directed by Woody Allen which had finished as runner-up for the NBR prize (NYT "virtually non-stop exhilaration ... a dramatic comedy not quite like any other ... warm-hearted, wise and fiercely funny ... another extraordinary Allen original"; NYP "a masterpiece"; LAT "just may be a perfect movie ... mellow, beautiful, rich and brimming with love ... the best Woody Allen yet and quite simply, a great film [of] emotional complexity"; CT "a joy to behold, a complex film that never loses either its sense of purpose or sense of humor"; V "one of Woody's great films ... a major achievement"; G "[a] fluid, engaging if often dark-hued romantic comedy"; Sp "something of a pain ... not to be recommended to the easily bored").

Hannah and Her Sisters triumphed again another two days later when the New York Film Critics Circle gathered to cast their annual votes. Allen's comedy polled nearly twice as many points as the runner-up, Oliver Stone's Vietnam War drama *Platoon* (NYT "[a] singular achievement ... vivid, terse, exceptionally moving ... one of the best films yet made about the fighting in Vietnam ... it could be the best"; CT "shattering"; WP "a triumph ... alive with authenticity ... dark and unforgettable"; V "an intense but artistically distanced study"; MFB "moving"; Time "impressive").

All three films were listed by The New York Times as among the ten best of the year, and on 4 January 1987, the National Society of Film Critics named another of the paper's listees as Best Picture: David Lynch's drama *Blue Velvet*, which had earlier finished as runner-up in Los Angeles (NYT "an instant cult classic ... it's one of a kind ... startling, powerfully imaginative ... arresting ... as fascinating as it is freakish"; NYP "one of the sickest films ever made"; LAT "brilliantly disturbing ... shocking, visionary"; CT "a thoroughly unpredictable, frequently disturbing and sometimes jaw-droppingly funny film ... there isn't anything else quite like it, and it's pretty wonderful"; WP "[a] cynical, sadistic mystery ... gruelling, as intense as a film can possibly be, but it is certainly far from satisfying"; BG "a riveting, complex, layered film ... will be too pungent and bizarre for the reassurance-seeking mainstream, but it's genuinely provocative – the American underworld film of the decade"; V "compelling"; TT "dark and curious and original"; MFB "striking"; Time "demands respect").

The stage seemed set for these four contrasting films to contest the Best Picture Oscar. *Hannah and Her Sisters* appeared most likely to win as only twice before had the same film been selected by both the east and west coast critics' groups (in 1979 and 1983) and each had gone on to win the Academy Award.

1986

The day after the NSFC winners were announced, the Hollywood Foreign Press Association revealed the Golden Globe nominees. *Hannah and Her Sisters* topped the list of contenders with five nominations, including Best Picture (Comedy/Musical). Unexpectedly, its tally was matched by a new Oscar contender, *The Mission*, an expensive historical drama about Jesuit priests in South America which had won the Palme d'Or at Cannes but then garnered a mainly negative response from critics when released commercially (NYT "a singularly lumpy sort of film"; NYP "pretentious hokum"; LAT "haunting spectacle"; WP "hamstrung by an unworkable script [and] disastrous casting, [the film is] an indigestible lump of sanctimony ... a thinly veiled fable"; BG "dramatically hollow, morally smug, fatally stodgy"; V "serious flaws ... doesn't come together comprehensively"; G "tries to be all things to all men – and that may be its central flaw"). The Oscar hopes of *Blue Velvet* meanwhile, were shaken by its exclusion from the top Globe categories, even though the HFPA listed twelve films in the Best Picture categories rather than the usual ten.

When the Globes were presented at the end of January, *Hannah and Her Sisters* won the Best Picture (Comedy/Musical) award, but its Oscar frontrunner status came under threat because *Platoon* won more Globes than any other film (three in total), including Best Picture (Drama) and, in a surprise, Best Director.

The Academy announced its list of nominees less than a fortnight later. *Platoon* and *A Room with a View* led the field with eight nominations, including Best Picture and Best Director. Also cited in both categories were *Hannah and Her Sisters* and *The Mission*, each with seven nominations. Although Lynch was included in the Best Director category, *Blue Velvet* was overlooked in favour of *Children of a Lesser God*, a drama about a speech therapist and a stubborn, hearing-impaired woman (LAT "an exceptionally adroit adaptation ... a classic love story – romantic, passionate [with] vibrant characters"; WP "romance the way Hollywood used to make it, with both conflict and tenderness"; V "touching"; TGM "worth seeing"; S&S "long and slow-moving").

Among the other films overlooked were: the sci-fi action blockbuster *Aliens*, which received seven nominations (NYT "a flaming, flashing, crashing, crackling blow-'em-up show that keeps you popping from your seat despite your better instincts"; CT "it's like being on some kind of hair-raising carnival ride that never stops"; WP "a wow ... gets you in its grip very early, and never lets go ... it doesn't get any better than this"; PI "[a] powerhouse sequel"); *The Color of Money*, a sequel to the 1961 Oscar-nominated drama *The Hustler* (NYT "a most entertaining, original film with its own vivid, very contemporary identity"; LAT "bold, exhilarating, nearly perfect ... quick, keen, astonishing-looking and full of the joys and the juices of acting and movie making ... one of the year's most interesting films"; CT "a disappointment"; PI "jazzy and profound, vibrant and vital"; S&S "an exciting, brilliantly filmed coda to 'The Hustler'"); the 1985

British film *My Beautiful Laundrette* (NYT "a fascinating, eccentric, very personal movie ... the most surprising, most satisfying hit of the year – a brilliant, cutting social comedy"; NYer "startlingly fresh"; LAT "an irresistible contemporary satirical romance"; BG "fresh, gritty, quirky and immediate"; TT "clever, funny and incisive"; G "ground-breaking, extraordinarily intriguing and undoubtedly controversial"; MFB "provocative and entertaining ... critical and sympathetic at the same time"); the Australian hit *Crocodile Dundee* (NYT "has become the movie phenomenon of the year"; LAT "an expert crowd-pleaser ... has such a sure, easy, confident touch that it's almost failure-proof"; CT "there are moments of real amusement"; PI "hilarious"; TT "comedy of the most simple, good-natured, old-fashioned sort"); *Down by Law* (NYT "engaging ... by far the most original, most bold, most organically cinematic American film of the year ... darkly comic"; LAT "an inkily comic dream of a film"; CT "has a self-conscious, formulaic feel"; TGM "fabulous"); the coming of age film *Stand by Me* (LAT "a compassionate, perfectly performed look at the real heart of youth ... it's one of those treasures absolutely not to be missed ... a quiet, lyrical odyssey"; CT "the show-biz embellishments end by turning a simple tale into something strained and synthetic"; WP "has a quality of seriousness that you hardly ever see in movies made about kids"; TGM "not a masterpiece, but it is an evocative and cheerily amusing movie about growing up"); the British film *Mona Lisa* (NYT "less a true film noir as a comment on one ... [it] is hardly ever involving; it is fun to watch, mostly for its performances... the excitement doesn't build"; LAT "rueful and funny; brutal, beautiful and lushly romantic"; BG "the best romantic gangster movie in years ... loaded with style ... [it] rides the performances of Hoskins and the others to movie heaven"; PI "extraordinary"); and the French drama *Sans Toit ni Loi (Vagabond)*, winner of the Golden Lion at the 1985 Venice Film Festival (NYT "disturbing ... so effective it can be gruelling to sit through"; WP "disturbing [and] disheartening [but] a movie that virtually shines with integrity"; LAT "gravely intelligent and unsentimental"; BG "will disturb you and stay with you ... fresh, startling, prickly and poignant, it's one of the year's best films"; PI "lacerating and unexpectedly profound").

Platoon became the clear Oscar frontrunner in early March when it rose to the top of the North America box office and the Directors Guild of America presented its annual plaudit to Stone.

At the Academy Awards at the end of the month, *Platoon* received four statuettes, including the Best Picture Oscar. The early frontrunner, *Hannah and Her Sisters*, earned three awards. Also garnering three Oscars was *A Room with a View*, which a week earlier added the Best Film BAFTA to the top prize from the London Film Critics. Surprisingly, *Platoon* was not even nominated for the BAFTA the following year.

BEST DIRECTOR

ACADEMY AWARDS
Woody Allen for *Hannah and Her Sisters*
James Ivory for *A Room with a View*
Roland Joffe for *The Mission*
David Lynch for *Blue Velvet*
• **Oliver Stone for *Platoon***

GOLDEN GLOBE AWARDS
Woody Allen – *Hannah and Her Sisters*
James Ivory – *A Room with a View*
Roland Joffe – *The Mission*
Rob Reiner – *Stand by Me*
• **Oliver Stone – *Platoon***

DIRECTORS GUILD AWARD
Woody Allen
   – Hannah and Her Sisters
Randa Haines
   – Children of a Lesser God
James Ivory – *A Room with a View*
Roland Joffe – *The Mission*
• **Oliver Stone – *Platoon***

BRITISH ACADEMY AWARDS
• **Woody Allen**
   – *Hannah and Her Sisters*
James Ivory – *A Room with a View*
Roland Joffe – *The Mission*
Neil Jordan – *Mona Lisa*

NEW YORK – **Woody Allen – *Hannah and Her Sisters***
LOS ANGELES – **David Lynch – *Blue Velvet***
BOARD OF REVIEW – **Woody Allen – *Hannah and Her Sisters***
NATIONAL SOCIETY – **David Lynch – *Blue Velvet***
LONDON – **Akira Kurosawa – *Ran***

The early favourite for the Best Director Oscar was Woody Allen for *Hannah and Her Sisters* (LAT "stunning"; CT "an achievement equal to his very finest seriocomedies … has struck a marvelous balance between the sacred and the silly"; G "very beautifully made"). Allen was honoured as Best Director by the New York Film Critics Circle for the third time in a decade, won the National Board of Review accolade, and finished as runner-up for the Los Angeles Film Critics Association prize.

While the west coast circle named *Hannah and Her Sisters* as Best Picture, they handed their Best Director award to David Lynch for *Blue Velvet* (NYT "confirms Lynch's stature as an innovator [and] a superb technician"; LAT "visionary [and] rapturously controlled ... has become a master at giving form to what is not permitted"; CT "pushes the clichés he's put together until they explode, opening a passageway to new sensations that don't yet have names"; BG "[a] film with a distinctive and highly vivid directorial signature"; TT "undeniable skill"). Lynch also collected the plaudit from the National Society of Film Critics, garnering nearly three times as many points as his nearest rival.

Allen and Lynch were both nominated by the Academy; Allen for a third time and Lynch for a second time. Each mentioned for the first time were: James Ivory for *A Room with a View* (NYT "[has] created an exceptionally faithful, ebullient screen equivalent to a literary work that lesser talents would embalm"; LAT "a certain studied pace dogged [his previous films] but it's gone [replaced with] a contagious sureness which makes [the film] glorious"; TT "remarkable"; G "[directed] not only with enthusiasm and affection but also with enough sheer skill to make the inevitable financial compromises virtually invisible"; Sp "[the film] has the bravura which comes equally from creative conviction and from tight formal control"); Roland Joffe for *The Mission* (WP "neither [the writer] nor director Joffe is particularly adept at weaving [the story's threads] together"; G "Joffe's work has a force and commitment about it that renders most other epics of the year pale by comparison"); and the runner-up in the New York voting, Oliver Stone for *Platoon* (NYT "[a] singular achievement"; LAT "movie-making with a zealot's fervor ... he succeeds with an immediacy that is frightening"; WP "a triumph for Oliver Stone ... [his] visceral approach to violence is balanced by classical symmetries and a kind of elegiac distance").

While the other four Oscar nominees were all candidates for the Golden Globe and Directors Guild of America accolade as well, Lynch was overlooked for both. The Hollywood Foreign Press Association snubbed him in favour of Rob Reiner for *Stand by Me* (NYT "hammers in every obvious element in an obvious script"; LAT "has seen that his cast stays honest and his movie marvelously restrained"; CT "handles his central image well and discreetly ... but there's nothing natural in the way Reiner has overloaded his film with manufactured drama"; WP "[the film] is no masterpiece of story construction, but it is redeemed by Reiner's flair for humor [and] mastery of mood") while the Guild excluded Lynch in favour of Randa Haines for her directorial debut *Children of a Lesser God* (NYT "slick ... [but] there's scarcely a single moment in [the film] that seems to be spontaneous"; LAT "flows beautifully under Randa Haines' direction"; WP "demonstrates a remarkable mastery of tone, modulating [the film] through its moments of humor and tension ... quite an achievement"; TGM "briskly efficient"; TT "sensitive direction").

Others by-passed for the Oscar were: the late Andrei Tarkovsky, a surprise runner-up for the NSFC prize, for *Offret (The Sacrifice)* (LAT "[his] finest work

... creates some of the most piercingly beautiful images ever captured on film [but] his wearying, deliberately languorous pace places the utmost demands on our powers of concentration"); Martin Scorsese for *The Color of Money* (LAT "[directed with] energy and inventiveness"; PI "made memorable by [his] verve ... dazzling"; S&S "brilliantly filmed"; TGM "the picture's good will is won by Newman's performance rather than earned by the writing and directing"); James Cameron for *Aliens* (LAT "taut, inexorably paced"; CT "I have never seen a movie that maintains such a pitch of intensity for so long"; WP "paces his movie along a perfectly accelerating curve ... a marvelously tactile director"; PI "he goes for broke and, against all the odds, he's surprisingly successful"); BAFTA nominee Neil Jordan for *Mona Lisa* (NYT "smooth and distinctive"; LAT "[a] controlled flight of lyricism matched by [a] lush command of image"; S&S "[made with] confidence and economy"); Stephen Fears for *My Beautiful Laundrette* (NYT "without showing off, [the film] has courage as well as artistry"; LAT "[he has] given it vitality, directness and astonishing reverberations"; TT "unobtrusively skilled handling"; S&S "[he] must take major credit"); Jim Jarmusch for *Down by Law* (NYT "we are seeing a true film maker at work, using film to create a narrative that couldn't exist on the stage or the printed page"; TGM "paints [shadows] on the screen, sadly and with beauty"); Bertrand Tavernier for *'Round Midnight* (NYT "lovely, elegiac pacing ... masterly"; LAT "the first film about jazzmen to be made in their own rhythms ... with consummate tact, intelligence and passion, Tavernier lets us understand [the exploration that is jazz]"; BG "the thing that makes [the film] special is Tavernier's sensitivity to his lead"; V "superbly crafted"; S&S "scores high marks"); and Agnes Varda for *Sans Toit ni Loi (Vagabond)* (NYT "[her] experience as a documentary film maker frames the story ... [she] has created a world too painfully real to ignore"; LAT "dares everything [here] and succeeds ... it is [her] evenhandedness, her unjudging presentation that are at the core of her art"; WP "directs dispassionately without a shred of compassion, a moment's sympathy ... the images have a remarkable clarity, vibrant with Varda's hard, merciless white light"; BG "not only remains true to the aesthetic of the French New Wave, she renews its emphasis on documentary-like spontaneity, its avoidance of moral judgments ... wonderful"; PI "Varda's unsparing and unsentimental dramatization [shows] exceptional restraint"; TGM "a marvel of metaphorical construction").

In late January, Stone was a surprise winner at the Globes. He became the Oscar frontrunner when he was honoured at the Berlin Film Festival and was presented with the DGA plaudit. On Oscar night *Platoon* was named Best Picture, and Stone received his first statuette as Best Director.

The week prior to the Oscars, Allen won his second Best Director BAFTA. Stone collected the same prize for *Platoon* the following year.

1986

BEST ACTOR

ACADEMY AWARDS
Dexter Gordon as 'Dale Turner' in *'Round Midnight*
Bob Hoskins as 'George' in *Mona Lisa*
William Hurt as 'James Leeds' in *Children of a Lesser God*
• **Paul Newman as 'Eddie Felson' in *The Color of Money***
James Woods as 'Richard Boyle' in *Salvador*

GOLDEN GLOBE AWARDS

(Drama)
Harrison Ford – *The Mosquito Coast*
Dexter Gordon – *'Round Midnight*
• **Bob Hoskins – *Mona Lisa***
William Hurt
  – *Children of Lesser God*
Jeremy Irons – *The Mission*
Paul Newman – *The Color of Money*

(Comedy/Musical)
Matthew Broderick
  – *Ferris Bueller's Day Off*
Jeff Daniels – *Something Wild*
Danny DeVito – *Ruthless People*
• **Paul Hogan – *Crocodile Dundee***
Jack Lemmon – *That's Life!*

BRITISH ACADEMY AWARDS
Woody Allen – *Hannah and Her Sisters*
Michael Caine – *Hannah and Her Sisters*
Paul Hogan – *Crocodile Dundee*
• **Bob Hoskins – *Mona Lisa***

NEW YORK – Bob Hoskins – *Mona Lisa*
LOS ANGELES – Bob Hoskins – *Mona Lisa*
BOARD OF REVIEW – Paul Newman – *The Color of Money*
NATIONAL SOCIETY – Bob Hoskins – *Mona Lisa*
LONDON – Bob Hoskins – *Mona Lisa* and William Hurt – *Kiss of the Spider Woman*

"It has been 54 years," observed Jack Mathews in The Los Angeles Times in late August, "since Fredric March won an Oscar for 'Dr Jekyll and Mr Hyde', the only moment in Academy Award history where a person was nominated for best actor for work in a horror film. By the full moon of next February's nominations, perhaps the spell will be broken. Jeff Goldblum's performance in 'The Fly', a genre-spliced story of romantic tragedy and horror, has been scaring up that kind of talk [and] it is hard to imagine finding five more effective or moving male acting performances in one season." Goldblum's work in the remake *The Fly* was widely acclaimed by critics (NYT "Goldblum's fly-man has heart and humor ... the one consistently strong element in the midst of Mr Cronenberg's haywire, tone-deaf direction is Jeff Goldblum's performance, a just-controlled mania that fills the screen without threatening to jump off it"; LAT "[a] wonderful performance ... brings out the film's underlying compassion and its edgy, ironic spirit"; CT "[the] transformations require him to develop from a gawky child into a commanding sexual presence and then into a monster of rage and paranoia ... [he] inhabits each stage fully, while still retaining our sympathy – no easy task"; TGM "a peerless portrayal") but despite finishing runner-up for the NSFC plaudit he received neither Golden Globe nor Academy Award nominations. It would be another five years before a performance in a horror film was rewarded with a golden statuette.

Throughout the awards season, the main contenders for the year's Best Actor accolades turned out to be Bob Hoskins and Paul Newman. Although Hoskins reaped the lion's share of accolades, sentiment prevailed at the Academy Awards and the Best Actor Oscar was won by Paul Newman.

Twenty-five years earlier, Newman had been lauded by critics and received his second nomination for the Best Actor statuette for his performance as Eddie Felson, a young pool shark, in *The Hustler*. For reprising the role in the sequel, *The Color of Money*, Newman earned even greater acclaim from critics and garnered his seventh mention from the Academy (NYT "appears certain to receive another Oscar nomination for his performance ... wonderfully funny [and] canny ... the film belongs to Mr Newman ... gives a rich, effortlessly commanding, funny performance"; NYP "electrifying"; LAT "it's virtually impossible to look at anyone else when Newman commands a scene ... the picture is in the pocket of the old pro"; PI "[this] is Newman's movie ... Newman regenerates before our eyes"; V "exceptional ... quietly commanding without overstating"; TGM "the performance should win him a deserved Oscar"; MFB "effortless excellence"). Newman was not in attendance at the Oscar ceremony. Having gone home empty-handed six times before, he had decided to stay away and see if his luck changed – and the tactic worked. Bette Davis opened the envelope and declared that Newman had won the Academy Award. His victory came twenty-nine years after his wife, Joanne Woodward, had won the Best Actress Oscar and, ironically, just a year after the Academy had presented him with an honorary award for lifetime achievement. Prior to the Oscars, Newman also collected the National Board of Review prize, finished runner-up in the balloting by the New York Film Critics Circle and placed third in the voting for the National Society of Film Critics accolade.

The overwhelming choice amongst the critics' groups, however, was Hoskins. The Jury at the Cannes Film Festival were the first to recognise him for his performance as a chauffeur who falls in love with a beautiful prostitute in *Mona Lisa* (NYT "splendid ... in their scenes together, Mr Hoskins and Miss Tyson come very close to making the preposterous appear to be both significant and moving"; LAT "formidable ... dominates the film, fulminating with moral outrage, energy pouring from him"; WP "playing a character who's a little stupid, without patronizing him, is one of the hardest things for a smart actor to do, and part of what makes Bob Hoskins' work in 'Mona Lisa' so terrific is that he pulls it off"; BG "the performance of his career"; PI "[a] mesmerizing portrait ... a performance of flawless and intuitive skill"; V "another memorable performance"; TT "magnificent"; G "astonishing ... what makes [the film] work as a cinematic experience is the acting"; MFB "a strong central performance"; S&S "[a] notably assured and sustained performance"). Hoskins won the New York Film Critics Circle award (ahead of Newman 41 points to 35), the Los Angeles Film Critics Association honour, the National Society of Film Critics plaudit, the Golden Globe (Drama), the London Film Critics and, a week before the Oscars, the British Academy Award.

Also nominated for the Oscar were: the previous year's winner William Hurt as a speech therapist in *Children of a Lesser God* (NYT "another serious, carefully thought-out performance"; NYP "a marathon performance"; LAT "[a] finely drawn portrayal [that is] intelligently acted"; WP "there's something subtle in Hurt's performance"; V "another seamless performance ... superbly played"; TT "a sound, fluent performance"; MFB "excellent"); jazz musician Dexter Gordon as an alcoholic saxophone player in *'Round Midnight* (NYT "becomes the very embodiment of music itself"; LAT "Gordon, moving serenely to his own inner rhythms, is complex and magnificent"; BG "Gordon is more than unforgettable; he's haunting ... Tavernier gets a magnificent performance from him simply by waiting him out ... Gordon fills the screen with authority"; TGM "phenomenal ... there's never been anything remotely like what Dexter Gordon brings to the screen ... [his] performance seems to have been captured rather than acted"; TT "admirable [and] uncompromising"; MFB "miraculously, [he] escapes the stereotyping of the film's conception ... [although] he is more a presence in the film than an actor"; S&S "dominates the picture physically ... in [his] slow speech there is wit and common sense"); and James Woods as a photo-journalist in *Salvador* which opened in some parts of North America in late 1985, but didn't have Oscar-qualifying screenings in Los Angeles until early the following year (NYT "puts nervous energy and self-mocking wit into the part, and it is not his fault if the [contradictory qualities of the character] don't quite stick together"; LAT "Woods is great in this part ... his nerviest, tightest, gutsiest performance"; WP "[his] work is chaotic and undisciplined, and in another context, he might seem hit or miss; but his anything-goes style melds perfectly with what's messy and lunatic about 'Salvador'"; BG "riveting"; V "it is unimaginable that any actor could be more convincing").

Although the film scored a Best Picture nomination, the Academy's acting branch shunned both previous winner Robert De Niro (LAT "gives [him] another of those nearly impossible physical challenges he thrives on"; WP "his most somber and withdrawn performance yet ... about as expressive as a church icon ... his contemporary acting approach and New York accent are comically inapt"; BG "his style, his energies, and even his speech patterns seem all wrong in period drama"; V "a bland, uninteresting performance") and Jeremy Irons (LAT "provides [him] with a chance for his purest and most searing film performance"; WP "Irons is a believable idealist but Bolt hasn't written a real character for [him]"; BG "bland"; V "[a] solid, technically accomplished performance") for their performances in *The Mission* (NYT "though played with self-effacing earnestness by Mr Irons and Mr De Niro, neither character has any dramatic identity"; BG "the problem is that there's no chemistry between Irons and De Niro"; G "the acting is more problematic ... De Niro looks fundamentally ill at ease, though still producing a performance of considerable power ... Irons has intensity and skill but less of that commodity"). Irons was a Best Actor (Drama) nominee at the Golden Globes for his performance.

Other Golden Globe contenders left off the Oscar ballot included: Paul Hogan, winner of the Best Actor (Comedy/Musical) trophy, in the Australian box office smash *Crocodile Dundee* (NYT "delightful ... pulls off [the role] with wonderful deadpan forthrightness and humor"; PI "has a charm and instant likability"); Harrison Ford in the drama *The Mosquito Coast* (NYT "played with a good deal of eccentric force"; LAT "Ford's power – even with his back to the camera, even when we can't read his face – is terrifying"; CT "[the character's] inner drives elude him completely ... the part requires a touch of steely obsession that lies beyond Ford's easygoing range"; PI "stakes unfamiliar dramatic ground"; V "stunning"; TGM "[a] surprisingly witty performance – he's certain to be in the running for an Oscar ... spectacularly acted"; Time "a hypnotizing portrayal"); and Jack Lemmon in the comedy *That's Life!* (NYT "[a] legitimately comic performance"; LAT "Lemmon and Andrews play their roles with such brilliance, wit and feeling, that they erase any imbalance [in the script]"; CT "[an] excessive, actorish performance"; PI "Lemmon, who has resorted to mannerisms in similar parts, comes into his own with a distraught, funny piece of work ... will doubtless [get] another Oscar nomination").

In addition to Goldblum, actors overlooked for both the Globes and the Oscar included: Woody Allen in *Hannah and Her Sisters* (NYT "never before has Allen been so comically serious ... we've seen the grandly neurotic, possibly suicidal side [of this character] in other films, but never the genuinely (if still comically) compassionate lover he also becomes here"; NYer "[the film] would be lifeless without Allen's presence"; LAT "Allen is his quite reliable old self, with less of a lemon twist"; CT "he's playing a real guy – and not just a cartoon character"; TT "makes Mickey at the same time richly comic and a figure of real tragedy and terror"; G "splendidly acted"); Gary Oldman in *Sid and Nancy* (NYT "played vividly"; LAT "a compelling portrait ... Oldman could easily have played Sid as a cartoonish lout, but he gives us a much more unsettling view of his escapades, capturing Sid's ambivalent yearnings for glory and his crude, almost childlike innocence"; CT "vivid and energized"; WP "[a] remarkable impersonation, but not performance ... captures Vicious' giddy daze and loose-limbed recklessness but plays that same note till the end"; BG "pulsates with the raw, uncensored force of a boy gone mad"; V "fits the part like a glove ... beyond praise"; TT "extraordinary"; S&S "[a] relentlessly whingeing performance"); Charlie Sheen in the Best Picture winner *Platoon* (NYT "plays the central role beautifully"; CT "[a] fine performance"; WP "exerts a quiet authority as the film's center ... he anchors the more florid performances of the two sergeants warring for his soul ... [a] strong and seething performance"); previous winner Jack Nicholson in *Heartburn* (NYT "brings humor and force to his part, but the part is barely there"; WP "gives Mark a sympathetic dimension that he didn't have in the novel"; V "flawless [and] impressive"; TT "polished"; Obs "Nicholson's charm is not quite up to it"); previous winner Paul Scofield in *Nineteen Nineteen* (NYT "played with remarkable sensitivity ... [a] brilliant, finely tuned performance ... Scofield's character is as detailed, as painstakingly woven as [an] intricate Oriental carpet"; TGM "performed with appropriate frigidity"); Gabriel Byrne in *Defence of the Realm* (LAT "emerges as a crackingly fine actor"; WP "impenetrable ... rarely registers an emotion"; TT "a real star performance"; S&S "convincingly played"; Sp "consistently good ... his studied and dispassionate style adds an element of affecting realism"); Roberto Benigni for *Down by Law* (NYT "extraordinary"; LAT "inspired"; MFB "he provides the film with most of its funniest moments"); Marcello Mastroianni as an ageing Fred Astaire impersonator in *Ginger e Fred (Ginger and Fred)* (NYT "hugely funny and affecting ... triumphant"; LAT "these [two] great star-actors offer a lesson in expressiveness as they toss of a look, a shrug, a gesture, each of them perfect"; CST "we never really get a sense of the person behind this performance"; PI "no praise is too extravagant for Mastroianni, whose performance is the acting achievement of an inspired career"; V "outdoes himself"); and Sean Connery in *The Name of the Rose* for which he would win the following year's British Academy Award as Best Actor (NYT "does his best to find the film's proper tone [and] doesn't have an easy time of it"; LAT "few actors can fight their way through [all the film's flaws, but] Connery does, firmly, with intelligence and a notable ring of irony and humanism"; CT "it's an empty role, yet it lets you see what a consummate film actor Connery has become"; TGM "gives a warmly mischievous portrayal that may be remembered as the highlight of his career"; Sp "bland").

1986

BEST ACTRESS

ACADEMY AWARDS
Jane Fonda as 'Alex Sternbergen' in *The Morning After*
• **Marlee Matlin as 'Sarah Norman' in *Children of a Lesser God***
Sissy Spacek as 'Babe Magrath Botrelle' in *Crimes of the Heart*
Kathleen Turner as 'Peggy Sue Kelcher Bodell' in *Peggy Sue Got Married*
Sigourney Weaver as 'Lieutenant Ellen Ripley' in *Aliens*

GOLDEN GLOBE AWARDS
(Drama)
Julie Andrews – *Duet for One*
Anne Bancroft – *'night Mother*
Farrah Fawcett – *Extremities*
• **Marlee Matlin**
  – *Children of a Lesser God*
Sigourney Weaver – *Aliens*

(Comedy/Musical)
Julie Andrews – *That's Life!*
Melanie Griffith – *Something Wild*
Bette Midler
  – Down and Out in Beverly Hills
• **Sissy Spacek**
  – *Crimes of the Heart*
Kathleen Turner
  – Peggy Sue Got Married

BRITISH ACADEMY AWARDS
Mia Farrow – *Hannah and Her Sisters*
• **Maggie Smith – *A Room with a View***
Meryl Streep – *Out of Africa*
Cathy Tyson – *Mona Lisa*

NEW YORK – Sissy Spacek – *Crimes of the Heart*
LOS ANGELES – Sandrine Bonnaire – *Sans Toit ni Loi (Vagabond)*
BOARD OF REVIEW – Kathleen Turner – *Peggy Sue Got Married*
NATIONAL SOCIETY – Chloe Webb – *Sid and Nancy*

Seven years after she had starred in Ridley Scott's science-fiction thriller *Alien*, Sigourney Weaver reprised her role in James Cameron's sequel *Aliens*, earning strong reviews and Academy Award and Golden Globe nominations (LAT "Cameron has shaped his film around the defiant intelligence and sensual athleticism of Weaver, and that's where 'Aliens' works best ... she's [the film's] white-hot core"; WP "gives Ripley's exploits a remarkable intimacy and conviction ... [Ripley is] the most memorable warrior figure of this movie generation [because Weaver is] an actress who can reconcile the tender with the ferocious ... [her] best performance to date"; V "a smashing job"). As her role was not the kind which typically received recognition from the Academy, several historians have promulgated the myth that Weaver was only included on the Oscar ballot because the field of candidates was weak. In his book 'Oscar Stars from A to Z', for example, Roy Pickard commented, "Destroying monsters on other planets has never been regarded as a serious occupation, and she was in the lists basically to make up the numbers." In truth, the Best Actress competition that year was particularly strong and, as Jack Mathews reported in The Los Angeles Times on 2 December 1986, Weaver was the one actress "who is routinely included in many people's lists" of likely Best Actress nominees.

The performances of two of the year's critics' prize-winners did not even rate a mention from the Academy: Los Angeles Film Critics Association winner and National Society of Film Critics runner-up Sandrine Bonnaire in *Sans Toit ni Loi (Vagabond)* (NYT "presents Mona's inconsistencies with brilliant subtlety"; LAT "[a] ferocious performance ... searing and complete [and] unforgettable"; CT "manages to be a commanding presence without doing anything to command our attention – there's no trace of technique in her gestures, no actorly self-consciousness in her presentation"; WP "an effective portrayal"; BG "vividly and unforgettably inscribed"; TGM "invests a character written as [a] generalized symbol with an individual sensitivity ... Bonnaire gives [the film] poetry"; TT "[an] uncompromising portrait"; MFB "convincing") and NSFC honouree Chloe Webb in *Sid and Nancy* (NYT "played vividly"; LAT "impressive ... lending compassion to what is otherwise a deeply unsympathetic character"; CT "vivid and energized"; WP "[a] remarkable impersonation, but not performance"; V "beyond praise"; TT "extraordinary"; S&S "[a] relentlessly whingeing performance"; Sp "particularly good").

Also excluded were the stars of two of the year's Best Picture nominees: BAFTA nominee Mia Farrow in *Hannah and Her Sisters* (NYT "splendid"; LAT "absolutely splendid"; CT "utterly natural"; G "splendidly acted") and Helena Bonham Carter in *A Room with a View* (NYT "the real star of the film ... a remarkably complex performance"; LAT "perhaps the only quibble [among the cast] ... she has no resources to match her fellow cast members' classical training [and] her attack on her lines is sometimes flat [but] on the other hand, you certainly believe her"; WP "[Ivory expertly uses] Carter's high-forehead earnestness for comedy: she becomes a master of the double take"; V "outstanding"; TT "perfectly cast"; G "excellent ... sharply observed"; MFB "touching"; Sp "excellent").

Oscar-voters also by-passed highly-anticipated performances by several previous winners: Julie Andrews for her two Globe nominated performances in the comedy *That's Life!* (NYT "the heart of the movie ... a performance that skirts sentimentality to work in easy, amused counterpoint to Mr Lemmon's"; LAT "Lemmon and Andrews play their roles with such brilliance, wit and feeling, that they erase any imbalance [in the script]"; WP "has little to do"; PI "the very inhibitions and reticence that have marred some of her other roles push [this characterization] to another level ... admirable") and the drama *Duet for One* (NYT "often a good deal better than the material ... forceful and affecting"; LAT "as improbable as the frequent emotional fireworks seem, Andrews strives to bring conviction to them"; CT "moving in a way a more demonstrative actress would not be"; WP "reaches successfully for greater range as an actress, but one is forced to wonder – to what end?"; TGM "resolutely superficial ... not convincingly [performed]"); both Globe nominee Anne Bancroft (NYT "[a] busy performance ... much too broad"; LAT "overly projected, not quite to the point of caricature but approaching it"; WP "all by herself [she] tries to pull this mess up to a level of acceptable drama, and if her Oscar-grabbing histrionics don't exactly fit the rest of [the movie] they're at least an enjoyable exercise in old-fashioned, big-canvas character work"; TGM "when not indulging her distressing tendency to mug, Bancroft is splendid") and Sissy Spacek (NYT "so persuasive that she never seems miscast"; WP "struggles with a difficult part ... solid but uninspiring"; TGM "miscast ... she is not capable of communicating in full emotional force [her character's] anger, depression and despair") in *'night Mother*; and Meryl Streep in *Heartburn* (NYT "finds a remarkable number of ways to register domestic happiness, unhappiness and in-betweens"; LAT "one of her loveliest characterizations"; WP "[she] inhabits Rachel in every detail"; V "flawless ... handles urban neurotic comedy without missing a beat").

Also overlooked were: Globe nominee Melanie Griffith in *Something Wild* (NYT "good ... plays with the sort of earnest intensity that is the basis of comedy at its best"; LAT "[a] first-class performance"; WP "takes the elements of a traditional comedienne and yokes them to an untraditional woman"; V "falls a little short in putting across all the aspects of this complicated woman"; S&S "beautifully played"); Globe nominee Farrah Fawcett in *Extremities*, a role she had played off-Broadway (NYT "gives a taut display of terror shading into hysterical hate ... [a] striking performance"; LAT "she makes the woman so thoroughly individual and believable in her fright and her outrage ... impressive"; WP "overwrought"; PI "[a] triumph"); Giulietta Masina as an ageing Ginger Rogers impersonator in *Ginger e Fred (Ginger and Fred)* (NYT "hugely funny and affecting ... triumphant"; LAT "these [two] great star-actors offer a lesson in expressiveness as they toss of a look, a shrug, a gesture, each of them perfect"; WP "what Masina does most is pose for Fellini's reaction shots"; BG "[Fellini] gives Masina quite the best of it; she's the one who holds everything together"); Maria Schell in *Nineteen Nineteen* (NYT "played with remarkable sensitivity ... [a] brilliant, finely tuned performance ... wonderful"; TGM "delineated with wise sensitivity"; S&S "strong"); Catherine Mouchet in *Thérèse* (NYT "played radiantly and with a good deal of humor"; LAT "played with a smiling, steely implacability"; WP "radiates a serene innocence"; S&S "a performance of marvellous candour"); and Gcina Mhlophe in *Place of Weeping (A Place for Weeping)* (NYT "a moving performance").

Having been surprisingly overlooked for the previous two years for her Globe (Comedy/Musical) winning performances in *Romancing the Stone* and *Prizzi's Honor*, Kathleen Turner earned an Oscar nod as a woman transported back in time in *Peggy Sue Got Married* (NYT "Turner's self-assured comic timing goes a long way toward salvaging the film, providing both moral and physical dimensions to a role that scarcely exists"; LAT "grand ... bites into the role with bravura"; WP "showcases [her] remarkable flair for comedy ... throws herself into the fun [and] finds a rich vein of double takes, put-downs and pauses"; BG "steadily affecting"; V "terrific"; TGM "sharp, classy, funny and sexy"; TT "carries off [the role] with conviction"). Turner had been expected to collect a third consecutive Globe, but she lost to Sissy Spacek (who had earlier outpolled Turner for the New York Film Critics Circle accolade) as the sister accused of murdering her husband in *Crimes of the Heart* (NYT "works hard but futilely"; LAT "somehow Spacek, with the most fey role and the most outrageous physical action, comes through unscathed; just how is one of the miracles of cinema"; BG "gives herself over to the good of the material"; V "superbly acted"; TGM "towers over everything else in and about the movie"). The Academy also nominated previous winner Spacek, for a fifth time.

Another previous winner, Jane Fonda, made the Oscar list for a seventh time as an alcoholic actress in *The Morning After* (NYT "winning ... played with a kind of intense intelligence"; LAT "pushes herself to the limit ... she's terrific at delineating Alex's mercurial mood swings ... a virtuoso job"; WP "makes [the film] seem like a lot more than it is ... takes [the writer's] zingers and gives them a bitter edge ... what's extraordinary is the number of levels she gives to Alex, the way she goes behind the bitterness to pathos, beyond the pathos to self-pity and back again"; MFB "beautifully played").

The frontrunner in this field was the Los Angeles runner-up and Globe (Drama) winner Marlee Matlin for her film debut as the strong-willed young woman in *Children of a Lesser God* (NYT "believable"; NYP "a remarkable debut"; LAT "[a] finely drawn portrayal [that is] intelligently acted"; CT "strong and wonderful ... she holds her own against the powerhouse she's acting with, carrying scenes with passion"; WP "she's a natural"; V "superbly played"; TGM "terrific ... connects the dots of Sarah's psychology with extraordinary economy"; TT "excellently played"; MFB "excellent").

On Oscar night, the previous year's Best Actor winner William Hurt presented the Best Actress statuette to his co-star and real-life partner at the time, Marlee Matlin. At just twenty-one years of age, Matlin became the youngest Best Actress winner in Oscar history.

1986

BEST SUPPORTING ACTOR

ACADEMY AWARDS
Tom Berenger as 'Sergeant Barnes' in *Platoon*
• **Michael Caine as 'Elliot' in *Hannah and Her Sisters***
Willem Dafoe as 'Sergeant Ellis' in *Platoon*
Denholm Elliott as 'Mr Emerson' in *A Room with a View*
Dennis Hopper as 'Shooter' in *Hoosiers*

GOLDEN GLOBE AWARDS
• **Tom Berenger – *Platoon***
Michael Caine – *Hannah and Her Sisters*
Dennis Hopper – *Blue Velvet*
Dennis Hopper – *Hoosiers*
Ray Liotta – *Something Wild*

BRITISH ACADEMY AWARDS
Klaus Maria Brandauer – *Out of Africa*
Simon Callow – *A Room with a View*
Denholm Elliott – *A Room with a View*
• **Ray McAnally – *The Mission***

NEW YORK – Daniel Day-Lewis – *My Beautiful Laundrette* and *A Room with a View*
LOS ANGELES – Dennis Hopper – *Blue Velvet* and *Hoosiers*
BOARD OF REVIEW – Daniel Day-Lewis – *My Beautiful Laundrette* and *A Room with a View*
NATIONAL SOCIETY – Dennis Hopper – *Blue Velvet*

The overwhelming favourite for the Academy Award was Dennis Hopper. He had been expected to be in consideration for his comeback role as a sadistic drug dealer in *Blue Velvet* (NYT "Mr Hopper and Miss Rossellini are so far outside the bounds of ordinary acting here that their performances are best understood in terms of sheer lack of inhibition; both give themselves entirely over to the material, which seems to be exactly what's called for ... [a] chilling performance"; LAT "superlative ... this part may be the ultimate Hopper; he certainly can't top it, and it is his fierce, febrile energy which keeps this constellation of actors in place"; WP "one-dimensional"), but he was instead nominated for a less daring and flashy role in a smaller movie, as an alcoholic basketball fan in *Hoosiers* (NYT "it's a sentimental role, but Mr Hopper manages to seem no less at home than he did in 'Blue Velvet'. That alone is enough to make his Oscar nomination well deserved"; LAT "Hopper is again demonically good"; WP "convincing"; V "a showy turn"). Hopper had been nominated for both performances at the Golden Globes and had won the Los Angeles Film Critics Association and National Society of Film Critics prizes.

Surprisingly, the Academy overlooked the year's other critics' prize-winner Daniel Day-Lewis. The twenty-nine-year old Englishman had received both the New York Film Critics Circle accolade and the National Board of Review plaudit for his sharply contrasting portrayals of a young gay punk in *My Beautiful Laundrette* (NYT "a performance that has both extraordinary technical flash and emotional substance ... the year's most expert performance"; LAT "taut, intelligent, erotic ... an emerging star"; BG "offers the most stunningly faceted performance by an actor so far this year") and a dull, aristocratic suitor in *A Room with a View*, one of the year's Best Picture nominees (NYT "spectacular"; WP "exceedingly badly acted ... spells prissy with capital letters"; TT "faultless"; G "precise"; S&S "most memorable of all [the film's characters] ... the performance is a gem"). He had also finished as the runner-up to Hopper for the NSFC trophy.

The dark horse in the Oscar field was one of Day-Lewis' lauded co-stars in *A Room with a View*: BAFTA nominee Denholm Elliott, who played a kind, middle-class intellectual (NYT "splendidly acted"; LAT "marvelous ... can almost bring tears to the eyes"; CT "holds the key to the film's serious side [and it works] thanks to the performance of Elliott, for far too long one of the English-speaking world's most underrated actors"; WP "exceedingly badly acted ... [he] walks through the old Denholm Elliott curmudgeon number"; V "outstanding"; TT "faultless"; MFB "polished"; Time "marvelous"). Elliott had also been eligible for consideration for his 1985 BAFTA winning turn in *Defence of the Realm* (NYT "not a great performance but he's better than anyone else [in the cast]"; LAT "there cannot be enough of [his] rueful, world-weary intelligence"; V "an extraordinary performance"; TGM "another simultaneously comic and pathetic portrait"; TT "admirable"; S&S "convincingly played"; MFB "magnificent"; Sp "a convincing performance").

According to most observers, however, the main challenger to Hopper was Globe winner Tom Berenger, mentioned for playing the scarred platoon sergeant in *Platoon*. Some commentators, however, believed that Berenger's Oscar chances were undermined by the inclusion on the ballot of his co-star Willem Dafoe, who had not been among the nominees when Berenger won the Globe. Many Hollywood insiders predicted that they would split the vote between them. Most reviewers had commented jointly on their pair of performances (NYT "excellent ... it's a measure of how well both roles are written and played that one comes to understand the astonishing cruelty of Barnes and the almost saintly goodness of Elias"; LAT "magnificent ... the actors [are] a fine match for each other"; CT "fine"; WP "the more florid performances of the two sergeants") with The Los Angeles Times and Variety among those adding additional comments about Dafoe's performance (LAT "it is particularly fine to see Dafoe as something other than a psychopath"; V "comes close to stealing the picture")

In a surprise, however, the Oscar was won by Englishman Michael Caine as a husband having a mid-life crisis in *Hannah and Her Sisters* (NYT "it's a measure of the way the film works that [he] has never before been so seriously comic"; LAT "lovely"; CT "played superbly ... comes across as a regular, living, breathing human being for the very first time ... he's given many fine performances before but never has Caine seemed so fresh and credible"; G "splendidly acted"; Sp "endearing").

At the British Academy Awards, Caine was in contention for the Best Actor award for *Hannah and Her Sisters* and many had expected Elliott to collect an unprecedented fourth consecutive prize as a result. In a surprise, the BAFTA was won by Ray McAnally in *The Mission* (NYT "the film's most interesting, most complex character [who is] played as well as possible by McAnally"; LAT "exceptionally good"; BG "comes closest to contributing the kind of ambivalence the film so sorely needs"; V "fine"; G "the one obvious triumph ... the most complete portrait of all, and it pulls the film in the right direction"). McAnally was a notable absentee from the list of Oscar candidates, even though *The Mission* was a Best Picture nominee.

Also by-passed were: Max von Sydow in *Hannah and Her Sisters* (NYT "brilliantly done"); the surprise runner-up for the New York critics' prize Andy Garcia in the critically-savaged *Eight Million Ways to Die* (NYT "the acting is loud and aimless ... Garcia does a lot of necktie straightening and shoulder twitching"); both Keith David (NYT "[a] particular standout"; LAT "vivid"; WP "big and magnificent [in] a staggeringly good performance") and Dale Dye (LAT "a performance that stands out for its veracity") in *Platoon*; River Phoenix in *The Mosquito Coast* (NYT "as good as the screenplay and direction allow him to be"; LAT "played with exquisite gradation"; PI "a remarkable, underplayed performance"; V "believable"; TGM "spectacularly acted"; TT "astonishing ... acting of a range and truth that trained grown-ups might envy"); 1985 BAFTA nominee Saeed Jaffrey in *My Beautiful Laundrette* (NYT "fine"; LAT "superb ... extraordinary"; WP "effortlessly amusing"; V "[a] standout"; G "marvellously played"; S&S "Jaffrey's ebullience is cunningly moulded"); Lance Henriksen in *Aliens* (LAT "particularly fine"); and both BAFTA nominee Simon Callow (NYT "noteworthy"; LAT "memorable"; V "skillful support"; TT "faultless") and Rupert Graves (V "skillful support"; TT "faultless") in *A Room with a View*.

BEST SUPPORTING ACTRESS

ACADEMY AWARDS
Tess Harper as 'Chick Boyle' in *Crimes of the Heart*
Piper Laurie as 'Mrs Norman' in *Children of a Lesser God*
Mary Elizabeth Mastrantonio as 'Carmen' in *The Color of Money*
Maggie Smith as 'Charlotte Bartlett' in *A Room with a View*
• **Dianne Wiest as 'Holly' in *Hannah and Her Sisters***

GOLDEN GLOBE AWARDS
Linda Kozlowski – *Crocodile Dundee*
Mary Elizabeth Mastrantonio – *The Color of Money*
• **Maggie Smith – *A Room with a View***
Cathy Tyson – *Mona Lisa*
Dianne Wiest – *Hannah and Her Sisters*

BRITISH ACADEMY AWARDS
Rosanna Arquette – *After Hours*
• **Judi Dench – *A Room with a View***
Barbara Hershey – *Hannah and Her Sisters*
Rosemary Leach – *A Room with a View*

NEW YORK – Dianne Wiest – *Hannah and Her Sisters*
LOS ANGELES – Cathy Tyson – *Mona Lisa*
BOARD OF REVIEW – Dianne Wiest – *Hannah and Her Sisters*
NATIONAL SOCIETY – Dianne Wiest – *Hannah and Her Sisters*

The overwhelming favourite for the Best Supporting Actress Oscar was Dianne Wiest as the neurotic, showbiz sister trying to start up a catering business in *Hannah and Her Sisters* (NYT "splendid"; LAT "absolutely splendid … at last comes into her own in a brilliant, brash, only slightly comic definition of today's up-to-the-minute New Yorker"; NYer "does all she can with her role"; V "steals the show"; G "splendidly acted"). Wiest had convincingly won three of the major critics' prizes and finished as runner-up for the fourth.

In the voting by the New York Film Critics Circle, for example, Wiest polled 42 points to win comfortably over both Mary Elizabeth Mastrantonio as the girlfriend of a young poolplayer in *The Color of Money* (NYT "the film's revelation … sharing honors with Mr Newman … [her] best work in films to date; V "a hot and disturbing performance"; Time "fascinating"; TGM "valiantly wrests more from less") and Cathy Tyson, the British niece of previous Best

Actress nominee Cicely Tyson, in her first film role, as the prostitute in *Mona Lisa* (NYT "a magical film personality ... in their scenes together, Mr Hoskins and Miss Tyson come very close to making the preposterous appear to be both significant and moving"; NYer "remarkable control"; LAT "formidable [in] a memorable debut ... more than holds her own with Hoskins"; WP "[she has] an ease before the camera that can erupt into a frightening intensity"; BG "Tyson makes us feel the reason for the deadness in Simone's eyes ... her face keeps the film from turning into a tapestry of lush pop imagery, kitschy sentiment, and set pieces"; TT "admirable"; S&S "[a] notably assured and sustained performance"). Mastrantonio and Tyson each polled just 14 points. Wiest claimed the National Society of Film Critics accolade by a similar margin (43 points to 16) over her *Hannah and Her Sisters* co-star Barbara Hershey (NYT "splendid"; LAT "splendid ... radiant"; NYer "a luscious presence"; CT "has never been better"; V "a revelation ... never before has she seemed so natural and humanly appealing").

The only actress to outpoll Wiest for a critics' award was New York prize runner-up Tyson, who collected the Los Angeles Film Critics Association accolade. Despite her win and a Golden Globe nomination, however, Tyson was a glaring omission from the list of Oscar nominees. Her exclusion might have been partially caused by uncertainty about whether to consider her as a leading or supporting candidate. In contrast to the Hollywood Foreign Press Association, the British Academy nominated Tyson for the Best Actress BAFTA.

With Tyson omitted from the Oscar ballot, observers declared previous winner Maggie Smith as the dark horse at her fifth nomination. Smith had been an unexpected winner at the Golden Globes (her second Globe win) for her performance as the heroine's spinster aunt and chaperone in *A Room with a View* (NYT "splendidly acted"; LAT "a veritable study in genteel self-denial"; V "outstanding"; Time "marvelous"; TT "a marvel"; G "the kind of jewelled and precise portrait which advertises English acting as about the best in the world"; MFB "another triumph"; Sp "excellent"). Ironically, at the British Academy Awards it was Smith who outpolled Tyson to claim the Best Actress award. It was her third BAFTA (and her second in three years).

Surprise nominees for the Academy Award were Tess Harper as the cousin in *Crimes of the Heart* (LAT "of all the women [in the cast], it is the fine Tess Harper who should sue; wound up even higher than Keaton, she has the additional burden of a camera lens peering into her face for every overblown moment"; BG "outstanding"; TGM "nothing can be done about Tess Harper's hysterical performance except to ignore it") and Piper Laurie (nominated for a third time) as the mother in *Children of a Lesser God* (NYT "appears briefly but effectively"; LAT "beautifully underplayed").

In addition to Tyson and Hershey, the other most obvious absentee from the Academy's short-list was Isabella Rossellini in *Blue Velvet* (NYT "Mr Hopper and Miss Rossellini are so far outside the bounds of ordinary acting here that their performances are best understood in terms of sheer lack of inhibition; both give themselves entirely over to the material, which seems to be exactly what's called for"; LAT "Rossellini, who has the film's greatest physical demands, is tormented and deeply touching"; WP "[the cast's] performances are one-dimensional, one and all").

Also passed over by Oscar voters were: both BAFTA winner Judi Dench (NYT "noteworthy"; V "skillful support"; TT "faultless"; SP "excellent … brought a certain majesty to the pseudo-romantic imagination") and Rosemary Leach (NYT "noteworthy"; LAT "memorable"; V "skillful support") in *A Room with a View*; both Carrie Fisher (NYT "[a] big performance in a small, vividly written role") and Julie Kavner (LAT "outstanding") in *Hannah and Her Sisters*; Jenette Goldstein in *Aliens* (V "makes a striking impression"); Linda Kozlowski in *Crocodile Dundee* (NYT "plays the reporter very well … gives her character a soft candy center that is appealing enough to make the characterization completely inoffensive and quite amusing"); Helen Mirren in *The Mosquito Coast* (NYT "her role here is so self-effacing it disappears into the foliage"; LAT "admirable … Mirren's quiet sturdiness grows on you by the film's end"); and Shirley Anne Field in *My Beautiful Laundrette* (LAT "especially memorable"; S&S "graceful and comic").

On Oscar night, as expected, Wiest claimed her first statuette as Best Supporting Actress. "Gee," she exclaimed as she held her award at the podium, "this isn't like what I imagined it would be in the bathtub!"

Wiest was surprisingly overlooked by the Academy the following year for her BAFTA nominated turn in *Radio Days*, but made the lists a second time in 1989 for her role in *Parenthood*. In 1994, for her role as an over-the-top movie star in another Woody Allen comedy, *Bullets Over Broadway*, she became only the second person to twice win the Best Supporting Actress Oscar (following Shelley Winter's second win in the Best Supporting Actress category in 1965).

BEST PICTURE

ACADEMY AWARDS

Broadcast News
(Twentieth Century-Fox, 131 mins, 16 Dec 1987, $51.2m, 7 noms)
Fatal Attraction
(Jaffe, Paramount, 119 mins, 18 Sep 1987, $156.6m, 6 noms)
Hope and Glory
(Davros, Columbia, 113 mins, 9 Oct 1987, $10.0m, 5 noms)
• *The Last Emperor*
(Hemdale, Columbia, 160 mins, 20 Nov 1987, $43.9m, 9 noms)
Moonstruck
(Palmer & Jewison, M-G-M, 102 mins, 16 Dec 1987, $80.6m, 6 noms)

GOLDEN GLOBE AWARDS

(Drama)

Cry Freedom
Empire of the Sun
Fatal Attraction
La Bamba
• *The Last Emperor*
Nuts

(Comedy/Musical)

Baby Boom
Broadcast News
Dirty Dancing
• *Hope and Glory*
Moonstruck

BRITISH ACADEMY AWARDS

Cry Freedom
Hope and Glory
• *Jean de Florette*
Radio Days

NEW YORK – *Broadcast News*
LOS ANGELES – *Hope and Glory*
BOARD OF REVIEW – *Empire of the Sun*
NATIONAL SOCIETY – *The Dead*
LONDON – *Hope and Glory*

Four different films were named Best Picture by the four major American critics' groups but, interestingly, none of them claimed the Best Picture Oscar.

The National Board of Review was the first group to announce its prize-winners, presenting its top award to *Empire of the Sun*, Steven Spielberg's drama about a young English boy in Japanese-occupied China during the Second World War (NYT "spectacular [and] unforgettable ... the best film made about childhood by a director born and bred [in the United States]"; LAT "for all its good intentions, for all the thrillingly staged moments and for all its not-inconsiderable craft, the film's grave problem is a lack of central heating: we don't have a single character to warm up to"; CT "sober, serious-minded [and] heavy"; WP "some of it is brilliant, but the psychological aspects of the film are stunted [making it] a profoundly perplexing, frustrating object [but with] things in it to marvel at and enjoy"; TGM "an elephantine beast fully outfitted in state-of-the-art cinematic bells and whistles, a lumbering behemoth with a magisterial magnificence that cannot be denied").

The New York Film Critics Circle gathered two days later and bestowed an unprecedented five accolades, including Best Picture, on James L. Brooks' television news satire *Broadcast News* (NYT "very funny ... [a] bright new comedy"; LAT "diabolically clever ... insightful and understanding and marvelous fun"; WP "ingratiatingly high-spirited"; V "enormously entertaining"). The film managed its record tally only because Best Actor winner Jack Nicholson was cited for his cameo in *Broadcast News* as well as for his leading performances in *Ironweed* and *The Witches of Eastwick*.

The Los Angeles Film Critics Association, meanwhile, selected John Boorman's *Hope and Glory*, a nostalgic comedy-drama about life in London during the Second World War (NYT "radiant ... invitingly nostalgic [and] warmly personal without being private"; NYer "great"; LAT "brilliantly evocative and warmly comic"; CT "a rich, funny, bracing film ... the best of the current season"; WP "exquisite"; Sp "consistently diverting"; S&S "singular"; SMH "nostalgic, certainly, but not sentimental or overtly patriotic").

Finally, in early January, the National Society of Film Critics honoured *The Dead*, an adaptation of a James Joyce short story about an Irish family gathering for an important feast. It was the last film directed by John Huston, who died prior to its release (NYT "magnificent ... close to faultless ... [a] wonderful film"; NYP "an exquisite film"; LAT "impeccable"; WP "has a mellifluous simplicity ... rapturous, consuming and sublime ... a movie of exquisite, overwhelmingly passionate moments ... couldn't be more perfect – a work of great feeling and beauty"; BG "poignantly exquisite ... extraordinary ... radiant ... profoundly, sublimely satisfying on every human level"; V "a well-crafted miniature"; TT "as magical as it is mysterious"; Time "sublimely moving"). *The Dead* had earlier finished as the runner-up in the voting in New York (it was outpolled by *Broadcast News* 42 points to 26 on the second ballot). *Hope and Glory* was the NSFC runner-up (the final vote was 44 points to 37 in favour of *The Dead*).

Two days after the NSFC winners were declared, the Hollywood Foreign Press Association announced the Golden Globe nominees. *Broadcast News* led the field of contenders with five nominations, a tally matched by two other films:

the NBR and Los Angeles runner-up *The Last Emperor*, a lavish historical epic about the last Chinese Emperor (NYT "arthritic, occasionally spectacular ... ultimately it's a let-down ... the eye is frequently entertained, while the center of the screen remains dead"; LAT "an intoxicating visual rush [but] as coolly lavish an epic as we may ever see ... its core is cool and distant"; WP "meticulously composed [but] no drama"; V "a film of unique, quite unsurpassed visual splendor ... fascinating [but] remote and untouchable"; TGM "everything human or political in this film is secondary to its aesthetics"; PI "a triumph ... the finest work on this scale we have seen since 'Gandhi'"; Time "astonishing"; MFB "huge, sumptuous, intelligent"; SMH "the spectacle is marvellous, but it isn't really enough to sustain [the film] for nearly three hours ... never as emotionally powerful as it should be") and *Moonstruck*, a comedy about a Brooklyn widow (NYP "guaranteed to make you feel warm all over"; LAT "it satisfies every hunger"; TGM "an intelligent comedy that is simultaneously modern in feeling but classical in structure ... easy to love"; SMH "an old-fashioned romantic comedy ... thoroughly charming and warmly recommended"). *Empire of the Sun* and *Hope and Glory* were each nominated in the Best Picture categories, but in a major surprise, Huston's *The Dead* was shut-out of contention entirely.

For the second year in a row, the Globe ceremony drastically changed the Oscar race. The pre-Globe Oscar favourite, *Broadcast News*, did not win a single award. It was most notably outpolled for the Best Picture (Comedy/Musical) category: the winner was *Hope and Glory*. In sharp contrast, *The Last Emperor* emerged with four trophies, including Best Picture (Drama), Best Director and Best Screenplay. The epic was suddenly the Oscar frontrunner and its status was confirmed three weeks later when it topped the Academy's list of nominees with nine mentions, including Best Picture, ahead of *Broadcast News* with seven nods, including Best Picture, but critically without a Best Director nomination.

The remaining Best Picture nominees were *Hope and Glory*, *Moonstruck* and the thriller *Fatal Attraction*, which had been the year's third most successful film at the box office (NYT "powerful [and] brilliantly manipulative"; NYP "spellbinding"; LAT "an exciting thriller, soaked in chic"; V "suspenseful"; SMH "exceptionally gripping"). *Empire of the Sun* received five nominations and *The Dead* earned two mentions, all in minor categories.

Hope and Glory topped the list of BAFTA contenders with thirteen nominations, including Best Film. With *Broadcast News*, *Empire of the Sun*, *The Last Emperor* and *Moonstruck* all ineligible for consideration by the British Academy until the following year, the other three Best Film nominees in London were all films notably omitted from the top Oscar shortlist: the biopic *Cry Freedom* (NYT "the year's most majestic anti-climax ... bewildering at some points and ineffectual at others"; LAT "earnest, clunky, awkward"; WP "a heraldic pageant ... less a portrait of the real person than the canonization of a modern saint ... the proficiency of the actors powers the movie despite a stiff script"; TGM "never boring [and] is frequently stirring"; MFB "a curious mixture but one that gels remarkably successfully across its vast canvas"; Sp "makes a huge emotional impact"; SMH "fails"); the French drama *Jean de Florette* (NYT "irresistible ... has the delicacy of something freshly observed"; LAT "heavily satisfying"; BG "a rare kind of pleasure ... its resolutely old-fashioned nature is its great strength"; PI "at once engrossing and slightly disappointing"; TGM "an immaculate film ... compelling"; V "affecting"; TT "a classic, superbly crafted"; SMH "enormously moving ... on no account should it be missed"); and Woody Allen's nostalgic comedy *Radio Days* (NYT "buoyant, comic and poignantly expressed ... as funny as it is moving"; CT "[a] masterpiece ... one of the best films of the year"; WP "immediately forgettable"; TGM "an occasionally charming trifle, a cinematic bauble"; V "one of Woody Allen's most purely entertaining pictures"; TT "charming").

Other films overlooked by the Academy were: *The Untouchables* (NYT "smashing ... violent, funny and sometimes breathtakingly beautiful ... superior mass-market entertainment"; LAT "[the film's] technical side is exemplary"; CT "does not have a great script, great performances or great direction"; WP "never brings its moral conflicts into focus ... has no atmosphere, no grit ... only marginally entertaining"; V "beautifully crafted"); *Prick Up Your Ears* (CT "a good film, sturdily and somberly made, but it never catches fire"; WP "a joyless, inconclusive affair"; BG "a witty, harrowing roller-coaster of a film"; V "a fine film"; TGM "[an] exceptional film"; G "witty, humane and understanding"; SMH "one of the freshest, most intelligent films of the year"); *The Princess Bride* (NYT "has sweetness and sincerity on its side ... and a cheery, earnest style that turns out to be ever more disarming as the film moves along"; LAT "dazzling and delightful ... derring-do tempered with wisecracks"; CT "generates a certain warmth and pleasure"; V "tedious ... totally lacking in momentum and magic"; SMH "[a] cheerfully silly fairytale"); the Swedish drama *Mitt Liv som Hund (My Life as a Dog)*, for which Lasse Hallström was a Best Director nominee (NYT "funny and moving"; LAT "a sterling film ... should be cherished"; WP "isn't as fully realized or satisfying as it should be ... it's undone by its own sweetness and charm"; TGM "it is difficult to imagine anyone of any age or background who will remain unmoved and undelighted"; TT "bristles with character and charm"; SMH "wonderful"); *Full Metal Jacket* (NYT "harrowing ... intense, schematic, superbly made"; LAT "a powerful and centered statement of outrage"; CT "has the power to fascinate ... a nearly perfect film"; WP "a disturbing, indelible movie"; BG "an honorable work, at times a striking one ... but it's powered by craft and dedication, not indignation or the kind of sustained passion 'Platoon' gives us ... it's almost abstract ...

seems to have lost any compelling overview"; TGM "strong stuff ... may be the best war movie ever made"); *House of Games* (NYT "[an] entertaining, deadpan, seriocomic melodrama [and] a wonderfully devious comedy"; LAT "coldly absorbing"; WP "a clever intelligent piece of work with an impulse to surprise and entertain [but] also a crock ... the tricks are fun but the sermon is a bore"; TGM "[it] is so bad it seems reasonable to conclude that God was out of town and Mamet's muse was in a coma"; S&S "compelling"); *Ochi Chyornye (Dark Eyes)* (NYT "enchanting and enchanted, a triumph"; LAT "a lush, bittersweet romance [which is] full of magnificent set-pieces"; BG "magical ... [a] gorgeously rueful, elegantly funny comedy of weakness ... charming"); *Manon des Sources*, the sequel to *Jean de Florette* (LAT "a landmark ... an extraordinarily rewarding experience"; WP "appealing"; BG "an instant classic, building on the richness of 'Jean de Florette' [and] bringing it full circle ... powerful"; PI "the superior movie"; V "poignant"); and Louis Malle's *Au Revoir les Enfants*, winner of the top prize at the Venice Film Festival (NYT "a work that has the kind of simplicity, ease and density of detail that only a film maker in total command of his craft can bring off, and then only rarely ... moving without ever being sentimental"; LAT "superb ... flawless and overwhelming ... one of the best films of this or any other year ... unforgettable"; CT "a quietly stunning film"; BG "overwhelming ... there isn't a false note"; V "moving" and "powerful"; TGM "shapeless and pat; TT "wonderful").

On Oscar night, *The Last Emperor* claimed all nine statuettes for which it had been nominated, including Best Picture. It was only the fourth film to claim nine or more Academy Awards and was the most honoured film since 1961. It repeated its win at the British Academy Awards the following year.

In London, *Hope and Glory* was unexpectedly outpolled for the BAFTA by *Jean de Florette*.

BEST DIRECTOR

ACADEMY AWARDS
• **Bernardo Bertolucci for *The Last Emperor***
John Boorman for *Hope and Glory*
Lasse Hallström for *Mitt Liv som Hund (My Life as a Dog)*
Norman Jewison for *Moonstruck*
Adrian Lyne for *Fatal Attraction*

GOLDEN GLOBE AWARDS
Richard Attenborough – *Cry Freedom*
• **Bernardo Bertolucci – *The Last Emperor***
John Boorman – *Hope and Glory*
James L. Brooks – *Broadcast News*
Adrian Lyne – *Fatal Attraction*

DIRECTORS GUILD AWARD
• **Bernardo Bertolucci**
  – *The Last Emperor*
James L. Brooks – *Broadcast News*
Lasse Hallström
  – *Mitt Liv som Hund*
  (My Life as a Dog)
Adrian Lyne – *Fatal Attraction*
Steven Spielberg – *Empire of the Sun*

BRITISH ACADEMY AWARDS
Richard Attenborough
  – *Cry Freedom*
Claude Berri – *Jean de Florette*
John Boorman – *Hope and Glory*
• **Oliver Stone – *Platoon***

NEW YORK – James L. Brooks – *Broadcast News*
LOS ANGELES – John Boorman – *Hope and Glory*
BOARD OF REVIEW – Steven Spielberg – *Empire of the Sun*
NATIONAL SOCIETY – John Boorman – *Hope and Glory*
LONDON – Stanley Kubrick – *Full Metal Jacket*

For the first time, all the nominees for the Best Director Oscar were non-Americans. Italian Bernardo Bertolucci, who had earlier won the Golden Globe and Directors Guild of America accolade, won the Academy Award for the lavish historical epic *The Last Emperor* (NYT "if it were a more poetically conceived movie, one might respond to everything of consequence that is not on the screen"; PI "marks the restoration of one of the world's most gifted directors to his rightful place … bends time and moves seamlessly between past and present").

Also nominated for the Academy's golden statuette were: Englishman John Boorman, who won the Los Angeles Film Critics Association and National Society of Film Critics prizes for *Hope and Glory* (NYT "[shows] a fine eye for the magical details that a little boy might notice ... makes the film seem open and involving at every turn ... the pacing [is] almost dreamlike"; CT "makes you wish this movie would go on forever"; MFB "splendid ... intelligently cast and directed"; Sp "the film is so consistently diverting that it is only afterwards that one sees how skilfully [he] has developed his themes"; S&S "[he] knows how to write and direct scenes which play in the cinema ... the sentimentality rarely gets out of hand"); Englishman Adrian Lyne for *Fatal Attraction* (NYT "as directed by Mr Lyne, it has an ingeniously teasing style that overrules substance at every turn ... [he] takes a brilliantly manipulative approach to what might have been a humdrum subject and shapes a soap opera of exceptional power"; LAT "Lyne's direction here is the tightest and most effective of his career"; TGM "always stylish [but] sometimes careless ... [the film] lures us in with an artful blend of stately pacing and caressing close-ups and brooding silences"); Swede Lasse Hallström, the surprise nominee, for *Mitt Liv som Hund (My Life as a Dog)* (LAT "Hallström shines"; WP "his approach is cloyingly tender"); and Canadian Norman Jewison for *Moonstruck* (LAT "[shows] what the craft of movie making is all about"; TGM "exemplary").

The most unexpected omissions from the category were all highly-favoured Americans: New York Film Critics Circle prizewinner and previous winner James L. Brooks, who had been the early Oscar frontrunner for *Broadcast News*, one of the year's Best Picture nominees (NYT "has so balanced the movie that no one performer can run off with it"; WP "masterfully interconnects this human triangle [and] shifts the mood from romantic to farcical, the comedy from broad to subtle"); National Board of Review prize-winner Steven Spielberg for *Empire of the Sun* (NYT "art and artifice play equal parts in the telling of this tale, and the latter is part and parcel of the film's overriding style ... gives [the film] a visual splendor, a heroic adventurousness and an immense scope that make it unforgettable"; LAT "thrillingly staged [with] not-inconsiderable craft"; CT "paced like a funeral march"; WP "there isn't a moment in the film that is blandly or routinely directed ... you feel his technical mastery in every frame, and the sheer raw energy he packs into his compositions can make you feel breathless ... Spielberg is a virtuoso performer, and virtuosity can't be dismissed ... but too much of the film has been conceived as a showcase for his brilliance; it's overburdened with epiphanies"; TGM "a technical tour de force [that becomes] grandiose technique"); the late John Huston, who had been the posthumous runner-up in New York for his final film *The Dead* (NYT "remarkable [and] astonishing"; LAT "a work which flows like music"; CT "[made with] intelligence, sensitivity and craftsmanship ... a work of great poise and tact"; WP "the images flow so easily and the film-making is so self-effacing, so direct and economical, that you don't expect it to affect you as powerfully as it does ... Huston's approach here is so assured that it verges on the serene"; BG "a radiant, triumphant work ... Huston saved his best, most intimate work until this valedictory"); and previous winner Woody Allen for *Radio Days* (NYT "never has Mr Allen been so steadily in control"; WP "stilted").

Other contenders overlooked by the Academy were: Brian De Palma for *The Untouchables* (NYT "shows off Mr De Palma's bravura technique to its best advantage"; WP "frame by frame the movie is exquisite, and perhaps the viewer is more impressed here by his mastery of the camera than ever before. But it's the human side of things that gives him fits"; V "beautifully crafted"); Stanley Kubrick for *Full Metal Jacket* (WP "breathtaking"; TGM "artistry and control"); Claude Berri for both *Jean de Florette* (NYT "Berri's control remains sure and firm"; LAT "superlative storytelling"; CT "a thoroughly professional job"; SFC "vividly told"; PI "top-flight directing"; TGM "Berri has done his work faithfully and well"; SMH "masterly") and its sequel *Manon des Sources* (CST "moves with a majestic pacing"); James Ivory for *Maurice* (NYT "Ivory's direction ably conveys Maurice's growing attraction to Clive"; LAT "well-nigh flawless"; G "beautifully made ... see it if only for its craftsmanship"); Nikita Mikhalkov for *Ochi Chyornye (Dark Eyes)*; David Mamet for *House of Games* (NYT "a fine, completely self-assured debut"; LAT "coldly skilful [but] the movie is too stylized"; TGM "as a director, Mamet is lumpen and inexperienced); Richard Attenborough for *Cry Freedom* (NYT "[the film] comes on so clumsily with such a casual, opportunistic disregard for facts and chronology that it may alienate more audiences than it converts ... [he] isn't an especially subtle movie director ... what come through most strongly is the ponderousness of the Attenborough style"; WP "[shows a] preference for choreographed crowd scenes over intimacy"; MFB "sometimes rather heavy-handedly"); and Stephen Frears for *Prick Up Your Ears* (SMH "superb execution").

At the BAFTAs the following year, Bertolucci was outpolled by a foreign director that the Academy had not nominated in 1987: Frenchman Louis Malle for *Au Revoir les Enfants* (NYT "in total command of his craft"; LAT "masterful [and] understated"; TGM "stylistically spare"). Jewison, meanwhile, won the Best Director prize at the Berlin Film Festival that year for *Moonstruck*.

1987

BEST ACTOR

ACADEMY AWARDS
• **Michael Douglas as 'Gordon Gekko' in *Wall Street***
William Hurt as 'Tom Grunick' in *Broadcast News*
Marcello Mastroianni as 'Romano Santoni' in *Ochi Chyornye (Dark Eyes)*
Jack Nicholson as 'Francis Phelan' in *Ironweed*
Robin Williams as 'Adrian Cronauer' in *Good Morning, Vietnam*

GOLDEN GLOBE AWARDS
(Drama)
• **Michael Douglas – *Wall Street***
John Lone – *The Last Emperor*
Jack Nicholson – *Ironweed*
Nick Nolte – *Weeds*
Denzel Washington – *Cry Freedom*

(Comedy/Musical)
Nicolas Cage – *Moonstruck*
Danny DeVito
  – *Throw Momma from the Train*
William Hurt – *Broadcast News*
Steve Martin – *Roxanne*
Patrick Swayze – *Dirty Dancing*
• **Robin Williams**
  – *Good Morning, Vietnam*

BRITISH ACADEMY AWARDS
• **Sean Connery – *The Name of the Rose***
Gérard Depardieu – *Jean de Florette*
Yves Montand – *Jean de Florette*
Gary Oldman – *Prick Up Your Ears*

NEW YORK – Jack Nicholson – *Broadcast News* and *Ironweed* and *The Witches of Eastwick*
LOS ANGELES – Steve Martin – *Roxanne* and Jack Nicholson – *Ironweed* and *The Witches of Eastwick*
BOARD OF REVIEW – Michael Douglas – *Wall Street*
NATIONAL SOCIETY – Steve Martin – *Roxanne*
LONDON – Gary Oldman – *Prick Up Your Ears* and Sean Connery – *The Untouchables*

Bernardo Bertolucci's *The Last Emperor* topped the list of Oscar contenders with nine nominations. Surprisingly, the epic was not mentioned in the acting categories and The Times in London singled out Golden Globe (Drama) nominee John Lone, as the "glaring omission" from the Academy's list (WP "Lone, an intense, energetic actor, is dispassionate here by necessity"; PI

"Lone's achievement in his absorbing account of Pu Yi is to place him at a distance and yet make his plight totally involving"; V "dominates the picture with his carefully judged, unshowy delineation"; SMH "it's his performance that sustains the film ... seems to be completely submerged in the role").

In Britain, where Lone was not eligible for consideration until the following year, the British Academy nominated four other actors overlooked for the Oscar short-list: Gary Oldman in *Prick Up Your Ears* (NYT "very good ... surpasses his fine work in 'Sid and Nancy'"; LAT "stunningly well played ... a wonder"; CT "keeps his scenes consistently lively"; WP "detailed and subtle ... an uncanny impersonation"; BG "mesmerizingly authoritative ... sensational, giving us affecting glimpses of the alienation beneath the bravado"; V "excellent"; TGM "expertly incarnated"; S&S "utterly convincing"); and both Gérard Depardieu (NYP "superb"; LAT "zestfully well acted ... the lodestar of this first film ... it's almost unendurable to watch him"; BG "sweeps us along"; TGM "superb ... works sensitive wonders with the title character"; MFB "stunning ... surpasses all his previous performances"; SMH "one of the best roles of his brilliant career ... he makes you weep") and Yves Montand (NYT "the role of his career"; NYP "superb ... quite possibly the performance of his lifetime"; LAT "one of the richest performances in memory"; BG "amazing"; PI "a performance of extraordinary richness"; TGM "brilliant"; MFB "stunning ... totally convincing") in *Jean de Florette*. Montand also earned praise that year for the film's sequel *Manon des Sources* (NYT "splendid"; LAT "caps a remarkable career with a portrayal that will rank high in screen annals"; WP "a fine performance"; BG "amazing ... startlingly compelling"; PI "[an] extraordinary portrait") as did co-star Daniel Auteuil (NYT "splendid"; LAT "tears you apart with his Ugolin"; WP "he gives the guileless farmer a sad dignity"; BG "not surprisingly, Auteuil, walked away with most of the important French acting awards ... he alone is the film's moral battleground"; SFC "performs wonders with the unsympathetic figure of Ugolin ... touching").

Perhaps the most glaring snub, however, was that of Los Angeles Film Critics Association and National Society of Film Critics prizewinner Steve Martin in *Roxanne* (NYT "Martin gives a sweet and serious performance ... thoroughly charming [and] touching"; LAT "Martin seems unfettered, expansive, utterly at ease ... there's a tenderness to him that's magnetic"; CST "charming"; CT "has never been better"; WP "nothing that Steve Martin does in 'Roxanne' is run-of-the-mill ... every gesture is blessed, inspired"). It was the second time in four years that Martin had been honoured by leading critics groups only to be ignored by the members of the Academy's acting branch.

Other notable contenders passed over by the Academy were: thirteen-year old Christian Bale in *Empire of the Sun* (NYT "eminently able to handle an ambitious and demanding role"; NYP "outstanding"; LAT "an anxious, edgy, very creditable Jim"; V "carries this massive production on his small shoulders ... superb"; Time "splendid"; TGM "competent"; TT "a finely rounded characterization"); Nicolas Cage in both *Moonstruck* (LAT "attacks the role with a nice balance between unbridled romanticism and tongue-in-cheek seriousness; he's marvelous"; V "solid and appealing"; TGM "brings to [the role] an off-the-wall but on-the-mark hysteria, goofy yet real"; TT "extraordinary") and *Raising Arizona* (NYT "[Cage and Hunter] go at their roles with a tenacity that the film itself never makes adequate use of"; LAT "Cage has crammed every ounce of sweet earnestness into [the role] and that is the sole quality that makes the character work"; WP "engagingly off the wall"; V "fine"); Mickey Rourke in *Barfly* (NYT "a big, broad, mesmerizing performance"; LAT "played with lots of sodden sparkle ... this performance may seem like a stunt but you're won over by [his] canny, lazy attack"; CST "Rourke and Dunaway take their characters as opportunities to stretch as actors, to make changes and do extreme things"; WP "triumphs"; V "quirky, unpredictable, mostly engaging"; TGM "wonderful"; MFB "startling"); Joe Mantegna in *House of Games* (NYT "splendidly in touch, not only with [the] character but also with the sense of the film"; LAT "it is only when [he] enters the scene that the movie really ripens up and connects"; CST "so perfectly and brilliantly attuned to [the character] that he would own the role no matter what adjustments he was asked to make [by his director]"; WP "Mantegna's performance here is the main reason to get excited ... [he] has the perfect delivery for Mamet's artificial, tough-guy style"); Anthony Hopkins in *84 Charing Cross Road* (LAT "some of the warmest and most winning moments of [his] screen career"; V "perfect"; TGM "Hopkins is marvellously eloquent with the sub-text"; MFB "[Hopkins, Bancroft and Dench] fit their parts to perfection"; Sp "the major pleasure of this film is Hopkins's performance"); Michael Caine in *The Whistle Blower* (NYT "a full and affecting performance well above his usual high level"; LAT "beautifully portrayed ... one of his best performances"; WP "has a handful of wonderful moments but ultimately his performance cannot transcend the material"; BG "anchors the film ... projects a lot more conviction than in most of his recent roles ... an object lesson in how to use underplaying"; V "excellent"); Richard E. Grant in *Withnail and I* (NYT "super"; LAT "sublime"); and Venice co-honouree James Wilby in *Maurice* (NYT "he very convincingly presents Maurice's dilemma"; LAT "[a] portrayal of intelligence and subtlety ... wonderfully unaffected"; WP "an accomplished performance"; BG "played with astonishing grace and sensitivity"; TT "deft"). Ahead of these candidates, the Academy nominated four of the Globe finalists and the Cannes Best Actor winner.

Seventeen years after he won an Oscar as the producer of the Best Picture winner *One Flew Over the Cuckoo's Nest*, Michael Douglas, the son of previous Best Actor nominee Kirk Douglas, was nominated for his performance as an insider trader in *Wall Street* (NYT "the funniest, canniest performance of his career"; LAT "played with icy ferocity ... a wizardly turn"; WP "[the film's] principal equity is a bullish performance from Michael Douglas ... bravura ... plays Gekko with a terrible intensity"; TGM "Douglas's portrayal of Gordon Gekko is an oily triumph"; SMH "[a] mesmerizing performance"). He had also starred as the adulterous husband in *Fatal Attraction*, a box office success and Best Picture Oscar nominee (LAT "complements [Close] superbly"; WP "played convincingly"; TGM "Douglas handles his chores with the expected aplomb").

Previous winner William Hurt was mentioned for a third consecutive year as a television anchorman in *Broadcast News* (NYT "smashing [and] terrific"; WP "[a] crisp performance ... gives his role the perfect blend of arrogance and awkwardness"; TT "excellent"), while previous winner Jack Nicholson was recognised for a ninth time as a homeless man in *Ironweed* (NYT "extremely well-acted"; LAT "[an] unsparing performance ... touching [and] shattering"; CT "doesn't disgrace himself [but] there isn't much he or anyone can do [with the script]"; WP "a disappointment ... both [he] and Streep remain deep down inside their characters but neither is able to communicate much on an interior life"; BG "what little success 'Ironweed' achieves comes from [his] resourcefulness in its central role ... he rises to the challenge"; PI "one can only watch [him] in awe ... absolutely heartbreaking"; TGM "a demonstration of Jack Nicholson's limits as an actor"; MFB "artful"). Nicholson had also starred in *The Witches of Eastwick* (NYT "[his] high spirits and madman antics are always a treat"; V "larger than life ... ferocious magnetism").

Marcello Mastroianni garnered his third nod as a man who gave up on his youthful ambitions when he married a wealthy woman in *Ochi Chyornye (Dark Eyes)* (NYT "remarkable ... both heart-breaking and farcical ... one of the highlights of his career"; NYP "superb"; LAT "beautifully faceted"; BG "[a] career-capping performance"; TGM "holding the loosely organized material together from beginning to end"; TT "[an] effortlessly unflawed performance"; SMH "perfectly cast"), while Robin Williams completed the list with his first nod as disc jockey in *Good Morning, Vietnam* (NYT "gets a chance to exercise his full-frontal comic intelligence ... Williams's performance, though it's full of uproarious comedy, is the work of an accomplished actor"; LAT "blazingly brilliant ... he's transformed"; CST "dazzling and funny"; V "impressive"; TGM "never before has he had this opportunity to integrate stand-up comedy and a fully developed character").

Nicholson received a record sixth award from the New York Film Critics Circle and his third honour from the west coast circle, yet the favourite for the Oscar was Douglas, who had only narrowly been outpolled by Nicholson in New York and had subsequently received the Globe (Drama). On Oscar night, as expected, Douglas received the Best Actor statuette.

1987

BEST ACTRESS

ACADEMY AWARDS
• **Cher as 'Loretta Castorini' in** *Moonstruck*
Glenn Close as 'Alex Forrest' in *Fatal Attraction*
Holly Hunter as 'Jane Craig' in *Broadcast News*
Sally Kirkland as 'Anna Radkova' in *Anna*
Meryl Streep as 'Helen Archer' in *Ironweed*

GOLDEN GLOBE AWARDS

(Drama)
Glenn Close – *Fatal Attraction*
Faye Dunaway – *Barfly*
• **Sally Kirkland – *Anna***
Rachel Levin – *Gaby: A True Story*
Barbra Streisand – *Nuts*

(Comedy/Musical)
• **Cher – *Moonstruck***
Jennifer Grey – *Dirty Dancing*
Holly Hunter – *Broadcast News*
Diane Keaton – *Baby Boom*
Bette Midler – *Outrageous Fortune*

BRITISH ACADEMY AWARDS
• **Anne Bancroft – *84 Charing Cross Road***
Emily Lloyd – *Wish You Were Here*
Sarah Miles – *Hope and Glory*
Julie Walters – *Personal Services*

NEW YORK – Holly Hunter – *Broadcast News*
**LOS ANGELES – Holly Hunter – *Broadcast News* and Sally Kirkland –
*Anna***
**BOARD OF REVIEW – Lillian Gish – *The Whales of August* and Holly
Hunter – *Broadcast News***
NATIONAL SOCIETY – Emily Lloyd – *Wish You Were Here*

"If there is any justice in Heaven, Christine Lahti and Anjelica Huston will be
the major contenders for this year's best actress Oscar," declared Vincent Canby
in The New York Times on 31 December 1987. Two weeks earlier, Lahti had
been runner-up for the Best Actress award from the New York Film Critics
Circle for her performance as an eccentric aunt in *Housekeeping* (NYT
"spellbinding ... gives one of the year's most haunting performances ...
illuminates every frame of the movie ... should be an automatic Oscar
nomination"; LAT "does a wonderful job, giving one of her sturdily natural,
hyper-aware performances"; CST "brings a delightful naturalism to the role ...
an honest, human characterization"; WP "beautifully conveys [the character]";

BG "flat-out wonderful") while Anjelica Huston had been in contention for her father's last film *The Dead* (NYT "splendid"; LAT "beyond the perfect ensemble is the haunting memory of Anjelica Huston's performance, simple and deeply stirring"; WP "pours such emotion into this story that her lines seem like a scraping away of the soul; it's almost unendurably painful"). Despite the support from The New York Times, neither Lahti not Huston were nominated for the Golden Globe or the Oscar.

The early frontrunner for the Academy Award was Holly Hunter as a reporter in *Broadcast News* (NYT "smashing ... a delight"; LAT "sensational ... no less than magnificent"; WP "[a] crisp performance [which is] a joy to watch"; V "simply superb"; TT "excellent"). Hunter, who had also starred in *Raising Arizona* (NYT "[Cage and Hunter] go at their roles with a tenacity that the film itself never makes adequate use of"; LAT "needs to be monumental, titanic in her hunger for maternity in order to set this plot in motion believably [but] is small and brown-wrenish"), won accolades from the New York Film Critics Circle and Los Angeles Film Critics Association, shared the National Board of Review prize and received a nomination for the Globe (Musical/Comedy).

Hunter was unexpectedly outpolled for the Globe, however, by Cher as a Brooklyn widow in *Moonstruck* (NYT "has evolved into the kind of larger-than-life movie star who's worth watching whatever she does"; LAT "finally has a role that lets her comic sensibilities out for a romp"; V "solid and appealing"; TGM "terrific ... her performance is the stuff of Oscar nominations, handling the tricky accent well and the subtle comedy flawlessly"; TT "beautifully vibrant and funny"; SMH "impeccable"). Both actresses were recognised by the Academy, and by Oscar night, Cher was considered the favourite.

The dark horses for the Oscar were Glenn Close (nominated for a fourth time in six years) as a psychotic woman in the box office hit *Fatal Attraction* (NYT "especially startling"; NYP "terrifying and yet always plausible"; LAT "infernally brilliant ... this is the most dangerous kind of role for an actor, yet she cuts so close to the bone that every emotion stays in focus"; WP "Close gives Alex dimension ...[she] should take pride in her performance"; V "genuinely frightening"; TGM "it's left to Close to provide the shadings [to the part] ... superb ... produces a wondrous metamorphosis ... her every scene is scorching"; Time "beautifully calibrated descent into lunacy"; SMH "simply magnificent") and the surprise Globe (Drama) champ Sally Kirkland, who mounted her own campaign for her turn as a former Czech film star in *Anna* (NYT "immensely dignified"; NYP "very effective, haunting"; LAT "an unparalleled, audacious original"; CT "her performance represents the Method at its most elevated ... a fully developed, unselfconscious characterization that emerges with amazing clarity and force"; WP "superb ... manages to be convincing even when [the film] becomes downright ridiculous"; BG "riveting ... the kind of large, bold, headlong, chance-taking performance that doesn't know the meaning of the word safe ... my favourite performance by an actress this year"; V "brilliant ... remarkably shades the character"; TGM "a performance so vigorously theatrical and narcissistic, it's bound to win awards"; TT "astonishing"; MFB "expansively actressy without the loss of a detailed individuality").

The only outsider in the field was previous winner Meryl Streep, who received a seventh nomination as a homeless woman in *Ironweed* (NYT "stunning ... she's a marvel ... a rich, invigorating, spellbinding [performance] ... would be an automatic Oscar nomination [if it] were a more cohesive movie ... her work is the equal of what she did in 'Sophie's Choice'"; LAT "[an] unsparing performance ... Streep has constructed a character with a thousand tiny adjustments ... shattering"; CST "well acted"; CT "faced with an underwritten part, she runs wildly out of control"; WP "does an even more accomplished vanishing act than usual ... becomes painfully real"; BG "[her] performance, while technically impressive, is seldom more"; PI "heartbreaking ... I can't think of any other major actress brave enough to take on the physical ruin of Helen and still make her moments of clarity and fantasy so touching"; V "too distant"; TGM "a demonstration of [her] limitless capacity for discovering accents even in characters who don't need them"; MFB "artful" TT "noticeable rather than notable").

The most surprising omission from the list of Oscar candidates was eighty-seven-year old Lillian Gish, who had shared the NBR plaudit with Hunter, as one of the widowed sisters in *The Whales of August* (NYT "[a] beautiful, very characteristic performance ... there's not a gesture or a line-reading that doesn't reflect her nearly three-quarters of a century into front of a camera"; LAT "she carries off [the role] with a star's authority"; CT "compelling"; WP "never less than archetypal"; V "superior [and] a delight"; S&S "splendid"; MFB "effective"). Observers had believed that sentiment would carry either Gish or her co-star, previous winner Bette Davis (NYT "[a] beautiful, very characteristic performance"; LAT "one of Davis' most crisp and disciplined performances"; CT "less impressive [than Gish] ... she is undone by [the] script"; WP "ripostes with vinegary familiarity"; V "superior [and] restrained; S&S "splendid"; MFB "effective"), to a nomination.

Another critics' prize-winner overlooked by the Academy was National Society of Film Critics honouree Emily Lloyd as the future British madam Cynthia Payne in *Wish You Were Here* (NYT "captivating ... capturing the full emotional range of this complicated young girl"; LAT "one of the those extraordinary fusions of actress and character that defy you to pry them apart ... shiveringly perfect"; CST "the key to the movie ... Lloyd is so fresh that she carries us past the tricky parts [in the screenplay] on the strength of personality alone ... one of the great debut roles for a young actress"; V "played with exasperating charm"; TGM "sensational"; MFB "she is the incarnation of what she is supposed to be portraying, but the portrayal bleeds off the edges of the screenplay and threatens to result in something truly dangerous"). She was, however, a BAFTA nominee.

Interestingly, also in contention for the BAFTA was Julie Walters, who played an older version of Payne in *Personal Services* (NYT "an energetic, blustery performance"; LAT "brings a vibrant, thorny toughness to her role"; TGM "this is Julie Walters' picture to steal and it's a deft theft, indeed ... [the screenwriter] gives the character a sadness that [she] can't admit, but that Walters can convey"; MFB "Walters' performance veers towards camp without ever falling into the trap of condescension").

Also nominated for the BAFTA were Anne Bancroft in *84 Charing Cross Road* (NYT "blunt"; LAT "some of the warmest and most winning moments of [her] screen career ... what a pleasure it is to watch [her] in a role that fits her like a glove"; CT "overacts a little ... projects her emotions so fiercely and broadly that her performance would probably seem overscaled on stage"; WP "[a] fine performance"; V "fantastic"; TGM "superbly realized"; MFB "[Hopkins, Bancroft and Dench] fit their parts to perfection") and Sarah Miles in *Hope and Glory* (V "overdoing things and projecting little inner feeling"; Sp "imaginative ... develops a warm and original portrayal"; S&S "her performance, in particular, has an affecting, old-style confidence").

Several observers had expected previous winner Barbra Streisand to garner a nomination for *Nuts*, her first film since she had been controversially overlooked by the Academy as both director and actress for *Yentl* (NYT "her shrewd, well-delivered retorts provide the film with its liveliest moments"; LAT "sails into the role with nothing held back"; CT "Streisand is too strong for the role as written"; WP "a bravissimo performance ... dazzling ... the performance of a lifetime"; TGM "the best non-musical performance of her career ... wonderful"). But as Aljean Harmetz observed in The New York Times, the film has been "negatively perceived as the kind of star vehicle that is produced simply to win awards." His colleague, Janet Maslin, wrote, "Streisand has the kind of downscale role that has been known to win Oscars, a role in which a star forsakes her usual cocoon [and] prove[s] she has grit ... [her] performance is better than that, but it's the showboating aspects of 'Nuts' that attract the most attention." In the Orlando Sentinel, meanwhile, Jay Boyar, had quipped, "Is Oscar lust the force behind 'Nuts'? No other explanation seems possible".

Among those also by-passed for Oscar consideration were several other previous winners, including: NSFC runner-up Diane Keaton in *Baby Boom* (NYT "a devilishly good performance ... [her] comically exaggerated toughness and absurd self-confidence make the performance a delight"; LAT "a dream part"); Faye Dunaway in *Barfly* (NYT "most affecting ... rediscovers the reserves of talent that in recent years have been hidden"; LAT "Dunaway's Wanda is the intense, passionate, beating heart of 'Barfly'"; WP "convinces ... [a] touching, deeply felt performance"; BG "eschewing her usual outsize volatility for affecting vulnerability [she] nicely balances comedy and fatalism ... the kind of role of which comebacks are made"; TGM "wonderful ... a muted and sensual characterization"); Joanne Woodward, reprising her stage success, in *The Glass Menagerie* (NYT "Woodward makes a fluttery, garrulous Amanda"; LAT "a brave and controversial reading [of the part] ... her performance grows within the film until she is transcendent"; WP "leaves out the tragic dimension to the character; her Amanda isn't moving – she's a prattling bore ... Woodward's performance is all empty declamation and artificiality"; V "brilliant"); Cannes Film Festival prizewinner Barbara Hershey in *Shy People* (NYT "technically first-rate, but limited by the melodramatic context"; LAT "only Hershey emerges unscathed ... the right actress in the right role but in the wrong movie ... allows Hershey to dig deeper than ever before into her resources as an actress"; CST "it's to Hershey's credit that she is able to play the role to the hilt and yet still make it real"; WP "applies herself diligently to her work here, and to some extent she can't be blamed for the results ... she is never playing anything more than a collection of attitudes") and Maggie Smith in *The Lonely Passion of Judith Hearne* (NYT "almost too good ... [her] subtlety only calls attention to the obviousness of the story"; LAT "gives a complicated, gently shaded reading to the role ... Smith's performance is elegant in every detail"; WP "perfectly cast [but] there's something too practiced and predictable about her Judith ... Smith's work is sound but without spontaneity"; V "[an] exceptionally detailed performance"; TGM "an unstudied, unmannered characterization that ranges from precise wit to harrowing anguish"; MFB "outshines the material"). Ignored by the Academy in Hollywood, Smith went on to win the Best Actress BAFTA for her performance the following year.

Also overlooked were: Karen Allen in *The Glass Menagerie* (LAT "gives the role a simple, lovely reading"; CST "the real revelation in the cast"; WP "she's the still, poetic center of the production ... her performance has such enthralling quietness and intimacy ... I've never before seen the character of Laura played convincingly, on stage or on screen"); 1986 Cannes winner Barbara Sukowa in *Rosa Luxemburg* (NYT "a fine, soberly intelligent performance [that] at the end becomes genuinely moving ... it is difficult to imagine anyone else in the part"; LAT "a performance that heats up as it unfolds, becoming electrifying in its final third ... [a] towering performance [and] a tour de force"; V "outstanding"; TT "convincing"; S&S "[a] charismatic rendition"; FQ "unquestionably intelligent and sincere"; MFB "brilliantly portrayed"); Mia Farrow in *Radio Days* (NYT "hilariously common-sensical ... flawless timing ... one of the more memorable performances of the year"; CT "memorable"; WP "never has time to develop a rhythm"); Lindsay Crouse in *House of Games* (NYT "splendidly in touch, not only with [the] character but also with the sense of the film"; LAT "seems to be tamping down the passion too hard"; CST "has there been a more mechanical performance this year, however artfully it is presented?"; WT "unfortunately, only draws your attention to the fact that nobody ever, every talks this way ... there's no tension in the performance"); Rachel Levin in *Gaby: A True Story* (NYT "her performance has a blunt, unsentimental quality"; LAT "radiant"; TGM "etches a remarkably complex portrait ... in short, she is the character, credibly, completely"); both Bette Midler (NYT "at her own raucous best ... flawless phrasing and timing"; BG "she warms the screen and puts a winning spin on her zaftig assertiveness") and Shelley Long (NYT "does this bluestocking role to perfection ... delightful") in *Outrageous Fortune* (NYT "hilarious, both separately and together"; LAT "sensational together and as individual presences ... [the film] is anchored in the reality that [they] bring so smashingly to Lauren and Sandy"); and Catherine Deneuve in *Le Lieu du Crime (Scene of the Crime)* (NYT "a subtle, superbly controlled performance"; LAT "provides Deneuve with one of the best roles of her career, one that demands far more of her than her fabled beauty [and] she in turn creates something more important than mere sympathy for the troubled woman she plays so persuasively"; CT "her slow transformation over the course of the film proceeds through subtle, imaginative steps").

The members of the Academy's acting branch also passed over the performance of Judy Davis in the Australian film *High Tide* which was given an Oscar qualifying run in Los Angles in the week before Christmas (NYT "brings the character to life ... an extraordinarily vivid screen presence ... she is also able to communicate all of Lilli's powerfully mixed feelings about her child in purely physical terms"; LAT "a genuinely great performance"; CST "sensitive acting"; WP "It's Davis who allows us to see Lilli's interior life ... [she] may convey mixed-up emotions with greater lucidity than any other actress working today ... yet there's never anything of the bravura performer in her work ... her performance is built out of smallish details and little moments"; V "[a] powerful performance ... [she] provides great depth and subtlety, making her character come vividly alive"; FQ "[a] complex characterization ... brings so much more to this estranged mother role than might seem possible"). The film opened elsewhere in North America progressively from February 1988 and Davis was ultimately named Best Actress for that year by the National Society of Film Critics, too late for the accolade to translate into an Oscar nomination.

On Oscar night, as expected, Cher was presented with the Best Actress Academy Award. She was unsuccessfully nominated by the British Academy the following year. Hunter, meanwhile, was honoured at the 1988 Berlin Film Festival for her performance in *Broadcast News*.

BEST SUPPORTING ACTOR

ACADEMY AWARDS
Albert Brooks as 'Aaron Altman' in *Broadcast News*
• **Sean Connery as 'Jim Malone' in *The Untouchables***
Morgan Freeman as 'Fast Black' in *Street Smart*
Vincent Gardenia as 'Comso Castorini' in *Moonstruck*
Denzel Washington as 'Steve Biko' in *Cry Freedom*

GOLDEN GLOBE AWARDS
• **Sean Connery – *The Untouchables***
Richard Dreyfuss – *Nuts*
R. Lee Ermey – *Full Metal Jacket*
Morgan Freeman – *Street Smart*
Rob Lowe – *Square Dance*

BRITISH ACADEMY AWARDS
• **Daniel Auteuil – *Jean de Florette***
Ian Bannen – *Hope and Glory*
Sean Connery – *The Untouchables*
John Thaw – *Cry Freedom*

NEW YORK – Morgan Freeman – *Street Smart*
LOS ANGELES – Morgan Freeman – *Street Smart*
BOARD OF REVIEW – Sean Connery – *The Untouchables*
NATIONAL SOCIETY – Morgan Freeman – *Street Smart*

After going home empty-handed from seven Best Actor nominations, many observers felt that Peter O'Toole would at last receive an Oscar for his supporting role in the epic *The Last Emperor* (NYT "not a great performance … [he] rattles off his lines with speed and what often seems to be a comic disregard for what they mean"; NYP "superb"; LAT "wonderfully dry"; WP "not a grand performance"; MFB "subtly over the top"). Surprisingly, however, O'Toole was not even nominated for either the Globe or the Academy Award.

Instead the Oscar was presented to another sentimental choice: Sean Connery as a police officer in *The Untouchables* (NYT "[his] fine performance provides the film with its moral center"; V "commands one's attention during every moment of his screen presence ... one of his finest performances"; CT "the best performance in the movie"; WP "has real brio and authenticity … he steals the show"). Connery was cited in both categories by the British Academy and took home the main prize for his work in *The Name of the Rose* for which he had been overlooked by the Academy in Hollywood the previous year. In the lead up to the Oscars, where he won the statuette at his first nomination, Connery won the Golden Globe and the National Board of Review accolade, and finished as the runner-up for each the other three major critics' prizes.

Also receiving his first nomination from the Academy was Morgan Freeman, who collected the accolades from the New York Film Critics Circle, the Los Angeles Film Critics Association and the National Society of Film Critics for his turn as a charismatic pimp in *Street Smart* (NYT "extremely good"; LAT "[a] devastating performance ... [a] commanding and terrifying portrait ... should be taken seriously when the next Oscars are thought about"; WP "the most convincing acting [in the film] ... gives his character an indelibly ugly and disturbing edge"; BG "[a] fine performance"; V "a strong and disturbing performance").

Also nominated were: Albert Brooks as an aspiring television anchorman in *Broadcast News* (NYT "smashing ... comes very near to stealing [the film]"; LAT "unparalleled"; WP "perfect"; V "an insightful performance"; TT "excellent"); Vincent Gardenia as a Brooklyn widow's father in *Moonstruck* (LAT "marvelous"; TGM "deliciously sly"; TT "wonderful"); and Best Actor (Drama) Globe nominee Denzel Washington as political activist Steve Biko in *Cry Freedom* (NYT "particularly good ... played with great magnetism and given an air of true heroism by Washington [even] though the role is badly underdeveloped in [the] screenplay"; NYP "played with quiet power"; LAT "a triumph"; WP "a zealous, Oscar-caliber performance"; V "remarkable"; Sp "plays Biko with great intelligence and charm, but the black activist has been made into a saintly figure").

The British Academy gave its award to Daniel Auteuil for his portrayal of the accomplice in *Jean de Florette* (WP "magnificently gormless"; BG "emerges as the first half's most compelling character ... a fascinating study"; PI "brilliantly done"; TGM "brilliant"; MFB "amazing"; SMH "unforgettable"). Also considered were: Connery in *The Untouchables*; Ian Bannen in *Hope and Glory* (NYT "especially entertaining"; CT "Bannen's crotchety performance is a little too calculatedly theatrical"; WP "some inspired gallery-playing"; Sp "charges theatrically, but enjoyably, through the latter part of the film"); and John Thaw in *Cry Freedom*. Connery was the only BAFTA finalist recognised by the Academy in Hollywood.

Also passed over by Oscar voters were: both Globe nominee and previous Best Actor Oscar winner Richard Dreyfuss as the lawyer (NYT "Dreyfuss is sharp, honest, incisive and greatly underutilized in this supporting role"; WP "impressive"; TGM "exhilarating in [his] perfection") and James Whitmore as the judge (NYT "has some nice moments"; WP "played with gentle brilliance

... a standout even amid this fine supporting cast"; TGM "exhilarating in [his] perfection") in *Nuts*; Globe nominee R. Lee Ermey in *Full Metal Jacket* (NYT "stunning"; LAT "exceptional"; BG "harrowingly convincing"; V "mesmerizing"); previous winner Robert De Niro as 1930s gangster Al Capone in *The Untouchables* (NYT "a rich performance"; WP "De Niro lends his presence but none of his talent ... going for a broad, theatrical style of acting he creates a satire on the idea of Capone"); Globe nominee Rob Lowe as a mentally challenged youth in *Square Dance* (NYT "[a] most arresting performance ... he's good"; LAT "a good job"; TGM "incongruously cast but surprisingly effective"); John Malkovich both as a prisoner in a Japanese PoW camp in *Empire of the Sun* (NYT "brings lot of fire to the role") and the brother in *The Glass Menagerie* (NYT "brings him fully to life"; LAT "a great, shattering and definitive interpretation of the role"; WP "unconvincing [and] theatrical"); Tom Waits in *Ironweed* (CST "well acted"; BG "only Waits conveys the woozy vision and simple belief in brotherhood of lost souls that Nicholson otherwise shoulders alone"); John Gielgud in *The Whistle Blower* (NYT "a marvel"; LAT "one of his best performances ... wonderful"; WP "this is not one of [his] better cameos"); Bob Hoskins in *The Lonely Passion of Judith Hearne* (NYT "is quiet paralyzed by the crude Americanisms of his character"; LAT "marvelous"; WP "exact but flat"); John Goodman in *Raising Arizona* (WP "magnificent"; V "outstanding"); François Négret in *Au Revoir les Enfants* (NYT "especially memorable"); and both Hugh Grant (NYT "so good in the film's early sections"; LAT "[a] portrayal of intelligence and subtlety"; WP "makes a virtually flawless metamorphosis from an exuberant college boy to frigid, rigid neo-Victorian prig"; TT "deft") and Rupert Graves (NYT "grittily authentic"; LAT "well-nigh flawless"; V "superlative [in a] notable [and] earthy portrayal"; TT "[a] rich and subtly shaped [performance]"; G "perfect") in *Maurice*, for which they had shared the Best Actor award at the 1987 Venice Film Festival along with James Wilby (TT they "deserved to share the honour").

1987

BEST SUPPORTING ACTRESS

ACADEMY AWARDS
Norma Aleandro as 'Florencia' in *Gaby: A True Story*
Anne Archer as 'Beth Gallagher' in *Fatal Attraction*
• **Olympia Dukakis as 'Rose Castorini' in *Moonstruck***
Anne Ramsey as 'Momma Lift' in *Throw Momma from the Train*
Ann Sothern as 'Tisha Doughty' in *The Whales of August*

GOLDEN GLOBE AWARDS
Norma Aleandro – *Gaby: A True Story*
Anne Archer – *Fatal Attraction*
• **Olympia Dukakis – *Moonstruck***
Anne Ramsey – *Throw Momma from the Train*
Vanessa Redgrave – *Prick Up Your Ears*

BRITISH ACADEMY AWARDS
Judi Dench – *84 Charing Cross Road*
Vanessa Redgrave – *Prick Up Your Ears*
Dianne Wiest – *Radio Days*
• **Susan Wooldridge – *Hope and Glory***

NEW YORK – Vanessa Redgrave – *Prick Up Your Ears*
LOS ANGELES – Olympia Dukakis – *Moonstruck*
BOARD OF REVIEW – Olympia Dukakis – *Moonstruck*
NATIONAL SOCIETY – Kathy Baker – *Street Smart*

Three actresses contested the major American critics' prizes at the end of the year: Vanessa Redgrave, who won the New York Film Critics Circle award and finished as the runner-up for the National Society of Film Critics prize, for her portrayal of literary agent Peggy Ramsey in *Prick Up Your Ears* (NYT "refreshingly staunch and common-sensical"; LAT "marvelously cast"; WP "absorbing"; BG "unreels witty lines with dry style"; V "takes top honors"; S&S "masterly"; MFB "endearingly mannered"); Olympia Dukakis, who collected the Los Angeles Film Critics Association and National Board of Review accolades, as the mother of a Brooklyn widow in *Moonstruck* (NYT "manages to have some good moments"; LAT "Dukakis seems to have an extra sheen of maturity and wisdom that moves her work from authoritative into memorable"; TGM "first among equals ... brilliant ... she's a dazzling force"; V "solid and appealing"; TT "wonderful"); and Kathy Baker, who won the NSFC plaudit (by one point over Redgrave) as a prostitute in *Street Smart* (NYT "played very memorably"; LAT "[a] devastating performance ... brilliant [and] compelling ... should be taken seriously when the next Oscars are thought about"; WP "does a good turn"). All three prize-winners were expected to contest the Oscar stakes, but in the end only one was recognised by the members of the Academy.

Both Dukakis and Redgrave were nominated for the Golden Globe, but Baker was overlooked in favour of Anne Archer as the wife of an adulterous man in *Fatal Attraction* (NYP "wonderful"; V "comes out shining"), Anne Ramsey as the senile, tough-as-boots old mother in *Throw Momma from the Train* (NYT "played as the ultimate grotesque ... belts out insults and motherly pleasantries with equal enthusiasm"; TGM "indescribable ... invests hideousness with humanity"), and Norma Aleandro, in her first English-language performance, in *Gaby: A True Story* (NYT "a superb performance ... a real standout ... Aleandro is a marvel"; V "radiant"). In The New York Times, Aljean Harmetz observed, "Since there are thousands of eligible performances, it is in the supporting-actor categories that advertising, publicity, or critical anointment can have the greatest effect. The producers of 'Gaby – A True Story" sent a video cassette of the movie to every member of the Academy and were rewarded with a nomination for Norma Aleandro, for her performance as Gaby's nurse."

Dukakis won the Globe and became the strong favourite to collect the Oscar when she was included on the ballot but her rivals for the critics' prizes, Baker and Redgrave, were both excluded. The Academy made one change from the list of Globe nominees: seventy-eight-year old Hollywood veteran Ann Sothern was mentioned, ahead of Redgrave, for her performance as the friend of a pair of elderly widowed sisters in *The Whales of August* (V "winning"). It was Sothern's first Oscar nomination after fifty years in Hollywood films.

The omission of Redgrave from the Academy's list of contenders was highlighted by her inclusion by the British Academy, which also named three other notable absentees from the Oscar ballot: Judi Dench in *84 Charing Cross Road* (TGM "colors in the background hues admirably"; MFB "[Hopkins, Bancroft and Dench] fit their parts to perfection"; Sp "her performance is impeccable"); Dianne Wiest as the unmarried aunt in *Radio Days* (NYT "[a] performance-without-price"; V "delicious"; TGM "exemplary ... singlehandedly adding layers of rich complexity to the essentially flat stereotype of the maiden aunt"); and Susan Wooldridge in *Hope and Glory*.

Other notable candidates snubbed by the Academy in Hollywood were: Joan Chen in *The Last Emperor* (V "exquisite"); Sammi Davis in *Hope and Glory* (NYT "especially fine"; CT "a wonderfully brassy, howling performance"); Miranda Richardson in *Empire of the Sun* (NYT "grows more beautiful as her spirits fade"; TGM "her wings have been clipped"); Elaine Stritch in *September*

(NYT "terrific … in a beautifully controlled performance, [she] delivers the film's best lines with rich irony"; LAT "wonderful [in a] blowzy, brassy, bravura performance as an aging movie star"; TGM "the audience gets the gloom relieved only by the glimmer of Elaine Stritch … [she is] the one lively frog in this golden pond … [she] brings such vitality to the lugubrious proceedings it's easy to forget that she's supposed to be unsympathetic"); Frances McDormand in *Raising Arizona* (NYT "very funny"); Shelley Duvall in *Roxanne* (NYT "another oddly realistic presence is that of Shelley Duvall, who fits surprisingly well into the role of [the] confidante"; CT "strikes the film's grace note"); Joan Cusack in *Broadcast News* (WP "the sidewinder touch that the deliciously gawky Cusack gives to her line readings causes you to rock in your chair with delight"); Carroll Baker in *Ironweed* (CST "well acted"; BG "plays with poignant delicacy"; TGM "a splendidly low-key appearance"); previous winner Wendy Hiller in *The Lonely Passion of Judith Hearne* (NYT "commanding"); and Jane Alexander in *Square Dance* (NYT "plays [the part] without going overboard, but also without being especially interesting"; LAT "[a] great performance … [makes her] scenes, simple in outline, soar with emotion … Alexander rarely tries roles like this, but she never makes a false step"; TGM "she manages to humanize the inhumane, without once stooping either to false sympathy or cheap sentimentality").

In London, Wooldridge won the BAFTA for Best Supporting Actress for her turn in *Hope and Glory*, while in Hollywood, the Oscar was presented to Dukakis for *Moonstruck*. She repeated her win at the British Academy Awards the following year.

BEST PICTURE

ACADEMY AWARDS
The Accidental Tourist
  (Warner Bros., 121 mins, 23 Dec 1988, $32.6m, 4 noms)
Dangerous Liaisons
  (Lorimar, Warner Bros., 120 mins, 21 Dec 1988, $34.7m, 7 noms)
Mississippi Burning
  (Zollo, Orion, 128 mins, 9 Dec 1988, $34.6m, 7 noms)
• *Rain Man*
  (Guber-Peters, United Artists, 16 Dec 1988, $172.8m, 8 noms)
Working Girl
  (Twentieth Century-Fox, 21 Dec 1988, $64.0m, 6 noms)

GOLDEN GLOBE AWARDS

(Drama)
The Accidental Tourist
Evil Angels
  (A Cry in the Dark)
Gorillas in the Mist
Mississippi Burning
• *Rain Man*
Running on Empty
The Unbearable Lightness of Being

(Comedy/Musical)
Big
A Fish Called Wanda
Midnight Run
Who Framed Roger Rabbit?
• *Working Girl*

BRITISH ACADEMY AWARDS
Au Revoir les Enfants
Babettes Gæstebud (Babette's Feast)
A Fish Called Wanda
• *The Last Emperor*

NEW YORK – *The Accidental Tourist*
LOS ANGELES – *Little Dorrit*
BOARD OF REVIEW – *Mississippi Burning*
NATIONAL SOCIETY – *The Unbearable Lightness of Being*
LONDON – *House of Games*

"The film of greatest potential interest to the voting membership of the Academy of Motion Picture Arts and Sciences this year will go unseen by them," predicted film critic Sheila Benson in the Los Angeles Times in late November. "'Little Dorrit' is hardly an unheralded film, [but] it was conceived as a major film in two parts – six hours in all … Well, six hours. That's a pretty steep investment of time. Academy members won't be seeing it after dinner at one another's houses." Arriving from across the Atlantic with great fanfare, *Little Dorrit* was among the best reviewed releases of the year (NYT "fluent, intelligent and atmospheric … remarkable"; LAT "a pungent, hilarious film with a lovely intelligence … pure astonishment, start to finish … perfection … [a] most stunning achievement"; CT "a genuine motion picture, made with the big screen in mind … capturing not only [the book's] complex plot and myriad characters but its monumental shape and exquisite texture as well"; V "a remarkable achievement ... astounding"). While it was named Best Picture by the Los Angeles Film Critics Association, Benson glumly concluded, "a membership used to being importuned and catered-to at every turn" is unlikely to actively seek out a six-hour two-part drama "at its sole commercial location" in the whole of the Los Angeles area. "To get Academy members' attention, you have to screen a movie over and over and over again," said Benson.

Little Dorrit took out the Los Angeles prize ahead of the thriller *Dead Ringers* (NYT "mesmerizing [and] terrifically unnerving"; LAT "spellbinding"; WP "a creepy thriller … disquieting [and] visceral … [but] becomes ridiculous, painful, unbelievable and tedious"; TGM "[a] gelid masterpiece … a nightmarish parable of the human condition"; Sp "enigmatic [and] disturbing").

Three days later, the National Board of Review announced its list of the year's ten best films and neither *Little Dorrit* nor *Dead Ringers* were mentioned. The group's Best Picture winner was the civil rights drama *Mississippi Burning* (NYT "first-rate … one of the toughest, straightest, most effective fiction films about bigotry and racial violence … mesmerizing"; LAT "powerful … a shattering experience"; CST "a gritty police drama, bloody [and] passionate"; WP "a thrilling drama"; BG "ambitious [and] a compelling detective story [but] flawed"; V "one of the most potent and insightful views of racial turmoil yet produced"; Time "powerful"; SMH "outstanding"). The runner-up for the prize was *Dangerous Liaisons* (NYT "[a] handsome, intelligent adaptation"; LAT "a glidingly cinematic version of [the] play"; WP "tantalizingly wicked [and] highly diverting but ultimately unsatisfying"; BG "flat … technically well done [but] it lacks tension and layering"; V "good but incompletely realised"; TT "very polished and absorbing"; SMH "a satisfying film and a valid Oscar contender").

Two days later, another two films that had not appeared on the NBR list finished first and second in the voting by the New York Film Critics Circle. The political drama *A World Apart* led on the second ballot (NYT "a beautifully acted, maddening movie that, while expressing all the right sentiments, never goes quite far enough"; LAT "enthralling"; CST "strong and heartbreaking"; CT "this is devastating stuff, and unforgettable"; WP "where [the film] falters artistically, it gains emotionally"; BG "moving, profound, grippingly performed ... one of the year's most dramatically powerful films ... should figure in more than one Oscar category"; V "absorbing"; FQ "powerful and unusual") but was ultimately beaten narrowly by the romantic comedy-drama *The Accidental Tourist* (NYT "brings virtually nothing – no color, no nuance, not even much liveliness – to bear upon the novel on which it is based"; LAT "irresistibly funny"; CT "not a completely successful movie"; V "slow, sonorous and largely unsatisfying"). Film critic Janet Maslin slammed the outcome in The New York Times writing, "the critics' votes were scattered far and wide ... which is how this nondescript dark-horse candidate managed – quite accidentally – to emerge a winner ... 'The Accidental Tourist' doesn't speak to anyone or anything in particular [and] isn't a film that will be remembered very long".

The National Society of Film Critics, meanwhile, selected *The Unbearable Lightness of Being* (NYT "settles down to recapitulate [the novel] with fidelity and an accumulating heaviness, as well as immense length"; LAT "a fine-looking film ... [but] ultimately adds up to the unbearable heaviness of movie-making"; CST "an erotic, rambling rumination"; CT "anything but light, though it very nearly is unbearable"; BG "grand, fiery, and liberating"; V "stunning"; TGM "an unprecedented Hollywood movie: a romantic and political epic without the faintest tinge of conventional moralizing [and] also overwhelmingly, unapologetically erotic"; MFB "over-long"; Sp "quite absorbing [and] well worth seeing"). The runner-up was the Spanish comedy *Mujeres al Borde de un Ataque de Nervois (Women on the Verge of a Nervous Breakdown)*, which had earlier been named Best Foreign-Language Film by the NBR and New York circle (NYT "most entertaining ... delightful"; LAT "a funny movie, full of sly comic touches"; WP "wonderful").

Yet more contenders entered consideration when the Hollywood Foreign Press Association announced the Golden Globe nominations. Topping the list was the comedy *Working Girl*, which received six nods (NYT "enjoyable even when it isn't credible, which is most of the time"; LAT "[a] sparkling success"; WP "[a] scrumptious romantic comedy [that is] easy to watch"; V "enjoyable"; TGM "can't quite get its funny act together"). The leading drama (with five nods) was *Running on Empty* (LAT "remarkably successful ... sophisticated, uncompromising and refreshingly original ... [an] impassioned and graceful film [that] achieves a heartbreaking believability"; CT "quietly hysterical, a series of tense, clenched scenes"; V "fresh and powerful").

Among the other films overlooked by the critics' groups, but nominated for the two Best Picture Globes, were: the Australian drama *Evil Angels (A Cry in the Dark)* (NYT "suspense wars with impatience ... becomes a virtually one-character movie"; LAT "[a] masterly and resonating film"; WP "compelling"; V "[a] classy, disturbing drama"; TGM "good"; TT "realistic [and] remarkable";

SMH "a terrific piece of work ... intimate and moving and deeply disturbing"); the biopic *Gorillas in the Mist* (NYT "an engrossing but long film with a tendency to meander"; LAT "tense, vigorous, thrilling and satisfying"; WP "crashes on a rocky and meandering script"; CST "technically accomplished but the screenplay has been skimped on"; V "admirable"; TGM "visually competent but narratively thin and psychologically barren"); the road movie *Rain Man* (LAT "will disappoint no one ... [it's] singularity lies in the [acting] challenge [Dustin] Hoffman has set himself"; CT "though it's well directed, written and performed, 'Rain Man' still slips irreversibly into the so-what category ... heart-sinking predictability"; WP "never really succeeds"; BG "Hoffman's performance is what makes 'Rain Man' special"; V "quite moving [but] uneven ... never builds a great deal of momentum"; TT "succeeds with sensitivity"; SMH "immensely moving"); the comedy *Big* (NYT "engaging"; LAT "funny, warm, sophisticated and imaginative"; WP "disarming ... has a warmhearted sweetness that's invigorating"); the popular British heist comedy *A Fish Called Wanda* (NYT "it's not easy to describe the movie's accumulating dimness or to understand what went wrong"; LAT "a convulsively funny affair ... a smart farce"; CST "has one hilarious scene after another"; WP "a wonderfully zany farce"; BG "frequently hilarious"; MFB "remarkable"; S&S "a resounding success"); and the year's biggest box office smash *Who Framed Roger Rabbit?* (NYT "a film whose best moments are so novel, so deliriously funny and so crazily unexpected that they truly must be seen to be believed ... a technical marvel"; NYP "sheer enchanted entertainment"; LAT "dense, satisfying, feverishly inventive and a technical marvel ... a film that no one sees just once"; WP "an instant slapstick classic"; V "an unparalleled technical achievement"; TT "exhilarating"; Obs "a milestone ... witty, imaginative, original and intelligent [and] breathtaking [in its] technical virtuosity"; MFB "a technical and logistical landmark"; S&S "the success of the film springs principally from the seamlessness with which the live action and animation are integrated").

The HFPA avoided nominating the year's most controversial drama *The Last Temptation of Christ*, which explored the notion of Christ's human weaknesses (NYT "exceptionally ambitious, deeply troubling and, at infrequent moments, genuinely transcendent"; LAT "an intense, utterly sincere, frequently fascinating piece of art"; CST "bold ... stirs the mind and the soul"; BG "a powerful and serious film ... at times painfully earnest, often fascinating, sometimes moving"; V "powerful"; Time "[a] masterpiece"; TGM "a serious, intense, wide-ranging exploration of the conflict played out in the soul between spirit and flesh ... a courageous film"; SMH "moving and powerful").

At the Globes ceremony, *Working Girl*, as expected, claimed the Best Picture (Comedy/Musical) award. In the Best Picture (Drama) category, the winner was *Rain Man*, a film which had not even appeared on either the annual NBR or The

New York Times lists of the ten best films of the year. *Rain Man* also won the Best Picture trophy at the 1989 Berlin Film Festival. At the same time as *Rain Man* was gaining momentum with these accolades, NBR winner *Mississippi Burning* was becoming embroiled in a public debate about its historical accuracy. "'Mississippi Burning' is now on trial," declared Vincent Canby in a piece in The New York Times on 8 January, "The film is being treated with everything from seriously reasoned outrage to the sort of lazy contempt one hears expressed at cocktail parties ... Alan Parker, the film's director, must be wondering what hit him."

The Academy announced its list of nominees on 14 February, and a frontrunner finally emerged: Globe (Drama) winner *Rain Man* led the field of contenders with eight mentions, including Best Picture.

Also in contention for the top statuette were: New York winner *The Accidental Tourist*; NBR winner *Mississippi Burning*; NBR runner-up *Dangerous Liaisons*; and Globe (Comedy/Musical) winner *Working Girl*.

Among the foreign-language films overlooked by both the critics' groups and the Academy were: the Palme d'Or winner *Pelle Erobreren (Pelle the Conqueror)* (NYT "a vividly re-created, minutely detailed panorama"; LAT "a towering achievement ... an exhilarating experience unlikely to be forgotten ... [a] masterful film"; TGM "a dark work with a light touch"); BAFTA nominee *Babettes Gæstebud (Babette's Feast)* (NYT "a very handsome, very literary movie"; LAT "delectable ... told with passion, intelligence and sumptuousness"; CT "a nearly perfect art film"; WP "precise and elegant"; TGM "sumptuous cinematic fare"; S&S "near flawless"; MFB "ironic and finely judged"); *Hong Gao Liang (Red Sorghum)*, which won the Best Picture prize at the 1988 Berlin Film Festival (LAT "a movie lover's thrill ... amazing"; WP "has structural shortcomings [but it's] images intoxicate your eyes"); and *Der Himmel über Berlin (Wings of Desire)* (NYT "startlingly original at first [it] is in the end damagingly overloaded"; LAT "a magnificent movie of sublime beauty and contagious optimism"; WP "[a] soaring, soul-searching film"; BG "a spellbinder [and] a classic"; TGM "bloated transcendence"; Sp "spectacular ... mysterious and distinctive, both powerful and insubstantial ... has more surface than substance, more technique than theme").

The frontrunner status of *Rain Man* was confirmed on 11 March when the Directors Guild of America handed its annual accolade to the film's director, Barry Levinson. On Oscar night, the Academy declared *Rain Man* to be the year's Best Picture.

The Oscar champ was released in Britain just weeks before its victory in Hollywood, making it eligible for BAFTAs in the following awards season. The British Academy, however, did not even nominate *Rain Man* for 1989 Best Film BAFTA.

1988

BEST DIRECTOR

ACADEMY AWARDS
Charles Crichton for *A Fish Called Wanda*
• **Barry Levinson for *Rain Man***
Mike Nichols for *Working Girl*
Alan Parker for *Mississippi Burning*
Martin Scorsese for *The Last Temptation of Christ*

GOLDEN GLOBE AWARDS
• **Clint Eastwood – *Bird***
Barry Levinson – *Rain Man*
Sidney Lumet – *Running on Empty*
Mike Nichols – *Working Girl*
Alan Parker – *Mississippi Burning*
Fred Schepisi – *Evil Angels (A Cry in the Dark)*

DIRECTORS GUILD AWARD
Charles Crichton
  – *A Fish Called Wanda*
• **Barry Levinson – *Rain Man***
Mike Nichols – *Working Girl*
Alan Parker – *Mississippi Burning*
Robert Zemeckis
  – *Who Framed Roger Rabbit?*

BRITISH ACADEMY AWARDS
Gabriel Axel
  – *Babettes Gæstebud*
  (Babette's Feast)
Bernardo Bertolucci
  – *The Last Emperor*
Charles Crichton
  – *A Fish Called Wanda*
• **Louis Malle
  – *Au Revoir les Enfants***

NEW YORK – Chris Menges – *A World Apart*
LOS ANGELES – David Cronenberg – *Dead Ringers*
BOARD OF REVIEW – Alan Parker – *Mississippi Burning*
NATIONAL SOCIETY – Philip Kaufman – *The Unbearable Lightness of Being*
LONDON – John Huston – *The Dead*

Each of the major pre-Oscar accolades in the United States were won by different directors: former Oscar-winning cinematographer Chris Menges for *A World Apart* (NYT "Menges is an efficient, intelligent director but not a very exciting one"; LAT "told with an empathy that is strengthened by [his] refusal to sentimentalize his characters"; CT "keeps his distance"; TGM "directed sparely"); David Cronenberg for *Dead Ringers* (NYT "sleek, icy elegance ... a mesmerizing achievement"; LAT "assured"; CT "has now acquired the fluency of style, the deep sense of character and the rhetorical distance necessary to transform his obsessions into art"; TGM "a precision worthy of a classic touring car"; Sp "ham-fisted ... he fails"); Alan Parker for *Mississippi Burning* (NYT "relentless in the way [he] maintains [the film's] focus"; LAT "Parker makes sure [the mood of realism] permeates every frame of his film"; WP "Parker never lets subtlety, or the facts, hobble his moral high horse"); Philip Kaufman for *The Unbearable Lightness of Being* (CT "the film has no vision"; MFB "blunt"; Sp "has failed almost entirely to catch the book's tone"); and Clint Eastwood for *Bird* (NYT "'Bird' is less moving as a character study than it is as a tribute and as labor of love"; TGM "darkly photography, loosely constructed"; V "impressive").

Surprisingly, Parker was the only one of these directors mentioned by the Directors Guild of America, who also named: Charles Crichton for *A Fish Called Wanda* (LAT "keeps his cast's intricate comings and goings in impeccable order with a minimum of attention called to his exquisite stewardship"; CST "understands why is it usually funny to not say something, and let the audience know what is not being said, than to simply blurt it out and hope for a quick laugh ... he is a master"; WP "it has a classic madcap grace, thanks no doubt to its legendary director"; BG "skillfully makes the film appear to have more shape and drive than it has"; MFB "an expert piece of comedy packaging"; S&S "miraculously unforced ... assured"); Barry Levinson for *Rain Man* (CT "adopts a distanced, contemplative tone, allowing the dialogue to develop its own easy rhythms ... also shows a nice flair for an evocative yet non-picturesque use of locations and a swift way of establishing minor characters without resorting to caricature"; WP "has fashioned a handsome, emphatic style for the film, but it's impossible to determine what he meant it to convey"; SMH "directs with tremendous skill"); Mike Nichols for *Working Girl* (NYT "displays an uncharacteristically blunt touch"; LAT "adroit direction"); and Robert Zemeckis for *Who Framed Roger Rabbit?* (NYT "consistently cheering [due to] the direction by Robert Zemeckis"; LAT "Zemeckis has had careful hold of the thread of movie memory and cartoon delight that strings together all of [the film's] action"; TGM "as wrought by Zemeckis, the animation blend is technically brilliant"; Obs "sensitively directed").

The Academy made only one change from the Guild list: Los Angeles Film Critics Association runner-up Martin Scorsese for *The Last Temptation of Christ* (NYT "stilted ... [the film is] often more apt to announce its ideas than to illustrate them"; LAT "varies his calm moments with swirling ones, brimming with visual rapture"; V "made with tremendous cinematic skill") was named ahead of Zemeckis.

Also overlooked by the Academy were: Lawrence Kasdan for *The Accidental Tourist* (CT "deserves some credit"; WP "directed tenderly"); Stephen Frears for *Dangerous Liaisons* (LAT "notable"; CT "something cloddish and naïve still comes through in Frears' direction"; SMH "stylish"); Sidney Lumet for *Running on Empty* (NYT "has directed the film in a crisp, handsome style"; LAT "graceful"; CT "artificial ... he destroys the natural contours of the storyline"; WP "Lumet grinds [the narrative's] significant gears"); Christine Edzard for *Little Dorrit* (NYT "fluent ... a remarkable achievement"; LAT "brilliant"; CT "does a most impressive job"; BG "solidly crafted"); Penny Marshall for *Big* (NYT "minimizes the sentimentality and keeps things mercifully sweet"; LAT "directed with verve and impeccable judgment"; WP "an assured comic rhythm"; MFB "smooth and unobtrusive"); Fred Schepisi for *Evil Angels (A Cry in the Dark)* (NYT "Schepisi may have followed the facts of the case, but he has not made them comprehensible in terms of the film"; LAT "masterly"; CT "using superbly evocative widescreen compositions to evoke the tension"; WP "dilutes the drama with excessive cutaways"); Gabriel Axel for *Babettes Gæstebud (Babette's Feast)* (NYT "treats the text with self-effacing but informed modesty"; LAT "guides his cast delicately ... subtle"; WP "interprets [the novel] with great charm and gentle comedy"; TGM "a model of understatement"; MFB "finely judged"); Cannes Film Festival Best Director winner Wim Wenders for *Der Himmel über Berlin (Wings of Desire)* (NYT "enchanting, but [he] allows it to become terribly overripe ... there's a relentlessness to the direction that keeps [the film] earthbound"; LAT "the film's power is that its poetry can soar to include the miraculous"; WP "has taken all the cinematic seraphim and made them novel again"); Pedro Almodóvar for *Mujeres al Borde de un Ataque de Nervois (Women on the Verge of a Nervous Breakdown)* (NYT "farce isn't easy to pull off, but [he] is well on his way to mastering this most difficult of all screen genres"; LAT "amazingly cinematic [and] as theatrical as this film gets it never seems contrived"); Zhang Yimou for *Hong Gao Liang (Red Sorghum)* (NYT "uses a lot of compositions that may look stirring to some but just self-conscious to others"; LAT "everything seems to work on this young director's sensibilities ... amazing"; WP "you marvel at Yimou's visceral brilliance"); and Bille August for *Pelle Erobreren (Pelle the Conqueror)* (NYT "disciplined ... never indulges the pathos that is built into the story"; LAT "masterful"; WP "doesn't have the talent or the empathy to transcend the familiarity ... the film's drama seems far away").

Once again, the DGA accolade proved to be the crucial key to the Oscar race. Levinson became the thirty-seventh director in forty years to win the golden statuette after receiving the Guild honour.

BEST ACTOR

ACADEMY AWARDS
Gene Hackman as 'Rupert Anderson' in *Mississippi Burning*
Tom Hanks as 'Josh Baskin' in *Big*
• **Dustin Hoffman as 'Raymond Babbitt' in *Rain Man***
Edward James Olmos as 'Jaime Escalante' in *Stand and Deliver*
Max von Sydow as 'Pappa Lasse' in *Pelle Erobreren (Pelle the Conqueror)*

GOLDEN GLOBE AWARDS

(Drama)
Gene Hackman – *Mississippi Burning*
• **Dustin Hoffman – *Rain Man***
Tom Hulce – *Dominick and Eugene*
Edward James Olmos
    – *Stand and Deliver*
Forest Whitaker – *Bird*

(Comedy/Musical)
Michael Caine
    – *Dirty Rotten Scoundrels*
John Cleese – *A Fish Called Wanda*
Robert De Niro – *Midnight Run*
• **Tom Hanks – *Big***
Bob Hoskins
    – *Who Framed Roger Rabbit?*

BRITISH ACADEMY AWARDS
• **John Cleese – *A Fish Called Wanda***
Michael Douglas – *Fatal Attraction*
Kevin Kline – *A Fish Called Wanda*
Robin Williams – *Good Morning, Vietnam*

NEW YORK – Jeremy Irons – *Dead Ringers*
LOS ANGELES – Tom Hanks – *Big* and *Punchline*
BOARD OF REVIEW – Gene Hackman – *Mississippi Burning*
NATIONAL SOCIETY – Michael Keaton – *Beetlejuice* and *Clean and Sober*
LONDON – Leo McKern – *Travelling North*

"One of the scandals at the Cannes festival," declared Vincent Canby in The New York Times, "was that Max von Sydow did not win the best actor award." For his turn as a widower in *Pelle Erobreren (Pelle the Conqueror)*, which won the Palme d'Or, von Sydow did, however, later win Best Actor at the inaugural European Film Awards (NYT "another highlight in an already extraordinary career ... splendid"; LAT "played superbly ... with this film he crowns his career ... as splendid a portrayal as we're likely to see this or any other year"; WP "astoundingly evocative ... has so completely entered the body of this old man that he seems physically transformed"; TGM "gives the performance of a career already marked with career-making performances, painting a complex portrait of a simple man"; TT "one of the finest, most shaded characterizations of von Sydow's career"). He was later rewarded with his first Oscar nomination.

The winner in Cannes, meanwhile, was Forest Whitaker for playing jazz great Charlie Parker in *Bird* (NYT "[his] performance is acceptable, possibly limited by its rather commonplace context … he doesn't convey much of the man's legendary charm"; NYP "extraordinary"; V "excellent"; TGM "holds the camera with a towering performance that misses only one aspect of the musician's personality, his legendary sexual charisma"; TT "excellent"). Whitaker was nominated for the Golden Globe (Drama) but was overlooked when the Oscar nominations were announced.

Nominated for the Oscar alongside von Sydow, each for the first time, were both Edward James Olmos as an inspirational teacher in *Stand and Deliver* (NYT "has transformed himself so completely … seems to be living and breathing this role rather than merely playing it"; LAT "Olmos' self-effacing magnetism is at the center of a rousing true story"; CT "[a] superior performance [that is] Oscar-calibre"; V "commanding"; MFB "superbly persuasive") and Los Angeles Film Critics Association honouree and Globe (Comedy/Musical) winner Tom Hanks as a young boy in a man's body in *Big* (NYT "[a] funny, flawless impression … wide-eyed, excited and wonderfully guileless, [he] is an absolute delight"; NYP "finds a vulnerability and sweetness for his character that's quite appealing"; LAT "a personal triumph"; WP "shows us what a generous, likable performer he can be … Hanks makes Josh's tentative bluffing seem like high-wire improvisation … astoundingly deft … his performance has an endearing, lost-innocent quality and without indulging himself, he never lets us lose sight of the fact that we're watching a kid"; V "completely engaging"; MFB "brilliant").

Included for a fourth time was previous winner Gene Hackman, who had received his third National Board of Review accolade, finished runner-up in Los Angeles and been honoured at the Berlin Film Festival, for his portrayal of an FBI agent in *Mississippi Burning* (NYT "sensational … a sure Oscar nominee and, very likely, a winner [in] possibly the best-written role of his career"; NYP "marvelous"; LAT "played exquisitely"; V "steals the picture").

Recognised for a sixth time was previous winner Dustin Hoffman, who had finished runner-up in voting by the New York Film Critics Circle after leading on the first ballot, as an autistic savant in *Rain Man* (NYT "a display of sustained virtuosity … remarkable"; LAT "hypnotically interesting, and, through impeccable timing, sometimes terribly funny"; CT "may have found the perfect role for his late career"; WP "in shaping the character, Hoffman concentrates on the externals [and consequently] Raymond never becomes accessible to us as a character … it's Hoffman's failure that sinks the picture"; BG "a staggering performance ... a little stagy, a little self-consciously virtuosic and utterly self-aware ... it's a technique performance [but] what Hoffman does with that technique is extraordinary"; TT "outstanding ... truly extraordinary"; MFB "careful, discreet and scrupulously detailed"; Time "meticulously observed"; SMH "a formidably sustained piece of acting ... certain to put Hoffman in the front running for an Oscar").

In addition to Cannes winner Whitaker, the Academy overlooked other prize-winning performances such as: New York winner Jeremy Irons as twins in *Dead Ringers* (NYT "impressive ... [a] seamless performance, a schizophrenic marvel ... Irons invests these bizarre, potentially freakish characters with so much intelligence and so much real feeling"; LAT "plays the two with throwaway brilliance [and] creates details of character so clear that without clue of clothes or words, we only need to scan his face to know which twin we have in front of us"; CT "a brilliant dual performance"; TGM "magnificent"; WP "creepy"; V "first-rate"; TT "[a] virtuoso [performance]"; Sp "subtle"); National Society of Film Critics winner Michael Keaton as both a demon in *Beetlejuice* (NYT "Keaton could have save 'Beetlejuice' for me, but he's really a supporting character, not on screen long enough to pull things together"; LAT "exuberant"; CT "showcases a funny Keaton"; WP "the juice that makes it go"; TGM "steals the movie") and a cocaine addict in *Clean and Sober* (NYT "terrific and convincing"; LAT "daringly and consummately played"; CT "energetic but uninspired, going through the standard moves with an extra edge of jangling freneticism"; WP "a surprisingly nimble dramatic debut"; BG "this is Keaton in his first serious role, and he brings it off handily, thanks to the shrewd way in which it's been tailored to his manic persona ... harrowingly convincing"; TGM "too limited to suggest what the screenplay does not and yet he does manage to hold our interest ... there's compelling tension to his performance"); and BAFTA winner John Cleese in *A Fish Called Wanda* (NYT "[a] sense of elevated madness is missing from his performance"; LAT "[on television] Cleese was wizardly at uncovering and railing against the qualities in the British character that most appalled him ... [here] he throws those qualities in bas relief"; CST "flawless"; S&S "gives full measure ... plays with a gangly and masterfully shell-shocked sincerity").

Others by-passed for a nomination included: Willem Dafoe as both Christ in *The Last Temptation of Christ* (NYT "overwhelming"; LAT "his growth over the course of the film is steady and powerful"; V "utterly compelling"; MFB "stylised"; Time "perfect") and an FBI agent in *Mississippi Burning* (NYT "functional"; NYP "wooden"; LAT "played exquisitely"; V "a disciplined and noteworthy portrayal"); John Malkovich in *Dangerous Liaisons* (NYT "unexpectedly fine"; LAT "seems to have been born with irony in his veins"; CT "seems to be constantly straining for [his] role"; WP "brings a fascinating dimension to his character"; BG "composure is what's most sorely lacking in [his] performance"; V "unconvincing"; S&S "superb"; SMH "particularly effective"); Tom Cruise in *Rain Man* (LAT "Cruise gives his loosest, most authoritative performance since 'Risky Business' but one with far greater range and maturity"; WP "a passable performance, but he can't supply the insight into Charlie that we need"; SMH "has created a full-blooded, memorable character"); William Hurt in *The Accidental Tourist* (NYT "played dourly"; LAT "finely observed"; V "remains expressionless"; MFB "pitched at just the right note"; Time "monotonous"); Globe nominee Bob Hoskins in *Who Framed Roger Rabbit?* (NYT "funny"; LAT "the treasure of the piece is Hoskins' pungent, visceral comic performance ... modulates his performance here from the subdued to the cartoon-manic to remain the absolute linchpin of the piece"; WP "wonderful"; Obs "wonderfully endearing ... [played with] total conviction"; S&S "Hoskins pitches his performance dead right ... he treats the rabbit like a spoilt, fractious child, but never makes the mistake of trying to upstage him"); Daniel Day-Lewis in *The Unbearable Lightness of Being* (NYT "surprisingly fine"; LAT "beautifully played"; MFB "affects a mannered smile [and] lacks that aura of openness to other possibilities that would have enriched, say, Warren Beatty or Dustin Hoffman in his part"; Sp "his performance is thoughtful and interesting"); both Ray Liotta (WP "plays respectably against type"; BG "convinces"; V "impresses") and Globe nominee Tom Hulce (CT "couldn't be more brazen in his begging for the audience's love"; WP "compelling"; V "believable") in *Dominick and Eugene* (NYT "the two leading actors do a superb job of bringing these characters to life ... they play their roles forthrightly, without any tendency to tearjerk"; LAT "rich, unsentimental, finely detailed characterizations"); and both Globe nominee Michael Caine (NYT "don't mistake what [he] does with the work of a straight man ... this is a superb comic performance ... Caine nearly walks off with the movie"; LAT "it's the droll snap with which Caine executes [his character's] manoeuvres that makes watching him such pleasure"; BG "a marvel of economy, unreeling exactly as much technique as he needs"; TGM "terrific ... an impeccable bit of comedy"; MFB "deft") and Steve Martin (NYT "splendidly funny ... a performance of inspired goofiness"; BG "virtuosically controlled blatancy"; TGM "balances things perfectly"; MFB "inspired") in *Dirty Rotten Scoundrels* (NYT "work together with an exuberant ease that's a joy to watch").

The four major critics' groups had all honoured a different actor, but none were the Oscar frontrunner. As expected, at the Academy Awards, the Globe (Drama) winner Dustin Hoffman received his second statuette as Best Actor.

At the British Academy Awards Cleese, who had been snubbed in Hollywood, was named Best Actor. Hoffman was nominated for the BAFTA the following year, but was outpolled by that year's Best Actor Oscar winner.

1988

BEST ACTRESS

ACADEMY AWARDS
Glenn Close as 'the Marquise de Merteuil' in *Dangerous Liaisons*
• **Jodie Foster as 'Sarah Tobias' in *The Accused***
Melanie Griffith as 'Tess McGill' in *Working Girl*
Meryl Streep as 'Lindy Chamberlain' in *Evil Angels (A Cry in the Dark)*
Sigourney Weaver as 'Dian Fossey' in *Gorillas in the Mist*

GOLDEN GLOBE AWARDS

(Drama)
• **Jodie Foster – *The Accused***
Christine Lahti – *Running on Empty*
• **Shirley MacLaine**
  – *Madame Sousatzka*
Meryl Streep
  – Evil Angels (A Cry in the Dark)
• **Sigourney Weaver**
  – *Gorillas in the Mist*

(Comedy/Musical)
Jamie Lee Curtis
  – A Fish Called Wanda
• **Melanie Griffith – *Working Girl***
Amy Irving – *Crossing Delancey*
Michelle Pfeiffer
  – Married to the Mob
Susan Sarandon – *Bull Durham*

BRITISH ACADEMY AWARDS
Stéphane Audran – *Babettes Gæstebud (Babette's Feast)*
Cher – *Moonstruck*
Jamie Lee Curtis – *A Fish Called Wanda*
• **Maggie Smith – *The Lonely Passion of Judith Hearne***

NEW YORK – Meryl Streep – *Evil Angels (A Cry in the Dark)*
LOS ANGELES – Christine Lahti – *Running on Empty*
BOARD OF REVIEW – Jodie Foster – *The Accused*
NATIONAL SOCIETY – Judy Davis – *High Tide*
LONDON – Stéphane Audran – *Babettes Gæstebud (Babette's Feast)*

In an unprecedented (and somewhat ridiculous) result, three actresses shared the Golden Globe (Drama): National Board of Review winner and New York Film Critics Circle runner-up Jodie Foster as a gang rape victim in *The Accused* (NYT "splendid [in a] devastating performance ... Foster makes her a startling character with plenty of tough realism and no self-pity"; LAT "an extraordinary performance, bolstered by an innate gallantry, a tensile strength of skill and an observation of physical detail that completely outclass her vehicle ... powerful"; CT "Sarah [is] given a seething intensity by Foster"; WP "[a] vibrant performance … creates the ultimate victim without ever becoming a wimp, mixing dignity with defenselessness"; BG "she remains interesting even after the script's heavy-handed message is delivered … a terrific performance"; V "is edgy and spunky in by far her most impressive adult performance to date"; TGM "[a] brilliant performance … [she] should win an Academy Award for her strutting, tightly-coiled, trembling portrayal"; TT "both aggressive and vulnerable"; MFB "a tough, sympathetic performance"); previous winner and Venice Film Festival honouree Shirley MacLaine as an eccentric piano teacher in *Madame Sousatzka* (NYT "plays this to the hilt and beyond, which is just what the role requires … [she] rivets the attention at every turn … [she is] liable to be laughing all the way to the Academy Awards"; NYP "one of the best performances of the year"; LAT "goes right to the edge but never quite falls off … no question about it, MacLaine triumphs as Sousatzka"; CT "can't really be described as acting … never succeeds in convincing the audience that she is the title character, but then, she never seems to want to … somehow it's the sheer obviousness of the performance that's most entertaining … she doesn't act as much as she exudes"; MFB "a parade of mannerisms rather than a character in action"; Time "the sort of acting that wins Oscars"; SMH "a scene-stealing, slightly over-the-top performance"); and Sigourney Weaver as anthropologist Dian Fossey in *Gorillas in the Mist* (NYT "[a] fine performance"; LAT "an absolutely stunning performance"; CST "makes [Fossey] passionate and private, and has an exquisite tenderness and tact in her delicate scenes with wild animals"; WP "is in her element here, and singlehandedly propels [the film] with a winning portrayal"; V "utterly believable and riveting … outstanding"; BG "riveting when she's with the primates [but her later] explosions seem stagy, not the real thing"; TGM "has no base to build on"; TT "convinces totally"; S&S "[her] resourceful performance gives considerable strength to what would otherwise be a lightweight allegory"; MFB "carefully played"; Time "strong").

The two unrewarded nominees were the Los Angeles Film Critics Association and New York Film Critics Circle winners: Christine Lahti as a 1960s activist on the run from the FBI in *Running on Empty* (NYP "[a] superb lead performance"; LAT "[a] superlative performance"; CT "seems strained and obvious"; WP "another Christine Lahti experiment in diffident eccentricity"; V "superb") and Meryl Streep as the Australian woman tried for murder after her baby daughter was taken by a dingo in *Evil Angels (A Cry in the Dark)* (NYT "another stunning performance … the kind of virtuosity that seems to redefine the possibilities of screen acting … one of the best performances of her career"; LAT "Streep dares monumentally … it's a performance to annihilate those who see her facility with accents as 'all' there is to her art"; WP "Streep – yes, with another perfect accent – brings her customary skilfulness to the part. It's not a showy performance, but the heroine's internal struggle seems to come from the

actress' pores"; V "a highly self-effacing performance"; TGM "she's good …
[her] remoteness and self-conscious technique work to her advantage here"; TT
"remarkable"; Time "no actress has ever played a victim more austerely … she
refuses to force this character on us"; SMH "extraordinary").

In a major shock, one of the three Globe (Drama) winners was subsequently
omitted from the list of Oscar nominees: previous winner MacLaine, who had
been favoured by many observers to claim a second statuette. She was the first
winner of the Best Actress (Drama) Globe to be overlooked by the Academy.
The unexpected exclusion of MacLaine overshadowed the omission of Lahti,
who had also been backed by some as a dark horse chance for the Oscar.

Also passed over for consideration were: European Film Award winner and
NSFC runner-up Carmen Maura in *Mujeres al Borde de un Ataque de Nervois
(Women on the Verge of a Nervous Breakdown)* (NYT "superb [and] wonderful
[in a] grand performance"; LAT "a splendid showcase for the wonderfully
expressive Maura … remarkable"); Cannes Film Festival co-winner Barbara
Hershey in *A World Apart* (NYT "beautifully acted … splendid"; CT "a marvel
of balance"; BG "grippingly performed"; V "naturalistic and believable"; FQ
"unflinching, masterfully controlled"; MFB "strong and dignified"; SMH
"totally convincing"); London Film Critics winner Stéphane Audran in *Babettes
Gæstebud (Babette's Feast)* (NYT "dominates the movie"; WP "perfection"; V
"warm and witty"; TGM "a letter-perfect performance"; S&S "one of her finest
hours"); Whoopi Goldberg in *Clara's Heart* (NYT "prize-worthy [but]
unfortunately Goldberg operates in a vacuum … her performance might well
have emerged as a sentimental favourite [for the Oscar] if the film itself weren't
so thin"; LAT "[a] sturdy, exquisitely shaded character study"; CT "[the] lone
bright spot in [the film] … [has] one of those tremulous but brave monologues
that win Oscar nominations"); Juliette Binoche in *The Unbearable Lightness of
Being* (NYT "surprisingly fine – both modest and intense"; LAT "beautifully
played"; V "enchanting"; MFB "endows her character with a full emotional
spectrum"); Natasha Richardson in the title role in *Patty Hearst* (NYT
"absolutely smashing … one of the year's three or four top performances by an
actress"; LAT "exemplary … the one solid virtue of [the film]"; CST "[a]
visceral, intuitive portrayal … remarkable"; WP "[her] performance is as good
as [the director] will allow it to be"; TT "convincing"); Susan Sarandon in *Bull
Durham* (NYT "she takes control of the film"; LAT "[played with] warmth and
brightness … [but] for all the tough/soft dimension that Sarandon gives her, is
really a paper-thin vehicle for a man's warmest imaginings"; WP "she makes it
more than just a film about baseball"; V "never believable"); Gena Rowlands in
Another Woman (NYT "a riveting screen image"; LAT "struggles prodigiously";
CT "the main victim of 'Another Woman' is Rowlands … throughout, [she] can
be seen straining at the limitations that Allen has imposed upon her"; CST "to

see [the film] is to get an insight into how good an actress [she] has been all along"; V "luminous and absorbing"; MFB "flawlessly performed"); Michelle Pfeiffer in *Married to the Mob* (NYT "turns Angela's plight into something funny, but [she is] readily upstaged"; LAT "could not be improved on ... her performance is the picture's linchpin – warm, delicately timed and utterly infectious"; WP "has the pivotal role of the movie and perhaps of her career ... shedding her WASP identity completely"); and Gong Li in *Hong Gao Liang (Red Sorghum)* (LAT "seems to grow in maturity and command before our eyes"; WP "exquisite").

National Society of Film Critics winner Judy Davis was ineligible for Oscar consideration for the Australian film *High Tide* as it been given a limited release in Los Angeles in December 1987 to qualify for the Academy Awards prior to its wide release elsewhere in North America the following February.

The Academy nominated previous winner and Globe (Drama) nominee Streep for an eighth time in eleven years along with Globe (Drama) co-winners Foster and Weaver, and Globe (Comedy/Musical) winner Melanie Griffith in *Working Girl* (NYT "[a] pure pleasure"; NYP "inflects every sentence with vulnerability, strength, sly humor and sex appeal ... mesmerizing"; LAT "[the film] is the sparkling success that it is because of the sheer irresistibility of Griffith"; WP "luminous ... the movie glows from her"; TGM "[the film's] one flawless note ... an impeccably tuned performance"; TT "[a] warm and supple performance"; S&S "delightfully played").

The frontrunner for the Academy Award, however, was an actress who had not featured in the critics' voting or been nominated for the Globe: Glenn Close as a scheming French aristocrat in *Dangerous Liaisons* (NYT "nothing Miss Close has done on the screen before approaches the richness and comic delicacy of her work as the Marquise ... an elegant performance"; LAT "has made Merteuil so overbearingly majestic that she very nearly swamps the picture"; CT "seems to be constantly straining for [her] role"; BG "Close has moments [and] she's the closest any of the cast come to projecting the requisite composure"; V "clearly relishes the role and handles it adroitly"; S&S "superb"; MFB "beautifully acted"; SMH "makes the Marquise a genuinely chilling character"). Close had been among the nominees the previous year for *Fatal Attraction* and was a sentimental (as well as a respected and acclaimed) favourite as she had gone home empty-handed four times over the previous six years.

On the big night, however, Close's fifth nomination proved no more productive than her previous bids. The winner of the Oscar was Foster.

At the British Academy Awards the following year, Close, Foster and Griffith were all nominated as Best Actress but lost to Pauline Collins in *Shirley Valentine*, an unsuccessful Oscar nominee that year. Streep, meanwhile, won the Best Actress prize at the Cannes Film Festival for *Evil Angels*.

BEST SUPPORTING ACTOR

ACADEMY AWARDS
Alec Guinness as 'William Dorrit' in *Little Dorrit*
• **Kevin Kline as 'Otto' in *A Fish Called Wanda***
Martin Landau as 'Abe Karatz' in *Tucker: The Man and His Dream*
River Phoenix as 'Danny Pope' in *Running on Empty*
Dean Stockwell as 'Tony "the Tiger" Russo' in *Married to the Mob*

GOLDEN GLOBE AWARDS
Alec Guinness – *Little Dorrit*
Neil Patrick Harris – *Clara's Heart*
Raul Julia – *Moon Over Parador*
• **Martin Landau – *Tucker: The Man and His Dream***
Lou Diamond Phillips – *Stand and Deliver*
River Phoenix – *Running on Empty*

BRITISH ACADEMY AWARDS
Joss Ackland – *White Mischief*
Peter O'Toole – *The Last Emperor*
• **Michael Palin – *A Fish Called Wanda***
David Suchet – *A World Apart*

NEW YORK – Dean Stockwell – *Married to the Mob* and *Tucker: The Man and His Dream*
LOS ANGELES – Alec Guinness – *Little Dorrit*
BOARD OF REVIEW – River Phoenix – *Running on Empty*
NATIONAL SOCIETY – Dean Stockwell – *Married to the Mob* and *Tucker: The Man and His Dream*

In a major surprise, Kevin Kline won the Oscar as an unstable criminal prone to insane jealousy in the comedy *A Fish Called Wanda* (LAT "deliriously dotty"; CST "flawless"; WP "Kline is worth the price of admission ... plays the character gleefully ... an outrageous performance on the ledge"; BG "turns in a very funny over-the-top performance"; V "hilarious"; S&S "a perfect over-energised foil to Cleese"). Kline, who had not been considered for the critics' prizes or nominated for the Golden Globe, outpolled the four actors who had collected all the major critics' accolades and the Golden Globe.

Previous Best Actor winner Alec Guinness won the Los Angeles Film Critics Association award (and was runner-up for the New York Film Critics Circle and

National Society of Film Critics plaudits) and received his fourth Oscar nomination as a debtor in *Little Dorrit* (NYT "he has rarely given a more finely judged performance ... unforgettable"; LAT "the towering achievement of his later years ... infinitely subtle shadings"; CT "has the great role of his late career ... he paints the portrait of his character stroke by considered stroke"; V "quite brilliant ... should reap awards when prize-giving time comes around"). He was the only one of the nominees to be absent from the Oscar ceremony.

Martin Landau claimed the Globe, was runner-up in the voting in Los Angeles and received his first Oscar nod as the title character's business partner in *Tucker: The Man and His Dream* (LAT "impressive ... there doesn't seem to be any emotion or subtlety he can't express"; WP "unrecognizable ... perfect"; V "highly sympathetic, sometimes moving").

Dean Stockwell won the New York and NSFC prizes for his performances in *Tucker: The Man and His Dream* (WP "Stockwell's delightfully demented Howard Hughes makes his throwaway cameo practically worth the price of admission") and as a Mafia boss in *Married to the Mob* (NYT "the film's biggest treat"; LAT "another of [his] indispensable contributions to current films"; V "a hoot"; TGM "exceptional"). He garnered his first mention from the Academy for the latter.

Eighteen-year old River Phoenix won the National Board of Review prize and his only Oscar nomination for his performance in the arguably leading role of the musically talented son in the drama *Running on Empty* (NYT "played outstandingly well"; LAT "[a] superlative performance"; CT "[Lumet] does considerable damage to River Phoenix, who has been instructed to fiddle with his glasses as often as possible"; WP "only River Phoenix [shows] signs of life"; V "superb [and] convincing"; TT "attractively played").

In London, Kline was nominated for the Best Actor BAFTA, but lost to co-star John Cleese. The supporting prize was won by one of his other co-stars, Michael Palin as a stammering, animal-loving criminal (CST "flawless").

Palin was overlooked in Hollywood, as were: Joss Ackland in *White Mischief* (NYT "excellent"; LAT "especially strong"; CT "a fine performance"; MFB "excellent"); fifteen-year old Globe nominee Neil Patrick Harris in *Clara's Heart* (NYT "does a good job [and] really holds his own"; LAT "delightful"; WP "impressive"; V "a smashing screen debut"); Globe nominee Lou Diamond Phillips in *Stand and Deliver* (NYT "good"; S&S "good"); Tim Robbins in *Bull Durham* (NYT "extremely funny ... has what could be the dream part of a career"; LAT "played with goofy, young-stud bravado and residual honesty"; V "good"; TT "makes the film sparkle"); Morgan Freeman in *Clean and Sober* (NYT "terrific"; TGM "splendid"); and Peter Capaldi in *Dangerous Liaisons* (LAT "excellent").

BEST SUPPORTING ACTRESS

ACADEMY AWARDS
Joan Cusack as 'Cyn' in *Working Girl*
• **Geena Davis as 'Muriel Pritchett' in *The Accidental Tourist***
Frances McDormand as 'Mrs Pell' in *Mississippi Burning*
Michelle Pfeiffer as 'Madame de Tourvel' in *Dangerous Liaisons*
Sigourney Weaver as 'Katherine Parker' in *Working Girl*

GOLDEN GLOBE AWARDS
Sonia Braga – *Moon Over Parador*
Barbara Hershey – *The Last Temptation of Christ*
Lena Olin – *The Unbearable Lightness of Being*
Diane Venora – *Bird*
• **Sigourney Weaver – *Working Girl***

BRITISH ACADEMY AWARDS
Maria Aitken – *A Fish Called Wanda*
Anne Archer – *Fatal Attraction*
Judi Dench – *A Handful of Dust*
• **Olympia Dukakis – *Moonstruck***

NEW YORK – Diane Venora – *Bird*
LOS ANGELES – Geneviève Bujold – *Dead Ringers* and *The Moderns*
BOARD OF REVIEW – Frances McDormand – *Mississippi Burning*
NATIONAL SOCIETY – Mercedes Ruehl – *Married to the Mob*

Sigourney Weaver won the Best Supporting Actress Golden Globe as a vain and double-crossing broker out-witted by her secretary in the comedy *Working Girl* (LAT "with impregnable self-confidence, Weaver slips deliciously into the role, playing the shrewd corporate shrew as though the role had been molded on her"; Time "brilliant") and was a co-winner of the Best Actress (Drama) Globe for her performance in *Gorillas in the Mist*. She subsequently earned Oscar nominations for both performances. As the previous four people to earn such double nominations had all received the supporting statuette, the double Golden Globe winning Weaver was considered a certainty to claim the Oscar in the secondary category, even though she had not been considered for any of the critics' prizes.

In what The New York Times later called "a major surprise", however, the Academy Award was won by another actress who had not featured in the critics' votes and who had not even been nominated for the Globe: first-time nominee

Geena Davis as the optimistic dog-trainer in *The Accidental Tourist* (NYT "tries hard but is sandbagged by her role"; CT "brings great charm, energy and singularity to [the] role"; WP "is like a crack of lightning in this bracing performance"; V "compelling"; SMH "steals the movie").

Also nominated for the Oscar (all for the first-time) were: Joan Cusack as a secretary in *Working Girl* (NYT "[goes] beyond simple caricature"; NYP "very funny"; TT "striking"); National Board of Review winner Frances McDormand as the battered wife in *Mississippi Burning* (NYT "surprisingly moving"; NYP "very fine"; LAT "brilliantly performed"; V "[a] glowing performance"; TT "[a] nicely shaded performance"); and Michelle Pfeiffer as the virtuous noblewoman in *Dangerous Liaisons* (NYT "[a] happy surprise"; LAT "touching [and has] the genuine trembling eroticism that this film must have"; WP "nothing is harder to play than virtue and Pfeiffer embodies it"; V "touching").

Overlooked were: New York Film Critics Circle winner Diane Venora in *Bird* (NYT "[a] smart, no-nonsense characterization"; NYP "strong and capable"; LAT "an almost eerily flawless performance"; V "riveting"; TT "excellent"); Los Angeles Film Critics Association winner Geneviève Bujold in *Dead Ringers* (NYT "[the character] is given real substance by [Bujold]"; LAT "splendid"; WP "spookily played"; V "first-rate"; TGM "[has] created a character sensually mysterious yet paradoxically transparent"; MFB "gives an almost somnambulist performance at times"); National Society of Film Critics winner Mercedes Ruehl in *Married to the Mob* (WP "hilarious [and] majestic … stealing scenes but never the show"; TGM "exceptional"); thirteen-year old New York prize runner-up and Cannes co-honouree Jodhi May in *A World Apart* (NYT "remarkably fine"; BG "riveting … strikes just the right balance"; V "naturalistic and believable"; SMH "gives one of those performances that linger in the memory"); NSFC runner-up Lena Olin in *The Unbearable Lightness of Being* (NYT "surprisingly fine – both modest and intense"; LAT "beautifully played"; V "enchanting"; MFB "duly energetic"); Barbara Hershey as Mary Magdalene in *The Last Temptation of Christ* (NYT "played in fiery style"; LAT "the picture's next strongest characterization [after that by Willem Dafoe]"); previous winner Anjelica Huston in *A Handful of Dust* (NYT "stunning"); Kathy Baker in *Clean and Sober* (NYT "terrific … combines toughness and tenderness in unexpected ways"; LAT "daringly and consummately played"; CST "superb"; BG "terrific … you can't take your eyes off her"); previous winner Peggy Ashcroft in *Madame Sousatzka*, for which she'd be a BAFTA nominee the following year (NYT "wonderful"); and Catherine O'Hara in *Beetlejuice* (LAT "shows us Delia is so funny because she is absolutely humorless"; TGM "at her most deliciously mannered").

Weaver was nominated for the BAFTA the following year, but was outpolled again, by Michelle Pfeiffer in *Dangerous Liaisons*.

BEST PICTURE

ACADEMY AWARDS

Born on the Fourth of July
  (Ho & Ixtlan, Universal, 145 mins, 20 Dec 1989, $70.0m, 8 noms)
Dead Poets Society
  (Touchstone, Buena Vista, 128 mins, 2 Jun 1989, $95.8m, 4 noms)
• Driving Miss Daisy
  (Zanuck, Warner Bros., 99 mins, 13 Dec 1989, $106.5, 9 noms)
Field of Dreams
  (Gordon Co, Universal, 107 mins, 21 Apr 1989, $64.4m, 3 noms)
My Left Foot
  (Ferndale, Granada, Miramax, 98 mins, 23 Sep 1989, $14.7 noms, 5 noms)

GOLDEN GLOBE AWARDS

(Drama)

• Born on the Fourth of July
Crimes and Misdemeanors
Dead Poets Society
Do the Right Thing
Glory

(Comedy/Musical)

• Driving Miss Daisy
The Little Mermaid
Shirley Valentine
War of the Roses
When Harry Met Sally...

PRODUCERS GUILD AWARD

Born on the Fourth of July
Dead Poets Society
• Driving Miss Daisy
Field of Dreams
Glory
Henry V
My Left Foot
When Harry Met Sally...

BRITISH ACADEMY AWARDS

• Dead Poets Society
My Left Foot
Shirley Valentine
When Harry Met Sally...

NEW YORK – *My Left Foot*
LOS ANGELES – *Do the Right Thing*
BOARD OF REVIEW – *Driving Miss Daisy*
NATIONAL SOCIETY – *Drugstore Cowboy*
LONDON – *Distant Voices, Still Lives*

At the Cannes Film Festival, the favourite for the Palme d'Or was the race relations drama *Do the Right Thing* (NYT "one terrific movie ... both funny and surrealistically sorrowful ... a remarkable piece of work"; LAT "stunning ...

complex, bravura movie making [and] also hugely entertaining"; CT "superior ... a sumptuous work"; BG "the year's most accomplished piece of American film making so far ... a complicated, metaphorical movie"; V "combines a forceful statement with solid entertainment"). In an upset, however, the prestigious accolade was presented to *sex, lies and videotape* (NYT "astonishing ... one of the freshest American films of the decade"; LAT "electrifying ... compelling"; V "one of the best American independent films in quite a long while"; TT "fully deserves its Cannes prize"; MFB "a modest chamber piece in which necessity has given birth to invention ... an intimate essay in which an elliptical, observation style, improvisatory performances and perceptive script combine to both entertain and unsettle"; SMH "impressive"). Controversially, neither film was nominated by the Academy.

At the end of the year, the National Board of Review selected *Driving Miss Daisy*, a drama about an elderly Southern widow with an African-American chauffeur (NYT "most successful"; LAT "musty and schematic"; WP "[a] lovely comedy"; TGM "wonderful"; SMH "a charmer"). The runner-up was *Henry V*, a British film version of the William Shakespeare play (NYT "exceptional ... a genuine triumph"; LAT "splendid ... thrilling ... [has a] biting, complex intelligence"; WP "[an] audacious, resonant, passionate film ... everything about this remarkable production is exhilaratingly unexpected"; BG "astonishing"; V "stirring, gritty and enjoyable'"; TT "clear, swift-moving"; SMH "impressive [and] compelling"). *sex, lies and videotape* polled third.

Two days later, the Los Angeles Film Critics Association championed *Do the Right Thing*, which had been a surprising absentee from the NBR's top ten list. The runner-up was *Drugstore Cowboy*, an independent drama about young drug addicts (NYT "absorbing"; LAT "an electrifying movie without one misstep or one conventional moment ... alert, razor-funny and compulsively watchable"; CST "one of the best films in the long tradition of American outlaw road movies ... poignant and effective"; WP "[a] stunningly bold and eccentric film ... it keeps coming at you in surprising, dazzling ways"; BG "fresh, gutsy"; V "provocative"; TGM "an exceptionally courageous film").

In New York, *Do the Right Thing* led after the first and second rounds of voting by the critics' circle, but eventually finished third with 24 points. The circle presented its top plaudit to the biopic *My Left Foot* which scored 36 points (NYT "an intelligent, beautifully acted adaptation"; NYer "exhilarating"; WP "the most passionately empathetic film about a physical affliction ever made"; BG "exhilarating ... there isn't a false note or a sentimental one in this joy of a film"; V "moving" and "excellent"; Sp "one of the most remarkable films of the year") ahead of *Enemies, A Love Story* with 31 points (NYT "deeply felt, fiercely evocative ... presents a very full spectrum of complicated and sometimes darkly funny emotions"; LAT "stunning ... a richly, satisfying, perfectly realized work

... may be the year's finest and most complex [movie]"; CST "an intriguing film"; WP "sophisticated ... develops into a heartbreakingly resonant [farce] ... a deeply, fully human work"; V "haunting, mordantly amusing, deliciously sexy"; TGM "esthetically sophisticated [and] psychologically rich").

Early in the new year, the Los Angeles runner-up *Drugstore Cowboy* claimed the National Society of Film Critics Best Picture prize with 35 points, ahead of *Enemies, A Love Story* with 20 points.

Leading the field of Golden Globe contenders, each with five nominations were: *Born on the Fourth of July*, a drama about Vietnam veterans (NYT "a film of visceral power ... harrowing and inspiring ... it's a film drawn on a very broad canvas, a rolling, furiously turbulent work of social history"; V "the most gripping, devastating, telling and understanding film about the Vietnam War ever"; TGM "always honest and it frequently moves the audience to tears [but fails] to reify the excessively familiar"); *Glory*, a drama about the African-Americans who fought for the North in the U.S. Civil War (NYT "a good, moving, complicated film"; LAT "splendid ... an eloquent, heart-tugging Civil War epic [although] a touch self-congratulatory"; WP "art with its convictions showing ... great clanking liberal movie-making ... as manipulative as it is uplifting"; V "stirring"; TGM "wonderful ... a rousing, disturbing, inspiring and occasionally depressing war movie"); and *When Harry Met Sally...*, a popular romantic comedy (NYT "funny but amazingly hollow ... cute and sentimental rather than romantic and charming"; WP "a sweet, embracable comedy ... a movie that walks on air"; TGM "warm and witty"; TT "ingratiating").

At the Globe ceremony, *Driving Miss Daisy* won the top three awards in the Comedy/Musical categories, but the evening's big winner was *Born on the Fourth of July*, winning Best Picture (Drama), Director and two other trophies.

When the Oscar nominees were announced nearly a month later, *Driving Miss Daisy* led the field with nine mentions, including Best Picture, but in a major surprise was overlooked for Best Director. This appeared to rule it out of contention for the Academy's top statuette as no film had won the Best Picture Oscar without a nomination for its director since 1931/32. This left *Born on the Fourth of July*, which had garnered eight nods, as the apparent frontrunner.

Also nominated for the Best Picture Oscar were: New York winner *My Left Foot*; the drama *Dead Poets Society*, about students at a New England boys' school in the 1950s (NYT "dim, sad ... too heavy for its own good"; LAT "impressive ... commands respect and affection"; CT "an oppressively tasteful, self-important melodrama ... refreshing but obvious"; WP "touching ... solid, smart entertainment"; V "lyrical, gorgeous"; MFB "has no convincing atmosphere at all"); and *Field of Dreams*, an inspirational baseball drama (NYT "a work so smartly written, so beautifully filmed, so perfectly acted, that it does the almost impossible trick of turning sentimentality into true emotion"; LAT "about as heartfelt a movie as any major studio has given us recently … but there's something missing"; CST "a delicate movie, a fragile construction of one goofy fantasy after another … but it has the courage to be about exactly what it promises"; CT "shrewd and accomplished [but] there's still something uncomfortably manipulative about it"; TGM "a daring movie … to deny the film its charm would be to deny ourselves our hopes"; MFB "essentially a charming fantasy"; S&S "slow-footed flummery lacking inner conviction"; Sp "effusive sentimentality [and a] determination to manipulate its audience's emotions").

In addition to the Academy's omission of *Do the Right Thing* and *sex, lies and videotape*, The New York Times called *Glory* "the most startling omission in the best picture category." Among the other acclaimed films by-passed by Academy members were: *The Fabulous Baker Boys* (NYT "[a] rapturously moody romance"; LAT "salty and sexy"; CT "smooth and smoky"; WP "at once smart and nostalgic … stunning"; BG "a delight"; TGM "smart, funny, schmaltzy, sexy, endearing"); *Casualties of War* (NYT "earnest, troubling [and] riveting"; LAT "a superb film"; WP "unflinching, masterly … a film of great emotional power and great seriousness … one of the most punishing, morally complex movies about men at war ever made"; TGM "a searing tale effectively told"; S&S "the strongest, the simplest and the most painful of all the Vietnam movies … extraordinary"); *Crimes and Misdemeanors* (NYT "[Woody] Allen's most securely serious and funny film to date"; LAT "poignant"; WP "relentless … feels like a tug of war between [the films' two halves]"; BG "brilliant"; TGM "flagrantly flawed but never less than fascinating"); *Parenthood* (LAT "[a] very real comic delight"; WP "[a] feel-good family comedy"; BG "funny, gritty, filled with surprising stabs of feeling"; V "keenly observed and often very funny"); and *The Little Mermaid* (NYT "Disney reverts to its trademark sweetness – with phenomenal success – in a film ingeniously tailored to be as appealing to adult viewers as it will be to children … a triumph"; LAT "impudent, grandiose [and] a multi-level crowd-pleaser … Disney's new triumph").

Also ignored was the year's biggest box office success, *Batman* (NYT "shapeless … neither funny nor solemn … has the personality not of a particular movie but of a product"; LAT "a murky, brooding piece … [but] is it fun? Not much"; WP "dark, haunting and poetic … a magnificent living comic book … as rich and satisfying a movie as you're likely to see all year"; BG "dark, brooding … grand opera for the eyes").

A fortnight before the Academy Awards, the Director's Guild of America handed its accolade to Oliver Stone for *Born on the Fourth of July*, confirming the director and his film as the Oscar favourites.

On 26 March, however, *Driving Miss Daisy* surprised observers and claimed the Best Picture statuette. It went on to earn more money at the North American box office than any of the other nominees.

BEST DIRECTOR

ACADEMY AWARDS
Woody Allen for *Crimes and Misdemeanors*
Kenneth Branagh for *Henry V*
Jim Sheridan for *My Left Foot*
• **Oliver Stone for *Born on the Fourth of July***
Peter Weir for *Dead Poets Society*

GOLDEN GLOBE AWARDS
Spike Lee – *Do the Right Thing*
Rob Reiner – *When Harry Met Sally...*
• **Oliver Stone – *Born on the Fourth of July***
Peter Weir – *Dead Poets Society*
Edward Zwick – *Glory*

DIRECTORS GUILD AWARD
Woody Allen
  – Crimes and Misdemeanors
• **Oliver Stone**
  – *Born on the Fourth of July*
Rob Reiner
  – When Harry Met Sally...
Phil Alden Robinson – *Field of Dreams*
Peter Weir – *Dead Poets Society*

BRITISH ACADEMY AWARDS
• **Kenneth Branagh – *Henry V***
Stephen Frears
  – Dangerous Liaisons
Alan Parker – *Mississippi Burning*
Peter Weir – *Dead Poets Society*

NEW YORK – Paul Mazursky – *Enemies, A Love Story*
LOS ANGELES – Spike Lee – *Do the Right Thing*
BOARD OF REVIEW – Kenneth Branagh – *Henry V*
NATIONAL SOCIETY – Gus Van Sant – *Drugstore Cowboy*
LONDON – Terence Davies – *Distant Voices, Still Lives*

When the Academy announced the Oscar nominees on Valentine's Day 1990, *Driving Miss Daisy* received more nominations than any other film. But its nine nods did not include a mention for its Australian director, Bruce Beresford (WP "the story holds a potential for sap that is mostly unfulfilled thanks to Beresford's stately approach"; CT "matches [the writer's] reserve and tastefulness [using] a quiet, restrained tone ... does an excellent job of balancing his cast"; BG "subtle helming"; V "sensitive direction"). Beresford had not been a contender for the Golden Globe or Directors Guild of America accolade either.

1989

The outcry over Beresford's absence from the Oscar ballot eclipsed three other notable omissions: Los Angeles Film Critics Association prize-winner Spike Lee for *Do the Right Thing* (NYT "riveting proof of the arrival of an abundantly gifted new talent ... sheer cinematic wizardry"; LAT "bravura movie making"; BG "bold, vivid, in your face ... the year's most accomplished piece of American film making so far ... Lee has absolutely refused to tailor [the film] even slightly to white expectations"); Edward Zwick for *Glory* (NYT "brilliantly realized"; LAT "directed passionately ... an impressive achievement"; CT "does not seem entirely at ease ... comes up with compositions that are too cramped and shallow to take full advantage of the visual resources standing before him"; WP "does not hesitate to play with our sympathies ... tends to select the stalest perspectives"; TGM "directed with a visual mastery on the level of David Lean"); and Steven Soderbergh for his directorial debut, the Palme d'Or winner *sex, lies and videotape* (LAT "it's [his] elegant manner that creates the film's tranquil spell ... his control is mesmerizing"; V "highly impressive directorial debut ... beautifully controlled").

Also passed over were: New York Film Critics Circle winner Paul Mazursky for *Enemies, A Love Story* (NYT "remarkably understated ... clearly invests a lot of energy in staging these scenes"; LAT "so clearly understands the knife edge between laughter and tears on which [the source material] constantly balances"; CST "[he] tells [the film's] story without compromise"; WP "keeps everything in equilibrium ... masterfully precise"); National Society of Film Critics winner Gus Van Sant for *Drugstore Cowboy* (CST "avoids both lush romanticism and picturesque exoticism ... he's interested in character more than attitude ... in setting out a level-headed approach to his protagonists, he's able to locate the higher impulses that animate them"; WP "gives his material shape and an invigorating, syncopated style"; BG "while stylized, it's refreshingly inscribed, often with arresting loping rhythms ... adroit"); DGA finalist Phil Alden Robinson for *Field of Dreams* (NYT "the film is anchored by [his] direction"; TGM "doesn't overplay his hand"); DGA and Globe nominee Rob Reiner for *When Harry Met Sally...* (V "directs with deftness and sincerity"; TGM "shows his usual light touch here"); Brian De Palma for *Casualties of War* (LAT "easily his best [work]"; WP "all the filmmaker's talents and interests are in balance ... a breakthrough work"; TGM "his visual style is straightforward ... the tension [is] allowed to surface naturally"; S&S "his vision has a bracing clarity"); and Tim Burton for *Batman* (WP "[his] grasp of his material is remarkably sure"; BG "takes what might merely have been a comic book and infuses it with psychological depth").

In the absence of Beresford, previous winner and Los Angeles runner-up Oliver Stone became the frontrunner for the three main Best Director awards for *Born on the Fourth of July* (NYT "reaches out instantly to his audience's hut-level emotions and sustains a walloping impact for two and a half hours ... [but] Stone's penchant for busy, jittery camera movements and cutting do not help"; LAT "when his film needs to lower its voice and make crucial points clear, Stone turns up the volume ... he uses bombast [and] overkill ... because [he] pulls out all the stops almost all the time, he undermines the story he wishes to fervently to tell"; CST "unflinching ... is to be commended"; TGM "beautifully and sometimes brilliantly made [but] never the most subtle of directors, Stone brings a jackhammer brutality to [the film] that the material no longer needs").

While Beresford had been snubbed for the Globe, DGA prize and Oscar, the only director alongside Stone to be in contention for all three accolades was another Australian, Peter Weir for *Dead Poets Society* (NYT "cannot resist tarting up the movie with the fancified effects that pass for art"; WP "adroit direction"; TT "great skill"). The remaining Oscar nominees were: previous winner Woody Allen for *Crimes and Misdemeanors* (NYT "never before has he made the leap [between comedy and drama] with more self-assurance"; CST "never before has he found such a confidant tone"; CT "leaden direction"); Kenneth Branagh for his directorial debut *Henry V*, for which he won the BAFTA as well as the following year's European Film Award (NYT "has transformed what initially seemed to be a lunatic dare into a genuine triumph"; LAT "his skill and passion equal his daring"; CST "Branagh's direction wisely goes for realism"; WP "inspired [and] forthright and articulate ... the work the young actor director does here is steeped in powerful emotion; a more auspicious, more thrilling debut could not be imagined"; BG "triumphs"; SMH "little short of miraculous"); and Jim Sheridan for *My Left Foot* (NYT "blunt and tough"; WP "underplays ... [the film] has a pitch-perfect dryness and simplicity; there's never a misstep or false note in the way [he] recreates [this world]"; TGM "skilful direction"; MFB "conventional ... shoots in a clean, functional manner"; Sp "competently and conventionally directed").

For the second time in four years, Stone won the Globe, DGA award and Oscar for a drama about the Vietnam War.

The Academy Awards, however, belonged to Beresford. Best Actress winner Jessica Tandy referred to Beresford in her acceptance speech as "that forgotten man", and later, when accepting the Best Picture award for *Driving Miss Daisy* producer Richard Zanuck said, "we're up here for one very simple reason – the fact that Bruce Beresford is a brilliant director."

In Australia, the morning after the ceremony, the headline across the front page of The Sydney Morning Herald declared "Beresford: he wins Oscars ... for other people." Beneath were photos of Tandy and Robert Duvall, who had won the Best Actor Oscar in 1983 for *Tender Mercies*, a film directed by Beresford, and for which the Australian film-maker had been unsuccessfully nominated for the Globe, DGA accolade and Academy Award.

1989

BEST ACTOR

ACADEMY AWARDS
Kenneth Branagh as 'King Henry V of England' in *Henry V*
Tom Cruise as 'Ron Kovic' in *Born on the Fourth of July*
• **Daniel Day-Lewis as 'Christy Brown' in *My Left Foot***
Morgan Freeman as 'Hoke Colburn' in *Driving Miss Daisy*
Robin Williams as 'John Keating' in *Dead Poets Society*

GOLDEN GLOBE AWARDS

(Drama)

• **Tom Cruise**
  – *Born on the Fourth of July*
Daniel Day-Lewis – *My Left Foot*
Jack Lemmon – *Dad*
Al Pacino – *Sea of Love*
Robin Williams – *Dead Poets Society*

(Comedy/Musical)

Billy Crystal
  – *When Harry Met Sally...*
Michael Douglas – *War of the Roses*
• **Morgan Freeman**
  – *Driving Miss Daisy*
Steve Martin – *Parenthood*
Jack Nicholson – *Batman*

BRITISH ACADEMY AWARDS
Kenneth Branagh – *Henry V*
• **Daniel Day-Lewis – *My Left Foot***
Dustin Hoffman – *Rain Man*
Robin Williams – *Dead Poets Society*

NEW YORK – Daniel Day-Lewis – *My Left Foot*
LOS ANGELES – Daniel Day-Lewis – *My Left Foot*
BOARD OF REVIEW – Morgan Freeman – *Driving Miss Daisy*
NATIONAL SOCIETY – Daniel Day-Lewis – *My Left Foot*
LONDON – Daniel Day-Lewis – *My Left Foot*

For his portrayal of Christy Brown, an Irish writer with cerebral palsy, in *My Left Foot*, English actor Daniel Day-Lewis won accolades from the New York Film Critics Circle, the Los Angeles Film Critics Association and the National Society of Film Critics, and received his first nomination from the Academy (NYT "beautifully acted … exemplary … technical facility can go a long way toward the creation of what appears to be a performance, thus it takes a while for the full measure of [his] work [here] to be appreciated"; NYP "[a] miraculous performance"; LAT "ferociously brilliant acting … one of the year's tour de force performances"; WP "this astounding young actor spares himself nothing

... takes the intensity of Christy's emotions to a point almost past belief, and way past the point where we expect most actors to stop ... he confronts us with Christy's physical wretchedness and asks for not one shred of mercy, not one tear ... the results are devastating and unforgettable"; BG "brilliant and impassioned"; V "brilliant"; Time "brilliant"; TGM "superbly acted ... impressive, physically and emotionally"; MFB "[an] immensely skilled, physically strenuous performance"; Sp "a tour de force of acting ... he dominates the screen [with] an amazing central performance"). Despite these awards, Day-Lewis was far from considered a runaway favourite for the golden statuette. In the Los Angeles Times, film critic Charles Champlin predicted that Day-Lewis' portrayal "is likely to go to the wire in the Oscar sweepstakes with Tom Cruise's powerful role as paraplegic Ron Kovic".

In the lead-up to the Academy Awards, many critics and bookmakers predicted that twenty-seven-year old Cruise would become the youngest man to win the Best Actor statuette. Over the previous couple of years, the popular star of the box office hits *Risky Business* and *Top Gun* had been gaining respect from critics for his performances in serious films such as *The Color of Money* and *Rain Man* (for which Paul Newman and Dustin Hoffman, respectively, won Best Actor Academy Awards). Cruise earned rave reviews for his portrayal of a Vietnam War veteran confined to a wheelchair in *Born on the Fourth of July* (NYT "fiery ... a performance that defines everything that is best about the movie"; LAT "Cruise delivers fierce physicality, empathy and the ability to work full throttle for virtually every scene [and also] a quality of defenselessness that is terribly touching ... [but] Cruise is not deep and you never catch a watchful intelligence lurking in his eyes"; CST "watching Cruise disappear into character carries the picture over its rough spots"; V "stunning"; TGM "tops even his delicate, excellent performance in 'Rain Man' ... believable [and] tremendously touching ... but an unknown actor might have been equipped to knead something fresh into the stale [material]"; SMH "plays Kovic with the kind of intensity that marks a career watershed"). He finished as the runner-up in the New York critics' vote, won the Globe (Drama) and earned his first nomination from the Academy.

Another serious contender for the Oscar was thought to be Morgan Freeman, who earned his second mention for reprising his stage performance as the chauffeur of an elderly Southern woman in *Driving Miss Daisy* (NYT "a tough performance ... laid-back and graceful, the work of an actor who has gone through all of the possibilities"; LAT "extraordinary ... the performance is not an apologia, it's a tribute"; WP "extraordinary"; V "[a] guaranteed Oscar nomination for a career-crowning performance"; SMH "[a] performance of splendid depth and restraint"). Freeman finished as the runner-up for the Los Angeles and NSFC prizes, won the National Board of Review accolade and the

Globe (Comedy/Musical) and was honoured at the Berlin Film Festival. His Oscar chances were also helped by his well-received supporting performance in *Glory*. Many critics had been predicting that he would be nominated in both the lead and support categories.

The outsiders for the Academy Award were Robin Williams (his second nod) as an inspirational teacher at a New England boys' school in the 1950s, in *Dead Poets Society* (NYT "exceptionally fine"; LAT "played with a fine lyric-comic frenzy"; CT "[the film] gives him some wonderful bits ... it's a part, and really a whole movie, designed to win him the love and adoration of the audience"; WP "[he] turns in an acting performance – and a nicely restrained one at that") and Kenneth Branagh as the eponymous English King in *Henry V*, a role for which Laurence Olivier had been nominated for playing in 1946 (NYT "[an] excellent [although] not especially lyric performance"; WP "astounding ... with each speech he throws down the gauntlet, challenging all comers ... in addition to billowing emotion, there is a bracing intelligence at work that fortifies the [line] readings and heightens their meaning"; BG "the dominant presence ... [plays with] tenacious directness and barely concealed ferocity [and] makes them work"; TT "correct, passionless, all intelligence"). Branagh was also a Best Director nominee for *Henry V*, which was his feature directorial debut.

Missing from the Academy's line-up was perhaps the most talked about performance of the year: Jack Nicholson's Golden Globe nominated turn as the Joker in *Batman* (NYT "brilliantly played"; LAT "Nicholson's Joker will be the pivotal point for many. It's his energy that keeps the picture alive ... a performance of draining intensity"; CST "really the most important character in the movie – in impact and screen time"; WP "seems to be having a blast ... he brings a sense of dangerous hilarity to the character ... [his] acting here is dexterous [and] he's brilliantly bonkers"; V "steals every scene ... he makes a glorious style of playing the most extravagantly psychotic character"). Observers speculated that Academy members had been divided about whether to vote for Nicholson in the lead or supporting category. He had received top-billing, but his character was not the centre of the film and had less screen time than the title character.

Other Golden Globe nominees left off the Oscar short-list included: previous winner Jack Lemmon in *Dad* (NYT "does a superlative job that is limited only by the tacky material ... a performance that is often something of a wonder"; LAT "Lemmon's work is extraordinary; notably unsentimental [and] something of a marvel physically"; CST "utterly convincing"; WP "uncharacteristically restrained ... he underplays the physical side of his performance ... his work is credible, even laudable"; BG "a career-capping performance"; V "memorable"); Al Pacino in *Sea of Love* (NYT "tears into a role make out of rice paper, for messy results"; CT "plays an empty shell so authentically he seems at times to be acting in a vacuum"; WP "a marvel ... he's great in the role ... the character is a cliché [but] as Pacino plays him, it's the character's cagey intelligence and tenacity that register and not the cliches"; V "superlative"; TGM "[a] strong lead performance"); Billy Crystal in *When Harry Met Sally...* (NYT "appealing and sometimes even unpredictable ... has the wittiest lines and snappiest delivery, but he also shows Harry to be remarkably gentle"; TGM "always disciplined and a consistent hoot, fleshing out a character who amounts to a brawnier version of the [Woody] Allen nebbish"; TT "convincing"; MFB "splendidly played"; Sp "the two leads have to carry the film, and it is hard to imagine them better cast ... [they] offer us two believable, likeable and idiosyncratic individuals, and they are never heavy-handed with the script"); and Steve Martin in *Parenthood* (NYT "[a] winning portrayal"; WP "ingratiating"; V "impressive").

Also overlooked for consideration were: Matt Dillon in *Drugstore Cowboy* (NYT "the role of his career ... perfect"; LAT "[a] hauntingly beautiful performance"; CST "very well played"; WP "a perfect role for Dillon; it makes use of that trace of torpor in him [and] gives him a chance to show some of his hang-dog charisma too"; TGM "an exceptionally courageous characterization ... faultless"); Jeff Bridges in *The Fabulous Baker Boys* (LAT "couldn't be improved upon"; CT "excellent ... highly convincing"; BG "an enormously sympathetic performance"; TGM "superb ... weaves his allusive magic"); Kevin Costner in *Field of Dreams* (NYT "perfectly acted ... does not make one false move"; TGM "[he and Madigan] both walk a delicate path between ingenuousness and strength, keeping the fantasy earthbound until it's ready to soar"; MFB "perfectly played"); Cannes winner James Spader in *sex, lies and videotape* (NYT "a tremendously subtle performance ... flawless"; LAT "bravura"; WP "superlative ... hypnotizing"); Matthew Broderick in *Glory* (NYT "superior ... mature and controlled performance"; LAT "a flawless performance"; V "beautifully acted ... perfectly judged"); both Michael J. Fox (NYT "plays [him] as best he can ... the role is a difficult one and , to his credit, [he] remains firmly in character ... it's not easy dramatizing this degree of moral righteousness"; LAT "his best dramatic performance to date"; WP "marvelous"; TGM "superbly acted ... his performance deepens in perfect harmony with the rising tension"; S&S "quietly astonishing") and Sean Penn (NYT "extremely fine ... plays Meserve with terrific élan ... there is plausibility in every movement and gesture"; LAT "bursts the boundaries of his role with his gargoyle intensity"; WP "striving for big effects, Penn plays him too boldly ... at times seems mannered and cartoonish"; V "riveting"; TGM "rivetingly intense ... rescues the sergeant from two-dimensional villainy"; SMH "steals the show") in *Casualties of War*; previous winner Robert De Niro in *Jacknife* (NYT "[a] powerhouse performance ... De Niro gives Megs the kind of rollicking good-old-boy manner that masks a heart of gold ... [the role] provides the most marvellous opportunities for De Niro to continually surprise with his portrayal"; CST "superb"; CT "the drama is affecting because of the quality of the performances [by De Niro and Baker]"; BG "gives us a brilliant screenful of acting pyrotechnics ... its generous, full-bodied acting"; MFB "magnificent ... suggesting intense vulnerability beneath the non-stop bluster and banter"); and John Hurt in *Scandal* (NYT "exceptionally fine work ... Hurt invests his lightweight character with the heft of a rich performance"; LAT "crackingly well-acted ... the film holds because of the brilliance of Hurt"; CST "one of the best performances of his career"; V "excellent").

On Oscar night, Jodie Foster opened the evening's second last envelope and announced that Day-Lewis had won the Academy Award. Day-Lewis also won the Best Actor BAFTA, outpolling Branagh and Williams as well as the previous year's Best Actor Oscar winner, Dustin Hoffman in *Rain Man*. The following year, Branagh won the European Film Award for *Henry V*.

BEST ACTRESS

ACADEMY AWARDS
Isabelle Adjani as 'Camille Claudel' in *Camille Claudel*
Pauline Collins as 'Shirley Valentine' in *Shirley Valentine*
Jessica Lange as 'Ann Talbot' in *Music Box*
Michelle Pfeiffer as 'Susie Diamond' in *The Fabulous Baker Boys*
• Jessica Tandy as 'Miss Daisy Werthan' in *Driving Miss Daisy*

GOLDEN GLOBE AWARDS

(Drama)

Sally Field – *Steel Magnolias*
Jessica Lange – *Music Box*
Andie MacDowell
   – *sex, lies and videotape*
• Michelle Pfeiffer
   – *The Fabulous Baker Boys*
Liv Ullmann – *The Rose Garden*

(Comedy/Musical)

Pauline Collins – *Shirley Valentine*
Meg Ryan
   – *When Harry Met Sally...*
Meryl Streep – *She-Devil*
• Jessica Tandy
   – *Driving Miss Daisy*
Kathleen Turner – *War of the Roses*

BRITISH ACADEMY AWARDS
Glenn Close – *Dangerous Liaisons*
• Pauline Collins – *Shirley Valentine*
Jodie Foster – *The Accused*
Melanie Griffith – *Working Girl*

NEW YORK – Michelle Pfeiffer – *The Fabulous Baker Boys*
LOS ANGELES – Andie MacDowell – *sex, lies and videotape* and Michelle Pfeiffer – *The Fabulous Baker Boys*
BOARD OF REVIEW – Michelle Pfeiffer – *The Fabulous Baker Boys*
NATIONAL SOCIETY – Michelle Pfeiffer – *The Fabulous Baker Boys*

In 1944 husband and wife Hume Cronyn and Jessica Tandy won acclaim from critics for their supporting performances as a German factory worker and his wife in *The Seventh Cross*. The Academy nominated Cronyn as Best Supporting Actor, but Tandy was overlooked. Seven years later, despite winning a Tony Award, Tandy was the only principal from the Broadway production of 'A Streetcar Named Desire' not to be signed for Elia Kazan's film version. The role of the faded Southern belle, Blanche DuBois, was instead played by Vivien Leigh, who received her second Best Actress Academy Award for her performance.

1989

It was not until 1989, forty-five years after her husband made the Academy's list, that Jessica Tandy received her first nomination, ironically, for playing another faded Southern belle – the elderly Jewish widow in *Driving Miss Daisy*, a role originated on stage by Dana Ivey (NYT "brings to [the role] her mastery of selective understatement ... Tandy creates a most particular woman"; LAT "Tandy is almost astringent in her denial of easy emotion"; CT "never playing for sympathy, she earns it completely"; WP "extraordinary ... [played] with unaffected grace"; V "[a] guaranteed Oscar nomination for a career-crowning performance ... touching"; SMH "[a] performance of splendid depth and restraint"). Prior to the Oscars, Tandy finished as the runner-up for the New York Film Critics Circle and National Society of Film Critics prizes, won the Golden Globe (Comedy/Musical) and was honoured at the Berlin Film Festival. She was considered the frontrunner for the statuette.

The other strong contender for the Oscar was the critics' choice and Globe (Drama) winner, Michelle Pfeiffer as a piano-bar singer in *The Fabulous Baker Boys* (NYT "electrifyingly right ... spectacular ... she just plain brings down the house"; LAT "fills the screen vividly ... couldn't be improved on"; CST "quite simply has one of the roles of a lifetime"; CT "excellent"; WP "burns an image on the screen"; BG "an enormously sympathetic performance ... erases any doubt that she has become one of Hollywood's major players"; V "hits the nail right on the head ... she's dynamite"). Pfeiffer was the first actress in seven years to win a clean sweep of the four critics' prizes, but she had only narrowly outpolled Tandy for the New York prize (39 points to 38) and the NSFC award (37 points to 31) and in Los Angeles she had shared the plaudit with Andie MacDowell in *sex, lies and videotape* (NYT "flawless"; LAT "supple, shaded brilliance"; WP "superlative ... exquisite ... plays Ann with a Diane Keatonish flourish, an orgy of elipses"; V "convincing"). MacDowell was subsequently overlooked by the Academy prompting the New York Times to comment, "it seems incomprehensible that Andie MacDowell should not have been nominated".

The other nominees for the Oscar were: Isabelle Adjani (her second mention) as the tragic sculptor involved with Auguste Rodin in the biopic *Camille Claudel*, for which she won the 1989 Berlin Film Festival prize (LAT "played with bravura and bristling intelligence ... [one of her] best performances"; CT "Adjani supplies a textbook bad performance, once that annihilates the character by forcing all of the audience's attention on the actress – her passion, her commitment, her technique ... Adjani devours [the film] almost entirely"; WP "a powerful performance that does not prettify Claudel's descent into madness ... Adjani shows not the slightest trace of restraint [in] a performance full of spirited, feminine turbulence from an actress with great stores of violent emotion at her disposal"; V "throws herself into a role worthy of her abilities, giving intense relief, if not enough pathos, to a strong-willed femme artist"; TGM "superb as the spirited young woman [but] as the mature Camille she is less convincing "; TT "becomes more interesting as Camille grows madder"; S&S "well acted"; MFB "fine"); BAFTA winner Pauline Collins for reprising her Tony award-winning stage performance as the eponymous British woman in *Shirley Valentine* (NYT "Collins brings as much energy and warmth to the role as ever, but on screen the strength of her performance is shattered by being chopped into tiny, disconnected bits; LAT "without Collins' waves of honesty, her enveloping warmth and the unhurried, confiding way about her delivery, we might well be left to wonder what all the fuss was about in this comedy-drama"; V "Collins is Shirley Valentine, the perfect match of actress and character"; S&S "a calculated if rather hollow triumph"; MFB "confident"); and previous Best Supporting Actress winner Jessica Lange (recognised for a fifth time in eight years) as a lawyer defending her father in *Music Box* (NYT "gives her best performance since 'Frances' ... her portrayal is so nuanced that we can sense the growing confusion as Ann's belief [is] challenged ... Lange comes as close to inventing a character out of thin air as any screen actor can"; LAT "there are flashes of brilliance [in her] performance"; CT "projects a combination of strength and sensitivity"; BG "Lange is sure to get an Oscar nomination for her gritty, high-voltage performance"; V "does a fair job but fails to flesh out a terribly one-dimensional character"; TGM "Lange's excellence is unquestionable ... charts the character's evolution from self-righteousness to doubt to agony to rage with commendable clarity").

In addition to MacDowell, Oscar voters overlooked: Sally Field in *Steel Magnolias* (WP "rolls out her ain't-gonna-cry-now Oscar-nomination skills"; BG "rises to her big emotional scene"); Liv Ullmann in *The Rose Garden* (LAT "an impassioned performance"; V "convincing"); Meg Ryan in *When Harry Met Sally...* (WP "finally finds a showcase for her sheer exuberance"; TGM "does her best work yet"; TT "convincing"; MFB "splendidly played"; Sp "the two leads have to carry the film, and it is hard to imagine them better cast ... [they] offer us two believable, likeable and idiosyncratic individuals, and they are never heavy-handed with the script"); Meryl Streep in *She-Devil* (NYT "hilarious ... Streep dives into this thimble-sized comedy and makes one believe that it is an Olympic-sized swimming pool of wit ... she is almost worth the price of admission"; LAT "Streep is such a studied, meticulous actress that, at times, her performance here seems like an impersonation of funniness rather than true funniness ... but she's so adroit that it's tough to tell the difference ... [it's] a biting caricature"; WP "unimaginative, straight-down-the-middle acting"; BG "[the film] has its moments, thanks chiefly to Streep's way with the comic role of a la-de-da writer of romance novels"; V "punctuates her lines with adroit, inventive physical comedy"; MFB "Streep relishes her [part, playing] with exactly the right degree of exaggeration required by a film in which characters represent stereotypes rather than people"); Winona Ryder in *Heathers* (NYT "manages to be both stunning and sympathetic"; LAT "[the director] has been beautifully served by Ryder"; WP "makes us love her teen-age murderess"; V "utterly fetching and winning"; TT "plays with assurance"); Ellen Barkin in *Sea of Love* (NYT "does her level best to seem simultaneously sexy, homicidal and innocent, which is not easy"; LAT "[the film] works because Barkin has the skill to keep us guessing"; CT "exceeds expectations"; TGM "[a] strong lead performance"); Nicole Kidman in *Dead Calm* (LAT "brilliant ... a magnificent discovery ... seems to approach [this non-stop action film] from a reservoir of intelligence and with an arc of her character's growth clearly in her mind"; CST "Kidman and Zane do generate real, palpable hatred in their scenes"; V "excellent ... she gives the character real tenacity and energy"; TGM "plays with intensity and conviction"); and European Film Award winner Ruth Sheen in the 1988 British film *High Hopes* (NYT "outstanding"; LAT "miraculously deft at erasing that line between performing and being ... masterly"; CT "vivid"; V "attractively played"; TT "beautifully played"; Sp "among the performances one singles out Ruth Sheen as Shirley; but all are inventive, energetic and precise").

On Oscar night, eighty-year old Tandy became the oldest person to win a statuette in the acting categories when she received the Best Actress Academy Award. She repeated her win at the BAFTAs the following year where Pfeiffer was also a nominee.

BEST SUPPORTING ACTOR

ACADEMY AWARDS
Danny Aiello as 'Sal' in *Do the Right Thing*
Dan Aykroyd as 'Boolie Werthan' in *Driving Miss Daisy*
Marlon Brando as 'Ian McKenzie' in *A Dry White Season*
Martin Landau as 'Judah Rosenthal' in *Crimes and Misdemeanors*
• Denzel Washington as 'Trip' in *Glory*

GOLDEN GLOBE AWARDS
Danny Aiello – *Do the Right Thing*
Marlon Brando – *A Dry White Season*
Sean Connery – *Indiana Jones and the Last Crusade*
Ed Harris – *Jacknife*
• Denzel Washington – *Glory*
Bruce Willis – *In Country*

BRITISH ACADEMY AWARDS
Marlon Brando – *A Dry White Season*
Sean Connery – *Indiana Jones and the Last Crusade*
• Ray McAnally – *My Left Foot*
Jack Nicholson – *Batman*

NEW YORK – Alan Alda – *Crimes and Misdemeanors*
LOS ANGELES – Danny Aiello – *Do the Right Thing*
BOARD OF REVIEW – Alan Alda – *Crimes and Misdemeanors*
NATIONAL SOCIETY – Beau Bridges – *The Fabulous Baker Boys*

Many observers believed that the Academy would make amends for the omission of *Do the Right Thing* from the top categories by presenting the Best Supporting Actor Oscar to Los Angeles Film Critics Association winner Danny Aiello for his performance as the owner of a Brooklyn pizzeria (NYT "superb ... [the] solidly dramatic center [of the film]"; V "[a] standout"; TT "admirable").

Other critics, however, favoured Denzel Washington, who earned his second nomination in three years, as an embittered former slave in *Glory* (NYT "beautifully acted ... superior ... an actor clearly on his way to a major screen career"; NYP "outstanding"; LAT "involving"; CT "[a] strong, simple performance"; WP "transcends the cliches"; V "a great performance"). Washington had won the Golden Globe and finished as runner-up for the New

York Film Critics Circle and National Society of Film Critics Association awards (both of which he lost by just a single point).

The dark horse in the field was one of the previous year's unsuccessful nominees, Martin Landau, nominated for his co-lead role as an ophthalmologist trying to get rid of his mistress in *Crimes and Misdemeanors* (NYT "splendid in the key role"; LAT "[gives] the story a dark, pathetic edge"; CT "Landau is cast adrift in a leading role no actor could play plausibly ... there's nobody home in the character as written"; WP "potent"; V "another career milestone").

The outsiders were Dan Aykroyd as the son in *Driving Miss Daisy* (NYT "a notably self-effacing performance"; CT "victimized by age makeup that doesn't always work [but] a solid presence"; TGM "stunningly excellent") and previous Best Actor Oscar winner Marlon Brando as a human rights lawyer in *A Dry White Season* (NYT "a sly and enormously funny"; LAT "[an] ironic and subtle [performance]"; BG "a wonderful performance"; TGM "Brando is in the movie scant minutes, but he creates a character in three dimensions instantly and nearly every line he reads engenders a titter of delight, not because he is over acting, but because he is acting so well"). It was Brando's eighth Oscar nod.

Overlooked were: Best Actor nominee Morgan Freeman in *Glory* (NYT "superior"; NYP "outstanding"; LAT "involving"); New York and National Board of Review winner Alan Alda in *Crimes and Misdemeanors* (NYT "priceless"); NSFC winner Beau Bridges in *The Fabulous Baker Boys* (LAT "couldn't be improved upon"; CT "highly convincing"; BG "an enormously sympathetic performance"; TGM "superb ... carving out a sympathetic portrait"); Peter Gallagher in *sex, lies and videotape* (NYT "flawless"; WP "superlative"); Ed Harris in *Jacknife* (NYT "has some absolutely shattering moments"; CST "superb"; WP "doing what he can with a one-note role"; BG "[Baker and Harris] give us characters who make us share their immersion in them... its generous, full-bodied acting"; MFB "a remarkable performance, ranging from near-catatonia to extreme physical violence"); both the late Ray McAnally, who posthumously won a BAFTA, as the father (NYT "fine"; WP "[a] burly and robust [performance]"; BG "reminds us of how it's possible to be unforgettable without saying much"; V "excellent"; TGM "superbly acted"; TT "admirable") and Hugh O'Connor as the young Christy Brown (NYT "though he is not on screen as long as Mr Day-Lewis, [he] is equally good"; TGM "superbly acted ... heartbreaking"; MFB "[an] immensely skilled, physically strenuous performance") in *My Left Foot*; Ian Holm (NYT "[a] stand out"; WP "engaging"), Robert Stephens (BG "richly drawn") and Paul Scofield (WP "[Branagh] urges a consummately forlorn performance out of Scofield") in *Henry V*; and Ethan Hawke in both *Dead Poets Society* (NYT "very good"; TT "sensitive and charming") and *Dad* (NYT "good"; V "splendid").

On Oscar night, Washington won the Academy Award.

BEST SUPPORTING ACTRESS

ACADEMY AWARDS
• **Brenda Fricker as 'Mrs Brown' in** *My Left Foot*
Anjelica Huston as 'Tamara' in *Enemies, A Love Story*
Lena Olin as 'Masha' in *Enemies, A Love Story*
Julia Roberts as 'Shelby Latcherie' in *Steel Magnolias*
Dianne Wiest as 'Helen' in *Parenthood*

GOLDEN GLOBE AWARDS
Bridget Fonda – *Scandal*
Brenda Fricker – *My Left Foot*
• **Julia Roberts – *Steel Magnolias***
Laura San Giacomo – *sex, lies and videotape*
Dianne Wiest – *Parenthood*

BRITISH ACADEMY AWARDS
Peggy Ashcroft – *Madame Sousatzka*
• **Michelle Pfeiffer – *Dangerous Liaisons***
Laura San Giacomo – *sex, lies and videotape*
Sigourney Weaver – *Working Girl*

NEW YORK – Lena Olin – *Enemies, A Love Story*
LOS ANGELES – Brenda Fricker – *My Left Foot*
BOARD OF REVIEW – Mary Stuart Masterson – *Immediate Family*
NATIONAL SOCIETY – Anjelica Huston – *Enemies, A Love Story*

As the sex-hungry mistress of a ghost-writer in *Enemies, A Love Story*, Lena Olin won the New York Film Critics Circle award (NYT "makes [her] a steamy and dangerous siren, as well as a tragic one"; LAT "hilarious"; WP "magnificent [in a] provocative, husky-voiced performance ... she seems almost uncannily invested in her emotions"). She later finished runner-up for the National Society of Film Critics prize to her co-star, Anjelica Huston (who'd earlier been runner-up for the Los Angeles Film Critics Association prize) as a long-presumed dead woman who suddenly reappears (NYT "Huston, commanding as ever, gives the film its most drolly articulate voice"; LAT "the film's strongest asset ... a performance which makes her Academy Award-winning [one] seem anemic by comparison"; WP "magnificent ... she's a mordant, sexy comedian, firing off angry zingers"; V "delightfully cynical and courageous"). Both Olin and Huston received nominations from the Academy.

Also nominated were: Los Angeles winner and New York runner-up Brenda Fricker as the mother in *My Left Foot* (NYT "fine"; WP "[a] burly and robust [performance]"; V "excellent"; TGM "superbly acted"; TT "admirable"; Sp "excellent ... copes with sonorous lines that would defeat many actresses"); Golden Globe champ Julia Roberts as a young woman with diabetes in *Steel Magnolias* (NYT "plays with the kind of mega-intensity the camera cannot always absorb"; V "has real freshness and charm"); and previous winner Dianne Wiest as a divorcee in *Parenthood* (LAT "has the movie's tartest lines and most spirited character, and she does them both proud"; BG "the best performance [in the film]"; V "vastly compelling"; S&S "[a] grand performance").

Notably absent from the Oscar list were: National Board of Review winner Mary Stuart Masterson in *Immediate Family* (NYT "so sharp and fresh that she stands out as the film's most urgently appealing figure"; LAT "her smallest emotion is pure and real"; BG "remarkable ... [her] performance is Oscar-calibre"; V "simply superb"; TGM "makes us believe in this girl's considerable inner resources"); European Film Award winner Edna Doré in *High Hopes* (LAT "exceptional"; CT "vivid"; V "a lovely performance"); and previous winner Olympia Dukakis in *Dad* (NYT "good"; WP "wickedly funny").

Others overlooked for consideration were: Bridget Fonda in *Scandal* (NYT "plausible and funny"; LAT "crackingly well-acted"; V "perfect"); Laura San Giacomo in *sex, lies and videotape* (NYT "flawless"; WP "superlative"); Mia Farrow in *Crimes and Misdemeanors* (NYT "[a] standout"); Amy Madigan in *Field of Dreams* (NYT "perfectly acted"; TGM "[Costner and Madigan] both walk a delicate path between ingenuousness and strength, keeping the fantasy earthbound until it's ready to soar"; MFB "perfectly played"); both Ruby Dee (NYT "fine"; V "[a] standout") and Rosie Perez (NYT "should have earned a nomination") in *Do the Right Thing*; Winona Ryder in *Great Balls of Fire* (NYT "[an] enormously poised performance"; LAT "[a] delicate portrait"; CT "enjoyable"; WP "Ryder's solid sense of character and even better sense of humor play paperweight to this flighty material"; BG "[an] extraordinarily nuanced portrayal"; MFB "it is [her] beautiful performance as Myra that seduces the story"); Kathy Baker in *Jacknife* (NYT "very effective ... [she] finds countless ways to keep Martha from becoming the stereotype of a spinster schoolteacher"; CST "superb"; CT "the drama is affecting because of the quality of the performances [by De Niro and Baker]"; WP "spectacularly natural ... she's so disarmingly assured, she's seductive" BG "[Baker and Harris] give us characters who make us share their immersion in them ... its generous, full-bodied acting"; MFB "magnificent"); and both Judi Dench as Mistress Quickly (NYT "[a] stand out"; WP "heartbreaking"; BG "richly drawn") and Emma Thompson as Princess Katherine of France (LAT "notable") in *Henry V*.

In something of a surprise on Oscar night, the statuette was won by Fricker.

BEST PICTURE

ACADEMY AWARDS

Awakenings
  (Columbia, 121 mins, 20 Dec 1990, $52.0m, 3 noms)
• *Dances with Wolves*
  (Tig, Orion, 183 mins, 9 Nov 1990, $184.2m, 12 noms)
Ghost
  (Koch, Paramount, 128 mins, 13 Jul 1990, $217.6m, 5 noms)
The Godfather Part III
  (Zoetrope, Paramount, 162 mins, 25 Dec 1990, $66.6m, 7 noms)
GoodFellas
  (Warner Bros., 146 mins, 19 Sep 1990, $46.8m, 6 noms)

GOLDEN GLOBE AWARDS

(Drama)	(Comedy/Musical)
Avalon	*Dick Tracy*
• *Dances with Wolves*	*Ghost*
The Godfather Part III	• *Green Card*
GoodFellas	*Home Alone*
Reversal of Fortune	*Pretty Woman*

PRODUCERS GUILD AWARD   BRITISH ACADEMY AWARDS

PRODUCERS GUILD AWARD	BRITISH ACADEMY AWARDS
Avalon	*Crimes and Misdemeanors*
Awakenings	*Driving Miss Daisy*
• *Dances with Wolves*	• *GoodFellas*
	Pretty Woman

NEW YORK – *GoodFellas*
LOS ANGELES – *GoodFellas*
BOARD OF REVIEW – *Dances with Wolves*
NATIONAL SOCIETY – *GoodFellas*
LONDON – *Crimes and Misdemeanors*

A decade after the financial disaster of *Heaven's Gate* had ended studio production of serious, large-scale Westerns, actor Kevin Costner ambitiously chose to make his directorial debut with *Dances with Wolves*, a lavish, epic Western about a US army officer who befriends a Lakota Sioux tribe during the US Civil War. Many in Hollywood scorned the highly personal project not only for indulging in a genre considered dead, but for its cost, running time and lengthy sub-titled sequences. Against all expectations, however, the film was a huge success with audiences and many critics (NYT "it is never exactly boring, only dulled ... a movie in acute need of sharpening"; NYP "there isn't a frame of this movie that's boring ... strangely intimate ... a grand, beautiful Western"; LAT "beautiful and memorable ... stirringly fine"; CT "a three-hour delight"; WP "stunning ... one of the year's most satisfying and audaciously entertaining films ... a gigantic achievement"; PI "superb ... a long-downtrodden genre is uplifted to heights it has not known in decades ... thoughtful and provocative"; V "elegiac"; TGM "a classic Western – morally absolute, emotionally nostalgic, shamelessly romantic ... a big picture in which the smallest detail has been handled with care ... a rhapsodic epic for the eyes"; FQ "a well-crafted film ... powerful"; SMH "a triumph on all levels ... a magnificent achievement"). In mid-December, *Dances with Wolves* was named Best Picture by the National Board of Review and became a major Academy Award contender.

On the same day as the announcement of the NBR winners, the Los Angeles Film Critics Association revealed the results of their balloting: *Dances with Wolves* finished as runner-up to Martin Scorsese's acclaimed gangster film *GoodFellas*, which had placed third in the NBR vote (NYT "breathless and brilliant ... the most politically serious and most evilly entertaining movie yet made about organized crime ... galvanizing"; LAT "extraordinary"; CST "the best mob movie ever"; WP "[a] masterpiece, but not the usual kind ... dazzlingly exhilarating ... stunning ... an incredible, relentless experience"; BG "immediately claims a place high on the list of great American gangster movies"; V "simultaneously fascinating and repelling ... colorful but dramatically unsatisfying"; SMH "a bravura display of film-making").

Two days later *GoodFellas* was also named Best Picture by the New York Film Critics Circle, 47 points to 19 over the Merchant Ivory drama *Mr and Mrs Bridge* (NYT "singularly bold, weird and offbeat ... a movie of marvelous and very dramatic density"; LAT "the film puts such a premium on tastefulness that it never threatens to become exciting"; TGM "a surprisingly risky film ... cerebral without being dry, delicate without being dull"; MFB "brilliantly retains the irony of the original [source material] ... immensely watchable"). Early in the new year, Scorsese's drama won the National Society of Film Critics plaudit by a similar margin (43 points to 23) over another crime drama *The Grifters*, which had polled third in New York (NYT "viciously entertaining ... smashing ... taut, tough and funny, and, at the end, sorrowful to a degree that takes the breath away"; LAT "the best film of the year"; CST "one of the best films of the year"; CT "a dark, offbeat drama ... highly recommended"; WP "keeps your attention riveted ... fascinating").

Dances with Wolves and *GoodFellas* were both nominated for the Best Picture (Drama) Golden Globe. They were overshadowed, however, by *The Godfather Part III*, the final part in Francis Ford Coppola's Mafia trilogy, which received seven nods from the Hollywood Foreign Press Association to lead the field of contenders (NYT "deeply moving ... stately, ceremonious ... irresistible"; NYP "it is not a masterpiece ... the disappointment can be crushing"; LAT "though [it] is definitely one of the best American movies of the year – a work of high ensemble talent and intelligence, gorgeously mounted and crafted, artistically audacious – it's still a disappointment"; CT "strangely insubstantial"; WP "a failure of heartbreaking proportions"; BG "while honorable, it frankly hasn't got the power, energy, inventiveness or richness of the first two films"; TGM "more than merely another bad movie"). Surprisingly, *The Grifters* was overlooked in favour of *Avalon* (NYT "a generous and touching film that is essentially smaller than its own sweeping ambitions"; LAT "an unusually ambitious work ... a superbly well-turned-out film, but something is missing ... has an uncomfortably generic quality"; CST "a warm and funny film, but also a sad one [that is ultimately] heartbreaking"; CST "superb"; CT "an episodic, sentimental saga ... soft-edged and synthetic"; WP "a rich, graceful work of lulling sentiment"; V "a lifeless experience devoid of central conflict or purpose") and *Reversal of Fortune* (NYT "lively, provocative, exquisitely acted ... a serious, invigorating American comedy about class, money, greed and the possibility of justice"; NYP "wildly entertaining"; LAT "brilliant"; V "riveting"; TGM "mesmerizing"; Sp "an enjoyable melodrama").

At the Globes ceremony, *Dances with Wolves* emerged as the winner and Oscar frontrunner. There was, however, a major surprise in the Best Picture (Comedy/Musical) category. The modest romantic comedy *Green Card* (NYT "as breezily escapist as a film this facile can be"; LAT "effortless engaging"; CT "disappointingly slight"; WP "instantly forgettable [but] nonetheless pleasing ... pleasant but lightweight"; BG "more romantic than comedic, but there isn't an abundance of either"; V "a genial, nicely played romance"; TGM "[a] gossamer comedy") unexpectedly outpolled *Dick Tracy* (NYT "thoroughly entertaining ... [a] stylish real-life cartoon ... simply the most deliriously stylish and inventive comedy to come out of Hollywood in years ... oddball and matchless"; NYP "an immaculate, numbingly dull piece of filmmaking"; LAT "brash, irresistible fun ... a film of enormous style"; CT "a panoply of set design and primary colors ... if this film doesn't sweep the technical craft Oscars next year, it will be a crime ... [but is] Beatty's least adventurous and least satisfying work as a filmmaker, a flimsily constructed, emotional inert movie ... a visual delight and a dramatic letdown"; WP "an ambitiously vainglorious effort, expensive, beautifully appointed, but at its core empty as a spent bullet"; V "a major disappointment ... curiously remote, uninvolving"; Time "not a great movie, but great moviemaking"; TGM "everything an excellent summer movie should be, and its visually one of the most astonishingly beautiful films in the history of the medium"; SMH "bright, imaginative and thoroughly entertaining") and the year's three biggest box office successes: *Ghost* (NYT "too slow moving at times, and a few of its special effects look incongruously silly [but it's] eccentric enough to remain interesting even when its ghost story isn't easy to believe"; LAT "a production prettified to the point of stickiness"; WP "an old-fashioned fantasy shot through with sentiment [which] sometimes verges on the laughable"; BG "a charmer ... beguilingly atmospheric ... an original"; V "light-weight romantic fantasy"), *Home Alone* (NYT "surprisingly charming"; LAT "delivers enough laughs"; WP "rambunctiously funny"; V "entertainment just right for the holiday season"; TGM "a perfect kids' movie, blending humor and adventure, fantasy and sentimentality, and it also has plenty of stuff for parents") and *Pretty Woman* (NYT "it is something special ... giddy, lighthearted escapism"; LAT "nothing works ... [a] frail comedy"; CT "thoroughly winning"; WP "a slick, instantly and entertainingly digestible Cinderella fable [but with] lurid aspects ... its unconsciously corrupt"; BG "an astonishingly self-oblivious piece of woman-bashing").

A month after winning the Globe, *Dances with Wolves* topped the list of Oscar candidates with twelve nominations (the highest tally in nearly a decade). *The Godfather Part III* trailed with seven, while *GoodFellas* garnered six. Also short-listed were the popular romantic drama *Ghost* and, in a major surprise, the drama *Awakenings* (NYT "both sentimentalizes its story and oversimplifies it"; LAT "never rises much above the level of a grade-A tear-jerker"; CT "manipulative ... a series of insistent emotional climaxes ... will [thus] certainly be a force to be reckoned with at Oscar time ... a canny piece of false art, one that consistently swaps meaning for superficial effect"; WP "a cause for rejoicing, a literate and compassionate film").

Despite nominations for directors Stephen Frears and Barbet Schroeder, respectively, both *The Grifters* and Globe nominee *Reversal of Fortune* were excluded from Best Picture consideration. Other prize winners and critics' awards contenders by-passed were: New York prize runner-up *Mr and Mrs Bridge*; Globe nominee *Dick Tracy*; NBR runner-up *Hamlet* (NYT "[a] sometimes slick but always lucid and beautifully cinematic version of the play"; WP "populist ... swift, respectable and decidedly not for the ages"); and the controversial Cannes winner *Wild at Heart* (NYT "the year's biggest anti-climax"; LAT "a comedy of a very special sort ... the violence in it, like the sentimentality, is so over-the-top"; CST "too long, slow-moving and soporific (in between the moments of sensation) and it's certainly not original ... it is actually reactionary"; CT "a mind-bending mix of comedy and violence"; WP "unlike anything that's ever been made before ... subversive [and] perversely original ... [but] lacking in the dreamlike irrevocability of [Lynch's] most brilliant work ... it's empty at heart"; BG "the grotesquerie is insubstantial"; TGM "bizarre to the bone ... stylistically hyperthyroid, exploitively violent, corrosively campy ... there has never been anything like it"; V "joltingly violent, wickedly funny and rivetingly erotic"; SMH "the year's most frustrating film").

Notable omissions among English-language releases included: *Alice* (NYT "marvelous ... splendid and sometimes uproariously funny"; LAT "not one of his weightier escapades [but] charming"; WP "displays a vital playfulness [but overall] continues [Woody] Allen's endless, banal quest for the Big Answers": BG "playful ... it isn't one of the best Allen films, but it's one of the better ones"); *Metropolitan* (NYT "a comedy of manners of a very high order that has a most unparochial wit and sense of fun ... a singular pleasure"; LAT "very gentle irony"; CT "soft and tentative"; WP "[this] modern comedy of manners is designed for urbane smirks [and] there is something tragic and tender between the lines"; V "strikingly original"); *Postcards from the Edge* (NYT "funny and well observed"; LAT "wickedly funny [but] amazingly thin ... defiantly underwritten"; CT "entertainingly malevolent"; TGM "it's brisk, it's funny, and it's surprisingly subtle"); *Miller's Crossing* (NYT "weightless [and] without much point at all ... a movie of random effects and little accumulative impact"; LAT "[an] elegiac, stylish gangster movie"; WP "brooding, dark ... a grim classic to admire if not to love"; BG "handsome, moody, potent, tactile ... hauntingly bountiful"; V "[a] standout"; TGM "gorgeously filmed, supremely well-acted, intricately written [but also] cynical and despairing ... brilliant ... a masterpiece, but of a unique kind"; G "striking"); *To Sleep with Anger* (NYT "a very entertaining, complex film"; LAT "[a] pungent and richly comic drama"; CT "a film of tremendous vitality, sensitivity, insight and, ultimately, mystery ... the first great film to come our way in quite a while"; WP "small, warm and unpretentious ... gratifying"; TGM "a complex, seamlessly acted study"); *Men Don't Leave* (NYT "a film that doesn't quite add up on its own ... gets by mostly on [Jessica] Lange's exceptional ability to hold an audience's attention"; LAT "a tender, beautifully acted, diabolically droll film"; CT "a magnificent piece of work – fresh, intelligent, funny and extremely moving ... a reminder of what movies can be"; WP "subtle, complex, fully and deeply felt ... I doubt you will see a better movie this year"); and *The Cook, The Thief, His Wife and Her Lover* (NYT "elegant, stylized and brutal ... a work so intelligent and powerful [and] so esthetically brilliant that it expands the boundaries of film itself"; NYP "grotesque and pretentious melodrama"; LAT "repulsive ... pointless self-indulgence ... sensational, all right, but hardly entertaining"; BG "overwhelming in terms of sheer visual style [and] overwhelmingly horrific"; G "magnificent ... one of the finest films to come out of Britain in the last decade"; SMH "extraordinary").

Foreign-language movies overlooked for consideration in the Academy's Best Picture category included: *Nuovo Cinema Paradiso (Cinema Paradiso)* (NYT "evokes nothing more substantial than sentimental B-movies made by hacks in Hollywood and abroad"; LAT "a shining valentine to the movies ... an almost unabashedly sentimental film"; WP "lovely ... exquisite"; BG "endearing"; MFB "a dewy-eyed portrait ... a self-indulgent film, probably a crowd-pleaser but essentially empty"); *Das Schreckliche Mädchen (The Nasty Girl)* (NYT "savagely original [but] becomes somewhat confused [and is] too carefully structured"; LAT "[a] stylized, satiric comedy ... one of the best films of the year ... exhilarating"; WP "lightheartedly original ... the movie engrosses us ... compelling"; BG "invigorating"; V "viciously funny ... well-crafted"; Time "bold, ironic and great fun"; Obs "funny, exciting, frightening and intellectually tough"; SMH "innovative and funny"); the 1989 Canadian film *Jésus de Montréal (Jesus of Montreal)* (NYT "intelligent, audacious"; LAT "a soaring, multifaceted delight"; CT "full of wonderful associations, intriguing ideas and penetrating wit [but] doesn't know where to stop ... in its excess it turns exasperating"; BG "affecting [but] too schematically simplistic"; V "audaciously conceived and brilliantly executed"; TGM "so much fun"; MFB "an impeccably post-modern version of the greatest story ever told"; Sp "strikingly original ... provocative, thoughtful"); and *Cyrano de Bergerac* (NYT "a physically elaborate period spectacle ... memorable"; LAT "glorious [and] well-nigh flawless"; CST "a splendid movie ... visually delightful"; TGM "lavishly appointed [and] decidedly handsome").

In the lead up to the Oscars, *GoodFellas* was named Best Film by the British Academy, but *Dances with Wolves* won the coveted accolades from the Producers and Directors Guilds. As a result, the Los Angeles Times said the only question left about the Oscars was just "how big a sweep will develop for 'Dances with Wolves'?" The answer was a haul of seven statuettes, including Best Picture – it was the first Western to claim the top Oscar since *Cimarron* in 1930/31.

Following its success at the Academy Awards, *Dances with Wolves* enjoyed such commercial and critical success that an even longer version of the film – with a running time of 224 minutes – was released in cinemas, consequently generating substantial repeat business with audiences that had already seen the original three-hour version.

BEST DIRECTOR

ACADEMY AWARDS
Francis Ford Coppola for *The Godfather Part III*
• **Kevin Costner for *Dances with Wolves***
Stephen Frears for *The Grifters*
Barbet Schroeder for *Reversal of Fortune*
Martin Scorsese for *GoodFellas*

GOLDEN GLOBE AWARDS
Bernardo Bertolucci – *The Sheltering Sky*
Francis Ford Coppola – *The Godfather Part III*
• **Kevin Costner – *Dances with Wolves***
Barbet Schroeder – *Reversal of Fortune*
Martin Scorsese – *GoodFellas*

DIRECTORS GUILD AWARD
Francis Ford Coppola
   – *The Godfather Part III*
• **Kevin Costner**
   – *Dances with Wolves*
Barry Levinson – *Avalon*
Martin Scorsese
   – *GoodFellas*
Guiseppe Tornatore
   – *Nuovo Cinema Paradiso*
   (Cinema Paradiso)

BRITISH ACADEMY AWARDS
Woody Allen
   – *Crimes and Misdemeanors*
Bruce Beresford
   – *Driving Miss Daisy*
• **Martin Scorsese**
   – *GoodFellas*
Giuseppe Tornatore
   – *Nuovo Cinema Paradiso*
   (Cinema Paradiso)

NEW YORK – Martin Scorsese – *GoodFellas*
LOS ANGELES – Martin Scorsese – *GoodFellas*
BOARD OF REVIEW – Kevin Costner – *Dances with Wolves*
NATIONAL SOCIETY – Martin Scorsese – *GoodFellas*
LONDON – Woody Allen – *Crimes and Misdemeanors*

At the Academy Awards Kevin Costner won Best Director for his directorial debut, *Dances with Wolves* ((NYT "what breaks through [here] is not genius but competence … commonplace"; LAT "a clear-eyed vision"; WP "[a] most impressive directorial debut … it's clear that the new director has a thrilling command of his tools … [it] isn't just competently directed, it's masterfully directed"; PI "a directing debut rich with promise"; V "fresh and assured"; TGM "on screen, he's Dances With Wolves; behind the camera, he's Directs With the Best"). In The New York Times, Janet Maslin called his win over veteran filmmaker Martin Scorsese "the evening's single biggest outrage."

Scorsese had dominated the early stages of the annual awards season for his handling of the acclaimed gangster film *GoodFellas* (NYT "there is flash in some of [his] directorial choices"; LAT "an artist working at the peak of his power"; WP "no director making films today has the visceral command of the movie camera that Scorsese has ... and there's exuberance, originality and a disquieting, stomach-wrenching brilliance in every frame of 'GoodFellas' ... in terms of sheer movie mechanics, of camera style and the shape and drive of his scenes, he's outstripped the work he did in his greatest films"; BG "gloriously and idiomatically right in every move ... stylistically innovative"). In mid-December, he outpolled Costner to win the Los Angeles Film Critics Association plaudit and convincingly claimed the New York Film Critics Circle accolade ahead of, respectively, Bernardo Bertolucci for *The Sheltering Sky* (NYT "the sort of dark, romantic movie that only [he] could pull off"; CT "brilliantly successful ... creates an elaborate, breathtakingly beautiful rhetoric of space") and Barbet Schroeder for *Reversal of Fortune* (LAT "under [his] direction the film may be morally ambiguous, but its performances and observations are absolutely on-target"). Early in the new year, Scorsese was named by the National Society of Film Critics for a third time with another overwhelming victory, this time over Stephen Frears for *The Grifters*, 49 points to 21 (LAT "a masterful display of control"; WP "renders that cutthroat universe [of professional tricksters] with adept strokes ... precision craftsmanship").

During the early part of the awards season, Costner, in contrast, only secured the National Board of Review prize. However, in the immediate lead-up to the Academy Awards, Costner emerged as the Oscar favourite by claiming the Golden Globe and the Directors Guild of America honour.

On Oscar night, Costner triumphed over a field comprised of Scorsese (who went home empty-handed for the third time), previous winner Francis Ford Coppola for *The Godfather Part III* (NYT "Coppola's deliberate invocation of the earlier [instalments] adds gravity without succumbing to the perils of repetition"; LAT "the brilliance and fertility of Coppola's talents pulls him through"; CT "fails to discover any new perspectives or to recreate the intensity of his original treatment ... Coppola cuts back and forth between these two main plots, yet never manages to place them in a meaningful dialectic ... instead, the film moves in spurts and spasms"; WP "the work of an artist estranged from his talent"), and two first-time contenders whose films were not in contention for Best Picture – NSFC runner-up Frears and New York runner-up Schroeder.

Several previous winners were overlooked for consideration: New York prize runner-up Bertolucci; Barry Levinson for *Avalon* (NYT "skilfully drawn";

LAT "telegraphs everything"; CT "[his] pumped-up scenes may be touching for a moment [but] his effects evaporate almost immediately"; WP "made with a master's confidence ... has never worked with the anything like the assurance he shows here"); Mike Nichols for *Postcards from the Edge* (LAT "speeds the movie by"; WP "finely attuned ... [but] while Nichols is servicing his star, he lets the other areas of the film go slack"; TGM "never strays too far from the humorous centre of things"); and Woody Allen for *Alice* (NYT "confirms [his] safe arrival on a whole new plateau of film-making").

Also by-passed were: David Lynch for *Wild at Heart* (LAT "what's disturbing about Lynch's work is that he unbinds the safety net"; WP "seems to misstep ... there are flashes of virtuosity but too much of what he's created here verges on self-parody"; BG "reveals too much self-awareness"); Joel Coen for *Miller's Crossing* (WP "the Coens are playing a controlling game and control frustrates passion, irrevocably"; BG "[their] stylistic virtuosity is finally hitched to [a] story"); Charles Burnett for *To Sleep with Anger* (NYT "accomplished"; CT "wonderfully light and understated, even at its most sinister, thanks to Burnett's delicate direction"; BG "artfully enriches the mix ... with imagination, assurance and originality"; TGM "he works wonders ... dazzling"); Peter Greenaway for the controversial drama *The Cook, The Thief, His Wife and Her Lover* (NYT "turns this tale into something profound and extremely rare: a work so intelligent and powerful that it evokes our best emotions ... creates such intensity that it is impossible to turn away from the screen ... [his] stroke of genius is to create a self-consciously false world peopled with character types who slowly become real ... deft"; LAT "deliberately theatrical"; CST "visceral"; CT "[his] contributions as a director seem largely negative ones ... his framing is highly inexpressive in its monotonous symmetry"); Whit Stillman for his debut, *Metropolitan* (LAT "Stillman is a pointillist, working in the tiniest, most meticulous ... [his] gift for quiet, scrupulous observation grows on you"; WP "has captured a world ... but in his microcosmic zeal [he] leaves [this] a one-joke movie"); and Franco Zeffirelli for his version of *Hamlet* (NYT "he creates a fluid and atmospheric style that keeps the camera moving but does not call attention to it"; WP "though he hasn't trashed the play, he has robbed it of its more resonant dimensions ... what [he] has lost in depth he's attempted to recover in immediacy"; BG "knows exactly how to drape 'Hamlet' around Gibson on the big screen").

Overlooked for their direction of foreign-language films were: Giuseppe Tornatore for the Italian drama *Nuovo Cinema Paradiso (Cinema Paradiso)* (NYT "his methods are commonplace and false"; WP "primarily a maker of documentary and television films, [this] heralds a new beginning [for him]"; BG "surprisingly potent in view of its obvious manipulativeness"); Denys Arcand for the Canadian film *Jésus de Montréal (Jesus of Montreal)* (NYT "as the film weaves in and out of the characters' lives [he] loses the wily, contemporary grip that makes his material effective"; LAT "[his] invention seems effortless ... ingenious"; WP "a movie from a director with intelligence and refined sensibilities [but] labored too"; BG "filled with powerful images and affecting acting"; V "brilliantly executed"; TGM "technically perfect ... simple in definition, complex in execution"); Jean-Paul Rappeneau for the lavish screen version of *Cyrano de Bergerac* (LAT "exceptionally graceful"; BG "he's shrewd enough to take advantage of film's intimacy to allow Depardieu's facial expressions and modulations to show the inner Cyrano beneath the bravado and bravura"; MFB "steers [the verse] with an exciting eloquence"); and Michael Verhoeven for *Das Schreckliche Mädchen (The Nasty Girl)*, for which he won the Best Director prize at the 1990 Berlin Film Festival (LAT "he tells his story in a theatrical mixture of colors and styles ... gives [the film] its darkly comic effect"; WP "tells this story with a surreal, ironic sense of humor and a grab bag of styles ... [he] points tacitly to the moral questions with disarming effectiveness"; BG "stylistically audacious [and] stingingly inventive"; TGM "the gentle irony here is unique, doubling as both an enticement and a trap. It gives the picture a breezy likeability, but, once we're lured in, turns purposeful and serious").

The most glaring omission, however, was Penny Marshall for the Best Picture nominee *Awakenings*, which had also earned a Best Actor nomination (NYT "mundane and inadequate"; LAT "has a gift for reticence [and] the taste to cut short most of the big moments ... but her sense of reserve also keeps the film from truly engaging us"; CT "seems determined to keep the eyes of her viewers perpetually misted over, which is a serious mistake"; WP "wins a chain of lustrous performances from an eclectic cast [and] masterfully plays our strings without becoming either melodramatic or maudlin"). Marshall, a former TV sitcom actress, was also notably absent from the both the Golden Globe and Directors Guild ballots.

1990

BEST ACTOR

ACADEMY AWARDS
Kevin Costner as 'Lt. John Dunbar' in *Dances with Wolves*
Robert De Niro as 'Leonard Lowe' in *Awakenings*
Gérard Depardieu as 'Cyrano de Bergerac' in *Cyrano de Bergerac*
Richard Harris as '"Bull" McCabe' in *The Field*
• **Jeremy Irons as 'Claus von Bulow' in *Reversal of Fortune***

GOLDEN GLOBE AWARDS

(Drama)
Kevin Costner – *Dances with Wolves*
Richard Harris – *The Field*
• **Jeremy Irons**
 – *Reversal of Fortune*
Robin Williams – *Awakenings*
Al Pacino – *The Godfather Part III*

(Comedy/Musical)
Macaulay Culkin – *Home Alone*
• **Gérard Depardieu – *Green Card***
Johnny Depp
 – *Edward Scissorhands*
Richard Gere – *Pretty Woman*
Patrick Swayze – *Ghost*

BRITISH ACADEMY AWARDS
Sean Connery – *The Hunt for Red October*
Tom Cruise – *Born on the Fourth of July*
Robert De Niro – *GoodFellas*
• **Philippe Noiret – *Nuovo Cinema Paradiso (Cinema Paradiso)***

NEW YORK – Robert De Niro – *Awakenings* and *GoodFellas*
LOS ANGELES – Jeremy Irons – *Reversal of Fortune*
**BOARD OF REVIEW – Robert De Niro – *Awakenings* and Robin
 Williams – *Awakenings***
NATIONAL SOCIETY – Jeremy Irons – *Reversal of Fortune*
LONDON – Philippe Noiret – Nuovo Cinema Paradiso (Cinema Paradiso)

Two years after being overlooked for an Oscar nomination for his New York
Film Critics Circle prize-winning performance as twins in *Dead Ringers*, Jeremy
Irons was again an early frontrunner for the Academy Award. He won the Los
Angeles Film Critics Association plaudit and the award from the National
Society of Film Critics, and finished as a close runner-up in the balloting in New
York, for his portrayal of Claus von Bulow, a man on trial for attempting to
murder his wealthy wife in *Reversal of Fortune* (NYT "exquisitely acted ... a
fine, devastating performance, affected, mannered, edgy, though seemingly ever
in complete control ... comes very close to being too good to be true ... makes

[the film] instructively entertaining"; LAT "a glittering performance that remains behind, an enigmatic after-image"; V "memorable"; TGM "elegantly ghoulish"; TT "a masterly interpretation"; Sp "has to sustain the whole [film] almost single-handed and he comes close to doing it").

Outpolling Irons in New York (by 35 points to 29) was Robert De Niro, who received his fourth accolade from the New York critics (his third as Best Actor) for his performances as a gangster in *GoodFellas* (LAT "flawless"; WP "stunning ... at his seamless best ... fascinating, entertaining, sometimes astounding [but] empty"; BG "terrific") and as a catatonic patient briefly revived by a new drug treatment in *Awakenings* (NYT "a skillful and ambitious performance but often a less than fully effective one"; NYP "skillfully played"; LAT "has the more technically difficult role ... sweet and full of feeling [but] a little wan"; CT "[his] usual meticulously observed performance"; WP "a physical wonder"). Two days earlier, De Niro had also been selected as Best Actor by the National Board of Review (his second trophy from the group) for *Awakenings*, sharing the honour with his co-star, Robin Williams as the doctor (NYT "very persuasive"; CT "an immediate problem, pushing himself forward in an ingratiating, show-biz manner that completely undermines the supposed shyness of his character ... another egregiously ego-stroking performance"; WP "comically tentative").

Surprisingly, however, De Niro was overlooked for a nomination at the Golden Globes. The momentum for the Oscar thus swung firmly behind Irons who claimed the Best Actor (Drama) Globe ahead of nominees: Kevin Costner as a US soldier who befriends a Lakota Sioux tribe during the US Civil War in *Dances with Wolves* (NYT "there's nothing wrong with the performance [but] Costner may not be the best person to direct himself ... flat, naturalistic screen behaviour"; LAT "charming"; WP "simultaneously the film's anchor and leavening agent"; PI "a commanding, resilient screen presence who disdains mannerism and affectation"; FQ "sensitive and convincing"); Richard Harris as a stubborn Irish farmer in *The Field*, his first screen role in eight years (NYT "a big, actory performance"; NYP "extraordinary"; LAT "sometimes confuses grandstanding with acting"; BG "Harris' performance takes sheer presence to realms of great power and force"; V "superb acting ... a resonant, domineering performance"); Al Pacino in *The Godfather Part III*, reprising the role of the Mafia boss for which he had received two Globe mentions in the early 1970s (NYT "mesmerizing"; WP "flails around inside his character"; V "magnificent"; TGM "has moments of excellence"); and Williams in *Awakenings*.

When the Academy announced its list of Oscar contenders on 13 February 1991, Irons was recognised for the first time and was identified by most observers as the favourite for the statuette. Previous winner De Niro, the other main contender for the critics' prizes, was cited for a fifth time, but for his turn in *Awakenings* rather than the more favoured *GoodFellas*. In a major shock, Pacino, who had been considered a sentimental dark horse, was not included (he was instead mentioned for the supporting award for his turn in *Dick Tracy*).

Ahead of Pacino, Oscar voters shortlisted: Costner for the year's most nominated film, *Dances with Wolves*, for which he was favoured to win the Best Director statuette; Globe nominee Harris, for a second time; and French star Gérard Depardieu, who had won the Globe (Comedy/Musical) for the romantic comedy *Green Card*, his first English-language film (NYT "the language barrier makes him seem not quite himself"; LAT "[the film's] ace in the hole is the almost indecent magnetism of Depardieu … plays this hand-tailored character with presence enough to stop a tank"; CT "pulls off the transition with aplomb [with much] charm and personal charisma"; WP "an amusing performance"; BG "gives a convincing account of himself … inordinately affecting"; TCM "devours the screen … impeccable"), but was nominated by the Academy for his Cannes prizewinning French-language performance as the poet soldier in *Cyrano de Bergerac* (NYT "[a] magical achievement ... a discipline whirlwind of conflicting emotions … Depardieu's must be the definite Cyrano … brings astonishing humor and pathos to the play's big set-pieces"; NYP "stunning ... pulls out all the stops"; LAT "brings together the right man at the right time of his life and career with one of the juiciest roles in European drama, one he was born to play … taps Depardieu's incredible inner reserves, his passion, intellect and physicality"; BG "fascinating to watch … intuitive, feeling, keenly attuned … has all the splash and panache you could hope for"; V "[a] grand performance"; Time "glorious"). José Ferrer won the Best Actor Oscar for playing the role in an English-language film version in 1950.

In addition to Pacino the Academy also by-passed: Philippe Noiret for his pair of 1989 European Film Award-winning performances in *Nuovo Cinema Paradiso (Cinema Paradiso)*, for which he also won the BAFTA (NYT "overacted"; LAT "memorably and beautifully played"; TGM "wonderful"; MFB "plays with his usual professionalism") and *La Vie et Rien d'Autre (Life and Nothing But)*, for which he also finished as the runner-up for the accolade in Los Angeles (NYT "[his character] never emerges as much more than a figure in a war-scarred landscape"; LAT "Noiret's priceless hangdog look, his mix of melancholy and affectionate irascibility here seem charged with heroic dignity"; WP "makes an engaging rugged camera subject, and though he gives an authoritative performance, it's not a terribly penetrating or affecting one"; BG "the depth beneath Noiret's angry cynicism [is] overpowering"); Danny Glover in *To Sleep with Anger*, for which he was NSFC runner-up and placed third in the voting in New York (NYT "a splendid character, richly written and played with great, insinuating ease"; LAT "gets straight down into the soul of Harry with a generous, brilliantly detailed performance"; CT "perfect"; BG "a rich, layered performance, quite the best [he] has been allowed to bring to the screen, worthy of recognition at Oscars time"; V "a powerfully unsettling presence"); previous winner Paul Newman in *Mr and Mrs Bridge* (NYT "splendid ... [he and Woodward] give the most adventurous, most stringent performances of their careers"; LAT "[an] uncompromising performance ... impeccably self-contained"; V "controlled"; TGM "subtle"; TT "distinguished"; MFB "stunning"); Mel Gibson as the eponymous tragic Danish prince in *Hamlet* (NYT "strong, intelligent ... he is by far the best part of [the film] ... extraordinarily convincing ... compelling"; NYP "very good"; LAT "a creditable Hamlet; even, in some of his showcase scenes, a more than creditable one [but] doesn't really bring anything extraordinary to the part"; WP "most of the credit must go to the film's star ... [his] Hamlet is deeply felt, electric and made very much for the camera ... there's nothing held back in his performance yet at the same time it's subtly calibrated"; BG "beats the odds ... heartfelt [as] he projects becomingly unpretentious straightforwardness and a surprising lack of self-consciousness in the famous soliloquies"; V "uninteresting"); Sean Penn in *State of Grace* (LAT "marvellous ... [a] complete and complex character"; BG "throws himself forcefully, and with heart, into the role"; WP "[an] affecting performance, a strong and silent struggle with his warring emotions"; V "excellent"); Gabriel Byrne in *Miller's Crossing* (NYT "[a] legitimate performance [but] not charismatic"; LAT "an opaque actor playing impenetrability"; BG "one of the most intriguingly complex crooks put on screen [and we can] trust Byrne to convey through his character's taciturnity his predilection for guilt and his own moral code"; TGM "supremely well-acted"); Nick Nolte in *Q&A* (NYT "one of the richest performances of his career"; LAT "[his] boldest, most spellbinding performance; his subtleties in playing this [role] are profound"; CT "adopts a trick voice and a theatrically menacing attitude that never let us forget that he's acting"; WP "[a] great performance ... doesn't flinch from his character's unsavoriness ... Nolte gives Brennan a kind of monumental brutishness – he makes him seem utterly indomitable"; BG "makes [the character] human, saves him from caricature even as [the] script self-destructs ... convincing"; V "bravura thesping"); Michael Gambon as the thief in *The Cook, The Thief, His Wife and Her Lover* (NYT "allows himself to be thoroughly despicable"; CT "stylized"; BG "Gambon, wallowing flamboyantly in the gangster's florid excesses, stands at the pinnacle of contemporary English acting"; SMH "hard to forget"); and Lothaire Bluteau in *Jésus de Montréal (Jesus of Montreal)* (NYP "excellent"; WP "lacks fire ... seems anything but the charismatic spiritual leader"; BG "affecting"; V "sensitive").

On Oscar night, as expected, Best Actor nominees Costner and Irons both won Academy Awards – Costner as Best Director and Irons as Best Actor.

BEST ACTRESS

ACADEMY AWARDS
• **Kathy Bates as 'Annie Wilkes' in** *Misery*
Anjelica Huston as 'Lilly Dillon' in *The Grifters*
Julia Roberts as 'Vivian Ward' in *Pretty Woman*
Meryl Streep as 'Suzanne Vale' in *Postcards from the Edge*
Joanne Woodward as 'Mrs Bridge' in *Mr and Mrs Bridge*

GOLDEN GLOBE AWARDS

(Drama)
• **Kathy Bates** – *Misery*
Anjelica Huston – *The Grifters*
Michelle Pfeiffer – *The Russia House*
Susan Sarandon – *White Palace*
Joanne Woodward
   – *Mr and Mrs Bridge*

(Comedy/Musical)
Mia Farrow – *Alice*
Andie MacDowell – *Green Card*
Demi Moore – *Ghost*
• **Julia Roberts** – *Pretty Woman*
Meryl Streep
   – *Postcards from the Edge*

BRITISH ACADEMY AWARDS
Shirley MacLaine – *Postcards from the Edge*
Michelle Pfeiffer – *The Fabulous Baker Boys*
Julia Roberts – *Pretty Woman*
• **Jessica Tandy** – *Driving Miss Daisy*

NEW YORK – **Joanne Woodward** – *Mr and Mrs Bridge*
LOS ANGELES – **Anjelica Huston** – *The Grifters* and *The Witches*
BOARD OF REVIEW – **Mia Farrow** – *Alice*
NATIONAL SOCIETY – **Anjelica Huston** – *The Grifters* and *The Witches*

Three Oscar frontrunners emerged from the critics' votes in mid-December.

The National Board of Review named Mia Farrow for her performance as the eponymous Manhattan socialite who discovers the truth about herself and her life through magical herbal medicines in *Alice*, her eleventh film with her then partner, director Woody Allen (NYT "has never been more surprisingly funny and affecting ... the kind of performance that, if there is any justice, will win her an Oscar nomination this year, maybe even an award"; WP "she may have her moments, but she never rises majestically to the occasion"; V "subtly spectacular"; Time "wonderful"; TGM "faultless").

The Los Angeles Film Critics Association gave their accolade to Anjelica Huston for her performances as a con-artist in *The Grifters* (NYT "spectacular";

NYP "breathtaking"; NYer "astounding"; LAT "Huston is the motor of the piece ... a perfect piece of work, mature and composed"; CT "one of her very best performances"; WP "[her] hard-edged performance is right on the money ... her emotions are precisely tailored and exact ... brings a vital conviction to her scenes"; Time "splendid ... [a] sure shot for an Oscar nomination") and as a witch planning to transform all children into mice in *The Witches* (NYT "the perfect glamorous villain"; LAT "a gem of strutting, swaggering monster camp, done with a sneering, Nazi commandant accent"; CST "[her] energy dominates the film ... worth seeing just for [her] obvious delight in playing a completely uncompromised villainess"; WP "the highlight [of the film]"). The association had previously given her their Best Supporting Actress award in 1985.

The runner-up for the Los Angeles award was sixty-year old Joanne Woodward as a Kansas wife in the Merchant Ivory film *Mr and Mrs Bridge*, which also starred her husband Paul Newman (NYT "splendid ... [she and Newman] give the most adventurous, most stringent performances of their careers"; LAT "the best reason to see the film is for the emotional shadings Woodward gives to the prim, needy Mrs Bridge"; V "she should be in the Oscar running this year for a nuanced, often funny portrayal"; Time "poignant"; TGM "subtle [and] impressive ... Woodward beautifully shades in the darker colours of both her [character's] vulnerability and culpability"; TT "marvellously enacted"; MFB "stunning").

Two days after the announcement of the NBR and Los Angeles winners, the west coast result was reversed in the balloting by the New York Film Critics Circle – Woodward narrowly outpolled Huston (35 points to 32) to win her third east coast honour. Early in the new year, the two actresses were the main contenders for the National Society of Film Critics honour, but the result was not as close: Huston won the plaudit 57 points to 25 ahead of Woodward.

When the Golden Globe nominees were announced two days after Christmas, the three critics prize-winners were all mentioned. When the trophies were presented a month later, however, all three went home empty-handed. Huston and Woodward were among those outpolled for Best Actress (Drama) by Kathy Bates as a romance novelist's deranged fan in the thriller *Misery*, for which she had placed third in the voting in New York (NYT "Bates is so good that she makes even Annie's open-faced enthusiasm somehow disconcerting ... memorable"; NYP "great"; LAT "she shows us the disgust and the fear of rejection and the demandingness that is the other side of Annie's googly-eyed adulation"; CT "a career-making performance ... displays an amazingly broad range of effects, moving from comedy to menace with a facility and truth far beyond [her director's] abilities"; WP "Bates is such an exceptional actress that we not only sympathize with her mad Annie, we also understand her better than we do Caan's dried-up hero"; BG "[a] terrific over-the-top performance ...

simultaneously comical and scary"; V "has a field day with her role, creating a quirky, memorable object of hate"; Time "simply spectacular"). Farrow, meanwhile, was one of the nominees outpolled by Julia Roberts for her performance as a prostitute in the box office smash *Pretty Woman* (NYT "a complete knockout ... this performance will make her a major star ... [she is] so funny, so natural and such an absolute delight that it is hard to hold anything against this movie"; LAT "stunning but cool as plastic"; CT "remarkably winning"; BG "charming"; V "a star-making performance").

When the Academy announced its list of nominees, the two Globe winners were both included and became dark horse contenders. New York and Los Angeles winners Huston and Woodward were both mentioned (for a third and fourth time, respectively) and were equal favourites for a second Oscar: Huston had won as Best Supporting Actress in 1985 while Woodward had won as Best Actress in 1957. Despite her NBR win, Farrow was overlooked in favour of Meryl Streep, who was recognised by the Academy for a ninth time in thirteen years. Streep played a recovering drug-addict film star who has a stormy relationship with her moviestar mother in *Postcards from the Edge*, a comedy written by Carrie Fisher and loosely based on her own relationship with her mother Debbie Reynolds (NYT "marvelous"; NYP "Streep is sublime"; LAT "it is clear now that there is nothing Streep cannot do"; CT "one of her most effective, least actressy performances ... her comic timing is extremely sharp"; WP "the most fully articulated comic performance of her career ... she flashes her steely wit like a saber"; TGM "understated ... beautifully in character and sardonically comfortable with the comedy").

Other contenders overlooked by the Academy were: Michelle Pfeiffer in *The Russia House* (NYT "gives the film's most persuasive performance ... brings to it a no-nonsense urgency that is missing from the rest of the movie"; LAT "brings [a] lyrical tenderness to her role"; CST "splendid"; WP "[an] enjoyable contribution ... entirely believable"; BG "believably Russian"; V "very believable"); Susan Sarandon in *White Palace* (NYT "gives a zesty, spirited, fully-formed performance that easily transcends the story's many preconceptions and cliches"; LAT "searingly well-acted ... with gusto [she creates] a raunchy, fallible, wounded real person"; WP "puts all her considerable talents into a rather trite pursuit [and] does what she can to triumph over the crudities in the material ... she makes [the character] tougher [than she is written and] gives her a sense of common-sense earthiness and sensuality, and she's brilliantly vital doing it"); Debra Winger in *The Sheltering Sky* (NYT "extraordinarily fine"; LAT "superb"; CT "performing at a level of profound physical involvement she takes [the characters'] quest into a startlingly different dimension"; G "[a] strong performance"; MFB "subtle in the way it catches variations in the character as she changes"; Sp "remarkable ... inhabiting the role rather than playing it"); Jessica Lange in *Men Don't Leave* (NYT "Lange makes Beth a moving and sympathetic figure ... but once again, [she] finds herself holding together a film that doesn't quite add up on its own"; LAT "emerges as a performance of heart, complexity and enormously subtle shading, [her] best since 'Tootsie'"; CST "altogether too good to be wasted on [such a character]"; CT "what may be the most modest and subtle performance of her career"; WP "I doubt you will see a better performance than Lange's this year"; TGM "her scope as an actress is beginning to seem limitless ... Lange is appropriately drab and listless – she doesn't ask approval for [the character], merely understanding"); Laura Dern in *Wild at Heart* (NYT "there's nothing phony or self-deceiving about Miss Dern's performance ... [a] triumph"; NYP "a larger-than-life performance"; WP "cuts loose as Lula in a way that few actresses have ever attempted; she's passionately uninhibited and without a shred of vanity or self-protection ... but her performance works more as spectacle than as anything else"; TGM "sweet and sizzling"); Helen Mirren as the wife in *The Cook, The Thief, His Wife and Her Lover* (NYT "astonishing as she gradually allows the wife's defensive facade to fall away"; CT "psychologically meticulous"; BG "unforgettable"; V "simply superb"; SMH "elegantly played"); European Film Award winner Carmen Maura in *Ay, Carmela!* (LAT "[her] performance, without ever losing its comic delicacy, steers the film into its deepest moments"; CT "only able to make sporadic use of her bounce and charm"; WP "plays the title role with her usual flash and earnestness"; BG "the incandescent Maura not only carries [the film], but wraps it around her like a flag"; V "memorable"; TGM "fitfully amusing ... [the] script merely serves to expose her flaws as a dramatic actress – she's great at extremes, not so hot at normal behaviour"; G "a bravura role ... goes the gamut from flamenco and flirtation through to the full tragedy of a civil war"); and Lena Stolze as a young German woman who decides to investigate the history of her town during the Second World War in *Das Schreckliche Mädchen (The Nasty Girl)* (NYT "the best thing in the movie"; LAT "irresistible"; WP "a perky performance"; V "deftly handles her character"; Obs "brings to the role of Sonja warmth, good humour and a sparkling intelligence ... makes the film glow").

On Oscar night, the highly-favoured pair of previous Oscar-winners Huston and Woodward were outpolled by Bates.

BEST SUPPORTING ACTOR

ACADEMY AWARDS
Bruce Davison as 'David' in *Longtime Companion*
Andy Garcia as 'Vincent Mancini' in *The Godfather Part III*
Graham Greene as 'Kicking Bird' in *Dances with Wolves*
Al Pacino as 'Big Boy Caprice' in *Dick Tracy*
• **Joe Pesci as 'Tommy DeVito' in *GoodFellas***

GOLDEN GLOBE AWARDS
Armand Assante – *Q&A*
• **Bruce Davison – *Longtime Companion***
Hector Elizondo – *Pretty Woman*
Andy Garcia – *The Godfather Part III*
Al Pacino – *Dick Tracy*
Joe Pesci – *GoodFellas*

BRITISH ACADEMY AWARDS
Alan Alda – *Crimes and Misdemeanors*
• **Salvatore Cascio – *Nuovo Cinema Paradiso (Cinema Paradiso)***
John Hurt – *The Field*
Al Pacino – *Dick Tracy*

NEW YORK – Bruce Davison – *Longtime Companion*
LOS ANGELES – Joe Pesci – *GoodFellas*
BOARD OF REVIEW – Joe Pesci – *GoodFellas*
NATIONAL SOCIETY – Bruce Davison – *Longtime Companion*

The major American end of year critics' awards were split between the two main Oscar contenders. For his performance as the gay lover of a television scriptwriter in *Longtime Companion*, Bruce Davison claimed the New York Film Critics Circle and National Society of Film Critics awards and finished as the runner-up in the voting by the Los Angeles Film Critics Association (NYT "each [character] tends to more of a type than a particular personality [with] the notable exception [of] Davison's David ... very moving"; LAT "the superlative cast forms an ensemble, but Davison's calm, quietly devoted, increasingly mature and selfless David dominates the entire film"; WP "sleekly modulated in his responses"; V "tremendously sensitive, compassionate"; TGM "poignant"; MFB "excellent [and] superb"; Sp "his scenes are honest and might have been honest, except that he is the least interesting of the unmemorable characters").

Meanwhile, Joe Pesci, who was outpolled by Davison in the New York vote (48 points to 34) and the NSFC ballot (38 points to 22), secured the Los Angeles and National Board of Review plaudits for his portrayal of a psychotic gangster in *GoodFellas* (LAT "truly chilling"; WP "stunning ... gives the film's deepest, most volatile performance ... unforgettably alarming and endearing"; BG "unerringly acted").

When the two critics' prize-winners lined up against one another at the Golden Globe Awards, it was Davison who emerged with the trophy and a slight edge going into the Oscar race.

Both Davison and Pesci were shortlisted by the Academy (Pesci for a second time) and were considered the strongest candidates in a strong field of nominees, whom observers argued all had a genuine chance of claiming the statuette. Surprisingly overlooked in the Best Actor category for *The Godfather Part III*, Al Pacino was something of a sentimental favourite as gang-leader "Big Boy" Caprice in *Dick Tracy* (NYT "astonishing ... a triumph ... heavyweight hilarity of a high order"; LAT "Pacino's Big Boy Caprice has to be one of the screen's most extravagantly funny creations ... 'Dick Tracy' is Pacino's movie, not Beatty's ... is likely to wow the world with pure, inspired comic invention"; CT "the film's best, boldest performance ... the major acting presence in the film ... comic vulgar, violent, and funny ... wonderful"; WP "Pacino gleefully steals Beatty's thunder"; V "virtually runs away with the show"; TGM "a tour de force of villainous comic acting hilariously imprisoned in a masterpiece of bestial make-up"; SMH "most impressive of all"). It was Pacino's sixth nod and his first in over a decade. Each nominated for the first time were: Cuban-born Andy Garcia as the illegitimate nephew and heir apparent of a Mafia boss in *The Godfather Part III* (NYT "[a] high-voltage performance"; LAT "Garcia seizes the screen here, and gives an explosive, tigerishly self-confident performance"; CT "has a few moments of forcefulness"; WP "seems to be the only actor in the film who knows what he's playing ... he gives a thrilling, feral performance"; BG "the one to watch ... plays in career-breakthrough fashion") and Canadian Graham Greene as a Lakota Sioux chief in *Dances with Wolves*, the year's most nominated film (LAT "[a] stand out"; WP "dazzling ... gives resonance to his character's anxiety over the coming of the whites"; V "vivid, transfixing"; TGM "marvellous"; FQ "poised and convincing").

Pacino was also a contender for the BAFTA, alongside three performances overlooked by the Academy: Alan Alda in *Crimes and Misdemeanors* (by-passed in Hollywood the previous year); John Hurt in *The Field*; and Salvatore Cascio as the little boy in the Italian film *Nuovo Cinema Paradiso (Cinema Paradiso)* (NYT "at the director's bidding, his gives an enthusiastic but awful miniature-adult performance"; TGM "adorable"; MFB "[played] with commendable naturalness"). Surprisingly, the winner was nine-year old Cascio.

Pacino was equally unsuccessful at the Academy Awards in Hollywood. A decade after he was first touted as an Oscar favourite, Pesci claimed the statuette for *GoodFellas*. It was the only award that the film received on the night.

Notable omissions from the field of Oscar finalists were: Armand Assante in *Q&A* (NYT "[a] stand out"; LAT "[a] great breakthrough ... a rich, ripe performance that never slips into overripeness ... Assante mesmerizes us ... it's bravura stuff"; WP "[a] great performance"); Hector Elizondo as the hotel manager in *Pretty Woman* (NYT "particularly winning"; CT "fine supporting work"; WP "[does] a great deal with [a] little role"; BG "charming"; V "outstanding"); Australian Anthony LaPaglia as a Mafia boss' nephew attracted to a policewoman in *Betsy's Wedding* (NYT "uproariously dominates the movie"; LAT "hilarious"; CT "doing a fairly droll De Niro impression"; WP "artfully played ... just about the movie's salvation ... he manages to be at once mannered and genuine"; TGM "gives the lines a hilarious De Niro inflection"; MFB "a fastidious, low-key comic performance"); Dustin Hoffman as Mumbles in *Dick Tracy* (NYT "[a] rare and funny contribution"; CT "scores a few laughs in a small role"; WP "brief [but] funny"; SMH "hilarious"); Pat Hingle in *The Grifters* (NYer "probably his best performance ever"; WP "his presence drops a little gravel into the mix"); Armin Mueller-Stahl in *Avalon* (NYT "outstanding"; LAT "a rare example of a folkloric performance that doesn't seem any less human for being larger-than-life"; WP "played brilliantly ... he gives the movie its soulful plaintiveness"); both Albert Finney (LAT "a grand turn ... breathtaking"; BG "[a] tough exterior and pained interior are deliciously conveyed in his slightly stiff, closed manner"; V "outstanding"; TGM "supremely well-acted") and John Turturro (NYT "gives the film's most interesting performance"; LAT "at the peak of smarmy perfection"; BG "juicily played"; TGM "supremely well-acted") in *Miller's Crossing*; Klaus Maria Brandauer in *The Russia House* (NYT "good"; LAT "a splendid cameo"); Willem Dafoe in *Wild at Heart* (WP "achingly mannered"; BG "indescribably and intentionally repulsive"); Chris O'Donnell in *Men Don't Leave* (LAT "stunning ... subject to a barrage of conflicting emotions, O'Donnell is sensitive, funny and furious, by degrees"; V "superb"); Alan Bates as Claudius in *Hamlet*, a performance for which he'd be a BAFTA nominee the following year (NYT "a solid performance"; BG "Close and Bates command what screen time they're given"; V "solid"); and Gary Oldman in *State of Grace* (NYT "phenomenal ... an electrifying performance"; NYP "amazing"; LAT "has been allowed to start his performance somewhere in the stratosphere and spiral upward from there"; CST "Oldman's performance is the best thing about [the movie]"; WP "shrill shenanigans ... a parody of an Irish souse"; BG "remarkable ... adds another unforgettable loose cannon to his impressive gallery of screen characterizations"; SMH "scares the living daylights out of you").

BEST SUPPORTING ACTRESS

ACADEMY AWARDS
Annette Bening as 'Mya Langtree' in *The Grifters*
Lorraine Bracco as 'Karen Hill' in *GoodFellas*
• **Whoopi Goldberg as 'Oda Mae Brown' in *Ghost***
Diane Ladd as 'Marietta Pace' in *Wild at Heart*
Mary McDonnell as 'Stands with a Fist' in *Dances with Wolves*

GOLDEN GLOBE AWARDS
Lorraine Bracco – *GoodFellas*
• **Whoopi Goldberg – *Ghost***
Diane Ladd – *Wild at Heart*
Shirley MacLaine – *Postcards from the Edge*
Mary McDonnell – *Dances with Wolves*
Winona Ryder – *Mermaids*

BRITISH ACADEMY AWARDS
• **Whoopi Goldberg – *Ghost***
Anjelica Huston – *Crimes and Misdemeanors*
Shirley MacLaine – *Steel Magnolias*
Billie Whitelaw – *The Krays*

NEW YORK – Jennifer Jason Leigh – *Last Exit to Brooklyn* and *Miami Blues*
LOS ANGELES – Lorraine Bracco – *GoodFellas*
BOARD OF REVIEW – Winona Ryder – *Mermaids*
NATIONAL SOCIETY – Annette Bening – *The Grifters*

Seven actresses contested the major critics' prizes, but none claimed the Oscar.

The National Board of Review named Winona Ryder as the elder daughter in *Mermaids* (NYT "enchanting and funny, and firmly in control of every scene not handed to Cher ... so good"; LAT "this is not one of the roles in which she's being challenged to do anything new"; CST "generates real charisma"; WP "perfect ... makes the fantastical side of Charlotte's inner life entirely plausible ... her richest performance"; V "delightful").

The Los Angeles Film Critics Association selected Lorraine Bracco as a cocaine-addicted gangster's wife in *GoodFellas* (LAT "plays [the role] perfectly"; WP "stunning ... a source of dark turbulence in the film"; V "inadequate") ahead of Dianne Wiest as the Avon lady in *Edward Scissorhands*

(LAT "[a] marvelous, spine-tinglingly funny caricature"; BG "played with just the right pitch of good-hearted twitter"; V "a smash").

Jennifer Jason Leigh won the New York Film Critics Association accolade as prostitutes in *Last Exit to Brooklyn* (NYT "nearly perfect"; LAT "remarkable ... [a] particular standout"; BG "steals the film"; MFB "manages convincingly the transition from street-corner vamp to used-up drudge") and *Miami Blues* (NYT "steals every scene"; LAT "Leigh's fine, lived-in performance extends our sympathies ... makes us understand Susie's yearnings"; CT "so deeply inside her character the effect is almost frightening"; WP "she is all wistfulness and freckled sincerity in Leigh's hands"; TGM "expertly observed"). The runner-up was Joan Plowright as the matriarch of an immigrant family in *Avalon* (NYT "warmly and broadly acted"; LAT "astonishing"; CT "[a] likeable turn"; WP "movingly expert").

The National Society of Film Critics winner was Annette Bening as a con-artist in *The Grifters* (NYT "absolutely right"; NYer "stunning"; LAT "perfection"; WP "exudes an appropriately floozy quality but ultimately lacks the acting machinery to make her role soar"; Time "splendid ... [a] sure shot for an Oscar nomination"). Bening outpolled Uma Thurman as both a homeless teenager in *Where the Heart Is* and as the wife of writer Henry Miller in *Henry and June* (NYT "takes a larger-than-life character and makes her even bigger, though her performance is often as curious as it is commanding"; LAT "June should be a femme fatale of mystical proportions but [she] plays her like a sultry '60s hippie co-ed"; BG "sympathetic"; TGM "the staggeringly charismatic Uma Thurman transforms June").

From this group, the Academy recognised only Bening and Bracco. The others were overlooked along with: Shirley MacLaine as an ageing star in *Postcards from the Edge* (NYT "marvelous"; NYP "amusing"; CT "a devastating parody"; TGM "wonderful ... her performance is luminous"); Glenn Close, both as heiress Sunny von Bulow in *Reversal of Fortune* (NYT "terrific"; LAT "flawless [and] icily splendid"; V "excellent"; Sp "seems to be miscast") and Queen Gertrude in *Hamlet* (NYT "makes her troubled without being monstrous ... but there is too much posturing in her performance"; LAT "there is one performance I liked very much ... Close brings something electrifying to her scenes ... she figures out a way to make the lines breathe and soar"; WP "stirring"; BG "full-blooded ... Close and Bates command what screen time they're given"); the previous year's winner, Brenda Fricker, in *The Field* (LAT "her underplaying is sometimes a relief in the din [but essentially] a colossal waste"; BG "conviction"); both Blythe Danner (NYT "exceptionally good"; TGM "splendid") and Kyra Sedgwick (V "smashing") in *Mr and Mrs Bridge*; Marcia Gay Harden in *Miller's Crossing* (BG "another plus [for the film]"; TGM "supremely well-acted"); Bernadette Peters in *Alice* (NYT "particular mention must be made of [her]"; WP "has a funny cameo"; BG "a kick"); Joan Cusack in *Men Don't Leave* (NYT "manages to be more amusing than bizarre"; LAT "at the very top of her form"; CT "unforgettable"; WP "a wonderfully ditzy performance"); Kathy Baker as the sexpot neighbour in *Edward Scissorhands* (NYT "played with funny flamboyance"; LAT "[a] marvelous, spine-tinglingly funny caricature"; BG "funny") and Billie Whitelaw as the mother of mobster twins in *The Krays* (LAT "great"; V "superb"; TGM "wondrously acted"; MFB "remains sympathetic in the role"; Sp "in the hands of an actress less able and sensitive the portrait of Violet would have been a disaster"; SMH "imposing").

Nominated alongside Bening and Bracco were: Whoopi Goldberg as a fake medium in *Ghost* (NYT "has found a film role that really suits her, and she makes the most of it ... though at first see seems to exist for comic relief, she has the most crucial role"; LAT "Goldberg in her element, giving the film its kick and energy ... gleefully, wickedly funny"; WP "a robust, gold-hearted performance ... put spiritual oomph into an otherwise strained tea-reading role"; BG "hearteningly full of her old comic sass"); Diane Ladd as a possessive mother in *Wild at Heart* (LAT "amazingly over-the-top, perhaps too much so"; WP "achingly mannered"; BG "an over-the-top performance"; TGM "presumably meant to out-baroque the late Geraldine Page"); and Mary McDonnell as a white woman raised in a Lakota Sioux tribe in *Dances with Wolves* (NYT "stand out"; WP "of all the performances, [her's] is the most complex ... this is forceful, stirring acting ... in painting this portrait, the actress has wet her brush with tears"; V "impressive"; TGM "manages [the] stereotype without a second of stagy behaviour"; FQ "skillful").

On Oscar night, fifty-one years after Hattie McDaniel won for *Gone with the Wind*, Golden Globe and BAFTA winner Goldberg claimed the statuette to become the second African-American woman to win an Academy Award in the acting categories. Three years later, she became the first African-American to host the Oscar ceremony.

1991

BEST PICTURE

ACADEMY AWARDS
Beauty and the Beast
  (Disney, Buena Vista, 84 mins, 22 Nov 1991, $145.8m, 6 noms)
Bugsy
  (Tri-Star, 135 mins, 13 Dec 1991, $49.1m, 10 noms)
J.F.K.
  (Camelot, Warner Bros., 190 mins, 20 Dec 1991, $70.4m, 8 noms)
The Prince of Tides
  (Barwood/Longfellow, Columbia, 132 mins, 25 Dec 1991, $74.7m, 7 noms)
• *The Silence of the Lambs*
  (Strong Heart, Orion, 118 mins, 14 Feb 1991, $130.7m, 7 noms)

GOLDEN GLOBE AWARDS
(Drama)   (Comedy/Musical)
• *Bugsy*   • *Beauty and the Beast*
J.F.K.   *City Slickers*
The Prince of Tides   *The Commitments*
The Silence of the Lambs *The Fisher King*
Thelma and Louise   *Fried Green Tomatoes*

PRODUCERS GUILD AWARD **BRITISH ACADEMY AWARDS**
At Play in the Fields of the Lord • *The Commitments*
Boyz n the Hood   *Dances with Wolves*
The Commitments   *Thelma and Louise*
J.F.K.   *The Silence of the Lambs*
The Prince of Tides
• *The Silence of the Lambs*

NEW YORK – *The Silence of the Lambs*
LOS ANGELES – *Bugsy*
BOARD OF REVIEW – *The Silence of the Lambs*
NATIONAL SOCIETY – *Life is Sweet*
LONDON
  (Best Film) *Thelma and Louise*
  (Best British Film) *Life is Sweet*

The short-list for the Academy's top prize was unusually diverse and in the Los Angeles Times, David Fox declared, "the stage is set for the most wide open Oscar race for Best Picture in years". Film historian Danny Peary subsequently recalled, "If you listened to the confounded Hollywood pundits prior to the Oscar telecast in March of 1992, you would have thought that none of the five nominees had a chance".

Topping the list of candidates with ten nominations was the Los Angeles Film Critics Association and Golden Globe (Drama) winner *Bugsy*, a gangster biopic (NYT "vastly entertaining"; LAT "glossy ... overall a satisfying film that delivers a full measure of stylish entertainment"; CST "a movie that vibrates with optimism and passion"; WP "exuberantly elegiac ... a great gangster picture, with all the visceral excitement of a classic mob saga [and] a salute to old Hollywood glamour ... one of the year's most bracing, entertaining movies ... near perfect: violent, sexy and knowingly smart"; BG "suave, outrageous, flamboyant, knowing and above all playful"; V "absorbing"; FQ "brash, bold-faced entertainment"; Time "riveting"). However, enthusiasm for the film was reportedly weak among Oscar voters and its director, Barry Levinson, won neither the Globe nor the Directors Guild of America accolade.

Garnering eight nods was *J.F.K.*, a drama which explored claims of a conspiracy behind the assassination of President Kennedy (NYT "the film's insurmountable problem is the vast amount of material it fails to make coherent sense of ... as busy and as full of exposition as it is, the conspiracy remains far more vague than the movie pretends ... simultaneously arrogant and timorous"; NYP "nearly great"; LAT "disturbing, infuriating yet undeniably effective, less a motion picture than an impassioned, insistent information barrage ... relentless"; CST "overwhelming"; CT "[a film of] hysteria, speediness and manic self-importance"; WP "a riveting marriage of fact and fiction, hypothesis and empirical proof in the edge-of-your-seat spirit of conspiracy thriller ... compelling viewing"; Time "electrifying"; SMH "impassioned, over-the-top, intense ... extremely powerful [but] overlong").

An early favourite was *The Prince of Tides* (NYT "a film that is gratifyingly lean"; LAT "mainstream film-making at its main-streamest, smooth and glossy"; CT "part Oscar bid, part vanity project and all pretty silly"; BG "a big, bold, slightly old-fashioned film carried by its heartfelt conviction"; V "deeply moving"; TGM "a good movie [but falters] at the two-thirds mark"; S&S "effective, middle-of-the-road entertainment"). The film earned seven nominations, but no recognition for its director, Barbra Streisand. Several observers predicted that her exclusion would help the film's chances, just as the omission of Bruce Beresford had helped *Driving Miss Daisy* two years earlier.

Also up for seven Oscars was the box office hit *The Silence of the Lambs*, a thriller about serial-killers (NYT "[a] swift, witty new suspense thriller ... pop film making of a high order"; NYP "intelligent ... chillingly effective"; LAT "stunning"; WP "a masterly suspense thriller"; BG "works in a mode that is comparatively flat"; V "mesmerizing"; TGM "becomes annoyingly predictable"; TT "brilliantly devised but repellent"; Sp "very artful ... a superior thriller"; SMH "a classic"). The film had been the first to win Best Picture, Director, Actor and Actress from the New York Film Critics Circle, and had also won the National Board of Review prize and the top accolades from both the Producers and Directors Guilds. Academy Awards voters, however, usually shunned films with disturbing subject matter. Furthermore, the film had been released well over a year earlier and was already available on home video.

The dark horse was Disney's *Beauty and the Beast*, the first fully-animated feature considered for Best Picture (NYT "fresh and altogether triumphant ... combines the latest computer animation techniques with the best of Broadway"; NYP "funny, enchanting"; LAT "sure to charm a wide audience"; WP "a delightfully modern fable, a near-masterpiece that draws on the sublime traditions of the past while remaining completely in sync with the sensibility of its time ... a giant step forward for Disney's animation unit"; V "ranks with the best of Disney's animated classics"; TGM "delightful"). *Beauty and the Beast* had won the Globe (Comedy/Musical) and was regarded a positive, family-oriented alternative to the other four nominees.

Arguably the most notable absentees from the list of contenders were: *Thelma and Louise* (NYT "hugely appealing ... reimagines the buddy film with such freshness and vigor that the genre seems positively new"; NYP "joyous, boisterous, edgy"; LAT "provocative, poignant and heartbreakingly funny"; WP "exhilarating"; BG "breathes new life into an old genre"; V "thumpingly adventurous"; Sp "fresh, provocative and, above all, funny"); *Boyz n the Hood* (NYT "gripping [and] disturbing"; NYP "remarkable ... a thoughtful, powerful, skillful movie"; LAT "striking"; CST "one of the best movies of 1991"; WP "unflinching, often funny, always compassionate"; V "absorbing"); and *An Angel at My Table* (NYT "a fine, rigorous adaptation"; LAT "too blankly enigmatic ... [but has] extraordinary moments"; CST "engrossing from beginning to end"; CT "excellent ... massively rich in emotions and associations"; WP "a big, sprawling, unshapely thing ... insufferably verbose and, at the same time, touched with magnificence"; V "touching and memorable"; TGM "a humanist biography filled with compassion"; G "one of the very best films of the year"; SMH "deeply moving ... brilliant").

Several winners of major awards, as well as runners-up, were overlooked including: Cannes Film Festival winner *Barton Fink* (NYT "an unqualified winner ... a fine dark comedy of flamboyant style"; LAT "exhilarating and frustrating at the same time ... enormously amusing [but] perplexing"; WP "rapturously funny, strangely bittersweet, moderately horrifying ... certainly one of the year's best and most intriguing films"; BG "a frantic comedy of emptiness [but] hellishly funny"; V "eccentric"; Time "just plain weird [and] intrinsically problematic"; G "lurches from parody into nightmare and back again"); New York runner-up *My Own Private Idaho* (NYT "invigorating ... blunt, uncompromising and nonjudgmental"; LAT "manages to confound all expectations"; CT "superb ... beautifully wrought, darkly funny and finally devastating ... almost single-handedly revives the notion of personal filmmaking in the United States ... a very rich, very sympathetic piece of work"; WP "the most ambitious mainstream film of the year ... gets you below the emotional belt in a searing, delicate way ... no movie this year approaches such magnificent imagery, such delectable poetry"; TGM "there are flaws [but the film] achieves more than most movies dream of attempting"); Los Angeles runner-up *The Fisher King* (NYT "a big, messy, exuberant movie [but it] pulls off its improbable success with a healthy dose of irreverence"; WP "a poignantly redemptive tale"; BG "too long [and] uneven [but it is] the kind of film that keeps you wanting to believe in it, and it delivers the big payoff it promises"; V "compelling"; Time "[a] long, dark and handsome – disorientating comedy"; TGM "a literate, visually attractive romantic comedy ... a fantasy that makes you feel good without leaving you coated in glucose"; S&S "a film that takes itself far too seriously [with] an unwieldy narrative, alternately garbled and contrived, cluttered with diversions of dubious effect"); National Society of Film Critics and London Film Critics prize winner *Life is Sweet* (NYT "very special ... a movie that breathes"; LAT "marvelously eccentric ... at once surreal and very real"; WP "blissfully funny"; V "highly sympathetic"; TGM "comic and quirky"); NSFC runner-up *Naked Lunch* (NYT "smashingly funny [and both] brilliant and vile"; LAT "it's a movie for people who really dig Croenenberg's mulchy fixations – and probably for no one else"; CT "a thrilling, astounding, devastating piece of work"; WP "[a] masterpiece"; V "fascinating, demanding, mordantly funny"; TGM "monumentally daring ... a sensual and intellectual feat"); BAFTA winner *The Commitments* (NYT "exuberant [but] becomes repetitive after a while"; LAT "there's no resisting 'The Commitments'"; CST "a loud, rollicking, comic extravaganza ... filled with life and energy"; CT "joyful but empty"; WP "sexy, hilarious, exuberantly energetic"; V "swell-executed and original"; TGM "terrifically engaging"); and 1990 Venice Film Festival winner *Rosencrantz and Guildenstern are Dead* (NYT "on the stage this sort of thing can be great fun [but] in the more realistic medium of film, so many words can numb the eardrums ... this is the effect of [this] new movie"; NYP "wonderfully witty"; LAT "a jewel of a movie ... both eloquently impish and brilliant"; WP "a thuddingly dull botch of a brilliant script"; S&S "too long, too slow, and ponderous when it is trying to be humorous"; Sp "an enchanting film, clever, funny, tense, touching and terrific to look at").

Other films overlooked were: *Jungle Fever* (NYT "consistently invigorating"; LAT "strong and powerful"; CT "a failure, but it is the kind of failure that engenders hope"; WP "funny, political, stirring and sentimental, often at the same time"); *Prospero's Books* (NYT "initially splendiferous and finally numbing"; CST "[an] experiment worth watching"; WP "qualifies more as an impressive technological novelty than a coherent work of art ... truly an aesthetic breakthrough"; BG "[its] sensory overload and essential superficiality steadily erode its impact"; G "nothing quite like it has been seen before"; SMH "stunning ... extraordinarily inventive"); *Trust* (NYT "droll ... richly detailed [with] no frills or grace notes"; LAT "a comedy for the new, white, suburban blitzed-out generation of smart, disaffected youth"; CT "consists of moments without continuity, of inventions without a context"; WP "absorbing ... comes in bursts of satiric success – but also pretension"); *Rambling Rose* (WP "hangs on the screen like a web spun out of glistening memories ... funny, moving [and] spectacularly acted"; BG "one of the year's very best films ... a joy"); the 1990 war drama *Europa, Europa* (NYT "brings new immediacy to the outrage by locating specific, wrenching details that transcend cliche"; LAT "[a] gruesomely comic movie"; CST "masterful"; WP "[a] darkly ironic masterpiece ... passionate, subtly intelligent [and] universal"; BG "stunning"; TGM "seems to lack the power of its own truthfulness"); *La Double Vie de Véronique (The Double Life of Veronique)* (NYT "alternately haunting and opaque ... a magnificent visual and aural experience ... it bewitches the eye"; LAT "bound to be overrated"; CT "mysterious, beautiful and passionate ... [a] seductive, challenging film"; BG "elegant, enigmatic and haunting ... mesmerizing"; Obs "haunting ... a transcendental experience"; Sp "the art house film par excellence – elusive and mystifying"); and *Daddy Nostalgie* (US: *Daddy Nostalgia*, UK: *These Foolish Things*) (NYT "handsomely elegiac [and] sophisticated"; LAT "elegant ... a shimmeringly beautiful film"; BG "moving ... as sweetly rueful as film gets"; TGM "a thing of beauty ... once in a long while a film comes along to remind you just how good a film can be").

While it was highly-anticipated as a potential Oscar contender, the chances of *Fried Green Tomatoes* were scuppered by mixed reviews (NYT "has some good performances and a measure of homespun appeal"; LAT "an ordinary film blessed with a number of out-of-the-ordinary performances ... a compendium of soap-opera clichés, simplistic and sentimental and drawn in the broadest of strokes"; BG "contrived and sentimental [yet] downright irresistible"; CT "never quite shakes off its stiff, studied feel ... it's meant to be uplifting [but] the material is so undernourished [and] none of the characters has been filled out beyond the underlying conventions"; SFC "deliciously funny"; V "absorbing and life-affirming"; TGM "rudimentary").

On Oscar night, it was *The Silence of the Lambs* which emerged victorious from this unpredictable field. It not only won the statuette for Best Picture, but became the third film to sweep the top five awards: Best Picture, Director, Actor, Actress and Adapted Screenplay.

BEST DIRECTOR

ACADEMY AWARDS
• **Jonathan Demme for** *The Silence of the Lambs*
Barry Levinson for *Bugsy*
Ridley Scott for *Thelma and Louise*
John Singleton for *Boyz n the Hood*
Oliver Stone for *J.F.K.*

GOLDEN GLOBE AWARDS
Jonathan Demme – *The Silence of the Lambs*
Terry Gilliam – *The Fisher King*
Barry Levinson – *Bugsy*
• **Oliver Stone – *J.F.K.***
Barbra Streisand – *The Prince of Tides*

DIRECTORS GUILD AWARD
• **Jonathan Demme**
 – *The Silence of the Lambs*
Barry Levinson – *Bugsy*
Ridley Scott – *Thelma and Louise*
Oliver Stone – *J.F.K.*
Barbra Streisand
 – *The Prince of Tides*

BRITISH ACADEMY AWARDS
Kevin Costner
 – *Dances with Wolves*
Jonathan Demme
 – *The Silence of the Lambs*
• **Alan Parker – *The Commitments***
Ridley Scott – *Thelma and Louise*

NEW YORK – Jonathan Demme – *The Silence of the Lambs*
LOS ANGELES – Barry Levinson – *Bugsy*
BOARD OF REVIEW – Jonathan Demme – *The Silence of the Lambs*
NATIONAL SOCIETY – David Cronenberg – *Naked Lunch*
LONDON
 (Director) **Ridley Scott – *Thelma and Louise***
 (British Director) **Alan Parker – *The Commitments***

The early frontrunners for the Best Director Oscar were the winners of the New York Film Critics Circe and Los Angeles Film Critics Association prizes. Jonathan Demme won the New York accolade for the thriller *The Silence of the Lambs* (NYT "meets most of the obligations of a suspense melodrama with great style [and] handles the big set pieces with phenomenal skill"; NYP "expertly crafted"; WP "adroitly directed"; BG "Demme's almost reportorial style defeats his aim to deliver exciting diversion"; S&S "avoids exploiting potentially sensational material") while Barry Levinson was honoured in Los Angeles for the gangster biopic *Bugsy* (NYT "stylish"; LAT "very assured ... Levinson's sensibility comes into his own ... [his] understated elegance [and] his very human touch make [the film] more real and more affecting"; CST "[the film] moves with a lightness that belies its strength"; WP "a lofty, intoxicating achievement, smoothly polished ... [his] direction is as expert as it is self-effacing ... without Levinson in charge it might have been a tragically flawed movie"; BG "elegance and control").

Both men were nominated for the Golden Globe, as were Los Angeles runner-up Terry Gilliam for *The Fisher King* (LAT "he throws so much into the stew that it loses its savor"; WP "fancifully and inventively put together"; V "well-directed"; S&S "[at times] displays cinematic élan [but many] scenes strain for fanciful significance"), previous winner Oliver Stone for *J.F.K.* (NYT "[a] hyperbolic style of film making ... lots of short, often hysterical scenes tumbling one after another"; LAT "a skillful director working at the peak of his craft"; CST "masterful"; CT "subverts [his] own best points by adopting a rhetoric so extreme and so manipulative ... sensory overload"; WP "he should feel more than mere craftsman's satisfaction at the result ... [the film] is almost always absorbing to watch"; SMH "dazzling direction") and Barbra Streisand for *The Prince of Tides* (NYT "expert handling ... [a] triumphantly good job"; NYP "has overextended herself"; LAT "a handsome, seamless piece of very traditional Hollywood direction"; CT "Streisand's sole visual trope is to frame her character against glowing courses of light"; BG "painstaking direction ... proves herself a potent director"; TGM "shines, rescuing the flashback from cliché, integrating these sequences seamlessly into the body of the film"). On the night, *Bugsy* was named Best Picture (Drama), but the surprise winner in the Best Director category was Stone, who collected his third Globe in six years.

The Directors Guild of America made one change from the Globe list: named in place of Gilliam was Ridley Scott for *Thelma and Louise* (NYT "reveals previously untapped talent for exuberant comedy and for vibrant American imagery"; LAT "[has] the panache to handle the characters' action sequences [and for] maintaining just the right tone for their more intimate moments"; BG "who had any idea that Scott – whose reputation mostly rests on his visuals – could get this far with a character-based film in classic American mold?"; SMH "stylishly directed") ahead of Gilliam. Previous winners Levinson and Stone were each mentioned for a third time, while Demme, Scott and Streisand (only the third woman ever short-listed by the DGA) were all first-time contenders.

The Academy, meanwhile, named previous winners Stone and Levinson along with Demme, Scott, and John Singleton for his directorial debut, *Boyz n the Hood* (NYT "terrifically confident"; LAT "a strong and striking debut"; CST "holds a mirror up to everyday black life"; CT "straightforward"; WP "is not one for subtleties"; V "impressive [and] effective"; S&S "directed with bold certainty"). At twenty-three years of age Singleton was the youngest person as well as the first African-American ever considered for Best Director.

The only Guild finalist to be overlooked by the Academy was Streisand. Her exclusion was met with an even greater outcry than when she had been passed over for *Yentl* eight years earlier. Several critics suggested that the Guild would honour her as a result of the Oscar snub. With *Bugsy* topping the list of contenders, however, others predicted that Levinson would claim the DGA and Academy prizes for a second time in four years.

Several other female directors were also absent from the Oscar list, including: Randa Haines for *The Doctor* (NYT "shows a talent for tugging at the heartstrings in unexpected ways"; LAT "shows how far quality work can go in redeeming a plot that is pat and predictable ... most of the credit for this must go to Haines ... in her hands [the film] becomes a study in even-handed assurance"; CT "sensitive ... [she is able to] coax a fair amount of emotion from [the script] without falling into tastelessness ... this is very good, very smart filmmaking"; BG "Hurt and the entire film, thanks to Haines, unreel beautifully calibrated and nuanced performances in which powerful emotions reach us through understatement"); Agnieszka Holland for *Europa, Europa* (NYT "[her] smooth direction is appealing ... [she has a] determinedly blithe directorial style"; LAT "lays [the] story out without any fuss or editorializing ... [her] neutral tone takes some getting used to, but it turns out to be a remarkably judicious approach"; CST "masterful, but sometimes heavy-handed"; WP "[has] a deft ability to capture the absurd aspects of her material and keep them in balance with the tragic"; TGM "seems to think that her hands-off method is intrinsically allusive and resonant [but the story] can't stand alone; it needs esthetic support, needs authorial interpretation"); Martha Coolidge for *Rambling Rose* (WP "delicacy and control"; BG "unerring and inspired direction"); and, most notably, Jane Campion for *An Angel at My Table* (NYT "succeeds"; LAT "there are extraordinary moments in the film that probably no one but Campion could come up with"; CST "told with clarity ... [the film] doesn't call attention to its qualities"; CT "deft ... Campion is really going where no filmmaker has gone before"; WP "the movie has power, and a great deal of its impact comes from the manner in which Campion forces us to suffer through Frame's defeats with her"; BG "there's a heightened vividness in her every frame ... arresting ... Campion succeeds unforgettably"; TGM "Campion's pace can be painfully slow, but her insights into the life of author Janet Frame are painstakingly precise").

Also by-passed were: National Society of Film Critics winner David Cronenberg for *Naked Lunch* (LAT "mostly, [he] jacks up his own career-long obsessions with glop and grunge and decay to fever pitch"; CT "brilliant [and] shrewd"; WP "the cool clinicism of [his] direction"; TGM "the product of a master chef"); New York prize runner-up Gus Van Sant for *My Own Private Idaho* (NYT "[his] control is such that the movie accommodates the artifice of [its] allusion without embarrassment and, indeed, to its own profit"; CT "a film of breathtaking free and constant movement ... [his work here is] graceful, elegant and expressive"; WP "in Phoenix – and in the movie around him – Van Sant has achieved a perfect synthesis ... [his] style is pillowy and caressing; it makes you feel as if you were gently hypnotized"; TGM "filmed with hypnotic, elegant surrealism"; S&S "shifts fluidly between close-up and panorama, intimacy and distance, symbiosis and alienation"); NSFC runner-up Mike Leigh for *Life is Sweet* (LAT "impeccable"; WP "discovers the tragic beauty in the mundane"); Cannes winner Joel Coen for *Barton Fink* (NYT "seemingly effortless technique"; LAT "[shows] considerable ability"; G "illustrates [the central character's] dilemma in purely cinematic terms"); Spike Lee for *Jungle Fever* (NYT "adept ... with 'Jungle Fever' [he] joins the ranks of our best"; LAT "his work is less strident here, more controlled, less in-your-face explosive"; CT "by far Lee's most accomplished work"); Hal Hartley for *Trust* (LAT "[has] a spare, controlled touch"; WP "Hartley's approach works beautifully"); Krzysztof Kieślowski for *La Double Vie de Véronique (The Double Life of Veronique)* (NYT "poetic in the truest sense"; LAT "has fallen into some bad habits here"; CT "a striking achievement"); and Bertrand Tavernier for *Daddy Nostalgie* (US: *Daddy Nostalgia*, UK: *These Foolish Things*) (LAT "[the film moves] effortlessly [with] graceful ease"; CT "beautifully constructed and delicately filmed"; BG "exquisitely directed"; V "directed with exceptional subtlety"; TGM "[the film has] strength that comes from realism, a slice of family life captured in riveting detail, and there is the power that comes from artfulness, the detail carefully selected and allusively arranged").

In March, neither Streisand, Stone, Scott nor Levinson won the Guild honour. Instead the accolade was awarded to Demme, who became the Oscar favourite as a result since the DGA winner had claimed the statuette thirty-nine times over the previous forty-two years. On Oscar night, this strong DGA record was further extended, when Demme was named Best Director.

In London, Demme and Scott and the previous year's Oscar winner, Kevin Costner for *Dances with Wolves*, were outpolled for the BAFTA by another director overlooked in Hollywood: Alan Parker for *The Commitments* (NYT "a mixture of annoying glibness and undeniable high-voltage style"; WP "Parker's sense of comedy is organic; he never lets the jokes elbow the comedy, or the music, out of the spotlight ... [he] keeps all the film's elements in balance ... every nuance is on beat"; TGM "the film is paced beautifully ... Parker doesn't let us down").

1991

BEST ACTOR

ACADEMY AWARDS
Warren Beatty as 'Bugsy Siegel' in *Bugsy*
Robert De Niro as 'Max Cady' in *Cape Fear*
• **Anthony Hopkins as 'Dr Hannibal Lecter' in *The Silence of the Lambs***
Nick Nolte as 'Tom Wingo' in *The Prince of Tides*
Robin Williams as 'Parry' in *The Fisher King*

GOLDEN GLOBE AWARDS

(Drama)
Warren Beatty – *Bugsy*
Kevin Costner – *J.F.K.*
Robert De Niro – *Cape Fear*
Anthony Hopkins
 – *The Silence of the Lambs*
• **Nick Nolte – *The Prince of Tides***

(Comedy/Musical)
Jeff Bridges – *The Fisher King*
Billy Crystal – *City Slickers*
Dustin Hoffman – *Hook*
Kevin Kline – *Soapdish*
• **Robin Williams**
 – *The Fisher King*

BRITISH ACADEMY AWARDS
Kevin Costner – *Dances with Wolves*
Gérard Depardieu – *Cyrano de Bergerac*
• **Anthony Hopkins – *The Silence of the Lambs***
Alan Rickman – *Truly, Madly, Deeply*

NEW YORK – Anthony Hopkins – *The Silence of the Lambs*
LOS ANGELES – Nick Nolte – *The Prince of Tides*
BOARD OF REVIEW – Warren Beatty – *Bugsy*
NATIONAL SOCIETY – River Phoenix – *My Own Private Idaho*
LONDON
 (Actor) **Gérard Depardieu – *Cyrano de Bergerac***
 (British Actor) **Alan Rickman – *Truly, Madly, Deeply***

The favourite for the Best Actor Oscar was Nick Nolte, who earned his first nomination as a man traumatised by childhood abuse in *The Prince of Tides* (NYT "superlative"; LAT "truly splendid ... the most moving acting of his career ... a full and deeply felt performance"; CT "a performance of skill and commanding sympathy"; BG "the performance of his career ... seems a shoo-in [for the Oscar] for the depth and fullness with which he negotiates [the character's] emotional gamut"; V "Nolte's performance of a lifetime"; Time "a force-of-nature performance"; TGM "an impeccable performance ... captures

247

[him] with eerie precision … expect [him] and Warren Beatty to vie for next year's Oscar"). In the lead up to the Academy Awards, Nolte had won the Los Angeles Film Critics Association prize and the Golden Globe (Drama).

The other main contender for the statuette was Warren Beatty in *Bugsy* (NYT "the role of his career … [a] brilliantly seductive and funny performance … handles [his] lines so flawlessly that their many layers are apparent"; NYP "the most daring acting Beatty has done in many years"; LAT "a great deal of the fun is seeing with what energetic panache [he] takes on the mantle of the mobster"; WP "brings out the absolute best in Beatty … has never shown as much sheer delight in performing … completely uninhibited"; BG "smooth"; V "a dynamite performance"; FQ "his best performance in years"). The previous Best Director Oscar winner was mentioned in the acting categories for a fourth time. He had finished as the runner-up for the Los Angeles Film Critics Association, National Board of Review and National Society of Film Critics accolades.

The dark horse was Anthony Hopkins, who was recognised for the first time as an imprisoned serial killer in *The Silence of the Lambs* (NYT "grandly played"; NYP "Hopkins will just blow you away with the quiet energy in his portrayal"; LAT "[an] insinuating performance … he very nearly owns the film"; WP "relishes his portrait"; BG "[an] intense portrait"; V "makes the role the personification of brilliant, hypnotic evil"; S&S "played with steely-eyed relish"). Hopkins had won the BAFTA and the New York Film Critics Circle award, but his performance, while memorable, was arguably a supporting role with limited screen time. The NBR had honoured him as Best Supporting Actor.

Also in contention were Globe (Comedy/Musical) winner Robin Williams as a homeless man in *The Fisher King* (NYT "creates a jolting but effective character [with] a disarming warmth and gentleness"; LAT "bafflingly off-putting"; WP "endearingly funny and mostly stays in character"; BG "does engaging riffs on his scatty persona"; TGM "[his] comparatively gaudy role has been closely tailored to his roomy talents"; S&S "draws on all his resources of manic energy [and] pixie charm") and previous winner Robert De Niro as a vengeful ex-convict in *Cape Fear* (NYT "[one] of the year's most accomplished performances"; WP "throws himself into the part with unmistakable relish … fully committed … a tremendously entertaining performance"; V "memorable"; TGM "mesmerizingly embodied"; SMH "[a] tour de force").

The most notable absentee from the list of candidates was Venice Film Festival and NSFC winner and New York runner-up River Phoenix as a narcoleptic gay hustler in *My Own Private Idaho* (NYT "surprising… sure … [and] very fine"; NYP "especially good"; LAT "[a] performance of great delicacy and humor"; WP "[gives] the movie a powerful, emotional center … haunting, deeply affecting"; V "believable, sometimes compelling"; TGM "[a] complex characterization"; FQ "heartbreakingly perfect").

An early favourite for the statuette had been Harrison Ford in *Regarding Henry* (NYT "a ponderous, toned-down golly-gee-whiz performance ... a bore"; LAT "effective ... poignant, amusing and always believable"; CT "displays some genuine dignity and restraint"; WP "irresistible"; BG "seems a diligent actor patiently applying himself to the demands of his far from altogether demanding role"; V "acutely well-acted ... first-rate"). Despite a major campaign, however, Ford was not nominated for either the Globe or the Oscar.

Also overlooked for consideration were: Kevin Costner in *J.F.K.* (NYP "some of his finest acting to date"; LAT "[a] comfortingly straight-arrow presence"; CST "a measured yet passionate performance"; CT "at his most blandly all-American"; WP "many of Stone's dramatic effects are dulled by Costner ... he's a dead, vacant performer"; V "a low-key but forceful performance"; SMH "acceptable"); Cannes honouree John Turturro in *Barton Fink* (NYT "superb"; LAT "Turturro is right on the money"; Time "superb"; G "keeps a commendably straight face throughout"; SMH "superb"); Wesley Snipes in *New Jack City* (NYT "played commandingly"; LAT "stunning, so good, in fact, that he tends to unbalance the movie"; WP "Snipes's work is lustrous and threatening"; V "commanding"); William Hurt in *The Doctor* (NYT "[a] beautifully precise characterization ... affecting"; LAT "[reaches] a high standard of believability"; WP "played brilliantly ... his performance is densely layered and detailed"; BG "[a] beautifully calibrated and nuanced performance"; V "moving"); both Gary Oldman (Sp "plays him with beguiling sweetness") and Tim Roth in *Rosencrantz and Guildenstern are Dead* (NYT "enthusiastically acted"; LAT "played to rare perfection"; V "cleverly acted ... splendid"); John Gielgud in *Prospero's Books* (NYT "[played] with the full relish and authority that only [he] can command"; WP "gives glorious voice [to the characters]"; BG "spellbinding"; V "mesmerizing"; Sp "wonderful"); Cuba Gooding, Jr. in *Boyz n the Hood* (NYT "most affecting"; CT "first-rate"); Martin Donovan in *Trust* (NYT "knows how to make [the] pared-down, stylized dialogue express the essence of his character"; V "excellent"); Val Kilmer in *The Doors* (NYT "nowhere is this attention to detail more astonishing that in [his] performance, which is so right it goes well beyond the uncanny ... unerringly good"; LAT "pulls a 'Raging Bull'-style metamorphosis ... impressive"; CST "[his] performance is the best thing in the movie – and since nearly every scene centers on Morrison, that is not small praise"); BG "does an uncanny job"); and Dirk Bogarde in *Daddy Nostalgie* (US: *Daddy Nostalgia*, UK: *These Foolish Things*) (NYT "beautifully captures the full range of frustration and awe that such a man might generate"; BG "exquisitely acted ... measured [and] touching"; V "a beautifully modulated performance"; TGM "masterful").

On Oscar night, the highly-favoured Beatty and Nolte were outpolled by Hopkins, who was the third non-American in a row to win as Best Actor.

1991

BEST ACTRESS

ACADEMY AWARDS
Geena Davis as 'Thelma Dickinson' in *Thelma and Louise*
Laura Dern as 'Rose' in *Rambling Rose*
• **Jodie Foster as 'Clarice Starling' in *The Silence of the Lambs***
Bette Midler as 'Dixie Leonard' in *For the Boys*
Susan Sarandon as 'Louise Sawyer' in *Thelma and Louise*

GOLDEN GLOBE AWARDS

(Drama)
Annette Bening – *Bugsy*
Geena Davis – *Thelma and Louise*
Laura Dern – *Rambling Rose*
• **Jodie Foster**
  – *The Silence of the Lambs*
Susan Sarandon – *Thelma and Louise*

(Comedy/Musical)
Ellen Barkin – *Switch*
Kathy Bates
  – *Fried Green Tomatoes*
Anjelica Huston
  – *The Addams Family*
• **Bette Midler – *For the Boys***
Michelle Pfeiffer
  – *Frankie and Johnny*

BRITISH ACADEMY AWARDS
Geena Davis – *Thelma and Louise*
• **Jodie Foster – *The Silence of the Lambs***
Susan Sarandon – *Thelma and Louise*
Juliet Stevenson – *Truly, Madly, Deeply*

NEW YORK – Jodie Foster – *The Silence of the Lambs*
LOS ANGELES – Mercedes Ruehl – *The Fisher King*
**BOARD OF REVIEW – Geena Davis – *Thelma and Louise* and Susan
    Sarandon – *Thelma and Louise***
NATIONAL SOCIETY – Alison Steadman – *Life is Sweet*
LONDON – Susan Sarandon – *Thelma and Louise* and *White Palace*

Both Geena Davis (NYT "Davis may have already won an Oscar, but for her the gorgeous, dizzy, mutable Thelma still amounts to a career-making role"; LAT "makes the greatest impression by departing furthest from the kookie types she's previously played"; WP "dazzling") and Susan Sarandon (WP "fiercely hard-boiled") won acclaim for their performances as the titular characters in one of the most talked about films of the year, *Thelma and Louise* (NYT "[the film] discovers unexpected resources in both its stars ... perfectly teamed ...

flawless"; LAT "[they] run through a gamut of emotions – from agony and hysteria to tears and laughter – that is formidable in its richness"; BG "terrific"; SMH "wonderful"; Sp "it is up to the actresses to hold our sympathy and they do"). The New York Film Critics Circle and the National Board of Review each considered them as a duo. They shared the NBR prize and were joint runners-up in New York. At the Golden Globes, the BAFTAs and the Academy Awards, however, Davis and Sarandon were in competition with one another, which contributed to the success of another of the nominees on all three occasions.

The beneficiary of the split vote between Davis and Sarandon was Jodie Foster. She played a trainee FBI investigating a serial killer in the box office hit *The Silence of the Lambs* (NYT "[she and Hopkins] give exciting substance to [their] roles ... so good"; NYP "Foster's ability to let Clarice's vulnerability barely bleed through her alert, no-nonsense facade is within the dizzying upper limits of acting"; LAT "subtle, intelligent ... steadfast, controlled, heartbreakingly insightful"; BG "[an] earnest, low-definition portrayal ... Foster's not in her best form"; V "strong"; TGM "flawless"; S&S "remarkable"; Sp "particularly good ... plays with painstaking naturalism and riveting low-key intensity"). Foster's performance earned her the New York accolade, the Globe (Drama), the BAFTA and the Oscar. It was her second Globe and second Oscar in three years. At age twenty-nine, she was the second person to receive a second statuette in the acting categories before the age of thirty (Luise Rainer was twenty-eight when she earned her second award in 1937).

Overshadowed were the two other nominees: Laura Dern, the daughter of previous nominees Bruce Dern and Diane Ladd (who was herself nominated again that year for her supporting role in the same film), as a promiscuous teenager in *Rambling Rose* (NYT "superb"; WP "completely uninhibited and without affection ... Dern accomplishes her effects so invisibly and with such graceful ease that her skills may be under-appreciated, but pay attention"; BG "Oscar-worthy ... far and away Dern's best work"; V "memorable"); and Bette Midler as a singer who entertains US troops in wartime in *For the Boys* (NYT "a role in which screen character and offstage persona are powerfully intertwined ... even in a role as patently flattering and theatrical as this one, [she] has an edge of candor that keeps her seeming very real ... [she is given] some remarkable opportunities for heartstring-pulling"; WP "the real shame is how recklessly Midler squanders her own abundant talents ... it's the crusty-broad approach to the character – the unsentimental toughness that manages somehow to be even more cloying and dishonest than outright weepy nostalgia – that's truly galling"; BG "by sheer force of personality, she elevates the film beyond a soap opera plot ... gets to command centre stage with her brassy extroversion, ripe vocalism and raunchy warmth"; TGM "the finest performance of her career – she's funny, scathing, scatological, touching and (rare for her) controlled").

Even though Midler won the Globe (Comedy/Musical), her inclusion was a surprise ahead of Annette Bening in the gangster biopic *Bugsy*, the year's most nominated picture (NYP "excellent"; LAT "Bening as always does excellent work"; WP "superb ... the classiest of the bunch ... she shows something new"; BG "looks like a series of airbrushed '40s postcards, a string of pouty pinups").

Also overlooked were: National Society of Film Critics winner Alison Steadman in *Life is Sweet* (NYT "a joy to watch"; WP "touching"; V "superb"; TGM "superb"; TT "marvellous"); Anjelica Huston in *The Addams Family* (NYT "a scene-stealing delight ... [her] seductive, deadpan manner sets the tone for the rest of the film"; LAT "looks perfect and brings tremendous polish to [the role]"; WP "terribly funny"); Mary Stuart Masterson in *Fried Green Tomatoes* (NYT "magnetic ... seems to be bursting at the seams of her role [with] furious honesty"; LAT "[her] burning vitality ends up leaving everyone but Tandy in the shade"; SFC "superb"); Ellen Barkin in *Switch* (NYT "extraordinarily convincing"; LAT "a truly original, sometimes hair-raising performance"; CT "a dazzling performance"; WP "[her] lively performance makes 'Switch' funnier than it deserves to be"; V "overdoes the grimacing and macho posturing"); Michelle Pfeiffer in *Frankie and Johnny* (NYT "a fine-tuned, deeply persuasive performance"; LAT "[her] realistic yet gently comic performance is a study in empathy and grace"); Annabelle Sciorra in *Jungle Fever* (NYT "in a cast of equals, Ms Sciorra may be just a little more equal than everyone else ... she shines"; CT "seems pleasant but insubstantial, a sketch that hasn't quite been completed"); Lili Taylor in *Dogfight* (NYT "touchingly played ... hides herself in the character"; LAT "adept"; BG "winning"; V "brings engaging enthusiasm and vigor to the part"); Adrienne Shelly in *Trust* (NYT "makes Maria's transformation both poignant and credible"; BG "appealing"; V "tangibly right"; TGM "plays Maria with intelligence and sympathetic conviction"); Kerry Fox in *An Angel at My Table* (NYT "remarkably vivid and strong"; WP "a towering, naked performance ... brilliantly delivers what an actress must – her character's behaviour"; V "quite remarkable"; TGM "remarkably portrayed ... gradually exposes the character from the outside in"); Gong Li in *Jou Du* (LAT "she makes the transition from frightened wife to vengeful adulterer without missing a beat ... it's a seamless, full-scale performance"; V "superb"); and Cannes Film Festival winner Irène Jacob in *La Double Vie de Véronique (The Double Life of Veronique)* (NYT "engaging"; BG "her performance is brilliantly internalized"; LAT "doesn't really give a performance; she poses expressively"; V "imbues both roles with an innocent but powerful magic"; TGM "in a performance that mixes bafflement with wonder, she proves herself worthy of the Cannes accolade"; Obs "entrancing").

Mercedes Ruehl, the winner of the Los Angeles Film Critics Association prize, was nominated in the supporting category for her work in *The Fisher King*.

BEST SUPPORTING ACTOR

ACADEMY AWARDS
Tommy Lee Jones as 'Clay Shaw' in *J.F.K.*
Harvey Keitel as 'Mickey Cohen' in *Bugsy*
Ben Kingsley as 'Meyer Lansky' in *Bugsy*
Michael Lerner as 'Jack Lipnick' in *Barton Fink*
• **Jack Palance as 'Curly' in *City Slickers***

GOLDEN GLOBE AWARDS
Ned Beatty – *Hear My Song*
John Goodman – *Barton Fink*
Harvey Keitel – *Bugsy*
Ben Kingsley – *Bugsy*
• **Jack Palance – *City Slickers***

BRITISH ACADEMY AWARDS
Alan Bates – *Hamlet*
Derek Jacobi – *Dead Again*
• **Alan Rickman – *Robin Hood: Prince of Thieves***
Andrew Strong – *The Commitments*

NEW YORK – Samuel L. Jackson – *Jungle Fever*
LOS ANGELES – Michael Lerner – *Barton Fink*
BOARD OF REVIEW – Anthony Hopkins – *The Silence of the Lambs*
NATIONAL SOCIETY – Harvey Keitel – *Bugsy* and *Mortal Thoughts* and *Thelma and Louise*

The New York Film Critics Circle named Samuel L. Jackson as Best Supporting Actor in *Jungle Fever* (CT "emerges of the film's most inventive actor") ahead of Steven Hill in *Billy Bathgate* (CT "[played with] a great deal of professionalism"; S&S "thanks to the performance of Steven Hill, the film very nearly slips through [the problems with its structure] ... effortlessly eloquent") and then John Goodman in *Barton Fink* (BG "the best performance of his career"; V "marvelous"). While Goodman was included on the Golden Globes ballot by the Hollywood Foreign Press Association, all three were overlooked by the Academy.

In London, Alan Rickman was honoured with the BAFTA for his comic portrayal of the Sherriff of Nottingham in *Robin Hood: Prince of Thieves* (NYT "overplays ... he isn't funny, just an actor who is desperate to create a little screen life ... he seems to be acting in another movie entirely"; LAT "funny enough, but his clowning has the regrettable effect of making him useless as a credible villain, severely crippling that side of the film"; CT "the witty disdain department has been placed entirely in the hands of Alan Rickman, who makes his Sheriff of Nottingham a withering camp figure ... [he's] funny, but such campy asides don't do much to establish the credibility of the character's menace"; WP "steals the picture ... plays the evil sheriff as if he were warming up for a burlesque production of 'Richard III' ... every inch as flamboyantly surreal as Jack Nicholson in 'Batman', Rickman strips the gear box with his performance here; this is no-brakes, no-clutch acting ... he's priceless").

Also nominated by the British Academy were: Alan Bates in *Hamlet* (NYT "a solid performance"; BG "Close and Bates command what screen time they're given"; V "solid"); Derek Jacobi in *Dead Again* (NYT "very good and straightforward in a role that might easily have been hammed up"; CT "softly hammy"; V "a pure delight"; TGM "a real asset in the comedy department"); and sixteen-year-old Andrew Strong as the lead singer in *The Commitments* (CT "[a] stand out"; TGM "an extraordinary natural talent"). None of the BAFTA contenders were considered for the Academy Award (Bates having been overlooked the previous year).

Arguably the most notable omission from the Academy's short list was Los Angeles Film Critics Association runner-up Robert Duvall in *Rambling Rose* (NYT "superb"; LAT "one of Duvall's best performances"; WP "what Duvall does with the role of Daddy is sheer magic ... this is his most effusive, grandiloquent performance ... his presence as an actor has never been larger, or more generous, than it is here"; BG "Oscar-worthy ... I suspect that Duvall has the best shot at the statue [from among the cast] for his richest, most rivetingly textured and affecting work since 'Tender Mercies'").

Other candidates overlooked for Oscar consideration were: Glenn Scott in *The Silence of the Lambs* (NYT "stalwart ... but the role is no match for those of his two co-stars"; Sp "[a] nice performance"); Elliott Gould in *Bugsy* (NYP "excellent"; LAT "[a] fine performance"; WP "makes a swift but indelible mark"; BG "[a] surprisingly effective vignette"); Globe nominee Ned Beatty in *Hear My Song* (NYT "may not be entirely comfortable lip-synching 'Sorrento', but he shows his versatility and fits in admirably with the story's overall spirit"; LAT "Beatty, ever a wonderful character actor who here gets to emerge as a romantic leading man"; BG "it's nice to see the versatile and underappreciated Beatty get a shot at something different"); both Gary Oldman as Lee Harvey Oswald (NYP "extremely subtle"; CT "the film's most magnetic performance"; WP "strong ... makes a believably nutsy Oswald"; SMH "impressive") and Joe Pesci as his associate (NYT "good"; WP "[a] strong supporting performance") in *J.F.K.*; Dustin Hoffman as Captain Hook in *Hook* (NYT "a hugely funny bravura performance"; LAT "a technically expert and convincing performance that at times plays more lifeless than it intends to"; CT "played with the accent and much of the attitude of Jeremy Irons' Klaus von Bulow in 'Reversal of Fortune'"; WP "it's Dustin Hoffman who takes us by storm ... a delicious portrait of lip-smacking evil, a vain, pompous, sublimely narcissistic swine ... [his] performance is unapologetically theatrical, and perfectly suited to the stylized quality of the film"; BG "plummily played like a combination of Charles II and William F. Buckley, Jr."); Michael Jeter in *The Fisher King* (NYT "heartbreakingly funny"; LAT "a show-stopper"; WP "brings down the house"; TGM "hilarious"); and Richard Dreyfuss in *Rosencrantz and Guildenstern are Dead* (NYT "enthusiastically acted"; LAT "splendid"; CST "memorable ... and becomes memorable in the time-honored way, by stealing his scenes"; WP "provides a bit of much-needed energy with hammy acting aplomb"; Sp "manages to be flamboyant, threatening, ingratiating and authoritative by turns – a magnetic performance"; S&S "over-acts wildly but appropriately").

Instead, the Academy short-listed: Tommy Lee Jones as a New Orleans businessman in *J.F.K.* (NYT "good"; WP "highly memorable"; "particularly noteworthy"; SMH "impressive"); both National Society of Film Critics winner Harvey Keitel (NYP "excellent"; LAT "especially effective"; WP "superb"; BG "brings a refreshing streetwise flavour to the prevailing sleekness [of the film]"; V "impressive"; FQ "flawless") and previous Best Actor Oscar winner Ben Kingsley (NYP "excellent"; LAT "especially effective"; WP "superb ... drolly subdued"; BG "potent"; V "impressive"; FQ "flawless") as gangsters in *Bugsy*; Los Angeles prize winner Michael Lerner as an old-fashioned Hollywood studio boss in *Barton Fink* (NYT "superb"; LAT "brings eye-popping gusto to the role"; G "you'll certainly appreciate [his] impression of Louis B. Mayer"; S&S "very funny"); and Golden Globe winner Jack Palance as an ageing cowboy in the popular comedy *City Slickers* (NYT "provides off-the-wall incongruity as well as some unexpectedly touching moments"; LAT "gives the movie its comic high points"; WP "even though he's doing a parody of himself, Jack Palance is as welcome as the cavalry"; BG "raises the level of the film a notch, contributing a beautifully shaped and modulated supporting performance, anchoring the bumbling trio [of leading actors]"; S&S "a masterly performance").

For his performance as an imprisoned serial killer in *The Silence of the Lambs*, Anthony Hopkins was named Best Supporting Actor by the National Board of Review. Although he appeared on screen for less than thirty minutes, or one quarter of the film, he was nominated in the lead performer category at both the Golden Globes, the BAFTAs and the Academy Awards.

On Oscar night, more than thirty-five years after he had last been an unsuccessful nominee, seventy-two-year old Palance won the golden statuette.

BEST SUPPORTING ACTRESS

ACADEMY AWARDS
Diane Ladd as 'Mother Hillyer' in *Rambling Rose*
Juliette Lewis as 'Danielle Bowden' in *Cape Fear*
Kate Nelligan as 'Lila Wingo Newbury' in *The Prince of Tides*
• **Mercedes Ruehl as 'Anne Napolitano' in *The Fisher King***
Jessica Tandy as 'Ninny Threadgoode' in *Fried Green Tomatoes*

GOLDEN GLOBE AWARDS
Nicole Kidman – *Billy Bathgate*
Diane Ladd – *Rambling Rose*
Juliette Lewis – *Cape Fear*
• **Mercedes Ruehl – *The Fisher King***
Jessica Tandy – *Fried Green Tomatoes*

BRITISH ACADEMY AWARDS
Annette Bening – *The Grifters*
• **Kate Nelligan – *Frankie and Johnny***
Amanda Plummer – *The Fisher King*
Julie Walters – *Stepping Out*

NEW YORK – Judy Davis – *Barton Fink* and *Naked Lunch*
LOS ANGELES – Jane Horrocks – *Life is Sweet*
BOARD OF REVIEW – Kate Nelligan – *Frankie and Johnny*
NATIONAL SOCIETY – Jane Horrocks – *Life is Sweet*

Non-Americans won the four major critics' prizes: Australian Judy Davis won the New York Film Critics Circle accolade for both *Barton Fink* (BG "played with enticingly husky ambiguity ... [she] catches exactly the mix of nightmarishness and mockery on which the Coens thrive") and *Naked Lunch* (NYT "wonderfully dry and unflappable in two different, bizarre incarnations"; LAT "preserves her hawk-like intensity in the midst of the splattery rumpus"; CT "droll and charismatic"; WP "superb ... shows a different side of her cyclonic talent here"; V "outstanding"; TGM "a pair of terrific performances"); Englishwoman Jane Horrocks won the Los Angeles Film Critics Association and National Society of Film Critics awards for *Life is Sweet* (NYT "a joy to watch"; WP "touching"; TGM "superb"); and Canadian Kate Nelligan won the National Board of Review plaudit for *Frankie and Johnny* (NYT "Nelligan, nearly unrecognizable, is outstandingly enjoyable").

Surprisingly, none of these winners were considered for the Golden Globe. In contention were: Nicole Kidman in *Billy Bathgate* (LAT "looks right and she works very hard at the role, but without a strong script to help her, she doesn't have the experience or the strength of personality to give Drew the substance she needs"; V "comes on strongly"); Diane Ladd in *Rambling Rose* (NYT "superb"; CT "Oscar-worthy ... [with] a hypnotically quavery softness [she tells] us volumes about the woman's background and character in every gesture, every phrasing"; WP "great"; S&S "a whimsical characterisation in keeping with the film"); New York and NSFC prize runner-up Juliette Lewis in *Cape Fear* (NYT "[one] of the year's most accomplished performances ... reveals [herself] to be a new young actress of stunning possibilities"; WP "a revelation ... she's superb"; V "excellent"; TGM "extraordinary"; SMH "brilliant"); Mercedes Ruehl in *The Fisher King* (NYT "proves herself to be a fiery comedian graced with superb timing"; LAT "a full-scale creation"; WP "[Williams] and Ruehl takes turns stealing the show"; BG "sensational ... a sure Oscar nominee"; V "sizzles"); and Jessica Tandy in *Fried Green Tomatoes* (LAT "very watchable ... watching her effortlessly animate her character, bringing Ninny fully to life, is the most enjoyable of privileges"; BG "her dignity and pared-down toughness of spirit carry her triumphantly past an overly contrived and sentimental ending"; SFC "beautifully acted"; V "at her sparkling best"; TGM "does what she can").

Ruehl, who had won the Los Angeles Film Critics Association's Best Actress award for her role in *The Fisher King*, won the Globe. She became the Oscar frontrunner when the Academy made only one change from the Globe list: Kidman was overlooked in favour of Nelligan, who was named not for her NBR award-winning turn in *Frankie and Johnny* but rather for her performance as a strong-willed Southern matriarch in *The Prince of Tides* (NYT "adds substantially to the film's vivid sense of [the protagonist's] life"; WP "fine").

In addition to Davis, Horrocks and Kidman, Oscar voters by-passed: Los Angeles prize runner-up Amanda Plummer in *The Fisher King* (BG "the women steal the film ... [she] is just as good [as Ruehl]"; V "terrific"; TGM "sometimes the funniest member of the [cast]"; S&S "perfect"); Elizabeth Perkins in *The Doctor* (NYT "very affecting"; NYP "wonderful"; BG "affectingly acted"; V "wonderfully good"); Kathleen Quinlan in *The Doors* (NYT "especially effective"; LAT "puts some witchy hauteur into British pop critic Patricia Kennealy"; BG "is a plus"); Tyra Ferrell in *Boyz n the Hood* (NYT "vibrant"; LAT "a fine, edgy performance"; CT "first-rate"); and Maureen O'Hara in *Only the Lonely* (NYT "[a] real scene-stealer ... succeeds in making Danny's mother a funny and engaging figure without stinting on the character's truly noxious side"; LAT "makes a genuinely spectacular comeback"; TGM "a high point ... she steals every scene she's in"; S&S "attacks her role with venomous relish").

On Oscar night, Globe winner Ruehl claimed the Oscar.

1992

BEST PICTURE

ACADEMY AWARDS

The Crying Game
   (Palace, Miramax, 113 mins, 26 Sep 1992, $62.5m, 6 noms)
A Few Good Men
   (Castle Rock, Columbia, 138 mins, 11 Dec 1992, $141.3m, 4 noms)
Howards End
   (Merchant Ivory, 140 mins, 13 Mar 1992, $25.9m, 9 noms)
Scent of a Woman
   (City Lights, Universal, 157 mins, 23 Dec 1992, $63.8m, 4 noms)
• *Unforgiven*
   (Warner Bros., 131 mins, 7 Aug 1992, $44.4m, 9 noms)

GOLDEN GLOBE AWARDS

(Drama)	(Comedy/Musical)
The Crying Game	*Aladdin*
A Few Good Men	*Enchanted April*
Howards End	*Honeymoon in Vegas*
• *Scent of a Woman*	• *The Player*
Unforgiven	*Sister Act*

PRODUCERS GUILD AWARD

• *The Crying Game*
A Few Good Men
Howards End
Scent of a Woman
Unforgiven

BRITISH ACADEMY AWARDS

(Best Film)	(Best British Film)
The Crying Game	• *The Crying Game*
• *Howards End*	
The Player	
Strictly Ballroom	
Unforgiven	

NEW YORK – *The Player*
LOS ANGELES – *Unforgiven*
BOARD OF REVIEW – *Howards End*
NATIONAL SOCIETY – *Unforgiven*

1992

LONDON

(Best Film) *Unforgiven*

(Best British Film) *Howards End*

The same two films closely contested the Best Picture prizes from the New York Film Critics Circle and the Los Angeles Film Critics Association, and appeared likely to each claim a Golden Globe before squaring off for the Academy Award. The west coast circle honoured the revisionist Western *Unforgiven* (NYT "most entertaining [but] never quite fulfils the expectations it so carefully sets up"; NYP "dark, brooding and very skilful"; LAT "a film that resonates with the spirit of films past while staking out a territory quite its own"; CT "an adult Western that can stand with the great accomplishments of the genre … dark, melancholic … mature, morally complex and challenging"; V "a classic ... a tense, hard-edged, superbly dramatic yarn ... compelling"; Time "a dark, passionate drama"; TT "a slow, reflective epic … powerful"; S&S "distinguished"). Finishing as runner-up was the Hollywood satire *The Player* (NYT "entertaining [and] irreverent"; NYP "sharp but affectionate"; LAT "a great Hollywood movie … artful [and] biting"; CT "a haphazard, uneven piece of work"; WP "[a] masterly, deadly funny satire of Hollywood power elite … the picture works on every level … a miracle"; BG "brilliantly provocative, sinfully enjoyable"; V "enormously entertaining"; FQ "it isn't really great ... doesn't have a lot of bite [but is nonetheless] amusing"; TT "delicate and corrosive"). Five days later, the east coast circle reversed the order of the Los Angeles vote, awarding their prize to *The Player* by just two points over *Unforgiven*.

Another two Best Picture contenders emerged from the vote by the National Board of Review, which took place the day before the balloting in New York. The winner was *Howards End*, a Merchant Ivory adaptation of a novel by E. M. Forster (NYT "[a] triumph … entertaining, richly textured ... elegant, funny and romantic [as well as] intensely serious … a great pleasure"; LAT "[a] most assured motion picture ... striking ... exceptional … most affecting … easily the film of the year"; V "compelling"; TGM "a great movie"; TT "resplendent"). Finishing as runner-up was *The Crying Game*, a drama about an IRA operative, which had become an unexpected sensation at the US box office following a careful, targeted campaign by Miramax (NYT "brilliant ... dazzling ... quite literally amazing"; LAT "an unusually satisfying film ... suspenseful and emotionally complex … sophisticated entertainment"; WP "exquisitely unique ... one of the most challenging, surprising films of the year … it deserves to be called great"; V "astonishingly good and daring"; TGM "simultaneously a tough, haunting, lyrical, hopeful film"; TT "dynamic, surprising").

1992

When the National Society of Film Critics voted, *Unforgiven* again emerged as the winner with 47 points. *The Crying Game* finished as the runner-up with 26 points, followed by *The Player* with 23.

All four of these contenders were named by the Hollywood Foreign Press Association, but leading the field with five nods was the courtroom drama *A Few Good Men* (NYT "entertaining"; NYP "pretty silly stuff"; LAT "more contrived than creditable [but] an uncomplicated piece of entertainment"; WP "riveting"; BG "the best-made safe Hollywood film of the year ... conventional enough to score big at Oscar time"; Time "extraordinarily well-made"; TGM "the performers are powerless to bring life to this moribund courtroom drama").

On Globes night, *The Player* was named Best Picture (Comedy/Musical) as expected. In the Drama category, however, there was a massive upset. *The Crying Game*, *A Few Good Men*, *Howards End* and *Unforgiven* were all outpolled by *Scent of a Woman* (NYP "pedestrian"; LAT "remarkable"; WP "an unholy mess ... the heavy hand of the studio script conference makes itself felt ... creeping phoniness"; TGM "bloated ... [a] failure ... a character study lacking in character"). As the film had been considered a surprise nominee given its mixed reviews, its victory was unexpected. Accusations of corruption soon followed when it was revealed that many HFPA members had been flown to New York during the voting period to see the film and meet its star, Al Pacino.

Despite the scandal, the Academy also included *Scent of a Woman* on its Best Picture ballot. In fact, the Oscar ballot exactly matched the lists of both Globe (Drama) and Producers Guild of America nominees, with the result that *The Player* was glaringly excluded.

Other highly-anticipated contenders were also overlooked, most notably: *Malcolm X* (NYT "an ambitious, tough, seriously considered biographical film ... Lee has attempted the impossible, and almost brought it off"; NYP "an exceptional biography ... first-rate filmmaking"; LAT "powerful"; BG "a great film"; V "disappointingly conventional and sluggish"); *Husbands and Wives* (NYT "a very fine, sometimes brutal comedy ... strong, wise and exhilarating"; NYP "sensitive, compact and funny"; LAT "a lacerating comedy"; CT "sharp"; BG "one of Allen's best ... holds us from start to finish – a rueful, ironic, wrenchingly funny study"; V "richly satisfying"; Time "a damn fine film"); and *A River Runs Through It* (NYT "one of the most accomplished films of the year ... beautiful and deeply felt ... an unsentimental film about a past that is ripe for cheap nostalgia"; LAT "loving and well-intentioned though this film is, it never convinces you that its subject matter merits this kind of idealized, worshipful attention"; WP "a loving work of embracing nostalgia ... a serious and, at times, moving film ... it's thoughtful and beautiful, but also a little stodgy"; BG "a conventional piece of movie-making"; TGM "perfectly admirable, absolutely controlled").

Other acclaimed releases overlooked for Best Picture consideration by the Academy that year were: the Disney animated hit *Aladdin* (NYT "beyond first-rate"; LAT "a film of wonders ... amazing ... generates as much on-screen magic as any film all year"; CT "a genuine charmer, filled with wit, feeling and verve"); *Reservoir Dogs* (NYT "dazzling ... aggressively brutal"; LAT "brash ... a showy but insubstantial comic opera of violence ... [but it's] so determinedly one-dimensional"; WP "gritty, bone-chilling, powerfully violent"; V "undeniably impressive"; TGM "you watch it with mesmerized fascination"; TT "startling"; S&S "a film of considerable acuity and power"); *Bob Roberts* (NYT "fiendishly funny ... hilarious"; NYP "clever, funny and deceptively complicated"; LAT "a shrewd and scathingly funny piece of pointed political satire ... audacious, bracing, uncommonly timely"; CT "promises much but fails to deliver"; WP "brilliantly witty"; BG "devilishly clever"; HRp "devastatingly sharp"; S&S "wants to manipulate its audience with satire, but for fear of being thought manipulative, it cops out by telling us point blank what to think"); *Glengarry Glen Ross* (NYT "[a] splendid film adaptation ... here is a movie for which everybody deserves awards ... mordantly funny"; CT "a well written, well staged and well acted piece, though there is something musty in its aesthetic"; BG "what we've got here is a play I wouldn't have thought filmable filmed pretty potently with Oscar-worthy performances"); *Gas Food Lodging* (NYT "a keenly observed character study ... not easily forgotten"; LAT "a rare exception ... there's a real shrewdness and compassion in its depiction of ordinary lives – but also a curious, lyrical sense of romance and mystery"; CT "appealingly quirky [but] uneven"; BG "impressive ... a delight"; V "[a] rich, multilevel work"; TGM "highly entertaining"; S&S "quite moving"); and *Edward II* (NYT "extravagant visual elegance and sexual politics mix with a powerful contemporary resonance"; LAT "direct but nevertheless stylized ... a timely, fiery attack on homophobia"; CT "manages the remarkable feat of being completely faithful to its source while standing as something unshakably contemporary ... a strikingly original creation in its own right ... in its scrupulous austerity and sensitivity to its materials, one of the most exquisite movies ever made"; BG "exchanges majestic language for arresting visuals and provocative gay activism"; V "provocative and challenging"; TGM "a complex consideration of the relationships between class, sex, wealth, power and privilege").

Landmark foreign-language releases excluded from the Academy's top category included: the 1991 Chinese drama *Da Hong Deng Long Gao Gao Gua (Raise the Red Lantern)* (NYT "beautifully crafted and richly detailed ... as visually striking as it is dramatically effective"; NYP "rarely is a film so visually memorable ... powerful"; LAT "a film of astonishing beauty and terror ... [a] calmly shattering film"; WP "breathtaking"; BG "gets high marks for artistry and restraint ... beautiful"; Time "brave, passionate and highly entertaining"; TGM "virtually perfect ... remarkable"; SMH "the highest realm of film-making art ... superb ... powerful"); the 1991 French black comedy *Delicatessen* (NYT "[a] lightweight but sometimes subversive stylish farce"; LAT "a nightmare comedy ... a fearsomely intense movie that mixes mood with formidable assurance ... a nasty, childlike, murderously funny show"; BG "stylish"; TT "wonderfully bizarre"; G "[an] extraordinarily freaky film"); and *Indochine*, the Best Foreign-Language Film Oscar winner (NYT "second-rate fiction ... it's not easy for any movie to cover so much time and history and still maintain its coherence as a drama"; LAT "lush and poignant ... a sweepingly romantic historical saga, at once intimate and epic"; CT "a maddeningly dry and tasteful exercise, without the hot blood of melodrama or its thrilling extremes"; WP "a lethargic opium dream of colonial Vietnam ... dramatically deadening"; BG "a big handsome sprawl of a movie"; V "riveting"; TT "spectacular").

Howards End and *Unforgiven* led the field of Academy Awards contenders, each with nine nods, but the Western became the strong favourite when Clint Eastwood won the Directors Guild of America award for his helming of the film. The dark horse in the Best Picture line-up was *The Crying Game* which had unexpectedly claimed the Producers Guild of America honour.

On Oscar night, there was no upset win: *Unforgiven* became the second Western in three years to be named Best Picture by the Academy.

At the British Academy Awards, *The Crying Game*, *Howards End*, *The Player* and *Unforgiven* were all nominated for Best Film, alongside the popular Australian film *Strictly Ballroom*, which was a Best Picture nominee at the Golden Globes the following year, but not at the Academy Awards. The winner was *Howards End*. However, *The Crying Game* did not go home empty-handed. The British Academy re-introduced its Best British Film award as a special honour for the film.

BEST DIRECTOR

ACADEMY AWARDS
Robert Altman for *The Player*
Martin Brest for *Scent of a Woman*
• **Clint Eastwood for *Unforgiven***
James Ivory for *Howards End*
Neil Jordan for *The Crying Game*

GOLDEN GLOBE AWARDS
Robert Altman – *The Player*
• **Clint Eastwood – *Unforgiven***
James Ivory – *Howards End*
Robert Redford – *A River Runs Through It*
Rob Reiner – *A Few Good Men*

DIRECTORS GUILD AWARD
Robert Altman – *The Player*
• **Clint Eastwood – *Unforgiven***
James Ivory – *Howards End*
Neil Jordan – *The Crying Game*
Rob Reiner – *A Few Good Men*

BRITISH ACADEMY AWARDS
• **Robert Altman – *The Player***
Clint Eastwood – *Unforgiven*
James Ivory – *Howards End*
Neil Jordan – *The Crying Game*

NEW YORK – **Robert Altman – *The Player***
LOS ANGELES – **Clint Eastwood – *Unforgiven***
BOARD OF REVIEW – **James Ivory – *Howards End***
NATIONAL SOCIETY – **Clint Eastwood – *Unforgiven***
LONDON
    (Director) **Robert Altman – *The Player***
    (British Director) **Neil Jordan – *The Crying Game***

Robert Altman became the early frontrunner for the year's Best Director accolades when he was honoured at the Cannes Film Festival for *The Player* (LAT "supremely deft ... [his] overlapping sound techniques have never seemed more appropriate"; CT "Altman's technical abilities are strained to the limit by the film's clearly minimal budget"; WP "playfully dead-on in his critique of Hollywood fatuity ... with consummate ease of a veteran showman, Altman keeps an awesome number of balls in the air"; BG "with a masterly touch"). At the end of the year he won the New York Film Critics Circle prize (for a second time), finished runner-up for both the Los Angeles Film Critics Association and

National Society of Film Critics plaudits and earned nominations for the Golden Globe, the Directors Guild of America award, the BAFTA and the Oscar.

During the awards season, however, actor-director Clint Eastwood emerged as the Oscar favourite for *Unforgiven* (NYT "doesn't play it safe as a director but there are times that the sheer scope of the narrative seems to overwhelm him"; LAT "he has infused [the film] with his sure, laconic, emotionally involving style"; V "impressive"). Outpolled by Altman in New York by just one vote, Eastwood claimed the Los Angeles and NSFC prizes, the Globe (for a second time) and the DGA honour. On Oscar night, he was presented with the Best Director statuette.

The other Oscar nominees included National Board of Review winner James Ivory for *Howards End* (LAT "[has] raised [his] work to a new level of accomplishment"; TT "his fastidious approach pays dividends [as he] orchestrates [everything] with delicate skill") and Neil Jordan, who polled third in the NSFC vote, for *The Crying Game* (LAT "confidently directed"; WP "[his] touch is so gracefully gentle"; TGM "he got everything working beautifully here"). Surprisingly, despite Best Film BAFTAs for both their films Ivory and Jordan were passed over for the Best Director BAFTA in favour of Altman.

Somewhat unexpectedly, the Academy's fifth nominee was Martin Brest for *Scent of a Woman* (NYT "meandering … [he] could well have created the impression of greater coherence by simply picking up the pace"; LAT "responds to the humanity in Goldman's script"; TGM "the pace makes the ice age seem hasty"). Brest had not been considered for the critics' prizes, the Guild award or the Globe.

Brest's inclusion came ahead of several high-profile contenders such as: DGA nominee Rob Reiner for *A Few Good Men* (LAT "has more than enough professionalism at his command as well as a shrewd feel for the mechanics of mass entertainment to involve us in his tale"; CT "cleanly told"; WP "what's missing is anything of Reiner himself"; BG "virtuosically directed … Reiner's direction here will catapult him to the top of the A list"; TGM "sloppy"; S&S "adopts the unassuming, sit-back-and-let-the-actors-talk approach"); previous winner Robert Redford for *A River Runs Through It* (NYT "accomplished"; LAT "presented in such an earnest and well-mannered style that much of the potential emotion feels bleached out of the proceedings"; WP "his studied sincerity robs the story of some of its natural vitality"; TGM "Redford is a master of avoidance [and] his omissions pay off handsomely"); previous winner Woody Allen for *Husbands and Wives* (LAT "accomplished"; CT "almost comically studied … he's done better"; BG "generous … one of [his] best"; TGM "well crafted"); and Spike Lee for *Malcolm X* (NYT "has attempted the impossible, and almost brought it off … Lee's method is almost self-effacing … the moments of confrontational melodrama, something for which [he] has a particular gift, are quite consciously underplayed"; LAT "very accomplished ... remarkable").

Also overlooked were: Quentin Tarantino for *Reservoir Dogs* (NYT "[the film] moves swiftly and with complete confidence"; LAT "as much a calling card as a movie, an audacious high-wire act announcing that he is here and to be reckoned with ... Tarantino does have the filmmaking flair to go along with his zeal ... it's impossible not to appreciate the undeniable skill and élan [he] brings to [the film]"; WP "does a righteous job for a first-time director"; TGM "Tarantino, in a gripping feature debut, packages a master's thesis on criminality in the wrappings of pulsating entertainment"); Allison Anders for *Gas Food Lodging* (NYT "keeps her film expertly balanced [and] directs in a spare, laconic style that keeps the material from degenerating into soap opera"; CT "establishes a nice feel for desolate, Southwestern small-town life [and] gets good performances out her cast ... Anders decidedly is a director worth watching"; BG "her head-on way of photographing [the film] sits well alongside her refusal to sentimentalize these women ... impressive"; S&S "assured ... [her] technique is by and large impressively unaffected"); Derek Jarman for *Edward II* (NYT "powerful"; CT "Jarman gives the words new meaning by presenting them in an unconventional and quite beautiful visual context ... [and] is almost magically able to select and highlight the single movement or set of the face that defines a character in one perfect stroke"; BG "boldly assertive"; TGM "the intentionally anachronistic production wonderfully updates Marlow's sensibility without altering his sense [or] sacrificing [his] poetry"); Regis Wargnier for *Indochine* (LAT "adroit at turning the heady personal melodrama of 'Indochine' against itself, shifting focus"; WP "has a fondness for extended metaphors, preferring intellectual artifice over character development"; BG "deserves credit for doing as much as he does to braid political and personalized convulsions"); Marc Caro and Jean-Pierre Jeunet for *Delicatessen* (NYT "[they do not] aspire to much more than simply flinging these characters together and intercutting their exploits in a quick, stylish fashion [yet] the results can be weirdly hilarious"; LAT "[their style] mixes mood with formidable assurance"; CT "show off a flair for offbeat sight gags and hilarious effects with cresting rhythms"; G "this is primarily a film-maker's film, belonging not so much to its cast as to its orchestrators"); and Zhang Yimou for *Da Hong Deng Long Gao Gao Gua (Raise the Red Lantern)* (NYT "beautifully crafted ... works with an exquisite simplicity ... [he directs] in a quiet, observant style"; LAT "every frame is expressive ... Zhang reveals himself as a supreme colorist"; BG "gets high marks for artistry and restraint"; TGM "classically composed ... the work of a man with utter confidence in his techniques").

BEST ACTOR

ACADEMY AWARDS
Robert Downey, Jr. as 'Charlie Chaplin' in *Chaplin*
Clint Eastwood as 'William Munny' in *Unforgiven*
• **Al Pacino as 'Lt-Col. Frank Slade' in *Scent of a Woman***
Stephen Rea as 'Fergus' in *The Crying Game*
Denzel Washington as 'Malcolm X' in *Malcolm X*

GOLDEN GLOBE AWARDS
(Drama)
Tom Cruise – *A Few Good Men*
Robert Downey, Jr. – *Chaplin*
Jack Nicholson – *Hoffa*
• **Al Pacino – *Scent of a Woman***
Denzel Washington – *Malcolm X*

(Comedy/Musical)
Nicolas Cage
– *Honeymoon in Vegas*
Billy Crystal – *Mr Saturday Night*
Marcello Mastroianni – *Used People*
Tim Robbins – *Bob Roberts*
• **Tim Robbins – *The Player***

BRITISH ACADEMY AWARDS
Daniel Day-Lewis – *The Last of the Mohicans*
• **Robert Downey, Jr. – *Chaplin***
Stephen Rea – *The Crying Game*
Tim Robbins – *The Player*

NEW YORK – Denzel Washington – *Malcolm X*
LOS ANGELES – Clint Eastwood – *Unforgiven*
BOARD OF REVIEW – Jack Lemmon – *Glengarry Glen Ross*
NATIONAL SOCIETY – Stephen Rea – *The Crying Game*
LONDON
    (Actor) **Robert Downey, Jr. – *Chaplin***
    (British Actor) **Daniel Day-Lewis – *The Last of the Mohicans***

All five Best Actor Oscar nominees won awards ahead of Hollywood's big night.

First-time Oscar nominee Robert Downey, Jr. won the BAFTA and a London Film Critics award for his portrayal of previous Oscar nominee Charlie Chaplin in *Chaplin* (NYT "good and persuasive as the adult Charlie when the material allows, and close to brilliant when he does some of Charlie's early vaudeville and film sketches"; NYP "with incredible skill, grace and unmocking mimicry, Downey is a superb Chaplin"; LAT "does more than master the man's celebrated duck walk and easy grace … Downey becomes Chaplin"; CT "an eerily accurate bit of mimicry"; WP "played with heart ... brings hard-won grace to his performance, but not the panache of a matinee idol nor the wistfulness of a gifted clown"; BG "does a pretty good job of staying focused on Chaplin's melancholy temperament and balletic grace ... an acceptable replica"; V "uncanny, truly remarkable ... a toweringly great performance"; FQ "striking").

Clint Eastwood, another first-time Oscar nominee, received the Los Angeles Film Critics Association prize and was runner-up for the National Society of Film Critics award as an ageing gunfighter in *Unforgiven* (NYT "splendid ... his richest, most satisfying performance"; LAT "exactly right for the role"; WP "if Eastwood had any emotional depth as an actor, the character's anguish might come through [but he] has little more than a paint-by-numbers approach to acting"; TT "wears the genre like the old pro he is").

Al Pacino was recognised by the Academy for a seventh and eighth time with mentions in both the acting categories. He was short-listed as Best Actor as a blind, retired army officer in *Scent of a Woman* (NYT "flamboyant ... the sort of role for which Oscar nominations were made ... [he] roars through this story with show-stopping intensity"; NYP "Pacino's grandstanding performance is not just hard to ignore; it takes the whole movie crashing down with it"; LAT "amazing ... a tour de force"; CT "a major piece of work"; WP "a masterful job"; V "[a] theatrical, virtuoso star turn ... one of his most energetic, emotionally open performances"; TGM "issued an actor's challenge, [he] responds with a great actor's performance"; TT "a showy, unyielding star turn"; SMH "one of those capital performances custom built to snatch Academy Awards"). Pacino placed third in the voting by the New York Film Critics Circle, was runner-up for the National Board of Review award and won his second Golden Globe (Drama).

Stephen Rea won the NSFC plaudit and subsequently made the Oscar list for the first time as an IRA gunman in the surprise hit *The Crying Game* (NYT "exceptionally well-acted ... intelligent, stylish and intriguing ... in a big, very complex role"; LAT "splendidly acted").

Finally, Denzel Washington became the first African-American nominated in the acting categories for a third time with his portrayal of the eponymous civil rights leader in *Malcolm X* (NYT "does for Malcolm X what Ben Kingsley did for Gandhi ... has the psychological heft, the intelligence and the reserve to give the film the dramatic excitement that isn't always apparent in the screenplay"; NYP "an Oscar nomination shoo-in"; LAT "a heroic performance ... makes all [the man's] transformations believable"; BG "[a] magnificently arch performance"; V "[a] forceful, magnetic and multi-layered lead performance"). Prior to the Oscars, Washington was honoured at the Berlin Film Festival, won the New York critics' accolade and finished runner-up in Los Angeles.

The two most glaring omissions from the list of candidates were Venice Film Festival and NBR winner Jack Lemmon in *Glengarry Glen Ross* (NYT "deserves awards ... among the cast of equals, [he and Pacino] stand out"; NYP "magnificent ... Lemmon will be nominated for an Oscar"; LAT "flawless ... [a] fine, intelligently showy performance ... should get nominated again ... even in a film like this, where fine acting is the rule not the exception, his work stands out"; CST "has a scene in this movie that represents the best work he has ever done"; BG "[an] Oscar-worthy performance") and Cannes Film Festival and Globe (Musical/Comedy) winner Tim Robbins in *The Player* (CT "[a] superb performance"; V "superb"). Robbins had also earned acclaim for *Bob Roberts* (NYT "a career-defining achievement"; LAT "[makes] him someone we can't take our eyes off"; CT "continues to show his versatility"; V "impressive").

Also overlooked were: Jack Nicholson in *Hoffa* (NYT "spookily compelling ... the performance is composed less of superficial tricks than of the actor's crafty intelligence and conviction"; NYP "a vital, full-bodied performance"; LAT "convincing [in a] strong performance"; CT "struggles to give a serious, committed performance ... fails to convince"; WP "[an] entertaining portrait"; V "[a] powerhouse performance"); New York runner-up Harvey Keitel in *Bad Lieutenant* (NYT "gives the role his all"; LAT "he keeps us watching his descent without wanting to look away [and] only an actor with tremendous reserves of power could accomplish that"; CST "plays this man with such uncompromised honesty that the performance can only be called courageous"; BG "maintains a blast-furnace level of intensity ... pulling out all the stops"; TT "his performance is remarkably naked and honest, ripe for an Oscar ... no actor's tricks here: this characterisation is built up from the inside"; G "[a] devastating, almost desperate, performance"; S&S "played to the hilt by Keitel in a shockingly brilliant performance"); Tom Cruise in *A Few Good Men* (LAT "rather than walk through the part, he attacks it with vigor"; CT "should prove that [he] is a fine actor capable of a laser intensity that overrides his good looks"; BG "when he stops acting cute and bright-eyed, Cruise burns up the screen"); Anthony Hopkins in *Howards End* (NYT "splendid"; LAT "remarkable acting"; V "can do no wrong in the acting department"; TGM "wonderfully delicate acting"; TT "excellent"); London Film Critics winner Daniel Day-Lewis in *The Last of the Mohicans* (NYT "dominating every scene"; LAT "beautifully creates a romantic character ... proves once again that he is one of those chameleons who can play absolutely anything with complete conviction"; WP "just a little bit Hollywood"; G "[played] with dignity and considerable presence"; S&S "an astonishing array of bad choices"); and Eric Stoltz in *The Waterdance* (NYT "a fine, self-assured, carefully measured performance"; LAT "[a] knockout ... makes [him] not only believable but sympathetic as well"; BG "[an] involvingly faceted portrayal").

Despite one of the strongest Best Actor fields in Oscar history, sentiment meant that the winner was never in any doubt. Jodie Foster opened the Best Actor envelope and declared Al Pacino the winner of the Academy Award.

1992

BEST ACTRESS

ACADEMY AWARDS
Catherine Deneuve as 'Éliane Devries' in *Indochine*
Mary McDonnell as 'Mary-Alice Culhane' in *Passion Fish*
Michelle Pfeiffer as 'Lurene Hallett' in *Love Field*
Susan Sarandon as 'Michaela Odone' in *Lorenzo's Oil*
• **Emma Thompson as 'Margaret Schlegel' in *Howards End***

GOLDEN GLOBE AWARDS

(Drama)	(Comedy/Musical)
Mary McDonnell – *Passion Fish*	Geena Davis
Michelle Pfeiffer – *Love Field*	– *A League of Their Own*
Susan Sarandon – *Lorenzo's Oil*	Whoopi Goldberg – *Sister Act*
Sharon Stone – *Basic Instinct*	Shirley MacLaine – *Used People*
• **Emma Thompson – *Howards End***	• **Miranda Richardson**
	– *Enchanted April*
	Meryl Streep – *Death Becomes Her*

BRITISH ACADEMY AWARDS
Judy Davis – *Husbands and Wives*
Tara Morice – *Strictly Ballroom*
Jessica Tandy – *Fried Green Tomatoes*
• **Emma Thompson – *Howards End***

NEW YORK – Emma Thompson – *Howards End*
LOS ANGELES – Emma Thompson – *Howards End*
BOARD OF REVIEW – Emma Thompson – *Howards End*
NATIONAL SOCIETY – Emma Thompson – *Howards End*
LONDON – Judy Davis – *Barton Fink* and *Husbands and Wives* and *Naked Lunch*

"Emma Thompson is considered a sure thing for best actress by default," declared Caryn James in The New York Times. "And though she deserves great honors for her deep and subtle performance in 'Howards End', it's not as if she has much competition ... it's a scramble to come up with five roles meaty enough to fill Oscar's best actress category." The nominees, James speculated, could include Michelle Pfeiffer in the box office smash *Batman Returns* (NYT "captivating ... an absolute hoot when she turns into the sexy, ambitious Catwoman"; LAT "the only exception to the overall doom and gloom is Michelle

269

Pfeiffer's stylish and funny performance ... [brings] energy and pizazz to the dual roles ... [she is] the best thing in the movie"; V "intimidating"; TGM "the film comes alive only when she's on camera") and Geena Davis in *A League of Their Own* (LAT "the clear standout ... handles herself exceptionally well giving the film a perhaps better performance than it deserves"; WP "[the film is] graced by Davis"; V "splendid"; TGM "is almost low-key, and her subtle performance serves as the perfect counterweight to Hanks's theatrics"). It would have been more accurate for James to say it was something of a scramble to come up with five roles played by Americans to fill the Best Actress category, as there were several worthy performances by foreign actresses for Oscar voters to consider.

English actress Emma Thompson had impressed critics with her performance as the elder sister in the drama *Howards End* (NYT "[an] expertly realized performance ... comes into her own"; LAT "remarkable acting ... impeccable ... acting of the most subtle, delicate sort ... the triumph of Thompson's performance is the way she gradually allows us to see past [the] surface and realize how wise and substantial Margaret is"; V "immensely sympathetic"; TGM "first among equals ... wonderfully drawn [and] beautifully measured ... Thompson captures every complicated facet"; TT "capably impersonated").

Critics had also praised two other English actresses: Helena Bonham Carter in *Where Angels Fear to Tread* (NYT "perform[s] flawlessly ... displays extraordinary intelligence and authority in a rewardingly delicate role"; NYP "excellent"; BG "impeccable"; V "her strongest performance to date") and Miranda Richardson in *Enchanted April* (NYT "is at the quiet center of this story and radiates a peaceful air"; Time "splendid"; SMH "impressive").

Meanwhile, critics had also praised Chinese star Gong Li in *Da Hong Deng Long Gao Gao Gua (Raise the Red Lantern)* (NYT "reveals unexpected sharpness as well as great depths of dignity and sorrow"; LAT "flawlessly portrayed"; SMH "commanding") and veteran French star Catherine Deneuve as the owner of a plantation in 1930s Vietnam in *Indochine* (NYT "lends the movie a lot of her own instinctive intelligence ... behind the movie-star façade, a real actress is at work"; LAT "such is Deneuve's presence that she dominates the film even when she is off-camera"; CT "only an actress with the regal bearing, glacial beauty and rich personal history of Catherine Deneuve could have carried off the central role of Elaine ... [her] magnificent composure and supreme self-confidence provide the main reasons for enduring 'Indochine'"; BG "makes us feel a mother's bereavement"; V "delivers a stunning portrait of a complex woman ... [an] impeccable performance"; TT "beguiling").

Of these acclaimed foreigners, the Academy named only Deneuve and Thompson, each for the first time. Globe (Comedy/Musical) winner Richardson was nominated in the supporting category for her performance in *Damage*.

Three Americans were shortlisted after their films were given qualifying runs near the end of the year: Mary McDonnell as a television soap star paralysed in an accident in *Passion Fish* (NYT "touching [and] vividly believable"; LAT "she does her best screen acting ... [an] Oscar-worthy performance"; WP "vividly acted"; V "effectively registers the thawing of her character, but doesn't exactly draw one in"); Berlin Film Festival winner Michelle Pfeiffer as a Dallas hairdresser determined to get to Washington D.C. for the funeral of President Kennedy in *Love Field* (NYT "plays Lurene with remarkable grace; NYP "does what she can with the part"; LAT "exceptional ... simply incandescent ... Pfeiffer's Lurene comes alive in a way that only the best actresses can manage ... [she] never condescends to her character but instead gives [her] the reality and emotional heft that she deserves"; WP "Pfeiffer's characterization of Lurene is a marvel"; V "memorable"; S&S "[a] superbly felt, astringent performance"); and Susan Sarandon as a mother determined to find a cure for her young son's debilitating disease in *Lorenzo's Oil* (NYT "hugely affecting"; NYP "the standout in the cast"; LAT "played with exceptional force"; CT "[her] manic intensity has never been better used in a film"; WP "played at full throttle ... an admirable performance"; V "convincingly conveys a fierceness and tenacity that is almost frightening"; TGM "superb"; S&S "astonishingly vivid"). Sarandon, in contention for a third time, was seen as the dark horse. She had finished runner-up to Thompson for both the New York Film Critics Circle and National Society of Film Critics accolades.

Other American actresses by-passed for consideration included: Sharon Stone in *Basic Instinct* (NYT "delivers Catherine's most heartless dialogue with chilling verisimilitude"; LAT "played with snooty insouciance"; WP "unforgettable"; V "a career-making role"; TGM "simultaneously sultry and vacant [but] comes off better than anyone else in the picture because her character is not meant to be real"); Whoopi Goldberg in *Sister Act* (NYT "one of her ultra-lovable roles"; LAT "[a] limber performance ... entertaining ... [she] drives 'Sister Act' from start to finish"; S&S "that it works is down to Goldberg's sassiness"); Shirley MacLaine in *Used People* (LAT "makes Pearl a character part ... this may be her best movie vehicle since 'Terms of Endearment' and her acting matches the chance"; WP "superlative"); and Julie Kavner in *This is My Life* (NYT "[played with] unfailing warmth and sturdiness"; WP "perfect"; TGM "[acts the role] with simplicity and sensitivity"; S&S "gives Dottie a wonderfully eccentric edge, and her timing is pristine").

On Oscar night, Emma Thompson won the statuette. She was the fifth person to win a clean sweep of the four critics' prizes, the Globe and the Oscar (she also won the BAFTA) and the first non-American to win the Best Actress statuette since Glenda Jackson in 1973.

1992

BEST SUPPORTING ACTOR

ACADEMY AWARDS
Jaye Davidson as 'Dil' in *The Crying Game*
• **Gene Hackman as 'Sheriff "Little Bill" Daggett' in *Unforgiven***
Jack Nicholson as 'Col. Nathan R. Jessup' in *A Few Good Men*
Al Pacino as 'Ricky Roma' in *Glengarry Glen Ross*
David Paymer as 'Stan Yankelman' in *Mr Saturday Night*

GOLDEN GLOBE AWARDS
• **Gene Hackman – *Unforgiven***
Jack Nicholson – *A Few Good Men*
Chris O'Donnell – *Scent of a Woman*
Al Pacino – *Glengarry Glen Ross*
David Paymer – *Mr Saturday Night*

BRITISH ACADEMY AWARDS
Jaye Davidson – *The Crying Game*
• **Gene Hackman – *Unforgiven***
Tommy Lee Jones – *J.F.K.*
Samuel West – *Howards End*

NEW YORK – Gene Hackman – *Unforgiven*
LOS ANGELES – Gene Hackman – *Unforgiven*
BOARD OF REVIEW – Jack Nicholson – *A Few Good Men*
NATIONAL SOCIETY – Gene Hackman – *Unforgiven*

Al Pacino was nominated by the Academy in both the Best Actor and Best Supporting Actor categories. Four of the five previous double nominees had claimed a statuette in the secondary category while the fifth (and most recent) had gone home empty-handed. As he was strongly favoured to win the Best Actor trophy, Pacino was considered a non-starter for his supporting turn as a real-estate salesman in *Glengarry Glen Ross* (NYT "deserves awards ... among the cast of equals, [he and Lemmon] stand out"; NYP "magnificent"; LAT "flawless ... [a] fine, intelligently show performance"; BG "[an] Oscar-worthy performance"; TT "excellent").

Also seen as only an outside chance was David Paymer as the brother and agent of a veteran stand-up comic in *Mr Saturday Night*, a performance few leading critics commented upon in their reviews of the film (NYT "deftly acted"; V "[a] standout performance"; TGM "a poignant performance").

The dark horse in the field was Jaye Davidson who had given the year's most talked about performance as a hairdresser involved with an IRA operative in the sleeper hit *The Crying Game*, his first screen role (NYP "memorable"; LAT "splendidly acted ... right on the money"; V "almost impossibly right"; TGM "a scintillating debut"). Although he had been by-passed for a Golden Globe nomination, Davidson had been mentioned by the British Academy and had featured strongly in the voting by the various critics' groups. He was runner-up for both the New York Film Critics Circle and National Society of Film Critics prizes.

The frontrunners for the Oscar, however, were two Hollywood veterans and previous Best Actor winners. Gene Hackman received his fifth nomination as a sadistic sheriff in a frontier town in *Unforgiven* (NYT "splendid ... [he] delights as Sheriff Daggett"; LAT "one of his most powerful and least mannered performances, displaying an implacable strength and controlled passion"; WP "does a worthy job"; TT "has the time of his life"). His performance had earned him the Los Angeles Film Critics Association plaudit, a second New York Film Critics Circle award, a second NSFC accolade, and a second Golden Globe. Meanwhile, Jack Nicholson's performance as a tough army colonel in *A Few Good Men* garnered him his fourth National Board of Review honour and a tenth Oscar nomination (NYT "superb ... Nicholson is in his own league"; NYP "highly entertaining"; LAT "a treat ... the kind of showy, self-confident acting that awards were made for"; BG "stunningly acted ... worth the price of admission"; V "spellbinds the viewer"; TGM "his relish of his exceptionally profane dialogue is palpable"). Nicholson was the fourth person and second man to be recognised by the Academy in the acting categories for a tenth time.

Among those overlooked were: Globe nominee Chris O'Donnell in *Scent of a Woman* (NYT "has the tough job of weathering [Pacino's performance] without jeopardizing his role as straight man, and he does this stalwartly"; LAT "plays him wonderfully"); New York runner-up Seymour Cassel as a gangster in *In the Soup*, a role written specifically for him (NYT "a hilarious turn ... is less an actor here than a one-man show ... the film's energy and humor are most sharply focused around [his] scene-stealing antics"; LAT "the year's largest, most robust piece of acting, a performance that no one can resist ... the kind of unstoppable performance that seems totally natural but has taken a lifetime of acting to prepare for ... [the] Sundance Film Festival gave him its first-ever special jury prize for acting, and a more deserved award you'll never see"; CT "throws everything into wild disorder ... unbridled emotionality"; TGM "superb"); Forest Whitaker in *The Crying Game* (NYT "strained and overwrought"; NYP "makes a strong impression"; LAT "splendidly acted"; V "[a] big-hearted, hugely emotional performance ... simply terrific"; TGM "powerfully affecting"); Kevin Bacon in *A Few Good Men* (TGM "a marvellous characterization"; S&S "[a] miraculously unswamped performance"); Wesley Snipes in *The Waterdance* (NYT "has the film's richest role and wastes none of it"; LAT "Snipes, projecting everything from bravado and despair to tenderness and angry tears, makes him close to unforgettable"; CT "[shows] several conflicting emotions simultaneously ... manages to be sparkle-eyed and broken down"; BG "Snipes' excellence achieves another dimension"; V "precisely and forcefully portrayed ... scene-stealing"); Graham Greene in *Thunderheart* (NYT "the film's outstanding performance ... Greene proves himself a naturally magnetic actor who deserves to be seen in other, more varied roles"; CT "has the juiciest role in the film"; WP "Greene, who stole Kevin Costner's thunder in 'Dances With Wolves', almost does it again [here] with Kilmer"); both Steve Buscemi (LAT "[a] stand out ... deadpan funny"; WP "masterful"; TGM "note perfect"; S&S "a distinctive performance") and Tim Roth (NYT "amazing"; TGM "note perfect") in *Reservoir Dogs*; Alan Rickman in *Bob Roberts* (NYT "over the edge one more time"; NYP "uproariously funny"; BG "depressingly funny as the lying CIA spook running Roberts' campaign"); and Vincent Perez in *Indochine* (V "handles his fast-changing role with great sensitivity").

Although he was presented with a special Golden Globe for his work, a campaign to secure Robin Williams an Oscar nomination for his voice acting as the Genie in the animated hit *Aladdin* was unsuccessful (NYT "[a] dizzying, elastic miracle"; LAT "what might turn out to be his most fondly remembered role ... he's never had a role that so showcased his genius, for that's what it is, for dizzying improvisational humor"; CT "pretty much takes over the last half of the film").

On Oscar night, it was Hackman who claimed the statuette. His victory set a new record length of time between Academy Award wins for a male actor: he had won his Best Actor Oscar twenty-one years earlier. Hackman was unexpectedly a winner in London as well, taking home the BAFTA ahead of the highly-favoured Davidson.

BEST SUPPORTING ACTRESS

ACADEMY AWARDS
Judy Davis as 'Sally' in *Husbands and Wives*
Joan Plowright as 'Mrs Fisher' in *Enchanted April*
Vanessa Redgrave as 'Ruth Wilcox' in *Howards End*
Miranda Richardson as 'Ingrid Fleming' in *Damage*
• **Marisa Tomei as 'Mona Lisa Vito' in *My Cousin Vinny***

GOLDEN GLOBE AWARDS
Geraldine Chaplin – *Chaplin*
Judy Davis – *Husbands and Wives*
• **Joan Plowright – *Enchanted April***
Miranda Richardson – *Damage*
Alfre Woodard – *Passion Fish*

BRITISH ACADEMY AWARDS
Kathy Bates – *Fried Green Tomatoes*
Helena Bonham Carter – *Howards End*
Miranda Richardson – *The Crying Game*
• **Miranda Richardson – *Damage***

NEW YORK – Miranda Richardson – *The Crying Game* and *Damage*
LOS ANGELES – Judy Davis – *Husbands and Wives*
BOARD OF REVIEW – Judy Davis – *Husbands and Wives*
NATIONAL SOCIETY – Judy Davis – *Husbands and Wives*

The mythology of popular culture has somehow incorporated the absurd idea that Jack Palance read out the wrong name when presenting the Best Supporting Actress Oscar. In what Variety described as "the biggest surprise of the night", the winner was unknown twenty-eight-year old Marisa Tomei as the fast-talking girlfriend of a small-time lawyer in *My Cousin Vinny* (NYT "gives every indication of being a fine comedian"; LAT "Tomei is so good at playing this svelte sharpie that she commandeers the screen whenever she's around"; CST "a high point"; BG "[the film is] carried by Tomei, who has her breakthrough here … her spunky sweetness is the only sign of life in the [movie]"; Time "wondrously sardonic"). Tomei had not been a contender for the critics' prizes nor a nominee for the Golden Globe. Even her inclusion on the ballot had been considered a surprise. Significantly, however, she was the only American performer in the category.

1992

Australian actress Judy Davis won the New York Film Critics Circle, National Board of Review and National Society of Film Critics awards and was runner-up for the Los Angeles Film Critics Association prize as a neurotic New Yorker recently separated from her husband in *Husbands and Wives* (NYT "remarkable ... nearly purloins the film"; NYP "excellent"; LAT "another exquisite performance"; CT "a brilliant comic performance ... the film's one edgy, inventive turn"; BG "on a level of brilliance all her own ... compelling ... she's the film's likeliest Oscar bet"; V "incandescent"). She had also earned praise for her contrasting role in *Where Angels Fear to Tread* (NYT "perform[s] flawlessly ... turns the exaggeratedly shrill and repressed Harriet into a lively comic caricature"; NYP "clever and finely tuned"; LAT "connoisseurs of elegantly nasty ham in the Bette Davis-Glenda Jackson tradition will relish Davis' fierce twitches, scowls and squall-like flare-ups"; WP "Davis is the high point of the film"; BG "impeccable"; TGM "shines ... her take on the hopelessly insular Harriet is a lampoon but not a cartoon ... hilarious"; S&S "stands out"). For her performance in *Husbands and Wives* along with her work in the previous year's *Barton Fink* and *Naked Lunch*, Davis had also been named Best Actress by the London Film Critics. Ahead of the ceremony, Davis was considered by most pundits as the favourite for the Oscar.

The other main contender was English actress Miranda Richardson, winner of the Los Angeles prize and runner-up in the balloting by the New York critics, the NBR and the NSFC, for her performance as the wife of an adulterous MP in *Damage* (NYT "Richardson's credible performance as Ingrid gives the film some spark"; NYP "affecting"; LAT "has some devastatingly potent scenes"; WP "[a] haunted performance"; V "puts frightening force behind her rage"). The critics' groups had also cited her as a ruthless IRA operative in *The Crying Game* (LAT "splendidly acted ... right on the money").

Richardson also appeared that year in a contrasting role in the period film *Enchanted April* and it was her co-star, English actress Joan Plowright, widow of previous Best Actor winner Laurence Olivier, who loomed as a dark horse for the Oscar. Plowright had unexpectedly won the Golden Globe as an elderly woman sharing an Italian villa in *Enchanted April* (NYT "uproariously funny ... Plowright's indignant hauteur makes for the film's most amusing moments"; NYP "priceless"; LAT "the sort of ripe grande dame turn at which British movies used to excel"; Time "splendid"; TGM "[a] masterful turn ... she gets the best lines and never misses a satiric beat"; SMH "impressive"). It was her first Oscar nomination.

Completing the list of nominees, meanwhile, was previous winner Vanessa Redgrave, who earned her sixth mention for *Howards End* (NYT "a strong performance"; LAT "remarkable acting"; TGM "etches an indelible cameo"; TT "quite moving").

Overlooked were: Helena Bonham Carter in *Howards End* (NYT "a breakthrough... gives a full-length portrait"; LAT "remarkable"; TT "appears to good effect"); Geraldine Chaplin as her grandmother, Hannah Chaplin in *Chaplin* (NYT "splendid"; CT "quite striking"; WP "tenderly played"; V "strong"); Angela Bassett in *Malcolm X* (LAT "excellent"; BG "tender"); Helen Hunt in *The Waterdance* (NYT "[a] finely drawn [characterization"; LAT "understated but very affecting work ... a performance that manages to project selflessness as strength and scrupulously avoids any hint of dishrag self-sacrifice"; CT "a warm, natural performance, mixing earthiness with a sense of the awkward"; V "exceptional"); 1991 Venice Film Festival winner Tilda Swinton in *Edward II* (NYT "turns in the most memorable performance, that of a love-starved woman whose iceberg exterior conceals a consuming sexual hunger"; TGM "exceptionally fine ... communicates meaning without sacrificing poetry"); both Kathy Najimy (NYT "[a] stand out"; LAT "could not be bettered") and Maggie Smith (LAT "the ideal foil for Goldberg's limber performance"; S&S "the most interesting character [in the film]") in *Sister Act*; and Sigourney Weaver in *1492: Conquest of Paradise* (NYT "surprisingly effective ... plays straight and true and looks regal"; LAT "brittle and artificial"; CT "contributes a saucy and intelligent Queen Isabel"; BG "does what she can"; TGM "superb ... although she is in only a few scenes, she invests them with humour and humanity").

Michelle Pfeiffer's supporting turn as Catwoman in the box office smash *Batman Returns*, meanwhile, was promoted by Warner Bros. in the Best Actress category and also went unrecognized.

The most surprising omission, however, was Globe nominee Alfre Woodard as the nurse in *Passion Fish* (NYT "played memorably ... [in a] cliche-free performance"; LAT "superb ... [she] gets all her character's false insouciance, confusion, tenacity and sense of displacement ... [an] Oscar-worthy performance"; WP "vividly acted"; TT "almost steals the show"; S&S "[a] superbly felt, astringent performance"). In the Los Angeles Times a month prior to the announcement of the nominations, Kenneth Turan had called Woodard's work, "the year's most overlooked supporting performance" and declared, "if there is any justice the academy will search it out and appropriately reward it."

BEST PICTURE

ACADEMY AWARDS

The Fugitive
   (Warner Bros., 133 mins, 6 Aug 1993, $183.8m, 7 noms)
In the Name of the Father
   (Hell's Kitchen, Universal, 125 mins, 29 Dec 1993, $25.0m, 7 noms)
The Piano
   (CIBY 2000, Miramax, 121 mins, 19 Nov 1993, $40.1m, 8 noms)
The Remains of the Day
   (Merchant Ivory, Columbia, 134 mins, 5 Nov 1993, $22.9m, 8 noms)
• *Schindler's List*
   (Amblin, Universal, 185 mins BW, 15 Dec 1993, $96.0m, 12 noms)

GOLDEN GLOBE AWARDS

(Drama)   (Comedy/Musical)
The Age of Innocence   *Dave*
In the Name of the Father   *Much Ado About Nothing*
The Piano   • *Mrs Doubtfire*
The Remains of the Day   *Sleepless in Seattle*
• *Schindler's List*   *Strictly Ballroom*

PRODUCERS GUILD AWARD

The Fugitive
In the Name of the Father
The Piano
The Remains of the Day
• *Schindler's List*

BRITISH ACADEMY AWARDS

(Best Film)   (Best British Film)
The Piano   *Naked*
The Remains of the Day   *Raining Stones*
• *Schindler's List*   • *Shadowlands*
Shadowlands   *Tom and Viv*

NEW YORK – *Schindler's List*
LOS ANGELES – *Schindler's List*
BOARD OF REVIEW – *Schindler's List*
NATIONAL SOCIETY – *Schindler's List*

1993

LONDON
(Best Film) *The Piano*
(Best British Film) *The Remains of the Day*

Schindler's List, a black and white epic about a Nazi industrialist who helped save over a thousand Jews during the Holocaust, became the first film to be named Best Picture by all four major American critics' groups, the Hollywood Foreign Press Association and both the Academies in London and Hollywood (NYT "dark, sobering and also invigoratingly dramatic"; NYP "extraordinary ... breathtaking [and] unforgettable ... one of the most gripping pictures of the year"; LAT "restrained and powerful ... an agonizing black-and-white tour de force ... quietly devastating"; WP "ruthlessly unsentimental"; TGM "a powerful and affecting piece of work [and a] deeply felt film").

The awards sweep by *Schindler's List* was complete, but not overwhelming. It won several trophies by only narrow margins over the New Zealand period drama *The Piano* (NYT "eerily beautiful ... moving [and] original ... it could be the movie sensation of the year"; NYP "astonishes ... an instant classic"; LAT "remarkable"; CST "compelling"; WP "evocative, powerful, extraordinarily beautiful"; BG "thematically, stylistically, emotionally, Jane Campion's exhilarating 'The Piano' is one of the richest films of the decade ... an instant classic ... lush, convulsive, impassioned, unforgettable ... a one-of-a-kind film"; V "visually sumptuous"; FQ "extraordinary"; Time "a triumph of dazzling movie art"; TT "magnificent ... extraordinarily powerful"; SMH "an undeniable masterpiece"). *The Piano* was one of two films to receive the Palme d'Or at the Cannes Film Festival. During the end-of-year awards season, it finished runner-up for the New York Film Critics Circle, Los Angeles Film Critics Association and National Society of Film Critics prizes (the New York result was 34 points to 31, while the NSFC tally was 44 to 36) and won the top prize from the London Film Critics.

Also considered by the Academy were: *The Remains of the Day*, winner of the Best British Film from the London Film Critics (NYT "a spellbinding new tragi-comedy of high and most entertaining order ... heart-breaking"; NYP "passionate ... magnificent [and] stunning ... a consummate masterpiece"; LAT "moving and carefully modulated"; CT "magnificent ... quality filmmaking with an emotional punch ... one of the year's best films"; TGM "splendid"; TT "exquisitely crafted"; G "luxuriously mounted and often brilliantly engineered"); *In the Name of the Father* (NYT "scathingly brilliant"; NYP "searing, unforgettable"; LAT "powerful"; WP "sluggish ... lacks focus and ultimately runs out of dramatic impetus"; TGM "the film is too eclectic on occasion"); and, surprisingly, the box office hit *The Fugitive* (NYT "a smashing success ... a juggernaut of an action-adventure saga"; NYP "so good it leaves you physically exhausted"; LAT "a crisp and jolting melodrama"; WP "a blistering adventure ... gripping"; BG "a hugely entertaining adrenaline rush"; S&S "remarkably successful"). It was the second year in a row that Oscar voters had considered the same five candidates as the Producers Guild of America.

Arguably, the two most glaring omissions from the Oscar shortlist were National Board of Review runner-up *The Age of Innocence* (NYT "intelligent"; NYP "compelling ... most moviegoers will be captivated [and yet] ultimately unsatisfying"; LAT "a beautifully done adaptation ... polished, elegant and completely cinematic [albeit] also a bit distant"; BG "visually magnificent, thematically rich, potently acted ... stunning"; TT "a major triumph"; S&S "a visual tour de force"; SMH "deeply moving") and the other Palme d'Or winner *Ba Wang Bie Ji (Farewell, My Concubine)* (NYT "extraordinary ... stunning ... a vastly entertaining movie"; NYP "a vibrant, visually exciting work"; LAT "superb ... [a] remarkable ... [a] gorgeous, intoxicating epic"; CT "a huge, gorgeous, crowd-pleasing spectacle ... eye-catching, adrenaline-churning, racy"; BG "impressive ... comes together with historical resonance and stirring, full-blooded sweep"; G "spectacular and intimate ... stunning ... a magnificent achievement").

Other award-winning films overlooked by Oscar voters were: Best British Film BAFTA winner *Shadowlands* (NYT "moving"; NYP "brilliant [and] heartbreaking"; LAT "a moving experience"; CT "artificial, overcalculated and strained"; WP "engaging"; G "first-class"); Venice Film Festival co-winner *Short Cuts* (NYT "a terrific movie"; LAT "a rich, unnerving film, as comic as it is astringent"; WP "a cynical, sexist and shallow work ... long, sour and ultimately pointless"; BG "brilliant, exhilarating ... a sublime and unflinching human comedy ... smart, funny and inventive"); Venice Film Festival co-winner *Trois Couleurs: Bleu (Three Colors: Blue)* (NYT "lyrically studied, solemn, sometimes almost abstract ... doesn't seduce the viewer into its very complex, musically formal arrangements ... represents an aridly intellectual kind of film making"; LAT "striking [and] haunting ... [an] artfully made film, dense with feeling, in which no shot is ordinary and no moment taken for granted"; TGM "provocative ... occasionally dazzling, often dizzying, always troubling"; S&S "anti-climactic"); Berlin Film Festival winner *Xi yan (The Wedding Banquet)* (NYT "funny and poignant"; NYP "unforgettable"; LAT "as poignant and pointed as it is funny (and it is very funny)"; CT "a touching, beautifully paced film in which the laughs are organic to the material"; BG "a surprising and delightful comedy ... one of the year's most joyful film discoveries"); and César winner *Les Nuits Fauves (Savage Nights)* (NYT "a landmark film ... provocative and poignant"; NYP "unflinching"; LAT "particularly disappointing"; WP "self-indulgent"; BG "unruly and jolting, but also alive and kicking [and] ultimately moving"; Time "sensational"; SMH "energy, style and emotional turbulence that marks it as one of a kind").

Other notable releases by-passed in the Best Picture category by the Academy were: *The Joy Luck Club* (NYT "both sweeping and intimate"; LAT "its deeply felt, straight-from-the-heart emotions and the unadorned way it presents them make quite an impact ... honest and compassionate"; WP "this sweeping movie is so immaculately dead-on that it nearly transcends criticism ... it's ravishing to look at, but it is not deep"; TGM "as a full-bore weepie, it succeeds "; S&S "[the] sentimentality becomes a little cloying"); *Searching for Bobby Fischer* (NYT "absorbing"; LAT "a beautifully calibrated model of honestly sentimental filmmaking, made with delicacy, restraint and unmistakable emotional power"; CT "uncommonly good"; TGM "a good movie that packs a great contemporary wallop"; WP "a wonderfully acted, heart-warming family film"); *Strictly Ballroom* (NYT "tells an enjoyable hokey story with flair"; LAT "close to irresistible"; BG "exhilarating"; V "light, breezy and immensely likeable"; TGM "buoyantly unique ... this picture is fun to be around ... a terrifically kinetic picture ... very likeable"); *Naked* (NYT "brilliant"; LAT "remarkable, unnerving"; BG "one of the most sorchingly compelling films in year ... [a] masterpiece [and] an epoch-defining film"); and *Orlando* (NYT "grand ... this ravishing and witty spectacle invades the mind through eyes that are dazzled ... could well become a classic of a very special kind ... [an] extraordinary film ... a triumph of intelligent, lyrical yet argumentative film making"; LAT "visually impressive [but] hollow"; BG "Sally Potter has brought [the novel] to the screen entertainingly and resourcefully"; V "exciting, wonderfully witty entertainment"; TT "wonderful").

BEST DIRECTOR

ACADEMY AWARDS
Robert Altman for *Short Cuts*
Jane Campion for *The Piano*
James Ivory for *The Remains of the Day*
Jim Sheridan for *In the Name of the Father*
• **Steven Spielberg for *Schindler's List***

GOLDEN GLOBE AWARDS
Jane Campion – *The Piano*
Andrew Davis – *The Fugitive*
James Ivory – *The Remains of the Day*
Martin Scorsese – *The Age of Innocence*
• **Steven Spielberg – *Schindler's List***

DIRECTORS GUILD AWARD
Jane Campion – *The Piano*
Andrew Davis – *The Fugitive*
James Ivory
 – *The Remains of the Day*
Martin Scorsese
 – *The Age of Innocence*
• **Steven Spielberg**
 – *Schindler's List*

BRITISH ACADEMY AWARDS
Richard Attenborough
 – *Shadowlands*
Jane Campion – *The Piano*
James Ivory
 – *The Remains of the Day*
• **Steven Spielberg**
 – *Schindler's List*

NEW YORK – Jane Campion – *The Piano*
LOS ANGELES – Jane Campion – *The Piano*
BOARD OF REVIEW – Martin Scorsese – *The Age of Innocence*
NATIONAL SOCIETY – Steven Spielberg – *Schindler's List*
LONDON
 (Director) **James Ivory – *The Remains of the Day***
 (British Director) **Ken Loach – *Raining Stones***

At the Cannes Film Festival, Jane Campion became the first woman to win the Palme d'Or, honoured for her period drama *The Piano* (LAT "captures attention confidently and absolutely … a writer-director whose command of the visual and emotional aspects of filmmaking is fearless and profound"; WP "the erotic tension that Campion brings to [the screen] is nearly excruciating … conveys as much through suggestion and implication as by direct statement"; BG "if there's any justice, Campion and Hunter will be showered with awards for their inspired work"; V "bold"; TT "Campion is now approaching cinema's mainstream yet her emotional daring, visual audacity and poetic impulse remain … Campion still thinks and feels afresh, and thinks in images"). She shared the festival's top accolade with Chen Kaige for *Ba Wang Bie Ji (Farewell, My Concubine)* (NYT "deft … Chen is a director who has as much command of the intimate moments as of the big scenes of crowds, chaos and confusion"; CT "the superb direction of the movie ensures that every scene is tense and lends definite importance to the storyline"; BG "consciously setting out to make a film more geared to universal popular taste than any he has made before, Chen succeeds beyond any Hollywood mogul's boldest hopes"; TGM "the film is clearly the work of a master director"). Both, however, were overlooked for the Cannes Best Director prize in favour of Mike Leigh for *Naked* (NYT "nothing that Mr Leigh has done in the past is adequate preparation for 'Naked'"; LAT "even Leigh has done nothing [before] as extreme, intense and daring as 'Naked'"; BG "Leigh's masterpiece").

In mid-December, many observers were surprised when Campion collected the Best Director accolades from both the New York Film Critics Circle and Los Angeles Film Critics Association. She was the first woman to have been so honoured by either group. She claimed the west coast prize ahead of Robert Altman for *Short Cuts* (BG "masterfully [directed] … a triumphant achievement") and the east coast plaudit by 34 votes to 31 over Steven Spielberg for *Schindler's List* (NYT "directed with fury and immediacy … rising brilliantly to the challenge of this material and displaying an electrifying creative intelligence … with every frame, he demonstrates the power of the film maker to distil complex events into fiercely indelible images"; NYP "an astonishing achievement"; LAT "Spielberg has had the nerve to simply let those dreadful scenes play, and as a consequence has created as indelible picture of the Holocaust as fiction film allows"; CT "what Spielberg has done in this Holocaust story is simply and forcefully place us *there*"; WP "Spielberg, so famous for emotional manipulation, here has let the material speak for itself"). Early in the new year, however, Spielberg bested Campion in the National Society of Film Critics voting to win the award 46 points to 33.

The Hollywood Foreign Press Association and the Directors Guild of America listed the same five nominees. Campion and Spielberg were mentioned, along with: Andrew Davis for *The Fugitive* (NYT "directed sensationally"; LAT "has done more than pack pounding energy into every sequence … has paid attention to the credibility of all the film's characters, involving us even more completely in the action in the process … marks Davis' coming of age as a crackling good action director"; WP "shot on the fly … taut"; BG "keeps things moving slickly and frantically, although his camerawork is a little arty"; Time "high energy directorial craftsmanship"); James Ivory for *The Remains of the Day* (NYT "exquisite work [by] one of our finest directors"; CT "quality filmmaking"; BG "impeccably crafted"; G "one of Ivory's finest"); and National Board of Review winner Martin Scorsese for *The Age of Innocence* (LAT "Scorsese impresses by how masterfully he has come up to the challenge [of filming the novel] ... beautifully done"; WP "deft"; BG "we expect beautiful craftsmanship from Scorsese, and it's there in an abundance that leaves no doubt that he's our foremost filmmaker today"). As expected, Spielberg was presented with both awards, and became the favourite for the Oscar.

Many predicted that the Academy would simply match the Globe and DGA list, but when the Oscar nominations were announced there were two changes. Davis and Scorsese were by-passed in favour of Los Angeles runner-up Altman (his fourth nomination and second consecutive nod) and Jim Sheridan, who made the list for a second time, for *In the Name of the Father* (NYT "shows [his] ability to tell a story both matter-of-factly and metaphorically ... his direction is plain and amazingly resonant ... sustains a devastating simplicity and a cool, watchful tone"; WP "cumbersome"; TGM "[the film ends up] a bit jumpy in its tone and its pacing"). Spielberg was recognised for a fourth time, Ivory for a third time (and second year in a row), while Campion was included for the first time becoming only the second woman nominated for the Best Director Oscar (the first had been Lina Wertmüller in 1976).

In addition to Davis and Scorsese, the Academy overlooked: previous winner Richard Attenborough for *Shadowlands* (NYT "directed in ripely sentimental fashion"; NYP "his greatest triumph"; CT "strained"; G "the best piece of direction he has ever accomplished"); the previous year's winner Clint Eastwood for *A Perfect World* (NYT "a deeply felt, deceptively simple film that marks the high point of [his] directing career thus far ... Eastwood's direction of this handsome film manages to be both majestic and self-effacing"; TGM "has opted to play it safe and commercial"); Wayne Wang for *The Joy Luck Club* (NYT "directed simply and forcefully"; LAT "evenhanded and caring direction"); Sally Potter for *Orlando* (NYT "breath-taking ... [her] achievement is in translating to film something of the breadth of Woolf's remarkable range of interests"; LAT "assured"; TGM "handles the transitions with fluid ease – the movie has a graceful flow"); Ang Lee for *Xi yan (The Wedding Banquet)* (LAT "handling the comedy and the seriousness with equal deftness"; CT "beautifully paced"; BG "there's nothing cramped or forced or compromised about Lee's filmmaking ... directed with finesse"); the late Cyril Collard for *Les Nuits Fauves (Savage Nights)* (NYT "impressive ... Collard's direction emphasizes the rawness of his story [and his] kaleidoscopic approach is involving"; LAT "was not a particularly adept filmmaker"; SMH "dynamically directed"); Krzysztof Kieślowski for *Trois Couleurs: Bleu (Three Colors: Blue)* (LAT "artfully made ... there is nothing ordinary or banal about the way [he] has gone about his business here"; TGM "his mastery of technique is such that you're compelled to watch even when you don't quite understand"; TT "'Blue' displays the brilliant technique of a great director"); and Australian Baz Luhrmann for *Strictly Ballroom* (NYT "gleefully flashy"; LAT "told with an unflagging energy and style"; TGM "his technique is stylized, almost over-the-top").

On Oscar night, Jane Campion won the statuette for Best Original Screenplay for *The Piano*, but was unable to cause an upset and become the first woman to win the Best Director Oscar. At his fourth nomination, eight years after he was controversially left off the ballot for *The Color Purple*, Spielberg won his first Best Director statuette.

1993

BEST ACTOR

ACADEMY AWARDS
Daniel Day-Lewis as 'Gerald Conlon' in *In the Name of the Father*
Laurence Fishburne as 'Ike Turner' in *What's Love Got to Do With It?*
• **Tom Hanks as 'Andrew Beckett' in *Philadelphia***
Anthony Hopkins as 'Stevens' in *The Remains of the Day*
Liam Neeson as 'Oskar Schindler' in *Schindler's List*

GOLDEN GLOBE AWARDS

(Drama)
Daniel Day-Lewis
 – *In the Name of the Father*
Harrison Ford – *The Fugitive*
• **Tom Hanks – *Philadelphia***
Anthony Hopkins
 – *The Remains of the Day*
Liam Neeson – *Schindler's List*

(Comedy/Musical)
Johnny Depp – *Benny and Joon*
Tom Hanks – *Sleepless in Seattle*
Kevin Kline – *Dave*
Colm Meaney – *The Snapper*
• **Robin Williams – *Mrs Doubtfire***

BRITISH ACADEMY AWARDS
Daniel Day-Lewis – *In the Name of the Father*
• **Anthony Hopkins – *The Remains of the Day***
Anthony Hopkins – *Shadowlands*
Liam Neeson – *Schindler's List*

NEW YORK – David Thewlis – *Naked*
LOS ANGELES – Anthony Hopkins – *The Remains of the Day* and *Shadowlands*
BOARD OF REVIEW – Anthony Hopkins – *The Remains of the Day* and *Shadowlands*
NATIONAL SOCIETY – David Thewlis – *Naked*
LONDON
 (Actor) **Anthony Hopkins – *The Remains of the Day***
 (British Actor) **David Thewlis – *Naked***

Three British actors dominated the end of year critics' prizes.

The New York Post said that the performance of Anthony Hopkins as a devoted butler in *The Remains of the Day*, was "one of the greatest acting achievements ever captured on film," and other critics were also impressed (NYT "wondrously played"; LAT "exceptional [and] little short of miraculous";

BG "exquisitely acted ... [an] unforgettable portrayal"; V "superbly observed and nuanced"; TGM "astonishing"; G "a virtual certainty for another Oscar nomination ... he can suggest a great deal more from what might otherwise seem a one-dimensional part ... no praise is too high" Sp "perfectly cast"). Less than two months later, Hopkins earned further praise for his portrayal of writer C.S. Lewis in *Shadowlands* (NYT "an amazingly versatile and moving performance ... acted with great tenderness"; NYP "perfect"; LAT "is in his element here"; CT "love and goodness are hard subjects to portray on screen [yet] Hopkins conveys them with such richness and truth that he may leave audiences too full for tears ... evocative minimalism ... this is great screen acting ... [he] triumphs"; WP "[the film] is illuminated from beginning to end by Hopkins ... may be the best thing he's ever done"; V "[a] towering performance"; Time "strong, unsentimental, exemplary"). Hopkins won the Los Angeles Film Critics Association, National Board of Review and London Film Critics Best Actor accolades, was runner-up for the New York Film Critics Circle prize and placed third in the voting by the National Society of Film Critics.

Runner-up for the Los Angeles and NSFC awards was Daniel Day-Lewis as both a nineteenth century gentleman in *The Age of Innocence* (NYT "excellent"; LAT "ideal"; BG "potently acted ... heartbreaking"; Time "superb"; S&S "excellent") and Gerry Conlon, a man wrongly imprisoned for an IRA bombing, in *In the Name of the Father* (NYT "another dazzling performance in what is so far the role of his career ... played so grippingly and unpredictably"; NYP "utterly compelling"; LAT "extraordinarily convincing [in] a blistering performance ... a piece of acting that makes us feel we are living those harrowing years right along with him"; WP "obviously relishes the opportunity"; V "first-rate"; TGM "convincing at every point in [the character's] journey").

Claiming the New York honour (by just two points) and the NSFC award (45 points to 25) was David Thewlis in *Naked*, for which he had been honoured at the Cannes Film Festival (NYT "staggeringly fine"; LAT "[a] searing performance"; BG "brilliant"; V "a tour-de-force"; FQ "a ferocious, luminous performance"; Time "a performance so perfectly perverse that you cannot look away"; TT "a terrific, highly charged performance"; S&S "[a] brilliant, fierce, intensely irritating near-monologue of a central performance").

When the Oscar nominations were announced, Thewlis became only the sixth winner of the New York critics' prize to be overlooked by the Academy. Included ahead of him were: previous winners Day-Lewis and Hopkins; Golden Globe (Drama) winner and Berlin honoree Tom Hanks as a lawyer with AIDS in *Philadelphia* (NYT "a brave, stirring, tremendously dignified performance"; NYP "will probably win an Oscar"; LAT "affecting ... [but] his performance, pitched to gain sympathy, manages that but not a great deal more"; WP "shows enormous courage and immense ability in the role ... heart-wrenchingly recreates the dreadful cost of the disease ... boldly acted"; V "dynamic"); Laurence Fishburne, the year's surprise nominee, as the abusive partner of singer Tina Turner in *What's Love Got to Do With It?* (NYT "[a] brilliant, mercurial portrayal ... elevates [the film] beyond the realm of run-on-the-mill biography"; NYP "truly terrifying"; LAT "beautifully played ... exceptional"; TGM "exemplary in [a] shallowly conceived role"); and Liam Neeson as the German industrialist who helped save over a thousand Jews from the Holocaust in *Schindler's List* (NYT "played with mesmerizing authority"; NYP "impressive"; TGM "Neeson creates in Schindler a chameleon who is both infinitely malleable and ultimately resolute ... his transcendent virtue comes alive").

Among the other contenders overlooked were: Globe (Comedy/Musical) winner Robin Williams in *Mrs Doubtfire* (NYT "William remains this film's main and only real attraction ... he is well worth seeing"; CT "his twin performances are predictably fine"; WP "at the top of his form ... he's downright irresistible"; BG "Williams is never going to leave you unentertained"); Michael Douglas in *Falling Down* (NYT "astonishing [and] terrific in what must be one of the richest and difficult roles of his career"; NYP "never been better"; CT "[shows] a far greater range of expressions than one has come to expect from [him]"; WP "his challenge was to play the character straight down the middle, and he meets this challenge so skillfully"; BG "arresting ... he's so internalized he practically isn't there ... some of his best acting"); Kevin Costner in *A Perfect World* (NYT "superb ... absolutely riveting, a marvel of guarded, watchful character revealed through sly understatement and precise details ... [a] vigorous screen performance"; NYP "deserves credit ... intriguing"; LAT "gives one of his most affecting performances ... surprisingly adept"; WP "he does spectacular things with [the role] ... he underplays the character's violence with such cunning skill that he becomes dangerously likeable"; TT "excellent"); Harrison Ford in *The Fugitive* (NYT "acted to steely perfection"; LAT "rare among action heroes, Ford is believable both in control and in trouble ... calls on his most distinctive trait, his vulnerability, to animate Dr Kimble"; CST "does just fine"; WP "breathes new life into the role [by taking] a darker, more gothic approach"; BG "invests [the character] with personality and faceting"); Jeff Bridges in *Fearless* (NYT "does well with a difficult role"; LAT "feels like a mistake to have cast him ... [makes the character] intolerable and impervious to empathy"; WP "a stellar performance"; BG "there's a certain Oscar nomination ahead of Bridges ... effortlessly, and with the most impressive display of emotional rawness in any Hollywood film so far this year, [he] compels us to identify with [his character] ... a performance of shadings and surprises"); Dennis Quaid in *Flesh and Bone* (LAT "the most moving performance of [his] career ... inhabits the role as he never has anything before ... an interior, laconic performance"; CT "terrific, understated and pungent"; WP "Quaid's moody performance holds more water [than that of co-star Meg Ryan] but he never attains the haunted depth he's supposed to"); Robert Duvall in *Wrestling Ernest Hemingway* (NYT "[an] intelligent but distant performance"; NYP "memorable"; LAT "overacts, but his way of overacting is to underact: he loads up on tiny gestures and vocal inflections"; WP "controlled"; BG "this is one of those bravura jobs that are meant to spell 'Oscar' … works beautifully"); Russell Crowe in *Romper Stomper* (NYT "exudes an antiheroic charisma"; NYP "superb"; WP "[a] harrowing performance"); and both Leslie Cheung (NYT "exceptionally good"; LAT "exceptional"; BG "runs the gamut of heartbreak in the film's most affecting and unceasingly fascinating performance"; S&S "[a] committed and highly threatening performance") and Zhang Fengyi (LAT "powerful"; BG "[a] strong central performance") in *Ba Wang Bie Ji (Farewell, My Concubine)* (NYP "first-rate"; CT "superb"; TGM "sublime … compelling").

The favourite for the Oscar was Hanks. An established comedy star, Hanks was admired for taking a controversial role in the first studio-made drama about HIV-AIDS. He was favoured despite criticisms that the film was unrealistic, conservative and timid. An interesting contrast was the lauded and controversial 1992 French film *Les Nuits Fauves (Savage Nights)* about a bisexual, HIV-positive film-maker, which won the Best Picture Cesar in Paris just three days after its star and director Cyril Collard died of AIDS (NYT "a brave, wrenching self-portrait"; LAT "[a] vivid presence"; SMH "dynamically acted"), but which the Academy ignored.

On Oscar night, Hanks won the statuette. Surprisingly he claimed a second Oscar the following year for *Forrest Gump*. In London, Hopkins won his second BAFTA in three years for *The Remains of the Day*. Hanks was not eligible until the following year, at which time he was unsuccessfully mentioned for *Forrest Gump* rather than *Philadelphia* (which the British Academy all but ignored).

1993

BEST ACTRESS

ACADEMY AWARDS
Angela Bassett as 'Tina Turner' in *What's Love Got to Do With It?*
Stockard Channing as 'Ouisa Kittredge' in *Six Degrees of Separation*
• **Holly Hunter as 'Ada McGrath' in *The Piano***
Emma Thompson as 'Miss Kenton' in *The Remains of the Day*
Debra Winger as 'Joy Gresham' in *Shadowlands*

GOLDEN GLOBE AWARDS
(Drama)
Juliette Binoche
   – *Trois Couleurs: Bleu*
   (Three Colors: Blue)
• **Holly Hunter – *The Piano***
Michelle Pfeiffer
   – *The Age of Innocence*
Emma Thompson
   – *The Remains of the Day*
Debra Winger
   – *A Dangerous Woman*

(Comedy/Musical)
• **Angela Bassett**
   – ***What's Love Got***
   to Do With It?
Stockard Channing
   – *Six Degrees of Separation*
Anjelica Huston
   – *Addams Family Values*
Diane Keaton
   – *Manhattan Murder Mystery*
Meg Ryan – *Sleepless in Seattle*

BRITISH ACADEMY AWARDS
• **Holly Hunter – *The Piano***
Miranda Richardson – *Tom and Viv*
Emma Thompson – *The Remains of the Day*
Debra Winger – *Shadowlands*

NEW YORK – Holly Hunter – *The Piano*
LOS ANGELES – Holly Hunter – *The Piano*
BOARD OF REVIEW – Holly Hunter – *The Piano*
NATIONAL SOCIETY – Holly Hunter – *The Piano*
LONDON
   (Actress) **Holly Hunter – *The Piano***
   (British Actress) **Miranda Richardson – *Damage***

For her performance as a voluntarily mute Scottish widow who travels to New Zealand for an arranged marriage in the nineteenth century in *The Piano*, Holly Hunter was named Best Actress at the Cannes Film Festival and earned widespread acclaim from critics (NYT "extraordinary ... there's not a sentimental moment in the movie, but she is heart-breaking"; NYP "[a] passionate and honest performance"; LAT "mesmerizing ... [an] unnerving performance [which] reaches a once-in-a-lifetime level of intensity ... exceptional acting"; WP "[Ada is] brought spectacularly to life by Holly Hunter ... exceptionally rich and detailed ... without a single line of spoken dialogue manages to give the most moving performance of her career as well as one of the best of the year"; BG "the performance of her career ... if there's any justice, Campion and Hunter will be showered with awards for their inspired work"; TT "remarkably good ... she has played gutsy girls in Hollywood before, but never with such inner strength and penetration"). At the end of the year she made a clean sweep of the five major critics' awards (her second wins from the New York Film Critics Circle, the Los Angeles Film Critics Association and the National Board of Review) and also collected the Golden Globe (Drama), the British Academy Award and the Oscar. She was also nominated for the Oscar and the BAFTA in the supporting category for her role in *The Firm*.

Also mentioned by the Academy in both the leading and supporting categories was Emma Thompson, who had won a similar end-of-year sweep of the major Best Actress accolades the previous year. Thompson earned her second consecutive Best Actress nod as the housekeeper in *The Remains of the Day* (NYT "in [her] performance, the film makes coherent a passion not really believable in the novel ... Thompson is splendid"; LAT "exceptional ... acting that is little short of miraculous"; BG "exquisitely acted"). She had also been commended by critics for her role in *Much Ado About Nothing*, a Shakespearian comedy directed by her then husband Kenneth Branagh (NYT "enchanting [and] moving"; LAT "thoroughly delightful"; Time "intense").

Another actress acclaimed for two performances was Debra Winger. She finished runner-up in Los Angeles for her portrayals of novelist Joy Gresham in *Shadowlands* (NYT "acted with great tenderness ... managing gracefully to avoid maudlin histrionics"; NYP "simply superb"; LAT "strong despite her role's built-in limits"; CT "overplays yet Winger's attack works"; Time "awfully good ... strong, unsentimental, exemplary") and as a mentally-challenged woman in *A Dangerous Woman* (NYT "sinks deeply into the role ... [an] eerily convincing performance [that is] furiously self-effacing"; NYP "[a] courageous performance in an underwritten part"; LAT "[is given] the space to create a full-out characterization ... wonderful without being showy"; CT "a highly detailed portrayal ... a virtuoso piece of work that manages to stop short of going over the top"; WP "theatrical"; S&S "brilliant"). She earned a Globe nomination for *A Dangerous Woman*, but the Academies in Hollywood and London recognised her for *Shadowlands*. In the Los Angeles Times, Kenneth Turan had predicted she would make the Oscar short-list for *Shadowlands* but asserted that her turn in *A Dangerous Woman* was "the stronger work".

Also nominated for the Oscar, each for the first time, were Angela Bassett as singer Tina Turner in *What's Love Got to Do With It?* (NYT "transforms herself memorably ... uncanny"; NYP "played with extraordinary intensity and passion"; LAT "exceptional ... the film rightfully belongs to Bassett ... [she] is more than equal to all the changes [of character over time]"; TGM "exemplary in [a] shallowly conceived role"; TT "takes on the challenge of impersonating an icon, and emerges triumphant"; S&S "convincing") and Stockard Channing for reprising her stage success as an art dealer in *Six Degrees of Separation* (NYT "a reprise of her fine [stage] performance as [the] hilariously brittle heroine ... deft"; NYP "excellent"; LAT "extraordinary ... makes Ouisa's gradual unfolding terrifying and beautiful"; TGM "played with a brittle poignancy").

The most surprising omission from the category was Globe nominee Michelle Pfeiffer as a woman scandalously estranged from her husband in nineteenth century New York City in *The Age of Innocence* (NYT "excellent ... she's the film's heart and conscience"; LAT "especially effective"; BG "potently acted ... Pfeiffer is superb"; S&S "excellent").

Also by-passed were: previous winner Jodie Foster in *Sommersby* (NYT "[a] romantic, resolute, elegant performance ... [she is] strong, passionate and mysterious ... beautifully self-possessed"; LAT "memorable ... losing herself totally in the period ... as completely thought-out a performance as you are likely to see"; CT "is given little to do except react and smile enigmatically"; BG "looks like next year's first sure-fire Oscar nominee"); New York and NSFC runner-up Ashley Judd in *Ruby in Paradise* (NYT "[played with] gravity and strength ... she gives substance to the film"; LAT "the focal point and sustaining force of the entire film"; CST "so good in this movie that her character stops being a performance and becomes someone you feel like you know"; CT "has none of the mannered intensity of a major actress"; TGM "[a] delicate performance"); Globe nominee Juliette Binoche in *Trois Couleurs: Bleu (Three Colors: Blue)* (NYP "compelling"; NYDN "brilliant"; LAT "startling ... [a performance of] glass-shattering honesty and integrity"; BG "a spellbinding tour de force"; G "[her] performance is deep and stronger than anything else she has given us"); Tara Morice in *Strictly Ballroom* (V "shines"; TGM "an esthetic chameleon, Morice is the perfect centrepiece"); Suzi Amis in *The Ballad of Little Jo* (NYT "the film is illuminated by [her] haunting performance"; NYP "a performance of subtlety and power"; LAT "most of the time she closes herself off"; BG "persuades"; S&S "extraordinary"); Tilda Swinton in *Orlando* (NYT "as important to the film's success as anything else are the bewitching face, figure and screen presence of Swinton"; NYP "phenomenal"; BG "unforgettable"; V "extraordinary"; TGM "exceptional acting"); and Romane Bohringer in *Les Nuits Fauves (Savage Nights)* (NYP "passionate, explosive"; LAT "[a] vital and accomplished debut"; SMH "dynamically acted").

1993

BEST SUPPORTING ACTOR

ACADEMY AWARDS
Leonardo DiCaprio as 'Arnie Grape' in *What's Eating Gilbert Grape?*
Ralph Fiennes as 'Amon Goeth' in *Schindler's List*
• **Tommy Lee Jones as 'Samuel Gerard' in *The Fugitive***
John Malkovich as 'Mitch Leary' in *In the Line of Fire*
Pete Postlethwaite as 'Guiseppe Conlon' in *In the Name of the Father*

GOLDEN GLOBE AWARDS
Leonardo DiCaprio – *What's Eating Gilbert Grape?*
Ralph Fiennes – *Schindler's List*
• **Tommy Lee Jones – *The Fugitive***
John Malkovich – *In the Line of Fire*
Pete Postlethwaite – *In the Name of the Father*

BRITISH ACADEMY AWARDS
• **Ralph Fiennes – *Schindler's List***
Tommy Lee Jones – *The Fugitive*
Ben Kingsley – *Schindler's List*
John Malkovich – *In the Line of Fire*

NEW YORK – Ralph Fiennes – *Schindler's List*
LOS ANGELES – Tommy Lee Jones – *The Fugitive*
BOARD OF REVIEW – Leonardo DiCaprio – *What's Eating Gilbert Grape?*
NATIONAL SOCIETY – Ralph Fiennes – *Schindler's List*

The same five actors contested both the Golden Globe and the Academy Award, and on each occasion the same contender claimed the prize.

Tommy Lee Jones won the Globe and the Oscar as the US Marshal in *The Fugitive* (NYT "acted to steely perfection"; NYP "a stunning achievement that may well earn him an Oscar nomination"; BG "stylishly keeps up his end of the cat-and-mouse ... invests [the character] with personality and faceting"). In the lead-up to the Globes and the Oscars, Jones won the Los Angeles Film Critics Association plaudit and finished as one of the joint runners-up for the National Society of Film Critics prize.

Also placing second in the NSFC voting, and finishing as the runner-up for the New York Film Critics Circle accolade as well, was nineteen-year-old Leonardo DiCaprio as the mentally-challenged younger brother in *What's

Eating Gilbert Grape? (NYT "the film's real show-stopping turn ... startling and vivid ... winds up capturing the enormous range of Arnie's raw emotions ... the performance has a sharp, desperate intensity from beginning to end"; NYP "remarkably convincing"; LAT "astonishing ... he's such a rigorously honest actor that he avoids all the obvious hokum"; BG "the film is stolen by DiCaprio ... impresses"; TGM "gives one of the most affectingly convincing impressions of an afflicted character [in over] 20 years"; TT "shines"). DiCaprio won the National Board of Review prize and received Globe and Oscar nominations for the first time. He had also earned kudos from critics for his turn in *This Boy's Life* (NYP "stunning"; LAT "expressive"; CT "the film's finest performance"; WP "the film draws its poignancy from [his] performance"; BG "memorable"; TGM "first-rate ... he perfectly captures [his] aggressive bravado and repressed vulnerability").

Outpolling DiCaprio and Jones for the New York and NSFC honours, but finishing runner-up in Los Angeles, was Ralph Fiennes as a Nazi concentration camp commander in *Schindler's List* (NYT "played fascinatingly"; NYP "makes an overwhelming impression"; TGM "it's to [his] credit that he shows how the flames scorch not only his many victims but also himself – Goeth is a satanic being consumed by his own evil"). In London, Fiennes outpolled a field of nominees that included Oscar-winner Jones to earn the British Academy Award.

Also making both the Globe and Oscar ballots were John Malkovich as a would-be Presidential assassin in *In the Line of Fire* (NYT "appears to be both maniacal and utterly ordinary"; NYP "a great performance ... one of the most memorable movie villains of recent years"; LAT "makes the best kind of villain for this piece ... insinuating, carefully thought out delivery"; TGM "terrific ... the picture springs to life whenever [he] hits the screen ... steals the show here") and Pete Postlethwaite as a man wrongly imprisoned as an accomplice to an IRA bombing in *In the Name of the Father* (NYT "steely naturalness"; NYP "a performance so profoundly impressive that it deserves consideration for the supporting actor Oscar"; LAT "persuasively played"; WP "perfect"; TGM "strong in a testing part").

The most unexpected omissions from Oscar contention were Harvey Keitel in *The Piano* (NYT "gives the performance of his career ... could be an Oscar performance"; LAT "exceptional acting ... adds an unexpected level of understated sensitivity to his work without losing any of its power"; WP "exceptionally rich and detailed"; BG "deserves high praise for his deeply felt work"; TT "creates an inevitably forceful impression") and Ben Kingsley as the book-keeper in *Schindler's List* (NYT "spectacularly fine"; NYP "impressive").

Also overlooked were: Sean Penn in *Carlito's Way* (NYT "truly unrecognisable ...Penn's strange, jarringly intense performances are infrequent these days, but this one was worth waiting for"; NYP "persuasive"; CST "a

virtuoso tour de force – one of those performances that takes on a life of its own";
Time "terrific"; TGM "barely recognizable [but] is done in by an ill-written
character"); Robert Duvall in *Falling Down* (NYT "excellent"; S&S "walks
away with the film ... slowly unveils a complex and real working class hero");
Donald Sutherland in *Six Degrees of Separation* (NYT "deft"; LAT
"extraordinary ... gives Flan a rehearsed sleekness that fits like armor"; BG
"unforgettable"; TGM "in top form"); Peter Vaughan in *The Remains of the Day*
(NYT "notable work"; G "[a] stand out ... a wonderfully tragi-comic
performance"); Jeff Daniels in *Gettysburg* (NYT "[his] luminous performance
as the heroic colonel dominates [the first] half of the film"; LAT "injects some
real feeling into all the historical posturing"; WP "[an] often moving portrayal
... achingly human"; BG "Oscar-worthy ... embodied with a touchingly stiff
mix of sensitivity and bravery"); Quentin Crisp as Queen Elizabeth I in *Orlando*
(NYT "elegantly realized"; WP "wonderful"; BG "exquisitely contained"); and
Carlos López in *Les Nuits Fauves (Savage Nights)* (SMH "dynamically acted").

BEST SUPPORTING ACTRESS

ACADEMY AWARDS
Holly Hunter as 'Tammy Hemphill' in *The Firm*
• **Anna Paquin as 'Fiona McGrath' in *The Piano***
Rosie Perez as 'Carla Rodrigo' in *Fearless*
Winona Ryder as 'May Welland' in *The Age of Innocence*
Emma Thompson as 'Gareth Pierce' in *In the Name of the Father*

GOLDEN GLOBE AWARDS
Penelope Ann Miller – *Carlito's Way*
Anna Paquin – *The Piano*
Rosie Perez – *Fearless*
• **Winona Ryder – *The Age of Innocence***
Emma Thompson – *In the Name of the Father*

BRITISH ACADEMY AWARDS
Holly Hunter – *The Firm*
• **Miriam Margolyes – *The Age of Innocence***
Winona Ryder – *The Age of Innocence*
Maggie Smith – *The Secret Garden*

NEW YORK – Gong Li – *Ba Wang Bie Ji (Farewell, My Concubine)*
LOS ANGELES – Anna Paquin – *The Piano* and Rosie Perez – *Fearless*
BOARD OF REVIEW – Winona Ryder – *The Age of Innocence*
NATIONAL SOCIETY – Madeline Stowe – *Short Cuts*

Two of the five Oscar nominees were considered non-starters. Holly Hunter was nominated as a private investigator's secretary in *The Firm* (NYT "[one of the film's] liveliest performances … [she] has a ball"; LAT "attention must be paid"; WP "primarily, the supporting cast drives the movie"; G "almost steals the film") but was the overwhelming favourite in the Best Actress category for *The Piano*. Emma Thompson was recognised as the lawyer in *In the Name of the Father* (NYT "steely naturalness"; NYP "another fine, ferocious performance"; WP "comes off as less a crusader than a fussy paper shuffler"; TGM "submits a sterling cameo") but had received the Best Actress statuette just the previous year. Like Hunter, she had also been nominated in both categories, earning a Best Actress nod for *The Remains of the Day*.

Most pundits saw the Academy Award to be a contest between three of the year's critics' prize-winners: Los Angeles Film Critics Association co-honorees

1993

Rosie Perez as plane crash survivor in *Fearless* (NYT "well-acted"; LAT "remarkable"; BG "heart-breaking"; Time "marvelously touching") and eleven-year old New Zealander Anna Paquin as the daughter in *The Piano* (CST "one of the most extraordinary examples of a child's acting in movie history"; WP "exceptionally rich and detailed"; BG "played with uncanny precocity"); and National Board of Review winner Winona Ryder as a society wife in *The Age of Innocence* (NYT "excellent"; NYP "outstanding"; LAT "captures May's genteel self-satisfaction exquisitely"; WP "[her] performance is as neatly turned as her ankle"; BG "potently acted"; S&S "excellent").

Perez, the runner-up in New York as well as a co-winner in Los Angeles, was the early favourite, but Ryder became the frontrunner when she won the Golden Globe. On Oscar night, however, in what Variety described as "the evening's biggest surprise", the winner was Paquin.

The most notable absentee from the Oscar ballot was New York honouree Gong Li as a former prostitute married to an Opera star in *Ba Wang Bie Ji (Farewell, My Concubine)* (NYT "splendid [in] the movie's most sophisticated performance"; LAT "excellent"; CT "superb ... reiterates her tremendous talent ... her performance finds a happy medium between independence and insecurity"; BG "[a] strong performance"; TGM "sublime ... compelling").

Also overlooked were: National Society of Film Critics winner Madeline Stowe in *Short Cuts* (NYT "astonishingly fine"; BG "finally gets the chance to inscribe a character of emotional complexity and utter believability"); NSFC runner-up Gwyneth Paltrow in *Flesh and Bone* (LAT "a striking performance"; CST "impressive"; WP "walks away with the movie"; BG "holds the screen impressively"; V "steals every scene she's in"); BAFTA winner Miriam Margolyes in *The Age of Innocence* (NYP "marvelous"; LAT "amusing"); Maggie Smith in *The Secret Garden* (NYT "her superbly measured performance gives the film a welcome tartness at times"; LAT "does best of all [the cast]"; S&S "on the right side of caricature"); both Tsai Chin and Tamlyn Tomita in *The Joy Luck Club* (NYT "the film is virtually stolen by [them]"; S&S "the strength of the performances, especially Tsai Chin's, ameliorates many of the film's faults"); Tantoo Cardinal in *Where the Rivers Flow North* (NYT "there isn't much to recommend [the film] beyond Ms Cardinal's performance ... [she] gives [her character] a freshness rarely seen on screen"; LAT "more than holds her own with [Rip] Torn ... a vibrant presence", WP "poignant [in an] authentic performance"); and both Piper Laurie (NYT "funny and buoyant"; CST "especially wonderful"; WP "exudes that customary offbeat radiance which seems to work every time ... a shimmering, unselfconscious performance") and Alfre Woodard (NYT "among the actors, it's no surprise to find that [she] shines, and that her vitality gives the film a noticeable lift"; WP "charmingly sassy") in *Rich in Love* (WP "fulfil their eccentric minor-character roles with dignity").

BEST PICTURE

ACADEMY AWARDS
• *Forrest Gump*
(Paramount, 142 mins, 6 Jul 1994, $329.6m, 13 noms)
Four Weddings and a Funeral
(Working Title, Gramercy, 118 mins, 9 Mar 1994, $52.7m, 2 noms)
Pulp Fiction
(Jersey, Miramax, 153 mins, 23 Sep 1994, $107.9m, 7 noms)
Quiz Show
(Hollywood Pictures, Buena Vista, 130 mins, 14 Sep 1994, $24.8m, 4 noms)
The Shawshank Redemption
(Castle Rock, Columbia, 142 mins, 23 Sep 1994, $28.3m, 7 noms)

GOLDEN GLOBE AWARDS

(Drama)
• *Forrest Gump*
Legends of the Fall
Nell
Pulp Fiction
Quiz Show

(Comedy/Musical)
The Adventures of Priscilla,
*   Queen of the Desert*
Ed Wood
Four Weddings and a Funeral
• *The Lion King*
Prêt-à-Porter (Ready to Wear)

PRODUCERS GUILD AWARD
• *Forrest Gump*
Four Weddings and a Funeral
Pulp Fiction
Quiz Show
The Shawshank Redemption

BRITISH ACADEMY AWARDS

(Best Film)
Forrest Gump
• *Four Weddings and a Funeral*
Pulp Fiction
Quiz Show

(Best British Film)
Backbeat
Bhaji on the Beach
Priest
• *Shallow Grave*

NEW YORK – *Quiz Show*
LOS ANGELES – *Pulp Fiction*
BOARD OF REVIEW – *Forrest Gump* and *Pulp Fiction*
NATIONAL SOCIETY – *Pulp Fiction*

1994

LONDON
(Best Film) *Schindler's List*
(Best British Film) *Four Weddings and a Funeral*

In The New York Times, Janet Maslin described 1994 as "an unusually strong year", an assessment borne out by the number of acclaimed films that didn't even make the shortlist for the Best Picture category at the Academy Awards.

Among the notable omissions were: the Disney animated film *The Lion King*, which was the year's biggest box office success and the Golden Globe (Comedy/Musical) winner (NYT "visually enchanting"; LAT "the greatest wonder of all is how approximately one million drawings ultimately turn into a film that lives and breathes"; CT "a modern masterpiece ... vast, ambitious, technically formidable ... delightful"; Time "a triumph"; CST "a superbly drawn animated feature"; WP "an impressive, almost daunting achievement ... spectacular"; TGM "an impressive feat of manufacturing, right down to the artistry"); *Little Women* (NYT "magical ... enchantingly pretty [and] touching ... the loveliest 'Little Women' ever on screen"; NYP "will melt the most granite of hearts"; LAT "beguiling ... [the film-makers] have got everything just right"; CT "splendid ... one of the year's best movies"; WP "graceful"; BG "warming, bountiful, brimful of high spirits, a glowing treat [and] a joy"; V "outstanding"; Time "entrancing ... the year's most unlikeliest triumph"; TGM "lively and thoughtful and beautifully formed"); *Bullets over Broadway* (NYT "a bright, energetic, sometimes side-splitting comedy"; NYP "a roaring good comedy"; WP "the most substantive, accessible – not to mention the funniest – film that [Woody Allen] has made in years"; Time "combines impeccable craftsmanship with a basic exuberance"; TGM "amiable"); *The Madness of King George* (NYT "splendid ... a deft, mischievous, beautifully acted historical drama with exceptionally broad appeal"; NYP "profoundly moving ... unequivocally one of the year's finest films"; LAT "one of the triumphs of the year – potent, engrossing and even thrilling"; WP "[a] riotous adaptation"; TGM "vivid [and] admirable"); *Ed Wood* (NYT "very good"; NYP "one of the year's funniest and most captivating films"; LAT "thoroughly entertaining if eccentric"; CT "glossy, giggling, darkly sympathetic"; BG "tenderly affecting"; TGM "flawed [and] clumsily sentimental"); *The Adventures of Priscilla, Queen of the Desert* (NYT "flamboyantly colorful [and] warmly entertaining ... outrageous [and] convention-flouting"; NYP "kitschy, kooky, camp"; LAT "the comic pizazz and bawdy dazzle of this film has a boisterous, addictive way about it"; CT "funny and compassionate, silly and sweet"; BG "campy and funny and joyous ... the feel-good movie of the year"; TGM "it's funny, it's endearing and it's strangely touching ... impressive"); and *Heavenly Creatures* (NYT "stylish and eerily compelling [but] overplays its campy excesses"; LAT "memorable ... an adventurous, accomplished piece of business, burning with cinematic energy"; CT "daring, revealing and, ultimately, entertaining"; WP "stunning ... [a] powerful, evocative movie"; BG "mesmerizing ... potent, daring invigorating filmmaking"; Time "thrilling"; TGM "disturbing ... devilishly clever").

Also overlooked for consideration in the Academy's most prestigious category were several acclaimed foreign-language films, including: *Belle Époque*, the surprise winner of the Best Foreign-Language Film Oscar at the Academy Awards ceremony in March 1994 (NYT "[a] warmly inviting film"; LAT "[a] sexy, bittersweet and contemplative comedy ... possesses a warm, universal appeal"; CT "stylish ... [has a] lilting charm"; BG "a sunny, delicious feel-good movie"); *Huozhe (To Live)* (NYT "extravagant and emotional ... [and] politically brave"; LAT "masterful, stirring ... superb ... a remarkable accomplishment"; CT "one of the most moving and important films of 1994 ... magisterial ... delicately structured and subtly articulated"; WP "a good movie [but] never strikes deep enough to reach our hearts"); *Yin Shi Nan Nu (Eat Drink Man Woman)* (NYT "wonderfully seductive [and] an uncomplicatedly pleasant experience"; LAT "[a] wise and rueful romantic comedy"; CT "a smart, sprightly, lip-smacking comedy ... it crackles with iridescent style and wit"; WP "[a] sumptuous comedy ... harmonious and poignantly funny"; TGM "a good film ... deceptively clever"; G "a constant delight and very funny"); and *La Reine Margot (Queen Margot)* (NYT "entertaining"; NYP "richly entertaining"; LAT "rich and full of verve"; BG "more broad than deep; it's melodrama, but on a grand scale – handsomely crafted"; TGM "motion everywhere, and the picture still seems dead at the centre").

The most glaring omission from the list was *Trois Couleurs: Rouge (Three Colors: Red)*, the final part of Krzysztof Kieślowski's trilogy about the ideals symbolised by the French flag (NYT "succeeds so stirringly ... seductive"; LAT "brilliant [and] profound"; CT "a phenomenon: gossamer and tough, sensitive and steely, a real cinematic event"; V "deft, deeply affecting"; HRp "haunting [and] brilliant"; TT "compelling"; G "outstanding ... the best of European cinema ... brilliantly stylish"; S&S "an elusive artefact, refracting different dramatic and emotional patterns according to viewpoint"). It was named Best Foreign-Language Film by the New York Film Critics Circle, the Los Angeles Film Critics Association and the National Society of Film Critics and was also the runner-up for the NSFC Best Picture award. When it was submitted for the Best Foreign-Language Film Oscar by Switzerland, however, the Academy declared it ineligible as its director was Polish and its stars were French. Encouraged by the ensuing outcry, Miramax mounted a major Best Picture campaign for the film. The Academy ultimately mentioned it in three categories, including Best Director, but not for the top Oscar. In London, it earned two BAFTA nominations, but was likewise overlooked for Best Film.

A high-profile campaign was also mounted for *Hoop Dreams*, a lauded documentary about inner city youths aspiring to be professional basketball players (NYT "brilliantly revealing"; NYP "remarkable"; LAT "a landmark of American documentary film"; WP "the most powerful movie about sports ever made ... extraordinary ... absorbing [and] genuinely profound"; Time "powerful"). Controversially, *Hoop Dreams* was not mentioned for either Best Picture nor Best Documentary, receiving a nomination only for Film Editing.

Over the more than two decades since its original release, the reputation of *The Hudsucker Proxy* has strengthened considerably. When it first opened in cinemas, however, it garnered generally unenthusiastic reviews and was another of the movies overlooked by the Academy (NYT "stylish and witty [but] has its problems"; LAT "a visual extravaganza [but the] highly polished surface leaves barely any space for an audience's emotional connection ... uninvolving"; CT "dark, startling, wittily extravagant"; WP "pointlessly flashy"; TGM "superficial"; G "the whole is somehow less than the sum of its parts ... the film lacks coherence if not complexity"; S&S "wholly delightful").

The acclaimed film noir *The Last Seduction* was ruled ineligible for Oscar consideration by the Academy because it screened on HBO in July, prior to securing a cinematic release in October (NYT "devilishly entertaining"; LAT "pleases audiences ... likes to play with people's minds and has the panache to pull it off"; CT "a smart, tough thriller ... a rare pleasure"; CST "ingenious and entertaining"; BG "a terrific little neo-noir ... exhilarating"; G "an extremely entertaining film").

The Los Angeles Film Critics Association, the National Board of Review and the National Society of Film Critics honoured *Pulp Fiction*, the winner of the Palme d'Or at the Cannes Film Festival and box office hit which The New York Times had declared to be the year's best movie (NYT "a work of depth, wit and blazing originality ... stunning"; LAT "doesn't merit sustained veneration ... noticeably uneven [and only] sporadically effective"; CT "astonishing"; WP "ingenious"; BG "one hell of a ride ... exhilarating"; V "spectacularly entertaining"; G "a bold combination of lowlife and dandyish posturing, of elegance and violence, of scatology and eschatology ... at every stage, we are surprised, shocked and astonished by the language, the wit, the formal invention, and the accidental mayhem").

The New York Film Critics Circle, meanwhile, gave their Best Picture accolade to *Quiz Show*, a drama about a scandal in the television industry in the 1950s (NYT "a rich, handsome, articulate film ... supremely elegant and thoughtful"; NYP "fascinating ... an unqualified triumph"; LAT "a thoughtful, absorbing drama ... impressive"; CT "absorbing ... one of the year's very finest films"; WP "mainstream American filmmaking at its very best ... engrossing, smart and morally complex ... nothing else out of Hollywood this year can hold a candle to it ... an exciting achievement"; V "engrossing"; Time "smart, hugely entertaining"; TGM "manages to be both terrifically entertaining and consistently thoughtful").

Both *Pulp Fiction* and *Quiz Show* were nominated by the Academies in Hollywood and London, but neither collected the top awards. Also nominated for the Oscar, but not the BAFTA where there were only four rather than five nominees, was the prison drama *The Shawshank Redemption* (NYT "a slow, gentle story of camaraderie ... eloquently restrained"; NYP "a hackneyed prison movie"; LAT "sentimental [and] overly long"; CT "simply marvelous entertainment ... surprisingly strong and engrossing"; WP "a sentimental yarn full of the darndest twists ... devoutly old-fashioned").

Ahead of these films, the Academies honoured two commercial successes.

In London, the winner was the comedy *Four Weddings and a Funeral*, which was the most commercially successful British film ever made and had led the BAFTA field with nine nominations (NYT "elegant, festive and very, very funny"; NYP "charming and seductive"; LAT "cheerful and witty ... [a] tasty, sophisticated romp"; CT "smart and ironic, perceptive and observant, witty and poignant, moving and sad, all at the same time ... a small miracle"; TGM "British humour at its eclectic best, a delicious heady mix of dry wit and ribald farce ... clever"; S&S "smarmy"). The film was also a Best Picture nominee in Hollywood, but was short-listed in only one other category and was regarded an outside chance for the top statuette.

The fourth BAFTA nominee was the film that triumphed at the Academy Awards: the comedy-drama *Forrest Gump* (NYT "feels less like a romance than like a coffee-table book celebrating the magic of special effects ... a loose string of vignettes, presented at an unemphatic, page-flipping pace ... superficial"; NYP "extraordinary"; LAT "a sweet piece of work [which] stumbles"; CT "easily the best major-studio movie of the year"; WP "as poignant as it is romantic"; BG "a one-of-a-kind treat ... remarkable"; TGM "doesn't have a lot to say ... the screenplay is loose and the chronology disjointed ... sentimental ... the film fails"; S&S "a feel-good movie for which it is hard to feel anything at all"; SMH "elegant and elegiac"). The film had unexpectedly been an enormous hit – by the time of Oscar voting, it was the fourth biggest money-earner in American history. The Globe (Drama) champ and NBR co-winner, *Forrest Gump* was the third film in history to be considered in thirteen categories at the Academy Awards and the most nominated picture since 1966.

On Oscar night, *Forrest Gump* collected six statuettes, including Best Picture. Ironically, given the number of notable films released that year, it was the first time the Academy had given its top prize to a picture listed by The New York Times as one of the year's ten worst films.

BEST DIRECTOR

ACADEMY AWARDS
Woody Allen for *Bullets over Broadway*
Krzysztof Kieślowski for *Trois Couleurs: Rouge* (*Three Colors: Red*)
Robert Redford for *Quiz Show*
Quentin Tarantino for *Pulp Fiction*
• **Robert Zemeckis for *Forrest Gump***

GOLDEN GLOBE AWARDS
Robert Redford – *Quiz Show*
Oliver Stone – *Natural Born Killers*
Quentin Tarantino – *Pulp Fiction*
• **Robert Zemeckis – *Forrest Gump***
Edward Zwick – *Legends of the Fall*

DIRECTORS GUILD AWARD
Frank Darabont
   – The Shawshank Redemption
Mike Newell
   – Four Weddings and a Funeral
Robert Redford – *Quiz Show*
Quentin Tarantino – *Pulp Fiction*
• **Robert Zemeckis – *Forrest Gump***

BRITISH ACADEMY AWARDS
Krzysztof Kieślowski
   – Trois Couleurs: Rouge
   (Three Colors: Red)
• **Mike Newell**
   – Four Weddings and a Funeral
Quentin Tarantino – *Pulp Fiction*
Robert Zemeckis – *Forrest Gump*

NEW YORK – Quentin Tarantino – *Pulp Fiction*
LOS ANGELES – Quentin Tarantino – *Pulp Fiction*
BOARD OF REVIEW – Quentin Tarantino – *Pulp Fiction*
NATIONAL SOCIETY – Quentin Tarantino – *Pulp Fiction*
LONDON
   (Director) **Steven Spielberg – *Schindler's List***
   (British Director) **Mike Newell – *Four Weddings and a Funeral***

At the Cannes Film Festival, Quentin Tarantino's second feature *Pulp Fiction* won the Palme d'Or but the young film-maker was overlooked for the Best Director award (NYT "brings [the script] to life with such exhilarating gusto"; CT "has craftily, artfully fashioned the buddy-buddy movie from hell"; WP "slyly assured"). At the end of the year, however, he became the first person to win a clean sweep of the four major American critics' Best Director prizes: the

New York Film Critics Circle, the Los Angeles Film Critics Association, National Board of Review and National Society of Film Critics awards. Tarantino was subsequently nominated for the Golden Globe, the Directors Guild of America accolade, the BAFTA and the Academy Award. While he received a Globe, BAFTA and Oscar for Best Adapted Screenplay, he collected none of the major Best Director honours.

The winner of the Globe, the DGA plaudit and Academy Award was Robert Zemeckis for the box office smash *Forrest Gump* (NYT "accomplished [but] remains much more successful at staging brilliant technical sleight-of-hand than at providing the dramatic basis for his visual inventions"; CT "shows an extraordinary mix of technological mastery and effervescent vision"; WP "deftly directed ... an undisputed master of film technology, [he here] shows off an equal aptitude for vivid storytelling"; BG "[achieves] an extremely delicate, graceful and finally virtuosic equilibrium"; V "elegantly made"). In London, the BAFTA was awarded to Mike Newell, who had been by-passed for Oscar consideration despite a DGA nod, for the hit comedy *Four Weddings and a Funeral* (NYT "this deft English comedy also constitutes a remarkable tightrope act on the part of Mike Newell"; TGM "brings off [the film's transitions] with admirable aplomb ... remarkably effective ... demonstrates a sure touch").

The other Oscar contenders were: previous winner Woody Allen for *Bullets over Broadway* (TGM "more the work of a seasoned pro than an inspired auteur"); previous winner Robert Redford for *Quiz Show* (NYT "directed with quietly dazzling acuity ... greatly surpassing the polite excellence of his past work"; LAT "an accomplished job of directing"; WP "the most accomplished film of Redford's directorial career"; TGM "Redford's best directorial effort since his debut with 'Ordinary People'"); and New York and NSFC runner-up Krzysztof Kieślowski for *Trois Couleurs: Rouge (Three Colors: Red)* (NYT "assured [and] deft"; LAT "tightly controlled ... brilliant"; CT "masterful"; TT "every scene proclaims a master director at work"; G "[the film shows] so much sheer film-making ability that it would be extremely difficult to fault it").

Overlooked for consideration were: Frank Darabont for *The Shawshank Redemption* (NYT "[his] direction [is] quiet and purposeful [and he] tells this tale with a surprising degree of loving care"; CT "with this one work, declares himself a special talent"; WP "[a] remarkable debut"); Tim Burton for *Ed Wood* (NYT "visual brilliance"; CT "time and time again, Burton and his cast rise above [the material] finding the anguish beneath the silliness"; WP "Burton has pulled it off with wit, imagination and something amazingly close to grace"); Nicholas Hytner for *The Madness of King George* (NYT "makes a vigorous film debut [as director] ... has no trouble explicating this chicanery in colourful, entertaining fashion"; LAT "so at home with film that it is difficult to believe this is his feature debut ... he has faultlessly opened up the play and made a distant world seem physically real"); Gillian Armstrong for *Little Women* (NYT "instantly demonstrates that she has caught the essence of this book's sweetness … [her] direction is sentimental without being saccharine [and she] reinvents 'Little Women' for present-day audiences without ever forgetting it's a story with a past"; LAT "[the film] says a great deal about [her] own character and integrity as an artist … [she has] got everything just right"; WP "glides over the more mawkish moments [and] applies a dusting of contemporary feminism"; BG "[has a] sympathetic and enlivening touch … the dynamic [between the sisters is] so successfully captured by Armstrong"); Joel Coen for *The Hudsucker Proxy* (LAT "you have to admire what [he and his brother] have accomplished … but its great filmmaking only from the wrists down"; WP "Coen's direction is brightly caricatured"; TGM "starts overdirecting sequences that [should] be expositional throwaways … misplaced bravura"); Stephan Elliott for *The Adventures of Priscilla, Queen of the Desert* (CT "for the most part Elliott manages to rein it in"; BG "skillfull"; TGM "impressive … brings it off quietly and unostentatiously"); 1993 London Film Critics winner Ken Loach for *Raining Stones* (LAT "[done] with great deftness"; CT "done with devastating realism and discretion"; WP "[he] examines the lives of his characters with the meticulousness of a documentarian, and the results are so unforced that they almost look as if they had been happened upon – found, rather than staged"; TGM "achingly naturalistic"); 1995 London Film Critics winner Peter Jackson for *Heavenly Creatures* (NYT "meticulous … gives [the film] a visual extravagance to match its characters' excitement"; LAT "accomplished … directs in a way that is both tightly controlled and highly emotional"; CT "stylish with ingenuity to spare"; WP "moves through each of [the film's] phases with daring and imagination … [his] style is poetic"; BG "[his] direction heightens the fatefulness hovering over [the lead characters] … [a] remarkable accomplishment"); Guillermo del Toro for *Cronos* (LAT "the real centerpiece of this film is writer-director del Toro … he knows how to convey his enjoyment [of the genre] and make the result distinctly his own"; TGM "edits the package skillfully"); Zhang Yimou for *Huozhe (To Live)* (NYT "the masterly Zhang knows he's creating melodrama and exaggerates to profound effect"; LAT "masterful"; CT "brilliant"; WP "provides an illuminating window on everyday Chinese life [with] moments of great beauty and overwhelming pathos"); and Ang Lee for *Yin Shi Nan Nu (Eat Drink Man Woman)* (BG "Lee's light hand with his timeless subjects, deftly, affectingly, ruefully and hilariously covers all the bases"; TGM "the movie glides nicely … he's a terrific technician").

Ruled ineligible for Oscar consideration by the Academy because his film was shown on cable television prior to securing a cinematic release was John Dahl for *The Last Seduction* (NYT "directs this film with stunning economy … [has] a tight, suspenseful style"; LAT "polished"; CT "[an] achievement").

BEST ACTOR

ACADEMY AWARDS
Morgan Freeman as 'Ellis Boyd Redding' in *The Shawshank Redemption*
• **Tom Hanks as 'Forrest Gump' in *Forrest Gump***
Nigel Hawthorne as 'King George III of Great Britain' in *The Madness of King George*
Paul Newman as 'Donald "Sully" Sullivan' in *Nobody's Fool*
John Travolta as 'Vincent Vega' in *Pulp Fiction*

GOLDEN GLOBE AWARDS

(Drama)
Morgan Freeman
   – *The Shawshank Redemption*
• **Tom Hanks – *Forrest Gump***
Paul Newman – *Nobody's Fool*
Brad Pitt – *Legends of the Fall*
John Travolta – *Pulp Fiction*

(Comedy/Musical)
Jim Carrey – *The Mask*
Johnny Depp – *Ed Wood*
• **Hugh Grant**
   – *Four Weddings and a Funeral*
Arnold Schwarzenegger – *Junior*
Terence Stamp
   – *The Adventures of Priscilla, Queen of the Desert*

SCREEN ACTORS GUILD
Morgan Freeman
   – *The Shawshank Redemption*
• **Tom Hanks – *Forrest Gump***
Paul Newman – *Nobody's Fool*
Tim Robbins
   – *The Shawshank Redemption*
John Travolta – *Pulp Fiction*

BRITISH ACADEMY AWARDS
• **Hugh Grant**
   – *Four Weddings and a Funeral*
Tom Hanks – *Forrest Gump*
Terence Stamp
   – *The Adventures of Priscilla, Queen of the Desert*
John Travolta – *Pulp Fiction*

NEW YORK – Paul Newman – *Nobody's Fool*
LOS ANGELES – John Travolta – *Pulp Fiction*
BOARD OF REVIEW – Tom Hanks – *Forrest Gump*
NATIONAL SOCIETY – Paul Newman – *Nobody's Fool*
LONDON
   (Actor) **John Travolta – *Pulp Fiction***
   (British Actor) **Ralph Fiennes – *Schindler's List***

The only man in Oscar history to win consecutive Best Actor statuettes had been Spencer Tracy in 1937 and 1938. Yet in 1994, the previous year's winner, Tom

Hanks, was the overwhelming favourite to win the Academy Award again for his performance as the slow-witted title character in *Forrest Gump* (NYT "[a] touching, imaginatively childlike performance"; NYP "a triumph ... creates a complete and utterly compelling human being"; LAT "convincingly played ... although [he] never breaks through to the point where we forget that we are watching a performance, however expert"; WP "vanishes inside the character"; BG "wonderful ... a character who allows Hanks to take his time, secure in the knowledge that the greater part of film acting is reacting ... deserves Oscar attention"; V "winningly acted"; TGM "for all that's wrong here, one thing is wonderfully, blissfully right, and his name is Tom Hanks ... never stoops to easy pathos ... his performance is rock solid ... Hanks single-handedly succeeds where the rest of the film fails"; SMH "a beautifully-judged, fine-grained performance"). Even though he had not been in serious contention for the New York Film Critics Circle, Los Angeles Film Critics Association or National Society of Film Critics accolades, Hanks won several key industry plaudits: the National Board of Review prize, a second consecutive Golden Globe (Drama) and the inaugural Best Actor trophy from the Screen Actors Guild.

The other main contenders for the Academy Award were the recipients of the Best Actor citations from the critics New York and Los Angeles.

The east coast circle named Paul Newman as Best Actor as a small-town handyman in *Nobody's Fool*, for which he was also honoured at the Berlin Film Festival (NYT "the single best [performance] of this year and among the finest he has ever given ... [his] approach [is] without cheap sentiment or self-pity"; NYP "astonishingly assured"; LAT "so right ... that he projects the excitement of an undiscovered new talent"; CT "Newman is the reason to see [this film]"; WP "Newman, already making room in his trophy case for Mr Oscar, is likable [but] we're always aware that we are in the presence of Great Actors"; V "splendid ... one of his most engaging performances"; TGM "Newman is enough of a movie actor to etch the character memorably, and enough of a movie star to make the icon likable ... his portrait of Sully is brought off with a minimalist's ease – it's a delight to watch"). It was the first time Newman had been honoured by the New York critics, although the circle had named him as Best Director in 1968. Newman also won the NBR honour and the Academy nominated him as Best Actor for an eighth time.

In Los Angeles, the winner was John Travolta for his turn as a hit man in the cult hit *Pulp Fiction* (NYT "acts with immense, long-overlooked charm"; LAT "memorable"; CT "has never seemed as nastily, lazily in control as he does here"; WP "manages to make Vincent sympathetic"; V "superb"). The comeback performance earned him a second mention from Oscar voters some seventeen years after he had first been included on the ballot.

Also in contention, but considered long-shots, were Morgan Freeman, recognised for a third time, as a prisoner in *The Shawshank Redemption* (NYT "quietly impressive ... commanding [and] moving ... [a] fine, circumspect performance"; NYP "[a] heartfelt performance"; WP "[proves to be] a master of comedic and poignant cadence ... [he] is sure to gain his third Oscar nomination") and Nigel Hawthorne for reprising his acclaimed stage performance as the temporarily unstable monarch King George III in *The Madness of King George* (NYT "grandly played ... for all his comic fireworks, [he] poignantly captures the [character]"; NYP "one of the finest cinematic performances I have ever seen"; LAT "a heroic performance that enlarges our understanding of what acting can accomplish"; WP "[delivers] side-splitting bits of bawdy physical comedy [and is] equally affecting in his mellower, more intimate scenes"; BG "[a] showy, funny and finally touching performance"; V "a touching performance"; TGM "by turn outrageous and pathetic and imperious and poignant and very funny ... most impressive"; S&S "exceptional"). Hawthorne would win the BAFTA and a London Film Critics prize for his performance the following year.

Although some commentators believed that sentiment would carry Newman to a second Oscar victory, on Academy Awards night, it was Hanks who received a second statuette as Best Actor. "I'm empowered to stand here thanks to the ensemble of actors who I shared the screen with, who made me a better actor," he humbly told the audience at the Shrine Auditorium.

In London, both Hanks and Travolta were among the nominees outpolled for the Best Actor BAFTA by Hugh Grant in the hit British comedy *Four Weddings and a Funeral* (NYT "turns [the part] into a career-making role"; LAT "a sunnily self-confident performance that anchors the film"; CT "near-flawless"; TGM "slips into the lead role easily and convincingly"; Sp "engaging"; S&S "does not exactly radiate sex appeal here"). Grant won the Globe (Comedy/Musical) but was excluded from the Best Actor Oscar short-list.

Also by-passed for Oscar consideration were: Ralph Fiennes in *Quiz Show* (NYT "underscores his astonishing range [with a] knowing, meticulous performance"; NYP "extraordinary"; LAT "his poignant and ravaged portrait ... provides [the film] with its center of gravity ... [the part is] beautifully played by Fiennes with a subtlety that is at least the equal of his Oscar-nominated performance in 'Schindler's List' ... dazzling [and] devastating"; CT "superb"; WP "ingratiating"; Time "played a little too stiffly"); Tommy Lee Jones in both *Blue Sky* (NYP "electrifying [and] explosive ... matches Lange's in strength and subtlety"; LAT "exceptional ... sensitive and emotionally vulnerable ... exceptional"; WP "gives as good as he gets back from Lange") and *Cobb* (NYT "captivating ... he easily inhabits this big, colourful role"; LAT "a performance too operatic and out of control"; CT "the major American movie acting feat of

1994 ... [it] is large and tempestuous ... we're clearly seeing an actor take a role to its limit ... there's a naked savagery, a fury and recklessness you rarely see in movies about legendary historical figures"); Tim Robbins in both *The Hudsucker Proxy* (NYT "projects a goofy appeal"; LAT "[a] brash comic performance that would have brought life to another film"; CST "right on target"; S&S "manages the change from sweetness to superficiality with expert ease") and *The Shawshank Redemption* (NYT "plays [the trickier of the two lead roles] intensely"; LAT "though [he] always seems to be playing a part, he is good at it"; WP "a performance that evolves with beautiful clarity"); Jim Carrey in the popular comedy *The Mask* (NYT "works very hard"; LAT "despite all this technology [the film] would be hard-pressed to love without the actor who plays both the cartoon and alter ego, Jim Carrey ... [he] is revealed here as a comic actor of charm and talent"; CT "progresses from traditional buffoonery to a king of high-voltage madness"; CST "demonstrates that he does have a genuine gift for comic invention"; BG "he's a pretty special effect on his own ... inventive [with] the ability to project vulnerability"); Johnny Depp in *Ed Wood* (NYT "witty and captivating"; CT "passionately acted ... remarkably sympathetic and engaging"; WP "does a brilliantly skilful job of portraying the filmmaker's engaging single-mindedness"; BG "Depp's performance is subtler than is seems ... quite the best thing he's put on film"); Willem Dafoe in *Tom and Viv* (NYT "[a] stunningly sharp, sympathetic portrait ... doesn't offer the flamboyant rant that usually captures Oscar voters, but in its brilliant restraint it is one of the finest performances of the year"; NYP "solid"; LAT "does surprisingly well"; G "beautifully acted"; S&S "[a] peculiar, monotone performance"); Albert Finney in *The Browning Version* (NYT "wonderfully restrained"; LAT "amazing ... his restraint really shines"; CT "defying traps of sentimentality or anachronism, he makes this part his own ... it's a great part that Finney handles superbly"; WP "[the film] is buttressed by Finney's brooding performance"; BG "magnificent"); Jorge Perugorría in *Fresa y Chocolate (Strawberry and Chocolate)* (NYT "especially good ... overt about his [character's] sexuality but he stops short of becoming a caricature"; LAT "[a] terrific portrayal"; G "wonderfully played"); Cannes Film Festival honoree Ge You in *Huozhe (To Live)* (NYT "magnificent ... a revelation, evoking sympathy and pity"; NYP "a performance of astonishing depth"; CT "his dry, masterly wit enables him to pull out darkness and pathos without seeming to strain"; WP "[a] rich and complicated [performance]"; S&S "masterly underplayed"); and Jean-Louis Trintignant in *Trois Couleurs: Rouge (Three Colors: Red)* (NYT "exceptionally fine ... moving from brusqueness to tenderness, transforms himself memorably"; LAT "remarkable [and] faultless"; TT "the performances of Jacob and Trintignant give the film a strong emotional core"; G "a wonderfully certain performance").

BEST ACTRESS

ACADEMY AWARDS
Jodie Foster as 'Nell' in *Nell*
• **Jessica Lange as 'Carly Marshall' in *Blue Sky***
Miranda Richardson as 'Vivienne Haigh-Wood' in *Tom and Viv*
Winona Ryder as 'Jo March' in *Little Women*
Susan Sarandon as 'Reggie Love' in *The Client*

GOLDEN GLOBE AWARDS

(Drama)
Jodie Foster – *Nell*
• **Jessica Lange – *Blue Sky***
Jennifer Jason Leigh
   – Mrs Parker and
   the Vicious Circle
Miranda Richardson – *Tom and Viv*
Meryl Streep – *The River Wild*

(Comedy/Musical)
• **Jamie Lee Curtis – *True Lies***
Geena Davis – *Speechless*
Andie MacDowell
   – Four Weddings and a Funeral
Shirley MacLaine – *Guarding Tess*
Emma Thompson – *Junior*

SCREEN ACTORS GUILD
• **Jodie Foster – *Nell***
Jessica Lange – *Blue Sky*
Meg Ryan
   – When a Man Loves a Woman
Susan Sarandon – *The Client*
Meryl Streep – *The River Wild*

BRITISH ACADEMY AWARDS
Linda Fiorentino
   – The Last Seduction
Irène Jacob
   – Trois Couleurs: Rouge
   (Three Colors: Rouge)
• **Susan Sarandon – *The Client***
Uma Thurman – *Pulp Fiction*

NEW YORK – Linda Fiorentino – *The Last Seduction*
LOS ANGELES – Jessica Lange – *Blue Sky*
BOARD OF REVIEW – Miranda Richardson – *Tom and Viv*
NATIONAL SOCIETY – Jennifer Jason Leigh – *Mrs Parker and the Vicious Circle*
LONDON
   (Actress) **Linda Fiorentino – *The Last Seduction***
   (British Actress) **Crissy Rock – *Ladybird, Ladybird***

Both the New York Film Critics Circle and the London Film Critics named Linda Fiorentino as Best Actress for her performance as a ruthless petty criminal in the independent film noir thriller *The Last Seduction* (NYT "[her] performance is flawlessly hard-boiled"; LAT "played with career-making gusto ... [her] diabolical performance is the delectable heart of [the film] ... beyond doubt one of the five top female performance of the year"; CST "the great quality of [the film] is the dry humor with which [she] puts across the role ... Fiorentino's performance [is] the best of the year"; Time "ferociously good"; TT "smartly performed"; G "a staggeringly apt performance ... [she] sustains her performance so well, tied to almost every frame of the movie, that you hardly notice or care when the story goes astray" S&S "it is entirely due to Fiorentino's performance that [the character] is as fascinating as she is rotten"). Fiorentino's chances for the Best Actress Oscar, however, were dashed when the Academy ruled the film ineligible because it had screened four times on the cable television service HBO prior to its release in North American cinemas.

Another notable absentee from the list of Oscar candidates was the National Society of Film Critics winner and New York runner-up Jennifer Jason Leigh as writer Dorothy Parker in *Mrs Parker and the Vicious Circle* (NYT "stunningly well-played ... dazzling – one of the year's rare performances worthy of a best actress prize"; NYP "memorable ... a sharp portrait"; LAT "an achievement"; CT "Leigh's performance demolishes the notion that there are no great roles for actresses in American movies ... [she] tears right into the juicy, boozy, burnt-out heart of the part ... [and] her voice is the triumph"; WP "played with skinless sensitivity ... a disturbing, emotionally raw performance"; BG "magnificent [and] heartbreaking"; TGM "her portrayal of Parker cuts no further than the script allows, yet the surface she skims is pleasing to watch ... touching"; G "mannered"; S&S "[a] formidable performance").

Also by-passed for consideration were: Sigourney Weaver in *Death and the Maiden* (NYT "sternly terrific [and] powerful"; NYP "moving [in] the performance of a lifetime"; LAT "plays the role in high-style heroic fashion"; WP "immensely powerful [but] the fundamental strength of Weaver's personality doesn't work here. Nor does her particular style of rage and sorrow"; TGM "struggles"); Meg Ryan in *When a Man Loves a Woman* (LAT "strongly and graphically portraying [an alcoholic]"; CT "the movie doesn't really give her enough room"; TGM "harrowing"; G "a convincing performance"); previous winner Meryl Streep in both the action film *The River Wild* (NYT "more than proves her mettle [in the action genre]"; LAT "a rip-roaring performance ... demonstrating such a radiant forcefulness, plus an easy facility with an impressive range of emotions, that she pretty much upstages even the on-rushing rapids ... convincing"; CST "adds a new dimension to her brilliant career"; TGM "opts to take the acting out of her act and put the motion into the picture") and the drama *The House of the Spirits* (NYT "[ages] with magnificent delicacy"; TGM "the best of the lot ... the character is virtually impossible to embody, but Streep comes impressively close to bringing it off"); Geena Davis in both *Angie*

(NYT "[her] performance is exhilaratingly funny and touching ... Davis's star turn anchors a film that might otherwise be dangerously adrift ... particularly good"; LAT "the film's comic centrepiece ... can't be faulted"; BG "a terrific vehicle for Geena Davis ... endearing ... she's a force of nature who carries the film past the broadness to which it sometimes succumbs") and *Speechless* (NYT "blusters especially hard ... is less at home [in this genre]"; LAT "[an] uninspired performance"; WP "sure delivery [of the script's] snappy patter ... [but is] completely unappealing"); previous winner Shirley MacLaine in *Guarding Tess* (NYT "does wonderfully"; LAT "adept ... underplays [and succeeds] in bringing [the film's] light-on-its-feet humor to life"; CT "filling in the edges of their broadly written roles, MacLaine and Cage commandeer the screen ... so good"); Berlin Film Festival honoree and London Film Critics winner Crissy Rock in *Ladybird, Ladybird* (NYT "acted with passionate intensity"; CT "a performance so wrenching and emotionally naked that barriers of the screen seem to dissolve ... this is great screen acting of a really unexpected kind ... pulls off a little miracle of sustained, re-created anguish ... without straining, she attains scary, fiery heights of torment and rage"; CST "brilliantly acted"; BG "[a] heartbreaking performance ... Rock's fire, authority and conviction as the unruly but loving mom is in a class by itself"; S&S "[an] unnerving and powerful performance"); both Melanie Lynskey (NYT "a particularly unsettling performance"; CT "special mention should go to Lynskey, who brings a frightening calm to the role of Pauline") and Kate Winslet (NYT "disturbingly effective"; CT "superb") in *Heavenly Creatures* (LAT "remarkable performances by its young actresses"); Lauren Valez in *I Like It Like That* (NYT "it is Ms Velez who is in almost every scene, holding the movie together and carrying off a flamboyant role with bright, scrappy style"; LAT "conveyed with striking confidence and sass"; BG "holds the screen appealingly"; TGM "superb"; S&S "movingly portrayed"); Gong Li in *Huozhe (To Live)* (NYT "magnificent ... carries the story's emotions"; WP "[a] rich and complicated [performance]"); Isabelle Adjani in *La Reine Margot (Queen Margot)* (LAT "burns a hole in the screen"; TGM "looks as photogenic as ever but doesn't enjoy much acting room"); and Irène Jacob as the fashion model in the drama *Trois Couleurs: Rouge (Three Colors: Red)* (NYT "exceptionally fine"; LAT "remarkable"; CT "wonderfully open and tender"; TT "the performances of Jacob and Trintignant give the film a strong emotional core").

The frontrunners for the Oscar were the winners of the Golden Globe (Drama) and the inaugural Screen Actors Guild trophy.

The Globe was won by Jessica Lange as the unstable wife in *Blue Sky*, a film which had been completed four years earlier but not released due to the financial collapse of the studio Orion (NYT "brings to [the role] fierce emotions and tact"; NYP "electrifying [and] explosive"; NYer "a stunning performance"; LAT "a great performance ... Lange doesn't hold anything back ... it's a fierce display ... intense, volatile [and] highly emotional yet controlled ... Lange's acting in 'Blue Sky' leaves you awe-struck"; WP "a plush, platinum star turn"; V "magnificent"). Lange received her sixth mention from the Academy.

Jodie Foster was presented with the SAG accolade for her performance as a young woman raised in isolation from civilisation in *Nell* (NYT "[an] intense, accomplished performance ... commands real interest"; NYP "seems a solid contender for another Oscar ... undeniably impressive acting"; LAT "a remarkable performance"; CT "mixes naturalism and theatrical poetry in an odd, entrancing way ... brings the part conviction and integrity"; CST "an effective film, and a moving one, largely because of the strange beauty of [her] performance"; WP "transcendent"; BG "they mint Oscars for the kind of performance [she] delivers ... Foster's performance is wondrous"; Time "on Oscar night they all may be applauding Foster ... a fearless, fierce, beautifully attuned performance"). She was recognised by the Academy for a fourth time.

Also nominated, but considered outside chances were: Miranda Richardson as the disturbed wife of poet T. S. Eliot in *Tom and Viv* (NYT "Richardson has been handed a role that approaches cliche"; NYP "merits an Oscar nomination for her passionate yet perfectly balanced performance"; LAT "superb ... the stand-out performance [of the film] "; TT "does her best to turn up the heat"; G "beautifully acted ... a veritable tour de force ... moves [through the character's changing moods] with a fluency and power that's wholly admirable ... a brave, if highly coloured performance ... dominates the film"; S&S "flawlessly acted ... [a] sympathetic, surprisingly humorous performance"); Susan Sarandon as a lawyer retained by a young boy in *The Client* (NYP "intriguing"; LAT "convincing"; WP "[a] strong performance"; BG "Sarandon is a plus [for the movie]"); and Winona Ryder as the novelist heroine in *Little Women* (NYT "plays Jo with spark and confidence ... her spirited presence gives the film an appealing linchpin"; NYP "delicious"; LAT "superbly acted ... perfectly cast"; CT "marvelous"; WP "energetic"; BG "ideal"; Time "luminous"). Ryder had also earned praise from critics for her work in *Reality Bites* (NYT "a fine comic performance"; LAT "couldn't be bettered ... it's a treat to see how much naturalness and assurance she brings to what could have been a pre-digested performance"; BG "the reason Ryder is so good is that she embraces Leilani's contradictions ... [she] keeps centering the film ... a delight").

On Oscar night, the winner was Lange. Referring to the years her film had spent in a New York City bank vault, she remarked, "This is such a wonderful honour, especially for a little film that seemed to have no future."

In London, the BAFTA was awarded to Sarandon for *The Client* over a field of nominees that included New York winner Fiorentino. Oscar winner Lange was not among those in contention for the prize.

BEST SUPPORTING ACTOR

ACADEMY AWARDS
Samuel L. Jackson as 'Jules' in *Pulp Fiction*
• **Martin Landau as 'Bela Lugosi' in *Ed Wood***
Chazz Palminteri as 'Cheech' in *Bullets over Broadway*
Paul Scofield as 'Mark Van Doren' in *Quiz Show*
Gary Sinise as 'Lieutenant Dan Taylor' in *Forrest Gump*

GOLDEN GLOBE AWARDS
Kevin Bacon – *The River Wild*
Samuel L. Jackson – *Pulp Fiction*
• **Martin Landau – *Ed Wood***
Gary Sinise – *Forrest Gump*
John Turturro – *Quiz Show*

SCREEN ACTORS GUILD
Samuel L. Jackson – *Pulp Fiction*
• **Martin Landau – *Ed Wood***
Chazz Palminteri
  – *Bullets over Broadway*
Gary Sinise – *Forrest Gump*
John Turturro – *Quiz Show*

BRITISH ACADEMY AWARDS
Simon Callow
  – *Four Weddings and a Funeral*
John Hannah
  – *Four Weddings and a Funeral*
• **Samuel L. Jackson – *Pulp Fiction***
Paul Scofield – *Quiz Show*

NEW YORK – **Martin Landau** – *Ed Wood*
LOS ANGELES – **Martin Landau** – *Ed Wood*
BOARD OF REVIEW – **Gary Sinise** – *Forrest Gump*
NATIONAL SOCIETY – **Martin Landau** – *Ed Wood*

For his portrayal of former horror film star Bela Lugosi in the comedy *Ed Wood*, Martin Landau received his third nomination for the Best Supporting Actor Oscar (NYT "played with hilarious crankiness by an outstandingly fine Landau ... as poignant as he is scabrously funny"; NYP "magnificent ... an obvious front-runner for the supporting actor Oscar ... more than an electrifying impersonation ... a hugely satisfying blend of pathos and hilarity"; LAT "a tasty, full-throttle performance ... wonderfully rousing yet poignant"; CT "passionately acted ... a stunning impersonation ... great acting"; WP "it's impossible to overestimate the job that Landau does here ... both vocally and physically, he's simply astounding"; BG "gives the film its emotional core ... Landau is a cinch Oscar nomination for his magnificent ruined Lugosi"; V "astonishing"; TGM "the one sharp edge in an otherwise dull offering"; S&S "marvellously incarnated"). During the awards season, Landau had collected the Los Angeles Film Critics Association plaudit, the inaugural Screen Actors Guild trophy and, each for the second time, the New York Film Critics Circle prize, the National Society of Film Critics award and the Golden Globe. He was the overwhelming favourite for the statuette.

The actor considered most likely to cause an upset on the night was Samuel L. Jackson, recognised as a hit man in *Pulp Fiction* (NYT "blisteringly fine ... never better ... manages to give the standout performance in a film in which every supporting actor deserves special mention"; LAT "a strong performance"; CT "has the tougher part [of the two leads, but] gets plenty of incandescent moments"; WP "looks the part, eyes burning"; V "superb"). Jackson placed second in the voting for the New York critics' Best Actor award and, surprisingly, was runner-up for both the NSFC Best Actor and Best Supporting Actor awards.

Also nominated were: Chazz Palminteri as a gangster in *Bullets over Broadway* (NYT "expert ... a terrific comic turn"; LAT "very well played"; WP "sublime"; TGM "[a] picture-stealing performance"); Gary Sinise as a soldier in the box office hit *Forrest Gump* (NYT "[his] dark, bitter performance offers an element of surprise"; NYP "impressive"; WP "fine"; BG "played with an impressive mix of bitterness and heart ... deserves Oscar attention"); and New York runner-up Paul Scofield, who earned his second mention from the Academy twenty-eight years after winning the Best Actor statuette, for his portrayal of poet and university literature professor Mark van Doren in *Quiz Show* (NYT "brilliantly nuanced ... a marvel"; LAT "dazzling ... gives his best performance since winning an Oscar for 'A Man for All Seasons'"; WP "played majestically"; Time "[a] great performance").

The most notable absentee from the list was Terence Stamp as an ageing transperson in the Australian comedy *The Adventures of Priscilla, Queen of the Desert* (NYT "spectacular ... marvellously ladylike and loaded with sly, acerbic wisecracks, he's worth the price of admission ... [he] captures this film at its most delicately droll"; NYP "lends depth and dignity to his character"; LAT "the movie's major surprise, gracefully convincing"; WP "the movie's chief asset"; TGM "superb ... Stamp's face (and what he does with it) is the entire movie in microcosm ... to be reckoned with and respected"). Stamp had been nominated as Best Actor at the Globes and the BAFTAs, but was overlooked by Oscar voters despite a campaign for him to be short-listed in the secondary category.

Also by-passed for consideration were: Mykelti Williamson in *Forrest Gump* (NYT "deserving of special mention"; WP "fine"); John Turturro in *Quiz Show* (NYT "played with such glee and fury by the scene-stealing Turturro that he becomes the film's most magnetic figure"; LAT "a tendency to exaggerate [his] performance"; WP "brilliantly abrasive"; Time "wonderfully played"); Campbell Scott as Robert Benchley in *Mrs Parker and the Vicious Circle* (NYT "a sweetly gallant performance ... played beautifully"; NYP "a revelation"; WP "impressive [in] an unexpectedly entertaining, true-to-life impersonation of Robert Benchley"; BG "affecting"; G "[a] beautifully reserved performance"; S&S "[an] elegant rendering"); both Robert Duvall (NYT "particularly appealing"; LAT "engaging"; WP "top-notch") and Spalding Gray (LAT "deliciously played"; WP "hilarious"; BG "played amusingly") in *The Paper*; Dennis Quaid in *Wyatt Earp* (NYT "the strongest part of [the film]"; LAT "worth seeing ... lost 43 pounds to amusingly portray the tubercular gambler Doc Holliday"; WP "spectacularly played"; BG "[a] colourful counterpoint to Costner's Earp"); Ian Hart as the young John Lennon in *Backbeat* (NYT "played furiously well"; LAT "phenomenal in the role"; CT "dominates the movie ... gives the movie its depth and jagged edges ... plays attitude more than mannerisms ... has made this role so much his own that you can't imagine anyone else today doing it"; WP "he's dead-on in his unbridled energy and the acerbic snap of his voice"; BG "electrifying ... no mere impersonation ... believable"; TT "best of the bunch ... brilliantly catches [the character] ... [he] has all the best (usually comic) lines ... but he also has the most interesting and complex response: his anger and generosity are finely poised"; S&S "an excellent performance"); both Ian Holm (BG "amusingly played") and Rupert Everett (NYT "flamboyantly memorable"; BG "makes the would-be regent quite amusing thanks to his ability to play dullness and stupidity with comic straightness") in *The Madness of King George*; and both Simon Callow (NYT "beautifully played ... a particularly vibrant presence"; CT "near-flawless ... should be remembered come Academy Award time for his performance") and John Hannah (NYT "beautifully played"; Sp "affecting") in *Four Weddings and a Funeral*.

On Oscar night, sixty-six-year old Landau finally received the Best Supporting Actor statuette. Unsuccessful Oscar nominee Jackson, however, did end up with an award for his performance in *Pulp Fiction*: he was a surprise winner of the BAFTA in London.

BEST SUPPORTING ACTRESS

ACADEMY AWARDS
Rosemary Harris as 'Rose Haigh-Wood' in *Tom and Viv*
Helen Mirren as 'Queen Charlotte' in *The Madness of King George*
Uma Thurman as 'Mia Wallace' in *Pulp Fiction*
Jennifer Tilly as 'Olive Neal' in *Bullets over Broadway*
• **Dianne Wiest as 'Helen Sinclair' in *Bullets over Broadway***

GOLDEN GLOBE AWARDS
Kirsten Dunst – *Interview with the Vampire*
Sophia Loren – *Prêt-à-Porter (Ready to Wear)*
Uma Thurman – *Pulp Fiction*
• **Dianne Wiest – *Bullets over Broadway***
Robin Wright – *Forrest Gump*

SCREEN ACTORS GUILD
Jamie Lee Curtis – *True Lies*
Sally Field – *Forrest Gump*
Uma Thurman – *Pulp Fiction*
• **Dianne Wiest**
  – *Bullets over Broadway*
Robin Wright – *Forrest Gump*

BRITISH ACADEMY AWARDS
Charlotte Coleman
  – *Four Weddings and a Funeral*
Sally Field – *Forrest Gump*
Anjelica Huston
  – *Manhattan Murder Mystery*
• **Kristin Scott Thomas**
  – *Four Weddings and a Funeral*

NEW YORK – Dianne Wiest – *Bullets over Broadway*
LOS ANGELES – Dianne Wiest – *Bullets over Broadway*
BOARD OF REVIEW – Dianne Wiest – *Bullets over Broadway*
NATIONAL SOCIETY – Rosemary Harris – *Tom and Viv*

Eight years after she had won the Best Supporting Actress Oscar for her performance in the Woody Allen comedy *Hannah and Her Sisters*, Dianne Wiest was the overwhelming favourite to claim a second statuette for her turn as a Broadway grande dame in another Allen comedy, *Bullets over Broadway* (NYT "wonderfully funny"; NYP "steals the show"; LAT "so gloriously over the top that she turns Helen into a sacred monster … Wiest doesn't try for pathos – she's having too much fun for that … every time you think she has gone too far, she redeems the foolery with her sozzled, spirited timing"; WP "sublime"). Wiest won her second Best Supporting Actress awards from both the New York Film Critics Circle and the National Board of Review, and also collected the Los

Angeles Film Critics Association accolade, the Golden Globe and the inaugural Screen Actors Guild trophy. Oscar voters short-listed her for a third time.

The only major prize that Wiest did not receive was the National Society of Film Critics plaudit, which was collected by sixty-four-year old English theatre legend Rosemary Harris as the mother of the unstable wife of poet T. S. Eliot in *Tom and Viv* (NYT "beautifully played"; LAT "a great and valiant small performance ... gives such delicacy and understanding to the role that it transforms the movie's meanings"; G "beautifully acted"). Harris was included on the Academy's short-list for the first time for her performance.

The dark horse in the Oscar field was Uma Thurman as a gangster's wife in *Pulp Fiction* (NYT "spirited"). While her performance went unremarked on by most leading newspaper film critics at the time of the film's release, Thurman finished runner-up for the New York and NSFC awards. In the voting for the east coast accolade, she was outpolled by just two points.

Also in contention for the statuette were Helen Mirren as Queen Charlotte in *The Madness of King George*, a performance that subsequently won her the Best Actress prize at the 1995 Cannes Film Festival (NYT "fine"; LAT "beautifully played"; BG "wonderful ... we don't see enough of her"; V "most touching"; TGM "a commendable cameo – no more, no less"), and Jennifer Tilly as a talentless gangster's moll in *Bullets over Broadway* (LAT "[a] scene-stealer ... genius"; WP "sublime"). Tilly's younger sister, Meg Tilly, had been a Best Supporting Actress nominee for *Agnes of God* in 1985.

Forrest Gump was nominated in a record-equalling thirteen categories, so it was surprising that Oscar voters recognised neither BAFTA nominee Sally Field (NYT "charges through the story in flowery, emphatically genteel Southern costumes [such that she] looks a little too good to be true") nor Robin Wright (NYP "[a] perfectly nuanced tour de force") for their performance in the film.

Similarly, even though *Four Weddings and a Funeral* garnered a Best Picture Academy Award nomination, BAFTA winner Kristin Scott Thomas was snubbed for her performance in the popular romantic comedy (NYT "beautifully played"; Sp "affecting"; S&S "makes a marvellously brittle Fiona").

Among those also overlooked were: Globe (Comedy/Musical) Best Actress winner Jamie Lee Curtis in *True Lies* (NYT "the visual transformation of Ms Curtis from schoolmarm to bombshell is especially well done [and while the striptease] scene has the potential to seem unpleasantly exploitative, [she] is much too deft a comedian to let that happen"; TGM "terrifically funny"; S&S "Curtis' role as Helen is disappointingly thin and facile – though Curtis has enough nuance to maintain a presence, she has little to do"); Sandra Bullock in the thriller *Speed* (WP "the only performer to stand out ... if it weren't for the smart-funny twist she gives to her lines – they're the best in the film – the air on that bus would have been stifling"); both Claire Danes as Beth (NYT "does a fine job"; NYP "performs with quiet strength"; LAT "superbly acted"; WP "simply vanishes into the part"; TGM "an assured presence every moment she's on screen") and Kirsten Dunst as Amy (NYT "scene-stealing") in *Little Women*; Jennifer Jason Leigh in *The Hudsucker Proxy* (NYT "wonderfully funny"; LAT "[a] brash comic performance that would have brought life to another film"; CST "right on target ... has the part down perfect"; S&S "a genuine, original performance"); Julianne Moore in *Vanya on 42nd Street* (NYT "[a] sly, delicately shaded performance"; NYP "stands out"; LAT "the surprise of the production ... utilizes all the opportunities this role provides"; BG "the most faceted Elena I've ever seen"; S&S "a triumph"); both Joanna Going (LAT "worth seeing"; BG "contributes a breakthrough performance") and Mare Winningham in *Wyatt Earp*; both Glenn Close (NYT "wickedly funny ... played devilishly"; WP "while the filmmaker's treatment of the character is downright sexist, Close gets even by stealing the movie"; BG "again gets stuck with a 'Fatal Attraction' variant and brings it off with the elegance, subtlety and grace we have come to expect from her") and Marisa Tomei (NYT "particularly appealing") in *The Paper* (WP "[Michael Keaton is] nicely foiled by Tomei and Close"); both Glenn Close (NYT "an especially powerful presence"; S&S "the film's one really strong performance") and Winona Ryder (NYT "captivating ... makes yet another radiant impression") in *The House of the Spirits*; Katharine Hepburn for her final screen role in *Love Affair* (NYT "Hepburn is ill served by this [film] ... [she] looks actually uncomfortable"; WP "hilarious"; BG "her presence does indeed stamp a certain imprimatur upon this enterprise"); Rain Phoenix in *Even Cowgirls Get the Blues* (NYT "has the best written part and is wonderfully natural"; TGM "Phoenix is ramrod stiff"; S&S "[an] exuberant performance"); Mirta Ibarra in *Fresa y Chocolate (Strawberry and Chocolate)* (LAT "[a] terrific portrayal"; G "[a] terrific performance"); and Cannes Film Festival winner Virna Lisi as the scheming dowager queen in *La Reine Margot (Queen Margot)* (NYT "entertaining ... [her] shockingly witchy appearance and evil mannerisms won her the best-actress prize at Cannes this year"; NYP "an Oscar-worthy performance"; LAT "unrecognisable ... gives a terrific dragon-lady performance ... her dark rage is almost comic in its magisterial meanness but Lisi doesn't camp it up"; WP "lends the film its only real substance ... she alone seems to believe that there's meaning in this sumptuous pageant"; BG "Lisi is never just a caricature"; G "devastating").

On Oscar night, Wiest was named the winner, becoming the second person to receive a second Best Supporting Actress statuette. "This is as surprising and marvellous as it was the first time," she told the audience at the Shrine Auditorium.

BEST PICTURE

ACADEMY AWARDS

Apollo 13
   (Imagine, Universal, 140 mins, 30 Jun 1995, $172.1m, 9 noms)
Babe
   (Kennedy Miller, Universal, 89 mins, 4 Aug 1995, $66.6m, 7 noms)
• ***Braveheart***
   (Icon/Ladd, Paramount, 177 mins, 24 May 1995, $75.6m, 10 noms)
Il Postino (The Postman)
   (Cecchi Gori, Miramax, 108 mins, 14 Jun 1995, $20.8m, 5 noms)
Sense and Sensibility
   (Mirage, Columbia, 136 mins, 13 Dec 1995, $42.7m, 7 noms)

GOLDEN GLOBE AWARDS

(Drama)
Apollo 13
Braveheart
The Bridges of Madison County
Leaving Las Vegas
• ***Sense and Sensibility***

(Comedy/Musical)
The American President
• ***Babe***
Get Shorty
Sabrina
Toy Story

PRODUCERS GUILD AWARD

• ***Apollo 13***
The American President
The Bridges of Madison County
Dead Man Walking
Leaving Las Vegas
Il Postino (The Postman)
Sense and Sensibility

CRITICS' CHOICE AWARDS

• ***Sense and Sensibility***

BRITISH ACADEMY AWARDS

(Best Film)
Babe
The Madness of King George
• ***Sense and Sensibility***
• ***The Usual Suspects***

(Best British Film)
Carrington
Land and Freedom
• ***The Madness of King George***
Trainspotting

NEW YORK – *Leaving Las Vegas*
LOS ANGELES – *Leaving Las Vegas*
BOARD OF REVIEW – *Sense and Sensibility*
NATIONAL SOCIETY – *Babe*

1995

LONDON

(Best Film) *Babe*

(Best British Film) ***The Madness of King George***

The early favourite for the Best Picture Academy Award was *Apollo 13*, a drama about the ill–fated moon mission which opened in North American cinemas just ahead of the Fourth of July holiday (NYT "the year's great thriller ... exciting, illuminating and inspiring ... spellbinding"; NYP "merits consideration as Best Picture"; LAT "engrossing [but] a successful failure ... an unnecessary phoniness [is allowed] to intrude on the proceedings"; CST "one of the year's best films"; CT "one of the most exciting adventure movies of the year ... a nail-biter and knuckle-whitener of the first rank ... gripping"; WP "soaring"; SFX "absorbing"; TT "plays boringly safe"; SMH "gripping ... a triumph"). Later in the year, however, other contenders emerged.

The New York Film Critics Circle and Los Angeles Film Critics Association both selected *Leaving Las Vegas*, an independent drama about a dying alcoholic (NYT "passionate and furiously alive [but] never rings entirely true"; LAT "a film laden with virtues but difficult to embrace"; CT "superior ... a sure bet to receive top Oscar nominations"; WP "touching ... one of the most powerful, honest pictures of the year"; TGM "leaves you gaping in admiration ... pure alchemy"; TT "poetic"; SMH "astonishing ... a masterpiece").

There were surprise winners of the other major established American accolades. The National Board of Review selected *Sense and Sensibility*, an adaptation of the novel by Jane Austen (NYT "grandly entertaining ... a sparkling, colourful and utterly contemporary comedy of manners"; NYP "near–perfect"; LAT "creates so much good feeling"; WP "abundant pleasures"; TGM "poised, delicate, powerful, hovering between poignancy and pealing laughter"; SMH "stylish"), while the National Society of Film Critics honoured *Babe*, an unexpectedly successful children's film about a pig who wants to be a sheep dog (NYT "endearing"; NYP "the year's most enjoyable film"; LAT "an unanticipated treat ... captivating ... charming and enchanting"; WP "a hilarious fantasy ... there's engaging vitality everywhere ... captivating"; TT "glorious"; S&S "funny, engaging and almost entirely uncloying"). *Sense and Sensibility* also claimed the inaugural Best Picture prize from the newly formed Broadcast Film Critics Association, while *Babe* also triumphed at the London Film Critics Awards.

Among the year's other most lauded movies and widely tipped for Best Picture nominations at the Oscars were: *Dead Man Walking* (NYT "exceptional ... [a] quietly courageous drama"; NYP "emotionally complex, intelligent, balanced"; CT "sophisticated ... you won't easily forget it"; WP "extremely affecting"; TT "powerful"); *The American President* (NYT "[has a] lighthearted charm"; LAT "genial and entertaining"; CT "crowd-pleasing ... a funny, sparkling show"; CST "great entertainment ... witty and warm"; NYDN "film making at its sparkling best"; BG "a smart, likable comedy filled with romantic charm ... hugely satisfying"); and *Toy Story* (NYT "miraculous, ground–breaking"; LAT "captivating ... although its computer-generated imagery is impressive, the major surprise of this bright foray into a new kind of animation is how much cleverness has been invested in story and dialogue"; CT "sparkles with fresh ideas, including, of course, its computer-based look ... a complete joy"; WP "a must–see movie ... ingenious [and] delightful"; BG "perfect holiday entertainment ... has instant classic written all over it").

At the Golden Globes, *Apollo 13* and *The American President* were the frontrunners for the Best Picture awards in the Drama and Comedy/Musical categories, respectively. In major surprises, however, both films were outpolled. In the Drama category, *Sense and Sensibility* was victorious, while sentimental favourite *Babe* scored a win in the Comedy/Musical category. Meanwhile, Globes night complicated the Best Picture Oscar race even further, when Mel Gibson unexpectedly won Best Director for *Braveheart*, a popular historical drama about a thirteenth century Scottish rebel released in the first half of the year (NYT "one of the most spectacular entertainments of the year ... an explosive action movie"; NYP "an hour too long ... predictable"; LAT "sumptuous and involving [but while it] may be rip-roaring, it isn't all that brave ... Gibson doesn't go beyond the good guys/bad guys war plan"; WP "a rambling disappointment"; BG "commands the screen ... a big, strapping medieval sword-and-arrow movie"). While the film's battle sequences were noted for their brutal realism, the movie's narrative was widely criticized for straying significantly from historical facts.

Unexpectedly, *Braveheart* topped the list of Best Picture Oscar nominees, garnering mentions in ten categories. However, most observers considered it too violent to be the eventual winner. *Apollo 13* and *Sense and Sensibility* were nominated for Best Picture, but in major surprises each were overlooked for Best Director. Also included on the ballot were *Babe* and the Italian film *Il Postino (The Postman)*, which was the top category's first foreign–language nominee since 1973 (NYT "a rueful, warmly affecting film"; LAT "a tender and wistful comedy"; SFC "unforgettable"; SFX "imperfect"; BG "more sentimental than profound, more anecdotal than dramatic"; TGM "blatantly sentimental [and yet] sublime"; S&S "its fundamental falsity and miscalculations are ever more evident").

Leaving Las Vegas was the first film to have won both the New York and Los Angeles prizes and then be overlooked for a Best Picture nomination at the Oscars. Although its director and stars were nominated, *Dead Man Walking* was also overlooked. *The American President* earned just a single nod, in the music categories.

Other films excluded from consideration included: *Nixon* (NYT "a bold feat of revisionism that veers unpredictably between turgidness and inspiration ... a huge mixed bag [but] attention must be paid"; LAT "impressive [but] the drama is hard to find"; CT "spellbinding"; CST "one of the year's best films"; WP "powerful ... an audacious biography rich in imagination and originality ... dense and challenging ... 'Nixon' dwarfs everything in American cinema since 'Schindler's List'"; BG "huge, brilliant, dark and cathartic ... more objective and restrained than any of Stone's previous films"); *The Bridges of Madison County* (NYT "remarkable ... a moving, elegiac love story"; LAT "surprising [and] appealing"; Time "intelligent"; S&S "enjoyable"); *Devil in a Blue Dress* (NYT "[an] unusually vibrant film noir [with] fresh energy"; LAT "a major accomplishment ... the most exotic crime entertainment of the season"; WP "stunning ... fast, absorbing and substantive"; TGM "a bland, workaday detective flick ... the movie is bloodless"); *Richard III* (NYT "swiftly paced, pictorially dazzling [and] sensationally flashy"; LAT "audacious ... made with gusto, daring and visual brilliance, this stripped-down, jazzed-up 'Richard' pulsates with bloody life, a triumph of both modernization and popularization") *Once Were Warriors* (NYT "ferocious [and] visceral ... brutally effective"; WP "an uncompromising, emotionally draining drama ... explosive"; V "excellent"; SFC "powerful"; BG "scaldingly convincing ... there's simply nothing like it"; TGM "a blunt, if moving, film"); *Persuasion* (NYT "lovey and subtle ... [the novel is] brilliantly captured"; LAT "literate, sophisticated, bitingly funny"; CT "a delight ... the film sparkles, its heart beats"; WP "lethally funny"; BG "transcendently rewarding ... a civilized joy"); *La Cité des Enfants Perdus (The City of Lost Children)* (NYT "provocative but impossibly convoluted"; LAT "stunningly surreal"; LAT "a stunningly surreal fantasy ... one of the most audacious, original films of the year"; CT "[a] spectacular visual treat ... this remarkable movie is really one-of-a-kind"; BG "a treat to watch [but] there's more visual payoff here than there is story to go with it"; V "dazzling"; G "what's lacking in the film is any real emotion"; S&S "all surface dazzle, no space for depth or resonance"); *Les Roseaux Sauvages (Wild Reeds)* (LAT "unexpectedly satisfying"; CT "an often painfully sensitive film [which] brims with affection, nostalgia and bittersweet resignation"; WP "always interesting and never conventional"; Time "one of the year's ten best"; TGM "superb ... elegant, painfully astute [and] moving"); and *Yao a Yao Yao Dao Waipo Qiao (Shanghai Triad)* (NYT "superb"; LAT "a great gangster film"; WP "poetic but perplexing"; TGM "a triumph"; TT "enthralling"; S&S "astonishing").

In the weeks before the Academy Award winners were announced *Apollo 13* again emerged as the Oscar favourite when it was named Best Picture by the

Producers Guild of America and Ron Howard won the Directors Guild of America prize.

On Oscar night, however, *Braveheart* won Best Picture. Los Angeles Times film critic Kenneth Turan described the result as "the single biggest surprise in an otherwise completely by the book evening".

At the BAFTAs the following month, *Braveheart* was not even nominated in the Best Film category. *The Madness of King George* won as Best British Film, while there was a tie for the Best Film award for only the second time in the history of the awards: *Sense and Sensibility* shared the award with the crime thriller *The Usual Suspects*, a sleeper hit at the North American box office which had been another notable absentee from the Best Picture Oscar category despite claiming the statuette for Best Original Screenplay (NYT "immensely stylish … the movie finally isn't anything more than an intricate feat of gamesmanship, but it's still quite something to see"; LAT "a polished exercise in pure virtuoso style"; CT "uncommonly thrilling … a nerve-shredding suspense movie"; WP "deliciously intricate"; BG "reminds us how entertaining deviousness can be"; G "a gripping, sophisticated thriller"; S&S "the most satisfyingly close-textured thriller for years").

BEST DIRECTOR

ACADEMY AWARDS
Mike Figgis for *Leaving Las Vegas*
• **Mel Gibson for *Braveheart***
Chris Noonan for *Babe*
Michael Radford for *Il Postino (The Postman)*
Tim Robbins for *Dead Man Walking*

GOLDEN GLOBE AWARDS
Mike Figgis – *Leaving Las Vegas*
• **Mel Gibson – *Braveheart***
Ron Howard – *Apollo 13*
Ang Lee – *Sense and Sensibility*
Rob Reiner – *The American President*
Martin Scorsese – *Casino*

DIRECTORS GUILD AWARD
Mike Figgis – *Leaving Las Vegas*
Mel Gibson – *Braveheart*
• **Ron Howard – *Apollo 13***
Ang Lee – *Sense and Sensibility*
Michael Radford
  – *Il Postino (The Postman)*

BRITISH ACADEMY AWARDS
Mel Gibson – *Braveheart*
Nicholas Hytner
  – *The Madness of King George*
Ang Lee – *Sense and Sensibility*
• **Michael Radford**
  – *Il Postino (The Postman)*

NEW YORK – Ang Lee – *Sense and Sensibility*
LOS ANGELES – Mike Figgis – *Leaving Las Vegas*
BOARD OF REVIEW – Ang Lee – *Sense and Sensibility*
NATIONAL SOCIETY – Mike Figgis – *Leaving Las Vegas*
CRITICS' CHOICE – Mel Gibson – *Braveheart*
LONDON
  (Director) **Peter Jackson – *Heavenly Creatures***
  (British Director) **Michael Radford – *Il Postino (The Postman)***

Former actor Ron Howard was the early frontrunner for the year's Best Director accolades for *Apollo 13* (NYT "efficient direction … a sure hand"; LAT "[he] is effective at putting the tension and bravery of that mission on screen"; CST "directed with a single–mindedness and attention to detail that makes it riveting"; CT "his clean, clear, good-humored, highly organized approach is ideal for material like 'Apollo 13'"; WP "excellent").

At the year's end, however, the critics groups by-passed Howard and honoured two other candidates. Winning both the New York Film Critics Circle and the National Board of Review prizes and finishing runner-up for the Los Angeles Film Critics Association plaudit was Ang Lee for *Sense and Sensibility* (LAT "does a more-than-credible job [but] isn't sharp on the nuances of British behavior"; TGM "deft ... has worked such alchemy"). Collecting the Los Angeles and National Society of Film Critics laurels and finishing runner-up in the voting in New York was Mike Figgis for *Leaving Las Vegas* (LAT "beautifully put together ... he has put a distinctive visual flourish into almost every scene"; TGM "fights hard to keep the entire movie from slipping into maudlin excess ... he wobbles a few times – but, in the main, victory is his"; G "[the] non-judgmental tone [he strikes] is one of [the film's] biggest strengths").

While the four main critics groups had shared their prizes between Lee and Figgis, observers still expected Howard to win the Golden Globe but in a shock result, the winner was Mel Gibson for *Braveheart* (NYP "accomplished"; LAT "as a filmmaker, he lacks the epic gift, but the movie works in a fairly basic level"; CST "given this material, I do not know anyone who could have directed it better"; WP "has proved that he is a competent director"; BG "fills [the movie] lively intelligence, red-blooded ardour ... cuts artfully between intimate clashes and mass patterns and takes a place alongside the directors he studied").

The biggest shock of the awards season, however, was the omission from the list of Oscar nominees of two of the three favourites, and the serious handicapping of the third. Although their films were named among the five best of the year, Lee and Howard were both snubbed. While he made the Oscar short-list, Figgis' chances of claiming the statuette were all but dashed when *Leaving Las Vegas* was excluded from the top category. The only time a director had won when his film had not been among the Best Picture contenders was in 1928/29.

Nominated alongside Figgis were Gibson, Michael Radford for *Il Postino (The Postman)* (SFE "well–directed"; TGM "poetry in motion"; G "what could have been a film of some charm but little substance is elevated to something better by both the director and [his leading] actor"; S&S "miscalculations"), Tim Robbins for *Dead Man Walking* (NYT "his direction is graceful and finally devastating"; LAT "wants to examine capital punishment with as much dispassion as possible"; CT "declares himself a director worth watching"; TGM "only competent") and, most unexpectedly, Chris Noonan for *Babe* (NYT "maintains a refreshingly light touch"; WP "has done a masterly job of pulling together this film's disparate elements ... [he has] transformed what could have been a passable kiddie picture into something alert and provocative"; TT "pitches the film, successfully, as a genial storybook fantasy").

Among the other notable candidates by-passed by Oscar voters were: previous winner Clint Eastwood for *The Bridges of Madison County* (NYT "has done the best imaginable job of directing [the material]"; LAT "Eastwood's sturdy utilitarianism, the sparseness and efficiency that characterize his style, are actually what this kind of material most needs"; TGM "competently directed"; S&S "the film's clean, technical efficiency makes it rather enjoyable"); previous winner Oliver Stone for *Nixon* (NYT "has the headstrong intelligence to make it work"; LAT "an impressive, well-crafted piece of work"; CT "has deliberately played the entire movie in a more somber, stately rhythm than usual"; BG "restrained [and] virtuosic"); Carl Franklin for *Devil in a Blue Dress* (NYT "he rises expertly to the occasion"; LAT "elegant control ... a fluid, persuasive piece of movie-making"; WP "confirms [he has] the directorial talent to bring [his vision] to life ... right now, he's right up there with the best"); Bryan Singer for *The Usual Suspects* (LAT "fine control ... shows Singer to be an uncommon kind of natural film-maker, disciplined rather than self-indulgent"; WP "directs with speed and dynamism"; BG "brings to the film a seductively velvety style"; S&S "tight direction"); John Lasseter for *Toy Story* (NYT "inspired direction"); Lee Tamahori for *Once Were Warriors* (WP "there's a documentary-like realism to the movie, thanks to its authentic Maori cast and Tamahori's semi-improvisational approach to direction"; BG "astonishingly assured"); Andre Techine for *Les Roseaux Sauvages (Wild Reeds)* (LAT "sensitive filmmaking ... has kept a firm but gentle hand on the proceedings, never letting the cast's uniformly fine actors stray from the truth"; CT "we sense that [he] is hiding little ... [made with] sheer open-hearted gentleness and ardor"); Marc Caro and Jean–Pierre Jeunet for *La Cité des Enfants Perdus (The City of Lost Children)* (LAT "true visionaries ... [they] never allow [the film's] unique dazzle to overwhelm its people ... they are no less creators of their own universe than they are storytellers who inspire the finest, most beautifully shaded performances from their distinctive actors"); and Zhang Yimou for *Yao a Yao Yao Dao Waipo Qiao (Shanghai Triad)* (NYT "immense grace"; TGM "masterly").

As they had done a decade earlier, the Directors Guild of America honoured a notable Oscar absentee when they handed their accolade to Howard. With the DGA winner excluded from the field, and the critics' choices either absent or undermined, Globe champ Gibson was the clear favourite. His win on Oscar night was no surprise.

Gibson was a nominee for the BAFTA as well, but the frontrunner was Lee whose *Sense and Sensibility* was favoured to win as Best Film. However, Lee faced strong competition from two English film-makers: Nicholas Hytner for *The Madness of King George* and unexpected Oscar nominee Radford for *Il Postino*. In a surprise result, the BAFTA went to Radford.

BEST ACTOR

ACADEMY AWARDS
• **Nicolas Cage as 'Ben' in *Leaving Las Vegas***
Richard Dreyfuss as 'Glenn Holland' in *Mr Holland's Opus*
Anthony Hopkins as 'President Richard M. Nixon' in *Nixon*
Sean Penn as 'Matthew Poncelet' in *Dead Man Walking*
Massimo Troisi as 'Mario Ruoppolo' in *Il Postino (The Postman)*

GOLDEN GLOBE AWARDS

(Drama)
• **Nicolas Cage – *Leaving Las Vegas***
Richard Dreyfuss
 – *Mr Holland's Opus*
Anthony Hopkins – *Nixon*
Ian McKellen – *Richard III*
Sean Penn – *Dead Man Walking*

(Comedy/Musical)
Michael Douglas
 – *The American President*
Harrison Ford – *Sabrina*
Steve Martin
 – *Father of the Bride Part II*
Patrick Swayze
 – *To Wong Foo, Thanks For Everything, Julie Newmar*
• **John Travolta – *Get Shorty***

SCREEN ACTORS GUILD
• **Nicolas Cage – *Leaving Las Vegas***
James Earl Jones
 – *Cry, the Beloved Country*
Anthony Hopkins – *Nixon*
Sean Penn – *Dead Man Walking*
Massimo Troisi
 – *Il Postino (The Postman)*

BRITISH ACADEMY AWARDS
Nicolas Cage – *Leaving Las Vegas*
• **Nigel Hawthorne
 – *The Madness of King George***
Jonathan Pryce – *Carrington*
Massimo Troisi
 – *Il Postino (The Postman)*

NEW YORK – Nicolas Cage – *Leaving Las Vegas*
LOS ANGELES – Nicolas Cage – *Leaving Las Vegas*
BOARD OF REVIEW – Nicolas Cage – *Leaving Las Vegas*
NATIONAL SOCIETY – Nicolas Cage – *Leaving Las Vegas*
CRITICS' CHOICE – Kevin Bacon – *Murder in the First*
LONDON
 (Actor) **Johnny Depp – *Don Juan DeMarco* and *Ed Wood***
 (British Actor) **Nigel Hawthorne – *The Madness of King George***

In 1962, Jack Lemmon was nominated as Best Actor for playing an alcoholic in *Days of Wine and Roses*. In an interview prior to the 1996 Oscar ceremony, he spoke about Nicolas Cage's Best Actor nominated portrayal of a drunk in *Leaving Las Vegas*. "Unlike anyone else who's played a drunk there is not a single scene in which Nic's character draws a sober breath," Lemmon said. "That is difficult to sustain for an entire film, and he did it with all these degrees and shadings." Film critics had also been almost unanimously impressed by Cage's work (NYT "played devastatingly ... digs deep to find his character's inner demons while also capturing the riotous energy of his outward charm ... astonishing, unsentimental"; LAT "sensitively acted"; CT "an Oscar-caliber performance"; WP "extraordinary"; SFC "watching him, it's hard to remember this is a healthy actor only pretending to be sick"; SFX "powerful"; BG "you won't soon forget Cage ... a terrific, classic end-of-the-line performance"; TGM "[a] most affecting portrait of an alcoholic ... [an] always observant never judgmental [portrait]"). Cage's bravura turn won him a clean sweep of the major American pre–Oscar accolades: the four top critics' prizes, the Golden Globe (Drama) and the Screen Actors Guild Award. On Oscar night, he was an unbackable favourite at his first nomination.

The only serious challenger to Cage amongst the Oscar nominees was Sean Penn, mentioned for the first time, as a death–row inmate in *Dead Man Walking* (NYT "astonishing ... Penn's mean, lean performance makes [the film's central] issues come furiously alive"; LAT "strong without even a breath of theatricality ... brings a renewed conviction and a skewered intensity to this part that makes his performance fresh and overpowering ... has the ability to make the character's emotional turmoil believable"; CT "a brilliant performance ... Oscar-calibre"; CST "proves again that he is the most powerful actor of his generation"; WP "you can't keep your eyes off him"; TGM "[a] glorious performance ... dominates the picture ... Penn unmasks him, very slowly, almost imperceptively, and with infinite subtlety").

Also nominated were: previous winner Richard Dreyfuss as a music teacher in *Mr Holland's Opus* (NYT "a warm and really touching performance ... firmly in control of the film's comic moments and just as comfortable delivering the film's calculatingly Capraesque payoff: a good cry"; NYP "a performance of truly breathtaking range and subtlety that makes him a major contender for another Oscar"; LAT "it is to Dreyfuss' credit that Holland is sympathetic at all ... plays the teacher likes an exposed nerve, alternatively agitated and soothed"; CT "precisely the kind of comeback role that earns Oscar nominations, if not awards"; V "quite effective and surprisingly restrained"; SFC "both touches and inspires"; TGM "this is Dreyfuss' picture to steal, and the theft is clean ... [he] is smart enough to play against the limp narrative"; G "a decent performance"; S&S "conveys an infectious enjoyment ... and negotiates the 30-year age span pretty convincingly"); previous winner Anthony Hopkins as President Richard M. Nixon in *Nixon* (NYT "overwhelmingly vivid"; LAT "does not satisfy"; CT "movingly played ... brings incredible empathy to the part"; WP "subtly magnificent ... [an] expert impersonation"; BG "first-rate ... a towering and complex performance that humanizes Nixon more than Nixon ever was able to humanize himself ... Hopkins and Allen will be Oscar faves"; Time "a failure"); and the late Italian actor Massimo Troisi for *Il Postino (The Postman)* (NYT "a wonderful performance"; LAT "with superb timing [and] an impressive variety of facial expressions, Troisi brings a truth and simplicity to his character that means everything"; WP "takes the potentially cheap situation and enriches it"; G "gives a performance which is so direct and so obviously sincere that even a slightly mannered style is easily forgivable"; S&S "he does not so much play as inhabit the role").

The most notable absentees from the list of Oscar candidates were Tom Hanks, the Oscar winner for the past two years, for *Apollo 13* (NYT "wonderful ... there's not a false move to anything he does on screen"; NYP "remarkable"; LAT "believable and involving"; CT "played to near perfection"; TT "never advances beyond being a nice family man") and Cannes Film Festival winner Jonathan Pryce in *Carrington* (NYT "an expertly clever, wonderfully sympathetic performance ... never reducing such flamboyance to caricature, [he] conveys Strachey's carefully measured public manner"; NYP "[an] arch yet aching portrayal"; LAT "a superb performance, theatrical in the best sense"; CT "a magnificent performance"; WP "[his] delicate mannerisms convey Strachey's wonderful sense of irony but avoid the pit of caricature ... a magnificent performance"; BG "one of the year's really few virtuosic characterizations ... a certain Oscar nominee"; SFC "brilliant"; Time "awfully good"; G "easily the best performance of his career on screen ... consistently watchable ... he fleshes out the character with quite fulsome detail").

Others shut out of the Oscar race were: Globe (Comedy/Musical) winner John Travolta in *Get Shorty* (NYT "played to suave perfection"; NYP "makes a strong claim to another Oscar nomination"; LAT "a splendid, old-fashioned star performance that pushes the picture to a level that would not have been possible without him"; WP "effortlessly seductive"; TGM "to his credit, Travolta turns this into something more than another criminal chic walk-through ... inspired"; G "the chief glory of the movie ... plays [the role] so deftly that the art of it is almost invisible"); Jack Nicholson in *The Crossing Guard* (NYT "lurches through this role with rekindled intensity"; LAT "[a] strong and emotional performance ... as impressive as he's been in years"; CT "[when he] plays anger [he] strikes every note with a molten grace ... rage pours out of him effortlessly, terrifyingly – yet with such flawless control"; WP "does a masterly job ... gives his most sustained, emotionally naked performance in a decade"; BG "a volcanic performance"); Denzel Washington in *Devil in a Blue Dress* (NYT "the role of Easy looks as tailor-made for [him] as his suit ... he's never had a part that fit him better"; LAT "a striking performance ... [he is] in complete charge of his resources"; WP "[he] is more grounded and charismatic than he has ever been ... [his] performance is rounded and melodic"; TGM "a character who suits [his] low-key intelligence"); both Robert De Niro (NYT "terrific"; G "De Niro is in complete and utter control [and] no one can touch him") and Al Pacino (G "over the top") in *Heat* (LAT "[both] give the kind of restrained yet powerful performance that ranks with the very best work of their careers"; CT "[they] redeem everything"; BG "arresting"); Michael Douglas in *The American President* (CT "[a] sparkling performance"; NYDN "a winning and carefully calibrated performance"); Temuera Morrison in *Once Were Warriors* (NYT "frighteningly credible"; WP "superbly performed"; TGM "powerfully played"; G "[a] towering performance ... excellent"); Linus Roache in *Priest* (NYT "played affectingly"; LAT "creates a quiet and believable portrait"; WP "a stirring performance [that is] beautifully sustained"; TT "[a] gutsy performance"); Leonardo DiCaprio in *The Basketball Diaries* (NYT "he's a stunning natural performer, who hides nothing ... wrenching expressiveness"; NYP "another ferociously fine performance"; LAT "the basic truth he brings [to the role] is in conflict with the film's essential bogusness ... [as a result, his] exertions come across as miming, not acting"; WP "a fierce, skinless performance ... [he] doesn't back off an inch [but] goes as far into the hell of drug abuse as any actor ever has – and comes out a star"; BG "never quite convinces"); Harvey Keitel in *Smoke* (LAT "wonderful ... gives another superb, detailed character turn"; CT "giving [his] absolute best ... [a] magnificent job"); Tim Roth in *Little Odessa* (NYT "a strong and subdued performance"; LAT "tense and cryptic"; CT "gives the film demonic intensity and a relentless kick"; TGM "[a] finely shaded performance"); and Ian McKellen in *Richard III*, for which he would win the European Film Award and earn a BAFTA nomination the following year (NYT "acted to the hilt"; LAT "[a] masterly performance"; WP "a shamelessly entertaining display of acting brilliance ... it's [his] florid mastery that dominates everything"; V "a vivid, finely honed characterization"; TGM "a superbly controlled yet monochromatic performance").

On Oscar night, Cage was named Best Actor. In collecting the statuette for the kind of low–budget, independent film he had supported throughout his career, he remarked, "I hope that there will be more encouragement for alternative movies where we can experiment," he said.

Cage was also nominated for the BAFTA, as was Oscar nominee Troisi and Cannes winner Pryce. Cage was denied the honour of a victory on both sides of the Atlantic, however, as the award went to one of the previous year's Best Actor Oscar nominees: Nigel Hawthorne for *The Madness of King George*.

BEST ACTRESS

ACADEMY AWARDS
• **Susan Sarandon as 'Sister Helen Prejean' in** *Dead Man Walking*
Elisabeth Shue as 'Sera' in *Leaving Las Vegas*
Sharon Stone as 'Ginger McKenna' in *Casino*
Meryl Streep as 'Francesca Johnson' in *The Bridges of Madison County*
Emma Thompson as 'Elinor Dashwood' in *Sense and Sensibility*

GOLDEN GLOBE AWARDS
(Drama)
Susan Sarandon – *Dead Man Walking*
Elisabeth Shue – *Leaving Las Vegas*
• **Sharon Stone –** *Casino*
Meryl Streep
  – *The Bridges of Madison County*
Emma Thompson
  – *Sense and Sensibility*

(Comedy/Musical)
Annette Bening
  – *The American President*
Sandra Bullock
  – *While You Were Sleeping*
Toni Collette – *Muriel's Wedding*
• **Nicole Kidman –** *To Die For*
Vanessa Redgrave
  – *A Month by the Lake*

SCREEN ACTORS GUILD
Joan Allen – *Nixon*
• **Susan Sarandon**
  – *Dead Man Walking*
Elisabeth Shue – *Leaving Las Vegas*
Meryl Streep
  – *The Bridges of Madison County*
Emma Thompson
  – *Sense and Sensibility*

BRITISH ACADEMY AWARDS
Nicole Kidman – *To Die For*
Helen Mirren
  – *The Madness of King George*
Elisabeth Shue – *Leaving Las Vegas*
• **Emma Thompson**
  – *Sense and Sensibility*

NEW YORK – Jennifer Jason Leigh – *Georgia*
LOS ANGELES – Elisabeth Shue – *Leaving Las Vegas*
BOARD OF REVIEW – Emma Thompson – *Carrington* and *Sense and Sensibility*
NATIONAL SOCIETY – Elisabeth Shue – *Leaving Las Vegas*
CRITICS' CHOICE – Nicole Kidman – *To Die For*
LONDON
  (Actress) **Nicole Kidman** – *To Die For*
  (British Actress) **Kate Winslet** – *Heavenly Creatures*

In early June, Meryl Streep earned some of the best reviews of her career as a farmer's Italian wife in *The Bridges of Madison County* (NYT "remarkable ... her best role in years"; LAT "a performance of exceptional strength ... she makes Francesca more real than she ever was on the page"; CST "wonderful"; SFC "completely arresting and true every moment"; Time "alchemizes literary mawkishness into intelligent movie passion"; TGM "beautifully acted"; TT "[a] vibrant performance"; S&S "on top form ... Eastwood lets Streep carry the picture"; SMH "the delight of the picture ... extraordinary [and] flawless").

October and November saw the North American release of three films in which lead actresses broke out of their familiar images and established themselves as serious talents: Nicole Kidman as a small–town woman who will do anything to be on television in *To Die For* (NYT "[a] smoothly hilarious performance"; NYP "her performance is an Oscar–worthy marvel ... unforgettably funny"; LAT "[her] perfectly pitched comic performance ends up being the kind of nervy knockout the film couldn't succeed without"; CT "she deserves an Oscar nomination for her work, completely disappearing into a mesmerizing character"; WP "what gives the movie its sharpest, sweetest edge is Nicole Kidman ... the finest role of her career ... playing mercilessly against her pinup girl image, she's an unforgettable comic archetype"; CST "superb ... inspired"; SFX "startlingly adept"; TGM "outstanding"); Elisabeth Shue as a prostitute in *Leaving Las Vegas* (NYT "a daring and affecting performance"; LAT "sensitively acted"; CT "faces a formidable challenge here, struggling in every frame to rescue Sera from the whore-with-the-heart-of-gold cliche ... amazingly, adroitly, she succeeds ... [it's] a career-making performance"; WP "extraordinary ... carves herself a new, dynamic career path"; BG "terrific"; G "a revelation"); and Sharon Stone as a gangster's wife in *Casino* (NYT "[a] spectacular, emblematic performance"; LAT "displays star quality and a feral intensity that is the equal of what the boys are putting down"; WP "surprisingly strong ... electric"; NYDN "impressive"; BG "her bravest performance yet").

In December, Emma Thompson received positive reviews for *Sense and Sensibility*, a film for which she adapted the screenplay from the novel by Jane Austen (NYT "wonderfully self–possessed"; NYP "[a] winning performance"; WP "masterfully acted"; SFX "strikingly perfect"; TGM "her particular brand of dry intelligence and emotional openness make her ideal to play the Austen heroine"; Time "superb"; SMH "excellent"). Thompson had already garnered praise the previous month for her performance as painter Dora Carrington in *Carrington* (LAT "a pulled-together, centered performance, the solid counterpoint to Pryce's necessary flamboyance ... has the presence capable of making Carrington's considerable emotional gyrations sympathetic at all times"; CT "breaks through her wholesome image wonderfully ... an intriguing mixture of innocence and impulsiveness"; G "transcends less than perfect casting").

Finally, at the very end of the year, two other actresses entered the Oscar race for their performances in films that went into limited release: Jennifer Jason Leigh for her struggling rock singer in *Georgia*, a film written by her mother (NYT "Leigh stunningly gives a piece of her heart to the main role ... a fierce, risk-taking performance ... scorching"; NYP "Leigh has a shot at an Oscar ... a performance so true it hurts"; LAT "exceptional ... what she accomplishes in 'Georgia' tears you apart ... she has taken a familiar characterization to another level so forcefully that we've never seen anything like it before ... excellent"; CT "a great, searing performance ... and she does it not by reaching out to the audience but by pulling us in"; SMH "astonishing"); and Susan Sarandon for her portrayal of a Catholic nun in *Dead Man Walking* (NYT "played with an unforced decency ... she's commandingly blunt, and she avoids cheapening her performance with the wrong kind of compassion"; NYP "a confident performance"; LAT "strong without even a breath of theatricality ... though her portrayal finally breaks through and gives the film much of its power, it is not as clear-cut or straightforward a success as Penn's work is"; CT "delivers one of her very best performances"; WP "leads [the viewer] gracefully into the belly of the beast [and] provides a perfect, understated counterpoint to Penn"; SFC "a stripped–down, gloriously effective performance"; TGM "Sarandon's performance is quietly reflective and hugely generous"; TT "infinitely subtle").

In the lead up to the Oscars, Shue won awards from the Los Angeles Film Critics Association and the National Society of Film Critics while Leigh took home the New York Film Critics Circle plaudit and Thompson collected the National Board of Review accolade. At the Golden Globes, meanwhile, Kidman and Stone received the Best Actress trophies. Kidman also won the inaugural Broadcast Film Critics Award (later known as the Critics Choice Award).

With the announcement of the Oscar nominations, however, the hopes of Leigh and Kidman were dashed. The Academy matched the Golden Globe (Drama) list with the result that both were overlooked. Previous winner Thompson was included for a fourth time while previous winner Streep earned her tenth nomination. Shue and Stone each received their first mention, and Sarandon was recognised for the fifth time (and the fourth time in the past five years). Yet to win a statuette, Sarandon was the strong favourite.

In addition to Leigh and Kidman, Oscar voters by–passed: previous winner Kathy Bates in *Dolores Claiborne* (NYT "[the film] revolves around [her] powerhouse of a performance ... does a walloping good job ... there's a big range of emotions within Dolores, and [she] finds them all"; LAT "gives a better performance than the film deserves"; WP "terrific ... as strong a performance as she's ever given"; TGM "superb"); Annette Bening in *The American President* (NYT "[has] the impossible job of delivering both heavyweight professionalism and adorableness [and she] isn't the contemporary actress for the job"; CT "[a] sparkling performance ... a revelation"; WP "effortlessly charming"; Time "ultimately winning"); Vanessa Redgrave in *A Month by the Lake* (NYT "one of her most delicious screen roles"; LAT "the actors are left to ham it up innocuously while their characters wait for the story to overtake them"; WP "[an] assured performance"; BG "startlingly touching"; TGM "nicely acted"); both Joely Richardson (LAT "superb ... dominates the film"; CT "brings a disquieting intensity to the role"; WP "intense ... [a] dominant force") and Jodhi May (NYT "masterly at capturing the psychological mystery behind this story"; CT "even better [than Richardson]") in *Sister My Sister* (G "[they] prove more than equal to difficult tasks"); Toni Collette in *Muriel's Wedding* (NYT "often veers towards caricature"; LAT "played with take-no-prisoners comic enthusiasm [and] the courage not to short-change Muriel's more off-putting qualities ... remarkable"; WP "Collette's performance is strong and fearless"; BG "excels ... she carries the film"; TGM "an elemental performance that you can't stop watching ... [she] resists the easy temptation to reduce Muriel's passage to a trite metamorphosis ... [Muriel is] never sentimentalized"); Rena Owen in *Once Were Warriors* (NYT "frighteningly credible"; NYP "[a] strong, gutsy portrayal ... unforgettable"; LAT "potent"; WP "[an] authoritative yet sympathetic performance"; BG "heart-rending and perfect, filling the screen not only with victimization but with miraculous depths of resilience and restorative energy"; TGM "powerfully played"; G "[a] towering performance ... excellent"; S&S "[the film gains] much of its dynamism from [her] sparky performance"); Amanda Root in *Persuasion* (NYT "perfectly portrayed"; LAT "an actress with the skill to win over an audience via quiet persuasiveness was necessary, and [she] does that beautifully"; CT "wonderful ... perfect"; BG "one of the decade's memorable breakthrough performances"); and Gong Li in *Yao a Yao Yao Dao Waipo Qiao (Shanghai Triad)* (NYT "superb ... a magnetic force, even in a role far outside her usual range ... [her] astonishing performance summons all the tawdriness, evil and eventual dignity the story demands ... extraordinarily sad and moving"; LAT "remarkable"; S&S "[her] greatest role so far ... sublime").

In the end, it finally proved to be Sarandon's year. The members of the Academy gave her a standing ovation as she received her Best Actress Oscar. "May all of us find in our hearts and in our homes and in our world a way to non–violently end violence and heal," she told the audience.

The previous year's BAFTA winner for *The Client*, Sarandon was not a contender at the British Academy Awards. The nominees were Helen Mirren in *The Madness of King George*, for which she'd been honoured at the Cannes Film Festival and been nominated at the Oscars the previous year in the Best Supporting Actress category, Oscar nominees Shue and Thompson and Globe winner Kidman. The winner was Thompson, who collected her second Best Actress BAFTA in four years.

1995

BEST SUPPORTING ACTOR

ACADEMY AWARDS
James Cromwell as 'Arthur Hoggett' in *Babe*
Ed Harris as 'Gene Kranz' in *Apollo 13*
Brad Pitt as 'Jeffrey Goines' in *Twelve Monkeys*
Tim Roth as 'Cunningham' in *Rob Roy*
• **Kevin Spacey as '"Verbal" Kint' in *The Usual Suspects***

GOLDEN GLOBE AWARDS
Ed Harris – *Apollo 13*
John Leguizamo – *To Wong Foo, Thanks For Everything, Julie Newmar*
• **Brad Pitt – *Twelve Monkeys***
Tim Roth – *Rob Roy*
Kevin Spacey – *The Usual Suspects*

SCREEN ACTORS GUILD
Kevin Bacon – *Murder in the First*
Kenneth Branagh – *Othello*
Don Cheadle – *Devil in a Blue Dress*
• **Ed Harris – *Apollo 13***
Kevin Spacey – *The Usual Suspects*

BRITISH ACADEMY AWARDS
Ian Holm
   – *The Madness of King George*
Martin Landau – *Ed Wood*
Alan Rickman
   – *Sense and Sensibility*
• **Tim Roth – *Rob Roy***

NEW YORK – **Kevin Spacey** – ***The Usual Suspects*** and ***Seven*** and
   Swimming with Sharks
LOS ANGELES – **Don Cheadle** – ***Devil in a Blue Dress***
BOARD OF REVIEW – **Kevin Spacey** – ***The Usual Suspects*** and ***Seven***
NATIONAL SOCIETY – **Don Cheadle** – ***Devil in a Blue Dress***
CRITICS' CHOICE – **Ed Harris** – ***Apollo 13*** and ***Nixon*** and **Kevin Spacey**
   – ***The Usual Suspects*** and ***Seven*** and ***Swimming with Sharks***

For his performance in *Devil in a Blue Dress*, Don Cheadle received rapturous reviews from critics who repeatedly described him a scene–stealer (NYT "the one to remember ... scene-stealing good company"; LAT "played with picture–stealing bravado"; WP "the real show–stopper [in a] jagged and rough [performance] ... he steals every scene he's in"; TGM "especially strong ... each time he's on screen, [he] lends the film the nervous edge it desperately needs"). Cheadle won plaudits from the Los Angeles Film Critics Association and the National Society of Film Critics and earned a nomination from the Screen Actors

Guild. In a stunning turn of events, however, Cheadle's name did not appear on either the Golden Globe or Academy Award nominations lists. Cheadle's shock omission contributed to the Rev. Jesse Jackson's targeting of the Oscar ceremony in protest at the lack of opportunities for peoples of colour in Hollywood. It was the first year since 1988 that no African–Americans were considered in the acting or directing categories.

Another highly-praised turn that failed to gain a mention from the Academy was Joaquin Phoenix's performance as a student seduced by his teacher in *To Die For* (NYT "rivetingly played with a raw, anguished expressiveness"; LAT "[the film is] given added poignancy by the off-center, sensitive performance of Phoenix"; CT "perfect"; WP "so tremulous and fragile that his compelling character distracts"; TGM "outstanding … [his] performance is so authentic, pitiful and funny, it seems found rather than acted"; FC "authentic").

Also overlooked were: Broadcast Film Critics Best Actor prizewinner Kevin Bacon in *Murder in the First* (NYT "[played] convincingly … [his] intense, tragic performance is the story's pivotal role"; LAT "[his] performance is adept technically and certainly a challenge physically"; TGM "without much help from the script, tries hard not to sentimentalize the victim-hero"); both Patrick McGoohan as King Edward I (NYT "played with delicious, coldblooded villainy"; LAT "Gibson has his ace in the hole: Patrick McGoohan is in possession of perhaps the most villainous enunciation in the history of acting"; WP "especially fun"; BG "brings stature to the role … convincing") and Angus MacFadyen as Robert the Bruce (NYP "memorable"; BG "brings a sentient awareness to the role") in *Braveheart*, the year's most nominated film; Gary Sinise in *Apollo 13* (NYT "terrific"; CT "convincing"); Paul Sorvino as Henry Kissinger in *Nixon* (NYT "uncannily impersonated"; NYP "altogether convincing"; BG "first-rate … rescues Kissinger from caricature"); both Delroy Lindo (NYT "played with insinuating power"; LAT "[a] strong and chilling performance"; WP "makes a prominent impression … terrific") and Thomas Jefferson Byrd (LAT "remarkable"; WP "burns himself on your memory") in *Clockers*; Robert Duvall in *Something to Talk About* (LAT "played with just the right insinuating swagger"; WP "the real standout … plays [the part] in full strut, filling in every corner of his character"; TGM "he mailed in his performance"); James LeGros in *Living in Oblivion* (NYT "an utter treat"; LAT "pointed [and] humorous"; WP "an inspired job"; SFC "LeGros is a scream"); David Morse in *The Crossing Guard* (NYT "captures the essential decency at the heart of the screenplay"; CT "lets us see how this once-reckless man's humanity has emerged from his prison ordeal"; WP "seems almost visibly imprisoned by his pain"); and Corin Redgrave in *Persuasion* (LAT "superbly played"; CT "wonderful"; BG "fun").

1995

The surprise inclusion on the Oscar short–list was James Cromwell as the owner of a pig determined to be a sheep dog in the Australian children's movie, *Babe* (WP "[a] wonderful, taciturn performance"). As he had been overlooked throughout the awards season his nomination was unexpected.

Also among the nominees were Tim Roth as a villainous English aristocrat in *Rob Roy* (NYT "does his malevolent best with the role ... does succeed in galvanizing the audience"; LAT "riveting ... when Roth's character is on screen, everyone's acting goes up a notch"; WP "I heartily recommend Tim Roth who is almost adorable in his utter loathsomeness ... makes such a wonderfully nasty villain"; BG "almost steals the movie"; TGM "wicked perfection"; SMH "played with a convincing sadistic edge") and Golden Globe winner Brad Pitt as a deranged mental patient in the science–fiction thriller *Twelve Monkeys* (NYT "giving a startlingly frenzied performance, he electrifies Jeffrey with a weird magnetism"; LAT "surprisingly funny"; CT "excellent [in] a deliberately alienating performance"; WP "wonderfully psychotic"; BG "Pitt's performance [is] surprising and entertaining").

The joint favourites for the Academy Award, however, were the BFCA co-winners: New York Film Critics and National Board of Review honoree Kevin Spacey as a partially–crippled, fast–talking criminal in *The Usual Suspects* (NYT "strong and fascinating ... the film's trickiest role is handled with supreme slyness"; NYP "[a] star–making performance"; WP "[a] rich character performance ... lets us in on the sly intelligence working behind [the character's] ineffectual pose"; SFC "[a] fine performance"; TT "particularly memorable"; G "very fine") and Screen Actors Guild winner Ed Harris as a NASA official in *Apollo 13* (NYT "terrific ... [a] tight, steely performance"; NYP "played fiercely well"; LAT "excellent [in a] linchpin performance"; CT "convincing"; WP "excellent"). Spacey's chances were aided by another flashy performance in the gruesome thriller *Seven*, for which he had also been cited by the New York critics and the NBR (BG "chilling ... if he'd shown up earlier, and there'd been more of him, he might indeed have been a match for Hannibal the Cannibal").

Oscar night proved to be a disappointment for *Apollo 13*. The film did not win the top award, and Harris went home empty–handed. The Best Supporting Actor Oscar went to Spacey.

In London, although *The Usual Suspects* shared the Best Film BAFTA, Spacey was surprisingly overlooked, failing even to garner a nomination. The British Academy instead shortlisted the previous year's Oscar winner, Martin Landau in *Ed Wood*, and three British actors: Ian Holm in *The Madness of King George*; Alan Rickman in *Sense and Sensibility* (WP "masterfully acted"); and Oscar nominee Roth. Despite strong support for their films, which both won Best Film BAFTAs, Holm and Rickman, who were both previous winners, were unable to claim a second trophy. The winner was Roth.

1995

BEST SUPPORTING ACTRESS

ACADEMY AWARDS
Joan Allen as 'Pat Nixon' in *Nixon*
Kathleen Quinlan as 'Marilyn Lovell' in *Apollo 13*
• **Mira Sorvino as 'Linda Ash' in *Mighty Aphrodite***
Mare Winningham as 'Georgia' in *Georgia*
Kate Winslet as 'Marianne Dashwood' in *Sense and Sensibility*

GOLDEN GLOBE AWARDS
Anjelica Huston – *The Crossing Guard*
Kathleen Quinlan – *Apollo 13*
Kyra Sedgwick – *Something to Talk About*
• **Mira Sorvino – *Mighty Aphrodite***
Kate Winslet – *Sense and Sensibility*

SCREEN ACTORS GUILD
Anjelica Huston – *The Crossing Guard*
Stockard Channing – *Smoke*
Mira Sorvino – *Mighty Aphrodite*
Mare Winningham – *Georgia*
• **Kate Winslet**
  – *Sense and Sensibility*

BRITISH ACADEMY AWARDS
Joan Allen – *Nixon*
Mira Sorvino – *Mighty Aphrodite*
Elizabeth Spriggs
  – *Sense and Sensibility*
• **Kate Winslet**
  – *Sense and Sensibility*

NEW YORK – Mira Sorvino – *Mighty Aphrodite*
LOS ANGELES – Joan Allen – *Nixon*
BOARD OF REVIEW – Mira Sorvino – *Mighty Aphrodite*
NATIONAL SOCIETY – Joan Allen – *Nixon*
CRITICS' CHOICE – Mira Sorvino – *Mighty Aphrodite*

Joan Allen "gives the best female performance of the year", declared Hal Hinson in The Washington Post about her turn as former U.S. First Lady Pat Nixon in *Nixon*. While critics were divided over the film, Allen's portrayal was almost universally lauded (NYT "played gracefully and touchingly"; NYP "moving [and] unforgettably well–played … heartfelt, professional work"; LAT "easily the most memorable performance in this film … exceptional work … able to get deeper into her character than anyone else [in the cast], Allen turns every scene she's in into eye-opening drama"; CT "stunningly played … adds such unexpected depth and dignity"; BG "wonderful [and] first-rate … Hopkins and Allen will be Oscar faves"; FC "beyond acting in its sureness – more like an incarnation than a performance"; SMH "[a] beautifully judged performance"). Allen won prizes from the Los Angeles Film Critics Association and the National Society of Film Critics, and was a strong Oscar contender.

The other early favourite was Mira Sorvino as a ditzy hooker with a grating voice and garish clothes in Woody Allen's *Mighty Aphrodite* (NYT "giving a breakthrough performance with sweet, flirty gusto"; NYP "bawdy, hilarious, genuinely touching ... she single–handedly saves the movie ... likely to get a supporting actress Oscar nomination for her efforts"; CT "dominates this movie so completely in its latter sections ... [the film is] a scrumptious showcase for [her]"; CST "Sorvino's performance is intriguing because, while never compromising Linda's exaggerated mannerisms, she subtly grows more sympathetic, until by the end we care for her, even though we still can't believe our eyes or ears"; BG "Sorvino realizes fully the comic potential she showed in 'Barcelona' holding the screen easily alongside Allen"; Time "wonderful"). Sorvino received the New York Film Critics Circle and the National Board of Review accolades for her work.

Sorvino also won the Golden Globe, but observers were uncertain whether the victory made her the Oscar frontrunner as her main rival was noticeably missing from the list of Globe candidates. Allen's absence was possibly due to uncertainty as to whether her role should be considered in the leading or supporting category. The Screen Actors Guild had defied the classification of Allen's part as a supporting role and nominated her as Best Actress.

In the supporting category, the Guild nominated Sorvino along with: Anjelica Huston in *The Crossing Guard* (LAT "[a] strong and emotional performance"; CT "the movie's high points include the scenes between Nicholson and Huston ... [she plays] effectively against [his sustained level]"; WP "as good as Nicholson is, Huston matches him"); Kate Winslet in *Sense and Sensibility* (NYT "wonderfully self–possessed"; LAT "best of the group ... impressive"; WP "masterfully acted"); Stockard Channing in *Smoke* (NYT "[a] good, sharp performance"; LAT "wonderful"; CT "excellent"; SFX "glorious"); and Mare Winningham in *Georgia* (NYT "admirably restrained in the more trickily muted of the two [sister] roles"; CT "a stunning performance"). Although Sorvino was expected to repeat her Globe win, the Guild unexpectedly chose Winslet.

Following her SAG win, Winslet became a serious challenger for the Oscar and was tipped to win the statuette by observers such as Kenneth Turan in the Los Angeles Times. The majority, however, continued to back Allen or Sorvino. The Academy nominated these three frontrunners along with SAG nominee Winningham and Globe nominee Kathleen Quinlan as an astronaut's wife in *Apollo 13* (NYT "played brightly and affectingly"; NYP "plays with balance and conviction"; WP "among the movie's best portrayed characters").

Oscar voters by-passed: Halle Berry in *Losing Isaiah* (NYT "impressive"; NYP "a characterization that is a triumph of both subtlety and substance"; LAT "[plays] with an all-out fervour"; WP "controlled in her transformation"; TGM "a knock out by any standard ... utterly convincing"); Ashley Judd in *Smoke* (NYT "[a] good, sharp performance"; LAT "wonderful [in a] brief, explosive cameo"; CT "excellent"; FC "[an] unnervingly raw tour–de–force"); 1994 Venice Film Festival honoree Vanessa Redgrave in *Little Odessa* (LAT "strong – although she overdoes the wailing"; CT "[infuses the film] with an openness and nervous dignity"; TGM "[a] finely shaded performance ... never lets the sick mother descend into cheap pathos"); Kyra Sedgwick in *Something to Talk About* (NYT "steals the show"; WP "has the picture's best lines, and she hits them dead-on"; TGM "mercifully, Sedgwick is on screen a lot, driving the movie between infrequent but potent comic highlights"); Uma Thurman in *A Month by the Lake* (NYT "a flashy performance"; WP "atrocious"; BG "amusingly played"; TGM "nicely acted"); Illeana Douglas in *To Die For* (NYT "played with terrific, snappish zest"; NYP "excellent"; LAT "a breakthrough role for Illeana Douglas"; WP "priceless"; TGM "[an] outstanding performance"); Catherine Keener in *Living in Oblivion* (WP "a hilarious study in subtle shifts of expression; nearly everything she does is a wonderful surprise"; SFC "brilliant"; TGM "a great performance"); Elizabeth Spriggs in *Sense and Sensibility* (NYT "uproariously blunt"); Amy Brennerman in *Heat* (BG "[an] arresting performance ... hypnotic"); and Mamaengaroa Kerr–Bell in *Once Were Warriors* (NYT "affecting"; LAT "potent"; TGM "this personification of generous innocence is carefully etched by Kerr-Bell in one of the film's finest performances ... heart-breaking"; G "excellent")

On Oscar night, it was Sorvino who emerged the winner. It was the second year in a row that the Best Supporting Actress statuette had been won for a performance in a film written and directed by Woody Allen.

Later the three main Oscar contenders – Allen, Sorvino and Winslet – lined up again for the prize from the British Academy. This time the home–ground advantage was with Winslet and the rising English star outpolled her American rivals and veteran English co–star Spriggs, to win the BAFTA.

1996

BEST PICTURE

ACADEMY AWARDS
• *The English Patient*
   (Miramax, 160 mins, 15 Nov 1996, $78.6m, 12 noms)
Fargo
   (Working Title, Gramercy, 97 mins, 8 Mar 1996, $25.8m, 7 noms)
Jerry Maguire
   (Tri–Star, 138 mins, 13 Dec 1996, $153.6m, 5 noms)
Secrets and Lies
   (CIBY 2000, October, 142 mins, 27 Sep 1996, $13.4m, 5 noms)
Shine
   (Monument, Fine Line, 105 mins, 22 Nov 1996, $35.8m, 7 noms)

GOLDEN GLOBE AWARDS
(Drama)
Breaking the Waves
• *The English Patient*
The People vs Larry Flynt
Secrets and Lies
Shine

(Comedy/Musical)
The Birdcage
Everyone Says I Love You
• *Evita*
Fargo
Jerry Maguire

PRODUCERS GUILD AWARD
Fargo
Hamlet
• *The English Patient*
The People vs Larry Flynt
Shine

CRITICS' CHOICE AWARDS
Big Night
The Crucible
The English Patient
Evita
• *Fargo*
Hamlet
Jerry Maguire
Lone Star
The People vs Larry Flynt
Shine

BRITISH ACADEMY AWARDS
(Best Film)
The English Patient
Fargo
Secrets and Lies
• *Shine*

(Best British Film)
Brassed Off
Carla's Song
• *Secrets and Lies*
Richard III

1996

Independent productions dominated the year's major Best Picture awards.

On 10 December, the National Board of Review awarded its top prize to *Shine* (NYT "powerful"; LAT "exhilarating ... popular filmmaking at its smartest and most persuasive"; WP "extraordinarily touching"; SFC "gripping"; BG "triumphant ... poignant and arresting at every turn ... it's not only one of the year's very best films; it's one of the most unforgettable"; Time "an Oscar contender"; TT "excellent"; G "[an] extraordinarily watchable and thoroughly commercial film that doesn't insult the intelligence ... direct, but not simplistic"; SMH "passionate [and] breathtaking").

Two days later, the New York Film Critics Circle honoured *Fargo*, which placed third in the voting by the NBR (NYT "stylish and entertaining"; NYP "a work of art ... mesmerizing"; LAT "something quite special"; CT "a scathingly funny, dark little crime comedy"; WP "works like a charm ... amusing, absorbing – but violent"; SFC "sure to become a classic"; BG "brilliant ... gruesome yet wildly, surrealistically funny"; V "very funny"; TGM "funny and fearsome in equal measure"; FQ "a fatuous piece of nonsense"). *Fargo* went on to win the Best Film prize from the London Film Critics.

On 14 December, *Fargo* finished runner-up in the voting by the Los Angeles Film Critics Association to *Secrets and Lies*, winner of the Palme d'Or at the Cannes Film Festival (NYT "tender and wrenching"; LAT "piercingly honest ... breathtaking"; WP "deeply touching ... reveals itself detail by searing detail"; CT "one of 1996's great films ... a beauty, a marvel ... a wonderful experience"; CST "funny ... magnificent"; SFC "heartbreaking"; BG "powerful, deeply felt and cathartic ... has a rare weight of cumulative impact ... easily one of the year's best movies"). *Secrets and Lies* was subsequently named Best British Film by the London Film Critics and finished runner-up in the National Society of Film Critics voting.

The winner of the NSFC plaudit was *Breaking the Waves*, which had earlier polled third in the voting by the critics in New York (NYT "a fierce, wrenchingly passionate film ... a bizarre and devastating experience ... visceral"; LAT "provocative"; WP "strangely banal and simplistic"; CST "emotionally and spiritually challenging"; BG "bold and brave").

1996

When the Hollywood Foreign Press Association announced the Golden Globe nominees on 19 December, all four prize-winners were mentioned for the Best Picture awards. The leading contender, however, with seven nods was *The English Patient*, which had been runner-up for the NBR prize (NYT "[a] fiercely romantic, mesmerizing tour de force … stunning … a purely cinematic triumph"; NYP "the most lavishly old–fashioned, satisfying romance of the year"; LAT "a mesmerizing romantic epic … captivates"; WP "awash in heart-rending emotions and gorgeous images, this is a movie to lose yourself in"; SFC "passionate and intelligent"; BG "a great epic romance … enthralling … magnificent"; Time "rapturous"). The film had been a Twentieth Century-Fox project, but the studio dropped it just weeks before filming was due to begin and Miramax took over. The New York Times and Time magazine both named it the year's best film.

The only studio film in contention for the Globe (Drama) was Columbia's *The People vs Larry Flynt* (NYT "a blazing, unlikely triumph … smart, funny, shamelessly entertaining and perfectly serious"; LAT "provocative and engrossing"; WP "enormously entertaining and surprisingly touching"; CT "winds up as a kind of screwy triumph"; CST "fascinating"; TGM "good dirty fun, flecked with enough wit to help you overlook the relatively barren characterization … [but ultimately] it's never fully convincing"). The film had been runner-up for the New York critics' plaudit.

At the Globes ceremony, Milos Forman was named Best Director for *The People vs Larry Flynt*, but *The English Patient* won Best Picture (Drama). In a surprise, Best Picture (Comedy/Musical) was won by the poorly reviewed *Evita* (NYT "breathless and shrill"; NYP "disappointing"; LAT "distant and devoid of emotional involvement"; CT "for all its coups and triumphs – the blazing performances, stunning cinematography, knockout crowd scenes and soaring songs – 'Evita' still seems less than a complete success, hollow somewhere at the center"; BG "more powerful on film than it was onstage"; TGM "extravagant, loud and long").

Three days after the Globes, the Producers Guild of America revealed its finalists. *The English Patient*, *Fargo*, *The People vs Larry Flynt* and *Shine* were shortlisted along with *Hamlet*, Kenneth Branagh's version of the great William Shakespeare tragedy which had never previously been filmed in its entirety (NYT "lavish … the style here is unabashedly flamboyant, but is works"; LAT "compelling [and] remarkable"; WP "intelligent [but] there's not a single thrilling moment in it"; CT "burningly imaginative"; CST "breathtaking … long but not slow, deep but not difficult"; SFC "extraordinary … a triumph"; BG "smashingly good"; Time "vigorous, thoughtful [and] thrilling"; TGM "audacious"). At 238 minutes in length, it was the second longest film ever released by a studio. Only the 1963 version of *Cleopatra* had been longer.

1996

On 11 February, the Academy announced its list of Best Picture nominees, and once again the independent releases dominated. Globe (Drama) winner *The English Patient* emerged as the Best Picture favourite when it led the field of contenders with twelve nominations. *Fargo, Shine* and *Secrets and Lies* were included, but *Breaking the Waves* and *The People vs Larry Flynt* were overlooked. The only studio film in contention was the romantic comedy *Jerry Maguire*, regarded by pundits as a surprise inclusion (NYT "bright, funny, tender ... disarming acting, colorful writing and true generosity of spirit keep it right on track"; LAT "a wholly unexpected film, as heady and surprising in its humor as in its emotional texture"; CST "a delight"; WP "good [but in the second half] the cuteness, comedy and poignancy are revved into overdrive ... cloying"; SFC "absorbing"; Time "altogether wondrous").

In early March, the frontrunner status of *The English Patient* was confirmed when it won the annual PGA accolade and Anthony Minghella was honoured by the Directors Guild of America. Less than a fortnight later, the tragic, romantic epic became the fifth film in history to collect nine or more statuettes from the Academy. Among its haul was the Academy Award for Best Picture. At their fifth consecutive attempt, Miramax had finally snared a Best Picture Oscar.

The four independent films that had been considered for the Oscar contested the Best Film BAFTA in London a month later and, surprisingly, *Shine* triumphed. The highly-favoured *Secrets and Lies* was presented with the Best British Film BAFTA.

The most notable independent film by-passed for Best Picture consideration was *Sling Blade* (NYT "indulgently long"; NYP "dull ... overlong and obvious"; LAT "mesmerizing ... stunningly original and powerful ... a strong, devastating film"; CT "a rich, emotionally complex tale"; CST "a work of great originality and fascination"; SFC "first-rate").

Other acclaimed but overlooked independents included: the previous year's European Film Awards Best Picture winner *Land and Freedom* (NYT "ambitious, often fascinating [but] also at times excruciatingly earnest and pedantically talky"; NYP "enthralling"; LAT "remarkable ... moving and thoughtful ... a passionate film"; CT "stunning"; WP "a bust in every respect – emotional, sensual and intellectual"; BG "there's nothing else like it around"; TGM "a grave disappointment"; TT "the nearest to greatness British cinema is likely to get this year"); *The Portrait of a Lady* (NYT "daring [and] a fascinating experiment"; NYP "compelling [but] static and posed"; LAT "impressive [and] never less than absorbing ... it succeeds"; CT "an odd, troubling film [yet] fascinating ... it has a gorgeous intensity, a haunting individuality, a reckless curiosity and a yen to avoid the conventional ... remarkable yet unsatisfying, stunning and tedious, beautiful yet labored"; WP "oddly un-charged, indistinct and even long-winded": SFC "a huge disappointment"; TT "fiercely stylised";

1996

SMH "a daring, intelligent and beautiful film"); *Lone Star* (NYT "[a] great, stirring epic ... perceptive and thoughtful ... gratifyingly complex and beautifully told; LAT "[a] triumph ... leisurely yet intense"; CST "a great American movie ... contains so many riches, it humbles ordinary movies"; WP "unapologetically literary ... lifeless"; BG "eloquent and richly layered"); *Big Night* (NYT "warm, funny and poignant"; LAT "a sensual feast"; WP "subtle, amusing... charming"; BG "bittersweet ... works perfectly as a piece of heartfelt naturalism"; Time "completely delicious"); *Welcome to the Dollhouse* (NYT "mordantly hilarious"; LAT "bitingly funny"; CST "intensely entertaining"; G "dark and bitingly funny"); *Flirting with Disaster* (NYT "a complete original ... fabulously funny ... side-splitting"; LAT "a beautifully balanced, frenetic comedy ... gets funnier and funnier as it goes along"; WP "deliciously hysterical"; TGM "one of the most inventive comedies in years ... wickedly funny"; G "the best example of modern screwball comedy that's come our way for a long time"); and *Dead Man* (NYT "a quirky allegory punctuated with brilliant visionary flashes that partially redeem a philosophic ham-handedness"; LAT "Jarmusch's best movie"; CT "strange and beautiful ... a visionary western ... watching this movie has an almost hypnotic effect ... a stunning picture: rich, eccentric, multi-layered and funny"; CST "strange, slow, unrewarding"; WP "offers many pleasures [but] unfortunately, the movie turns in on itself, becomes redundant [and] sluggish"; SFC "bizarre"; TGM "[a] sweet delight").

Notable studio films excluded from the top Oscar category included: *The Crucible* (NYT "vibrant ... handsome and impassioned ... succeeds so well"; LAT "this film is too frantic to be involving"; SMH "the obviousness of the material, its relentless inevitability, mars [the film]"); *Courage Under Fire* (NYT "gripping [but] conventional"; LAT "intelligent, involving and serious [and] honestly emotional"; WP "downright entertaining"; CST "fascinating"; WP "a downright entertaining combo of mystery, melodrama and action adventure"; TGM "as the film progresses, a certain amount of conventional garbage begins to seep into the narrative ... at the end, you feel torn between admiration and annoyance"); Venice Film Festival prizewinner *Michael Collins* (LAT "alive [and] provocative ... shows that history and drama make a powerful combination when the mix is right"; CT "stunning ... a shockingly brilliant picture"; BG "filled with compelling imagery and energized tragedy"); and *Romeo + Juliet* (NYT "fascinating [but] uneven ... a witty and sometimes successful experiment ... even at its startling best, it's as exhausting as it is bold"; NYP "breathless"; LAT "loud, exuberant and excessive [but] irresistible ... drenched in style"; CT "exciting and exasperating by turns"; WP "audacious [and] largely successful"; BG "[an] artistic disaster [but] seldom boring"; TGM "intriguingly wild [and] truly affecting"; G "it's the style of the piece that amazes"; S&S "extravagant [and] exhilarating").

BEST DIRECTOR

ACADEMY AWARDS
Joel Coen for *Fargo*
Milos Forman for *The People vs Larry Flynt*
Scott Hicks for *Shine*
Mike Leigh for *Secrets and Lies*
• **Anthony Minghella for *The English Patient***

GOLDEN GLOBE AWARDS
Joel Coen – *Fargo*
• **Milos Forman – *The People vs Larry Flynt***
Scott Hicks – *Shine*
Anthony Minghella – *The English Patient*
Alan Parker – *Evita*

DIRECTORS GUILD AWARD
Joel Coen – *Fargo*
Cameron Crowe – *Jerry Maguire*
Scott Hicks – *Shine*
Mike Leigh – *Secrets and Lies*
• **Anthony Minghella**
   – *The English Patient*

BRITISH ACADEMY AWARDS
Joel Coen – *Fargo*
Scott Hicks – *Shine*
Mike Leigh – *Secrets and Lies*
• **Anthony Minghella**
   – *The English Patient*

NEW YORK – Lars von Trier – *Breaking the Waves*
LOS ANGELES – Mike Leigh – *Secrets and Lies*
BOARD OF REVIEW – Joel Coen – *Fargo*
NATIONAL SOCIETY – Lars von Trier – *Breaking the Waves*
CRITICS' CHOICE – Anthony Minghella – *The English Patient*
LONDON
   (Director) **Joel Coen – *Fargo***
   (British Director) **Mike Leigh – *Secrets and Lies***

The New York Film Critics Circle and National Society of Film Critics each named Lars von Trier as Best Director for *Breaking the Waves* (NYT "stunning [and] hugely effective"). Despite these accolades, the Danish film-maker was overlooked for nominations from the Hollywood Foreign Press Association, the Directors Guild of America and the Academies in London and Hollywood.

Joel Coen won the plaudit from the National Board of Review and the London Film Critics for the comedy *Fargo*, for which he had earlier won his second Best Director prize at the Cannes Film Festival (WP "stylish"; BG "impressive"; G "there is hardly a false note").

When the Los Angeles Film Critics Association voted, Coen finished as runner-up to Mike Leigh for *Secrets and Lies* (NYT "expertly ... everything about this story unfolds beautifully, with a rueful, knowing intelligence"; LAT "unforced, confident and completely involving ... filmmaking to savor"; SFC "[a] marvelous achievement"; BG "at the top of his form"). Although overlooked at the Golden Globes, Leigh was mentioned for the DGA accolade, the BAFTA and the Oscar. Coen, meanwhile, was cited for all four awards, as was Scott Hicks for *Shine* (NYT "graceful ... [the film] has been so envelopingly directed that its emotional impact is powerful and real ... Hicks's direction has an elegance and dignity that rescue 'Shine' from the exploitative"; WP "has created a symphony of dramatic minor chords and major movements"; BG "told with restraint, fleetness and empathy ... stunning, electrifying filmmaking"; G "doesn't hesitate to tell the story as honestly as possible ... clearly Hicks knows to direct actors and make it seem as if they are hardly acting"; SMH "unsentimental [and] understanding").

While the recipient of the Globe was Milos Forman for *The People vs Larry Flynt*, who was included on the Oscar list despite being snubbed by the Guild (CT "keeps the story simple, lucid, plausible and human"), the winner of the DGA prize, BAFTA and Oscar was Anthony Minghella for *The English Patient* (LAT "delicately calibrated ... demonstrates [a] command of dreamlike mood and atmosphere on a large scale"; CST "a creative job"; SFC "astonishing").

Overlooked for Oscar consideration were: New York prize runner-up Jane Campion for *The Portrait of a Lady* (NYT "[her] approach [is] brilliantly eccentric even when it yields mixed results ... fascinating"; SMH "creates a beautiful atmosphere"); John Sayles for *Lone Star* (NYT "beautifully told ... every moment of the film is utterly right ... he handles this film's dozens of significant characters and the many interwoven strands of its story line with ease"; LAT "establishes himself in the top tier of American filmmakers"; WP "carefully crafted"; SFX "well-made"; BG "brilliantly and with assurance"); Billy Bob Thornton for *Sling Blade* (NYT "he directs with an abundance of long, flat medium shots that rob the film of intimacy and give it a sleepy pace"; LAT "[has] forcefulness as a filmmaker"; CT "his direction is artless, aiming his camera at his subjects and letting situations unfold at a natural, leisurely pace"; SFC "breathtaking"); Kenneth Branagh for *Hamlet* (NYT "solid showmanship"; LAT "brings the Bard's greatest tragedy passionately alive on the screen with remarkable clarity and meaning"; CT "in Branagh's hands, Shakespeare's great drama leaps to life ... he lets the play breathe, grow and sweep us away"; CST "dares to be bold"; SFC "[a] great achievement"; BG "astute"); Cameron Crowe for *Jerry Maguire* (NYT "a director with a distinctively touching, quirky style";

LAT "[the film] is fresh and refreshing due to Crowe's outstanding script and his ability as a director to bring everything to life on screen"; WP "has a heavy hand with it comes to feel-good pandering"; TGM "in sufficiently caring hands, it can be an attractive formula, but [he] appears to be wearing mitts here ... the rhythm is all stop-and-go, with too little 'go' to sustain a two-hour plus length"); Nicholas Hytner for *The Crucible* (NYT "vigorously staged ... is able to move the film with the dangerous momentum of a runaway train"; S&S "knows when to rest his story firmly on the shoulders of his cast"); Todd Solondz for *Welcome to the Dollhouse* (NYT "deft"; LAT "catches the unlooked-for humor in poignant, hurtful situations"; WP "extraordinarily sensitive"); David O. Russell for *Flirting with Disaster* (NYT "thanks to this film maker's fine comic acumen, the payoff is always there"; LAT "this is the hardest kind of comedy to do well, but you wouldn't know that from Russell's casual ease with the material"; WP "[his] direction is rough and jazzy"; TGM "directs the crowded proceedings with Swiss-watch timing and terrific verve"); Ken Loach for *Land and Freedom* (LAT "he exactly calibrates his emotional effects, avoiding over-dramatization and telling his story simply but with conviction"; CT "near the top of his form, bringing his diverse and sometimes astonishing talents to a rich and explosive subject"; WP "can't keep the story moving forward"; TGM "his anti-epic instincts are at odds with this purely epic rhetoric, and the film never quite finds a comfortable line between these competing extremes"; G "[his] depiction of [events] is direct, passionate and formidably informed by political conviction"); Jim Jarmusch for *Dead Man* (CT "creates a haunting atmosphere ... he distances us, replaces the usual tension and protracted action with sardonic humor and dry lyricism ... has never made a better film"); and 1995 Cannes Film Festival winner Mathieu Kassovitz for *La Haine (Hate)* (LAT "bold, even flashy style"; CT "has a vigorous, superreal style yet [the film] is done with such fire and conviction that it often seems real"; WP "does a terrific job"; TGM "stylish").

Arguably the most glaring omission from the Guild, Globe and Oscar short-lists was Baz Luhrmann for *Romeo + Juliet* (NYT "lets the camera swirl ... sustains a remarkable amount of fire [with some] striking inventions"; NYP "inspired"; LAT "well-planned, thought out to the smallest detail in the service of a unifying conception"; TGM "brilliantly kinetic, technically savvy ... achieves a truly affecting marriage of his splashy imagery to the original text"; G "a recipe for near-disaster which, somehow, [he] turns into near-triumph ... the adaptation works because Luhrmann knows how to tell a story, even if he pushes it along as fast and furiously as humanly possible"; S&S "elevates Shakespeare cinematically [and] makes the story a visceral epic"). The following year, Luhrmann won the Best Director BAFTA for his handling of the film.

1996

BEST ACTOR

ACADEMY AWARDS
Tom Cruise as 'Jerry Maguire' in *Jerry Maguire*
Ralph Fiennes as 'Count Laszlo de Almasy' in *The English Patient*
Woody Harrelson as 'Larry Flynt' in *The People vs Larry Flynt*
• **Geoffrey Rush as 'David Helfgott' in *Shine***
Billy Bob Thornton as 'Karl Childers' in *Sling Blade*

GOLDEN GLOBE AWARDS
(Drama)
Ralph Fiennes – *The English Patient*
Mel Gibson – *Ransom*
Woody Harrelson
  – *The People vs Larry Flynt*
Liam Neeson – *Michael Collins*
• **Geoffrey Rush – *Shine***

(Comedy/Musical)
Antonio Banderas – *Evita*
Kevin Costner – *Tin Cup*
• **Tom Cruise – *Jerry Maguire***
Nathan Lane – *The Birdcage*
Eddie Murphy
  – *The Nutty Professor*

SCREEN ACTORS GUILD
Tom Cruise – *Jerry Maguire*
Ralph Fiennes – *The English Patient*
Woody Harrelson
  – *The People vs Larry Flynt*
• **Geoffrey Rush – *Shine***
Billy Bob Thornton – *Sling Blade*

BRITISH ACADEMY AWARDS
Ralph Fiennes – *The English Patient*
Ian McKellen – *Richard III*
• **Geoffrey Rush – *Shine***
Timothy Spall – *Secrets and Lies*

NEW YORK – Geoffrey Rush – *Shine*
LOS ANGELES – Geoffrey Rush – *Shine*
BOARD OF REVIEW – Tom Cruise – *Jerry Maguire*
NATIONAL SOCIETY – Eddie Murphy – *The Nutty Professor*
CRITICS' CHOICE – Geoffrey Rush – *Shine*
LONDON
  (Actor) **Morgan Freeman – *Seven***
  (British Actor) **Ewan McGregor – *Brassed Off* and *Emma* and
    The Pillow Book and *Trainspotting***

Australian stage actor Geoffrey Rush was named Best Actor by both the New York Film Critics Circle and Los Angeles Film Critics Association and also claimed the prize from the Broadcast Film Critics Association. Consequently, he became the Oscar frontrunner for his portrayal of Australian pianist David

Helfgott in *Shine* (NYT "remarkable"; NYP "deserves Oscar consideration"; LAT "handles the challenge [of the part] superbly"; WP "deeply affecting [and] particularly memorable"; BG "stunning acting ... the performance of the year"; TGM "a serious candidate for a best-actor Oscar"; TT "brilliantly portrayed"; G "outstanding"; SMH "simply superb ... Helfgott has been so unsentimentally and frankly portrayed, so perfectly captured ... an Oscar-winning performance").

The National Board of Review selected Tom Cruise as a struggling sports agent in the romantic comedy *Jerry Maguire* (NYT "does some of his best real acting"; NYP "the best he's been in years"; LAT "shows a willingness to explore the darker implications of his usual persona"; WP "impressive ... at the top of his form"; V "one of his very best roles"; Time "brilliant"), while the National Society of Film Critics honoured Eddie Murphy, who played seven different characters in *The Nutty Professor*, a remake of the 1963 movie starring Jerry Lewis (NYT "[creates] a warm, fully-formed character [and] proves himself a surprisingly strong actor"; LAT "funny"; WP "[an] extraordinary comedic talent ... brings a tenderness and dignity to the performance that he has never shown before"; CST "very good ... he outdoes himself"; SFC "wonderful"; Time "astonishing ... terrific"). Murphy was a close runner-up to Rush in Los Angeles while Cruise came second to Rush in the voting for the BFCA honour.

At the Golden Globes, Rush and Cruise were victorious as Best Actor in a Drama and in a Comedy/Musical, respectively. Each was nominated for both the Screen Actors Guild accolade and the Academy Award.

Also nominated for the two prizes were: Ralph Fiennes as a burns victim recalling a love affair in the deserts of North Africa in *The English Patient* (LAT "[an] expert performance"; Time "especially superb"); former television star Woody Harrelson as porn magazine publisher Larry Flynt in *The People vs Larry Flynt* (LAT "Harrelson's intensity and charisma make Flynt magnetic"; SFC "the performance turns cartoony"; TGM "the script doesn't give Harrelson much room to round out the character"); and Billy Bob Thornton as a mentally–challenged man released from prison in *Sling Blade* (NYT "[an] arresting performance ... [he] is sadly affecting ... fully inhabiting this strange, lonely character"; NYP "[a] top–flight performance"; LAT "totally persuasive"; CT "a revelation ... transforms himself"; CST "memorable"; WP "stunning"; SFC "brilliantly played"; Time "[a] beautifully felt performance should earn Thornton an Oscar nomination"; TT "[his performance] sets the film apart").

Overlooked by the Guild and the Academy were: previous winner and New York prize runner-up Daniel Day-Lewis in *The Crucible* (NYT "beautifully acted ... played with a charismatic blend of guilt and fury"; LAT "gets to fully inhabit his part only in the film's later stages"; WP "well-acted"; S&S "faultlessly anguished"; SMH "full-on"); Venice Film Festival prizewinner

Liam Neeson in *Michael Collins* (NYT "roaringly good ... played with great magnetism and triumphant bluster"; LAT "perfectly suited"; CT "at his best playing Collins"; CST "a performance charged with zest and conviction"; SFC "commands almost every frame – he's taut, vital and intense"; BG "first-rate ... inhabits the character [with] physical authority and passion"); previous winner Anthony Hopkins in *Surviving Picasso* (NYT "played with superb swagger ... [a] vital performance"; LAT "equally frustrating and fascinating"; CT "has done a remarkable job with this role ... conveys an intellect and stature that suggest both master technician and artistic soul"; CST "another great biographical interpretation"; SFC "brilliant"; TGM "as a character study, the narrowness of this canvas leaves [him] with little room to act"); Antonio Banderas in *Evita* (NYT "an unexpectedly splendid job"; CT "even better [than Madonna] ... has a sardonic command of the role and the movie that helps pull the action into sharp focus"; BG "played with wonderful crackle and snarl"); both Robin Williams (NYT "mischievously funny"; WP "perfectly understated"; BG "underplays affectingly") and Nathan Lane (NYT "a solid but broad performance"; WP "inspired"; CST "a little too obvious and over-the-top"; BG "touching") in *The Birdcage* (LAT "[they] almost can't help being funny"); Chris Cooper in *Lone Star* (NYT "brings grit and dignity to the film's pivotal role, perfectly in keeping with the film's tacit style"); Johnny Depp in *Dead Man* (LAT "[a] riveting central performance"; CT "brilliantly played"; WP "[a] comically restrained performance"; TGM "fittingly ethereal in the title role"); Kenneth Branagh in *Hamlet* (NYT "[a] fine, robust performance"; LAT "soars theatrically ... has succeeded admirably"; WP "charges at the role fearlessly"; BG "exhilarating to watch"; TGM "superb ... a controlled, affecting performance – always evocative without ever floating up into tour de force bombast"); Leonardo DiCaprio in *Romeo + Juliet* (NYT "played radiantly"; NYP "mercurial"; BG "flat ... all listlessness and sullenness"; S&S "his performance is all raw emotion ... superb"); Stanley Tucci in *Big Night* (NYT "[his] comically reserved performance is a complete delight"; LAT "convincingly played"; SFC "entirely convincing"); Timothy Spall in *Secrets and Lies* (NYP "brilliantly underplayed"; CT "splendid"; WP "breathtakingly vulnerable"; BG "tender and sensitive"); and Ewan McGregor in *Trainspotting* (NYT "underplays Renton to dry perfection"; LAT "in McGregor the film has an actor whose magnetism monopolizes our attention no matter what").

Rush was victorious at the Screen Actors Guild Awards, and at the Oscars a month later he became the third SAG champ in as many years to claim the Academy Award. He was also honoured by the British Academy, winning the BAFTA ahead of Oscar nominee Fiennes, Spall, and European Film Award winner Ian McKellen in *Richard III* (who had been passed over for a nomination by the Academy in Hollywood the previous year).

1996

BEST ACTRESS

ACADEMY AWARDS
Brenda Blethyn as 'Cynthia Rose Purley' in *Secrets and Lies*
Diane Keaton as 'Bessie Wakefield' in *Marvin's Room*
• **Frances McDormand as 'Marge Gunderson' in *Fargo***
Kristin Scott Thomas as 'Katharine Clifton' in *The English Patient*
Emily Watson as 'Bess McNeill' *in Breaking the Waves*

GOLDEN GLOBE AWARDS

(Drama)
• **Brenda Blethyn**
  – ***Secrets and Lies***
Courtney Love
  – *The People vs Larry Flynt*
Meryl Streep – *Marvin's Room*
Kristin Scott Thomas
  – *The English Patient*
Emily Watson – *Breaking the Waves*

(Comedy/Musical)
Glenn Close – *101 Dalmatians*
• **Madonna – *Evita***
Frances McDormand – *Fargo*
Debbie Reynolds – *Mother*
Barbra Streisand
  – *The Mirror Has Two Faces*

SCREEN ACTORS GUILD
Brenda Blethyn
  – *Secrets and Lies*
Diane Keaton – *Marvin's Room*
• **Frances McDormand – *Fargo***
Gena Rowlands – *Unhook the Stars*
Kristin Scott Thomas
  – *The English Patient*

BRITISH ACADEMY AWARDS
• **Brenda Blethyn**
  – ***Secrets and Lies***
Frances McDormand – *Fargo*
Kristin Scott Thomas
  – *The English Patient*
Emily Watson – *Breaking the Waves*

NEW YORK – Emily Watson – *Breaking the Waves*
LOS ANGELES – Brenda Blethyn – *Secrets and Lies*
BOARD OF REVIEW – Frances McDormand – *Fargo*
NATIONAL SOCIETY – Emily Watson – *Breaking the Waves*
CRITICS' CHOICE – Frances McDormand – *Fargo*
LONDON
    (Actress) **Frances McDormand – *Fargo***
    (British Actress) **Brenda Blethyn – *Secrets and Lies***

Three major contenders for Best Actress Academy Award emerged at the Cannes Film Festival.

1996

Brenda Blethyn was honoured at the Festival for her performance as a lonely working class woman contacted by the daughter she gave up for adoption at birth in *Secrets and Lies* (NYT "unforgettable [in a] grand, heart–rending performance ... creating a central character so big and real she gives emotional life to an entire film"; LAT "exceptional acting"; CT "splendid ... [a] spellbinding turn ... with enormous skill and no hesitations, Blethyn is able to show us the woman and her emotionally threadbare present, while also suggesting the girl she was"; WP "breathtakingly vulnerable"; SFC "superb"; BG "[a] complex and heart-wrenching performance"; Time "bravura acting ... heroic work").

Also garnering acclaim was Emily Watson as a naive Scottish woman devoted to both God and her paralysed husband in *Breaking the Waves* (NYT "an astonishing screen debut ... [she] fervently and glowingly embodies Bess ... she creates Bess with a devastating immediacy ... a trusting, absolutely unguarded performance"; NYP "astonishing"; LAT "a terribly alive performance"; CST "touching"; SFC "transcendent ... unforgettable ... heartbreaking"; BG "the film belongs to Watson ... radiant ... unbearably vulnerable and touching ... raw and unprotected and heartbreaking ... astonishing"; V "extraordinary"; Time "acts volcanically ... she is pure emotion, naked, shameless, unmediated by discretion"; G "outstanding"; S&S "Watsons' performance, in which she seems to empty herself out onto the screen, is so believable") and Frances McDormand as a pregnant Minnesota police officer investigating a murder in *Fargo* (NYT "perfect ... wonderful"; NYP "nuanced"; LAT "a brilliant and unblinking comic performance"; WP "enjoys the comedic role of her career"; CST "should have a lock on an Academy Award nomination"; SFC "unforgettable"; TGM "played with luminous grace"; G "remarkable ... humanises the film").

At the end of the year, McDormand was named Best Actress by the National Board of Review and finished runner-up to Watson in New York and then to Blethyn in Los Angeles. Across the Atlantic, Watson was honoured at the European Film Awards while McDormand and Blethyn each received awards from the London Film Critics. In the voting by the National Society of Film Critics, meanwhile, Watson outpolled Blethyn for the Best Actress trophy.

At the Golden Globe Awards, Blethyn won Best Actress (Drama) ahead of Watson. Also nominated were: rock singer Courtney Love as a drug addicted former prostitute in *The People vs Larry Flynt*, a performance which Columbia promoted for the Best Supporting Actress Oscar (NYT "Love's performance is far too good to confuse one well-tended image with the other"; NYP "[a] revelation"; LAT "vivid ... one of the most original performances of the year"; WP "with an almost dangerous, steamy presence that almost fogs up the lens, she's the main reason to watch this movie"; V "impulsive, emotionally naked";

TGM "delivers a performance that doubles as an erupting volcano, all boisterous fire and decadent ash ... mesmerizing"); previous winner Meryl Streep as a single mother in *Marvin's Room* (NYT "impressive"; CT "plays the tightly wound Lee with expert brittleness"; CST "convincing"; WP "makes us acutely aware of her technique ... mannered [and] overstudied"; TGM "out of context, Streep's efforts could be an exercise in grandstanding [but] she gives the film the harsh edge it needs [and] the real measure of the quality of [her] work here is that she makes the other actors look good"); and Kristin Scott Thomas as the Englishwoman who has a tragic affair in *The English Patient* (NYT "played in a great, career-altering change of pace"; NYP "this is the performance that must make her a star"; LAT "radiant ... a gorgeous and magnetic performance ... makes the strongest impression [from among the cast]"; SFC "luminous"; Time "superb"). Thomas had also earned praise in the United States that year for the 1995 drama *Angels and Insects* (NYT "[a] precise, measured performance, perfectly in keeping with the story's tone"; LAT "especially well-acted"; TGM "first among equals ... her quiet intelligence steals the picture ... she breathes hard-suffering life into a feminist symbol ... note-perfect").

In a major surprise, McDormand was outpolled for Best Actress (Comedy/Musical) by singer-actress Madonna for her turn as Eva Peron in the musical *Evita* (NYT "does rise glitteringly to this strange occasion, fully inhabiting the role ... her performance is legitimately stellar and full of fire"; LAT "looks completely convincing"; CT "though the script and songs don't give [the part] enough depth or shading, she punches her numbers across with a star's confidence and force ... makes the show work"; CST "magnificent"; WP "unexceptional"; BG "she brings it off triumphantly ... in throwing herself at the role with a nonstop single-mindedness, Madonna does more than just merge with the icon"; V "superb"; Time "plays Evita with a poignant weariness"; TGM "serves her iconic purpose well"). The pop singer's unexpected victory resulted in a massive campaign to secure her recognition from the Academy.

One factor that seemed to work against Madonna's chances was her exclusion from the field of Screen Actors Guild contenders. Also absent from the Guild ballot was New York winner Watson. In contention were: Globe nominees Blethyn, McDormand and Thomas; Gena Rowlands in *Unhook the Stars*, a film directed by her son Nick Cassavetes (NYT "impressive acting ... delivers a wonderfully detailed portrait"; LAT "glows ... is in her usual top form"; WP "radiant"; SFC "compelling [and] moving"; TGM "the centrepiece ... impressive"); and BFCA prize runner-up Diane Keaton as the selfless spinster caring for her ailing relatives in *Marvin's Room* (NYT "a lovely performance ... works wonders"; NYP "[a] career–topping, incandescent portrait"; LAT "enormously touching"; CT "the movie's key is Keaton's open-hearted performance"; CST "convincing"; SFC "radiant [and] especially moving"; SFX "brings a depth to her portrayal rarely seen in movies"; TGM "one of the least affected performances of her career, an emotional transparency").

The Guild's choice of Keaton ahead of Globe nominee Streep for their performances as contrasting sisters in *Marvin's Room* was endorsed by the Academy, who nominated previous winner Keaton for a third time, but by-passed Streep. Also nominated were Los Angeles winner Blethyn, NBR winner McDormand, Globe and SAG nominee Thomas and New York winner Watson.

In London, the British Academy – which considered four candidates rather than five – also mentioned Blethyn, McDormand, Thomas and Watson. Keaton and Streep were not eligible for the BAFTA until the following year.

Absent from the Oscar list was Globe (Comedy/Musical) winner Madonna. Also shut-out of consideration were: Nicole Kidman in *The Portrait of a Lady* (NYP "accomplished ... sympathetic and charismatic"; LAT "the picture of clarity, purpose and single-minded intelligence as Isabel, but also colder than she perhaps needs to be"; WP "well acted ... bound to garner attention ... convincingly vulnerable"; SFC "a haunted, pained performance"; TT "played with tight control"); Laura Dern in *Citizen Ruth* (NYT "criminally negligent as Ruth is, she becomes outrageously funny and weirdly lovable thanks to Dern's sidesplitting performance ... [proves to be] a terrific physical comedian"; NYP "deserves some credit for her brave performance"; LAT "fearless ... plays her with gusto and absolutely no special pleading"; BG "[the film is] carried into some refreshingly nervy places by Dern's loose-cannon performance ... she never yields to any placating impulse"; SFC "never been better ... hysterically funny"; TGM "a disconcertingly real Method-deep performance"); Debbie Reynolds in *Mother* (NYT "played divinely"; LAT "returns to the screen triumphantly ... there's nothing cutesy in [her] performance [and her] self-confidence and old pro's perfect timing play beautifully"; CST "a triumph of perfect tone and timing"; WP "deft"; BG "[played] with such savvy and self-assurance ... [she has a] beautifully gauged way of etching a strong and independent older woman"; Time "she's the best reason for seeing this movie"); Gwyneth Paltrow in *Emma* (NYT "resplendent, gliding through the film with an elegance and patrician wit"; NYP "flawless comic timing"; LAT "engaging ... completely wins us over"; CST "sparkles"; WP "a breakthrough performance"; SFC "an intelligent performance"; BG "appealing"; Time "plays beautifully"); Meg Ryan in *Courage Under Fire* (NYT "unexpectedly tough and credible ... brings the right tricky nuances to the film's versions of her final battle, and makes each of them look possible"; LAT "Walden is not an easy role to play well and Meg Ryan brings to it skill plus the critical residue of accumulated likability that serves her well in the film's darker moments"; WP "transforms Walden from selfless warrior to blubbering coward without betraying the truth"; SFC "convincing"; TGM "completely credible"; S&S "with a commanding new tone, is as good as her underwritten role allows"); Claire Danes in *Romeo + Juliet* (NYT "played radiantly"; LAT "the performance of the film ... her Juliet has a freshness, directness and simplicity that is just what's called for"; BG "eyes alive with sentience and spirit, she alone brings Luhrmann's misconception to life"; TGM "does more than look her part ... striking straight at the ambiguous heart of the role, she offers alluring hints of a maturity far beyond her teen-age years"; G "about the best thing in the picture ... affecting"; S&S "brings a quiet resolution to her part, a maturity and pragmatism"); Lili Taylor in *I Shot Andy Warhol* (NYT "the film's extraordinary centerpiece, giving a great, funny, furiously alive performance"; LAT "a portrayal as luminous as it is gritty and fearless"; CT "a scaldingly brave, salty and funny job ... [her] acting often has a biting intelligence and nerviness, an almost clinical avoidance of cheap effects or sentimentality"; WP "entertaining"; SFC "her greatest performance to date"; G "perfect"; TGM "[an] evocative performance": S&S "plays it with seriousness [with] real moments of pathos"); Alison Elliott in *The Spitfire Grill* (NYT "she has a way of commanding vast empathy ... [she] stays fresh and captivating, sustaining her ability to surprise"; LAT "graceful acting ... uses her expressiveness to put a considerable amount of shading into this performance"; CST "a calm, strong presence"; WP "[a] haunting, almost feral performance"; BG "a beautiful and moving performance ... right on the money"); Amanda Plummer in *Butterfly Kiss* (NYT "[a] brave, blazing performance"; LAT "[a] galvanic portrayal"; CT "mesmerizing"; TGM "mesmerizing, doing what the script doesn't and grounding this craziness in a semblance of psychological reality"); Theresa Randle in *Girl 6* (NYT "by the end of the film, she's looking like a star"; CT "the film turns into a showcase for Randle's skills and range"; BG "enormously appealing ... holds the screen even when the thinness of [the] script becomes inescapably apparent"); eleven-year-old Heather Matarazzo in *Welcome to the Dollhouse* (NYT "poised and wonderfully deadpan"; CST "a dead-on performance"; WP "an astoundingly mature performance"; TGM "stolidly played"; G "an excellent performance"); and both Helen Mirren (NYT "scrupulously underplays"; CST "closely observed ... fascinating"; WP "imbues this movie with grace and assurance ... makes [her character's] evolution a credible, touching experience") and Fionnula Flanagan (NYT "magnificent ... conveys a mixture of ominous militancy and material vulnerability that is as compelling as it is utterly believable"; WP "provides [Mirren] with stunning support"; G "excellent") in *Some Mother's Son* (LAT "give wonderful performances"; TGM "both deliver powerful performances"; TT "powerful").

A month after being by-passed for the Globe, McDormand's Oscar chances were dramatically revived when she was named Best Actress at the Guild Awards. On Oscar night, as expected, she was named Best Actress for *Fargo*. In London, however, McDormand was outpolled for the BAFTA by Blethyn.

BEST SUPPORTING ACTOR

ACADEMY AWARDS
• **Cuba Gooding, Jr. as 'Rod Tidwell' in *Jerry Maguire***
William H. Macy as 'Jerry Lundegaard' in *Fargo*
Armin Mueller-Stahl as 'Peter Helfgott' in *Shine*
Edward Norton as 'Aaron Stampler' in *Primal Fear*
James Woods as 'Byron De La Beckwith' in *Ghosts of Mississippi*

GOLDEN GLOBE AWARDS
Cuba Gooding, Jr. – *Jerry Maguire*
Samuel L. Jackson – *A Time to Kill*
• **Edward Norton – *Primal Fear***
Paul Scofield – *The Crucible*
James Woods – *Ghosts of Mississippi*

SCREEN ACTORS GUILD
Hank Azaria – *The Birdcage*
• **Cuba Gooding, Jr. – *Jerry Maguire***
Nathan Lane – *The Birdcage*
William H. Macy – *Fargo*
Noah Taylor – *Shine*

BRITISH ACADEMY AWARDS
John Gielgud – *Shine*
Edward Norton – *Primal Fear*
Alan Rickman – *Michael Collins*
• **Paul Scofield – *The Crucible***

NEW YORK – Harry Belafonte – *Kansas City*
LOS ANGELES – Edward Norton – *Everyone Says I Love You* and *The People vs Larry Flynt* and *Primal Fear*
BOARD OF REVIEW – Edward Norton – *Everyone Says I Love You* and *The People vs Larry Flynt* and *Primal Fear*
NATIONAL SOCIETY – Martin Donovan – *The Portrait of a Lady* and Tony Shalhoub – *Big Night*
CRITICS' CHOICE – Cuba Gooding, Jr. – *Jerry Maguire*

The New York Film Critics Circle gave their Best Supporting Actor prize to Harry Belafonte as a gangster in *Kansas City* (NYT "brilliantly played ... the film's strongest dramatic moments belong to [him]"; NYP "played with relish"; CT "mesmerizing"; BG "played with an invigorating hardness he seldom has been allowed to display throughout his long career"). Finishing runner-up in the voting was Martin Donovan in *The Portrait of a Lady* (NYT "impressively provides warmth and focus"; CT "wonderful ... gives Ralph a true romantic quality"; CST "touching"; WP "sensitive"; SFC "touching") while Tony

Shalhoub placed third for *Big Night* (NYT "excellent"; BG "both mournfully funny and morally authoritative"). Donovan and Shalhoub were subsequently named as co-winners by the National Society of Film Critics but all three of these contenders were overlooked for nominations at the Golden Globes, the Screen Actors Guild Awards and the Oscars. The campaign for Belafonte had been left dead in the water when Fine Line Features opted not to finance any promotional ads or screenings for *Kansas City* which had been a commercial flop at cinemas.

The winner of the Los Angeles Film Critics Association and National Board of Review accolades was Edward Norton, cited for his first three film performances as an altar boy accused of murdering a bishop in *Primal Fear* (NYT "played with subtle cleverness"; LAT "strong"; CT "impressive ... he has to take his character through some bewildering changes [yet he] manages to keep us on edge, engrossed in the game"; CST "completely convincing in more ways than one"; WP "[a] brilliant debut"; SFC "brilliantly mixes timidity and rage in developing a character who is at once sympathetic and scary ... exceptional"; BG "compelling ... reminds us how mesmerizing a low-powered performance can be ... [a] dynamite performance"), as a groom-to-be in the musical *Everyone Says I Love You* and as a lawyer in *The People vs Larry Flynt*. Norton was victorious again at the Golden Globes for his debut in *Primal Fear* and became the Oscar frontrunner when the Academy included him on its shortlist.

The other serious contender for the statuette, also at his first nomination, was Cuba Gooding, Jr. as a talented football player in *Jerry Maguire* (NYT "an uproariously funny performance"; LAT "a brash success"; WP "brilliant ... playfully challenging Cruise at every turn ... just about walks off with the movie ... ebullient grandstanding"; CST "fine"; SFX "terrific"; Time "funny and flamboyant"; TGM "keeps it on the safe side of caricature – just barely at times, but he at least allows us to see beyond the cultural baggage and into the burdened man"). Gooding had become a serious candidate when he won the SAG award. Surprisingly, Norton had been overlooked for a SAG nomination.

Nominated alongside Norton and Gooding for the Oscar were: William H. Macy as the car salesman who arranges his wife's kidnapping in *Fargo* (NYT "perfect"; CST "brilliantly played"; SFX "wonderful"); Los Angeles runner-up Armin Mueller-Stahl as the domineering father in *Shine* (NYT "played devastatingly"; LAT "magnificently played ... when 'Shine' threatens to get gooey, the integrity of [his] chilling performance invariably stops it cold"; WP "modulates adroitly"; BG "riveting"; G "excellent"); and James Woods as a racist finally put on trial for murder in *Ghosts of Mississippi* (NYT "played with a fine panic-stricken timidity"; LAT "a showy performance"; WP "almost uncomfortable perfection"; CST "convincing"; SFC "chilling"). Many found Macy's shortlisting a surprise since he had more screen time in *Fargo* than Best Actress nominee Frances McDormand.

Overlooked were: Samuel L. Jackson in *A Time to Kill* (NYT "scorchingly terrific"; LAT "brings an anguish and an integrity to the role that no one else matches … his focus and intensity make even the most implausible speeches sound reasonable, and the film stops dead for all the right reasons when he's on screen"; CST "strong and convincing"; TGM "compelling … the best thing here, though the writing of his character is choppy"); both Hank Azaria (CT "outshines [his co-stars]"; WP "[the film's] best performance") and previous winner Gene Hackman (NYT "played with deadpan wickedness") in *The Birdcage* (LAT "[they] come off much better [than the two leads]"); Noah Taylor in *Shine* (NYT "played especially well"; WP "deeply affecting"; G "equally good [as Geoffrey Rush]"); Jonathon Pryce in *Evita* (CT "plays with silky expertise"; BG "works miracles with Peron, turning what onstage had been a crude caricature into a crafty operator, shrewdly weighing every exchange"; TGM "competent but largely wasted"); Gary Farmer in *Dead Man* (CT "brilliantly played"; WP "[an] amusing turn"; SFC "extraordinary"; TGM "it's Farmer's picture to steal, and the theft is immaculate – blending native reserve and Western irony, he strides the cultural divide with perfect aplomb"); Alan Alda in *Flirting with Disaster* (NYT "delivering wicked self-parody"); Derek Jacobi in *Hamlet* (NYT "stands out as a superb, quietly calculating Claudius"; CT "a beautifully worked out and infinitely subtle portrayal of weakness and cruelty masked by false solicitude"; WP "the movie's most interesting performance"; SFC "perfect"); Harold Perrineau in *Romeo + Juliet* (NYP "scene–stealing"); Ewan McGregor in *Emma* (NYT "gives the performance all the requisite flirtatious spark"; LAT "worth mentioning"); both Stephen Rea (NYT "stands out"; LAT "effective"; WP "played memorably") and Alan Rickman (LAT "impressive"; CST "played with shifty conceit"; BG "first-rate"; Time "wonderfully played") in *Michael Collins*; Matt Damon (NYT "memorable"; WP "impressive"; SFC "fine"; TGM "the stand out performance"), Michael Moriarty (LAT "impressive [and] convincing"; WP "excellent"; SFC "fine") and Lou Diamond Phillips (NYT "memorable"; LAT "an intense, focussed performance"; WP "stands out … excellent"; SFC "terrific"; S&S "it's only in [his] performance that the film offers any tellingly jagged edges") in *Courage Under Fire*; and Thomas von Brömssen in the 1995 Swedish drama *Lust och Fägring Stor (All Things Fair)* (LAT "beautifully acted"; TGM "touching").

On Oscar night, Gooding claimed the golden statuette. A month later at the BAFTAs, Paul Scofield was named Best Supporting Actor in *The Crucible* (NYT "beautifully acted … shrewdly plays"; LAT "impeccable work"; WP "well-acted"; SFC "remarkable"; S&S "[his] timing is awesome"). Scofield had been nominated for the Globe, but snubbed by Oscar voters.

1996

BEST SUPPORTING ACTRESS

ACADEMY AWARDS
Joan Allen as 'Elizabeth Proctor' in *The Crucible*
Lauren Bacall as 'Hannah Morgan' in *The Mirror Has Two Faces*
• Juliette Binoche as 'Hana' in *The English Patient*
Barbara Hershey as 'Madame Serena Merle' in *The Portrait of a Lady*
Marianne Jean-Baptiste as 'Hortense Cumberbatch' in *Secrets and Lies*

GOLDEN GLOBE AWARDS
Joan Allen – *The Crucible*
• Lauren Bacall – *The Mirror Has Two Faces*
Juliette Binoche – *The English Patient*
Barbara Hershey – *The Portrait of a Lady*
Marianne Jean-Baptiste – *Secrets and Lies*
Marion Ross – *The Evening Star*

SCREEN ACTORS GUILD
• Lauren Bacall
   – *The Mirror Has Two Faces*
Juliette Binoche
   – *The English Patient*
Marisa Tomei – *Unhook the Stars*
Gwen Verdon – *Marvin's Room*
Renée Zellweger – *Jerry Maguire*

BRITISH ACADEMY AWARDS
Lauren Bacall
   – *The Mirror Has Two Faces*
• Juliette Binoche
   – *The English Patient*
Marianne Jean-Baptiste
   – *Secrets and Lies*
Lynn Redgrave – *Shine*

NEW YORK – Courtney Love – *The People vs Larry Flynt*
LOS ANGELES – Barbara Hershey – *The Portrait of a Lady*
BOARD OF REVIEW – Juliette Binoche – *The English Patient* and Kristin
   Scott Thomas – *The English Patient*
NATIONAL SOCIETY – Barbara Hershey – *The Portrait of a Lady*
CRITICS' CHOICE – Joan Allen – *The Crucible*

The favourite for the Best Supporting Actress Oscar was seventy-two-year old Hollywood veteran Lauren Bacall who had won the Golden Globe and Screen Actors Guild accolade, and earned her first Academy Award nomination, as the mother in *The Mirror Has Two Faces* (NYT "elegant and sardonic"; WP "acerbic"; TGM "an arch turn"; TT "stylish"; G "a very nice performance").

   The dark horse in the field according to industry observers, was Barbara Hershey, recognised for the first time as the manipulative Madame Merle in *The*

Portrait of a Lady (NYT "fares outstandingly well here ... [a] brittle, poignant performance"; NYP "accomplished"; LAT "does magnificent work"; CT "wonderful ... she gives the character depth, sympathy and surprise"; CST "magnificent"; WP "delivers a superb dark-lady performance"; SFC "outstanding"). Hershey had won the Los Angeles Film Critics Association and National Society of Film Critics plaudits, finished as runner-up in the voting by the New York Film Critics Circle, and had been a nominee for the Globe.

Also nominated for the Oscar were: Joan Allen (for the second consecutive year) as the devoted wife in *The Crucible* (NYT "especially impressive ... [her] look of luminous simplicity suits the film's visual style and [her] immensely dignified performance captures the essence of Miller's concerns"; NYP "luminous"; LAT "impeccable work"; WP "well-acted"; SFC "remarkable"; Time "radiant"; S&S "a joy to watch"; SMH "top acting honours go to Joan Allen ... she steals the final scenes with her restraint"); NBR co-winner Juliette Binoche as the nurse in *The English Patient* (NYT "played with radiant simplicity"; LAT "[an] expert performance"; SFC "deft"; Time "superb"); and Marianne Jean-Baptiste for her feature film debut as the woman who meets her birth mother in *Secrets and Lies* (NYT "played with graceful reserve ... [she is] impressively strong and dignified in this pivotal role"; CT "splendid ... has the movie's most difficult role and she executes it perfectly ... the movie's grace note"; WP "breathtakingly vulnerable"; SFC "superb").

Despite a major campaign by Columbia, the Academy by-passed New York winner and Los Angeles and Broadcast Film Critics Award runner-up Courtney Love as a drug addicted former prostitute in *The People vs Larry Flynt* (NYT "Love's performance is far too good to confuse one well-tended image with the other"; NYP "[a] revelation"; LAT "vivid ... one of the most original performances of the year"; WP "with an almost dangerous, steamy presence that almost fogs up the lens, she's the main reason to watch this movie"; V "impulsive, emotionally naked"; TGM "delivers a performance that doubles as an erupting volcano, all boisterous fire and decadent ash ... mesmerizing").

Also overlooked for consideration were: Lynn Redgrave in *Shine* (BG "doesn't have much screen time to persuade us that she's the source of the emotional solidity and unconditional acceptance [Helfgott] needs [yet] without ever seeming to try too hard, she does"; G "excellent"); previous winner Dianne Wiest in *The Birdcage* (NYT "plays her hilariously"; LAT "[she and Hackman], both expert farceurs, come off much better [than the two leads]"; BG "makes something out of what was almost nothing in the original ... [she has] a marvelous way with comic subtleties"); Mary Tyler Moore in *Flirting with Disaster* (NYT "played deliciously"; NYP "hilarious"; WP "[an] exuberant, unrestrained performance"; TGM "it's a brave performance by Moore"); both Frances McDormand (NYT "outstanding"; LAT "effective") and Elizabeth Peña

(NYT "gives an especially vivid performance"; LAT "notable"; Time "touching") in *Lone Star*; both Juliet Stevenson (CT "perfectly played ... [deserves] a special hurrah"; SFC "vividly delineated") and Toni Collette (BG "has no peer at portraying the desperation of the chronically unmatched") in *Emma* (NYT both "vibrant"); Irma P. Hall in *A Family Thing* (NYT "portrayed with such zest and heart that she nearly steals the movie"; LAT "something to write home about ... brings such vivid life to the irascible, no-nonsense aunt ... clearly one of the most memorable supporting performances of the year"; CT "a breakthrough performance ... holding her own with two of the best actors in American movies, she imbues this crafty old woman with solidity, depth and a heroic quality"; WP "steals the show"; TGM "[the two stars] both are easily eclipsed by Hall ... [she] takes this cardboard figure and inflates her with dignity, bearing, pathos and charm, singlehandedly giving the movie much of its sharp humor and all of its emotional power"); Linda Henry in *Beautiful Thing* (NYT "wonderful"; LAT "fine acting ... a powerhouse"; TGM "works wonders as the battling mother"); both Julie Christie (NYT "heart–rendering"; LAT "perfect"; CT "poignant") and Kate Winslet (NYT "a fervent performance"; CT "bravura and modern"; CST "touchingly vulnerable") in *Hamlet*; both NSFC runner-up Renée Zellweger (LAT "with relaxed comic timing and the ability to glow without being glamorous, [her] way with the interplay of feeling and humor makes her the film's emotional center"; WP "captivating"; TGM "a revelation ... as written the role could be soft, but [she] redeems it with the most delicate of touches") and Bonnie Hunt (NYT "scene–stealingly good"; CST "a delight to watch"; TGM "a fetching cameo, turning what is potentially a man-hating stereotype into a warm, witty icon of sibling loyalty") in *Jerry Maguire*; and both Marion Ross (NYT "a warm, sturdy job"; BG "played in ways that project a touching envy") and Miranda Richardson (NYT "the film's one bright, funny turn"; CT "terrific"; BG "amusing") in *The Evening Star*.

Unsurprisingly, Miranda Richardson was also overlooked for *Kansas City* (NYT "a coolly understated performance"; LAT "has got all the shifts and unpredictability of this flighty, empty creature pat"). Following the film's disastrous performance at the box office, Fine Line Features decided against funding any promotional ads or screenings of the film during the awards season.

On Oscar night, sentimental choice Bacall was outpolled in a major shock. When Kevin Spacey opened the envelope, the winner was Binoche. Her award was one of nine Oscars awarded to Best Picture winner *The English Patient*. "I'm so surprised!" she told the audience as she accepted her statuette. "It's true I didn't prepare anything. I thought Lauren was going to get it ... and I think she deserves it." Binoche went on to win the Best Supporting Actress BAFTA, again ahead of sentimental favourite Bacall, and the European Film Award for Best Actress for her turn in *The English Patient*.

1997

BEST PICTURE

ACADEMY AWARDS
As Good As It Gets
  (Gracie, Tri–Star, 138 mins, 23 Dec 1997, $147.6m, 7 noms)
The Full Monty
  (Redwave, Fox Searchlight, 95 mins, 13 Aug 1997, $45.8m, 4 noms)
Good Will Hunting
  (Be Gentleman, Miramax, 126 mins, 5 Dec 1997, $138.3m, 9 noms)
L.A. Confidential
  (Warner Bros., 136 mins, 19 Sep 1997, $64.6m, 9 noms)
• *Titanic*
  (Lightstorm, Twentieth Century-Fox, Paramount, 194 mins, 19 Dec 1997, $600.7m, 14 noms)

GOLDEN GLOBE AWARDS
(Drama)
Amistad
The Boxer
Good Will Hunting
L.A. Confidential
• *Titanic*

(Comedy/Musical)
• *As Good As It Gets*
The Full Monty
Men in Black
My Best Friend's Wedding
Wag the Dog

PRODUCERS GUILD AWARD
Amistad
As Good As It Gets
Good Will Hunting
L.A. Confidential
• *Titanic*

CRITICS' CHOICE AWARDS
Amistad
As Good As It Gets
Boogie Nights
Donnie Brasco
The Full Monty
Good Will Hunting
• *L.A. Confidential*
Titanic
Wag the Dog
The Wings of the Dove

BRITISH ACADEMY AWARDS
(Best Film)
• *The Full Monty*
L.A. Confidential
Mrs Brown
Titanic

(Best British Film)
The Borrowers
The Full Monty
Mrs Brown
• *Nil By Mouth*
Regeneration
Twenty-Four Seven

NEW YORK – *L.A. Confidential*
LOS ANGELES – *L.A. Confidential*
BOARD OF REVIEW – *L.A. Confidential*
NATIONAL SOCIETY – *L.A. Confidential*
LONDON
> (Best Film) *L.A. Confidential*
> (Best British Film) *The Full Monty*

For many observers, it was a year in which the Academies in Hollywood and London each rewarded box office success ahead of artistic achievement.

The major critics groups all honoured the crime drama *L.A. Confidential* (NYT "resplendently wicked ... a vastly entertaining throwback ... nearly flawless"; NYP "fascinating"; LAT "compelling ... dark, dangerous and intoxicating"; CT "absolutely first-rate entertainment, a hardboiled thriller that breaks exciting new territory"; CST "seductive and beautiful, cynical and twisted, and one of the best films of the year"; WP "superb ... one of the most enjoyable shoot'em-ups of the year, a complex moral opera"; SFC "one of the best crime dramas to come along in years"; BG "steamy and riveting ... juicy dynamite"; Time "cinematic gold"; TT "sordid, brutal at times, but still darkly comic"; G "gets just about everything right"; S&S "triumphant"). It was subsequently nominated for the Golden Globe (Drama), the BAFTA and the Oscar, but was outpolled for all three accolades.

At the time, the special effects-laden romantic drama *Titanic* was the most expensive film ever made and the biggest money earner ever released. It received a record eight Globe nominations and a record-equalling fourteen Oscar nominations in an unprecedented fourteen categories. It took out both the Globe (Drama) and the Producers Guild of America prize, and later collected a record-equalling eleven statuettes from the Academy, including Best Picture. The film's success, however, was not entirely driven by its popularity. The blockbuster topped The New York Times list of the year's best films and finished third in the voting by the New York Film Critics Circle (NYT "the movie of the year ... magnificent [and] unforgettable"; NYP "utterly spell–binding ... [an] awesome spectacle ... unforgettable"; LAT "compels our interest absolutely [even though it is] hackneyed, completely derivative [and] a movie that reeks of phoniness"; CT "a wild mixture of delirious love story, exhilarating adventure and excitement"; WP "nearly inane melodrama ... the whole framing story is a cartoon ... [but] easily the most visually stunning experience of the year"; SFC "a fairly decent movie [but the script is] awkward and embarrassing"; BG "part of the impact comes from its sheer overdoneness").

Titanic and *L.A. Confidential* were each shortlisted for the BAFTA. The winner, however, was the English comedy *The Full Monty*, a surprise box office hit (NYT "irresistible ... casually hilarious"; LAT "heart–warming fun"; CT "refreshing ... takes a premise that seems ripe for broad, vulgar joking and turns it into a sly, even subtle, comedy"; CST "a lovable comedy"; WP "funny"; SFC "both funny and touching ... a wild and rousing crowd-pleaser"; TGM "a laugh and a half, a genial crowd-pleaser"). *The Full Monty* was an unsuccessful nominee for the Globe (Comedy/Musical) and the Oscar.

Also nominated for the Academy Award were the Globe (Comedy/Musical) winner *As Good As It Gets* (NYT "[a] tart, yet warmly entertaining film"; LAT "the best and funniest romantic comedy of the year"; WP "the episodes are wonderful ... but the movie loses all momentum"; SFC "almost as good as it gets"; Time "buoyant"; TGM "never quite as good as it could be") and the drama *Good Will Hunting* (NYT "smart and touching"; LAT "difficult entertainment to resist"; CST "smart, involving"; WP "[a] strikingly original drama"; SFC "powerful ... intimate, heartfelt and wickedly funny"; BG "[a] fresh Hollywood film ... brainy and heartfelt and right on target ... one of the year's best and most satisfying films"). The other nominee for the BAFTA, but overlooked in Hollywood, was *Mrs Brown* (LAT "a decorous, always involving costume drama"; CT "[a] fine new British film ... a dramatic portrait ... touching"; SFC "a first-rate historical drama").

Many observers expressed surprise at the exclusion from Oscar consideration of three highly-anticipated contenders: *Amistad* (LAT "engrossing ... [but not] the film it might have been, the film its director intended"; CST "a hollow triumph ... lacks emotional power"; SFC "admirable but disappointing"; BG "a big, bold, noble juggernaut of a film ... a powerhouse"); New York and National Society of Film Critics runner-up *The Sweet Hereafter* (NYT "wrenching ... mournfully beautiful ... brilliant"; NYP "passionate [and] emotionally charged ... a masterpiece of contemporary filmmaking"; LAT "exceptional ... [an] exquisite and overwhelming emotional tapestry ... powerful"; WP "superb"; SFC "intelligent"; BG "a shattering film, yet a cathartic one, hauntingly, unsettlingly beautiful"; TT "an unsettling film"); and *The Ice Storm* (NYT "[a] richly observed film ... elegant and deeply disquieting ... haunting"; LAT "does manage to have some affecting moments [but the filmmakers] can't succeed in making [the story] our concern"; WP "everything feels artificial"; SFC "impressive [but] never becomes the thoroughly satisfying psychological drama which it promises to be"; SFX "devastating"; BG "impeccable"; Time "[a] daring epic in miniature"; TT "brilliant ... thoughtful, beautiful and funny").

Also by-passed were: *Boogie Nights*, which placed third in the voting by the NSFC (NYT "everything about [the film] is interestingly unexpected"; LAT "a startling film ... impressive is the film's sureness of touch, its ability to be empathetic, nonjudgmental and gently satirical"; CT "a giddily trenchant drama and a weirdly engaging dark comedy"; CST "curiously touching"; WP "a stunning and powerful film"; SFC "great [and] impressive … a wonderful, sprawling, sophisticated film"; Time "compelling entertainment"); *In the Company of Men* (NYT "stunning … tremendously gutsy … a fascinating, divisive conversation piece"; LAT "not dramatically involving … [and] not satisfying enough to base an entire film on"; CST "remarkable"; WP "breathtaking … too compelling to ignore … pulls you in deeper and deeper … a fully realized movie, whose intelligence – despite its grim findings – dwarfs any Hollywood production"; Time "compelling-repelling"; TGM "an ingenious satire"); *Eve's Bayou* (NYT "every element of the film merges to create an atmosphere of extraordinary erotic tension and anxiety"; LAT "virtually unique … an inspired achievement … one of the year's best"; CT "deserves to be highlighted in a season of oversized action pictures"; CST "a film of astonishing maturity and confidence … if it is not nominated for Academy Awards, then the academy is not paying attention … one of the best films of the year"; BG "a languid, velvety dream of a film"); *The Apostle* (NYT "a lovely, heartfelt film … something unusual in cinematic turns"; NYP "heartfelt, funny and raw [but] short on dramatic tension"; LAT "something special"; CT "a unique movie, maybe a great one"; SFC "a warm, multi-faceted study"); *Wag the Dog* (NYT "swift, hilarious and impossible to resist"; LAT "a gloriously cynical black comedy"; CT "sharp, irreverent, fresh, glib and amusingly cynical [but] not a total success"; CST "absurd and convincing at the same time"; WP "a blithely unfunny comedy … a little too precious for its own good"); *The Wings of the Dove* (NYT "spellbinding … a magnificent film"; LAT "richly appointed and beautifully mounted [and] emotionally involving"; SFC "luscious, surprisingly complex"; Sp "luminous … a model of creative adaptation"; S&S "[a] skilful, graceful movie"); *Gattaca* (NYT "a handsome and fully imagined work"; NYP "fascinating … simultaneously stirs emotions and stimulates the mind"; CT "moving and subtle"; CST "one of the smartest and most provocative of science fiction films, a thriller with ideas … intelligent and thrilling … visually exciting"; WP "intriguing, eerily stylish but muddled"); *Oscar and Lucinda* (LAT "vibrant … audacious and unusual … has wit and style to burn"; CT "a strange, beautiful, intelligent and dissatisfying movie in which ravishing delights and memorable moments alternate with gorgeous tedium"; CST "charming"; BG "exotic and original … [a] magical experience"); and *Ma Vie en Rose (My Life in Pink)* (NYT "irresistible … a jolly modern fairy tale"; LAT "a remarkably assured first feature … a lively, high-spirited film that is at once light and serious, sentimental and smart … [a] graceful film"; WP "refreshingly direct, original and provocative"; TGM "[an] ingenious little film"; TT "marvellous"; S&S "a generous and at times gorgeous instance of cinema's true powers and promise").

BEST DIRECTOR

ACADEMY AWARDS
• **James Cameron for *Titanic***
Peter Cattaneo for *The Full Monty*
Atom Egoyan for *The Sweet Hereafter*
Curtis Hanson for *L.A. Confidential*
Gus Van Sant for *Good Will Hunting*

GOLDEN GLOBE AWARDS
James L. Brooks – *As Good As It Gets*
• **James Cameron – *Titanic***
Curtis Hanson – *L.A. Confidential*
Jim Sheridan – *The Boxer*
Steven Spielberg – *Amistad*

DIRECTORS GUILD AWARD
James L. Brooks
 – *As Good As It Gets*
• **James Cameron – *Titanic***
Curtis Hanson – *L.A. Confidential*
Steven Spielberg – *Amistad*
Gus Van Sant – *Good Will Hunting*

BRITISH ACADEMY AWARDS
Peter Cattaneo – *The Full Monty*
James Cameron – *Titanic*
Curtis Hanson – *L.A. Confidential*
• **Baz Luhrmann**
 – *Romeo + Juliet*

NEW YORK – **Curtis Hanson** – ***L.A. Confidential***
LOS ANGELES – **Curtis Hanson** – ***L.A. Confidential***
BOARD OF REVIEW – **Curtis Hanson** – ***L.A. Confidential***
NATIONAL SOCIETY – **Curtis Hanson** – ***L.A. Confidential***
CRITICS' CHOICE – **James Cameron** – ***Titanic***
LONDON
 (Director) **Curtis Hanson** – ***L.A. Confidential***
 (British Director) **Anthony Minghella** – ***The English Patient***

The choice of most of the major critics' groups was Curtis Hanson for the police drama *L.A. Confidential* (LAT "[has] a command of narrative drive … [his] clean, relentless storytelling sense [and] ability to draw us in [are the film's] quintessential asset"; WP "keeps a complex story coherent and absorbing"; BG "[the book is] transferred to the screen with visual style … Hanson wisely opts for narrative thrust instead of nostalgic noir flourishes"; G "against great odds, the director's ambition has been matched by his achievement"; S&S "manages to capture [the original novel's] uniquely raw and brutal tone within a much smoother and more elegant framework ... Hanson's real flair, however, is for casting").

Hanson was nominated for both the Golden Globe and the Directors Guild of America award. Also short-listed for both prizes were: James L. Brooks for *As Good As It Gets* (LAT "magically written, directed and acted"; CST "[a] supreme balancing act"; WP "has a gift for making life continue infinitely in entertaining episodes"); James Cameron for *Titanic* (NYT "succeeds magically ... rises to the occasion with a simple, captivating narrative style, one that cares little for subtlety but overflows with wonderful, well-chosen Hollywood hokum"; LAT "lacks the skills necessary to pull off his coup"; CST "flawlessly crafted"; WP "captures the majesty, the tragedy, the fury and the futility of the event in a way that supersedes his trivial attempts to melodramatize it"; BG "brings it off with high-tech bravura") and Steven Spielberg for *Amistad* (LAT "displays the director's impressive mastery of mainstream filmmaking [but] also show that [his] system is not working"). The final spot on the Globe ballot went to Jim Sheridan for *The Boxer* (NYT "[told with] stirring conviction"; LAT "strong direction"; CT "in the end, Sheridan squanders some of [the] mood, which is a shame"; WP "well-crafted"; TGM "its impossible to avoid the sense of manipulative overkill") while the DGA list was rounded out by Gus Van Sant for *Good Will Hunting* (NYT "directed with style, shrewdness and clarity"). Both honours were presented to Cameron.

In a major surprise, previous winner Brooks was overlooked for the Oscar even though his film was included on the Best Picture ballot and his leading stars were frontrunners for the Best Actor and Best Actress statuettes.

Others excluded from consideration were: Ang Lee for *The Ice Storm* (NYT "daring ... uses the mainstays of period filmmaking in subtly unexpected ways"; WP "[the film] has its moments, mostly thanks to Ang Lee's bright direction"; SFC "delicate"; SFX "studied"); Barry Levinson for *Wag the Dog* (NYT "directed in discreetly sidesplitting fashion"; BG "deadpan direction and pacing"); John Madden for *Mrs Brown* (LAT "careful direction"; CT "directs with a good sense of proportion and deference to his performers"; BG "guides the story deftly"; G "well-made"); Iain Softley for *The Wings of the Dove* (BG "precisely and acutely calibrated"; S&S "a smooth job ... skillful"); Robert Duvall for *The Apostle* (NYT "[his] unobtrusive direction moves the film at a leisurely pace that lets many scenes build the gentle, pleasing rhythms of small-town Southern life"; LAT "has been able to create drama that is no less gripping for being quiet and low-key"; CT "takes scrupulous care, uses rich observation [and] brilliantly, he brings out all the conflicts and contradictions"); Paul Thomas Anderson for *Boogie Nights* (LAT "impressive is the film's sureness of touch ... perhaps the most exciting thing about [the film] is the ease with which

[he] spins out this complex web ... he is a filmmaker definitely worth watching, both now and in the future"); Neil LaBute for *In the Company of Men* (NYT "startlingly assured work ... directs with such sparseness and precision"; WP "exceedingly well-made ... has a masterful hand"; TGM "using a static camera that stares from an impassive distance, he has the courage to stand back from his created characters"); Andrew Niccol for *Gattaca* (NYT "impressively fine-tuned ... presented with a cool, eerie precision"; CT "has a scintillating visual style"; CST "remarkable"; SMH "has a keen sense of the visual drama of it all"); Kasi Lemmons for *Eve's Bayou* (LAT "an inspired achievement ... there are no false notes [thanks to her] command of cinematic style"; CST "a remarkable directing debut"; WP "astute in documenting complex and contradictory emotions"; BG "beautifully crafted ... an impressive directing debut"); and Gillian Armstrong for *Oscar and Lucinda* (NYT "directed exquisitely"; LAT "highly assured"; CT "[the novel] has been transferred to the screen with meticulous care and dazzling craft"; BG "[the film] is the magical experience it is because she avoids polemic and connects instead with behavior ... masterfully inscribes the textures and ferment of a society").

The Academy recognised five first-time candidates. Globe nominees Cameron, Hanson and Van Sant were included along with Peter Cattaneo for *The Full Monty* (NYT "a splendid feature debut"; LAT "[the writer and he] balance broad humor with much affection"; WP "[the writer and he] handle this material with an engaging balance of good taste and outright slapstick"; TGM "shrewd enough to keep the broad farce on a short leash") and New York runner-up Atom Egoyan for *The Sweet Hereafter* (LAT "delicate and assured ... he directs [his cast] expertly [and] has done his best to suffuse this story with a sobering, almost stately restraint ...[he] understands how potent a deliberate pace can be, how effective it is in making already powerful material strong enough to tear at your heart"; BG "[moves him] from cerebral stylist to important filmmaker in full possession of a distinctive vision"; S&S "skilful and nuanced"). On Oscar night, as expected, the winner was Cameron.

In London, Cameron, Hanson and Cattaneo (whose movie was named Best Film), were all outpolled for the BAFTA by Baz Luhrmann for *Romeo + Juliet*. Luhrmann had not even garnered a nomination in Hollywood the previous year.

1997

BEST ACTOR

ACADEMY AWARDS
Matt Damon as 'Will Hunting' in *Good Will Hunting*
Robert Duvall as 'E. F. "Sonny" Dewey' in *The Apostle*
Peter Fonda as 'Ulee Jackson' in *Ulee's Gold*
Dustin Hoffman as 'Stanley Motss' in *Wag the Dog*
• **Jack Nicholson as 'Melvin Udall' in *As Good As It Gets***

GOLDEN GLOBE AWARDS
(Drama)
Matt Damon – *Good Will Hunting*
Daniel Day-Lewis – *The Boxer*
Leonardo DiCaprio – *Titanic*
• **Peter Fonda – *Ulee's Gold***
Djimon Hounsou – *Amistad*

(Comedy/Musical)
Jim Carrey – *Liar, Liar*
Dustin Hoffman – *Wag the Dog*
Samuel L. Jackson – *Jackie Brown*
Kevin Kline – *In & Out*
• **Jack Nicholson
– *As Good As It Gets***

SCREEN ACTORS GUILD
Matt Damon – *Good Will Hunting*
Robert Duvall – *The Apostle*
Peter Fonda – *Ulee's Gold*
Dustin Hoffman – *Wag the Dog*
• **Jack Nicholson
– *As Good As It Gets***

BRITISH ACADEMY AWARDS
• **Robert Carlyle – *The Full Monty***
Billy Connolly – *Mrs Brown*
Kevin Spacey – *L.A. Confidential*
Ray Winstone – *Nil by Mouth*

NEW YORK – Peter Fonda – *Ulee's Gold*
LOS ANGELES – Robert Duvall – *The Apostle*
BOARD OF REVIEW – Jack Nicholson – *As Good As It Gets*
NATIONAL SOCIETY – Robert Duvall – *The Apostle*
CRITICS' CHOICE – Jack Nicholson – *As Good As It Gets*
LONDON
   (Actor) **Geoffrey Rush – *Shine***
   (British Actor) **Robert Carlyle – *Carla's Song* and *Face* and *The Full
   Monty***

Twenty-seven-year old Matt Damon earned his first Oscar nomination in the
acting categories as a troubled loner with a gift for physics in *Good Will Hunting*
(NYT "Damon, very much the supernova, is mercurial in ways that keep his
character steadily surprising"; NYP "disarming"; LAT "charismatic ... strong

and believable"; WP "an impressive actor who makes Will's tormented problems very much his own"; SFC "a radiant performance ... sensational"; TT "mercurial"). Strongly favoured to win a statuette for Best Original Screenplay with co-star Ben Affleck, Damon was considered a rank outsider in the Best Actor category in which the other four candidates were all Hollywood veterans, three of whom were previous Oscar winners.

Dustin Hoffman received his seventh mention as a Hollywood producer in the political satire *Wag the Dog* (NYT "gives the kind of wonderfully funny performance that is liable to win prizes ... splendidly acted"; LAT "[he] is able to go way past caricature"; CT "[has] an actor's ball ... has rarely been funnier"; CST "his best performance in some time"; BG "'Wag the Dog' is mostly Hoffman's movie, and it's delicious to watch him pick it up and run with it"; TT "a characterization to cherish"; Sp "a beautifully pitched performance"). Robert Duvall, meanwhile, was nominated for a fifth time, as a Texan preacher in *The Apostle*, a film which he also wrote and directed (NYT "played with foxy charm and volcanic energy"; NYP "commands attention"; LAT "screen acting to cherish and remember ... has created as complete a person as the screen allows"; CT "powerfully and convincingly created ... if ever a performance in a recent American movie deserved to be called great, it's Duvall's as Sonny ... the performance of his life ... here is the rarest of movie achievements: a living, breathing human being, a character realized so expertly that we accept him as real ... convincing ... this performance glows with passion, seethes with emotion ... [there is] not one false, forced or shallow moment"; WP "Duvall's performance is not only flashy and expansive, it's delicate and finely tuned"; SFC "brilliantly played"; TT "subtle" and "complex"). Duvall had been named Best Actor by both the Los Angeles Film Critics Association and the National Society of Film Critics.

Considered the main contenders for the Oscar statuette were New York Film Critics Circle winner Peter Fonda as a beekeeper in *Ulee's Gold* (NYT "quietly astonishing ... the finest work of [his] career ... this film calls for deep reserves of backbone from its terse hero, and [he] supplies them with supreme dignity and grace"; LAT "a compelling performance ... his performance holds the film together"; WP "convincing"; CSF "reveals a depth of talent we did not suspect"; BG "magnificent ... he effortlessly projects integrity and idealism from beneath his gangly farmer's body language ... delivers a revelatory, deeply felt performance"; TGM "the performance of his career ... Fonda is a portrait of emotional repression"; TT "acting on one note – how did he ever win an Oscar nomination?"; S&S "Fonda wears his role as assuredly and naturally as if it were an old coat") and National Board of Review winner Jack Nicholson as an obsessive compulsive writer in *As Good As It Gets* (NYT "shameless scenery-chewing [but he is] delightfully reinvigorated by Melvin's miserableness"; NYP "winning"; LAT "to see Nicholson, who frequently gives the appearance of coasting through his roles, working as hard as he does here is a wonderful thing ... discarding almost all his familiar mannerisms, [he] takes more care than usual with this role, maintaining the mastery of bravura humor and timing that leads to big laughs while allowing his character to be honest and vulnerable"; BG "restraint and control [makes his] character so improbably engaging"). Winner of the Golden Globe (Drama), Fonda was the son of previous Best Actor winner Henry Fonda, and younger brother of previous Best Actress winner Jane Fonda. Winner of the Golden Globe (Comedy/Musical), Nicholson was the second person to earn an eleventh nod in the acting categories from the Academy.

When Nicholson was honoured by the Screen Actors Guild over the same slate of candidates shortlisted for the Oscar, many observers gave him the edge in the race for the Oscar. A fortnight later, he duly claimed his second Best Actor Academy Award. He was only the second man to have won a third statuette in the acting categories.

The BAFTA, meanwhile, was won by an actor overlooked in Hollywood: London Film Critics winner Robert Carlyle in *The Full Monty* (NYT "played with stellar presence and acerbic charm"; NYP "funny, edgy and painfully vulnerable"; CT "[his] performance is especially enjoyable ... vulnerably likable"; WP "turns on the charm"; SFX "touching"; G "the film is lucky to have [him] as its lead ... can play lightly but seldom misses a chance to get under the skin of his character").

Also mentioned for the BAFTA but snubbed in Hollywood were Billy Connolly in *Mrs Brown* (LAT "impressive"; CT "spectacularly played ... it's likely both Dench and Connolly will be well remembered in the year's-end film acting citations"; WP "marvelously well–acted ... wholly believable"; BG "[Dench and Connolly give] two of the year's most satisfying performances") and Kevin Spacey in *L.A. Confidential* (NYT "at his insinuating best, languid and debonair, in a much more offbeat performance than this film could have drawn from a more conventional star"; LAT "strong ... Spacey is the essence of corrupt charm"; CT "terrifically well-played"; BG "perfect, drolly superb ... there are a lot of facets to Spacey's suave, intelligence performance"). The remaining nominee, Ray Winstone in *Nil by Mouth*, was overlooked by Oscar voters the following year.

Arguably the most glaring omission from the Oscar list, however, was New York runner-up Ian Holm as a lawyer in *The Sweet Hereafter* (NYT "expertly playing a stubbornly benighted character"; NYP "brilliantly played"; LAT "masterful ... played with fluid precision"; CST "heartbreaking"; BG "played with tight-lipped messianic fervor"; SFC "masterful"; TT "overwhelming"). The most high-profile absentee, meanwhile, was Globe nominee Leonardo DiCaprio as the young hero in *Titanic* (NYT "played enchantingly"; CST "strong"). He was excluded despite the film's record-equalling fourteen nominations.

By-passed for their work in major awards-season contenders were: Djimon Hounsou in *Amistad* (NYT "he radiates extraordinary presence and fury ... acts his role quite movingly within the narrow confines of the screenplay"; LAT "projects a remarkable dignity and bearing that is exactly what the part calls for"; CST "depends largely on his screen presence, which is formidable"; SFC "magnificent"; BG "a powerhouse performance"); both Russell Crowe and Guy Pearce in *L.A. Confidential* (NYT "the two Australian actors qualify as revelations"; NYP "dazzling"; LAT "strong"; CT "terrifically well-played"; CST "convincing"; BG "jolting performances ... they set the pace for the film's explosive vitality"; G "a pair of nerve-tingling performances which deserve to stand in a parade of Oscar nominations"; S&S "they are both frighteningly driven"); previous winner Daniel Day-Lewis in *The Boxer* (NYT "impassioned acting ... once again breathes fire into the character ... his vitality lends real force to the film's moral arguments ... stirring"; LAT "believably hard and taciturn"; CT "seems both raw and fearsomely controlled ... lets his acting blaze"); Mark Wahlberg in *Boogie Nights* (NYT "the movie's special gift ... gives a terrifically appealing performance ... he does all [that's required] with captivating ingenuousness and not a single false note"; LAT "expertly acted ... is indispensable to the success of [the film] ... completely convincing"; WP "a remarkable centerpiece ... played with a perfect blend of dopiness and dash ... he owns this movie"; SFC "superb"); and Linus Roache in *The Wings of the Dove* (NYT "a calm, beautifully understated portrait"; BG "passionately acted"; TT "fine"; G "given a perfect veneer of lightweight sincerity"; Sp "riveting ...pulls off an effortless double-act of easy-going geniality and surging passion").

Also overlooked were: previous winner Al Pacino in *Donnie Brasco* (NYT "brings such color and pathos to a story that automatically invokes the breadth of his own career ... a character actor's field day"; LAT "an effective and modulated performance ... [he] shrewdly underplays Lefty, leaving us with an affecting portrait of an old warrior"; CT "excellent ... [in] the best acting part in the movie, [he] gives it everything the filmmakers could have wanted"; CST "poignant and subtle"; WP "tremendous ... dominates every scene he's in"; G "centerstage is almost always occupied by Pacino"; S&S "brings enormous dignity to the role"); both Andy Garcia (NYT "ingratiating ... but he doesn't rise comfortably to the intense pitch [the film] requires"; NYP "superb"; LAT "it is hard to imagine anyone doing a finer job"; CT "memorable"; WP "becomes ultimately tiresome"; SFC "fascinating"; BG "rises to the challenge") and previous winner Richard Dreyfuss (NYP "a riveting, Oscar–worthy performance"; WP "great"; BG "flawless") in *Night Falls on Manhattan*;

Cannes Film Festival prizewinner Sean Penn in *She's So Lovely* (NYT "[a] big, headstrong performance"; LAT "Penn does some of the best acting of his career"; CT "compelling [but the character] remains essentially elusive"; WP "terrific – the fact that he's so capable of exploding gives loaded presence to his understated moments"); Ralph Fiennes in *Oscar and Lucinda* (NYT "a courageous portrayal ... manages to make Oscar as bashfully likable as he is quaint"; LAT "[an] off-putting portrayal"; CT "it's also hard to swallow the tic-ridden performance of Fiennes ... becomes irritating to watch"; BG "[a] fiercely intense yet subtle performance ... unforgettable"; TT "extremely skilful [but] "cold""); Samuel L. Jackson in *Eve's Bayou* (NYT "powerfully acted ... in a performance that requires him to infuse the role of perfect father and dream lover with a demonic charge, [he] makes Louis at once irresistibly lovable and slightly terrifying"; LAT "[a] remarkably faceted portrayal"; CT "Jackson, in a tough role to play, is a standout"; WP "plays this role with a combination of charm and suavity that's hard to beat"; SFC "an assured, complex performance"); Aaron Eckhart in *In the Company of Men* (NYT "played shockingly well"; LAT "convincingly acted"; WP "brilliantly played ... is in chilling command ... played with unnerving presence"; SFC "compelling"; TGM "he's wonderful"); Martin Donovan in *Hollow Reed* (NYT "[an] exceptional performance"; LAT "a marvel of versatility"; SFC "[a] standout"; BG "the film pivots on the performance of Martin Donovan ... impressive"; TGM "[a] controlled, subtle performance"); John Lynch in *Angel Baby* (NYT "does a beautiful job of conveying Harry's mad love and terrible confusion"; WP "electrically convincing"; SFC "played with a heartbreaking vulnerability"; BG "as the gifted, troubled Harry, [he] is all razory sentience ... electrifying"; TGM "[a] riveting performance"); and Ian Hart in *Nothing Personal*, for which he was honoured at the 1995 Venice Film Festival (NYT "played with a wild, frightening fury ... [a] viscerally shocking performance"; BG "[a] potent performance")

1997

BEST ACTRESS

ACADEMY AWARDS
Helena Bonham Carter as 'Kate Croy' in *The Wings of the Dove*
Julie Christie as 'Phyllis Mann' in *Afterglow*
Judi Dench as 'Queen Victoria of Great Britain' in *Mrs Brown*
• **Helen Hunt as 'Carol Connelly' in *As Good As It Gets***
Kate Winslet as 'Rose DeWitt Bukater' in *Titanic*

GOLDEN GLOBE AWARDS

(Drama)
Helena Bonham Carter
– *The Wings of the Dove*
• **Judi Dench – *Mrs Brown***
Jodie Foster – *Contact*
Jessica Lange – *A Thousand Acres*
Kate Winslet – *Titanic*

(Comedy/Musical)
Joey Lauren Adams – *Chasing Amy*
Pam Grier – *Jackie Brown*
• **Helen Hunt – *As Good As It Gets***
Jennifer Lopez – *Selina*
Julia Roberts
– *My Best Friend's Wedding*

SCREEN ACTORS GUILD
Helena Bonham Carter
– *The Wings of the Dove*
Judi Dench – *Mrs Brown*
Pam Grier – *Jackie Brown*
• **Helen Hunt – *As Good As It Gets***
Kate Winslet – *Titanic*
Robin Wright – *She's So Lovely*

BRITISH ACADEMY AWARDS
Kim Basinger – *L.A. Confidential*
Helena Bonham Carter
– *The Wings of the Dove*
Kathy Burke – *Nil by Mouth*
• **Judi Dench – *Mrs Brown***

NEW YORK – Julie Christie – *Afterglow*
LOS ANGELES – Helena Bonham Carter – *The Wings of the Dove*
BOARD OF REVIEW – Helena Bonham Carter – *The Wings of the Dove*
NATIONAL SOCIETY – Julie Christie – *Afterglow*
CRITICS' CHOICE – Helena Bonham Carter – *The Wings of the Dove*
LONDON
(Actress) **Claire Danes – *Romeo + Juliet***
(British Actress) **Judi Dench – *Mrs Brown***

For the first time since 1971, four non-Americans were nominated for the Best Actress Academy Award; all of them English.

Included on the Oscar lists for the first time was Helena Bonham Carter as a scheming fortune hunter in *The Wings of the Dove* (NYT "the performance of her career"; LAT "outstanding ... subtle acting ... her most mature performance to date ... the success of this film rests on the work of Bonham Carter"; CST "played with bold imagination"; WP "her most mature performance yet"; SFC "her best performance to date"; BG "wonderfully alive ... passionately acted"; TT "subtle, appealing ... fine acting"; G "dominates the film"; Sp "riveting [with] a hard edge, a drive you rarely see from her"). In the lead up to the Academy Awards, Carter was the winner of the Best Actress awards from the Los Angeles Film Critics Association, the National Board of Review and the Broadcast Film Critics Association. She was also runner-up for the New York Film Critics and National Society of Film Critics prizes, and garnered nominations for the Golden Globe (Drama) and the Screen Actors Guild accolade.

Twenty-six years after she was last mentioned, previous winner Julie Christie received her third Oscar nomination as a former B-grade film star in *Afterglow* (NYT "radiant ... may be the best performance of her career"; NYP "persuasive"; LAT "brings her [character] alive in what is surely one of her finest roles"; CT "a performance full of soft contours, sharp edges and mysterious depths ... something really special"; WP "gets the Most Valuable Player award ... makes the greatest use of her moments [with her] gestures, tones and inflections"; BG "the film belongs to Julie Christie ... the greatest role of her career, playing a brokenhearted ruin with elegance, wit, self-possession, and more throwaway style ... one of the seasons' very best performances by any actress in any film"; TT "as moving and deeply textured as any [performance] in her entire career"). Christie narrowly outpolled Carter for the New York prize, which she had previously won in 1965, and also took home the NSFC plaudit.

Outpolling both Carter and Christie for the Globe (Drama) and earning her first Oscar nomination was theatre legend Judi Dench as the widowed Queen Victoria in *Mrs Brown* (NYT "played with splendid regal grace ... [she] melts Victoria's reserve with sly, wonderful delicacy"; LAT "[an] impressive, commanding performance ... [a] tour de force"; WP "marvelously well–acted"; CT "spectacularly played ... it's likely both Dench and Connolly will be well remembered in the year's-end film acting citations"; CST "wonderful"; WP "brings enormous dignity as well as a wealth of insecurities to the title role ... wholly believable"; SFC "[a display of] quiet intelligence and meticulous craft"; BG "[Dench and Connolly give] two of the year's most satisfying performances ... [she is] remarkable and affecting"; G "marvellously contained"). Dench finished third in the voting by the NSFC and won the Best British Actress award from the London Film Critics.

The fourth English actress nominated for the golden statuette was Kate Winslet, who garnered her second Oscar nomination as the wealthy woman who finds romance with a working-class artist aboard the titular luxury liner in

Titanic (NYT "played enchantingly"; NYP "superb ... perfect"; CST "strongly acted"; BG "convincing").

The British media was surprised when the Academy passed over these four nominees and presented the Oscar to Helen Hunt, a first-time nominee for her turn as a struggling waitress in *As Good As It Gets* (NYT "endearing"; LAT "excellent ... works beautifully with Nicholson's swooping highs and lows ... it's a class act"; SFC "gets high marks ... a tough, touching performance"; WP "is coming into her magnificent own; she plays fabulously off Nicholson"; BG "will win you over"; TGM "[a] breakthrough performance ... it's a subtle job of acting in less-then-subtle surroundings"). A relative unknown in Britain, Hunt was a major television star in the United States at the time having won numerous Golden Globes and Emmys for her performance on the long-running situation comedy 'Mad About You', and had made a successful transition to feature films with a starring role in the box office hit *Twister*. Although she had not received any of the major critics' accolades, Hunt had won the Globe (Comedy/Musical) and the Screen Actors Guild trophy prior to her win at the Academy Awards. Hunt was also helped by her status as the only American in the category. Over the previous twenty-five years the Best Actress statuette had been presented to a foreigner only twice: to Glenda Jackson in 1973 for *A Touch of Class* and to Emma Thompson in 1992 for *Howards End*.

In London, the British Academy presented the Best Actress BAFTA to Dench for *Mrs Brown* ahead of a field of nominees comprising Best Supporting Actress Oscar winner Kim Basinger in *L.A. Confidential*, Oscar nominee Carter, and Cannes Film Festival honouree Kathy Burke in *Nil by Mouth* whose performance would be overlooked in Hollywood the following year.

Many observers had predicted that Academy members would nominate Pam Grier, the former star of several 1970s blaxploitation films, for her role in *Jackie Brown* (NYT "an enjoyable comeback [but] she isn't an actress well served by quiet stretches of doing nothing before the camera"; CT "does a dazzling job ... she lives Jackie, fully convincing us"). Grier earned both Globe and SAG nominations, but was passed over by Oscar voters.

Other Americans overlooked included: previous winner Jodie Foster in *Contact* (NYT "a strong, fiercely intelligent portrayal"; LAT "an exceptional performance ... Foster is [the film's] lodestar, and when she is on screen, the film can't help but be engrossing"; CT "keeps pulling out her reserves of emotion, brains and commitment to bring Ellie alive ... an inspiring central performance"; WP "a lot of work goes into her performance, but the role is not an especially sympathetic or believably human one"; BG "ideal ... most of 'Contact' is played out on Foster's face ... she's a comet of purity and conviction"; TT "excellent, perfectly cast"); Joan Allen in *The Ice Storm* (NYT "beautifully acted ... especially poignant and graceful"; LAT "manages to make something real and human out of her character"; WP "splendid"; SFC "[a] nuanced performance"); Julia Roberts in *My Best Friend's Wedding* (NYT "dazzles, winning through sheer force of star personality"; LAT "especially good ... winning ... [a] relaxed and confident performance"; CST "does a skillful job"; SFC "at her vibrant best"; S&S "extremely engaging, showing restraint and range"); Jennifer Jason Leigh as Catherine Sloper in *Washington Square*, the role for which Olivia de Havilland had won her second Oscar in 1949 (NYT "fascinating ... [the character is] exposed with utter candor by the unstintingly gutsy Leigh"; LAT "[the role] is squarely within her range and interest, and [she] provides her with fine moments ... but even this performance as the film's solid center, could have used some modulation"; CT "movingly portrayed"; WP "a great role has found another great actress ... has the dedication, skill and lack of vanity to make this ultimate wallflower real ... a beautiful piece of work"; BG "throws herself into the role with abandon, playing Catherine's heightened emotions with the full force of something pent up, erupting awkwardly, but unstoppable ... initially heartbreaking in the nakedness of her emotional need, Leigh modulates beautifully the gathering strength beneath Catherine's all but hysterical release of emotion"); Joey Lauren Adams in *Chasing Amy* (NYT "fares better with frank, jousting dialogue than with shrill monologues"; LAT "[an] astonishing, selfless performance"; CT "strong ... a fearlessly emotional performance that's convincing even when it turns shrill ... startling intensity"; CST "a discovery"; S&S "[a] shrill performance"); and Robin Wright in *She's So Lovely* (NYT "[a] big, headstrong performance"; WP "exudes both toughness and vulnerability ... memorable"; BG "Wright's performance impresses with its bravery ... but her performance too seems merely a pale clone of Rowlands's in 'A Woman Under the Influence'").

Foreigners omitted from consideration included: both previous winner Emma Thompson (CT "yet another stirring performance") and her mother Phyllida Law (CT "wonderful") in *The Winter Guest* (NYT "polished and fine-tuned"; LAT "luminous portrayals"; WP "the result is stunning as the two play out a bickery drama ... exquisitely acted"; BG "the performances shine with the innate give-and-take of chamber music"); Emily Watson in *The Boxer* (NYT "impassioned acting ... beautifully conveys all of Maggie's melting ambivalence ... stirring"; LAT "an actress who is Day-Lewis' match ... especially effective"; V "[a] good, committed performance"; WP "brings an affecting mixture of frailty and strength to her role"; SFC "luminous"); Cate Blanchett in *Oscar and Lucinda* (NYT "marvelous [and] appealing ... [acts with] strength and vivacity"; LAT "beguiling"; BG "will firmly put [her] on the world map ... she blazes to idiosyncratic life ... unforgettable"; SFC "amusing"; Time "luminous"); and Michèle Laroque in *Ma Vie en Rose (My Life in Pink)* (SFC "excellent").

BEST SUPPORTING ACTOR

ACADEMY AWARDS
Robert Forster as 'Max Cherry' in *Jackie Brown*
Anthony Hopkins as 'President John Quincy Adams' in *Amistad*
Greg Kinnear as 'Simon Bishop' in *As Good As It Gets*
Burt Reynolds as 'Jack Horner' in *Boogie Nights*
• **Robin Williams as 'Sean McGuire' in *Good Will Hunting***

GOLDEN GLOBE AWARDS
Rupert Everett – *My Best Friend's Wedding*
Anthony Hopkins – *Amistad*
Greg Kinnear – *As Good As It Gets*
• **Burt Reynolds – *Boogie Nights***
Jon Voight – *The Rainmaker*
Robin Williams – *Good Will Hunting*

SCREEN ACTORS GUILD
Billy Connolly – *Mrs Brown*
Anthony Hopkins – *Amistad*
Greg Kinnear – *As Good As It Gets*
Burt Reynolds – *Boogie Nights*
• **Robin Williams**
   – *Good Will Hunting*

BRITISH ACADEMY AWARDS
Mark Addy – *The Full Monty*
Rupert Everett
   – *My Best Friend's Wedding*
Burt Reynolds – *Boogie Nights*
• **Tom Wilkinson – *The Full Monty***

NEW YORK – **Burt Reynolds – *Boogie Nights***
LOS ANGELES – **Burt Reynolds – *Boogie Nights***
BOARD OF REVIEW – **Greg Kinnear – *As Good As It Gets***
NATIONAL SOCIETY – **Burt Reynolds – *Boogie Nights***
CRITICS' CHOICE – **Anthony Hopkins – *Amistad***
LONDON (British Supporting Actor) **Rupert Everett – *My Best Friend's Wedding***

The early favourite for the Best Supporting Actor Oscar was sixty-one-year old Hollywood veteran Burt Reynolds as a 1970s pornographic film–maker in *Boogie Nights* (NYT "his best and most suavely funny performance in many years"; LAT "expertly acted ... especially good"; CT "wonderful ... has just the right aging charisma and frayed warmth"; CST "one of his best performances"; WP "a strong, benevolent force ... in top form"). Reynolds won plaudits from the New York Film Critics Circle, the Los Angeles Film Critics Association and the National Society of Film Critics, and also collected the Golden Globe.

Also nominated for the Globe were: Rupert Everett as the gay friend in *My Best Friend's Wedding* (NYT "things pick up when Mr Everett, who hasn't before had a role this buoyantly showy, arrives"; NYP "magnificent"; LAT "superb supporting work"; WP "wonderful, lively, spontaneous, brilliantly timed stuff"; Time "terrific"; TGM "brazenly swipes every scene he's in"; G "delivers some good lines with polished timing"; S&S "beautifully plays the role to the extent that he even survives the script's intentions to reduce him to an effete, camp clown"; Sp "virtuoso comic nimbleness ... shrugs off the performance with careless panache"); Anthony Hopkins as elderly former US President John Quincy Adams in *Amistad* (NYT "one of the most subtle performances of his career"; NYP "heavy–handed"; LAT "though his acting here is the kind of showy impersonation that exists largely on the surface, watching this masterful performer grumbling his way through the role of a cranky old galoot creates a surface that is satisfyingly rich and amusing"; CT "yet another fine character turn"; CST "powerful ... the heart of the film"; SFC "makes the most of his moments"); National Board of Review winner Greg Kinnear as the young gay artist in *As Good As It Gets* (NYT "affectingly played"; NYP "steals the movie"; LAT "does everything the part calls for"; SFC "[a] winning performance"; TGM "manages to elevate the gay-guy role somewhat above its usual function"); Jon Voight as a lawyer in *The Rainmaker* (NYT "another delicious bit of villainy ... a wicked delight"; LAT "he's terrific as Drummond"; CT "beautifully acted"; WP "Voight is a fabulous villain"; BG "Voight is enjoying a comeback on the strength of his zestful yet controlled character acting, and deserves to"); and Robin Williams as a psychiatrist in *Good Will Hunting* (NYT "wonderfully strong and substantial ... touching"; LAT "unconvincing"; CST "one of his best performances"; SFC "a soulfully rich performance"; BG "easily one of the best and most substantial roles of [his] career"; TT "[a] shapely performance").

When the Academy announced its list of nominees Globe nominee Everett was considered by many to be the most notable omission. Also overlooked were: John Travolta in *She's So Lovely* (NYT "terrific [in] a show–stopping performance"; LAT "irresistible"); James Cromwell in *L.A. Confidential* (NYT "mordantly good"; S&S "perfect"); Brian Cox in *The Boxer* (NYT "positively scary"; CST "played with a quiet, sad, strong center"); Jude Law in *Gattaca* (NYT "a sensational major movie debut"; SMH "scene-stealing"); Tobey Maguire in *The Ice Storm* (NYT beautifully acted"; WP "splendid"; SFC "[a] nuanced performance"; BG "flawless ... he gives the film its voice of unwarranted hope"); Jason Lee in *Chasing Amy* (NYT "darkly funny"; CT "strong"; TGM "gets the choicest [bon] mots ... [and] serves them up with lip-smacking relish"); Albert Finney in *Washington Square* (NYT "played splendidly, with caustic authority"; LAT "caricatured and overdone"; WP "gives us greater than a patriarchal tyrant ... gives us a human being"; SFC "effective"; BG "convinces"); and both Ian Holm (NYT "deft"; NYP "splendid"; LAT "one of his great screen roles"; CT "[a] superb, unimprovable performance"; WP "great"; BG "delivers the film's best performance") and James Gandolfini (SFC "terrific"; BG "squirmingly and affectingly played") in *Night Falls on Manhattan*.

Unexpectedly included on the Oscar ballot ahead of these contenders was Robert Forster, who earned his first mention as a bail bondsman in *Jackie Brown* (NYT "a wonderfully strong presence"; CT "shines"; CST "has the role of his career"). Critics' prize-winners Kinnear and Reynolds were each nominated for the first time, while Hopkins and Williams were each recognised for the fourth time.

Two weeks before the Academy Awards, Reynolds' frontrunner status was seriously challenged when the Screen Actors Guild presented its trophy to Williams ahead of Hopkins, Kinnear, Reynolds and comedian Billy Connolly for his performance in *Mrs Brown*, a role for which he was subsequently a Best Actor BAFTA nominee (LAT "impressive"; CT "spectacularly played ... it's likely both Dench and Connolly will be well remembered in the year's-end film acting citations"; WP "marvelously well–acted ... wholly believable"; BG "[Dench and Connolly give] two of the year's most satisfying performances").

Early on Oscar night, Mira Sorvino opened the envelope and announced that the winner was Williams. "This might be the first time I'm speechless," he joked as he collected the statuette.

Reynolds likewise went home empty-handed on the other side of the Atlantic. The winner of the BAFTA was Tom Wilkinson in *The Full Monty* (NYT "the film's most winning character"; NYP "nearly walks away with the movie"; CT "strong"; WP "quite touching"). Also nominated for the BAFTA were Everett, and Wilkinson's co-star in *The Full Monty*, Mark Addy (CT "strong"; WP "endearing"; Time "touching"). Despite honouring *The Full Monty* with four nominations, including Best Picture, the Academy in Hollywood had overlooked both Addy and Wilkinson for Best Supporting Actor nominations.

BEST SUPPORTING ACTRESS

ACADEMY AWARDS
• **Kim Basinger as 'Lynn Bracken' in *L.A. Confidential***
Joan Cusack as 'Emily Montgomery' in *In & Out*
Minnie Driver as 'Skylar' in *Good Will Hunting*
Julianne Moore as 'Amber Waves' in *Boogie Nights*
Gloria Stuart as 'Rose DeWitt Bukater' in *Titanic*

GOLDEN GLOBE AWARDS
• **Kim Basinger – *L.A. Confidential***
Joan Cusack – *In & Out*
Julianne Moore – *Boogie Nights*
Gloria Stuart – *Titanic*
Sigourney Weaver – *The Ice Storm*

SCREEN ACTORS GUILD
• **Kim Basinger – *L.A. Confidential***
Minnie Driver – *Good Will Hunting*
Alison Elliott – *The Wings of the Dove*
Julianne Moore – *Boogie Nights*
• **Gloria Stuart – *Titanic***

BRITISH ACADEMY AWARDS
Jennifer Ehle – *Wilde*
Lesley Sharp – *The Full Monty*
Zoë Wanamaker – *Wilde*
• **Sigourney Weaver**
 – *The Ice Storm*

NEW YORK – Joan Cusack – *In & Out*
LOS ANGELES – Julianne Moore – *Boogie Nights*
BOARD OF REVIEW – Anne Heche – *Donnie Brasco*
NATIONAL SOCIETY – Julianne Moore – *Boogie Nights*
CRITICS' CHOICE – Joan Cusack – *In & Out*
LONDON (British Supporting Actress) **Minnie Driver – *Big Night* and**
 Grosse Point Blank* and *Sleepers

"There must be some mistake," said Sigourney Weaver as she accepted the Best Supporting Actress trophy at the British Academy Awards. "It's not possible that 'Ice Storm' should receive a reward!" Her comment was a rebuke to the members of the Academy in Hollywood who had not recognised *The Ice Storm*, one of the year's most acclaimed films, with a single nomination. The most glaring omission from the Oscar ballot, Weaver won the BAFTA for playing a self-centred 1970s New England housewife who has an affair with her neighbour (NYT "beautifully acted … striking"; WP "splendid"; CST "[a] quietly observant performance"; SFC "[a] nuanced performance"; BG "flawless ... played with acid wit and ice-pick tongue").

Surprisingly, Weaver won the accolade in London ahead of three English nominees: Lesley Sharp in *The Full Monty* (CT "strong") and both Jennifer Ehle and Zoë Wanamaker in the biopic *Wilde*. Sharp, like Weaver, had been overlooked by Oscar voters earlier in the season. Ehle and Wanamaker, meanwhile, would be by-passed for consideration in Hollywood the following year.

While Weaver was the most notable absentee from the Oscar ballot, other worthy contenders passed over included: Sarah Polley in *The Sweet Hereafter* (NYT "particularly good ... an eerily incandescent performance"; NYP "luminous"; LAT "[played] most poignantly ... an especially subtle performance"; SFC "especially touching"; BG "especially unforgettable"); previous winner Maggie Smith in *Washington Square* (NYT "steals many a scene"; LAT "caricatured and overdone"; CT "a comic tour de force"; WP "ditheringly delicious"; SFC "indulges in blatant scene-stealing ... she'll probably win an Oscar nomination"); Debbi Morgan in *Eve's Bayou* (NYT "powerfully acted"; LAT "vivid ... [a] remarkably faceted portrayal"; Time "especially fine work"); and Alison Elliott in *The Wings of the Dove* (NYT "registers every nuance of Millie's doubt ... heartbreaking"; SFC "played beautifully"; TT "fine acting"; Sp "riveting ... pitches it absolutely right").

Also left out of consideration were: National Board of Review winner Anne Heche both as an undercover agent's wife in *Donnie Brasco* (NYT "does well with what could have been the thankless role of [the] wife") and a Presidential aide in *Wag the Dog* (NYT "splendidly acted ... ruthlessly effective"; BG "fun"); Pauline Collins in *Paradise Road* (NYT "strong"; LAT "stands out ... smoothly handles the role"; CT "excellent"; WP "[her] assured performance as a missionary with courage stands out the most [in the stellar cast]"); Christina Ricci in *The Ice Storm* (NYT "beautifully acted ... touchingly real"; WP "splendid"; SFX "does a good job"; BG "flawless ... the film's most faceted performance"); Claire Danes in *The Rainmaker* (NYT "first–rate, giving a stirring, wistful performance that is free of false ingenuousness"; LAT "[her] strength as Kelly Riker, and the sincere chemistry between her and Damon, offset the cliché [of the storyline]"; CT "beautifully acted"); Uma Thurman in *Gattaca* (NYT "bewitching"); Gena Rowlands in *She's So Lovely* (NYT "a brief but wonderful appearance"; WP "a nice, supporting performance"); Joely Richardson in *Hollow Reed* (NYT "[an] exceptional performance ... delivers a compellingly scary portrait of a determined woman driven by revenge"; LAT "wisely doesn't ask us to try to like Hannah"; BG "plays [the role] in acutely observed fashion"; TGM "the actors respond with controlled, subtle performances, especially Richardson"); and both Farrah Fawcett (NYT "played convincingly"; LAT "makes us believe") and Miranda Richardson (NYT "first rate"; NYP "brilliant"; CT "[a] letter-perfect portrayal"; SFC "good") in *The Apostle* (WP both "outstanding").

Two critics' prize-winners were included on the Academy's ballot. New York Film Critics Circle winner Joan Cusack earned her second nomination as the fiancée of a high school drama teacher in *In & Out* (NYT "especially good"; LAT "has the first role in a long time that she can really throw herself into ... [a] pleasure"; CT "gets to steal a few scenes, though you wish [the director] had encouraged her to tone down the cartoonishness instead of playing it up"; WP "dazzlingly endearing"; BG "[a] knockout ... one of the most reliably brilliant comedians around ... her way of putting together what in most hands would be routine ingredients makes you want to hug her – as soon as you stop laughing") while Los Angeles Film Critics Association and National Society of Film Critics winner Julianne Moore received her first nomination as a 1970s porn star in *Boogie Nights* (NYT "wonderful ... her studiously bad acting in movie-making scenes is perfect"; LAT "expertly acted ... provides Amber Waves with a sad and inescapable poignancy"; CT "looks and moves exactly right"; WP "has an almost sepulchral magnetism as the quietly tormented den mother"; SFC "astonishing").

Also nominated was Minnie Driver as a Harvard medical student in *Good Will Hunting* (NYT "adds further charm to an already wise, inviting story"). Named Best British Supporting Actress by the London Film Critics for performances in three other films, her turn in *Good Will Hunting* would earn her the same prize again the following year.

The frontrunners for the Oscar, however, were the first-time candidates who, just two weeks prior to the Academy Awards, had shared the Screen Actors Guild accolade: Kim Basinger as a Veronica Lake-lookalike prostitute in *L.A. Confidential*, a role for which she was considered for the Best Actress BAFTA (NYP "dazzling"; LAT "provides the film's emotional center"; CST "convincing"; SFC "a poignant performance"; Time "entrancing"; G "floods Lynn's soul with a bruised virtue") and Gloria Stuart as an elderly survivor of the sinking of the Titanic who recalls her on-board romance in *Titanic* (NYT "played spiritedly"; NYP "superb ... luminous"; CST "strongly acted").

Basinger took home the Golden Globe, but there was strong sentimental support for Stuart. At eighty-seven, she was the oldest person to receive a nomination in the acting categories as well as a respected Hollywood veteran who had been a founder member of the Screen Actors Guild in 1933.

On Oscar night, *Titanic* garnered eleven statuettes from fourteen nominations. One of the three categories in which it did not collect an award was Best Supporting Actress. The winner was Basinger.

1998

BEST PICTURE

ACADEMY AWARDS
Elizabeth
   (Working Title, PolyGram, 124 mins, 6 Nov 1998, $30.0m, 7 noms)
Saving Private Ryan
   (Amblin, DreamWorks, Paramount, 170 mins, 24 Jul 1998, $216.1m, 11 noms)
• *Shakespeare in Love*
   (Miramax, Universal, 122 mins, 11 Dec 1998, $100.24m, 13 noms)
The Thin Red Line
   (Phoenix, Twentieth Century-Fox, 170 mins, 23 Dec 1998, $36.4m, 7 noms)
La Vita è Bella (Life is Beautiful)
   (Cecchi Gori, Miramax, 118 mins, 23 Oct 1998, $57.6m, 7 noms)

GOLDEN GLOBE AWARDS

(Drama)
Elizabeth
Gods and Monsters
The Horse Whisperer
• *Saving Private Ryan*
The Truman Show

(Comedy/Musical)
Bulworth
The Mask of Zorro
Patch Adams
• *Shakespeare in Love*
Still Crazy
There's Something About Mary

PRODUCERS GUILD AWARD
Gods and Monsters
La Vita è Bella (Life is Beautiful)
• *Saving Private Ryan*
Shakespeare in Love
Waking Ned (Waking Ned Devine)

CRITICS' CHOICE AWARDS
Elizabeth
Gods and Monsters
La Vita è Bella (Life is Beautiful)
Out of Sight
Pleasantville
• *Saving Private Ryan*
Shakespeare in Love
A Simple Plan
The Thin Red Line
The Truman Show

1998

BRITISH ACADEMY AWARDS

(Best Film)
Elizabeth
Saving Private Ryan
• Shakespeare in Love
The Truman Show

(Best British Film)
• Elizabeth
Hilary and Jackie
Little Voice
Lock, Stock and
    Two Smoking Barrels
My Name is Joe
Sliding Doors

NEW YORK – *Saving Private Ryan*
LOS ANGELES – *Saving Private Ryan*
BOARD OF REVIEW – *Gods and Monsters*
NATIONAL SOCIETY – *Out of Sight*
LONDON
    (Best Film) *Saving Private Ryan*
    (Best British Film) *Lock, Stock and Two Smoking Barrels*

"It's just such a weak year," bemoaned Newsday critic Jack Matthews at the start of the awards season, "There's very little suspense in terms of the Oscars … it's as if everyone knew that 'Saving Private Ryan' was going to turn out to be this dominant film." On the back of rapturous reviews and strong box office returns, Steven Spielberg's *Saving Private Ryan* seemed certain to claim the Best Picture Oscar for the newly established DreamWorks for the first time (NYT "soberly magnificent … devastating … the finest war movie of our time"; LAT "a powerful and impressive milestone in the realistic depiction of combat … [but] the script is only workmanlike … [weakened by] obviously sentimental moments"; CT "this great World War II battle film – shot with all its director's famous technical genius and sense of wonder, but tempered with a new toughness and maturity – is a watershed picture … accomplishes something rare and extraordinary"; CST "powerful"; WP "searing, heartbreaking … this is simply the greatest war movie ever made"; SFC "overwhelming … extraordinary"; SFX "terrific"; Time "remarkable").

Saving Private Ryan was named Best Picture by both the New York Film Critics Circle and the Los Angeles Film Critics Association. On the west coast, it won narrowly over *The Butcher Boy* (NYT "audacious … disturbing [and] astonishing"; LAT "consistently amazing … a film destined to be a classic … a work of awesome power and passion … uniquely challenging"; CT "a wild, ecstatic piece of work … has an intensity and brilliance that can seem maddening, even monstrous … easily one of the year's best movies"; CST "original"; WP "challenging and ultimately dazzling ... remarkable"; SFC "bravely imaginative"; BG "vital and original ... a keenly felt, startlingly dark comedy"; SMH "[a] bold, tricky film ... shocking and exhilarating"). In New York, meanwhile, Spielberg's war film won with 37 points to 32 over *Affliction* (NYT "quietly stunning ... a searing tale ... strong and solid"; NYP "the best film of the year"; LAT "one of the year's strongest dramas ... intense, almost overwhelming"; BG "a harrowing film ... scathing and all-too-relevant").

Surprisingly, the National Board of Review placed Spielberg's film second on its list of the year's best films behind *Gods and Monsters*, an independent drama about early Hollywood director James Whale (NYT "an unalloyed success"; NYP "wonderful, engrossing, smart and touching"; LAT "none of [the film], frankly, rises to the levels of subtlety that McKellen's performance does"; CT "engaging"; CST "not great or powerful [but] good-hearted"; WP "fascinating ... marvelous"; BG "flawed"; TGM "confused"). Appearing on the list in third place was the historical drama *Elizabeth* (NYT "a new brand style of history, styled to catch the attention of restless modern youth"; CT "madly overwrought"; SFX "often riveting [but] occasionally ridiculous"; BG "vibrant ... dazzling entertainment"; Time "rich, old-fashioned historical spectacle"; G "the very model of a successful historical drama – imposingly beautiful, persuasively resonant, unfailingly entertaining"; SMH "dynamic").

In an even more surprising decision the National Society of Film Critics gave their top prize to *Out of Sight*, a crime drama-comedy which had been ignored by the NBR (NYT "[Soderbergh] makes it work like a dream"; LAT "engaging and consummately entertaining"; CT "a darky amusing and sly romantic comedy"; V "vastly entertaining"; SFC "if not a minor masterpiece, certainly an estimable achievement"; G "so good it gives you goosebumps ... a hip, romantic thriller ... clever and satisfying"; SMH "marvellously elegant and witty"). *Saving Private Ryan* had led by a wide margin on the initial ballot, but ultimately finished third with 24 points. *Affliction* polled second with 25 points, ten points adrift of *Out of Sight*.

When the nominees for the Golden Globes were announced, *Saving Private Ryan* received five mentions, but was eclipsed by two films which each garnered six nods: *The Truman Show*, which the Los Angeles Times named as the year's best movie (NYT "[a] must–see ... guaranteed Oscar bait and delectably clever entertainment"; LAT "emotionally involving ... as serious as it is funny ... adventurous, provocative, even daring [and] consistently moving"; CT "definitely one of the movies of the year ... unusual and delightfully offbeat ... delicately subversive, hypnotically sardonic"; SFC "wonderful ... an original, inspired piece of work ... compelling"; TT "[has] an elegant, intelligent and satirical edge now rarely encountered in Hollywood") and *Shakespeare in Love* (NYT "pure enchantment ... inspired [and] exhilarating"; LAT "one of those entertaining confections that's so pleasing to the eye and ear you'd have to be a genuine Scrooge to struggle against it"; CT "splendorous ... a grand, sumptuous entertainment, a movie that excites and entrances on so many levels that it takes your breath away"; WP "a witty, romantic, even bawdy romp"; BG "exhilarating ... the best backstage comedy ever made"; G "a remarkably astute packaging exercise ... an intriguing film, balancing precariously but successfully between silliness and brains").

When the Globe winners were announced in late January, the Oscar frontrunner status of *Saving Private Ryan* was confirmed with victories in the Best Picture (Drama) and Best Director categories. Meanwhile, *Shakespeare in Love* emerged as its main competition for Oscar glory, receiving three Globe trophies, including as Best Picture (Comedy/Musical).

Both Globe winners were nominated for the Best Picture Academy Award. Unexpectedly leading the field with thirteen nominations was *Shakespeare in Love*, followed by *Saving Private Ryan* with eleven. Joining them in the Best Picture category were *Elizabeth* and two films set in the Second World War that had been late entrants into awards season contention: the Italian comedy-drama *La Vita è Bella (Life is Beautiful)*, the Best Picture winner at the European Film Awards (NYT "entertaining [and] passionate ... an unpretentious, enormously likable film"; LAT "surprising [with] genuine poignancy"; V "sluggish, uneven and lacking in rhythm [but with] pathos and winning humor"; CT "one of the triumphs of the year"; CST "great"; WP "sad, funny and haunting ... something rare and extraordinary"; SFC "funny [and] harrowing"; BG "powerful [but] goes on a little too long to sustain its high-wire act"; TT "fantastic"; G "wonderful"; S&S "magnificent"; SMH "compelling ... a masterpiece"); and *The Thin Red Line* (NYT "intermittently brilliant ... will as easily fascinate those attuned to Mr Malick's artistry as it disappoints anyone in search of a plot"; LAT "an art film to the core ... poetic almost to excess ... an elliptical, episodic film, dependent on images and reveries ... almost hallucinogenic surrealism ... remains a stubbornly personal film"; V "a complex, highly talented work marked by intellectual and philosophical ambitions"; CT "poetic, violent and visually stunning ... a strong Academy Award contender"; CST "fascinating ... this is not a movie of conventional war cliches"; WP "symphonic"; SFC "great ... audacious and ambitious ... it may be counted as one of the few steps forward in cinema"; TT "a masterpiece ... staggering"). *The Thin Red Line* was the first feature directed by Terrence Malick since 1978, and many critics began to regard *Saving Private Ryan* as conventional, sentimental and overly patriotic by comparison. In The Washington Post, Michael O'Sullivan labelled *The Thin Red Line*, "the thinking person's 'Saving Private Ryan'".

With the announcement of the Academy Award shortlists, *Gods and Monsters* became the first NBR winner to be passed over for a Best Picture Oscar nomination since 1987. NSFC winner *Out of Sight* was also snubbed, as were Globe nominee *The Truman Show* and both New York and Los Angeles runners-up *Affliction* and *The Butcher Boy*.

Among the more highly-anticipated releases that ultimately failed to make the shortlist were: *Beloved*, a film version of Toni Morrison's Pulitzer Prize winning novel (NYT "transfixing, deeply felt ... a gripping, wildly imaginative film that's not quite like any other"; LAT "strange, troubling and powerfully imagined ... ungainly and hard to follow at times [but] once this film gets its bearings, the unsentimental fierceness of its vision brushes obstacles and quibbles from its path"; CT "majestically emotional and lyrical ... a spooky beauty and a natural wonder ... beyond question, this is one of the movies of the year, both a technical marvel and a triumph of imagination, bravery and artistry"; WP "a great film ... harrowing, breathtaking"; V "has power and impressive artistry"; CST "a remarkable and brave achievement"; SFC "majestic, confounding [and] heartbreaking ... a film that rewards mightily"); Globe nominee *Bulworth* (LAT "a chaotic but somehow endearing mishmash ... amusing ... a lively, undisciplined one-of-a-kind vanity project"; CT "a raucous, profane, bitingly funny rant"; CST "not a perfect movie"; WP "splendid ... daring [and] deliberately offensive"; SFC "a brilliant satire ... hilarious"; TGM "a hoot"); Globe nominee *The Horse Whisperer* (NYT "rapturously beautiful ... stirring"; LAT "impressive [but] excessive [and] uninvolving"; CT "subtle, languorous and understated"; CST "touching"; WP "tastefully understated"; SFC "appears to stretch on forever"); and *Primary Colors* (NYT "polished"; LAT "a smart and savvy piece of work ... delicious"; CT "a winner with flaws ... classy entertainment: a sharp-witted comedy"; CST "a superb film – funny, insightful and very wise"; SFC "an intelligent movie"; TGM "wonderfully adroit ... a sophisticated and unsentimental political film").

Also by-passed for consideration were: Producers Guild of America nominee *Waking Ned (Waking Ned Devine)* (NYT "delightful"; LAT "a roguish and delightful comedy of duplicity that's as entertaining as it is sly"; CT "nothing less than one of the year's best movies – funny, charming and clever"; WP "a delight"; SFC "a movie treat"; G "a likable comedy"); *Pleasantville* (NYT "[an] ingenious fantasy ... entertaining [but] has inspired more trickery than depth"; LAT "takes an unexpected dramatic turn and ends up having more on its mind than it can successfully handle"; CT "wildly ambitious"; WP "so ambitious, so clever and so satisfying"; CST "one of the year's best and most original films ... a social commentary of surprising power"; TGM "delightful as it often is, the film suffers from the same structural and thematic tidiness, even smugness, that it nominally opposes"; TT "something special ... delights"); *Henry Fool* (NYT "a great American film [of] brilliance and deep resonance ... astounding"; LAT "a career milestone and a film that could become a landmark in American independent cinema"; CT "an austerely funny, brilliantly written and acted serio-comic tale ... has wit and edge, compassion and sensibility ... one of the year's best American films"; WP "fascinating and often infuriating ... a bundle of contradictions, many of them lyrical, more of them utterly frustrating"; SFC "wise and amusing"; TGM "delectably weird and entertaining"; SMH "exhilarating"); *Hilary and Jackie* (NYT "insightful and wrenching [and] astoundingly rich and subtle"; NYP "moving, provocative, intelligent ... one of the best movies of the year"; LAT "compelling"; WP "profound and haunting"; CST "extraordinary"; G "a complex, ambivalent picture ... impressive"); *A Simple Plan* (NYT "[a] quietly devastating thriller"; LAT "chilling"; CT "surprisingly thrilling"; CST "one of the year's best films"; WP "brilliant complexity"; SFC "riveting [and] moving"); *The Opposite of Sex* (NYT "gleefully acerbic [and] laceratingly funny"; LAT "a brilliantly written black comedy"; CST "refreshing"; WP "a terrific movie"; SFC "very funny"; TT "biting satire"; G "a transgressive delight ... splendidly malicious [and] tautly written"; S&S "a delight on every conceivable level"); *The General* (NYT "canny, elegant"; CT "a near-masterpiece ... one of the most effective and convincing studies of a criminal ever put on screen ... ruthlessly chilling"; SFC "one of the liveliest, smartest and most surprising films in a long time"; S&S "a subtle and absorbing picture"); 1997 Best British Film BAFTA winner *Nil by Mouth* (NYT "brutally truthful ... powerful"; LAT "raw and vital ... very strong stuff"; CST "unflinching and observant"; WP "may be the most riveting drama you see this year ... the film has an impressive, yet disturbing rawness ... compelling viewing"; SFC "exhaustingly painful"; SMH "vivid"); *The Spanish Prisoner* (NYT "Mamet's craftiest and most satisfying cinematic puzzle"; LAT "the smoothest and most convincing of Mamet's elaborate charades"; CT "scintillatingly clever [and] pleasurably perverse ... a genuinely engrossing, continuously surprising intellectual puzzle"; WP "gripping"); and Berlin Film Festival winner *Central do Brasil (Central Station)* (NYT "beautifully observed ... [a] lovely, stirring film"; LAT "as beautiful as it is wrenching ... stunning ... a rich cinematic experience"; TGM "powerful").

In the weeks leading up to the Oscars, *Saving Private Ryan* seemed to firm as the favourite for the golden statuette with wins from the Producers Guild of America and the Directors Guild of America. And on Hollywood's big night, it received five statuettes, including Best Director. In an upset, however, *Shakespeare in Love* claimed the Best Picture Oscar to bring its tally to seven trophies. It was the first time since 1989 that the Academy had presented the Best Picture and Best Director Oscars to different films.

BEST DIRECTOR

ACADEMY AWARDS
Roberto Benigni for *La Vita è Bella (Life is Beautiful)*
John Madden for *Shakespeare in Love*
Terrence Malick for *The Thin Red Line*
• **Steven Spielberg for *Saving Private Ryan***
Peter Weir for *The Truman Show*

GOLDEN GLOBE AWARDS
Shekhar Kapur – *Elizabeth*
John Madden – *Shakespeare in Love*
Robert Redford – *The Horse Whisperer*
• **Steven Spielberg – *Saving Private Ryan***
Peter Weir – *The Truman Show*

DIRECTORS GUILD AWARD
Roberto Benigni
  – *La Vita è Bella*
  (Life is Beautiful)
John Madden – *Shakespeare in Love*
Terrence Malick
  – *The Thin Red Line*
• **Steven Spielberg**
  – *Saving Private Ryan*
Peter Weir – *The Truman Show*

BRITISH ACADEMY AWARDS
Shekhar Kapur – *Elizabeth*
John Madden – *Shakespeare in Love*
Steven Spielberg
  – *Saving Private Ryan*
• **Peter Weir – *The Truman Show***

NEW YORK – Terrence Malick – ***The Thin Red Line***
LOS ANGELES – Steven Spielberg – *Saving Private Ryan*
BOARD OF REVIEW – Shekhar Kapur – *Elizabeth*
NATIONAL SOCIETY – Steven Soderbergh – *Out of Sight*
CRITICS' CHOICE – Steven Spielberg – *Saving Private Ryan*
LONDON
  (Director) **Peter Weir – *The Truman Show***
  (British Director) **John Boorman – *The General***

The overwhelming favourite for the year's Best Director accolades was Steven Spielberg for the war drama *Saving Private Ryan* (NYT "the second pinnacle in a career of magical versatility … with stunning efficacy [he] seems to reimagine [the combat film genre] entirely, dazzling with breadth and intensity"; LAT "a startling reminder of exactly how spectacular a director [he] can be when he allows himself to be challenged ... [but] the hitch in Spielberg's otherwise problem-free direction is a tendency to be too insistent at obviously sentimental moments"; CT "a watershed ... accomplishes something rare and extraordinary"; SFC "Spielberg's accomplishment as a director is beyond praise ... extraordinary"; SFX "a wonderful job"). While many critics had reservations about the film's sentimentality and overt patriotism, there was almost universal acclaim for it's realistic battle sequences. Surprisingly, however, Spielberg collected only two of the major critics' prizes: the Los Angeles Film Critics Association prize, which he had previously won in 1982, and the Critics' Choice Award from the Broadcast Film Critics Association.

The runner-up for the Los Angeles award was Cannes Film Festival prizewinner John Boorman for the black-and-white drama *The General* (NYT "he tells this tale of an Irish underworld original with an unerring instinct for the captivating detail"; CT "at the peak of his powers, brilliantly executed on every level"; SFC "exemplary work"; G "every detail of the story and characterisation has clearly been weighed by a mature writer-director fully aware of his responsibility to balance dramatic entertainment with a care for historical truth").

The National Board of Review honoured Indian filmmaker Shekhar Kapur for the historical drama *Elizabeth* (NYT "Kapur's lusty, flamboyant approach does suit"; CT "overdirected in a frenzied self-conscious style"; BG "part of the reason for the success of the film is Kapur's bold conception and high-relief execution"; SMH "[he] is so sure of what he wants and so adroit at getting it"), ahead of writer-director Bill Condon for *Gods and Monsters* (NYT "creates a deeply resonant portrait ... graceful [and] deft"; LAT "Condon's writing and directing seem more alive and involving when [McKellen] is the focus of them"; CT "beautifully filmed ... exceedingly well-made").

In the voting by the New York Film Critics Circle, Spielberg was narrowly outpolled by Terrence Malick, who collected his second prize from the circle for *The Thin Red Line*, another Second World War drama (NYT "shows why being a great film director and directing a great film are not the same"; CT "the star of this picture is clearly Malick"; CST "masterful"; BG "hasn't lost his knack for impressive visuals, although he still has trouble summoning emotional or visceral immediacy"). The result of the final ballot was 37 points to 32 in favour of Malick.

Malick and Spielberg were joint runners-up for the National Society of Film Critics accolade, each garnering 25 points, three short of the tally attained by Steven Soderbergh for the crime drama *Out of Sight* (NYT "directed with terrific panache"; LAT "impeccable ... [he] has let it unfold with dry wit and great skill ... adroit"; CT "directed with almost palpable enjoyment ... sure-handed and solid, beautifully styled and shot"; WP "handles the time shifts adroitly, always keeping us on track"; SFC "top-notch"; BG "deft direction"; Obs "very well made"; G "so exquisitely rendered you can't help but be swept along ... Soderbergh's direction dances ... it dovetails into numerous flashbacks and fits together a cool jigsaw of rewinds, freeze-frames and zooms"; S&S "the real star of 'Out of Sight' is [its] director ... he rises to the challenge of his most mainstream assignment to date with a dazzling display of hip cinematic style"; SMH "[his] directing is a rich mix of studio gloss and independent spontaneity").

Of these various critics' prize-winners and runners-up, only two were mentioned by the Hollywood Foreign Press Association: Kapur and Spielberg. Also nominated for the Golden Globe were John Madden for *Shakespeare in Love* (LAT "smoothly executed"), Peter Weir for *The Truman Show* (NYT "must handle the tricky job with optimum timing"; LAT "directed with enviable grace and restraint ... [his] deliberate tone is essential to the film's multiple and almost contradictory successes"; CT "ranks with his best work"; CST "meticulous"; BG "Weir's direction plugs us seductively and then disquietingly into the virtual unreality of Truman's [world]"; G "brilliantly executed") and Robert Redford for *The Horse Whisperer* (NYT "has found his own visually eloquent way to turn the potboiler [novel] into a panorama ... the film sustains a careful, pensive tone"; LAT "has been made with too much sensitivity ... directs everything smoothly but from a distance, with too few natural moments"). In the end, the winner was Spielberg who collected his second Globe in six years.

For the first time since 1981, the Directors Guild of America and the Academy each selected the same five candidates. Spielberg was the frontrunner for both accolades. He was nominated for the Oscar for a fifth time, and was the first person considered for the Guild honour for a ninth time. The surprise inclusion was Italian actor-director Roberto Benigni for *La Vita è Bella (Life is Beautiful)* (NYT "never trivializes his material"; WP "handles it deftly"; BG "has created a film that is as powerful as the best fables ... [keeps] the spectres of sentimentality and bathos at bay with a masterly lightness and delicacy of touch"). Also in contention were: Madden, Malick and Weir.

The glaring omission from the Guild and Oscar ballots was NBR winner Kapur, and his exclusion was highlighted when he was nominated as Best Director by the British Academy alongside Oscar contenders Madden, Spielberg and Weir.

In addition to the by-passed Globe nominees and critics' choices, the Academy also overlooked: Neil Jordan for *The Butcher Boy* (NYT "does a remarkable job ... creates a riveting mixture of daydream and reality"; LAT "remarkable ... may just be his best [movie]"; CT "a film of flaming creativity and audacity"; WP "deftly balanced ... shifts perspective seamlessly"; BG "[there's] a controlled intensity on Jordan's part, which neatly stokes the tension"; SMH "Jordan manages to keep you with him on the terrible trip he's taking"); Jonathon Demme for *Beloved* (NYT "succeeds uncannily well"; CT "inspired work"; WP "gives the film its voluptuous sense of horror and its prowling currents of deviant sexuality … Demme plunges us into an elemental universe"); Warren Beatty for *Bulworth* (NYT "has directed this political satire with jubilant wit and energy"; WP "manages to pull it off by sheer force of will [and] clarity of vision"; SFC "deserves great credit"); Mike Nichols for *Primary Colors* (NYT "Nichols, who shows much skill in eliciting individual performances, doesn't often make them mesh"; CT "intelligently crafted"); Sam Raimi for *A Simple Plan* (NYT "makes a flawless segue into mainstream storytelling"; LAT "restrains his appetite for excess"; CT "exceedingly well-directed"; WP "disciplined … has a fine eye for imagery that amplifies character and mood"; SFC "tremendously successful"); Paul Schrader for *Affliction* (NYT "has made a film that needs to be watched carefully … gives it the deliberate plainness that makes every small exchange matter … guides 'Affliction' in a spare, sorrowful spirit that exposes their universality"); Gary Oldman for *Nil by Mouth* (NYT "[a] fierce debut … the domestic brutality seen here is sudden and shocking, and [he] makes its horror deeply felt"; LAT "does very well … not surprisingly molds his cast into a thoroughly convincing ensemble [and shows] a real feel for the cinematic"; SMH "an astonishing directorial debut … [his] camera is outstandingly fluid"); David Mamet for *The Spanish Prisoner* (LAT "the smoothest and most convincing of Mamet's elaborate charades"; CT "he pulls off the brainiest and most delightfully convoluted thriller since 'The Usual Suspects'"); Hal Hartley for *Henry Fool* (NYT "exacting … shows off such fine compositional sense … there are no casual details and absolutely no clutter"; LAT "Hartley has done something fairly unusual in American movies"); and Walter Salles for *Central do Brasil (Central Station)* (NYT "the wonder of [this] is all in the telling … beautifully observed … it is the filmmaker's elegant restraint that makes [the] sentiments so deeply felt … [he] directs simply and watchfully [and] brings great tenderness and surprise to the events"; LAT "profound scope and vision"; TGM "takes a bold approach [and directs with great] restraint").

Two weeks before the Oscar ceremony, Spielberg became the first person to be honoured by the DGA for a third time. The victory made him an overwhelming favourite for the Oscar and, as expected, on the big night he won his second statuette.

Three weeks later, however, Spielberg was surprisingly outpolled for the BAFTA by Weir, who was the second consecutive Australian director to be honoured in London.

BEST ACTOR

ACADEMY AWARDS
• **Roberto Benigni as 'Guido Orefice' in** *La Vita è Bella (Life is Beautiful)*
Tom Hanks as 'Capt. John H. Miller' in *Saving Private Ryan*
Ian McKellen as 'James Whale' in *Gods and Monsters*
Nick Nolte as 'Wade Whitehouse' in *Affliction*
Edward Norton as 'Derek Vinyard' in *American History X*

GOLDEN GLOBE AWARDS
(Drama)
• **Jim Carrey** – *The Truman Show*
Stephen Fry – *Wilde*
Tom Hanks – *Saving Private Ryan*
Ian McKellen – *Gods and Monsters*
Nick Nolte – *Affliction*

(Comedy/Musical)
Antonio Banderas
  – *The Mask of Zorro*
Warren Beatty – *Bulworth*
• **Michael Caine – *Little Voice***
John Travolta – *Primary Colors*
Robin Williams – *Patch Adams*

SCREEN ACTORS GUILD
• **Roberto Benigni**
  – *La Vita è Bella*
  (*Life is Beautiful*)
Joseph Fiennes
  – *Shakespeare in Love*
Tom Hanks – *Saving Private Ryan*
Ian McKellen – *Gods and Monsters*
Nick Nolte – *Affliction*

BRITISH ACADEMY AWARDS
• **Roberto Benigni**
  – *La Vita è Bella*
  (*Life is Beautiful*)
Michael Caine – *Little Voice*
Joseph Fiennes
  – *Shakespeare in Love*
Tom Hanks – *Saving Private Ryan*

NEW YORK – Nick Nolte – *Affliction*
LOS ANGELES – Ian McKellen – *Gods and Monsters*
BOARD OF REVIEW – Ian McKellen – *Gods and Monsters*
NATIONAL SOCIETY – Nick Nolte – *Affliction*
CRITICS' CHOICE – Ian McKellen – *Apt Pupil* and *Gods and Monsters*
LONDON
  (Actor) **Jack Nicholson** – *As Good As It Gets*
  (British Actor) **Brendan Gleeson** – *The General*

Nick Nolte won the New York Film Critics Circle and National Society of Film Critics prizes and also finished as close runner-up for the Los Angeles Film Critic Association plaudit as a stressed police officer in *Affliction* (NYT "played with fierce, anguished intensity ... the performance of his career ... devastating"; LAT "a great performance ... a sure bet for an Oscar nomination"; CT "[an] emotionally searing performance"; CST "magnificent"; BG "heart-wrenching in the best and most challenging role of his career"; TT "magnificent"; SFC has "never been better"). As a result, for the second time in eight years, he was the favourite for the Best Actor Academy Award.

Another frontrunner was Ian McKellen, who claimed the Los Angeles and National Board of Review plaudits and finished runner-up for the New York and NSFC honours, for his portrayal of film director James Whale in *Gods and Monsters* (NYT "a performance that richly deserves to be remembered at the end of the year ... splendid ... works wonders with the character"; NYP "sheer brilliance, quite probably the performance of the year"; LAT "his work, always impeccable, reaches a remarkable new plateau here ... better work by an actor will not be seen this year ... one of the things that makes [his] performance so spectacular is the subtlety and delicacy he brings to a role we think we've seen"; CT "superbly acted"; WP "a performance of enormous complexity and nuance"; BG "brilliant"; TGM "a vivid performance").

Only a few years after collecting back-to-back Best Actor Oscars, Tom Hanks was again a strong contender for the statuette as a US army officer leading an evacuation mission during the D–Day landings in *Saving Private Ryan* (NYT "never have [his] everyman qualities been more instantly effective than here ... gives the film such substance and pride"; LAT "gives an indelible performance as an elevated everyman"; CT "the actors – especially Hanks, Burns, Sizemore and Davies – transform and transcend [near-stock] types, give them blood, flesh and grit"; WP "another of his quietly brilliant everyman roles"; SFC "an honest, four-square performance"; SFX "sensitive"; Time "compelling").

These three frontrunners were all short-listed for the Golden Globe (Drama) and the Screen Actors Guild award, but were unexpectedly outpolled on both occasions. The Globe (Drama) went to Jim Carrey as a man who unknowingly grows up as part of a television series, in *The Truman Show* (NYT "[an] instantly iconic performance"; LAT "gives Carrey the role of his career ... it's hard to imagine another actor as effective"; CT "there's no doubt that Carrey makes the performance – and the movie – work"; CST "surprisingly good ... a well-planned performance"; SFC "funny and engaging ... touching"; BG "doing less than usual physically, Carrey accomplishes more than he ever has ... [his] muted yet feelingful clowning is brilliant and touching"; G "a performance to impress"). The Guild honour, meanwhile, was won by European Film Award winner Roberto Benigni as a Jewish man attempting to shield his son from the horrors of the Holocaust in *La Vita è Bella (Life is Beautiful)* (NYT "because [he] can be heart–rending without a trace of the maudlin, [the film] works"; LAT "irresistibly funny"; CST "the role he was born to play"; WP "in one bold stride,

[he] has set himself apart from the rank and file of funnymen, joining the elite class of clowns who know that humor and heartbreak are only a howl of pain apart"; SFC "funny and sad"; BG "compels belief in the childlike purity his character keeps alive"; TT "brilliant").

There was also an upset for the Globe (Comedy/Musical). Michael Caine took the trophy for his turn in *Little Voice* (NYT "[he and Blethyn] add humor and spice"; NYP "[an] exquisite performance"; LAT "solid work ... does a poignant job"; CT "[a] big, bravura comic performance"; WP "brings a brassy dignity to [the role]"; SMH "gives the film an interesting, abrasive edge") ahead of perceived frontrunners Warren Beatty in *Bulworth* (NYT "played by a magically revitalized Warren Beatty ... dominates virtually every scene"; LAT "the reason 'Bulworth' is more engaging than expected is Beatty's good-humored willingness to look completely silly"; WP "an effervescent performance that rivals his best work") and John Travolta in *Primary Colors* (LAT "it's no more than a turn, an amusing and light-fingered impersonation ... [but] an irresistible one"; V "effective"; CT "has charisma to spare ... but [he] misses something crucial"; CST "dominates the film").

Benigni, Hanks, McKellen and Nolte were all nominated for the Best Actor Oscar. Benigni also earned nominations in the Best Director and Best Original Screenplay categories and his film was short-listed for the Best Foreign-Language Film statuette. Surprisingly, for the fifth spot Oscar voters by-passed both Globe winners and cited a contender not previously mentioned during the awards season: Edward Norton as a neo–Nazi in *American History X* (NYT "fiery acting ... plays [the role] scaringly well"; LAT "a forceful, mesmerizing performance ... Derek cuts a compelling figure courtesy of Norton's bravura performance"; V "superbly acted ... outstanding"; WP "[an] intelligent and muscular performance"; CT "Oscar talk this early is grating, but [he] performs the role so well that he is the immediate front-runner"; CST "effective"; TGM "makes [the film] worth seeing ... a brilliant, career-high performance").

Also by-passed for consideration were: Stephen Fry in *Wilde* (NYT "[his] warmly sympathetic performance finds the gentleness beneath the wit"; LAT "perfect ... triumphant"; CT "not only resembles Wilde physically [but] grasps him intellectually ... convinces because he's able to show and clarify so many sides of the character"; WP "remarkable ... brings a quiet strength to a role whose victimhood would probably be easier to portray than its dignity"; TGM "the best thing about the movie"; SMH "remarkably appealing"); Bill Paxton in *A Simple Plan* (NYT "[a] fine, sturdy performance"; LAT "a perfectly transparent performance, at once shocking and believable, and for those who prefer their dramatic arcs on a gentle curve, it's one of the year's more memorable efforts"; CST "flawless"; WP "excellent"; SFC "[a] lovely, complex performance"); John Hurt in *Love and Death on Long Island* (NYT "simply wonderful – acerbic, funny and heartbreaking ... splendid"; LAT "[an] exquisite, nuanced performance ... Hurt's grasp of the role couldn't be surer ... one of the great performances of his career ... magnificent"; CT "wonderful ... a performance in which you marvel at the details"; WP "it's hard to imagine the movie without him ... perfect"; S&S "in top form ... bringing a real sense of poignancy, late-flowering passion and assured comic timing to a role that could easily have toppled into caricature"); Denzel Washington in *He Got Game* (NYT "a splendid, carefully measured performance"; LAT "his excellent performance carries the film ... convincing"; CT "towering over the cast ... easily exposes both sides of [the character] ... proves again he's an acting natural"; WP "the movie's best performance"; S&S "played superbly"); Sean Penn in *Hurlyburly* (NYT "burrows so deeply into Eddie that he almost vomits his character onto the screen"; LAT "absolutely galvanic"; CST "remarkable"; SFC "spectacularly intense"); Campbell Scott in *The Spanish Prisoner* (LAT "[an] intriguing performance"; CT "played with just the right resentful intelligence ... [he] gets every bit of Joe's crescendoing fear and desire"; SFC "a fine, complex performance"); Brendan Gleeson in *The General* (NYT "played magnificently"; LAT "has a high time playing [this] great role"; CT "stunning ... watching him, you're hardly aware of acting ... [he] makes Cahill live and burn on screen ... remarkable"; SFC "brilliant"; TT "terrific"; G "his performance is among the events of the year"; S&S "[a] towering performance [which] boasts a compelling snap of authenticity"); Derek Jacobi in *Love is the Devil* (NYT "[an] uncompromising, hard-edged performance"; LAT "uncanny"; CT "[his] performance ultimately provides much of the film's depth"; WP "played with glee and savage self-assurance ... [his] physical transformation into Bacon is remarkable"; G "[his] performance, in which affection, generosity, indifference and cruelty are juggled and nuanced to perfection [is] a miniature masterpiece"; S&S "mesmerising"); Ray Winstone in *Nil by Mouth* (LAT "thoroughly convincing"; CST "brilliant"; WP "outstanding [and] unforgettable"; SFC "terrifying"; SMH "superb ... deserves kudos"); and twelve-year old Eamonn Owens in *The Butcher Boy* (NYT "remarkably, almost every scene in the film is carried by [him]"; CT "Francie is one of the year's most memorable movie characters [and] Owens lights up the screen ... [he] gives a devilishly unbuttoned and exciting child performance"; WP "holding the center together is [his] performance ... a disturbing and menacing portrayal"; BG "astonishing ... so potently do [the director] and Owens put him on-screen that you never stop caring about him, or dreading what he might do next"; S&S "extraordinary").

On Oscar night, Benigni collected not only the Best Foreign-Language Film Oscar, but also the statuette for Best Actor. It was the first time that the Academy had honoured a performance in a non-English language film in the Best Actor category. He triumphed again in London a few weeks later.

1998

BEST ACTRESS

ACADEMY AWARDS
Cate Blanchett as 'Queen Elizabeth I of England' in *Elizabeth*
Fernanda Montenegro as 'Dora' in *Central do Brasil (Central Station)*
• **Gwyneth Paltrow as 'Viola De Lesseps' in *Shakespeare in Love***
Meryl Streep as 'Kate Gulden' in *One True Thing*
Emily Watson as 'Jacqueline du Pré' in *Hilary and Jackie*

GOLDEN GLOBE AWARDS

(Drama)
• **Cate Blanchett – *Elizabeth***
Fernanda Montenegro
   – Central do Brasil
   (Central Station)
Susan Sarandon – *Stepmom*
Meryl Streep – *One True Thing*
Emily Watson – *Hilary and Jackie*

(Comedy/Musical)
Cameron Diaz
   – There's Something About Mary
Jane Horrocks – *Little Voice*
• **Gwyneth Paltrow**
   – Shakespeare in Love
Christina Ricci
   – The Opposite of Sex
Meg Ryan – *You've Got Mail*

SCREEN ACTORS GUILD
Cate Blanchett – *Elizabeth*
Jane Horrocks – *Little Voice*
• **Gwyneth Paltrow**
   – Shakespeare in Love
Meryl Streep – *One True Thing*
Emily Watson – *Hilary and Jackie*

BRITISH ACADEMY AWARDS
• **Cate Blanchett – *Elizabeth***
Jane Horrocks – *Little Voice*
Gwyneth Paltrow
   – Shakespeare in Love
Emily Watson – *Hilary and Jackie*

NEW YORK – Cameron Diaz – *There's Something About Mary*
LOS ANGELES – Fernanda Montenegro – *Central do Brasil (Central Station)* and Ally Sheedy – *High Art*
BOARD OF REVIEW – Fernanda Montenegro – *Central do Brasil (Central Station)*
NATIONAL SOCIETY – Ally Sheedy – *High Art*
CRITICS' CHOICE – Cate Blanchett – *Elizabeth*
LONDON
   (Actress) **Cate Blanchett – *Elizabeth***
   (British Actress) **Helena Bonham Carter – *The Wings of the Dove***

1998

The frontrunners for the Best Actress Academy Award were the winners of the two Golden Globes. Each in contention for the Oscar for the first time.

For her portrayal of the young Queen Elizabeth I of England in *Elizabeth*, Cate Blanchett won the Globe (Drama), the Broadcast Film Critics prize and the London Film Critics accolade, and finished runner-up for the National Society of Film Critics citation (NYT "captivating ... brings spirit, beauty and substance to what otherwise might have been turned into a vacuous role"; LAT "the film's saving grace ... has a commanding grip on her character ... [making] a seamless transition from naive idealist to steely monarch"; CST "uncannily comes to resemble the great monarch"; WP "perfectly cast"; SFX "an exceptional performance"; Time "takes the title character from wariness to regality [with] subtle grace"; BG "the stuff the Oscar's dreams are made of ... she takes one of the juiciest roles and fills it with spirit and spine, pulse and purpose ... strong and transcendent ... Blanchett's name is surfacing in early pre-Oscar buzz, and well it should"; TGM "has both the poise and palpable intelligence to manage this mixture of the real and iconic ... [a] stellar performance"; TT "this is the film that will make her name"; Obs "conveys with some conviction [her] political growth and emotional hardening"; G "Blanchett's triumph is to a create a thoroughly convincing depiction of the journey from canoodling girlhood to the threshold of an imperial monarchy ... [she] is nothing short of electrifying"; SMH "a controlled and understated portrayal").

The winner of the Globe (Comedy/Musical) was Gwyneth Paltrow for her turn as a young aristocrat in the romantic comedy *Shakespeare in Love* (NYT "[a] fully realized starring performance ... so breathtaking that she seems utterly plausible"; NYP "breathtaking"; LAT "irresistible ... doing her best work since 'Emma'"; WP "played charmingly"; BG "[her] best roles in ages ... she burns with fevered emotions"; G "wryly unselfconscious, convincingly slipping in and out of a chatty version of blank verse").

Nominated for the Oscar alongside Blanchett and Paltrow were: Fernanda Montenegro, co-winner of the Los Angeles Film Critics Association award and winner of the National Board of Review accolade, who had been honoured at the Berlin Film Festival, for her performance as a retired teacher in *Central do Brasil (Central Station)* (NYT "a bravura performance ... superbly modulated"; LAT "one of the year's finest performances ... a personal triumph"; CST "successful"; SFC "a landmark performance ... sensational"; TGM "a revelation"); Emily Watson as cellist Jacqueline du Pré in *Hilary and Jackie* (NYT "[a] blazing performance ... beautifully acted ... mesmerizing"; LAT "superbly acted ... completely inhabits the role, living it as much as acting it"; CT "Watson's performance is high pitched when appropriate yet also composed of fine details"; CST "fiery and strong-willed"; TT "very impressive ... fierce ... strong, sensitive ... [a] fearless impersonation"; G "[an] edgy mixture of demureness and sexual mischief ... outstanding"); and previous winner Meryl Streep as a mother dying of cancer in *One True Thing* (NYT "Streep's performance is as uncompromised as any she has given"; LAT "one of the least self-consciously dramatic and surface showy [performances] of her career, but Streep adds a level of honesty and reality that makes it one of her most moving ... this performance is the equal of her best work because she doesn't condescend to [the character]"; V "expertly played"; CT "another top-notch performance ... letter-perfect in a wrenching role ... she doesn't deserve to have her excellence taken for granted"; WP "an honest, unaffected performance"; SFX "a magisterial performance"; TGM "exquisite ... taking the few notes at her disposal and crafting a dramatic symphony"). Streep's nomination was her eleventh from the Academy, and she was the third person to be so honoured. She had also earned praise for her turn as the stern eldest sister in the Irish drama *Dancing at Lughnasa* (NYT played "with supreme, heart–breaking economy"; LAT "convincingly unsympathetic").

The most glaring omissions from the list of candidates were: Los Angeles co-winner and National Society of Film Critics winner Ally Sheedy as a photographer in *High Art* (NYT "a fierce, tricky performance ... mesmerizing"; LAT "plays Lucy with a strength that gradually falls away as a facade over her vulnerability"; CT "interesting ... a very brave performance"; CST "on just the right note, scene after scene"; TGM "excels ... vibrant"); and Jane Horrocks as the shy but talented singer in *Little Voice*, originally a stage role written specifically as a showcase for her unique talents as a mimic and impersonator (NYT "uncanny ... phenomenal mimicry ... makes a splendid centerpiece"; NYP "brilliantly acted ... [an] exquisite performance"; LAT "a transfixing, tour de force performance ... as much as her singing, it's her skilful acting that turns L.V. into a strange, unnervingly spooky presence ... delicate work ... a genuine astonishment"; CT "demonstrates a thrillingly unexpected talent for mimicry [and] suggests a mind and soul behind the voice"; CST "an astonishing performance ... amazing"; WP "[the film] showcases [her] to perfection ... utterly believable [and] achingly well-acted, 'Little Voice' would collapse in a heap without Horrocks there to support it ... a miracle"; Time "Horrocks' metamorphosis from starling to star is worth cherishing"; TT "ideal"; SMH "[a] great performance ... quietly underplaying").

Despite a strong campaign, Oscar voters also by-passed actress and talk-show host Oprah Winfrey as a former slave in *Beloved* (NYT "[the film's] linchpin ... has the dramatic power to hold it together [but] however fiercely she plays the role of Sethe, she is more often a person acting than an intuitive actress"; LAT "convincing ... her untutored quality makes a good fit with the stoicism that is Sethe's touchstone"; CT "Winfrey shines as Sethe"; CST "a brave, deep performance"; WP "a remarkable performance … what a blaze of genius she is"; SFC "a credible, restrained performance").

Academy members also ignored the shock New York Film Critics Circle winner and Globe nominee Cameron Diaz in the popular comedy *There's Something About Mary* (NYT "played with a blithe comic style that makes her as funny as she is dazzling"; LAT "[the co-directors] have a secret weapon in [the film's] star, Cameron Diaz … [she] is irreplaceable here … more than being completely believable as the delight of all eyes … [she keeps] the film alive during those moments when it raggedly slows down"; G "the joke's impact is redoubled by the wholesome radiance Diaz brings to the part, and be her evident willingness to join in the fun"). The unexpected result from the east coast balloting apparently resulted from a deadlock among the circle's members in their support for Montenegro and Renée Zellweger for her performances as the daughter in *One True Thing* (NYT "understated and entirely credible … registers all the attendant emotions"; CT "gives Ellen some contradictory sweetness and softness that work well at times"; CST "not acting so much as fiercely possessing her character"; WP "outstanding"; TGM "easily holds her own in the film's most difficult role … traces [her character's] journey with nuanced precision") and as a young Jewish mother in *A Price Above Rubies* (NYT "serious [and] admirable"; LAT "showcases Zellweger in a challenging role … there's sufficient complexity to Sonia to allow Zellweger to make an impression"; CT "she has a hard task that she acquits admirably: portraying a woman consumed by sexuality and passion, and sporadically in communion with spirits, yet never letting her become absurd or pitiable"; CST "[a] ferociously strong performance"; TGM "plays Sonia straightforwardly and earnestly"). Zellweger was another notable absentee from the Oscar ballot.

Other contenders excluded from consideration were: previous winner Emma Thompson in *Primary Colors* (NYT "played keenly"; CT "projects the unamazed intelligence that has become her hallmark"; WP "so good is Thompson, in fact, that you feel her presence in a way you don't feel Travolta's … she's really the one that drives the movie"); Christina Ricci in *The Opposite of Sex* (LAT "remarkable [and] sensational"; CST "right on the money"; WP "plays Dedee with a deadpan venom"; SFC "delicious"; TT "delicious"; S&S "a central performance of jaw-dropping virtuosity … phenomenal"; SMH "irresistible to watch"); Alfre Woodard in *Down in the Delta* (LAT "[an] impressive portrayal … holds back resolutely in order to bring Loretta to new life in the smallest of increments … moving"; CST "a performance that is like an act of sympathy with the character"; WP "affecting"; SFC "a beautifully layered performance … magical"; TGM "stands out … a real pleasure to watch"); previous winner Holly Hunter in *Living Out Loud* (NYT "performs stiffly at times, but she brings intelligence, thwarted passion and obvious depth of feeling to Judith's struggle"; LAT "impressive [and] vivid ... in [her] accomplished hands, Judith begins to gradually, and believably reclaim her sense of self and her own life"; CT "easily slips under the skin of [her] character ... Hunter, in particular, is so complex and appealing"; WP "the film's greatest asset ... Hunter, enigmatic as a fragile social butterfly, also brings humor and daring to a character who might have been an irksome Upper East Sider"; SFC "a kick to watch"); 1997 Cannes Film Festival honoree Kathy Burke in *Nil by Mouth* (NYT "extraordinary ... [she] hauntingly conveys the contradictions that keep [the couple] together"; LAT "thoroughly convincing"; WP "outstanding ... carries suffering with touching, almost alarming stoicism"; SFC "heartbreaking ... an outstanding performance"; SMH "superb ... absolutely unrecognisable"); Vanessa Redgrave in *Mrs Dalloway* (NYT "[her] marvelous performance gives the film its grandeur"; LAT "transcendent ... she soars"; CT "provides a great actress with a role that eminently suits her ... the matchless Redgrave playing one of the dream roles of her career"; WP "fills [the film] with the fragility of life [and] the ache of lost possibility ... a rather lovely performance"; SMH "an engaging performance"); Samantha Morton in *Under the Skin* (NYT "plays the central role with incredible abandon ... embodies the role with furious intensity and with a raw yet waifness presence"; LAT "a scorching no-holds-barred, totally selfless portrayal"; CT "one of the year's finest movie performances ... fiercely unforgettable"; SFC "an unflinching performance"; SMH "superbly acted ... terrific"; TGM "[her] star turn is absolutely riveting ... Morton gets so far under the character's skin, so painfully deep, that we dearly want to believe in her eventual salvation"; TT "compels attention"); and 1997 Venice Film Festival winner Robin Tunney in *Niagara, Niagara* (NYT "her brutally repellent performance is a tour de force so uncompromising that your sympathy for the character periodically gives way to a sickening sense of disgust"; CT "has the showcase part, and you can see why she impressed the Venice jury ... with a wide-eyed intensity [she] turns Mary into a real-life Jekyll and Hyde"; CST "so good she's sometimes scary"; WP "[an] alarming but measured portrayal").

By Oscar night, Paltrow had emerged as the clear favourite for the statuette. Miramax had launched a massive publicity campaign aimed at winning prestigious statuettes for *Shakespeare in Love* and a fortnight out from the Academy Awards ceremony, Paltrow won the Guild accolade. Significantly, she was also aided by the fact her main rival was a foreigner. Over the previous twenty-five years, the Best Actress Academy Award had been won by only two foreigners (in 1973 and 1992). When Jack Nicholson opened the envelope, it was Paltrow who triumphed.

The result, however, was reversed in London a few weeks later. The British Academy awarded the Best Actress BAFTA to Blanchett ahead of a field of candidates that included Paltrow.

1998

BEST SUPPORTING ACTOR

ACADEMY AWARDS
• **James Coburn as 'Glen Whitehouse' in** *Affliction*
Robert Duvall as 'Jerome Facher' in *A Civil Action*
Ed Harris as 'Christof' in *The Truman Show*
Geoffrey Rush as 'Philip Henslowe' in *Shakespeare in Love*
Billy Bob Thornton as 'Jacob Mitchell' in *A Simple Plan*

GOLDEN GLOBE AWARDS
Robert Duvall – *A Civil Action*
• **Ed Harris – *The Truman Show***
Bill Murray – *Rushmore*
Geoffrey Rush – *Shakespeare in Love*
Donald Sutherland – *Without Limits*
Billy Bob Thornton – *A Simple Plan*

SCREEN ACTORS GUILD
James Coburn – *Affliction*
• **Robert Duvall – *A Civil Action***
David Kelly
   – *Waking Ned*
   (Waking Ned Devine)
Geoffrey Rush
   – *Shakespeare in Love*
Billy Bob Thornton – *A Simple Plan*

BRITISH ACADEMY AWARDS
Ed Harris – *The Truman Show*
Geoffrey Rush – *Elizabeth*
• **Geoffrey Rush**
   – *Shakespeare in Love*
Tom Wilkinson
   – *Shakespeare in Love*

NEW YORK – Bill Murray – *Rushmore*
LOS ANGELES – Bill Murray – *Rushmore* and ***Wild Things*** and **Billy Bob Thornton – *A Simple Plan***
BOARD OF REVIEW – Ed Harris – *Stepmom* and ***The Truman Show***
NATIONAL SOCIETY – Bill Murray – *Rushmore*
CRITICS' CHOICE – Billy Bob Thornton – *Primary Colors* and ***A Simple Plan***
LONDON (British Supporting Actor) **Nigel Hawthorne – *The Object of My Affection***

The ensemble cast of *Saving Private Ryan*, which included Tom Sizemore, Jeremy Davies, Barry Pepper, Matt Damon, Edward Burns and Giovanni Ribisi, was widely praised collectively by critics (NYT "played with seamless ensemble spirit … taking these standard-issue characters and making them unaccountably compelling"; LAT "Spielberg has adroitly cast these roles [leaving us] admiring these performances"; CT "the actors – especially Hanks, Burns, Sizemore and Davies – transform and transcend [near-stock] types, give them blood, flesh and grit"; CST "effective"; WP "all the actors [are] excellent"; SFC "extraordinary"). At the end of the year, DreamWorks focussed its campaign on Sizemore (LAT "the best, most controlled work of his career") but ultimately none of the film's cast received critics' prizes or nominations for any of the season's major accolades.

Similarly overlooked were both Nick Nolte (NYT "another ferocious performance"; LAT "the film's best performance") and Sean Penn (BG "especially arresting") for their parts in the year's other major Second World War combat drama, *The Thin Red Line*. Nolte, however, received a Best Actor nomination that year for the family drama *Affliction*.

Another of the year's Best Actor nominees, Edward Norton, had similarly been simultaneously been promoted for both categories. Nominated for his leading role in *American History X*, he was among those overlooked in the supporting category for *Rounders* (NYT "startling"; NYP "a sublime supporting performance … he is terrific"; LAT "the energy and confidence he brings to [this kind of role] makes the character the perfect foil for [Matt Damon]"; CT "fun to watch … beautifully played).

The most unexpected omission from the list of Oscar contenders was Bill Murray as the tycoon in *Rushmore* (NYT "played with all the right wiles"; LAT "a fine, bittersweet performance, one of his best ever"; CT "this is the best performance of his career"; CST "played with the right note"; WP "vulnerable, but wickedly funny"; SFC "a first-class performance … wonderful"). Murray was awarded the New York Film Critics Circle and National Society of Film Critics prizes, shared the Los Angeles Film Critics Association plaudit and was a Golden Globe nominee. Many in Hollywood had tipped him to win the coveted statuette.

Also by-passed for consideration were: NSFC runner-up and Globe nominee Donald Sutherland in *Without Limits* (NYT "played with great, wry authority"; LAT "a commanding, almost hypnotic performance that is among the actor's best"; CT "the film's great performance … makes Bowerman both accessible and mysterious, even, at times, a little frightening … it's a classic movie portrayal"; CST "Sutherland's performance is the film's treasure"; TGM "steals the picture … the movie jumps to life whenever [he] brings his raw-boned intensity to the screen, deftly turning Bowerman into victory's philosophic draftsman"); Paul Newman in *Message in a Bottle* (NYT "scene-stealing"; LAT "a gem of a performance as Newman makes things look easy that other actors couldn't begin to accomplish"; CT "easily steals the picture … though, in other hands, he might have become another cliché, Newman puts a charge behind his lines, getting laughs"; WP "milks a rather throwaway role with charm"; TT "coming within a wink of stealing the whole film"); Jon Voight in *The General* (NYT "beautifully embodied"; CT "another of his brilliant recent string of supporting performances"; G "fine acting ... his world-weary delivery suits the resonant economy of [the film's style] ... [a] substantial performance"); Brendan Fraser in *Gods and Monsters* (NYT "impressive"; LAT "does a respectable job"; CST "subtle and attuned to the role"; SFC "[a] real surprise"; WP "a touching, unselfconscious performance"; BG "played with more than a hint of 'Frankenstein' earnestness by a boxed-in Fraser"); Nigel Hawthorne in *The Object of My Affection* (NYT "played with refreshing worldliness ... he sounds the film's only notes of real poignancy"; LAT "engaging"; CT "[a] splendid performance ... brings unexpected depth to the picture"; CST "becomes the movie's center of interest"; WP "portrayed with poignancy"; SFC "touching"); New York runner-up Dylan Baker in *Happiness* (NYT "a brave and chilling performance"; LAT "[an] empathetic performance"); Jude Law in *Wilde* (NYT "riveting"; LAT "a full-dimensional performance ... triumphant"; SMH "Law's almost demonic looks give real life to Bosie"); Guy Torry in *American History X* (NYT "a fine, funny performance"; CT "most impressive"; CST "a wonderful performance"; WP "fills the role brilliantly"); Screen Actors Guild nominee David Kelly in *Waking Ned (Waking Ned Devine)* (NYT "[a] wonderful performance"; CT "a considerable part of the charm of the film"; CST "engaging [and] delightful"; SFC "a wonder"; G "a terrific performance ... he gurns and squirms to devastating effect"); William H. Macy in *Pleasantville* (NYT "brings a funny, touchingly naïve bombast to the father's role"; CT "gives him a touching quality"; WP "[a] superb performance"); Johnny Galecki in *The Opposite of Sex* (LAT "absolutely hilarious"; S&S "perfectly pinpointing the snide petulance of a certain type of smalltown queen"); and Christopher Eccleston in both *A Price Above Rubies* (NYT "a warily intense performance"; CT "has exactly the right merciless aura") and *Elizabeth* (BG "[a] strong presence"; TG "first-rate"; SMH "a big, beetle-browed performance which would be a scene-stealer in other company")

Ahead of these contenders, the Academy shortlisted: seventy-year old James Coburn as an abusive alcoholic in *Affliction* (NYT "in a shockingly savage performance, Coburn rampages through the film"; LAT "convincingly menacing ... there's a strong push for Coburn for best supporting actor"; CT "played with volcanic intensity"; CST "magnificent ... a performance of power"; BG "played with lacerating power ... a jolting performance"; TT "fabulous"); previous Best Actor winner Robert Duvall as a lawyer in *A Civil Action* (NYT "outstandingly deft"; LAT "superb"; CT "a great supporting performance ... plays him so cunningly well, you begin to smile at his every appearance"; WP "sly and amusing"; SFC "ultimately saves the film"); Ed Harris as an eccentric television producer in *The Truman Show* (NYT "plays this pivotal role with a sinister, laid–back authority that amounts to the film's most satirical aspect"; CT "super-real ... makes a palpable, believable and threatening character"; CST "finds the right notes"; G "a brilliant parody"); previous Best Actor winner Geoffrey Rush as a theatre owner in *Shakespeare in Love* (WP "particularly funny"; SFC "proves adept at comedy"; BG "has fun"); and previous Best Adapted Screenplay Oscar winner Billy Bob Thornton as one of the men who find a huge amount of money in a crashed plane in *A Simple Plan* (NYT "[many scenes] pivot on [his] haunting mix of menace and fragility in the film's showier role"; LAT "mesmerizing ... carries the film's moral compass ... Thornton makes him the most interesting character"; CT "the standout ... draws you in ... [a] strong performance"; CST "flawless"; WP "excellent"; SFC "[a] lovely, complex performance"). Thornton has also earned praised for his turn in *Primary Colors* (NYT "plays [the part] with sly finesse"; CT "the top performance in a movie of unusually good actors"; TGM "dead-on") and was honoured by the Broadcast Film Critics Association for both performances.

The favourites for the statuette were Globe and National Board of Review winner Harris and Los Angeles co-winner and Broadcast Film Critics honouree Thornton. The dark horse appeared to be Duvall, who unexpectedly claimed the Screen Actors Guild trophy just a fortnight before the Academy Awards.

In a surprise on Oscar night, however, the sentimental favourite Coburn was presented with the Academy Award. "I've been doing this for over half my life," the veteran told the audience at the Dorothy Chandler Pavilion, "I finally got one right, I guess!"

The British Academy, meanwhile, presented its prize to Rush for his comic turn in *Shakespeare in Love*. He had also been nominated in the same category for his role as a spymaster in the historical drama *Elizabeth* (LAT "seems more lost than menacing"; BG "if Blanchett weren't so strong and transcendent as Elizabeth, the film would be stolen by her Australian compatriot, Geoffrey Rush"; TG "first-rate ... particularly outstanding"; OBs "there are several other good performances, especially Geoffrey Rush"; G "[a] memorable portrayal").

1998

BEST SUPPORTING ACTRESS

ACADEMY AWARDS
Kathy Bates as 'Libby Holden' in *Primary Colors*
Brenda Blethyn as 'Mari' in *Little Voice*
• **Judi Dench as 'Queen Elizabeth I of England' in *Shakespeare in Love***
Rachel Griffiths as 'Hilary du Pré' in *Hilary and Jackie*
Lynn Redgrave as 'Hanna' in *Gods and Monsters*

GOLDEN GLOBE AWARDS
Kathy Bates – *Primary Colors*
Brenda Blethyn – *Little Voice*
Judi Dench – *Shakespeare in Love*
• **Lynn Redgrave – *Gods and Monsters***
Sharon Stone – *The Mighty*

SCREEN ACTORS GUILD
• **Kathy Bates – *Primary Colors***
Brenda Blethyn – *Little Voice*
Judi Dench
  – *Shakespeare in Love*
Rachel Griffiths – *Hilary and Jackie*
Lynn Redgrave
  – *Gods and Monsters*

BRITISH ACADEMY AWARDS
Kathy Burke – *Elizabeth*
Brenda Blethyn – *Little Voice*
• **Judi Dench**
  – *Shakespeare in Love*
Lynn Redgrave
  – *Gods and Monsters*

NEW YORK – Lisa Kudrow – *The Opposite of Sex*
LOS ANGELES – Joan Allen – *Pleasantville*
BOARD OF REVIEW – Christina Ricci – *Buffalo 66* and *The Opposite of Sex* and *Pecker*
NATIONAL SOCIETY – Judi Dench – *Shakespeare in Love*
CRITICS' CHOICE – Joan Allen – *Pleasantville* and Kathy Bates – *Primary Colors*
LONDON (British Supporting Actress) **Minnie Driver – *Good Will Hunting* and Kate Beckinsale – *The Last Days of Disco***

A year after she was unsuccessfully nominated for the Best Actress Oscar for playing Queen Victoria in John Madden's *Mrs Brown*, Judi Dench was the overwhelming favourite for the Best Supporting Actress Academy Award for her portrayal of Queen Elizabeth I in the romantic comedy *Shakespeare in Love*, another film directed by Madden (NYT "one of the film's utmost treats"; LAT "an unflappable Judi Dench as the one-woman armada Elizabeth I"; WP "shines"; BG "weighs in magnificently, with a full head of mischievous imperiousness"). In the lead-up to the Oscars, Dench won the National Society of Film Critics prize, and earned Golden Globe, British Academy Award and Screen Actors Guild nominations.

The main challenger for the statuette was Lynn Redgrave, who earned her second Oscar nomination as the loyal German housekeeper in *Gods and Monsters* (NYT "warmly attentive and unrecognizably plain"; LAT "amusing"; CST "very good"; WP "funny"; SFC "unrecognizable"; BG "Redgrave, avoiding sentimentality, is first-rate"). Redgrave did not collect any of the critics' prizes, but was the surprise winner of the Globe and was among those short-listed for the Guild accolade.

The dark horse in the field was SAG winner, Broadcast Film Critics co-winner and Los Angeles Film Critics Association runner-up Kathy Bates as a political adviser in *Primary Colors* (NYT "a showstopper"; LAT "her best performance since winning an Oscar ... good enough to practically steal the entire picture"; CT "well-acted"; WP "steals the movie"; TGM "Bates is the main provider not only of the picture's farcical humor but also, in a heart-rending final speech, of its surprising poignancy"). Bates was the only American in the category, a factor that often contributed to Oscar success, however, she was also the only previous Oscar winner in the category. Despite the Guild and BFCA honours, few observers considered her likely to claim a second statuette.

The chances of Dench were bolstered by the surprise exclusion of the year's other prize-winners: New York Film Critics Circle winner Lisa Kudrow in *The Opposite of Sex* (NYT "funniest and most touching [of the film's supporting characters] ... sustains her expert 'Friends' timing in a role that's a marked departure"; LAT "sensational ... walks away with the picture"; WP "perfectly capturing Lucia's snippy, prim frustration"; TT "fabulous"; S&S "turning Lucia into an impressively complex character"; SMH "an impressively sharp-tongued and believable portrayal"); Los Angeles winner and BFCA co-winner Joan Allen in *Pleasantville* (NYT "Allen truly does blossom ... a lovely performance"; LAT "especially good"; CT "makes Betty's transformation as convincing from the inside as outside"; WP "superb"; SFC "she's great in the part"; TGM "superb"); and National Board of Review winner Christina Ricci, who was cited for three arguably leading roles in *Buffalo 66*, *Pecker* and *The Opposite of Sex*.

Other notable omissions were: both Thandie Newton (NYT "played astonishingly"; LAT "with the appearance of Beloved, the film comes fully alive, and [her] performance in the role is the largest part of the reason ... [she] hits the right unnerving notes with her work ... her Beloved is a truly disconcerting, unfathomable presence"; WP "steals the show ... [a] great performance"; CT "played with truly scary abandon"; CST "interesting ... brings a difficult character to life"; SFC "wondrously scary and sometimes funny") and Beah Richards (NYT "radiant"; LAT "most satisfying of all [the cast] ... poignantly conveys the mystical, healing presence of Baby Suggs"; SFC "vivid ... imbues the film with tremendous warmth and forgiveness") in *Beloved*; and Laura Linney in *The Truman Show* (NYT "[her] dazzling domestic falseness is one of the film's most resonant ingredients"). Linney's chances appeared to be hurt by contradictory Paramount advertisements promoting her for consideration in both the Best Actress and Best Supporting Actress categories.

Also by-passed for consideration were: Sharon Stone in *The Mighty* (NYT "a game, down-to-earth performance ... brightens the movie"; LAT "does a solid job"; WP "as [the] mom, the talented Stone is wasted"; SFC "subdued and credible"; TGM "delivers a nicely muted cameo"); NSFC runner-up Patricia Clarkson in *High Art* (NYT "a devilish turn"; CT "the film's most entertaining player"; CST "succeeds in creating a complete, complex character"); Sissy Spacek in *Affliction* (NYT "luminous"; BG "plays the girlfriend so gently that we hold our breath"; TT "wonderfully understated"); Kathy Burke in *Elizabeth* (NYT "rages so vividly"; SMH "eye-catching ... [turns] Mary into a full-blown grotesque"); Toni Collette in *Velvet Goldmine* (LAT "good"; CT "only Collette as Mandy Slade has much depth"; TGM "technically expert, slipping effortlessly in and out of her American and affected British accents"); and Jennifer Ehle in *Wilde* (TGM "finding silent depths in an underwritten role"; SMH "does a masterly job").

Ahead of all these contenders, Oscar voters nominated Brenda Blethyn as the loud–mouthed mother in *Little Voice* (NYT "[she and Caine] add humor and spice"; NYP "[an] exquisite performance"; LAT "it's especially difficult to endure Blethyn's abrasive work"; CT "[a] big, bravura comic performance"; WP "astonishes in the role ... a great comic performance"; TT "monotonously loud"; SMH "[a] great performance ... enormous fun") and Rachel Griffiths as the sister of cellist Jacqueline du Pré in *Hilary and Jackie* (NYT "[a] calm, quietly anguished performance ... beautifully acted"; LAT "superbly acted ... brings a keen mixture of melancholy and resilience to the part"; CT "pulls off the more difficult feat ... provides the film's emotional core ... makes [her character's choices] believable"; WP "[an] accomplished performance"; TT "excellent ... [a] fierce ... strong, sensitive performance"; G "has perhaps the tougher part ... [she] opens up the whole package of complicity, indulgence and vicariousness ... outstanding"). Both had been SAG nominees and it was the first time that the Academy and Guild ballots for Best Supporting Actress had matched.

On Oscar night, as expected, Dench was presented with the Oscar. "I feel, for eight minutes on the screen, I should only get a little bit of him," she remarked. Dench was victorious again in London a few weeks later, collecting a competitive BAFTA for feature film work for the third time in her career.

1999

BEST PICTURE

ACADEMY AWARDS
• *American Beauty*
(DreamWorks, 121 mins, 1 Oct 1999, $130.0m, 8 noms)
The Cider House Rules
(Miramax, 126 mins, 17 Dec 1999, $57.5m, 7 noms)
The Green Mile
(Castle Rock, Warner Bros., 188 mins, 10 Dec 1999, $136.8m, 4 noms)
The Insider
(Touchstone, 157 mins, 5 Nov 1999, $28.9m, 7 noms)
The Sixth Sense
(Hollywood, Spyglass, 107 mins, 6 Aug 1999, $293.5m, 6 noms)

GOLDEN GLOBE AWARDS
(Drama)
• *American Beauty*
The End of the Affair
The Hurricane
The Insider
The Talented Mr Ripley

(Comedy/Musical)
Analyze This
Being John Malkovich
Man on the Moon
Notting Hill
• *Toy Story 2*

PRODUCERS GUILD AWARD
• *American Beauty*
Being John Malkovich
The Cider House Rules
The Hurricane
The Insider

CRITICS' CHOICE AWARDS
• *American Beauty*
Being John Malkovich
The Cider House Rules
The Green Mile
The Insider
Magnolia
Man on the Moon
The Sixth Sense
The Talented Mr Ripley
Three Kings

BRITISH ACADEMY AWARDS
(Best Film)
• *American Beauty*
East is East
The End of the Affair
The Sixth Sense
The Talented Mr Ripley

(Best British Film)
• *East is East*
Notting Hill
Onegin
Ratcatcher
Wonderland

1999

NEW YORK – *Topsy-Turvy*
LOS ANGELES – *The Insider*
BOARD OF REVIEW – *American Beauty*
NATIONAL SOCIETY – *Being John Malkovich* and *Topsy-Turvy*
LONDON
   (Best Film) *American Beauty*
   (Best British Film) *East is East*

Showered with the best notices of the year, the comedy-drama *American Beauty* was seen by DreamWorks as a strong candidate with which to claim the Academy's top accolade for the first time (NYT "hilarious [and] beautiful [with] haunting power"; NYP "a flatout masterpiece, surely the best movie of the year"; LAT "edgy and provocative ... distinctive [and] delicately balanced"; V "a real American original"; WP "hilarious, painful and brutally frank ... one of the year's finest pictures ... a triumph – adult, smart, involving, stylish ... a scalding satire"; SFC "a wonder of a film ... luminous, beautifully executed ... dazzling [and] wholly original ... the best American film of the year"; G "stunning ... intelligent, exhilarating, effervescent film-making"; SMH "unique and wonderful ... brilliant"). *American Beauty* was named Best Picture by the National Board of Review and the London Film Critics, and finished runner-up for the top accolades from the New York Film Critics Circle and the Los Angeles Film Critics Association.

The runner-up in the voting by the NBR was *The Talented Mr Ripley* (NYT "[a] hypnotic, sensually charged adaptation ... a scenic, voluptuously beautiful film"; NYP "seductive and stylish"; NYDN "a class act all the way"; LAT "a wonderfully accomplished work [yet] unexpectedly lacking in emotional depth"; V "intoxicating and involving"; CT "a partly brilliant, partly overreaching movie thriller"; CST "intelligent"; SFC "excellent"; SFX "shattering"; SMH "a sophisticated film"). Finishing third was the ensemble drama *Magnolia* (NYT "self-destructs spectacularly [but] is still too good to be missed"; NYP "an audacious, hilarious, deeply affecting three-hour tapestry"; LAT "[a] frantic, flawed, fascinating film ... both impressive and a bit out of control ... a level of nonstop emotional intensity that borders on the exhausting"; V "a remarkably inventive and audacious film"; CT "breathtaking ... as bracing as it is bleak ... marvelous"; CST "a great joyous leap into melodrama and coincidence"; WP "flawed and fascinating ... [an] edgy, messy, wildly ambitious portrait"; SFC "extraordinary [and] wonderful"; TGM "exuberant and exasperating ... it delights [but] is a little short on substance"). Both were expected to be among the contenders for the Best Picture Oscar.

1999

Taking the prize in Los Angeles ahead of *American Beauty* was the whistle-blower drama *The Insider* (NYT "enthralling"; LAT "exceptional ... a compelling drama"; CT "intelligent, gripping ... first-class"; WP "absorbing ... a well-orchestrated nightmare that keeps you on edge until the very end"; TGM "engrossing"; SMH "infinitely fascinating").

Meanwhile, the New York accolade was won by *Topsy-Turvy*, a film about Gilbert and Sullivan (NYT "grandly entertaining ... [a] delightful film"; NYP "charming, warm, witty ... and moving"; LAT "a bit longer than it might be"; CT "marvelous ... a feast of a film ... one of the cinema's great valentines to the theater"; CST "one of the year's best"; WP "a creaking, unfocused period piece"; SFC "a delight"; TGM "fascinating but occasionally frustrating ... disjointed"; G "funny, tender, sharp and moving"; SMH "good").

Finishing as runners-up in New York alongside *American Beauty* were both the independent comedy *Being John Malkovich* (NYT "endearing [and] irresistible ... very funny"; NYP "a must-see-more-than-once event"; LAT "a clever and outrageous piece of whimsical fantasy that is unique, unpredictable and more than a little strange"; CT "weird to the max, smart and sneaky ... the most original American movie of the year"; CST "endlessly inventive [and] dazzling ... either [it] gets nominated for best picture, or the members of the Academy need portals into their brains"; WP "full of creativity ... utterly, deliciously insane ... a fabulous movie ... certainly the year's most inventive and one of the most purely enjoyable"; SFC "a wonderfully demented fantasia ... tremendously entertaining"; TGM "strange and beguiling ... wonderfully inventive, wickedly funny, and thoughtful"; G "a screwball comedy from a parallel dimension ... your jaw may well drop with disbelief"; SMH "[a] wonderfully unhinged comic fantasy") and the drama *The Straight Story* (NYT "a slow-moving, folksy-looking, profoundly spiritual film that can hold an audience in absolute thrall ... a supremely improbable triumph"; NYP "lyrical, sweet and brimming with optimism"; LAT "too mannered and weird around the edges to be convincing"; CT "wonderful ... the year's most beautiful and simply moving film"; WP "cuts a path directly to the heart"; SFC "beautiful and surprisingly gentle"; G "a sweet and disarming tale"). *Topsy-Turvy* and *Being John Malkovich* later shared the National Society of Film Critics plaudit.

American Beauty led the field of Globe contenders with six mentions. Its competition for Best Picture (Drama) comprised: both *The Insider* and *The Talented Mr Ripley*, which each garnered five nominations; *The Hurricane* (NYT "stirring but schmaltzy [and] unabashedly sentimental ... blatantly manipulative"; NYP "deeply moving"; LAT "fairly standard middle-of-the-road fare, simplistic, conventional ... not up to the mark set by Washington's work ... [has a] tendency toward tedium"; CT "old-fashioned [yet] compelling ... a movie of real power, heartfelt emotion"); and the romantic tragedy *The End of the Affair* (NYT "intoxicating ... deeply stirring and elegantly concise ... a seamlessly engrossing film"; NYP "it's hard to feel anything but disappointment and boredom"; LAT "handsomely mounted, literate, emotionally sophisticated"; WP "an intelligent film, beautifully acted and stylishly made"; SFC "guaranteed to be mistaken for a first-rate picture ... a frustrating amalgam of the brilliant and the ponderous, the inspired and the fatuous"). New York and NSFC prizewinner *Topsy-Turvy* was a notable omission from the Globe short-list, which many considered a major blow to its chances of Oscar recognition.

The inclusion of *The Hurricane* on the Globe ballot was a surprise given the film had received mixed reviews from critics. Other highly-anticipated awards season contenders that subsequently failed to impress critics were: *Angela's Ashes* (NYT "the film isn't wrenching enough ... [makes] the deplorable and the sentimental one and the same"; LAT "missing something essential"; CT "a film of integrity, skill and compassion, lovingly produced, ambitiously designed, meticulously realized ... [yet] some crucial fire or magic is missing"; CST "lacking a heart"; WP "Parker's well-meaning adaptation is unrelentingly sodden"; SFC "doesn't work as entertainment ... deadening"; G "overblown"); *Snow Falling on Cedars* (NYT "admirably high-minded and visually gorgeous but fatally anesthetised by its own grandiosity"; LAT "has to fight to hold our attention and it doesn't always succeed ... too calculated"; V "impeccably crafted but dramatically dull"; CT "too reverent, too showy, too earnest ... falls short of Oscar-worthiness"; CST "a rich, multilayered film"; WP "mediocre"; SFC "plodding and self-serious"); *Man on the Moon* (NYT "a formidable piece of work [but] opaque"; NYP "one of the year's most entertaining movies"; CT "uninspired"; WP "less a story than a series of exhibits ... re-creates but never enters"; SFC "a near miss"; HRp "ultimately disappoints"); and *Any Given Sunday* (NYT "a mechanically contrived series of power struggles ... nothing subtle about it ... in the end the movie cops out"; NYP "predictable and blatantly commercial"; LAT "[an] energetic and diverting sports soap opera"; CT "an archetypal big-audience movie with the usual format ... this rowdy, high-impact movie lacks taste, decorum, sensitivity and humility"; CST "a smart sports movie almost swamped by production overkill"; WP "an exercise in bombast").

Perhaps the most high-profile of all the eagerly-awaited contenders to eventually divide critics and make no real impact on the awards season, however, was *Eyes Wide Shut*, the final film by Stanley Kubrick (NYT "astonishing [and] quietly devastating ... [a] brilliantly provocative tour de force ... stunning [and] literally spellbinding"; NYP "a letdown"; LAT "a strange, somber and troubling meditation of jealousy, obsession and (yes) sex and death ... half brilliant, half banal ... a film that is better at mood than substance [and yet] has the powerful, lacerating impact of inescapable nightmare"; HRp "challenging and richly rewarding"; WP "mesmerizing"; G "extraordinary ... captivating").

As the Golden Globes approached, *The Insider* and *The Hurricane* became embroiled in well-publicised controversies over historical accuracy, while *The Talented Mr Ripley* seemed to be abandoned ignominiously by distributor Miramax in favour of an alternative awards season contender with greater appeal to the Academy's membership: *The Cider House Rules*, an adaptation of John Irving's popular novel which had not earned Best Picture mentions from the NBR or the Hollywood Foreign Press Association (NYT "an unabashedly sentimental movie [and] its tone turns cloyingly sweet"; LAT "superb"; CT "a deliberately old-fashioned picture that succeeds in nearly everything it tries to do"; CST "a muddle ... absorbing and enchanting in parts [but] arrives nowhere in particular"; WP "a sensitive but not overly sentimental adaptation"; SFC "[the film] is no classic"; G "[a] combination of shameless, manipulative sentimentality and a bizarre deployment of adult issues"). It was thus no surprise when *American Beauty* collected four trophies, including Best Picture (Drama).

There was, however, a surprise winner in the Comedy/Musical category. The two favourites, the critically acclaimed *Being John Malkovich* and the box office hit *Notting Hill* (NYT "has lots of glossy charm"; NYP "enchanting"; LAT "consistently amusing"; CT "a romantic comedy that just flat-out works ... funny, sympathetic, mostly smart"; CST "bright"; WP "fabulous"; V "engaging"), were outpolled by the lauded animated hit *Toy Story 2* (NYT "has the power to enchant children while keeping adults entertained"; LAT "lively and good-humored with a great sense of fun"; V "satisfying in every respect"; HRp "a triumph at every level"; CT "a beginning-to-end joy ... quite thought-provoking and packs a surprising emotional wallop"; CT "you can't ask for a family film to do more ... smart and playful"; CST "enchanting"; WP "a sequel that eclipses the original ... hilarious [and] inventive ... our hearts are kept breathtakingly close to breaking").

Just days before the Globe ceremony, the Producers Guild of America announced its five finalists. As expected both *American Beauty* and *Being John Malkovich* were mentioned, while *The Cider House Rules* was included ahead of *The Talented Mr Ripley*. Despite mounting controversy, both *The Insider* and *The Hurricane* were also shortlisted.

Nearly a month later, the Academy announced its list of nominees. As expected, *American Beauty* led the field with eight nominations including Best Picture, while the strong campaign by Miramax succeeded in securing seven mentions for *The Cider House Rules* including a spot in the top category. Also recognised in seven categories, including Best Picture, was *The Insider*. Completing the Best Picture line-up were two films that had not been in contention for the Globe or the PGA honour: *The Green Mile*, a three-hour prison drama which had become a major box office hit despite dividing critics (NYT "extravagantly long ... does not truly warrant such a marathon ... could have been told with more economy"; NYP "a terrific, powerful movie"; LAT "[a] bloated film [which] moves with suffocating deliberateness"; CT "good, not great ... too overblown, too stylistically overripe"; WP "hardly a second of it seems convincing ... a shattering disappointment"; V "generally holds one's attention through the long journey"; SFC "three hours of overstatement and schmaltz ... inflated, self-important and often absurd"; TGM "[a] debacle ... an exercise in titanic self-importance"); and the year's surprise commercial smash *The Sixth Sense* (NYT "gaggingly mawkish supernatural kitsch"; NYP "a superb film"; LAT "so disarmingly eerie it's virtually guaranteed to rattle the most jaded of cages"; V "interesting"; CT "startling ... it's a rarity for a movie to be willing to try your patience and even more of one for your perseverance to be so amply rewarded ... an uncommonly serious-minded movie that's brave enough to engage our deepest emotions"; CST "intriguing"; TGM "too plodding to be a thriller, too one-dimensional to be psychological, and not nearly frightening enough to be chilling"; S&S "an attention-grabbing fusion of minimalism and overstatement"). Both films had appeared on the BFCA top ten list. Notably shut out of contention for the Academy's top honour were: *Being John Malkovich*, *The Hurricane*, *Magnolia*, *The Talented Mr Ripley* and *Topsy-Turvy*.

Also overlooked were: European Film Award winner *Todo Sobre Mi Madre (All About My Mother)* (NYT "marvelous"; LAT "a surprisingly satisfying combination of bawdy sexual humor [and] genuine emotion"; CT "a vividly colourful melodrama"; WP "great ... [a] richly, nuanced drama"; TT "impressive"; G "[an] accomplished and distinctive movie"); *Boys Don't Cry* (NYT "stunning ... transfixing"; NYP "a haunting, superbly made film"; LAT "an exceptional – and exceptionally disturbing – film ... unflinching, uncompromising ... powerful [and] wrenching"; CST "one of the best films of the year"; WP "heartbreaking"); *Onegin* (NYT "out of balance"; LAT "breathtaking in its beauty and authenticity ... a pleasure in all ways"; CST "the visuals are wonderful, but the drama is muted"; SFC "intelligent and sensitive [but] too deliberate"; Time "a handsome, well-acted, richly textured adaptation"; G "earnest but worthwhile"; S&S "consistently enthralling"); *Three Kings* (NYT "isn't nearly as successful as [the director's previous films]"; NYP "original and brilliant"; LAT "ambitious ... Hollywood with a twist"; CT "war movies never looked like this before ... amazingly pointed"; CST "one of the best movies of the year ... a dark, zesty, live-wire action-adventure comedy ... an exciting and funny movie"; WP "enormously entertaining ... brilliant, if somewhat flawed"; TGM "not a great picture, but it is a very good one"; TT "[a] rip-roaring action comedy"; SMH "a smart, slick, funny, action-packed, perfectly cast satire"); *Felicia's Journey* (NYT "brilliant ... hard to forget"; LAT "one of the year's riskiest yet most effective films"; CT "a psychological thriller of uncommon intelligence and compassion ... a subtle, heartbreaking film"; CST "astounding"; WP "hypnotic ... entrancing [and] richly drawn"; SFC "beautifully made"); *Lola Rennt (Run Lola Run)* (NYT "sheer cleverness ... a furiously kinetic display of pyrotechnics"; LAT "[a] hyperkinetic pop culture firecracker of a film ... cleverness is [the film's] greatest asset"; CT "a knockout ... the year's most playful feature ... a pure shot of adrenaline ... incredibly exciting and dazzlingly clever"; CST "a film of non-stop motion and visual invention"; SFC "fascinating"; S&S "exhilaratingly hyperactive ... stylish ... keeps us breathless"; SMH "astonishing [and] ingenious ... an original"); and *Bacheha-Ye Aseman (Children of Heaven)* (LAT "this film leaves you moved"; CT "wonderful ... one of the year's genuine crowd-pleasers: a movie both heart-warmingly innocent and rousingly exciting ... something unique and moving"; WP "charming, sometimes heart-rending ... unusually touching").

Also snubbed was the year's most unexpected critical and commercial success, *The Blair Witch Project* (NYT "skilfully spun out of thin air ... a most inventive departure from standard horror fare"; NYP "original"; LAT "a clever, entertaining stunt"; V "smart without feeling manipulative"; CT "chilling"; CST "extraordinarily effective"; WP "simple but devastatingly effective"; SFC "one-of-a-kind ... enormously successful"; G "stunningly effective ... inspired ... a vivisectional experiment in anxiety").

Through the Oscar voting period, Miramax continued to heavily promote *The Cider House Rules* and generated hype suggesting that the film might pull off an upset win. Despite such talk, however, *American Beauty* remained on track, collecting the PGA accolade and the Directors Guild of American plaudit for director Sam Mendes.

On Oscar night, the much-discussed Miramax upset failed to materialise. *American Beauty* triumphed in the Best Picture category, thus claiming the top Academy Award for DreamWorks for the first time. A few weeks later, the film repeated its win at the British Academy Awards over a field of nominees that included NBR runner-up *The Talented Mr Ripley*.

BEST DIRECTOR

ACADEMY AWARDS
Lasse Hallström for *The Cider House Rules*
Spike Jonze for *Being John Malkovich*
Michael Mann for *The Insider*
• **Sam Mendes for *American Beauty***
M. Night Shyamalan for *The Sixth Sense*

GOLDEN GLOBE AWARDS
Norman Jewison – *The Hurricane*
Neil Jordan – *The End of the Affair*
Michael Mann – *The Insider*
• **Sam Mendes – *American Beauty***
Anthony Minghella – *The Talented Mr Ripley*

DIRECTORS GUILD AWARD
Frank Darabont – *The Green Mile*
Spike Jonze – *Being John Malkovich*
Michael Mann – *The Insider*
• **Sam Mendes – *American Beauty***
M. Night Shyamalan
 – *The Sixth Sense*

BRITISH ACADEMY AWARDS
• **Pedro Almodóvar**
 – *Todo Sobre Mi Madre*
 (*All About My Mother*)
Neil Jordan – *The End of the Affair*
Sam Mendes – *American Beauty*
Anthony Minghella
 – *The Talented Mr Ripley*
M. Night Shyamalan
 – *The Sixth Sense*

NEW YORK – **Mike Leigh** – ***Topsy-Turvy***
LOS ANGELES – **Sam Mendes** – ***American Beauty***
BOARD OF REVIEW – **Anthony Minghella** – ***The Talented Mr Ripley***
NATIONAL SOCIETY – **Mike Leigh** – ***Topsy-Turvy***
CRITICS' CHOICE – **Sam Mendes** – ***American Beauty***
LONDON
 (Director) **Sam Mendes** – ***American Beauty***
 (British Director) **Lynne Ramsay** – ***Ratcatcher***

The overwhelming favourite for the Academy Award was Sam Mendes, a respected theatre director who had made his feature film directorial debut with the suburban comedy-drama *American Beauty* (NYT "directed with terrific visual flair ... brilliantly staged"; LAT "very accomplished ... delicately

1999

balanced"; V "displays a very sure hand"; SFC "remarkable [and] sensational";
G "a film of incredible flair and formal, compositional brilliance ... [he] shows
an awe-inspiringly precocious mastery of technique"). In the lead-up to the
Oscars, Mendes was honoured by the Los Angeles Film Critics Association, the
Broadcast Film Critics Association and the Directors Guild of America. He had
also won the Golden Globe.

Nominated for the Oscar alongside Mendes were: Michael Mann, the runner-
up for Los Angeles prize, for *The Insider* (NYT "directed with pulse-quickening
panache that heightens the tensions within the story ... he strikes a balance, and
he gets it right"; LAT "fiercely directed [with] riveting skill ... uses his instinct
for dramatic storytelling to fill every bit of this two-hour, 38-minute film with
passion and tension"; CT "directed and acted with unusual intelligence and
intensity"; WP "well-orchestrated"; TGM "the directorial inventiveness [is]
relentless"; SMH "never lets you lose your bearings ... adept"); Spike Jonze for
his directorial debut *Being John Malkovich* (NYT "endearingly nutty ...
irresistible"; LAT "displays the same kind of unexpected delight in playing with
reality that he used in music videos ... his gift here is being able to treat a highly
unusual scenario as if it were the most normal of situations"; CT "done in a
deceptively flat, deadpan style"; TGM "shoots [the surrealism] with a
nonchalant naturalism ... the point is all the more effective because it's casually
made ... Jonze treats the script like the treasure it is – with care and restraint ...
he underplays this wonky material, giving the surreal content a realistic outline";
G "favours melancholic downplaying, but isn't averse to stylistic digressions");
M. Night Shyamalan for the thriller *The Sixth Sense* (LAT "deft"); and Lasse
Hallström for *The Cider House Rules* (LAT "splendid ... astute ... can handle
the tragicomic with assurance"; CT "directed with such sensitivity and feeling
that it casts its narrative spell as affectingly as the old studio classics"; G "sure-
footed ... the film unfolds with confidence and pace"). Hallström, the only
previous nominee in the field, emerged as the dark horse even though he had not
featured during the awards season prior to his nomination by the Academy.

There were numerous notable omissions from the Oscar ballot, including:
New York Film Critics Circle and National Society of Film Critics winner Mike
Leigh for *Topsy-Turvy* (NYT "orchestrates this delightful film so well"; CT
"Leigh's methods yield dazzling results again"); National Board of Review
winner Anthony Minghella for *The Talented Mr Ripley* (NYT "directed with
acute attention to every nuance"; LAT "beautifully mounted and directed ... a
wonderfully accomplished work"; WP "ably written and directed"; SFC
"expertly poised"); Norman Jewison for *The Hurricane* (NYP "expertly
crafted"; CT "a wizardly job of compressing the story, tying all the strands
together: carrying us, in a tricky flashback structure"); Neil Jordan for *The End
of the Affair* (NYT "graceful"; LAT "has beautifully crafted this film"; WP

"stylishly made"); Frank Darabont for *The Green Mile* (LAT "ultra-leisurely storytelling by a filmmaker too fond of his own work to cut a drama, and too powerful to be amendable to changing his mind ... suffocating deliberateness"; CT "stylistically overripe"; WP "routinely competent but completely untransfigured by distinction"; TGM "seems blithely unaware"); David Lynch, runner-up for the prize in New York, for *The Straight Story* (NYT "rises to this challenge with exhilarating vigor ... bravely defying conventional wisdom ... precise and technically adept"; CT "Lynch does something rare"; WP "what a triumph this is for Lynch"); David O. Russell, runner-up for NSFC accolade, for *Three Kings* (NYT "experiments nervously [and] loses track of his narrative ... the film needs a cleaner start-to-finish line"; LAT "this chaotic war within a war is vividly captured by the high-energy, frenetic visual style used by Russell ... a further step in the evolution of an audacious and entertaining filmmaker"; CT "[the film] will surprise some audiences with its bravura technique"; SMH "beautifully constructed"); Kimberly Peirce for *Boys Don't Cry* (NYT "Peirce has found a way to tell [the story] brilliantly ... insightful overview"; NYP "superbly made"; LAT "made with complete conviction and rare skill"; CST "finds the right note"; WP "Peirce has created a deeply sympathetic story that transforms Brandon's tragic story into a sweetly textured metaphor for sexual identity and freedom"; SFC "amazing"; TGM "beautifully nuanced ... Peirce does more with less – she desensationalizes the tale in order to humanize its participants ... measured direction"); Paul Thomas Anderson for *Magnolia* (NYT "artfully orchestrated"; LAT "[the film] may occasionally overshoot its mark, but it's the kind of jumble only a truly gifted filmmaker can make ... constant [is] the energy, confidence and panache that mark [his] directing style"; CT "daring [but] at times undisciplined"; TGM "give [him] credit for his splendid nerve"); and the late Stanley Kubrick for *Eyes Wide Shut* (NYT "the film moves effortlessly ... one more brilliantly provocative tour de force"; LAT "the work of a master director ... virtuoso visual work ... uses pure cinematic technique to go to the core of his emotions"; G "from the very first frames, Kubrick's imperious command of his material is evident").

Also by-passed for consideration were: Atom Egoyan for *Felicia's Journey* (NYT "brilliantly bends this Gothic-flavored fable to express his own tricky cinematic vision"; LAT "wonderfully accomplished ... consolidating the Canadian filmmaker's status as a major director in contemporary world cinema"; CT "the best of Egoyan's films"; WP "deceptively casual style"; SFC "impeccably directed"); Martha Fiennes for *Onegin* (LAT "elegantly wrought [and] remarkably assured"; TT "though she shapes scenes conscientiously, [she] doesn't convey a sense of forward movement ... there's something frozen about her film"; G "adroit"); Julie Taymor for *Titus* (NYT "audacious ... pays dividends ... what was then, she forcefully reminds us, is also now"; LAT "a dynamic film directed with unflagging energy"; TGM "uses her production skills to create an eclectically evil world"); Guy Ritchie for *Lock, Stock and Two Smoking Barrels* (NYT "brash, ebullient direction"; CT "the pace of the storytelling shrieks 1990s, thanks to the frenzied cutting style of writer-director Guy Ritchie"; WP "most of [the style] is done in the editing room, where the director tries every trick ever invented"; TGM "bravura showiness"); David Fincher for *Fight Club* (NYT "finds subject matter audacious enough to suit his lightning-fast visual sophistication, and puts that style to stunningly effective use"; CT "directed with his usual stunning visual pyrotechnics ... shot with breathtaking bravura"; CST "very well made"; WP "fluid direction"); and Tom Tykwer for *Lola Rennt (Run Lola Run)* (NYT "visual virtuosity ... fuses lightning-fast visual tricks, tirelessly shifting styles and the arbitrary possibilities of interactive storytelling [and he] does this with a vigor and pizazz"; LAT "restless, inventive work ... impressive"; CT "has a fully developed, technically dashing, almost brazenly confident style"; SFC "dazzling technique"; S&S "that Tykwer maintains our flow of empathy while demonstrating and exploiting the potential of interactive cinema manqué is, in itself, an awesome achievement"; SMH "his control of narrative drive is perhaps the cleverest trick in his whole armoury").

On Oscar night, as expected, DGA honoree Mendes collected the Academy Award.

In London a few weeks later, however, Mendes was unexpectedly outpolled for the BAFTA. Instead, the British Academy chose to honour Spanish film-maker Pedro Almodóvar for *Todo Sobre Mi Madre (All About My Mother)*, a film for which he had been honoured at the Cannes Film Festival eleven months earlier (NYT "filmed by Mr Almodóvar with the sweeping visual assurance that binds this film together so firmly"; LAT "understands that true drama can be found in the heart of outrageous melodrama"; CT "adept"; WP "[his] mastery of the medium has never been so assured"; SFC "technically accomplished"; TT "impressive"; S&S "proves that [he] is one of the greats of European cinema"). Almodóvar had been among the glaring omissions from the list of Best Director Oscar nominees, although he collected a statuette as the director of the year's Best Foreign-Language Film.

1999

BEST ACTOR

ACADEMY AWARDS
Russell Crowe as 'Jeffrey Wigand' in *The Insider*
Richard Farnsworth as 'Alvin Straight' in *The Straight Story*
Sean Penn as 'Emmet Ray' in *Sweet and Lowdown*
• **Kevin Spacey as 'Lester Burnham' in *American Beauty***
Denzel Washington as 'Rubin "Hurricane" Carter' in *The Hurricane*

GOLDEN GLOBE AWARDS
(Drama)
Russell Crowe – *The Insider*
Matt Damon
 – *The Talented Mr Ripley*
Richard Farnsworth
 – *The Straight Story*
Kevin Spacey – *American Beauty*
• **Denzel Washington – *The Hurricane***

(Comedy/Musical)
• **Jim Carrey – *Man on the Moon***
Robert De Niro – *Analyze This*
Rupert Everett – *An Ideal Husband*
Hugh Grant – *Notting Hill*
Sean Penn – *Sweet and Lowdown*

SCREEN ACTORS GUILD
Jim Carrey – *Man on the Moon*
Russell Crowe – *The Insider*
Philip Seymour Hoffman – *Flawless*
• **Kevin Spacey – *American Beauty***
Denzel Washington – *The Hurricane*

BRITISH ACADEMY AWARDS
Jim Broadbent – *Topsy-Turvy*
Russell Crowe – *The Insider*
Ralph Fiennes
 – *The End of the Affair*
Om Puri – *East is East*
• **Kevin Spacey – *American Beauty***

NEW YORK – Richard Farnsworth – *The Straight Story*
LOS ANGELES – Russell Crowe – *The Insider*
BOARD OF REVIEW – Russell Crowe – *The Insider*
NATIONAL SOCIETY – Russell Crowe – *The Insider*
CRITICS' CHOICE – Russell Crowe – *The Insider*
LONDON
   (Actor) **Kevin Spacey – *American Beauty***
   (British Actor) **Jeremy Northam – *Happy Texas* and *An Ideal Husband*
      and *The Winslow Boy***

Thirty-five-year old Russell Crowe dominated the early part of the awards
season for his portrayal of fifty-seven-year old Jeffrey Wigand, a former tobacco
company employee who became an industry whistle-blower, in *The Insider*

(NYT "a subtle powerhouse in his wrenching evocation of Mr Wigand"; LAT "[a] memorable starring performance [and] marvelous"; CT "acted with unusual intelligence and intensity ... played with gray-haired, slightly frayed pugnacity – and refreshingly non-heroic vibes ... convincing"; WP "fantastic to watch ... virtually disappears inside [the role] ... [his] minimalist performance gives us clear insight into this opaque being"; HRp "excellent"; TGM "intense [a] vivid performance"; SMH "has transformed himself ... [he] effortlessly holds his place in the frame"). Crowe was named Best Actor by the Los Angeles Film Critics Association, the National Board of Review, the Broadcast Film Critics Association and the National Society of Film Critics. He was narrowly outpolled for the New York Film Critics Circle accolade, however, by seventy-nine-year old Hollywood veteran Richard Farnsworth as a retiree who travels interstate on a lawnmower to visit his dying brother in *The Straight Story* (NYT "played without a trace of artifice ... an amazingly stalwart performance that will not soon be forgotten"; LAT "exactly right [in] the role of a lifetime ... [a] dignified yet irascible performance"; CT "transfixing ... the performance of a lifetime"; WP "gives the performance of his life"; TT "touchingly played").

Both men were shortlisted for the Golden Globe (Drama) along with: Matt Damon in *The Talented Mr Ripley* (NYT "played with a fine, tricky mix of obsequiousness and ruthlessness"; LAT "does the best he can here, but this role is off-putting without playing to his strengths"; SFC "altogether amazing"); Kevin Spacey in *American Beauty* (NYT "played with heavenly finesse ... his wittiest and most agile screen performance yet"; LAT "faultless [in a] bravura performance"; CT "makes the transformation of Lester something wholly original"; WP "outstanding ... a performance that practically glows with vulnerability ... achingly tender"; SFC "his most impressive work yet"; Time "hands down the year's best performance"; G "superbly modulated"); and Denzel Washington in *The Hurricane* (NYT "an astonishing performance ... it is impossible not to be moved by the depth of [his] portrayal ... [he] leans into an otherwise schlocky movie and slams is out of the ballpark"; LAT "especially impressive ... [acts] with power, intensity, remarkable range and an ability to disturb that is both unnerving and electric ... a ferocious performance"; V "genuinely touching"; CT "terrific ... a great, transcendent portrayal, melding so completely with Carter that he can carry us easily through all his stages and changes ... a performance of depth and charisma, complexity and edge ... [a] knockout"; CST "one of [his] great performances"; WP "brilliantly played ... intense and tender ... a great performance, and sure Oscar bait"; SMH "brilliant"). When Julia Roberts opened the envelope at the Globe ceremony, neither of the critics' champs' names were inside. The winner was Washington, who became the second African-American to receive the Globe.

1999

On 1 February, the Screen Actors Guild shortlisted Crowe, Spacey and Washington, along with Philip Seymour Hoffman in *Flawless* (NYT "brings an angry heat to a stunt role ... makes you aware every second that he is giving a carefully shaped, larger-than-life performance"; LAT "fearless ... at once amusing and moving ... Hoffman could well be remembered in the upcoming awards season"; CT "plays the showier role with gusto ... a performancy performance that effectively communicates [the character's traits] yet never stops drawing attention to itself"; CST "shows he's one of the best new character actors") and Globe (Comedy/Musical) winner Jim Carrey as the late stand-up comic Andy Kaufman in *Man on the Moon* (NYT "an electrifying homage ... Carrey makes a flawless, uncanny impersonator [and then] adds his own stamp to the material"; LAT "a brilliant, almost terrifying impersonation ... seems to have an intuitive understanding of his bizarre subject"; CT "defying the notion that superstars only play themselves, gives a brilliantly askew, highly convincing impersonation"; CST "a heroic performance ... successfully disappears inside the character"; WP "astonishing ... [Kaufman] is exactly reconstructed [but] I'm not sure if this qualifies as acting"; SFC "does a meticulous job ... but a quality of mischief is absent").

Two weeks later Crowe, Spacey and Washington were also recognised by the Academy, but the fourth and fifth contenders were different from the Guild short list. Also nominated were Farnsworth and, in a major surprise, Sean Penn as a jazz guitarist in *Sweet and Lowdown* (NYT "while [he] makes Emmet a colorfully outrageous creation, the character himself isn't writ large enough to occupy the whole film"; LAT "brings an essential energy and a nice deadpan comic sensibility to his portrait"; CST "a master class in character development"; WP "splendidly acted ... Penn's performance is the movie's ultimate grace note ... Penn augments Emmet with a delicious combination of innocence, Panlike mischief and edginess"; TT "plays him with fetching boyish bravura ... [a] great performance").

The unexpected inclusion of Penn resulted in the exclusion of Globe winner Carrey for the second year in a row. The 1998 Cannes prize-winning performance of Peter Mullan in *My Name is Joe* (LAT "[played] with a compelling naturalism"; CT "an extraordinary performance ... makes Joe a raw yet sympathetic portrait of pain, hope and courage ... towering over everything is Mullan's portrayal of Joe"; WP "thoroughly engaging ... [a] charming, realistically moving performance ... he's full of passion and conviction"; SFC "beautifully acted") and the work of both NSFC runner-up Jim Broadbent (NYT "played with wonderful literate crankiness"; LAT "intense, captivating"; WP "towers over the rest of the cast"; SFC "wonderful") and his co-star Allan Corduner (NYT "excellent") in *Topsy-Turvy* (CT "show-stoppers"; G "outstanding ... superb performances") were also excluded.

Notable performances by previous Best Actor Oscar winners were also by-passed, including: Tom Hanks in *The Green Mile* (NYT "unaffectedly good ... helps ease the film into its just-folks storytelling mode"; LAT "excellent, elevating acting ... [his acting] can't completely rescue this bloated film, but it's certainly the best reason to see it"; CT "excellent ... supplies the right kind of moral center"; WP "very engaging"; SFC "played predictably"); Al Pacino in *The Insider* (NYT "one of Pacino's best, most alive characterizations"; LAT "[a] memorable starring performance"; CT "gives us an idealized but very exciting Bergman"; CST "always convincing"; WP "lends the right balance of heroic and antiheroic qualities"; HRp "excellent"; TGM "intense"; G "forgoes his usual grandstanding theatrics"); Nicolas Cage in *Bringing Out the Dead* (NYT "played soulfully ... gives a fine, haunting performance"; CT "for Cage, who gives the film a solid center, it's a partly thankless role ... without Cage's calm and bitterness, the film would be diminished"; G "played with great verve"); and Anthony Hopkins in *Titus* (NYT "his performance, one of his finest, is ghoulishly funny and emotionally devastating all at once"; LAT "a towering portrayal"; TGM "above them all, Hopkins rages and roars grandly").

Other acclaimed performances absent from the Oscar short-list were: Bob Hoskins in *Felicia's Journey* (NYT "a remarkably restrained and compassionate portrayal"; LAT "arguably Hoskins' finest performance"; CT "[an] awesomely moving performance ... should have had a lock on the Best Actor award [at Cannes] ... [a] powerful portrayal"; WP "what could be the finest performance of his career ... a master chef of nuance"); Terence Stamp in *The Limey* (NYT "plays the title role furiously, with single-minded intensity"; CT "he's perfect in the role"); Edward Norton in *Fight Club* (NYT "Norton, an ingenious actor, is once again trickier than he looks"; NYP "extraordinary"; LAT "Norton can disappear into anyone, but the spectacle of him disappearing into a barely-alive nobody is not particularly gratifying"; CT "Norton, a specialist in crookedly smiling, inwardly angry misfits, goes the limit here"); George Clooney in *Three Kings* (LAT "especially effective ... perfectly conveys the combination of capability, authority and a touch of larceny the film insists on"; CT "[his] best role ... he fits so well into this movie"; WP "tough and believable and full of a leader's charisma"; SMH "pitch-perfect ... a precise, deliberately reined-in performance"); and Nigel Hawthorne in *The Winslow Boy* (NYT "a wonderful performance, inhabits the role with wry urbanity and stirring conviction"; LAT "brings a humanity and a caring to his role that [the film] would be lost without"; WP "[an] impeccable, dignified performance ... he almost eclipses his uncanny performance as King George III in 'The Madness of King George' ... the greatness of his performance is evident immediately"; SFC "superbly played"; G "[a] cracking performance ... a joy to watch").

Finally, the acclaimed performance of Ralph Fiennes in *The End of the Affair* (NYT "[earns] high praise ... played with [an] intensely romantic aura"; NYP "mannered"; LAT "[a] passionate performance ... marvelously played ... seems almost born to the part"; WP "beautifully acted ... he saunters through the movie with sleek assurance ... [the character] fits him like a taut glove"), was perhaps unable to secure sufficient support from members of the Academy's Acting Branch because of his equally lauded turn in *Onegin*, a drama directed by his sister (NYT "almost everything that's good about 'Onegin' emanates from [his] complex portrayal"; LAT "at his most poised and least mannered ... one of his most effective, best-modulated portrayals to date"; Time "well-acted"; G "a finely, almost perfectly judged performance"; S&S "well acted ... [a] thoughtful performance").

Following his Globe win, Washington was the strong favourite for both the SAG trophy and the Oscar statuette. No African-American had won a statuette for a leading performance since Sidney Poitier in 1963. Washington, a previous Best Supporting Actor Oscar winner, had been recognised by the Academy in the acting categories for a fourth time, an unprecedented honour for an African-American. As the Oscars approached, however, Washington's frontrunner status came under serious threat when he was outpolled for the SAG award by Spacey, another previous Best Supporting Actor Oscar winner. All five previous Guild champs had subsequently collected the Academy's statuette.

At the Oscars a fortnight later, the flawless record of the Guild was preserved when Spacey was presented with the Best Actor Academy Award. He was also victorious at the British Academy Awards in London a few weeks later. It was his first BAFTA.

BEST ACTRESS

ACADEMY AWARDS
Annette Bening as 'Carolyn Burnham' in *American Beauty*
Janet McTeer as 'Mary Jo Walker' in *Tumbleweeds*
Julianne Moore as 'Sarah Miles' in *The End of the Affair*
Meryl Streep as 'Roberta Guaspari' in *Music of the Heart*
• **Hilary Swank as 'Teena Brandon/Brandon Teena' in *Boys Don't Cry***

GOLDEN GLOBE AWARDS
(Drama)
Annette Bening – *American Beauty*
Julianne Moore
  – The End of the Affair
Meryl Streep – *Music of the Heart*
• **Hilary Swank – *Boys Don't Cry***
Sigourney Weaver
  – A Map of the World

(Comedy/Musical)
• **Janet McTeer – *Tumbleweeds***
Julianne Moore – *An Ideal Husband*
Julia Roberts – *Notting Hill*
Sharon Stone – *The Muse*
Reese Witherspoon – *Election*

SCREEN ACTORS GUILD
• **Annette Bening**
  – *American Beauty*
Janet McTeer – *Tumbleweeds*
Julianne Moore
  – The End of the Affair
Meryl Streep – *Music of the Heart*
Hilary Swank – *Boys Don't Cry*

BRITISH ACADEMY AWARDS
Linda Bassett – *East is East*
• **Annette Bening**
  – *American Beauty*
Julianne Moore
  – The End of the Affair
Emily Watson – *Angela's Ashes*

NEW YORK – Hilary Swank – *Boys Don't Cry*
LOS ANGELES – Hilary Swank – *Boys Don't Cry*
BOARD OF REVIEW – Janet McTeer – *Tumbleweeds*
NATIONAL SOCIETY – Reese Witherspoon – *Election*
CRITICS' CHOICE – Hilary Swank – *Boys Don't Cry*
LONDON
    (Actress) **Annette Bening – *American Beauty***
    (British Actress) **Emily Watson – *Angela's Ashes* and *Hilary and Jackie***

Both the New York Film Critics Circle and the Los Angeles Film Critics Association named twenty-five-year old Hilary Swank as the year's Best Actress for her portrayal in the independent drama *Boys Don't Cry* of Brandon Teena, a young woman who was brutally raped and murdered after she was caught passing herself off as a man in a small town (NYT "astonishing ... [an] inspired performance ... deserves to be remembered at the end of the year for a devastating portrayal"; LAT "astonishing ... a piercing performance'"; V "flawless"; CT "a tremendous lead performance"; CST "deserves all praise for her performance ... a bravura piece of work"; WP "wonderfully portrayed ... [she and Sevigny give] performances of such luminous intensity that they break your heart"; SFC "so good it almost hurts ... inhabits the part so fully that it's nearly impossible to remember she's a woman ... Swank's performance crosses into a realm of veracity rare in any film acting"; TGM "wonderfully conveyed"). A relatively unknown actress, Swank had earned the year's strongest critical acclaim and her victories made her a strong frontrunner for the Oscar. The previous nine actresses to be named by both the east and west coast critics groups had all been nominated by the Academy, and six had taken home the statuette. In the early stages of the awards season Swank also collected the Best Actress award from the Broadcast Film Critics Association.

The National Board of Review presented Swank with its Best Breakthrough Performance award, and gave its Best Actress plaudit to another relative unknown in a small, independent drama: English actress Janet McTeer as an itinerant American single–mother in *Tumbleweeds* (NYT "an actor melting so deeply into a role that what is on the screen is not a performance at all but a kind of spontaneous alchemy ... [an] astoundingly vital portrayal ... extraordinarily nuanced"; LAT "superlative in every way ... persuades you instantly that to the core she is Mary Jo ... her performance ranks among the year's best"; CT "slips so completely into the skin of [the character] ... catches all the externals with such dazzling confidence that she can sail right past them [and] cut to the heart of Mary Jo"; WP "McTeer doesn't imitate Mary Jo Walker, and she doesn't act her. She becomes her. It's almost spooky ... [an] outsize performance"; TGM "what lends this wiry little film its piquancy is the performance of McTeer ... [her] performance is scintillating").

A performance in yet another independent film garnered the remaining critics' accolade. Reese Witherspoon was named by the National Society of Film Critics for playing an over-achieving student running for class president in the satire *Election* (NYT "charges through the film with all due comic monstrousness and turns her character into somebody everybody knows"; LAT "[an] expert performance ... completely delightful"; CT "a dead-on comic performance"; WP "plays Tracy so convincingly, I'm not sure I can look at her without a shudder again"). Twenty-three-year old Witherspoon had earlier been a surprise runner-up to Swank in the voting by the Los Angeles critics.

All three critics' prizewinners were recognised by the Hollywood Foreign Press Association. Swank was nominated for the Golden Globe (Drama) alongside: Annette Bening in *American Beauty* (NYT "scathingly funny, and also quite graceful"; LAT "faultless [in a] bravura performance ... [her character is] inhabited completely and convincingly"; WP "outstanding ... wires her role with such high-voltage archness and vitality, we'd swear we like her ... so convincing as this brittle Barbie with the tight smile that she seems in danger of shattering all movie long"; G "outstanding ... her best performance since 'The Grifters'"); Meryl Streep in *Music of the Heart* (NYT "boring as it may have become for Meryl Streep to show up for awards ceremonies, count on her to be doing it again [because] her performance here is strong and convincing [and] without undue sentimentality"; LAT "she's quite convincing here"; CT "soars ... conveys the essence of this stubborn mother and dedicated teacher without sentimentalizing her or condescending to us ... out-and-out great acting"; WP "fleshy, vulnerable, extraordinarily alive ... she's fabulous"; SFX "absolutely disappears into her role"; TGM "faultless ... another perfect Streep performance that mixes grit, vulnerability and repressed passion ... convincing"; TT "a remarkable performance"; SMH "convincing"); Sigourney Weaver in *A Map of the World* (NYT "she dominates virtually every scene ... [she] finds the rogue self-destructiveness that gives the character definition ... bares soul and body"; LAT "a luminous portrayal that misses no nuances or implications ... Alice requires nothing less than a heroic portrayal – and that is precisely what Weaver gives her"; CT "outstanding"; SFC "a great performance ... amazing [and] exceptional"; TT "one of those performances the Academy simply can't get enough of ... outstanding ... takes the intensity she poured into Ripley, her heroine from the Alien movies, and unleashes it on the inner demons of Alice's psyche"); and New York runner-up Julianne Moore in *The End of the Affair* (NYT "brings strength and rapturousness to her potentially melodramatic role, and casts a spell that is never broken"; NYP "mannered"; LAT "memorable ... [a] passionate performance"; WP "beautifully acted ... makes Sarah a flesh-and-blood object of hatred and desire, a vulnerable ideal ... unforgettable"; SFC "believable but bland"; SMH "persuasive").

Julianne Moore earned a rare double Globe nomination, when she was also included in the Globe (Comedy/Musical) category for *An Ideal Husband* (LAT "memorable"; SFC "admirable"; TGM "there's just not a false note"). Also in contention were McTeer and Witherspoon, Julia Roberts in *Notting Hill* (NYT "a lovely opportunity to poke fun at her own situation"; LAT "surprisingly effective"; CT "utterly convincing ... she does imbue Anna with a tangible sense of vulnerability"; G "Roberts is really very good, better than she has ever been") and Sharon Stone in *The Muse* (NYT "hilarious ... a delectable comic performance ... Sarah is played dreamily by Ms Stone"; LAT "sure-handed, gleeful work"; CT "Stone is perfect for Sarah ... shows some stunningly unexpected verbal and physical comedy gifts here").

As expected, Swank triumphed in the Drama category at the Globe ceremony, a victory that further strengthened her status as the Oscar frontrunner. In the Comedy/Musical category, meanwhile, the winner was McTeer and the result was equally important for her chances of receiving recognition from the Academy since many observers thought her work may have been overshadowed by Susan Sarandon's turn in a similar role in *Anywhere But Here* (NYT "show-stopping ... Sarandon makes her enormously funny and appealing"; LAT "Sarandon and her character do not make a good fit"; CT "hands Sarandon one of the richest comic-dramatic opportunities of her career ... she makes magic with a part that could easily sink into the over-cute ... [she] nails the character's brassy chutzpah, flirty energy, unabashed sexiness and hilarious posturing – as well as the kind heart beating beneath it all"; WP "Sarandon is the movie's most enduring pleasure").

In February, the Screen Actors Guild and the Academy both mentioned the same five candidates: Globe winners Swank and McTeer were nominated alongside Bening and Moore (who was cited for her role in *The End of the Affair*). Completing the line-up was Streep, whose inclusion on the Oscar ballot equalled Katharine Hepburn's all-time record for the acting categories.

Overlooked for Globe, Guild and Academy recognition were: Winona Ryder in *Girl, Interrupted* (NYT "her most penetrating screen performance, one that deserves extra credit for not pleading for our love"; LAT "not flashy or showy, Ryder's performance has an authenticity to it, and the actress knows how to make us care in the bargain ... what helps the film stay honest are the purity and grace of its lead performances by Ryder and Jolie"; CT "the movie never really uses her or her intensity well"; CST "intriguing and watchable"; WP "played powerfully"); Emily Watson, winner of the Best British Actress award from the London Film Critics, in *Angela's Ashes* (NYT "played with patience and backbone"; NYP "as good as ever"; CST "wonderful"; WP "Watson, as lively an actress as you'd ever want to see, is limp as an Irish dishrag as the whiny Angela"; LAT "compelling [but] she's mainly called on to suffer and endure"; G "there's not much for her to do"; SMH "a lived-in performance"); European Film Award winner Cecilia Roth in *Todo Sobre Mi Madre (All About My Mother)* (CT "Roth's performance is wonderful because it doesn't feel like a performance"; G "[a] magnificent and moving performance ... wonderful ... [she] really does deserve an Academy Award"; S&S "[a] brave performance ... at once fiercely emotional and unsentimental"); Anjelica Huston in *Agnes Browne*, a film which she also directed (NYT "wisely underplays her role"; LAT "radiates an irresistible earth-mother glow that all but spills off the screen"; CST "cannot be faulted"; SFC "terrific"); Glenn Close in *Cookie's Fortune* (NYT "played diabolically well"; LAT "played with a wonderfully focused daffiness"; CT "superb ... so grasps her character's looney viewpoint, that she can make us relish Camille, turn meanness into high comedy"; TGM "first-rate"; SMH "gloriously overwrought"); Kate Winslet in *Holy Smoke!* (NYT "Winslet is stunning in this role"; LAT "it's not easy to imagine a young actress who could so convincingly hold her own on all levels with [co-star Harvey Keitel]"; CST "interesting"); and Franka Potente in the unexpected German box office hit *Lola Rennt (Run Lola Run)* (SFC "exudes amazing electricity"; SMH "a good performance ... something more pure than acting").

Also eligible for recognition, but ultimately overlooked, was 1991 European Film Award winner Juliette Binoche in *Les Amants du Pont-Neuf (The Lovers on the Bridge)* (NYT "inhabits her role with a rare grace and conviction"; LAT "bravura ... [in] a far more demanding role than that of the nurse in 'The English Patient' that won [her] an Oscar"; CT "her soft, dazzlingly empathetic face and wounding beauty make this grim milieu sing"). Screenings of the film, which had never previously been released in the United States, were arranged in selected cities, including Los Angeles, by Martin Scorsese and Miramax.

Swank's status as the overwhelming Oscar favourite was severely shaken at the Guild Awards when she was unexpectedly outpolled by Bening, who was eight and a half months pregnant at the time. The surprise victory led many observers to predict a victory for Bening at the Oscars since the previous four SAG winners had also claimed the Oscar.

There was, however, no *American Beauty* clean sweep on Oscar night. When Roberto Benigni opened the envelope, the winner of the Best Actress Academy Award was revealed to be Swank. "We have come a long way," she told the audience at the Shrine Auditorium. "To think that this movie wouldn't have been made three and a half years ago ... and we've made it now for under two million dollars. And now, this! It's quite remarkable." Among those she singled out for recognition was Kimberley Peirce, who joined Randa Haines and Jane Campion as the only women to that date to have directed an Oscar-winning performance.

Bening was, however, victorious in London at the British Academy Awards (she had already claimed the Best Actress prize from the London Film Critics). Bening received the Best Actress BAFTA ahead of a field of nominees which included Oscar contender Moore, whose role in *The End of the Affair* had previously earned Deborah Kerr a Best British Actress BAFTA nomination in 1955.

Swank was nominated for the BAFTA the following year but was outpolled by that year's Oscar winner, Julia Roberts in *Erin Brockovich*.

BEST SUPPORTING ACTOR

ACADEMY AWARDS
• **Michael Caine as 'Dr Wilbur Larch' in *The Cider House Rules***
Tom Cruise as 'Frank T. J. Mackey' in *Magnolia*
Michael Clarke Duncan as 'John Coffey' in *The Green Mile*
Jude Law as 'Dickie Greenleaf' in *The Talented Mr Ripley*
Haley Joel Osment as 'Cole Sear' in *The Sixth Sense*

GOLDEN GLOBE AWARDS
Michael Caine – *The Cider House Rules*
• **Tom Cruise – *Magnolia***
Michael Clarke Duncan – *The Green Mile*
Jude Law – *The Talented Mr Ripley*
Haley Joel Osment – *The Sixth Sense*

SCREEN ACTORS GUILD
• **Michael Caine**
  – *The Cider House Rules*
Chris Cooper – *American Beauty*
Tom Cruise – *Magnolia*
Michael Clarke Duncan
  – *The Green Mile*
Haley Joel Osment – *The Sixth Sense*

BRITISH ACADEMY AWARDS
Wes Bentley – *American Beauty*
Michael Caine
  – *The Cider House Rules*
Rhys Ifans – *Notting Hill*
• **Jude Law**
  – *The Talented Mr Ripley*
Timothy Spall – *Topsy-Turvy*

NEW YORK – John Malkovich – *Being John Malkovich*
LOS ANGELES – Christopher Plummer – *The Insider*
BOARD OF REVIEW – Philip Seymour Hoffman – *Magnolia* and *The Talented Mr Ripley*
NATIONAL SOCIETY – Christopher Plummer – *The Insider*
CRITICS' CHOICE – Michael Clarke Duncan – *The Green Mile*
LONDON (British Supporting Actor) **Michael Caine – *Little Voice***

Three winners of major critics' prizes surprisingly failed to garner nominations for the Golden Globe, the Screen Actors Guild trophy or the Academy Award, despite strong campaigns by distributors.

John Malkovich won the New York Film Critics Circle award and was runner-up for the Los Angeles Film Critics Association plaudit for portraying a fictionalised version of himself in the independent comedy *Being John Malkovich* (LAT "a capital job of impersonating his haughty and distant public persona"; CT "despite his shallow part, has fun with it"; WP "brilliant ... this may be the first time in history that a man wins an Oscar for playing himself"; TGM "a comic marvel to behold"; G "relishes every moment"; SMH "perfect").

The Los Angeles and National Society of Film Critics honours were each presented to Christopher Plummer in *The Insider* (NYT "an acute Mike Wallace impersonation"; CT "good as he always is, seems the wrong actor to play [the role] ... oozing with suave theatrical polish and irony, he can't convey the gritty bulldog Wallace persona familiar to us"; WP "has a powerful ring of believability"; HRp "excellent"; G "played with brilliantined brio").

The National Board of Review accolade, meanwhile, was won by Philip Seymour Hoffman for his performances in *Magnolia* (NYT "splendid acting ... extremely memorable"; CT "wonderful ... incredibly strong"; SMH "superb") and *The Talented Mr Ripley* (NYT "scene-stealingly wonderful"; LAT "best of all [the cast] ... pitch perfect"; CT "top-notch ... acidly witty social portraiture"; WP "utterly superb ... if we remember this movie for nothing else, let's toss the acting wreath to Hoffman"). Hoffman garnered as many points as Plummer in the NSFC voting, but did not share the award due to a technicality in the group's complicated voting system.

The only winner of a major critics' prize to contest the Globe, SAG award and Oscar was Michael Clarke Duncan, who won the Broadcast Film Critics Association prize as a soft–hearted prisoner with mysterious powers in *The Green Mile* (NYT "[an] unassumingly strong, moving performance"; LAT "wonderfully played"; CT "though he does a good job, it's not enough to resolve the seeming cliches"; SFC "overstated").

Arguably, the most glaring omissions from the Oscars shortlist were SAG nominee Chris Cooper (NYT "wonderful"; LAT "faultless"; WP "outstanding... finds deft grace notes") and BAFTA candidate Wes Bentley (LAT "faultless ... brings a commanding but low-key intensity and intimacy to Ricky"; WP "outstanding"; CST "grounded"; SFC "not a false note ... eerie ... unusual") as the father and son in *American Beauty*, the year's most nominated film and the favourite for the Best Picture statuette.

Others overlooked for the Globe, Guild award and Oscar were: both Stephen Rea (NYT "played with quiet eloquence"; NYP "mannered"; LAT "wonderfully subdued and restrained"; SFC "a constrained, delicate performance") and Ian Hart (NYT "a memorably Dickensian performance ... effortlessly [played]"; LAT "excellently portrayed"; CST "the best turn [in the film]"; SFC "[played with] unexpected sensitivity") in *The End of the Affair*; Ving Rhames in *Bringing Out the Dead* (NYT "a joyously scene-stealing performance"; LAT "delightful"; G "riveting"); Timothy Spall in *Topsy-Turvy* (LAT "especially strong"; CT "[a] show-stopper"; TGM "both genuine and moving"; G "notable"); Rhys Ifans in *Notting Hill* (NYT "popping up just often enough to steal much of the movie"; CT "hilarious"; SFC "stands out"; G "an outrageous scene-stealer"); Jamie Foxx in *Any Given Sunday* (NYT "the movie's revelation ... a subtle performance"; CT "[a] standout"; CST "doesn't step wrong"); Max von Sydow in *Snow Falling on Cedars* (NYT "well-acted"; LAT "scene-stealing ... giving the film's best performance"; CT "gives the movie's best performance"; TGM "hams shamelessly"); both David Morse (NYT "shares Hanks' laid-back timing and sly delivery"; LAT "especially effective"; WP "brings a deep-seated integrity to Brutus") and Sam Rockwell (NYT "provides loads of local color"; LAT "convincingly played") in *The Green Mile* (CT "excellent"); and Jeffrey Wright in *Ride with the Devil* (LAT "excellent work"; CST "especially intriguing").

The frontrunners for the Academy Award were Globe winner Tom Cruise as a misogynist infomercial guru in *Magnolia* (NYT "splendid acting ... is allowed to come on like gangbusters and then reveal hidden uncertainty"; LAT "expertly performed ... almost steals the picture"; CT "wonderful ... gives his best performance since 'Born on the Fourth of July' ... a savagely comic turn ... show-stopping"; WP "[a] blistering turn"; SFC "amazing ... a mesmerizing performance"; TGM "dazzling ... hits some kind of career highpoint"; SMH "great ... enjoyably showy") and SAG winner Michael Caine as a New England doctor who runs an orphanage in *The Cider House Rules* (NYT "beautifully acted ... a coup for an actor who had seemed too often trapped in the role of snake-eyed British lotharios, con men and other sleazeballs"; LAT "a career-crowning portrayal ... understated yet towering"; WP "Caine is fabulous, easily the best thing in the film"; SFC "wonderful ... indelibly drawn"; Time "excellent"; G "Caine – though hampered by a frankly uncertain American accent – is watchable, as always").

The dark horse in the category was eleven-year old Haley Joel Osment in the surprise box office smash *The Sixth Sense* (LAT "easily gives the best kid performance of the year ... if he were to get an Oscar nomination, it would be both historic and just"; WP "remarkable ... brilliantly played"; SFC "extraordinary"; TGM "a five-star child-actor performance ... believable and engaging"; S&S "[an] exquisite performance"; TT "the real star of the show").

The Oscar ballot was rounded out by Jude Law as a jazz–loving playboy in *The Talented Mr Ripley* (NYT "a star-making role ... Dickie is pure eros and adrenaline, a combination not many actors could handle with this much aplomb"; LAT "brings the right kind of savoir-fare to Dickie"; WP "persuasive and likable"; TGM "terrific").

On Oscar night, sixty-one-year old Caine claimed his second Best Supporting Actor Academy Award. In London a few weeks later, he was among the nominees outpolled for the British Academy Award by Law, one of the unsuccessful Oscar nominees.

1999

BEST SUPPORTING ACTRESS

ACADEMY AWARDS
Toni Collette as 'Lynn Sear' in *The Sixth Sense*
• **Angelina Jolie as 'Lisa Rowe' in *Girl, Interrupted***
Catherine Keener as 'Maxine' in *Being John Malkovich*
Samantha Morton as 'Hattie' in *Sweet and Lowdown*
Chloë Sevigny as 'Lana Tisdel' in *Boys Don't Cry*

GOLDEN GLOBE AWARDS
Cameron Diaz – *Being John Malkovich*
• **Angelina Jolie – *Girl, Interrupted***
Catherine Keener – *Being John Malkovich*
Samantha Morton – *Sweet and Lowdown*
Natalie Portman – *Anywhere But Here*
Chloë Sevigny – *Boys Don't Cry*

SCREEN ACTORS GUILD
Cameron Diaz
  – Being John Malkovich
• **Angelina Jolie – *Girl, Interrupted***
Catherine Keener
  – Being John Malkovich
Julianne Moore – *Magnolia*
Chloë Sevigny – *Boys Don't Cry*

BRITISH ACADEMY AWARDS
Thora Birch – *American Beauty*
Cate Blanchett
  – The Talented Mr Ripley
Cameron Diaz
  – Being John Malkovich
• **Maggie Smith**
  – *Tea with Mussolini*
Mena Suvari – *American Beauty*

NEW YORK – Catherine Keener – *Being John Malkovich*
LOS ANGELES – Chloë Sevigny – *Boys Don't Cry*
BOARD OF REVIEW – Julianne Moore – *Cookie's Fortune* and ***An Ideal Husband*** and ***Magnolia*** and ***A Map of the World***
NATIONAL SOCIETY – Chloë Sevigny – *Boys Don't Cry*
CRITICS' CHOICE – Angelina Jolie – *Girl, Interrupted*
LONDON (British Supporting Actress) **Lynn Redgrave – *Gods and Monsters***

Julianne Moore seemed certain to earn simultaneous Oscar nominations in the Best Actress and Best Supporting Actress categories following her double nominations at both the Golden Globes and the Screen Actors Awards, and her Best Supporting Actress prize from the National Board of Review for her performances in four different films. The Academy, however, recognised her only in the lead category, overlooking her Guild nominated turn as the increasingly hysterical wife of a dying media tycoon in *Magnolia* (NYT "splendid acting ... wafts luminously through the film"; CT "wonderful ... incredibly strong"; TGM "dazzling ... starts her performance at an operatic pitch of hysteria and then keeps pushing it higher"). The other winners of the major critics' prizewinners, however, were all included on the Oscar ballot which comprised five first-time nominees.

The New York Film Critics Circle winner was Catherine Keener as a manipulative business woman in *Being John Malkovich* (NYT "Keener, an established indie queen whose funny, alluring work here will make her much more widely appreciated, turns conniving Maxine into the object of everyone's affections"; LAT "[enters] into the spirit of the piece with energy, daring and a zest for the unusual").

The Los Angeles Film Critics Association and National Society of Film Critics honoree was Chloë Sevigny as a young woman who does not initially realise that her boyfriend is really a woman in *Boys Don't Cry* (NYT "raw emotion ... on a par with Ms Swank's work"; LAT "played with haunting immediacy"; [she and Swank give] performances of such luminous intensity that they break your heart"; V "flawless"; SFC "outstanding"; TGM "compelling").

The Broadcast Film Critics Association award winner and also the recipient of the Golden Globe, was Angelina Jolie as a troubled patient in *Girl, Interrupted*, a role many critics considered to be a co-lead rather than supporting role (NYT "[a] ferocious, white-hot performance"; LAT "it's a mark of the strength of [her] performance that Lisa is in many ways the most individual and believable character ... what helps the film stay honest are the purity and grace of its lead performances by Ryder and Jolie"; CT "to say Jolie steals the movie is an understatement; when she's on the screen, it's hard to look away from her"; CST "intriguing and watchable"; WP "well-acted ... acting honors go to Angelina Jolie, splendidly menacing as Lisa ... [her] ferocious, white-hot performance captures the scary allure of this daredevil and brutal truth teller"; TGM "[the script] leaves Angelina Jolie to roar and bluster and steal the show").

Completing the Oscar short-list were: Samantha Morton, runner-up for the Los Angeles prize, as a mute woman in *Sweet and Lowdown* (NYT "Morton does this astonishing well, mixing the baleful loneliness of Buster Keaton with a Harpo Marx sweetness ... the film's most affecting performance without the benefit of music or voice"; LAT "as played by the wonderfully expressive British actress Samantha Morton, Hattie is able to say more with looks than most people can with words ... a very sweet virtuoso performance that can stand comparison to the classic playful ingenues of the silent screen"; WP "splendidly acted ... played with extraordinary sweetness and vulnerability"; SFC "there's nothing simplistic or condescending in her performance"; TT "although Morton doesn't utter a word, her doting waif brilliantly shows up the insecurities behind Penn's bluster"); and Toni Collette as a single mother in *The Sixth Sense* (LAT "a virtual revelation"; CT "strong work"; SFC "beautiful support ... plays [her character] with every nerve frayed, every emotion on the surface of her face"; S&S "[an] exquisite performance").

Two weeks prior to the Academy Awards, Jolie became the overwhelming favourite when she added the Screen Actors Guild accolade to her Golden Globe. On Oscar night, twenty-one years after her father Jon Voight won an Academy Award for *Coming Home*, Jolie was awarded the Best Supporting Actress statuette.

Jolie did not, however, have the chance to repeat her victory on the other side of the Atlantic. The British Academy nominated five candidates who had been overlooked for the Oscar: Cameron Diaz in *Being John Malkovich* (NYT "does a hilarious turn"; LAT "[enters] into the spirit of the piece with energy, daring and a zest for the unusual"; SFC "nearly unrecognizable"); Maggie Smith in *Tea with Mussolini* (NYT "the runaway winner of the acting derby [among the film's cast] in terms of attention-getting lines and haughty attitudinizing is Dame Maggie"; LAT "Cher and Smith play their big moment of truth scene with aplomb"; WP "[brings her] vividly to life"); both Thora Birch (LAT "faultless"; WP "outstanding"; CST "grounded") and Mena Suvari (LAT "convincing"; WP "outstanding"; SFC "terrific ... a major discovery") in *American Beauty*; and Cate Blanchett in *The Talented Mr Ripley* (NYT "played irresistibly"; LAT "excellent"; CT "top-notch ... acidly witty social portraiture"; SFX "deserves an Oscar"; SMH "she glows"). Blanchett had also earned praise for a notable, and sharply contrasting, supporting role in *Pushing Tin* (NYT "whatever possessed [her] to play Nick's spouse, a jaunty Long Island housewife with a strong local accent, has actually stood her in good stead ... she fits in so well here that it may be a while before you wonder why Elizabeth I is talking about tuna casseroles"; LAT "makes an unnervingly perfect transition from Elizabeth the queen to Long Island housewife"; CT "brilliant"; CST "astonishingly transformed"; WP "gives Connie a real presence ... it is almost worth watching this movie for her"; SFC "takes on a completely different body"). The winner of the BAFTA was Smith, who equalled the late Peter Finch's record of five British Academy Awards in the acting categories for work in feature films.

Overlooked by both the Academies in Hollywood and London were: Natalie Portman in *Anywhere But Here* (NYT "proving her mettle in a fully formed dramatic role ... [she] does a terrific job"; NYP "an Oscar-calibre performance"; LAT "Portman's work as 14-year-old daughter Ann is keenly empathetic"; CT "wins us over with her subtlety and natural grace"; WP "does as well as her role allows"); Patricia Neal in *Cookie's Fortune* (NYT "played touchingly"; LAT "played with such resonance and gusto"; CST "touching"); Nicole Kidman in *Eyes Wide Shut* (LAT "absorbing"; G "all too plausible"); Sissy Spacek in *The Straight Story* (WP "terrific"; S&S "the film's richest performance"; SMH "endearing"); Patricia Arquette in *Bringing Out the Dead* (NYT "Arquette's quietly credible performance helps center Frank's experiences"; Kimberly J. Brown in *Tumbleweeds* (NYT "extraordinarily nuanced ... the child performance of the year"; LAT "McTeer in turn is well matched by resourceful Kimberly J. Brown"; WP "superb ... makes a believably down-to-earth kid"); and Cherry Jones in *Cradle Will Rock* (LAT "her most impressive screen performance to date ... [her] controlled energy and charisma simultaneously drive the film and ground it in a reality it needs"; WP "brilliant").

Index

Index

Index

Index

Index

444

Index

Index

Index

Index

Index

Index

Index

451

Index

Index

Index

Index

Index

456

Index

Index

Index

Index

Index

Index

Index

Index

Index

Made in the USA
Middletown, DE
17 June 2019